SOCIETIES, NETWORKS, AND TRANSITIONS

A GLOBAL HISTORY

SOCIETIES, NETWORKS, AND TRANSITIONS

A GLOBAL HISTORY

Volume I: To 1500

Third Edition

Craig A. Lockard
University of Wisconsin—Green Bay

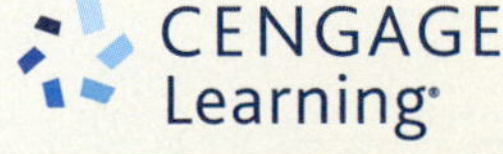

Australia • Brazil • Mexico • Singapore • United Kingdom • United States

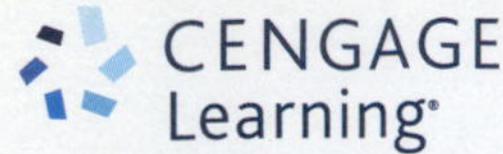

Societies, Networks, and Transitions: A Global History, Third Edition, Vol I: To 1500
Craig A. Lockard

Product Director: Suzanne Jeans

Product Manager: Brooke Barbier

Senior Content Developer: Tonya Lobato

Associate Content Developer: Cara Swan

Product Assistant: Andrew Newton

Media Developer: Kate MacLean

Marketing Development Manager: Kyle Zimmerman

Senior Content Project Manager: Carol Newman

Senior Art Director: Cate Barr

Manufacturing Planner: Sandee Milewski

Intellectual Property Analyst: Jessica Elias

Production Service/Compositor: Cenveo® Publisher Services

Text Designer: Alisha Webber/ Cenveo® Publisher Services

Cover Designer: Anne Bell Carter/ A Bell Design Co.

Cover Image: Roman mosaics from the "Luxurious Residence" in Sepphoris. Market scene: vendors bringing goods. 3rd–6th century C.E.

Library of Congress Control Number: 2013952675

Student Edition:

ISBN-13: 978-1-285-78308-6

ISBN-10: 1-285-78308-5

Cengage Learning
200 First Stamford Place, 4th Floor
Stamford CT 06902
USA

Printed in the United States of America
3 4 5 6 7 18 17 16 15

Brief Contents

Contents

Maps

Features

PROFILES

WITNESS TO THE PAST

HISTORICAL CONTROVERSIES

Preface

"Awareness of the need for a universal view of history—for a history which transcends national and regional boundaries and comprehends the entire globe—is one of the marks of the present. Our past [is] the past of the world, our history is the first to be world history."[1]

—Geoffrey Barraclough

British historian Geoffrey Barraclough wrote these words over three decades ago, yet historians are still grappling with what it means to write world history, and why it is crucial to do so, especially to better inform today's students about their changing world and how it came to be. The intended audience for this text is students taking introductory world history courses and the faculty who teach them. Many of these students will be taking world history in colleges, universities, and community colleges, often with the goal of satisfying general education requirements or building a foundation for majoring in history or a related field. Most others will take world history in secondary schools, often as Advanced Placement courses. Like the contemporary world, the marketplace for texts is also changing. Both students, many of whom have outside jobs, and instructors, often facing expanded workloads, have increasing demands on their time. New technologies are promoting new pedagogies and a multiplicity of classroom approaches. Hence, any textbook must provide a sound knowledge base while also enhancing teaching and learning whatever the pedagogy employed.

To make this third edition even more accessible and reader friendly than the first two editions, we have streamlined and shortened the narrative. Based on instructor feedback, we have also moved the popular *Societies, Networks, and Transitions* essay features from the end of each part to the beginning in order to give them more prominence. Like the core chapter narrative, these essays are also shorter, more streamlined, and are now organized by theme so that students can easily grasp the major parallels and changes that take place over the timeframe of the part. I believe that these changes and additions enhance the book's presentation and clarity and enable it to convey the richness and importance of world history for today's students and tomorrow's leaders while also making the teaching of the material easier for both high school and college instructors using this text.

Twenty-first-century students, more than any generation before them, live in multicultural countries and an interconnected world. The world's interdependence calls for teaching a wider vision, which is the goal of this text. My intention is to create a meaningful, coherent, and stimulating presentation that conveys to students the incredible diversity of societies from earliest times to the present, as well as the ways they have been increasingly connected to other societies and shaped by these relationships. History may happen "as one darn thing after another," but the job of historians is to make it something more than facts, names, and dates. A text should provide a readable narrative, supplying a content base while also posing larger questions. The writing is as clear and thorough in its explanation of events and concepts as I can make it. No text can or should teach the course, but I hope that this text provides enough of a baseline of regional and global coverage to allow each instructor to bring her or his own talents, understandings, and particular interests to the process.

I became involved in teaching, debating, and writing world history as a result of my personal and academic experiences. My interest in other cultures was first awakened in the multicultural Southern California city where I grew up. Many of my classmates or their parents had come from Asia, Latin America, or the Middle East. There was also a substantial African American community. A curious person did not have to search far to hear music, sample foods, or encounter ideas from many different cultures. I remember being enchanted by the Chinese landscape paintings at a local museum devoted to Asian art, and vowing to one day see some of those misty mountains for myself. Today many young people may be as interested as I was in learning about the world, since, thanks to immigration, many cities and towns all over North America have taken on a cosmopolitan flavor similar to my hometown.

While experiences growing up sparked my interest in other cultures, it was my schooling that pointed the way to a career in teaching world history. When I entered college, many undergraduate students in the United States, often as part of the general education requirement, were required to take a year-long course in Western Civilization that introduced students to Egyptian pyramids, Greek philosophy, medieval pageantry, Renaissance art, and the French Revolution, enriching our lives. Fortunately, my university expanded student horizons further by adding course components (albeit brief) on China, Japan, India, and Islam while also developing a study abroad program. I participated in both the study abroad in Salzburg, Austria, and a year-long student exchange with a university in Hong Kong, which meant living with, rather than just sampling, different customs, outlooks, and histories.

More teachers and academic historians now realize that the emphasis in U.S. education on the histories of the United States and western Europe, to the near exclusion of the rest of the world, was not sufficient for understanding the realities of the twentieth century nor is it today. For decades young Americans have been sent thousands of miles away to fight wars in countries, such as Vietnam and Afghanistan, that few Americans had ever heard of. Newspapers and television reported developments in places such as Japan and Pakistan,

[1]Main Trends in History. New York: Holmes and Meier, 1979, p. 153.

Egypt and Congo, Cuba and Brazil, which had increasing relevance for Americans. Over the past half century graduate programs and scholarship directed toward Asian, African, Middle Eastern, Latin American, and eastern European and Russian history also grew out of the awareness of a widening world, broadening conceptions of history. I attended one of the new programs in Asian Studies for my MA degree, and then the first PhD program in world history. Thanks to that program, I encountered the stimulating work of pioneering world historians from North America such as Philip Curtin, Marshall Hodgson, William McNeill, and Leften S. Stavrianos. My own approach, developed as I taught undergraduate world history courses beginning in 1969, owes much to the global vision they offered.

To bring some coherence to the emerging world history field as well as to promote a global approach at all levels of education, several dozen of us teaching at the university, college, community college, and secondary school levels in the United States and Canada came together in the early 1980s to form the World History Association (WHA), for which I served as founding secretary and later as a member of the Executive Council. The organization grew rapidly, encouraging the teaching, studying, and writing of world history not only in the United States but all over the world. The approaches to world history found among active WHA members vary widely, and my engagement in the ongoing discussions at conferences and in essays, often about the merits of varied textbooks, provided an excellent background for writing this text.

The Aims and Approach of the Text

Societies, Networks, and Transitions: A Global History provides an accessible, thought-provoking guide to students in their exploration of the landscape of the past, helping them to think about it in all its social diversity and interconnectedness and to see their lives with fresh understanding. It does this by combining clear writing, special learning features, current scholarship, and a comprehensive, global approach that does not omit the role and richness of particular regions.

There is a method behind these aims. For forty-five years I have written about and taught Asian, African, and world history at universities in the United States and, as a visiting professor, Malaysia. A cumulative seven years of study, research, teaching, or travel in Southeast Asia, East Asia, East Africa, and Europe gave me insights into a wide variety of cultures and historical perspectives. Finally, the WHA, its publications and conferences, and the electronic listserv, H-WORLD, have provided active forums for vigorously discussing how best to think about and teach world history.

The most effective approach to presenting world history in a text for undergraduate and advanced high school students, I have concluded, is one that combines the themes of connections and cultures. World history is very much about connections that transcend countries, cultures, and regions, and a text should discuss, for example, major long-distance trade networks such as the Silk Road, the spread of religions, maritime exploration, world wars, and transregional empires such as the Persian, Mongol, and British Empires. These connections are part of the broader global picture. Students need to understand that cultures, however unique, did not emerge and operate in a vacuum but faced similar challenges, shared many common experiences, and influenced each other.

The broader picture is drawn by means of several features in the text. To strengthen the presentation of the global overview, the text uses a short but innovative essay feature entitled "Societies, Networks, and Transitions." Appearing at the beginning of each of the six chronological parts, this feature analyzes and synthesizes the wider trends of the era, such as the role of long-distance trade, the spread of technologies and religions, and global climate change. The objective is to introduce and amplify the wider transregional messages developed in the part chapters and help students to think about the global context in which societies are enmeshed. The essays also make comparisons, for example, between the Han Chinese, Mauryan Indian, and Roman Empires, and between Chinese, Indian, and European emigration in the nineteenth century. These comparisons help to throw further light on diverse cultures and the differences and similarities between them during the era covered. Finally, each essay is meant to show how the transitions that characterize the era lead up to the era discussed in the following part. Furthermore, several chapters concentrate on global rather than regional developments.

However, while a broad global overview is a strongly developed feature of this text, most chapters, while acknowledging and explaining relevant linkages, focus on a particular region or several regions. Most students learn easiest by focusing on one region or culture at a time. Students also benefit from recognizing the cultural richness and intellectual creativity of specific societies. From this text students learn, for instance, about Chinese poetry, Indonesian music, Arab science, Greek philosophy, West African arts, Indian cinema, Latin American economies, and Anglo-American political thought. As a component of this cultural richness, this text also devotes considerable attention to the enduring religious traditions, such as Buddhism, Christianity, and Islam, and to issues of gender. The cultural richness of a region and its distinctive social patterns can get lost in an approach that minimizes regional coverage. Today most people are still mostly concerned with events in their own countries, even as their lives are reshaped by transnational economies and global cultural movements.

Also a strong part of the presentation of world history in this text is its attempt to be comprehensive and inclusive. To enhance comprehensiveness, the text balances social, economic, political, and cultural and religious history, and it also devotes some attention to geographical and environmental contexts as well as to the history of ideas and technologies. At the same time, the text highlights features within societies, such as economic production, technological innovations, and portable ideas that had widespread or enduring influence. To ensure inclusiveness, the text recognizes the contributions of many societies, including some often neglected, such as sub-Saharan Africa, pre-Columbian America, Southeast Asia, and Oceania. In particular, this text offers strong coverage of the diverse Asian societies. Throughout history, as today, the great majority of the world's population has lived in Asia.

Organizing the Text

All textbook authors struggle with how to organize the material. To keep the number of chapters corresponding to the twenty-eight or thirty weeks of most academic calendars in North America, and roughly equal in length, I have often had to combine several regions into a single chapter to be comprehensive, sometimes making decisions for conveniences sake. For example, unlike texts that may have only one chapter on sub-Saharan Africa covering the centuries from ancient times to 1500 C.E., this text discusses sub-Saharan Africa in each of the six chronological eras, devoting three chapters to the centuries prior to 1500 C.E. and three to the years since 1450 C.E. But this sometimes necessitated grouping Africa, depending on the era, with Europe, the Middle East, or the Americas. Unlike texts that may, for example, have material on Tang dynasty China scattered through several chapters, making it harder for students to gain a cohesive view of that society, I want to convey a comprehensive perspective of major societies such as Tang China. The material is divided into parts defined as distinct eras (such as the Classical and the Early Modern) so that students can understand how all regions were part of world history from earliest times. I believe that a chronological structure aids students in grasping the changes over time while helping to organize the material.

Distinguishing Features

Several features of *Societies, Networks, Transitions: A Global History* will help students better understand, assimilate, and appreciate the material they are about to encounter. Those unique to this text include the following.

Introducing World History World History may be the first and possibly the only history course many undergraduates will take in college. The text opens with a short essay that introduces students to the nature of history, the special challenges posed by studying world history, and why we need to study it.

Balancing Themes Three broad themes—uniqueness, interdependence, and change—have shaped the text. They are discussed throughout in terms of three related concepts—societies, networks, and transitions; they are also clearly identified in the text via the use of "S," "N," or "T" icons. These concepts, discussed in more detail in "Introducing World History," can be summarized as follows:

- **SOCIETIES** Influenced by environmental and geographical factors, people have formed and maintained societies defined by distinctive but often changing cultures, beliefs, social forms, institutions, and material traits.
- **NETWORKS** Over the centuries societies have generally been connected to other societies by growing networks forged by phenomena such as migration, long-distance trade, exploration, military expansion, colonization, the spread of ideas and technologies, and webs of communication. These growing networks modified individual societies, created regional systems, and eventually led to a global system.
- **TRANSITIONS** Each major historical era has been marked by one or more great transitions sparked by events or innovations, such as settled agriculture, Mongol imperialism, industrial revolution, or world war, that have had profound and enduring influences on many societies, gradually reshaping the world. At the same time, societies and regions have experienced transitions of regional rather than global scope that have generated new ways of thinking or doing things, such as the expansion of Islam into India or the European colonization of East Africa and Mexico.

Through exposure to these three ideas integrated throughout the text, students learn of the rich cultural mosaic of the world. They are also introduced to its patterns of connections and unity as well as of continuity and change.

"Societies, Networks, and Transitions" Minichapters A short, thematically organized feature at the beginning of each part assists the student in backing up from the stories of societies and regions to see the larger historical patterns of change and the wider links among distant peoples. This comparative analysis allows students to identify experiences and transitions common to several regions or the entire world and to reflect further on the text themes. Additionally, the feature provides an important overview of key developments in the subsequent set of chapters.

Historical Controversies Since one of the common misconceptions about history is that it is about the "dead" past, included at the end of each part is a brief account of a debate among historians over how an issue in the past should be interpreted and what it means to us today. For example, why are the major societies dominated by males, and has this always been true? Why and when did Europe begin its "great divergence" from China and other Asian societies? How do historians evaluate contemporary globalization? Reappraisal is at the heart of history, and many historical questions are never completely answered. Yet most textbooks ignore this dimension of historical study; this text is innovative in including it. The Historical Controversy essays will help show students that historical facts are anything but dead; they live and change their meaning as new questions are asked by each new generation.

Profiles It is impossible to recount the human story without using broad generalizations, but it is also difficult to understand that story without seeing historical events reflected in the lives of men and women, prominent but also ordinary people. Each chapter contains a Profile that focuses on the experiences or accomplishments of a woman or man, to convey the flavor of life of the period, to embellish the chapter narrative with interesting personalities, and to integrate gender into the historical account. The Profiles try to show how gender affected the individual, shaping her or his opportunities and involvement in society. Several focus questions ask the student to reflect on the Profile. For instance, students will examine a historian in early China, look at the spread of Christianity as seen through the life of a pagan female philosopher in Egypt, relive the experience of a female slave in colonial Brazil, and envision modern Indian life through a sketch of a film star. For this edition I have prepared three new Profiles.

Special Coverage This text also treats often-neglected areas and subjects. For example:

- It includes several regions with considerable historical importance but often marginalized or even omitted in many texts, including sub-Saharan Africa, Southeast Asia, Korea, Central Asia, pre-Columbian North America, ancient South America, the Caribbean, Polynesia, Australia, Canada, and the United States.
- It includes discussions of significant groups that transcend regional boundaries, such as the caravan travelers and traders of the Silk Road, Mongol empire builders, the Indian Ocean maritime traders, and contemporary humanitarian organizations such as Amnesty International and Doctors Without Borders.
- It features extensive coverage of the roots, rise, reshaping, and enduring influence of the great religious and philosophical traditions.
- It blends coverage of gender, particularly the experiences of women, and of social history generally, into the larger narrative.
- It devotes the first chapter of the text to the roots of human history. After a brief introduction to the shaping of our planet, human evolution, and the spread of people around the world, the chapter examines the birth of agriculture, cities, and states, which set the stage for everything to come.
- It includes strong coverage of the world since 1945, a focus of great interest to many students.

Witness to the Past Many texts incorporate excerpts from primary sources, but this text also keeps student needs in mind by using up-to-date translations and addressing a wide range of topics. Included are excerpts from important Buddhist, Hindu, Confucian, and Islamic works that helped shape great traditions. Readings such as a collection of Roman graffiti, a thirteenth-century tourist description of a Chinese city, a report on an Aztec market, and a manifesto for modern Egyptian women reveal something of people's lives and concerns. Also offered are materials that shed light on the politics of the time, such as an African king's plea to end the slave trade, Karl Marx's *Communist Manifesto*, and the recent *Arab Human Development Report*. Five new primary source readings are included in this edition. The wide selection of document excerpts is also designed to illustrate how historians work with original documents. Unlike most texts, chapters are also enlivened by brief but numerous excerpts of statements, writings, or songs from people of the era that are effectively interspersed in the chapter narrative so that students can better see the vantage points and opinions of the people then living.

Chapter Learning Aids

The carefully designed learning aids are meant to help faculty teach world history and students actively learn and appreciate it. A number of aids have been created, including some that distinguish this text from others in use.

Chapter Opening Features A chapter outline shows the chapter contents at a glance. The outlines include *focus questions* for each section to prepare students for thinking about the main themes and topics of the chapter. Chapter text then opens with a quotation from a primary source pertinent to chapter topics. An interest-grabbing vignette or sketch then funnels students' attention toward the chapter themes they are about to explore.

Thematic Icons Every major section within each chapter is now identified by helpful thematic icons that let students know which of the main themes, societies, networks, or transitions, are being discussed.

Timelines To help students grasp the overall chronological picture of the chapter, timelines highlight key dates and events for each of the major regions discussed in each chapter.

Special Boxed Features Each chapter contains a *Witness to the Past* drawn from a primary source, and a *Profile* highlighting a man or woman from that era. Questions are also placed at the end of the primary source readings and profiles to help students comprehend the material.

Maps and Other Visuals Maps, photos, chronologies, and tables are amply interspersed throughout the chapters, illustrating and unifying coverage and themes.

Section Summaries At the end of each major section within a chapter, a bulleted summary helps students to review the key topics.

Chapter Summary At the end of each chapter, a concise summary invites students to sum up the chapter content and review its major points.

Key Terms and Pronunciation Guides Important terms likely to be new to the student are boldfaced in the text and immediately defined. These key terms are also listed at the end of the chapter and then listed with their definitions at the end of the text. The pronunciation of foreign and other difficult terms is shown parenthetically where the terms are introduced to help students with the terminology.

New to This Edition

In developing this new edition, I have also benefited from the responses to the first two editions, including correspondence and conversations with instructors and students who used the text. Incorporating many of their suggestions, this third edition is somewhat shorter than the first and second editions. Each part now opens with the comparative "Societies, Networks, and Transitions" essays that provide students an overview of important themes in the coming set of chapters. The chapter structure is now streamlined by combining some materials and hence eliminating superfluous heads.

In addition to all these changes, I have updated the narrative to incorporate new scholarly knowledge and historical developments over the last three years and since the second edition was published. Hence, many chapters include new information. Paleontology, archaeology, and ancient history are lively fields of study that constantly produce new knowledge, and the chapters in Part I include updates on subjects such as human evolution, the spread of modern humans, the rise of agriculture, the emergence of states, and early human settlement in the Americas. Later chapters incorporate new material on such subjects as the development of Hinduism, Austronesian migrations, Ottoman naval expansion, the effects of climate change, and Native American revolts against colonialism. As most readers know, many important developments have occurred in the last few years, and hence the chapters in Part VI have required the most revision. As a result, Chapter 26 on the Global System includes, among other topics, new material on the global recession, increasing global warming, the rise of the BRICS nations, and the roles of social media. Chapter 27 on East Asia examines economic challenges, human rights protests in China, violence in Tibet and Xinjiang, changing Chinese and Japanese leadership, and North Korean developments and regional tensions. The discussion of Europe and Russia in Chapter 28 ponders recent economic challenges, immigration issues, separatist and rightwing movements, Vladimir Putin's government, and changing attitudes toward the European Union and euro currency. In Chapter 29 on the Americas, I have added material on such topics as the Barack Obama presidency, politics in various Latin American nations, and the first Latin American pope. New material in Chapter 30 on the Middle East and Africa includes Turkish politics, the "Arab spring" conflicts in Egypt and Syria, and politics in varied African nations. Finally, Chapter 31 addresses India's challenges, political transition in Burma, and politics and violence in various Southeast Asian nations such as Thailand. These chapters should give students a good introduction to the world in which they live.

Ancillaries

A wide array of supplements accompany this text to assist students with different learning needs and to help instructors master today's various classroom challenges.

Instructor Resources

Aplia™ is an online interactive learning solution that improves comprehension and outcomes by increasing student effort and engagement. Founded by a professor to enhance his own courses, Aplia provides automatically graded assignments with detailed, immediate explanations on every question. The interactive assignments have been developed to address the major concepts covered in *Societies, Networks, and Transitions* and are designed to promote critical thinking and engage students more fully in learning. Question types include questions built around animated maps, primary sources such as newspaper extracts, or imagined scenarios, like engaging in a conversation with a historical figure or finding a diary and being asked to fill in some blanks; more in-depth primary source question sets address a major topic with a number of related primary sources and questions that promote deeper analysis of historical evidence. Many of the questions incorporate images, video clips, or audio clips. Students get immediate feedback on their work (not only what they got right or wrong, but why), and they can choose to see another set of related questions if they want more practice. A searchable eBook is available inside the course as well so that students can easily reference it as they work. Map reading and writing tutorials are also available to get students off to a good start. Aplia's simple-to-use course management interface allows instructors to post announcements, upload course materials, host student discussions, e-mail students, and manage the gradebook; a knowledgeable and friendly support team offers assistance and personalized support in customizing assignments to the instructor's course schedule. To learn more and view a demo for this book, visit www.aplia.com.

MindTap Reader for *Societies, Networks, and Transitions* is an eBook specifically designed to address the ways students assimilate content and media assets. MindTap Reader combines thoughtful navigation ergonomics, advanced student annotation, note-taking, and search tools, and embedded media assets such as video and MP3 chapter summaries, primary source documents with critical thinking questions, and interactive (zoomable) maps. Students can use the eBook as their primary text or as a multimedia companion to their printed book. The MindTap Reader eBook is available within the MindTap and Aplia online offerings found at www.cengagebrain.com.

History CourseMate Cengage Learning's History CourseMate brings course concepts to life with interactive learning, study tools, and exam preparation tools that support the printed textbook. Use Engagement Tracker to monitor student engagement in the course and watch student comprehension soar as your class works with the printed textbook and the textbook-specific website. An interactive eBook allows students to take notes, highlight, search, and interact with embedded media (such as quizzes, flashcards, primary sources, and videos). Learn more at **www.cengage.com/coursemate**.

Instructor Companion Website This website is an all-in-one resource for class preparation, presentation, and testing for instructors. Accessible through Cengage.com/login with your faculty account, you will find an Instructor's Manual, Powerpoint presentations (descriptions below), and testbank files (please see Cognero description).

Instructor's Manual Prepared by Janet Jenkins of Arkansas Tech University, this manual contains for each chapter: instructional objectives, chapter outlines, lecture suggestions, discussion topics, primary source analysis, and suggested writing assignments.

PowerPoint® Lecture Tools Prepared by Janet Jenkins of Arkansas Tech University. These presentations are ready-to-use, visual outlines of each chapter. They are easily customized for your lectures. There are presentations of only lecture or only images, as well as combined lecture and image presentations. Also available is a per chapter JPEG library of images and maps.

Cengage Learning Testing, powered by Cognero® for Societies, Networks, and Transitions was prepared by David Burrow of University of South Dakota and is accessible through Cengage.com/login with your faculty account. This test bank contains multiple-choice and essay questions for each chapter. Cognero® is a flexible, online system that allows you to author, edit, and manage test bank content for Societies, Networks, and Transitions, third edition. Create multiple test versions instantly and deliver through your LMS from your classroom, or wherever you may be, with no special installs or downloads required.

The following format types are available for download from Instructor Companion Site: Blackboard, Angel, Moodle, Canvas, Desire2Learn. You can import these files directly into your LMS to edit, manage questions, and create tests. The test bank is also available in PDF format from the Instructor Companion Website.

Companion Website This website for instructors features an Instructor's Resource Manual (instructional objectives, chapter outlines, lecture suggestions, discussion topics, primary source analysis, and suggested writing assignments) and PowerPoint presentations (lecture outlines, images, and maps). In addition, access to ***HistoryFinder***, a searchable online database with thousands of assets, allows instructors to easily create exciting presentations for their classroom by downloading art, photographs, maps, primary sources, and audio/video clips directly into a Microsoft® PowerPoint® slide.

CourseReader CourseReader is an online collection of primary and secondary sources that lets you create a customized electronic reader in minutes. With an easy-to-use interface and assessment tool, you can choose exactly what your students will be assigned—simply search or browse Cengage Learning's extensive document database to preview and select your customized collection of readings. In addition to print sources of all types (letters, diary entries, speeches, newspaper accounts, etc.), their collection includes a growing number of images and video and audio clips. Each primary source document includes a descriptive headnote that puts the reading into context and is further supported by both critical thinking and multiple-choice questions designed to reinforce key points. For more information visit **www.cengage.com/coursereader**.

Cengagebrain.com Save your students' time and money. Direct them to **www.cengagebrain.com** for choice in formats and savings and a better chance to succeed in your class. Cengagebrain.com, Cengage Learning's online store, is a single destination for more than 10,000 new textbooks, eTextbooks, eChapters, study tools, and audio supplements. Students have the freedom to purchase a-la-carte exactly what they need when they need it. Students can save 50 percent on the electronic textbook, and can pay as little as $1.99 for an individual eChapter.

Reader Program Cengage Learning publishes a number of readers, some containing exclusively primary sources, others a combination of primary and secondary sources, and some designed to guide students through the process of historical inquiry. Visit Cengage.com/history for a complete list of readers.

Custom Options Nobody knows your students like you, so why not give them a text that is tailor-fit to their needs? Cengage Learning offers custom solutions for your course—whether it's making a small modification to *Societies, Networks, and Transitions* to match your syllabus or combining multiple sources to create something truly unique. You can pick and choose chapters, include your own material, and add additional map exercises along with the Rand McNally Atlas to create a text that fits the way you teach. Ensure that your students get the most out of their textbook dollar by giving them exactly what they need. Contact your Cengage Learning representative to explore custom solutions for your course.

Student Resources

Student Companion Site This website features an assortment of resources to help students master the subject matter. It includes chapter outlines, glossary, flashcards, and learning objectives.

CourseMate The more you study, the better the results. Make the most of your study time by accessing everything you need to succeed in one place. Read your textbook, take notes, review flashcards, watch videos, and take practice quizzes online with CourseMate.

MindTap Reader MindTap Reader is an eBook specifically designed to address the ways students assimilate content and media assets. MindTap Reader combines thoughtful navigation ergonomics, advanced student annotation, note-taking, and search tools, and embedded media assets such as video and MP3 chapter summaries, primary source documents with critical thinking questions, and interactive (zoomable) maps. Students can use the eBook as their primary text or as a multimedia companion to their printed book. The MindTap Reader eBook is available within the MindTap found at www.cengagebrain.com.

Reader Program Cengage Learning publishes a number of readers, some containing exclusively primary sources, others a combination of primary and secondary sources, and some designed to guide students through the process of historical inquiry. Visit Cengage.com/history for a complete list of readers.

Cengagebrain.com Save time and money! Go to www.cengagebrain.com for choice in formats and savings and a better chance to succeed in your class. Cengagebrain.com,

Cengage Learning's online store, is a single destination for more than 10,000 new textbooks, eTextbooks, eChapters, study tools, and audio supplements. Students have the freedom to purchase a-la-carte exactly what they need when they need it. Students can save 50% on the electronic textbook, and can pay as little as $1.99 for an individual eChapter.

***Writing for College History, 1e* [ISBN: 9780618306039]** Prepared by Robert M. Frakes, Clarion University. This brief handbook for survey courses in American history, Western Civilization/European history, and world civilization guides students through the various types of writing assignments they encounter in a history class. Providing examples of student writing and candid assessments of student work, this text focuses on the rules and conventions of writing for the college history course.

***The History Handbook, 2e* [ISBN: 9780495906766]** Prepared by Carol Berkin of Baruch College, City University of New York and Betty Anderson of Boston University. This book teaches students both basic and history-specific study skills such as how to read primary sources, research historical topics, and correctly cite sources. Substantially less expensive than comparable skill-building texts, *The History Handbook* also offers tips for Internet research and evaluating online sources.

***Doing History: Research and Writing in the Digital Age, 2e* [ISBN: 9781133587880]** Prepared by Michael J. Galgano, J. Chris Arndt, and Raymond M. Hyser of James Madison University. Whether you're starting down the path as a history major, or simply looking for a straightforward and systematic guide to writing a successful paper, you'll find this text to be an indispensable handbook to historical research. This text's "soup to nuts" approach to researching and writing about history addresses every step of the process, from locating your sources and gathering information, to writing clearly and making proper use of various citation styles to avoid plagiarism. You'll also learn how to make the most of every tool available to you—especially the technology that helps you conduct the process efficiently and effectively.

***The Modern Researcher, 6e* [ISBN: 9780495318705]** Prepared by Jacques Barzun and Henry F. Graff of Columbia University. This classic introduction to the techniques of research and the art of expression is used widely in history courses, but is also appropriate for writing and research methods courses in other departments. Barzun and Graff thoroughly cover every aspect of research, from the selection of a topic through the gathering, analysis, writing, revision, and publication of findings, presenting the process not as a set of rules but through actual cases that put the subtleties of research in a useful context. Part One covers the principles and methods of research; Part Two covers writing, speaking, and getting one's work published.

***Rand McNally Historical Atlas of the World, 2e* [ISBN: 9780618841912]** This valuable resource features over 70 maps that portray the rich panoply of the world's history from preliterate times to the present. They show how cultures and civilization were linked and how they interacted. The maps make it clear that history is not static. Rather, it is about change and movement across time. The maps show change by presenting the dynamics of expansion, cooperation, and conflict. This atlas includes maps that display the world from the beginning of civilization; the political development of all major areas of the world; expanded coverage of Africa, Latin America, and the Middle East; the current Islamic World; and the world population change in 1900 and 2000.

Formats

The text is available in a one-volume hardcover edition, a two-volume paperback edition, and as an interactive ebook. *Volume I: To 1500* includes Chapters 1–14; *Volume II: Since 1450* includes Chapters 15–31.

Acknowledgments

The author would like to thank the following community of instructors who, by sharing their teaching experiences and insightful feedback, helped shape the third edition and accompanying ancillary program:

Milan Andrejevich, Ivy Tech Community College
Maria Arbelaez, University of Nebraska at Omaha
Natalie Bayer, Drake University
William Burns, George Washington University
David Burrow, University of South Dakota
Brent Carney, Eastern Gateway Community College
William Collins, Salem State University
John Dennehy, Massachusetts Maritime Academy
Ross Doughty, Ursinus College
Ashley Duane, Wayne County Community College
Sherrie Dux-Ideus, Central Community College-Hastings
Randee Goodstadt, Asheville-Buncombe Technical Community College
Aimee Harris-Johnson, El Paso Community College
Gregory Havrilcsak, University of Michigan-Flint
Michael Hinckley, Northern Kentucky University
Donna Hoffa, Wayne County Community College
Janet Jenkins, Arkansas Tech University
Kenneth Koons, Virginia Military Institute
Raymond Krohn, Boise State University
Elizabeth Littell-Lamb, University of Tampa
Chrissy Lutz, Fort Valley State University
Mary Lyons-Carmona, University of Nebraska-Omaha
John McCannon, Southern New Hampshire University
David K. McQuilkin, Bridgewater College
Kyriakos Nalmpantis, Kent State University
Victor Padilla, Wright College
Dave Price, Santa Fe College
Marsha Robinson, Miami University
Shelley Rose, Cleveland State University
Julie Smith, Mount Aloysius College
Michael Swope, Wayne County Community College
Kelly Thompson, Wayne County Community College

Ann Tschetter, University of Nebraska-Lincoln
James Williams, University of Indianapolis
Bryan Wuthrich, Santa Fe College

The author would also like to acknowledge the following instructors who lent their insight and guidance to the previous editions: Siamak Adhami, Saddleback Community College; Sanjam Ahluwalia, Northern Arizona University; David G. Atwill, Pennsylvania State University; Susan Autry, Central Piedmont Community College; Ewa K. Bacon, Lewis University; Brett Berliner, Morgan State University; Edward Bond, Alabama A&M University; Bradford C. Brown, Bradley University; Gayle K. Brunelle, California State University, Fullerton; Clea Bunch, University of Arkansas at Little Rock; Rainer Buschmann, California State University, Channel Islands; Jorge Canizares-Esguerra, State University of New York–Buffalo; Bruce A. Castleman, San Diego State University; Harold B. Cline, Jr., Middle Georgia College; Simon Cordery, Monmouth College; Steve Corso, Elwood-John Glenn High School; Dale Crandall-Bear, Solano Community College; Gregory Crider, Winthrop University; Cole Dawson, Warner Pacific College; Hilde De Weerdt, University of Tennessee, Knoxville; Anna Dronzek, University of Minnesota, Morris; Jodi Eastberg, Alverno College; James R. Evans, Southeastern Community College; Robert Fish, Japan Society of New York; Eve Fisher, South Dakota State University; Robert J. Flynn, Portland Community College; Gladys Frantz-Murphy, Regis University; Timothy Furnish, Georgia Perimeter College; James E. Genova, The Ohio State University; Deborah Gerish, Emporia State University; Rick Gianni, Purdue University Calumet; Kurt A. Gingrich, Radford University; Candace Gregory-Abbott, California State University, Sacramento; Paul L. Hanson, California Lutheran University; A. Katie Harris, Georgia State University; Timothy Hawkins, Indiana State University; Linda Wilke Heil, Central Community College; Mark Hoffman, Wayne County Community College District; Don Holsinger, Seattle Pacific University; Mary N. Hovanec, Cuyahoga Community College; Bram Hubbell, Friends Seminary; Jonathan Judaken, University of Memphis; Thomas E. Kaiser, University of Arkansas at Little Rock; Frances Kelleher, Grand Valley State University; Carol Keller, San Antonio College; Patricia A. Kennedy, Leeward Community College–University of Hawaii; Kim Klein, Shippensburg University; Rachel Layman, Lawrence North High School; Jonathan Lee, San Antonio College; Thomas Lide, San Diego State University; Derek S. Linton, Hobart and William Smith Colleges; David L. Longfellow, Baylor University; Christine Lovasz-Kaiser, University of Southern Indiana; John Lyons, Joliet Junior College; Mary Ann Mahony, Central Connecticut State University; Erik C. Maiershofer, Point Loma Nazarene University; Afshin Marashi, California State University, Sacramento; Laurence Marvin, Berry College; Robert B. McCormick, University of South Carolina Upstate; Patrick McDevitt, University at Buffalo SUNY; Doug T. McGetchin, Florida Atlantic University; Bill Mihalopoulos, Northern Michigan University; W. Jack Miller, Pennsylvania State University—Abington; Edwin Moise, Clemson University; Kerry Muhlestein, Brigham Young University–Hawaii; Aarti Nakra, Salt Lake Community College; Peter Ngwafu, Albany State University; Monique O'Connell, Wake Forest University; Melvin Page, East Tennessee State University; Annette Palmer, Morgan State University; Nicholas C. J. Pappas, Sam Houston State University; Craig Patton, Alabama A & M University; Patricia M. Pelley, Texas Tech University; William Pelz, Elgin Community College; John Pesda, Camden County College; Paul Philp, John Paul II HS/Eastfield Community College; Jason Ripper, Everett Community College; Pamela Roseman, Georgia Perimeter College; Paul Salstrom, St. Mary-of-the-Woods; Sharlene Sayegh, California State University, Long Beach; Michael Seth, James Madison University; Rose Mary Sheldon, Virginia Military Institute; David Simonelli, Youngstown State University; Peter Von Sivers, University of Utah; Anthony J. Steinhoff, University of Tennessee–Chattanooga; Nancy L. Stockdale, University of Central Florida; Bill Strickland, East Grand Rapids High School; Robert Shannon Sumner, University of West Georgia; Kate Transchel, California State University, Chico; Sally N. Vaughn, University of Houston; Thomas G. Velek, Mississippi University for Women; Kurt Waters, Centreville High School; and Kenneth Wilburn, East Carolina University.

The author has incurred many intellectual debts in developing his expertise in world history, as well as in preparing this text. To begin with, I cannot find words to express my gratitude to the editors and staff at Cengage Learning—Brooke Barbier, Tonya Lobato, Carol Newman, and Jean Woy—who had enough faith in this project to tolerate my missed deadlines and sometimes grumpy responses to editorial decisions or some other crisis. I also owe an incalculable debt to my development editor on the first edition, Phil Herbst, who prodded and pampered and helped me write for a student, rather than scholarly, audience. Tonya Lobato adroitly supervised the second and third editions. Abbey Stebing ably handled photos; Charlotte Miller, maps; Yashmita Hota, general project management; and Cara Swan, the wealth of ancillary materials. I also owe a great debt to Pam Gordon, whose interest and encouragement got this project started, and Nancy Blaine, who skillfully oversaw the writing and revising of the first two editions. Ken Wolf of Murray State University prepared the initial drafts of several of the early chapters in the first edition and in other ways gave me useful criticism and advice. I am grateful to historians such as James Hastings, Edwin Moise, Michelle Pinto, Rick Gianni, and Ibrahim Shafie who pointed out factual errors in the first two editions. I would also like to acknowledge the inspiring mentors who helped me at various stages of my academic preparation: Bill Goldman, who introduced me to world history at Pasadena High School in California; Charles Hobart and David Poston, University of Redlands professors who sparked my interest in Asia; George Wong, Bart Stoodley, and especially Andrew and Margaret Roy, my mentors at Chung Chi College in Hong Kong; Walter Vella, Robert Van Niel, and Daniel Kwok, who taught me Asian studies at Hawaii; and John Smail and Philip Curtin, under whom I studied comparative world history in the immensely exciting PhD program at Wisconsin. My various sojourns in East Asia, Southeast Asia, and East Africa allowed me to meet and learn from many inspiring and knowledgeable scholars. I have also been greatly stimulated and influenced in my approach by the writings of many fine global historians, but I would single out Philip Curtin, Marshall Hodgson, L. S. Stavrianos, William McNeill, Fernand Braudel, Eric Hobsbawm, Immanuel Wallerstein, and Peter Stearns. Curtin, Hobsbawm, and McNeill also gave me personal encouragement concerning my writing in the field, for which I am very grateful.

Colleagues at the various universities where I taught have been supportive of my explorations in world and comparative history. Most especially I acknowledge the friendship, support, and intellectual collaboration over three and a half decades of my colleagues in the interdisciplinary Social Change and Development Department at the University of Wisconsin–Green Bay (UWGB), especially Harvey Kaye, Lynn Walter, Larry Smith, Andy Kersten, Kim Nielsen, Andrew Austin, and the late Tony Galt, as well as members of the History faculty. I have also benefited immeasurably as a world historian from the visiting lecture series sponsored by UWGB's Center for History and Social Change, directed by Harvey Kaye, which over the years has brought in dozens of outstanding scholars. My students at UWGB and elsewhere have also taught me much.

I also thank my colleagues in the World History Association (WHA), who have generously shared their knowledge, encouraged my work, and otherwise provided an exceptional opportunity for learning and an exchange of ideas. I am proud to have helped establish this organization, which incorporates world history teachers at all levels of education and in many nations. Among many others, I want to express a special thank-you to longtime friends and colleagues in the WHA from whom I have learned so much and with whom I have shared many wonderful meals and conversations.

Finally, I need to acknowledge the loving support and intellectual contributions of my wife Kathy, who patiently, although not always without complaint, for the many years of the project put up with my hectic work schedule and the ever-growing piles of research materials, books, and chapter drafts scattered around our cluttered den and sometimes colonizing other space around the house.

About the Author

Craig A. Lockard is Ben and Joyce Rosenberg Professor of History Emeritus in the Social Change and Development Department at the University of Wisconsin–Green Bay, where he taught courses on Asian, African, comparative, and world history from 1975 to 2010. He has also taught at SUNY-Buffalo, SUNY-Stony Brook, and the University of Bridgeport, and twice served as a Fulbright-Hays professor at the University of Malaya in Malaysia. After undergraduate studies at the University of Redlands, during which he was able to spend a semester in Austria and a year as an exchange student at a Chung Chi College in Hong Kong (now part of the Chinese University of Hong Kong), the author earned an MA in Asian Studies at the University of Hawaii and a PhD in Comparative World and Southeast Asian History at the University of Wisconsin–Madison. His published books, articles, essays, and reviews range over a wide spectrum of topics: world history; Southeast Asian history, politics, and society; Malaysian studies; Asian emigration and diasporas; the Vietnam War; and folk, popular, rock, and world music. Among his major books are *Southeast Asia in World History* (2009); *WORLD* (2009); *Chinese Society and Politics in Sarawak: Historical Essays* (2009); *Dance of Life: Popular Music and Politics in Modern Southeast Asia* (1998); and *From Kampung to City: A Social History of Kuching, Malaysia, 1820–1970* (1987). He was also part of the task force that prepared revisions to the U.S. National Standards in World History (1996). Professor Lockard has served on various editorial advisory boards, including the *Journal of World History*, *World History Connected*, and *The History Teacher*, and as book review editor for the *Journal of Asian Studies* and the *World History Bulletin*. He was one of the founders of the World History Association, served as the organization's first secretary and several terms as a member of the Executive Council. He has lived and traveled widely in Asia, Africa, and Europe.

Note on Spelling and Usage

Transforming foreign words and names, especially those from non-European languages, into spellings usable for English-speaking readers presents a challenge. Sometimes, as with Chinese, Thai, and Malay/Indonesian, several Romanized spelling systems have developed. Generally I have chosen user-friendly spellings that are widely used in other Western writings (such as *Aksum* for the classical Ethiopian state and *Ashoka* for the classical Indian king). For Chinese, I generally use the *pinyin* system developed in the People's Republic over the past few decades (such as *Qin* and *Qing* rather than the older *Chin* and *Ching* for these dynasties, and *Beijing* instead of *Peking*), but for a few terms and names (such as the twentieth-century political leaders *Sun Yat-sen* and *Chiang Kai-shek*) I have retained an older spelling more familiar to Western readers and easier to pronounce. The same strategy is used for some other terms or names from Afro-Asian societies, such as *Cairo* instead of *al-Cahira* (the Arabic name) for the Egyptian city, *Bombay* instead of *Mumbai* (the current Indian usage) for India's largest city, and *Burma* instead of *Myanmar*. In some cases I have favored a newer spelling widely used in a region and modern scholarship but not perhaps well known in the West. For example, in discussing Southeast Asia I follow contemporary scholarship and use *Melaka* instead of *Malacca* for the Malayan city and *Maluku* rather than *Moluccas* for the Indonesian islands. Similarly, like Africa specialists I have opted to use some newer spellings, such as *Gikuyu* rather than *Kikuyu* for the Kenyan ethnic group. To simplify things for the reader I have tried to avoid using diacritical marks within words. Sometimes their use is unavoidable, such as for the premodern Chinese city of *Chang'an;* the two syllables here are pronounced separately. I also follow the East Asian custom of rendering Chinese, Japanese, and Korean names with the surname (family name) first (e.g., *Mao Zedong, Tokugawa Ieyasu*). The reader is also referred to the opening essay, "Introducing World History," for explanations of the dating system used (such as the Common Era and the Intermediate Era) and geographical concepts (such as Eurasia for Europe and Asia, and Oceania for Australia, New Zealand, and the Pacific islands).

Introducing World History

"A journey of a thousand miles begins with the first step."

—Chinese Proverb

This introduction helps you take the important "first step" toward understanding the scope and challenge of studying world history, presenting the main concepts and themes of world history tot serve as your guide, while providing a foretaste of the lively debates among historians as they try to make sense of the past, and how societies' contacts with one another created the interconnected world we know today.

What Do Historians Do?

History, the study of the past, looks at all of human life, thought, and behavior. The job of the historian is to both describe *and* interpret the past. Most professional historians want to make sense of historical events. Two general concepts help in these efforts: continuity and change. The legal system in the United States, for example, is unlike any other in the world, but has also been shaped in part by both English and ancient Roman legal practices.

Historians face their greatest challenges in interpreting the past. Although most strive to support their generalizations with evidence, they often disagree on how an event should be interpreted, sometimes because of political differences. In 1992 a widely publicized debate marked the 500-year anniversary of the first cross-Atlantic voyage of Christopher Columbus to the Western Hemisphere in 1492. Some historians pictured Columbus as a farsighted pioneer who made possible communication between the hemispheres, while others saw him as an immoral villain who began a pattern of exploiting Native American peoples by Europeans. Similar debates raged about whether it was necessary for the United States to drop atomic bombs on Japan in 1945, killing thousands of Japanese civilians but also ending World War II.

Our understanding of the past often changes as historians both acquire new information and use old information to answer new questions. Only within the past sixty years, for example, have historians studied the diaries and journals that reveal the important role of women during the American Civil War. Recently some historians used long neglected sources to conclude that, a millennium ago, China had the world's most dynamic economy and sophisticated technology. Similarly, historians have recently discovered thousands of old books written in African languages, forcing a rethinking of literacy and scholarship in West African societies hundreds of years ago.

What history "tells us" is constantly evolving. New evidence, changing interests, and the asking of new questions all add up to seeing things in a new light. No text contains the whole or final truth. **Historical revision**, or changing understanding of the past, and the difficulties of interpretation also make history controversial. In recent years heated debates about what schools should teach about history have erupted in many countries, including Japan, India, France, Egypt, and the United States.

Historians bridge the gap between the humanities and social sciences. As humanists, historians study the philosophies, religions, literatures, and arts that people generated over the ages. As social scientists, historians examine political, social, and economic patterns, though frequently asking questions different from those asked by anthropologists, economists, political scientists, and sociologists, who are generally more concerned with the present and theoretical questions. Historians also study people in their many roles and stations in life, the accomplishments of the rich and famous as well as the struggles and dreams of common women and men.

Why Study World History?

World or global history, the broadest field of history, studies the human record as a whole and the experiences of people in all the world's inhabited regions—Africa, the Americas, Asia, Europe, and the Pacific Basin—and also helps us better understand individual societies by making it easier to look at them comparatively. Studying history on a global scale also brings out patterns of life, cultural traditions, and connections between societies that go beyond a particular region, such as the spread of Buddhism, which followed the trade routes throughout southern and eastern Asia. World history helps us comprehend both the "forest" ("big picture") and the "trees" (individual societies), allowing us to situate ourselves in a broader context.

This helps us understand our increasingly connected world. Decisions made in Washington, D.C., Paris, or Tokyo influence citizens in Argentina, Senegal, and Malaysia, just as events elsewhere often affect the lives of people in Europe and North America. World historians use the widest angle of vision to comprehend how diverse local traditions and international trends intermingle. Western phenomena such as McDonald's, Hard Rock Cafes, French wines, Hollywood films, churches, the Internet, cell phones, and text messaging have spread around the world but so have non-Western products and ideas, among them Mexican soap operas, Chinese food, Japanese cars, Indonesian arts, African rhythms, and the Islamic religion. We must remember that, for all their idiosyncrasies, each society develops in a wider world.

A global perspective also highlights the past achievements of all peoples. The history of science, for example, shows that key inventions—printing, sternpost rudders, the compass, the wheelbarrow, gunpowder—originated in China, and the modern system of numbering came from India, reaching Europe from the Middle East as "Arabic" numerals. Indeed, various peoples—Mesopotamians, Egyptians, Greeks, Chinese, Indians, Arabs—built the early foundation for modern science and technology; their discoveries moved along the trade routes. Importers of technology and ideas often modified or improved on them. For example, Europeans made good use of Chinese, Indian, and Arab technologies, as well as their own inventions, in their quest to explore the world in the fifteenth and sixteenth centuries. The interdependence among and exchanges between peoples is a historical as well as a present reality.

The World History Challenge

When we study world history, we see other countries and peoples, past and present, with which we may be unfamiliar. World history helps us to recognize how some of the attitudes we absorb from the particular society and era we live in shape, and may distort, our understanding of the world and of history. Coming to terms with this mental baggage means examining such things as maps and geographical concepts and acquiring intellectual tools for comprehending other cultures.

Broadening the Scope of Our Histories

During much of the twentieth century, many high school and college students in North America were taught some version of a course, usually called Western Civilization, that emphasized the rise of western Europe and the European contributions to modern North American societies. This course recognized the undeniably influential role of Western nations, technologies, and ideas in the modern world, but also reflected more available data on Europe and North America compared with the rest of the world. This approach often exaggerated the role that Europe played in world history before modern times, pushing Asian, African, and Native American peoples and their accomplishments into the background while underplaying the contributions these peoples made to Europe. Students usually learned little about China, India, or Islamic societies, and even less about Africa, Southeast Asia, or Latin America.

In the 1960s history teaching began to change in North America. The political independence of most Asian, African, and Caribbean nations from Western nations fostered a more sophisticated understanding of African, Asian, Latin American, Native American, and Pacific island history in North America and Europe, making it easier to write a history of the entire globe. As a result, world history courses, rare before the 1960s, became increasingly common in U.S. universities, colleges, and high schools by the late twentieth century and have proliferated in several other countries, such as Australia, Canada, South Africa, China, and the Netherlands.

Revising Maps and Geography

Maps not only tell us where places are; they also create a mental image of the world, revealing how peoples perceive themselves and others. For example, Chinese maps once portrayed China as the "Middle Kingdom," the center of the world surrounded by "barbarians," reflecting and deepening the Chinese sense of superiority over neighboring peoples. Similarly, 2,500 years ago, Greek maps showed Greece at the center of the inhabited world known to them.

Even modern maps can be misleading. For example, the Mercator projection (or spatial presentation) still used in many school maps and atlases in North America and elsewhere, is based on a sixteenth-century European model that distorts the relative size of landmasses, greatly exaggerating Europe, North America, and Greenland while diminishing the lands nearer the equator and in the Southern Hemisphere. Hence, Africa, India, Southeast Asia, China, and South America look much smaller than they actually are. In the United States, maps using a Mercator projection have often tellingly placed the Americas in the middle of the map, cutting Asia in half, suggesting that the United States, appearing larger than it actually is, plays the central role in the world. Some alternative maps give a more accurate view of relative size. For example, the oval-shaped Eckert projection uses an ellipse that shows a better balance of size and shape while minimizing distortion of continental areas. A comparison between the Mercator and Eckert world maps is shown on this page and the next.

Concepts of geographical features and divisions, such as continents, the large landmasses on which most people live, also shape mental images. The classical Greeks used the terms *Europe*, *Africa*, and *Asia* in defining their world 2,500 years ago; later Europeans transformed these terms into the names for continents. For centuries Western peoples have considered Europe a continent although Europe is not a separate landmass, and the physical barriers between it and Asia are not that significant. If towering mountain ranges and other geographical barriers mark off a continent, India (blocked off by truly formidable mountains) or Southeast Asia make better candidates than Europe. Seeing Asia as a single continent is also a problem, given its spectacular size and geographical diversity. Today world geographers and historians often consider Europe and Asia to constitute one huge continent, Eurasia, containing several subcontinental regions such as Europe, South Asia, and East Asia.

Popular terms such as *Near East*, *Middle East*, or *Far East* are also misleading. They were originally formulated by Europeans to describe regions in relationship to Europe. Much depends on the viewer's position; Australians, for example, often label nearby Southeast and East Asia as the "Near North." Few Western scholars of China or Japan today refer to the "Far East," preferring the more neutral term *East Asia*. This text considers the term *Near East*, long used for western Asia, as outdated, but it refers to Southwest Asia and North Africa, closely linked historically (especially after the rise of Islam 1,400 years ago), as the Middle East, since that term is more convenient than the alternatives. The text also uses the term *Oceania* to refer to Australia, New Zealand, and the Pacific islands.

Rethinking the Dating System

A critical feature of historical study is the dating of events. World history challenges us by making us aware that all dating systems are based on the assumptions of a particular culture. Many Asian peoples saw history as moving in great cycles of birth, maturation, and decay (sometimes involving millions of years), whereas Westerners saw history as moving in a straight line from past to future (as can be seen in the chronologies within each chapter). Calendars were often tied to myths about the world's creation or about a people's or country's origins. Hence, the classical Roman calendar was based on the founding of the city of Rome around 2,700 years ago.

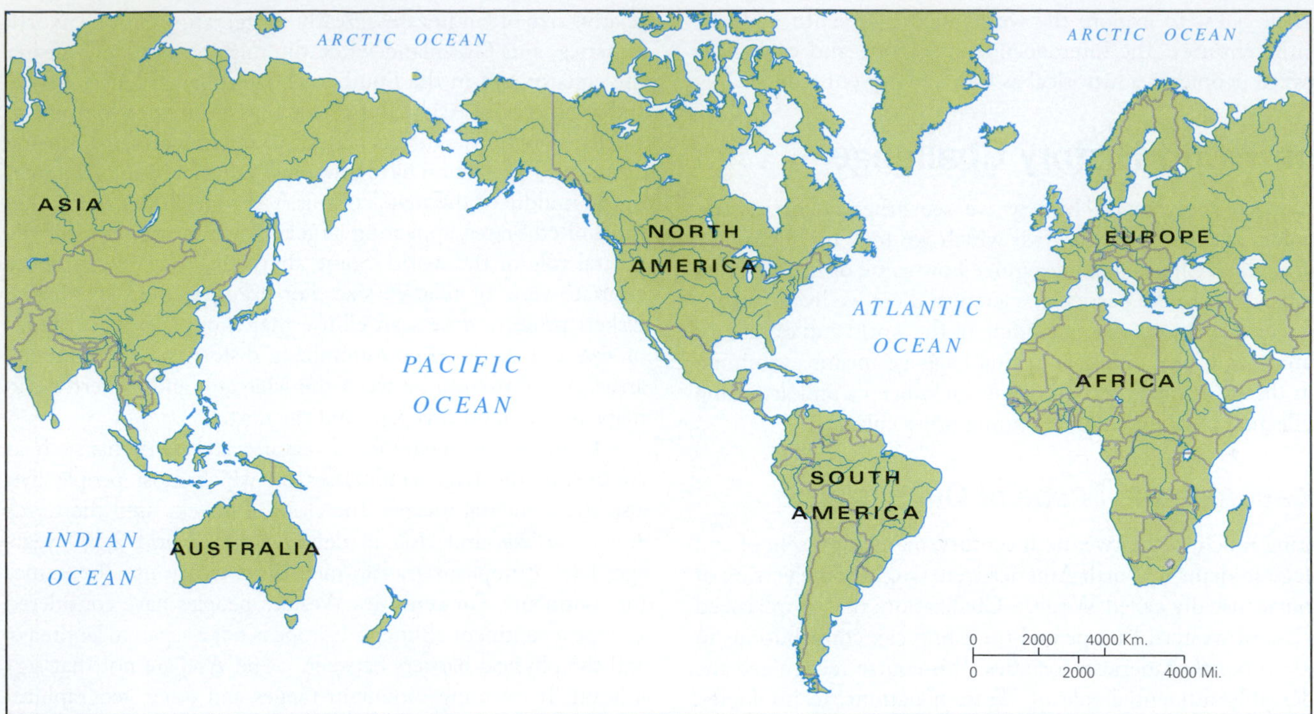

MERCATOR PROJECTION

The dating system used throughout the Western world today is based on the Gregorian Christian calendar, created by a sixteenth-century Roman Catholic pope, Gregory XIII. It uses the birth of Christianity's founder, Jesus of Nazareth, around 2,000 years ago as the turning point. Dates for events prior to the Christian era were identified as B.C. (before Christ); years in the Christian era were labeled A.D. (for the Latin *anno domini,* "in the year of the Lord"). Many history books published in Europe and North America still employ this system, which has spread around the world in recent centuries.

The notion of Christian and pre-Christian eras has no longer been satisfactory for studies of world history because it is rooted in the viewpoint of only one religious tradition, whereas there are many in the world, usually with different calendars. Muslims, for example, who consider the revelations of the prophet Muhammad to be history's central event, begin their dating system with Muhammad's journey, within Arabia, from the city of Mecca to Medina in 622 A.D. The Chinese chronological system divides history into cycles stretching over 24 million years. The Chinese are now in the fifth millennium of the current cycle, which corresponds more accurately than does the Gregorian calendar to the beginning of the world's oldest cities and states, between 5,000 and 6,000 years ago. Many other alternative dating systems exist. Selecting one over the others constitutes favoritism for a particular society or cultural tradition.

Therefore, most world historians and many specialists in Asian and African, and some in European, U.S., and Latin American history, have moved toward a more secular, or nonreligious, concept, the Common Era. This system still accepts as familiar, at least to Western readers, the dates used in the Western calendar, but it calls the period after the transition a "common" era, since many influential, dynamic societies existed two millennia ago throughout the world, not only in the Judeo-Christian Holy Land. Two millennia ago, the beginning of the Common Era, the Roman Empire was at its height, Chinese and Indian empires ruled large chunks of Asia, and many peoples in the Eastern Hemisphere were linked by trade and religion to a greater extent than ever before. Several African and American urban societies also flourished. Hence this period makes a useful and familiar benchmark. In the new system, events are dated as B.C.E. (before the Common Era) and as C.E. (Common Era, which begins in year 1 of the Christian calendar). This change is an attempt at including all the world's people.

Rethinking the Division of History into Periods

To make world history more comprehensible, historians divide long periods of time into smaller segments, such as "the ancient world" or "modern history," each marked by certain key events or turning points, a system known as **periodization**. For example, scholars of European, Islamic, Chinese, Indonesian, or U.S. history generally agree among themselves on the major eras and turning points for the region or country they study, but world historians need a system that can encompass all parts of the world since most historic events did not affect all regions. For instance, developments that were key to eastern Eurasia, such as the spread of Buddhism, did not directly affect western Eurasia and Africa in these centuries; the Americas remained isolated from the Eastern Hemisphere until about 500 years ago.

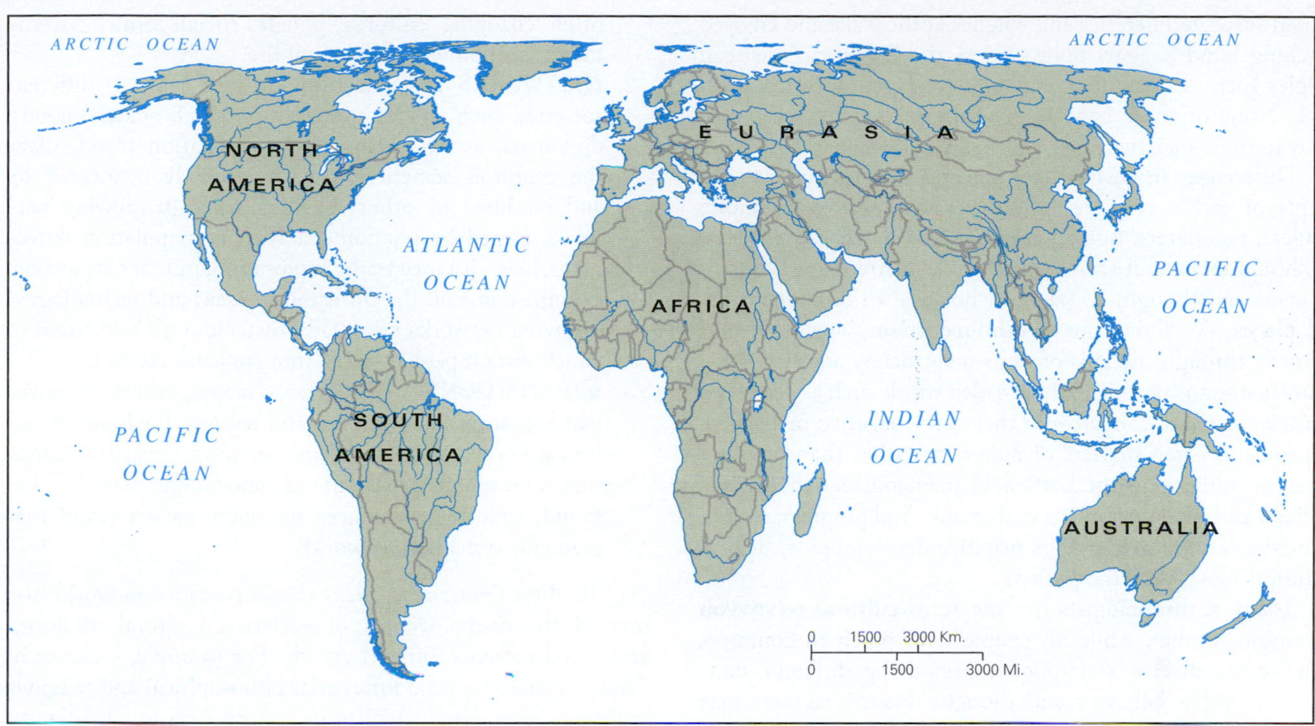

ECKERT PROJECTION

Given the need for an inclusive chronological pattern, this book divides history into periods, each notable for significant changes around the world:

1. **Ancient (100,000–600 B.C.E.)** The Ancient Era, during which the foundations for world history were built, can be divided into two distinct periods. During the long centuries known as Prehistory (ca. 100,000–4000 B.C.E.), Stone Age peoples, living in small groups, survived by hunting and gathering food. Eventually some of them began simple farming and living in villages, launching the era of agrarian societies. Between 4000 and 600 B.C.E., agriculture became more productive, the first cities and states were established in both hemispheres, and some societies invented writing, allowing historians to better study their experiences and ideas.
2. **Classical (600 B.C.E.–600 C.E.)** The creation of more states and complex agrarian societies, the birth of major religions and philosophies, the formation of the first large empires, and the expansion of long-distance trade, which linked distant peoples, marked the Classical Era.
3. **Intermediate (600–1500 C.E.)** The Intermediate Era, comprising a long middle period or "middle ages" of expanding horizons that modified or displaced the classical societies, was characterized by increasing trade connections between distant peoples within the same hemisphere, the growth and spread of several older religions and of a new faith, Islam, and oceanic exploration by Asians and Europeans.
4. **Early Modern (1450–1750 C.E.)** During the Early Modern Era, the whole globe became intertwined as European exploration and conquests in the Americas, Africa, and southern Asia fostered the rise of a global economy, capitalism, and a trans-Atlantic slave trade while undermining American, African, and some other societies.
5. **Modern (1750–1945 C.E.)** Rapid technological and economic change in Europe and North America, Western colonization of many Asian and African societies, political revolutions and ideologies, world wars, and a widening gap between rich and poor societies distinguished the Modern Era.
6. **Contemporary** (1945–present) In the Contemporary Era we see a more closely interlinked world, including the global spread of commercial markets, cultures, and communications, the collapse of Western colonial empires, international organizations, new technologies, struggles by poor nations to develop economically, environmental destruction, and conflict between powerful nations.

Understanding Cultural and Historical Differences

The study of world history challenges us to understand peoples and ideas very different from our own. The past is, as one writer has put it, "a foreign country; they do things differently there."[1] As human behavior changes with the times, sometimes dramatically, so do people's beliefs, including moral and ethical standards. For example, in Asia centuries ago, Assyrians and Mongols sometimes killed everyone in cities that resisted their conquest. Some European Christians seven hundred years ago

[1]P. I. Harley, quoted in David Lowenthal, *The Past Is a Foreign Country* (Cambridge: Cambridge University Press, 1985), p. xvi.

burned suspected heretics and witches at the stake and enjoyed watching blind beggars fight. Across the Atlantic, American peoples such as the Aztecs and Incas engaged in human sacrifice. None of these behaviors would be morally acceptable today in most societies.

Differences in customs complicate efforts to understand people of earlier centuries. We need not approve of empire builders, plunderers, human sacrifice, and witch burning, but we should be careful about applying our current standards of behavior and thought to people who lived in different times and places. We should avoid **ethnocentrism**, viewing others narrowly through the lens of one's own society and its values. Many historians perceive value-loaded words such as *primitive*, *barbarian*, *civilized*, or *progress* that carry negative or positive meanings as often matters of judgment rather than fact. For instance, soldiers on the battlefield may consider themselves civilized and their opponents barbarians. And progress, such as industrialization, often brings negative developments, such as pollution, along with the positive.

Today anthropologists use the term **cultural relativism** to remind us that, while all people have much in common, societies are diverse and unique, embodying different standards of proper behavior and thought. Hence, cultures may have very different ideas about children's obligations to their parents, what happens to people's souls when they die, or what constitutes pleasing music. We can still conclude that Mongol empire builders in Eurasia some eight hundred years ago were brutal; or that the mid-twentieth-century Nazi German dictator, Adolph Hitler, was a murderous tyrant; or that laws in some societies today that blame and penalize women who are raped are wrong. But cultural relativism discourages us from criticizing other cultures or ancient peoples just because they are or were different from us.

The Major Themes

This text uses certain themes to take maximum advantage of world history's power to illuminate both change and continuity as we move from the past to the present. Specifically, the author asked himself: What do educated students today need to know about world history to understand the globalizing era in which they live?

Three broad themes shaped around three concepts—societies, networks, and transitions—help you comprehend how today's world emerged.

1. **SOCIETIES** are broad groups of people that have common traditions, institutions and organized patterns of relationships with each other. Societies, influenced by environmental factors, were defined by distinctive but often changing cultures, beliefs, social forms, governments, economies, and ways of life.
2. **NETWORKS** are collections of links between different societies, such as the routes over which traders, goods, diplomats, armies, ideas, and information travel. Over the centuries societies were increasingly connected to, and modified by other societies, through growing networks forged by phenomena such as population movement, long-distance trade, exploration, military expansion, colonization, and the diffusion of ideas and technologies. Growing networks eventually fostered a global system in which distant peoples came into frequent contact.
3. **TRANSITIONS** are passages, changes, events, or movements that reshape societies and regions. Each major historical era was marked by one or more great transitions that were sparked by events or innovations that had profound, enduring influences on many societies and that gradually reshaped the world.

The first theme recognizes the importance in world history of the distinctiveness of societies. Cultural traditions and social patterns differed greatly. For example, societies in Eurasia fostered several influential philosophical and religious traditions, from Confucianism in eastern Asia to Christianity, born in the Middle East and later nourished both there and in Europe. Historians often identify unique traditions in a society that go back hundreds or even thousands of years.

The second theme acknowledges the way societies have contacted and engaged with each other through networks to create the interdependent world we know today. The spread of technologies and ideas, exploration and colonization, and global trade across Eurasia and Africa and then into the Western Hemisphere spurred this interlinking process. Today networks such as the World Wide Web, airline routes, multinational corporations, and terrorist organizations operate on a global scale. The third theme helps to emphasize major developments that shaped world history. The most important transitions include, roughly in chronological order, the beginning of agriculture, the rise of cities and states, the birth and spread of philosophical and religious traditions, the forming of great empires, the linking of Eurasia by the Mongols, the European seafaring explorations and conquests, the Industrial Revolution, the forging and dismantling of Western colonial empires, world wars, and the invention of electronic technologies that allow for instantaneous communication around the world.

With these themes in mind, the text constructs the rich story of world history. The intellectual experience of studying world history is exciting and will give you a clearer understanding of how the world as you know it came to be.

SOCIETIES, NETWORKS, AND TRANSITIONS

A GLOBAL HISTORY

SOCIETIES

PART I

Ancient Foundations of World History, to ca. 600 B.C.E.

CHAPTER OUTLINE

People today live in the shadow of the ancient peoples who began farming, learned to work metals, and founded the first cities in western Eurasia, Africa, and the Americas. These ancient centuries, and the transitions that marked them, constructed the foundations for much that came later, including organized societies and the growing networks that connected them.

With the first great transition in human history, the introduction of agriculture some 10,000 years ago, people began to deliberately cultivate plants and raise draft animals. Agriculture was the essential building block that stimulated other major developments, in particular the founding of cities and states and the invention of metalworking. We can thank early farmers in Eurasia and northern Africa for giving us, between 10,000 and 5000 B.C.E., valuable inventions such as pottery, cloth, and the plow. New developments then fostered other changes. For example, better means of transportation over land and sea allowed people, goods, ideas, and even diseases to travel longer distances in a shorter time. Expanded trade encouraged cities, and metal weapons and improved transportation allowed city rulers to build or expand states.

Transportation became the basis for networks of trade and cultural exchange linking distant societies. In turn, this wider sharing of ideas helped bring about further transformations in social and cultural patterns. Today, like the ancients, we still get our food mostly from intensive agriculture and livestock raising, work metals into useful products like tools, ride in wheeled vehicles and boats that allow us to travel over long distances, worship in religious buildings, and often live in cities, where people representing several classes and many occupations work and trade. These cities, like ancient cities, are located in powerful states that are administered by bureaucratic governments and protected by military forces. The Ancient Era built the framework for much that came later.

Transitions
Technological Foundations

We can thank the ancient peoples for inventing useful technologies such as metallurgy and for vastly improving transportation. Today we take these technologies for granted; indeed, they are basic to modern industrial life. In ancient times, however, people developed these technologies to help them solve particular problems. Once developed, they had many consequences and spurred many transitions. For example, metallurgy became a key to economic growth but also led to deforestation as forests were cut to make charcoal to fire the kilns. Bronze and, a few centuries later, iron aided agriculture, transportation, and communication (see Map: Metals and Great States ca. 1000 B.C.E.).

The Copper and Bronze Ages

The first metal to be worked was copper. Stoneworkers discovered that heating copper reduced it to liquid form and allowed it to be shaped in a mold. As it cooled, it could be given a good cutting edge. Many peoples in both hemispheres made copper tools and weapons, and they traded copper widely.

Beginning around 3000 B.C.E. in western Asia, metalworkers figured out how to mix copper with tin or arsenic to create bronze. This discovery launched the Bronze Age in the Eastern Hemisphere. The Sumerians were the first society known to use bronze in commerce. Between 2600 and 2000 B.C.E. bronze technology was adopted or invented in northern Africa (Egypt and Nubia), eastern Europe, India, China, and Southeast Asia. In South America, some peoples made use of another copper-arsenic alloy, as well as silver and gold.

Bronze technology affected life. Easier to make and more durable than copper, bronze was well suited for tools, drinking vessels, and weapons. In Hebrew tradition, the formidable biblical Philistine warrior Goliath had a bronze helmet, bronze armor on his legs, and a bronze javelin. Since many regions lacked adequate tin deposits, bronze making probably spurred both trade networks and warfare. Armies were formed in part to protect mines, markets, and trade routes. Metalsmiths were so valuable that invading armies often carried them home in captivity. Finally, copper and bronze, as well as gold and silver, were used for the first coins, which gradually became the major medium of exchange.

The Iron Age

The making of iron provided the next technological breakthrough. Western Asia had little tin but large quantities of iron ore. Iron was much harder to work than copper: artisans needed to produce higher temperatures, and heating produced a spongy mass rather than a liquid. Eventually inventive workers, possibly in the Hittite kingdom along the Black Sea or in Palestine, discovered a completely new but laborious technology that involved repeatedly heating and hammering the iron and plunging the result into cold water.

The Iron Age began in western Asia and Egypt by around 1600 B.C.E. Between 900 and 500 B.C.E., iron technology was also adopted or invented in Greece, India, western and central Europe, Central Asia, China, Southeast Asia, and West and East Africa. Some peoples acquired iron through trade, and others through contact with ironworking peoples. Since ironworking never developed in the Americas or Australia, these societies had no iron weapons or tools. Eurasians and Africans may have benefited from having societies close enough to each other to regularly exchange ideas. In contrast, many thousands of miles, much of it rain forest or desert, separated the societies of North and Mesoamerica from those in the Andes region, limiting contact.

Ironworking brought many advantages. The metal was cheaper to make than bronze and also more adaptable: with it people could produce better axes for cutting wood, plows for farming, wagon wheels for transport, and swords for warfare. For example, in Hebrew tradition, the Israelites could not drive the Canaanites out of the Palestinian lowland because they had iron chariots. Centuries later metalworkers learned how to add carbon to iron to make steel. But like many technologies, iron proved a mixed blessing. While it improved farming, it also made for deadlier weapons. Armies equipped with iron-tipped weapons enjoyed a strategic advantage over their neighbors. Although iron shields afforded some protection, more men may have died as warfare became more frequent.

Transitions

The Rise of Cities and Population Growth

Beginning around 3500 B.C.E. the social and cultural forms common to hunters and gatherers began to change as more and more people settled down to farming and developed more organized societies. Gradually some farming villages became towns and then cities. From the very beginning, ancient cities served a variety of functions. Some, like several Mesopotamian and South American cities, developed as centers for religious ceremonies. Cities in Egypt and China, by contrast, seem to have been founded chiefly as administrative centers to govern the surrounding territories. Many others, including those in India, Nubia, and Mexico, formed around marketplaces. The shift from the relatively egalitarian ethos of hunting and gathering to a more hierarchical social organization changed people's lives. Because trade was a major city activity, merchants became prominent members of urban society, making available products from near and far in their shops and stalls. Increasingly people were divided into social classes, with the wealthier groups controlling the distribution and consumption of economic resources.

Productive agriculture and urbanization fostered a dramatic increase in population around the world. Between 8000 and 500 B.C.E. the world's population jumped from 5 or 10 million up to an estimated 100 million. The great majority of these people lived in Mesopotamia (the most densely populated area), Egypt, India, China, and southeastern Europe. People were also living longer than during the Stone Age, when a third died before age twenty and only a tenth lived past forty. Bronze Age peoples lived into their early forties, and probably 5 to 10 percent lived past sixty.

Networks

Transportation Breakthroughs and Human Mobility

Metalworking was only one of several valuable technologies invented in ancient times. The invention and spread of wheeled vehicles and boats also made it easier for people to migrate or carry cargo over longer distances. The ancient era saw several great migrations involving large numbers of people over the centuries. Using carts and chariots, Indo-European peoples occupied large areas of Eurasia. Traveling by foot or in canoes, and also possessing iron technology, Bantu-speaking peoples from western Africa settled the forests and grasslands of the southern half of Africa. Boat sails had been invented in the Middle East by 5000 B.C.E., allowing wind to be harnessed to drive boats. Using seagoing boats, especially large outrigger canoes, peoples from Southeast Asia sailed to and settled most of the widely scattered Pacific islands. Increasingly better forms of transport made it easier for distant peoples to come into contact with one another and share their ways of life. Maritime trade networks, such as those linking Pacific islands with Southeast Asia and the eastern Mediterranean with northwest Europe, stretched over vast distances.

This increased travel inspired the first maps, drawn in Mesopotamia around 2300 B.C.E. These maps, drawn onto small tablets and then baked, recognized distant relationships in portraying agricultural land, town plans, and the world as known to Babylonians. Such a map from the sixth or seventh century B.C.E. reveals how trade and communication had

METALS AND GREAT STATES CA. 1000 B.C.E. The earliest states arose in river valleys—the Nile, Tigris-Euphrates, Indus, and Yellow—and these early states also worked metals, first bronze and then iron, to produce tools and weapons.

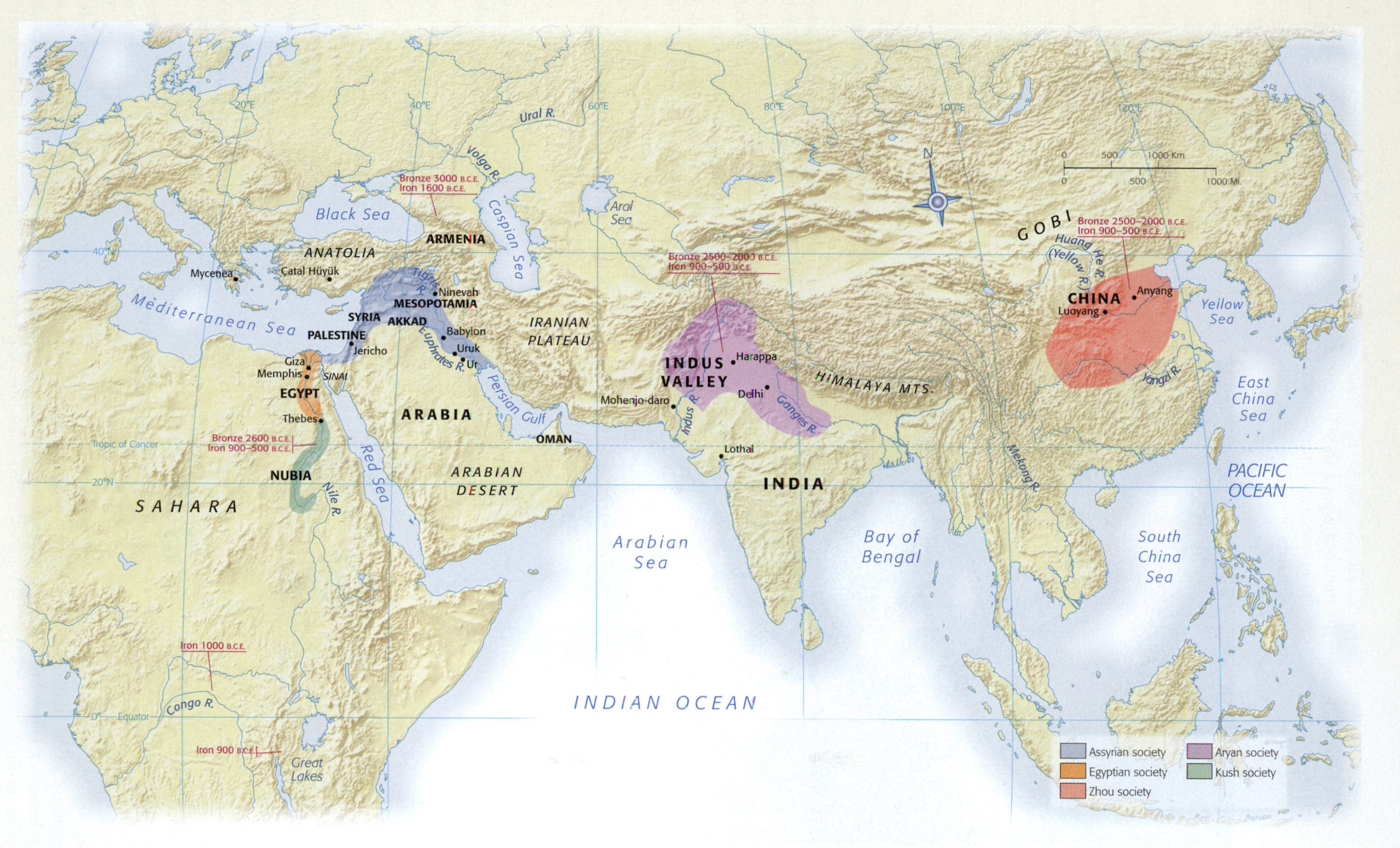

TERRACOTTA FIGURES FROM HARAPPAN CITIES These terracotta figures found in the ruins of Harappa show the diverse hairstyles and ornaments popular in the city. Archaeologists believe that these indicate the diversity of social classes and ethnic groups that inhabited Harappa.

De Agostini/Getty Images

expanded their horizons. The map shows the Babylonian world, including rivers, canals, cities, and neighboring states, in the center of a flat earth, with the remote lands on the fringe inhabited by legendary beasts. The mapmaker noted that his sketch showed the "four corners" of the earth.

Networks
Trade and Networks of Exchange

Trade networks moving objects of value, from raw materials to luxury goods, linked major cities and even distant societies. Between 4000 and 3000 B.C.E. traders began shipping minerals, precious stones, and other valued commodities over long distances, and Mesopotamia became a commercial hub linking southern Asia with Egypt. Beginning around 1200 B.C.E., the heavily urbanized Phoenicians, who lived in what is now Lebanon and Syria, established many trading ports around the Mediterranean, becoming the first known society to flourish mostly through interregional commerce rather than farming. Gradually trade routes expanded over long distances, increasing contacts between societies with different cultures and institutions.

Goods traveled initially by riverboat and by donkey or horse caravans. By 2000 B.C.E., however, sea trading in the Mediterranean Sea, Persian Gulf, and Indian Ocean had become more important. Some areas became trade centers. Mesopotamia was the center of a vast trade network, with links eastward to India and Central Asia and westward to Egypt and Italy. Its location as the hub of this network allowed it to draw ideas, produce, and people from a huge hinterland. Similarly, Egypt connected Africa and Eurasia. The Persian Gulf has served as a contact zone for over five millennia, with various cities serving as major trade hubs.

Trade fostered other innovations. The need to guide ships or caravans to distant destinations, as well as the belief that the changing skies could influence human activity (astrology), sparked the study of the stars. Babylonian astrological beliefs and the zodiac may have been spread by trade to western Asia and southern Europe, where they became popular. Growing trade also required the creation of currencies, without which our modern economic life would be impossible. Simple forms of money, mostly varied weights of precious metals like silver, were invented between 3000 and 2500 B.C.E. in Mesopotamian cities. Legal codes were then written that specified fines, interest rates, and even the ideal price of some common goods. By 600 B.C.E. the first gold coins were being struck in western Asia. Money made exchange easier, especially in cities, and it may have stimulated the development of mathematics as a tool for calculating wealth. Various ancient societies in both hemispheres developed some system of mathematics.

Transitions States, Political Hierarchies, and Warfare

Closely related to urbanization and trade was the emergence of the first states, hierarchically organized political and bureaucratic structures that were governed by powerful elites and that often comprised many cities. States marked a major transition to more complex and organized societies. Kings and emperors, and sometimes queens, ruled over many rural peasants and city dwellers who paid taxes, in money or in agricultural products, in acknowledgment of the ruler's ability to keep order, promote justice, and protect his subjects from harm. According to ancient Hindu sacred writings: "Him do ye proclaim, O men as kings and father of kings, the lordly power, the suzerain of all creation…the slayer of foes, the guardian of the law."[1] Opposition to the ruler and his policies was viewed as treason and could mean death or imprisonment.

The first known states formed in Mesopotamia around 3500 B.C.E. and in Egypt by 3000 B.C.E. Between 3000 and 1000 B.C.E. states were also established in India, China, Vietnam, Nubia, and southeastern Europe, as well as in Mesoamerica and South America. Today we take for granted the notion of large political units to whom people owe allegiance, but in the ancient world they were major innovations. By 2350 B.C.E. the first empires, formed by conquest, appeared in Mesopotamia. Among the consequences of states and empires was the rise of conflict between them as well as with nearby pastoral peoples, which resulted in increased warfare.

One of the chief tasks of the ruler was to protect and perhaps expand his state, and often rulers waged war to acquire land and people and thereby gain more resources and tax revenues. Warfare by settled peoples required a powerful state. To wage war, kings had to marshal resources such as food and metals as well as recruit soldiers. Rulers also had to discourage dissent and instill among the population a sense that warfare was worthwhile. Even today people remember the legends of great ancient warriors (real or mythical), such as Hercules at Troy. But soldiers experienced difficult lives. One Egyptian text reported that a soldier "is awakened when an hour has passed and he is driven like an ass. He works till the sun sets. He is hungry, his body is exhausted, he is dead while still alive. His body is broken with dysentery."[2]

Warfare became increasingly lethal as weaponry and strategy improved. When the powerful Assyrians, who built a great empire, swept through Mesopotamia in the ninth century B.C.E., their advanced cavalry and siege weaponry enabled them to level and burn the great city of Babylon. Later the Assyrians themselves experienced defeat, as their capital, Nineveh, fell to "the noise of the whip and of rattling wheels, galloping horses, clattering chariots!"[3] Even though many ancient cities were surrounded by defensive walls, they were still vulnerable to well-armed foes.

In Afro-Eurasia many wars matched states against pastoral nomads, who were attracted by the wealth of the farming societies and their cities. Often viewed by the farming peoples as "barbarians," nomads possessed many horses or camels and pioneered the development of chariot and cavalry warfare. Between 2000 and 1000 B.C.E. nomadic peoples occasionally conquered cities and states. As an example of how warfare could spawn cultural transitions, many of these pastoralists eventually adopted some of the ways of the conquered farmers, while the urban

[1]From the *Brahmanas*, quoted in F.R. Allchin, *The Archaeology of Historic South Asia: The Emergence of Cities and States* (New York: Cambridge University Press, 1995), 86–87.

[2]Quoted in Barbara Mertz, *Red Land, Black Land: Daily Life in Ancient Egypt*, rev. ed. (New York: Dodd Mead, and Company, 1978), 135–136.

[3]Nahum 3:2–3, *The Holy Bible*, New King James Version (Chicago: Thomas Nelson, 1983), 907.

FRAGMENTS OF EGYPTIAN-HITTITE TREATY This carved stone fragment contains a treaty, signed around 1250 B.C.E., between Egypt and the Hittite kingdom in Anatolia that ended a war between the two states. The treaty is inscribed in the widely used cuneiform script of the Akkadian language. It eloquently demonstrates the reality of ancient warfare but also expresses the age-old quest for peace.

peoples acquired the pastoralists' military technologies.

The costs of war, in treasure and people, also prompted rulers to make peace treaties with rival powers and prompted prophets to call for beating "their swords into ploughshares, their spears into pruning hooks; nation shall not lift up sword against nation."[4] The quest for peace was as old as the urge to wage war.

Societies
Institutionalized Religions

Institutionalized religions shaped the values and behavior of societies. The rise of agriculture and then cities gradually transformed the belief that nature was alive with spiritual forces (animism) to more systematic theologies and organized religious observances. These beliefs and practices gave order and meaning to people's lives and may have promoted cooperation and a sense of community. Ideas about the fate of individual humans after death as well as notions of right and wrong differed widely as societies developed unique traditions and beliefs. While most ancient peoples were polytheists or animists, believing in many gods or spirits, a few, such as the Hebrews and some African societies, were monotheists, believing in one high god who presided over the universe.

Religious views spread from one society to another, at first orally, through myths or stories about the interaction of gods with the human world. These myths explained the birth of the universe, the progression of seasons, the uncertainties of agriculture, the flooding of rivers, and human dramas such as battlefield losses and victories. Religious views and myths were later captured in sacred books, and several thousand years later many millions of people still revere some of these books, such as the Hebrew Bible and the Hindu Vedas. Oral traditions and sacred texts helped Egyptian and Mesopotamian ideas, such as an afterlife, Day of Judgment, and Garden of Eden, to become influential around the Mediterranean Basin and western Asia.

Full-time religious specialists evolved, often replacing the shamans, the part-time spiritual leaders associated with earlier times. With the rise of agriculture and larger communities, a priestly class was seen as able to communicate with the gods and interpret their will. Because they provided essential services such as writing or calculating the time of the annual floods and staffing temples serving thousands of believers, priests were the first social group to be freed from direct subsistence labor.

Institutionalized religions influenced societies. Since religious ceremonies and ideas provided supernatural sanction for the social and political order, they became a powerful force for social control. Challenging the political or social system, which was seen as divinely inspired, now constituted blasphemy and condemned one to eternal punishment after death. Many of the ancient religions, led by men and worshiping chiefly male gods, supported patriarchal attitudes.

Societies
Writing and Its Consequences

Writing, which allowed for recordkeeping and improved communication, was one of the most crucial cultural innovations. Although limited to a relatively small group of people for much of history, writing was a critical invention of several early societies that increased occupational specialization, including the emergence of clerks, scribes, bureaucrats, and eventually teachers, scholars, and historians. Initially developed chiefly to keep commercial accounts, codify legends and rituals, or record political proclamations, writing later gave birth to literature, historiography, sacred texts, and other forms of learning and culture that could now be transmitted and expanded. Hence the Sumerian epic of Gilgamesh influenced both the Hebrew book of Genesis and the stories of the Greek bard Homer many centuries later. Rulers used writing to communicate over long distances with district governors and foreign leaders, and merchants used it to make arrangements with merchants in other cities, enhancing the role of communication networks.

Writing, however, had contradictory consequences. On the one hand, it clearly stimulated creativity and intellectual growth while allowing for a spread of knowledge. But writing often became a tool for preserving the social and political order, especially when literacy was restricted to a privileged elite such as bureaucrats, lawyers, or priests. For example, a soldier in ancient China complained that he and his colleagues wanted to return home, but they "were in awe of the [official] orders in the tablets."[5] Sacred literature was also frequently closed to debate, since it supposedly came from the gods.

Societies
Social Inequality, Patriarchy, and Social Life

With less equality but more people, the potential for social conflict increased. Most communities included haves and have-nots, landlords and landless, free citizens and slaves. The gap between rich and poor made crime a serious problem. Theft was common in major Mesopotamian and Egyptian cities and was addressed through harsh law codes. In societies with large enslaved populations, which included debtors and prisoners of war, revolt was a possibility. Although more pervasive in Mesopotamia than in China, Egypt, and India, slaveholding was common in all ancient agricultural societies.

Patriarchy was another source of inequality and remains a feature of life today. Men increasingly believed that women were unsuited to run governments, and few of them were allowed to do so. Social changes that required heavy physical labor in farming, warfare, and long-distance trade influenced gender and family relations. Women became known as the "weaker sex" and were often assigned chiefly domestic tasks.

[4] Isaiah 2:4, *Holy Bible*, 683.

[5] Quoted in Herlee Glessner Creel, *The Birth of China: A Survey of the Formative Period of Chinese Civilization* (New York: Frederick Unger, 1961), 256.

An ancient Chinese saying asserted that "men plow and women weave."[6] Although women continued to produce some of the pottery and most of the cloth, they were no longer equal contributors to food needs because they now spent more time at home. In farming families, women were also encouraged to bear a larger number of children to help in the fields. In many places, men, especially rulers and the rich, had multiple wives or took concubines. Sexual options became more limited for women because men wanted to ensure that their personal wealth could be passed on to children of known paternity.

Despite the social inequality and long hours of toil, leisure activities developed that are familiar to us today. For example, the Sumerian city dwellers in Mesopotamia enjoyed dancing and music and invented beautiful, elaborate harps and lyres for their pleasure. Chinese music lovers preferred flutes and drums, and Egyptians preferred metal horns. Music was used for worship, festivals, and work, but the oldest known love songs had also appeared by 2300 B.C.E. in Egypt. Wrestling became a popular sport in many cultures.

Alcoholic drinks like beer and wine were also common, often consumed in public taverns, and in many societies drinking became an integral part of leisure and social relationships. Homer summed up the pleasures favored in early Greece: "The things in which we take a perennial delight are the feast, the lyre [a musical instrument], the dance, clean linen in plenty, a hot bath and our beds."[7] These are pleasures that most modern people share, indicating that some things have not changed much in three thousand years.

[6]Quoted in Merry Wiesner-Hanks, *Gender in History* (Malden, MA: Blackwell, 2001), 61.

[7]From Homer's *The Odyssey*, quoted in Rodney Castledon, *Minoans: Life in Bronze Age Crete* (New York: Routledge, 1993), 9.

BELL OF MARQUIES Music had a key function in the court life of Zhou China. This sixty-four-piece bell set was found in the tomb of a regional ruler, which also contained many flutes, drums, zithers, pan pipes, and chimes. Five men using mallets and poles were needed to play this set of bells.

Asian Art & Archaeology, Inc./Corbis

1 The Origins of Human Societies, to ca. 2000 B.C.E.

Pichugin Dmitry/Shutterstock

TASSILI ARCHERS Thousands of ancient paintings on rock surfaces and cave walls record the activities of African hunters, gatherers, and pastoralists. This painting of archers on a hunt was made in a rock shelter on the Tassili plateau of what is today Algeria, probably long before the Sahara region had dried up and become a harsh desert.

It takes a long time to build a mountain.

—Malay proverb

The human story was already very old when, at Abu Hureyra (AH-boo hoo-RAY-rah) in the Euphrates (you-FRAY-teez) River Valley of what is now Syria, a group of villagers became some of the first farmers, thus taking a large step in shaping world history. People who hunted game and gathered vegetables and nuts occupied Abu Hureyra 13,000 years ago, when the area was wetter and blessed with many edible wild plants and herds of Persian gazelles. But a long cold spell brought a drought; to survive, the Abu Hureyra villagers began cultivating the most easily grown grains and later raised domesticated sheep and goats. By 7600 B.C.E. they had shifted completely to farming and animal herding.

The Abu Hureyra farmers pursued a life familiar to rural folk for millennia afterwards. A village was composed of several hundred people crowded into narrow lanes and courtyards, with families dwelling in multiroom mud houses with plaster floors. At night family members studied the sky and pondered the mysteries of the universe. Men did much of the farm work while women carried heavy loads on their heads, prepared meals, and ground grain in a kneeling position, an activity that was hard on arms, knees, and toes. Work for both women and men called for muscle power, and many villagers suffered from arthritis and lower back injuries. Abu Hureyra was abandoned in 5000 B.C.E.

Prehistory includes a vast span of time during which all living creatures appeared and developed. Humans evolved physically, mentally, and culturally over many millennia, learning to make simple tools and then spreading throughout the world. Later most societies, like the Abu Hureyra villagers, made the first great historical transition from hunting and gathering to farming and animal herding, profoundly changing the relationship between people and the environment. The rise of agriculture all over the world made possible the emergence of larger societies with cities and states, which in turn stimulated long-distance trade and the rise of social, cultural, and economic networks linking distant societies.

IN THIS CHAPTER

Prehistory: The Cosmos, Earth, and the Roots of Humanity

According to most scientists, what were the various stages of human evolution?

Some scholars have promoted a "big history" that places the development of human societies and networks in a much longer and more comprehensive framework. We cannot comprehend the rise of complex societies without knowledge of prefarming peoples, human ancestors, and, before that, the beginning of life on earth and the formation of our planet within the larger cosmic order. Recurring patterns of balance and imbalance and of order and disorder in the natural world, such as global warming and cooling, have always played a role in human history. People have speculated about the origins of the cosmos, earth, life, and humanity for countless generations. Over the years their views have been integrated into religions.

Perceptions of Cosmic Mysteries

Human development on earth constitutes only a tiny fraction of the long history of the universe, which most astronomers think began in a Big Bang explosion some 13.7 billion years ago. As the universe expanded, matter coalesced into stars, which formed into billions of galaxies. Our solar system emerged about 4.5 billion years ago out of clouds of gas. On earth the developing atmosphere kept the surface warm enough for organic compounds to coalesce into life forms. This is the story presented by modern science.

Over the centuries most human societies, to explain their existence, crafted creation stories and cosmologies explaining the natural and supernatural worlds. While varying greatly, these explanations usually involved myths or legends of some divine creator or creators. The earliest known creation story, from Mesopotamia, claimed that heaven and earth were formed as one in a primeval sea and were separated by the gods, powerful human-like beings unperceivable to mortals. Mesopotamian beliefs influenced the seven-day creation story in the Hebrew book of Genesis.

Many cosmological traditions, however, were very different. Ancient Hindu holy books describe a universe emerging out of nothingness: "There was neither nonexistence or existence then . . . neither the realm of space nor the sky which is beyond. Darkness was hidden by darkness . . . emptiness."[1] Then a great heat formed the cosmos and generated life. The Chinese believed that the universe was created out of chaos and darkness when the creator Pan Ku fashioned the sun, moon, and stars to put everything in proper order, producing a unifying force in the universe, the "way," or dao (DOW). A related Chinese theory, *fengshui* (fung-SHWAY), suggests that the earth itself contains natural forces that people must comprehend in order to properly situate buildings and graves, ideas that recently gained a following in Western countries.

Early Life and Evolutionary Change

"Life," meaning organisms able to consume food, grow, and reproduce with a genetic code, has a long history. Simple, single-celled life emerged by perhaps 3.5 to 3.8 billion years ago and remained dominant until about a half billion years ago, when complex life forms proliferated in incredible variety.

[1]From the *Rig Veda*, quoted in Carolyn Brown Heinz, *Asian Cultural Traditions* (Prospect Heights, IL: Waveland, 1999), 132.

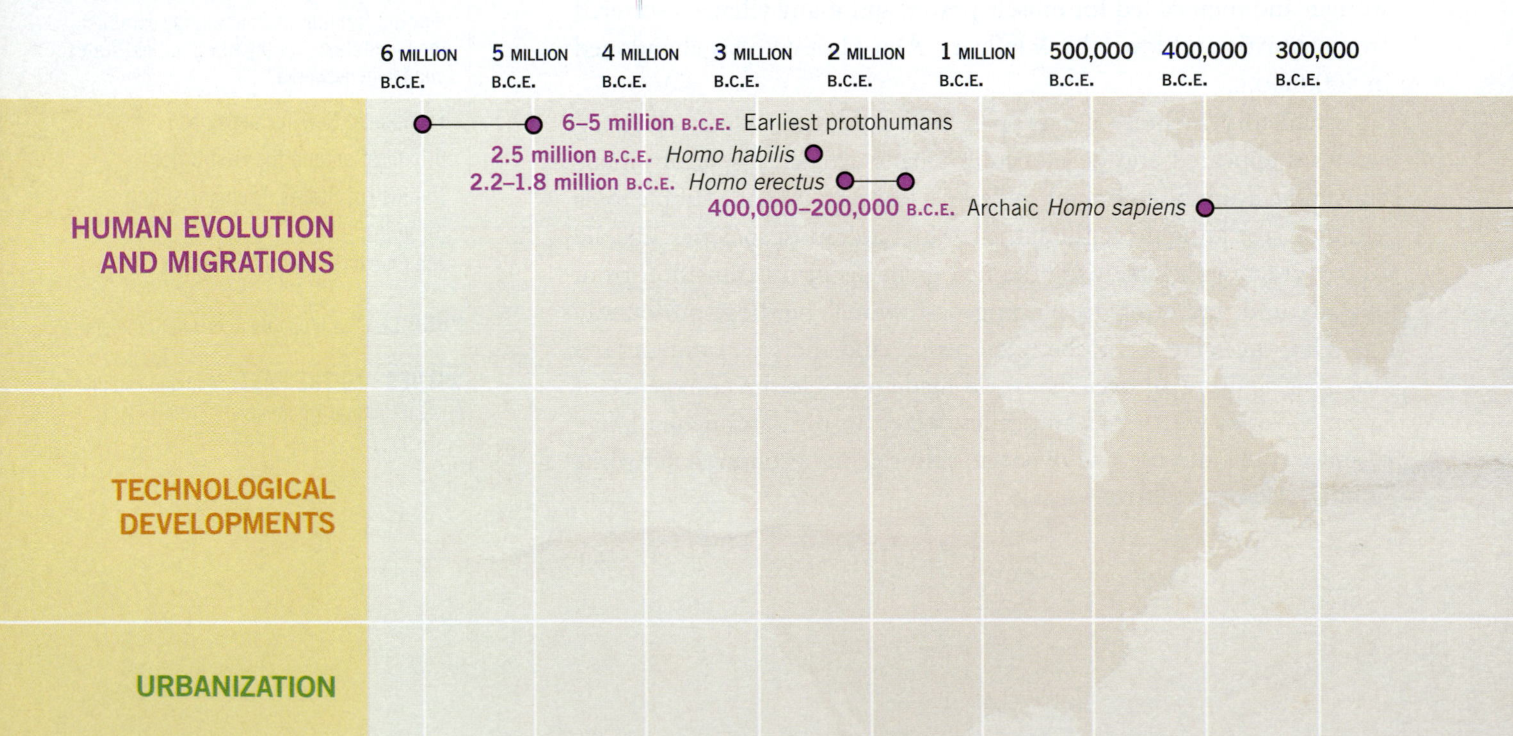

Animal life colonized the land between 400 and 500 million years ago and evolved into many species. Volcanic and earthquake activity caused by plate movements influenced human history, and sometimes intense volcanic eruptions dramatically altered regional climates. Warmer or cooler climates helped shape human societies and sometimes undermined them.

Most natural scientists agree that living things change over many generations through evolution, modifying their genetic composition to adapt to their environment. In the nineteenth century the British biologist Charles Darwin explained the process with his theory of natural selection: individuals developed variations that helped them to compete for food and domination within their own species and to triumph over rival species. Scientists still debate evolution's mechanisms but mostly confirm Darwin's basic insights that species, including humans, are shaped by their changing biological and physical environment.

A half dozen massive species extinctions have occurred in the past 400 million years. For example, 250 million years ago gigantic volcanic eruptions produced enough climate-changing gases to almost wipe out all life. The best-known extinction involved the dinosaurs, which flourished for 150 million years before dying out about 65 million years ago, probably from the cooling of the planet from increasing volcanic activity combined with the cataclysmic impact of one or several large asteroids or comets smashing into the earth, destroying food sources and killing off about 70 percent of all species. This occurrence gave mammals a chance to rise, and one group eventually evolved into humans. So far humans have been lucky. Scientists estimate that 99 percent of all species eventually became extinct when conditions changed dramatically. Yet species have died rapidly over the past two hundred years, most likely because of environmental changes such as pollution, habitat removal, and global warming generated by human activity.

Eventually evolutionary changes among one branch of mammals led to the immediate ancestors of humans, which are part of the primate order, the mammal category that includes the apes. Although human–chimp lines diverged sometime before 5 or 6 million years ago, over 98 percent of human DNA is the same as that of chimpanzees. By using their superior brain to gain an evolutionary edge, humans ultimately dominated other large animal species. They formed complex social organizations that emphasized cooperation for mutual benefit, developed tools, mastered fire, and learned how to use speech, all of which gave them great advantages. Ultimately they developed a more complex technology to manipulate the physical environment in many ways to meet their needs.

Hominids (HOM-uh-nids), a family including humans and their immediate ancestors, first evolved 5 to 6 million years ago from more primitive primates in Africa, where the span of human prehistory is much longer than anywhere else. The most extensive fossil evidence comes from the southern African plateau and the Great Rift Valley of East Africa, a wide, deep chasm stretching from Ethiopia south to Tanzania. Scientists vigorously debate fossil and artifact remains and whether teeth, skulls, and bones belong to ancestors of humans or apes, but fossil discoveries point to several stages and branches in early human evolution. A common ancestral, apelike group living in the woodlands and savannahs of East Africa developed occasional and then permanent bipedalism (walking upright on two feet), making more activity possible by leaving hands free for holding food or babies, making and manipulating objects such as tools, and carrying food back to camp. Bipeds, being higher off the ground, could also scan the horizon for predators or prey.

Several hominid groups apparently coexisted at the same time, but only one led to modern humans. Several branches of early

Hominids A family including humans and their immediate ancestors.

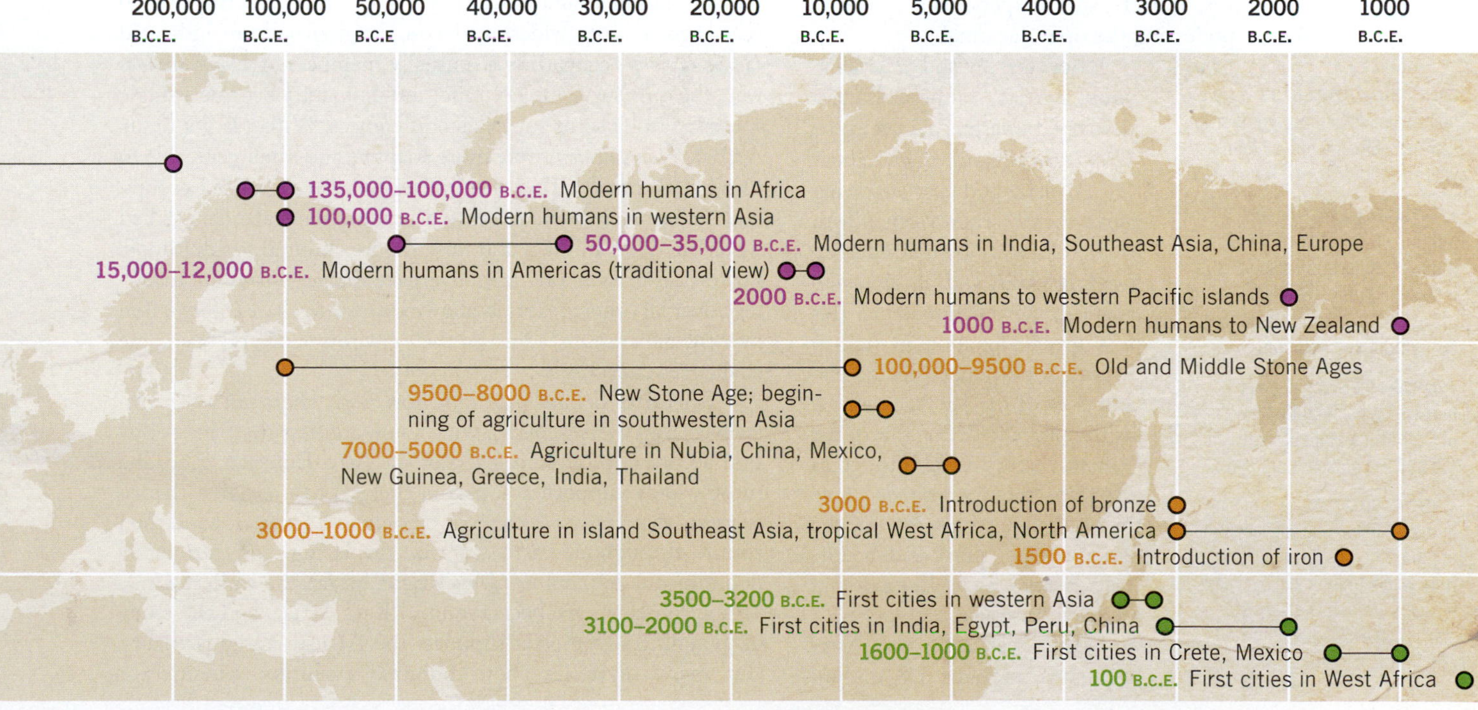

hominids known as **australopithecines** (aw-strah-lo-PITH-uh-seens) lived in eastern and southern Africa 4 or 5 million years ago with brains about one-third the size of our brains. In Ethiopia, archaeologists unearthed the bones of a small female, named Lucy by anthropologists, who probably walked mostly on her feet but also climbed trees. Scholars disagree as to whether these hominids might be the ancestors to modern humans.

Some 2.5 million years ago one branch of australopithecines evolved into our direct ancestor. The earth cooled, fostering the first of a series of Ice Ages, which covered large areas of northern Eurasia and North America with deep ice sheets and glaciers. As Africa and its hominid inhabitants experienced a drier climate and more open habitats, the challenges posed by this climate change encouraged increased intelligence. ***Homo habilis*** (HOH-moh HAB-uh-luhs) ("handy human") had a larger brain size and ability to make and use simple stone tools for hunting and gathering. Stone choppers and later hand axes made possible a more varied diet, more successful hunting, and larger groups that could cooperate to share food. The other branches of australopithecines died out.

As hominid societies developed, males increasingly became the hunters or scavengers for meat and females the gatherers of nuts and vegetables. Although meat became a more crucial protein source, gathering still probably brought more food than hunting or scavenging. These early humans were probably mainly vegetarians, like many primates today. Cooperation between the sexes and group members was the key to survival and probably involved communication through gestures and vocal cries.

Homo Erectus and Migrations Out of Africa

Probably between 1.8 and 2.2 million years ago, when their environment fluctuated, more advanced hominids, called ***Homo erectus*** ("erect human"), evolved from *Homo habilis* in East Africa. They had a brain about two-thirds the size of ours and eventually developed a more complex and widespread tool culture including hand axes, cleavers, and scrapers. They spread to other parts of Africa, preferring the open savannah.

australopithecines Early hominids living in eastern and southern Africa 4 to 5 million years ago.

Homo habilis ("handy human") A direct ancestor of humans, so named because of its increased brain size and ability to make and use simple stone tools for hunting and gathering.

Homo erectus ("erect human") A hominid that emerged in East Africa probably between 1.8 and 2.2 million years ago.

Homo sapiens ("thinking human") A hominid who evolved around 400,000 years ago and from whom anatomically modern humans (*Homo sapiens sapiens*) evolved around 100,000 years ago.

Between 1 and 2 million years ago, as southern Eurasia developed a warmer climate, some *Homo erectus* bands migrated out of Africa, perhaps following game herds. They carried with them refined tools, more effective hunting skills, and an ability to adapt to new environments. This first great migration in human history corresponded to the ebb and flow of the Ice Ages as well as the periodic drying out of the Sahara region. Over thousands of years these hominids came to occupy northern Africa, the Middle East, South and Southeast Asia, China, Europe, and perhaps Australia.

The earliest non-African sites, perhaps 1.8 million years old, have been found in the Caucasus (KAW-kuh-suhs) Mountains of western Asia. Bones and tools discovered in Chinese caves and skulls from the Indonesian island of Java, then connected to mainland Asia, have been dated at 1.6 to 1.9 million years ago, and *Homo erectus* may have been widespread in East and Southeast Asia by 1.5 million years ago. Fossils from frigid eastern Siberia date back 300,000 years, indicating how adaptable and resourceful the species had become. These hominids also lived in Spain by 800,000 B.C.E. However, their tool cultures differed somewhat from those of Chinese *Homo erectus*, indicating cultural diversity and perhaps major variation from the Asian species. By 500,000 years ago *Homo erectus* in China lived in closely knit groups, engaged in cooperative hunting, and used both wood and bamboo for containers and weapons. Most lived in caves, but some built simple wooden huts for shelter. Their hand axes were the Swiss army knives of their time, with a tip for piercing, thin edges for cutting, and thick edges for scraping and chipping. Scientists debate whether *Homo erectus* could use speech.

Discovering how to start and control fire was perhaps the most significant human invention. Where or when people first used fire or how many millennia it took for knowledge of fire to spread widely remains unclear; *Homo erectus* probably controlled fire at least 1 million years ago. Fire opened up many possibilities, providing warmth and light after sunset, frightening away predators, and making possible a more varied diet of cooked food, which fostered group living and cooperation as people gathered together around campfires. Fire also enabled ancestral humans to spread to cooler regions, such as Europe and northern Asia.

The Evolution and Diversity of *Homo Sapiens*

The transition from *Homo erectus* to archaic forms of ***Homo sapiens*** ("thinking human"), a species physically close to modern humans, began around 400,000 years ago in Africa. By 200,000 years ago a more widespread complex tool culture indicated *Homo sapiens* occupation. Eventually members of *Homo sapiens* were the only surviving hominids and humanity became a single species, despite some superficial differences. With a larger brain, Archaic *Homo sapiens* were more adaptive and intelligent, able to think conceptually. They lived in fairly large organized groups, built temporary shelters, created crude lunar calendars, killed whole herds of animals, and raised more children to adulthood. Possession of symbolic language gave *Homo sapiens* an advantage over all other creatures, allowing them to share information over the generations, adjust to their environment, and overcome challenges collectively.

Scientists debate precisely how and where *Homo erectus* evolved into *Homo sapiens*, with some arguing that the evolution occurred in different parts of the Afro-Eurasian zone. The most widely supported scenario, the African Origins theory, suggests that *Homo sapiens* evolved only in East Africa and then spread throughout Afro-Eurasia, displacing and ultimately dooming the remaining *Homo erectus*. So far, the earliest *Homo sapiens* remains have been found in East Africa, and the study of genetic codes mostly supports the African Origins theory. But many mysteries about hominid evolution remain. For

John Reader/Photo Researchers/Science Source

THE LAETOLI FOOTPRINTS Some 4 million years ago in Tanzania, three australopithecines walked across a muddy field covered in ash from a nearby volcanic eruption. When the mud dried, their tracks were permanently preserved, providing evidence of some of the earliest upright hominids.

example, the 18,000-year-old bones of diminutive but tool-using hominids, 3 to 3.5 feet tall as adults, on the small Indonesian island of Flores sparked debate as to where these fossils fit into the human family tree. The Flores people (nicknamed by observers "hobbits" because of their small stature) may have been miniature versions of *Homo erectus* or *Homo sapiens* or perhaps constituted some unknown, and more primitive, human-like species. Reflecting a mix of primitive and modern features, the venison-eating Red Deer Cave people who lived in China some 11,000–15,000 years ago present another puzzle.

However the evolution into *Homo sapiens* occurred, all humans came to constitute one species that could interbreed and communicate with each other. It remains unclear whether a few differences in physical features, such as skin and hair color and eye and face shape, developed earlier or later in *Homo sapiens* evolution. The diverse groupings were once labeled "races," meaning large groups that shared distinctive genetic traits and physical characteristics. But experts often dismiss the race concept for its inability to classify human populations. Observable physical attributes such as skin color reflect a tiny portion of one's genetic makeup and thus cannot always predict whether two groups are genetically similar or different. Since much genetic intermixing occurred, many people are difficult to classify. Humans are much more similar than different.

Sometime between 135,000 and 100,000 years ago in Africa, anatomically modern humans with slightly larger brains, known as *Homo sapiens sapiens*, developed out of *Homo sapiens*. With this biological change, language and culture expanded in new directions and developed many variations. Scholars debate whether creativity, intelligence, and even language abilities were innate to *Homo sapiens sapiens*, as suggested by engraved pigments and advanced stone tools in South African caves from 75,000 to 100,000 years ago, or arose only some 50,000 years ago, possibly as a result of a genetic mutation. With this great transition humanity reached its present level of intellectual and physical development, establishing the foundation for the constant expansion of information networks to a global level.

Modern human language development made possible complex cultures with shared learning and became the main method of communication for much of history. Some 5,000 or 6,000 languages emerged around the globe. Some, such as English and German, have a clear common ancestry, but scholars debate the relationships and origins of most of the world's languages. Human intellectual development also included abstract, symbolic thought, revealed early in decoration and art. Ocher (O-ker), for example, a natural red iron oxide, was mined in various African locations and probably used for body decoration. The gorgeous cave and rock art of southwestern Europe, Africa, western Asia, and Australia traces back at least 30,000 to 40,000 years and probably had magical, religious, or ritual purposes, such as the celebration of spirits or valued animals.

The Globalization of Human Settlement

Between 50,000 and 12,000 years ago restless modern humans settled much of the world. As people spread, genetic differences grew and *Homo sapiens sapiens* proved able to adapt to many environments. By 100,000 years ago some had already left Africa to settle in Palestine. Human settlement might not have expanded much beyond Africa and southwestern Asia until 50,000 years ago. But rising sea levels at the end of the last Ice Age may also have covered evidence that might allow us to trace migration routes along southern Asian coasts. Eventually modern humans reached central and eastern Eurasia, from where some moved on to Australia and the Americas.

Modern humans crossed to the eastern fringe of Asia, arriving in India and Southeast Asia between 40,000 and 50,000 years ago, China between 35,000 and 50,000 years ago, and Europe between 35,000 and 45,000 years ago (see Map 1.1). To reach Australia and New Guinea from Southeast Asia across a very shallow sea required rafts or boats, but modern humans may have settled there between 60,000 and 45,000 B.C.E. The peopling of the Pacific islands to the east began much later, around 2000 B.C.E.

Beginning around 200,000 years ago, a vibrant new tool culture emerged in Europe that has been identified with the **Neanderthals** (nee-AN-der-thals), hominids

Neanderthals Hominids who were probably descended from *Homo erectus* populations in Europe and who later spread into western and Central Asia.

MAP 1.1 SPREAD OF MODERN HUMANS AROUND THE GLOBE Most scholars believe that modern humans originated in Africa and that some of them began leaving Africa around 100,000 years ago. Gradually they spread out through Eurasia. From eastern Asia, some crossed to the Americas.

30°W
0°
30°E
60°E
90°E
120°E
150°E
180°
150°W
120°W
90°W
60°W
30°W
60°N
30°N
0°—Equator
30°S
60°S
ASIA
NORTH AMERICA
AFRICA
ATLANTIC OCEAN
PACIFIC OCEAN
INDIAN OCEAN
SOUTH AMERICA
ATLANTIC OCEAN
AUSTRALIA
N
ANTARCTICA

Areas of human occupation
100,000 years ago
100,000–40,000 years ago
40,000–10,000 years ago

Probable migration routes
Before 100,000 years ago
After 100,000 years ago

Probable coastline, 20,000 years ago
Ice sheets, 20,000 years ago

0 1500 3000 Km.
0 1500 3000 Mi.

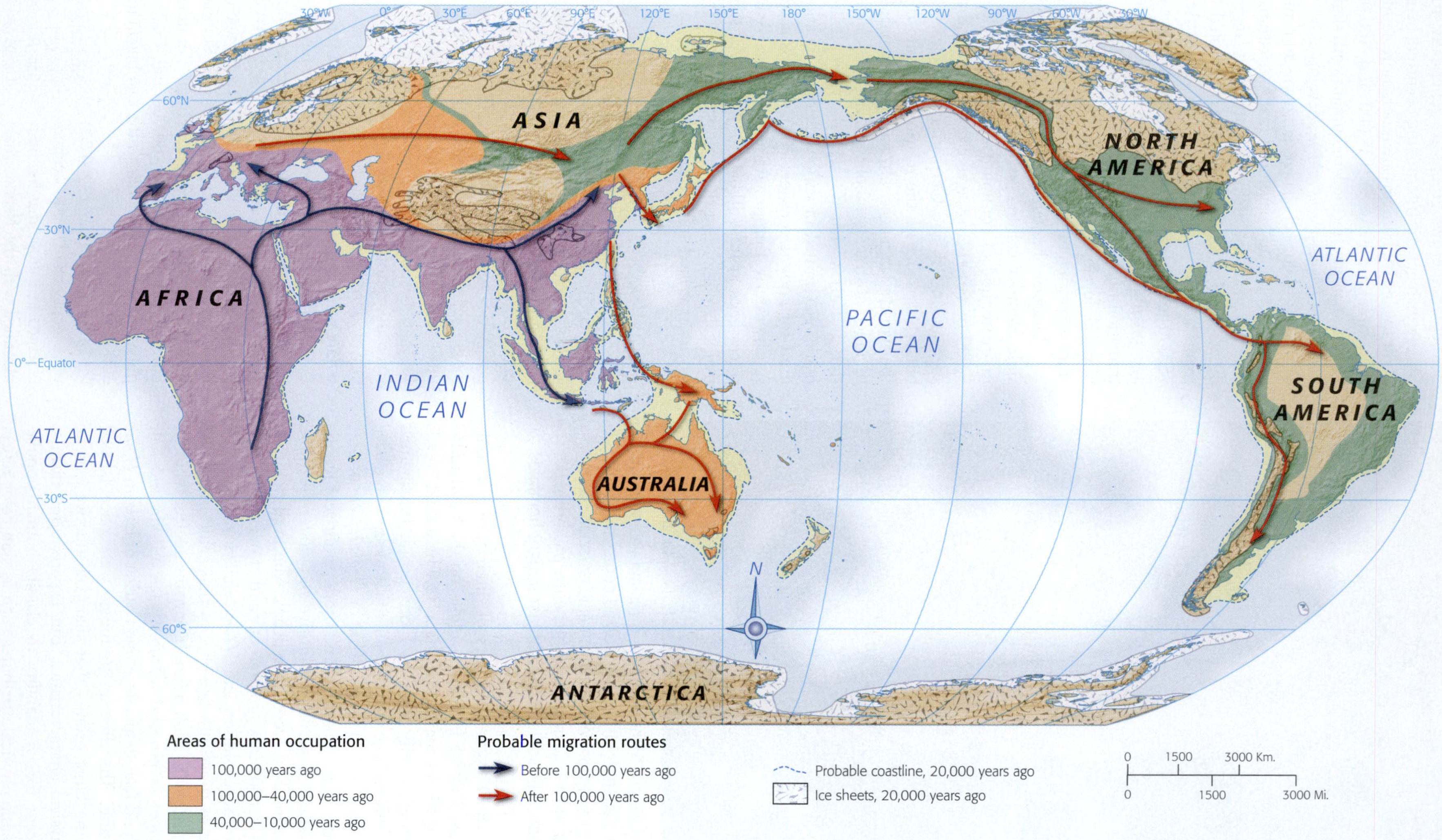

probably related to *Homo erectus* who gradually inhabited a wide region stretching from Spain and Germany to western and Central Asia to North Africa. Skillful hunters, the Neanderthals maintained social values, buried their dead, and cared for the sick. Their cranial capacity equaled or even exceeded that of *Homo sapiens*, and they had larger bodies. Scholars debate whether they possessed spoken language, but agree that they were capable of communication, used tools, made bone flutes, wore jewelry, and sailed boats to Mediterranean islands. Recent fossil discoveries in Siberia suggest that a species related to Neanderthals, known as **Denisovans** (dun-EE-suh-vinz), may have once been widespread in eastern Eurasia before the arrival of modern humans, but their exact relationship to the Neanderthals and to *Homo sapiens sapiens* is a matter of debate. By 70,000 years ago both Neanderthals and modern humans lived in Palestine. Whether Neanderthals in Europe died out before the modern, tool-using humans known as **Cro-Magnons** (krow-MAG-nuns) arrived in Europe from Asia or whether they coexisted with the newcomers for several millennia is again unclear. DNA studies suggest that Neanderthals were a rather different species from Cro-Magnons. However, recent and controversial studies suggest that modern humans in Europe and Asia (but not Africa) may have a small number of Neanderthal or Denisovan genes, suggesting some interbreeding. Whether Neanderthals were ultimately annihilated, outnumbered, outcompeted, or assimilated by the more resourceful and adaptable modern humans, who had better technology and warmer clothing, remains unknown.

Archaeologists long thought that the peopling of the Americas came very late, the earliest migration into North America occurring only 12,000 to 15,000 years ago. But recent discoveries suggest that the pioneer arrivals may have crossed from Northeast Asia, probably in very small numbers, as early as 20,000 or possibly even 30,000 or 40,000 years ago (see Chapter 4). At various times a wide Ice Age land bridge connected Alaska and Siberia across today's Bering Strait, and the evidence for a migration chiefly from Asia over thousands of years is strong. The first settlers moved by land or by boat along the coast. A few controversial studies suggest that some Stone Age settlers arrived in eastern North America from Spain. Nonetheless, gradually Asian migrants settled throughout the Western Hemisphere, becoming the ancestors of today's Native Americans. DNA research suggests that all modern Native Americans, from North America to Chile, are closely related to each other and to several peoples in eastern Siberia or the Altai region of Central Asia. Some Native American languages also have a distant but clear connection to several Siberian languages.

MAKE SURE YOU UNDERSTAND THESE KEY POINTS BEFORE MOVING ON

- **Early hominids first evolved in Africa (most likely East Africa) 4 to 6 million years ago.**
- **Of the early hominids, our direct ancestor, *Homo habilis*, was most successful because it used simple stone tools.**
- ***Homo erectus* developed more refined tools and migrated to Eurasia and throughout Africa; *Homo sapiens* had larger brains and evolved into modern humans, who developed language and spread throughout the world.**
- **Though humans from different parts of the world may have different appearances, their genetic differences are insignificant.**

The Odyssey of Early Human Societies

How did hunting and gathering shape life during the long Stone Age?

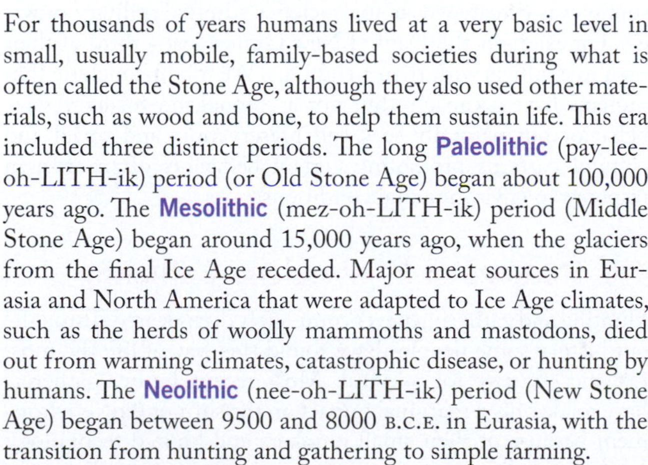

For thousands of years humans lived at a very basic level in small, usually mobile, family-based societies during what is often called the Stone Age, although they also used other materials, such as wood and bone, to help them sustain life. This era included three distinct periods. The long **Paleolithic** (pay-lee-oh-LITH-ik) period (or Old Stone Age) began about 100,000 years ago. The **Mesolithic** (mez-oh-LITH-ik) period (Middle Stone Age) began around 15,000 years ago, when the glaciers from the final Ice Age receded. Major meat sources in Eurasia and North America that were adapted to Ice Age climates, such as the herds of woolly mammoths and mastodons, died out from warming climates, catastrophic disease, or hunting by humans. The **Neolithic** (nee-oh-LITH-ik) period (New Stone Age) began between 9500 and 8000 B.C.E. in Eurasia, with the transition from hunting and gathering to simple farming.

Hunting, Gathering, and Cooperation

The earliest and simplest forms of society, small groups of twenty to sixty members, depended on members cooperating to fish, hunt live animals, scavenge for dead or dying animals, and gather edible plants, a subsistence way of life that depended on naturally occurring resources. Improved tools made possible more food options and better weapons against predators or rivals, and hunting became more important. When the bow and arrow were invented in Africa, Europe, and southwestern Asia at least 15,000 years ago, hunters could kill large animals at a safer distance. Although the main hunters, men, gained prestige, meat usually provided a small part of the diet. Some coastal peoples became skilled deep-sea fishermen by 40,000 years ago.

The gathering by women of edible vegetation such as

Denisovans Hominids related to Neanderthals who lived in eastern Eurasia.

Cro-Magnons The first modern, tool-using humans in Europe.

Paleolithic The Old Stone Age, which began 100,000 years ago with the first modern humans and lasted for many millennia.

Mesolithic The Middle Stone Age, which began around 15,000 years ago as the glaciers from the final Ice Age began to recede.

Neolithic The New Stone Age, which began between 10,000 and 11,500 years ago with the transition to simple farming.

fruits and nuts was probably more essential for group survival than obtaining meat, giving women status and influence. This is still true among many hunter-gatherers today. Furthermore, women probably helped develop new technologies such as grinding stones, nets (to catch small animals), baskets, and primitive cloth. Woven cloth clothing appeared by 28,000 years ago, and pottery at least 18,000 years ago in China.

The hunter-gatherer way of life may not have been as impoverished as we sometimes imagine. Many societies were creative, inventing fishhooks, harpoons, fuel lamps, dugout boats, and canoes. Twentieth-century hunter-gatherers, such as the Mbuti (em-BOO-tee) of the Congo rain forest and the !Kung of the Kalahari Desert, enjoyed varied, healthy diets, long life expectancies, considerable economic security, and a rich communal life. Many spent only ten to twenty hours a week in collecting food and establishing camps and had plenty of time for music, dance, and socializing. Yet hunter-gatherers always faced serious challenges. Early humans had to make their own weapons and clothing and construct temporary huts. For some groups, life remained precarious and many died young, since not all enjoyed access to adequate food resources.

Hunting and gathering generally encouraged cooperation, fostering closely knit communities based on kinship. Members communicated with one another and passed information from one generation to another, conveying a sense of the past and traditions. Personal relationships were paramount, while obtaining material wealth was devalued because the mostly nomadic way of life made individual accumulation of material possessions impractical. These small groups shared food resources among the immediate family and friends, thus helping to ensure survival and promoting an intense social life. But harmony and mutual affection were not guaranteed. Those who violated group customs could be killed or banished, and sometimes conflicts split groups apart. Most hunter-gatherer bands had no government or leader; social responsibilities linked people together in egalitarian relationships; and all members generally had equal access to resources. Yet groups often tended to reward the most resourceful members.

Women and men probably enjoyed a comparable status, as they do in many hunter-gathering societies today. As key providers of food, women may have participated alongside men in group decision making. They also likely held a special place in religious practice as bearers of life. Midwives were highly respected. **Matrilineal** (mat-ruh-LIN-ee-uhl) **kinship** patterns, which trace descent and inheritance through the female line, were probably common, as they are today in these societies. But stronger and often more assertive men enjoyed some advantages over women. Although childbearing influenced women's roles, women were not constantly pregnant. Since it was necessary to limit group size to avoid depleting environmental resources, most societies practiced birth control and abortion. Breastfeeding an infant for several years suppressed ovulation and created longer intervals between pregnancies. Paleolithic populations grew slowly, perhaps by only 10 percent a century.

Matrilineal kinship A pattern of kinship that traces descent and inheritance through the female line.

animism The belief that all creatures as well as inanimate objects and natural phenomena have souls and can influence human well-being.

polytheism A belief in many spirits or deities.

shamans Specialists in communicating with or manipulating the supernatural realm.

Cultural Life and Violence

Some aspects of culture that we might recognize today were taking shape, such as religious belief. As people sought to understand dreams, death, and natural phenomena, they developed both **animism** (ANN-uh-miz-um)—the belief that all creatures, as well as inanimate objects and natural phenomena, have souls and can influence human well-being—and **polytheism** (PAUL-e-thee-ism), the belief in many spirits or deities. Since spirits were thought capable of helping or harming a person, **shamans** (SHAW-mans), specialists in communicating with or manipulating the supernatural realm, became important; many shamans were women. Some social activities developed early, including music, dance, making and drinking beer or wine, and painting on rocks and cave walls. Primitive flutes can be traced back 45,000 years. Dancing and singing likely promoted togetherness.

Egalitarian, self-sufficient societies enriched by spirituality and leisure activities may sound appealing to many modern people, but violence between and within different societies has also been a part of human culture throughout history. Predators such as bears, wolves, and lions hunted people, perhaps instilling a terror of dangerous animals, apparent in myths and folklore, and a tendency to justify violence. Men proved their bravery to attract females.

Anthropologists debate whether humans are inherently aggressive and warlike or peaceful and cooperative. Today's hunter-gatherer or simple agriculture societies suggest that both patterns are common. Some peoples, such as the Hopi and Zuni Indians of the American Southwest, the Penan of Borneo, and many Australian Aborigines, have generally avoided armed conflict. But most societies have engaged in at least occasional violence, such as when their survival or food supply was threatened. Some societies admired military prowess. For example, the Dani of New Guinea lost a third of their men to conflicts with their neighbors. We might conclude that humans have a capacity but not a compulsion for aggressive behavior but naturally seek self-preservation, and social and cultural patterns promoting certain behaviors often arise in response to environmental conditions.

The Heritage of Hunting and Gathering

Hunting and gathering never completely disappeared. Throughout history some peoples have found this way of life the most realistic strategy for survival. Most recent hunter-gatherers have made only a marginal impact on the surrounding environment because of their small numbers and limited technology. Learning to live within environmental constraints, they were highly successful adapters. Although generating little material wealth, hunting and gathering remained viable for many societies, such as Australian Aborigines, until modern times.

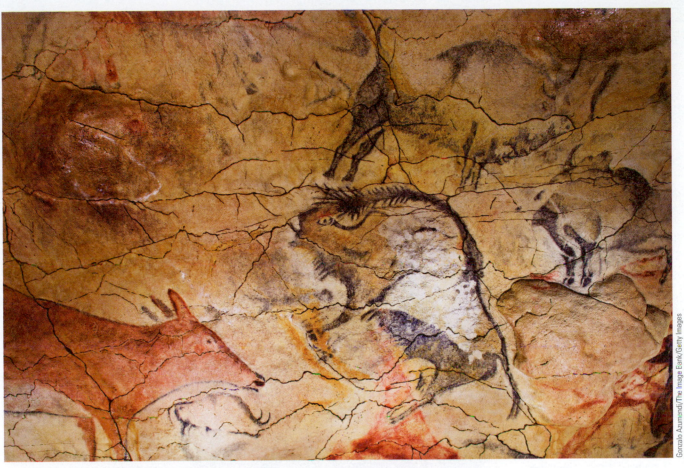

Gonzalo Azumendi/The Image Bank/Getty Images

CAVE PAINTINGS IN EUROPE. This Ice Age painting of bison and deer is from a cave in Altamira, Spain. Many paintings on cave walls have been found in France and Iberia. Paleolithic peoples all over the world painted pictures of the animals they hunted or feared as well as of each other, suggesting an increasing self-awareness.

Australia was the only inhabitable continent where agriculture never developed before modern times, largely because populations remained small, much of the continent was harsh desert, and the Aborigines were skillful hunter-gatherers. But trade routes spanned the continent, and many Aborigines developed notions of land management as well as rich mythologies about their origins and their relationship to the fragile environment.

Although we must be cautious in comparing modern hunters and gatherers to peoples who lived many millennia ago, today's few remaining hunter-gatherers can probably reveal something about ancient societies (see Profile: The !Kung Hunters and Gatherers). But this way of life may disappear during the twenty-first century. In recent decades many societies have been disrupted or destroyed by logging, commercial fishing, plantation development, dam building, tourism, and other activities that exploit their environments. For example, in the Amazon Basin, the burning of rain forests and opening of new land for farming or mining overwhelm many Native American groups. These peoples, defenseless against modern technology, may have to make the same transition to new survival strategies as other peoples did millennia ago.

MAKE SURE YOU UNDERSTAND THESE KEY POINTS BEFORE MOVING ON

- **During the Paleolithic and Mesolithic eras, people lived in small groups of hunters and gatherers.**
- **In general, women gathered fruits and nuts, which provided the majority of the food, while men hunted game.**
- **Hunting and gathering groups were usually close-knit and egalitarian, though violence was not unknown.**
- **Anthropologists are undecided as to whether humans have a natural tendency toward violence or peace.**

PROFILE

The !Kung Hunters and Gatherers

While all societies change over time, often in response to environmental conditions, the remaining hunter-gatherer peoples today may give us a glimpse of how some prehistoric peoples lived. The !Kung, a subgroup of the Khoisan people (once known as Bushmen), live in the inhospitable Kalahari Desert in southwestern Africa, in what is today Botswana and Namibia. Several thousand years ago the Khoisan were widespread in the southern half of Africa, and some probably adapted to desert life a long time ago.

The !Kung have become skilled hunter-gatherers. Women obtain between 60 and 80 percent of the food, collecting nuts, berries, beans, leafy greens, roots, and bird eggs, as well as catching tortoises, small mammals, snakes, insects, termites, and caterpillars. The men, who can follow animal tracks and other clues for many miles without rest, hunt animals, snare birds, and extract honey from beehives. The !Kung utilize some fifty species of plants and animals for food, medicine, cosmetics, and poisons. Although unfamiliar to Westerners, their food sources are highly nutritious.

The !Kung have adapted well to a harsh environment. Even during periodic drought conditions, the diversity of !Kung food sources ensures a steady supply. Furthermore, their diet is low in salt, carbohydrates, and saturated fats and high in vitamins and roughage. Combined with a relatively unstressful life, such a diet helps them avoid modern health problems like high blood pressure, ulcers, obesity, and heart disease. Living far from clinics, they die more easily from accidents and malaria. Nonetheless, !Kung life expectancy is similar to that in many industrialized countries.

Martin Harvey/Peter Arnold/Getty Images

A MODERN SAN FAMILY. A father embraces his two children, ages 10 and 14, in Nambia. Like the San in recent times, most people lived from hunting and gathering during the Stone Age.

Spending only fifteen to twenty hours a week in maintaining their livelihood, the !Kung have ample free time for resting, visiting friends, and playing games. Children have few responsibilities because their labor is not needed for the group's survival. The !Kung value gender interdependence and are willing to do the work normally associated with the opposite sex. Hence, fathers take an active role in child rearing. They prefer companionship to privacy, and their intense social life is symbolized by a large communal space in the midst of the camp surrounded by family sleeping huts. The !Kung strongly discourage aggressiveness. Their folk stories praise the animal tricksters who evade the use of force.

Throughout history farming peoples have affected hunter-gatherers. In recent decades the !Kung have faced many challenges that have altered the lives of many bands. Most are no longer completely self-sufficient, trading desert products to nearby farming villages for tools and food. Others have been drafted into the military, have taken up wage labor, or have been displaced because their territory has been claimed by governments or business interests. Today, forced or induced to abandon their traditional ways of life, some disoriented !Kung have moved to dilapidated, impoverished villages on the edges of towns. The future for their ancestral lifestyle is unpromising.

THINKING ABOUT THE PROFILE

1. What role does the gathering by women play in the !Kung economy?
2. How does the traditional !Kung way of life promote leisure activity?
3. What problems do the !Kung face today?

The Agricultural Transformation, 10,000–4000 B.C.E.

What environmental factors explain the transition to agriculture?

Between 10,000 and 11,500 years ago, some hunter-gatherers began to develop simple agriculture. This momentous change marked the beginning of the Neolithic period, when humans began to master the environment and alter the ecological system in unprecedented ways, cultivating the soil, selecting seeds, and breeding animals that could help them survive. The often-used term *Agricultural Revolution* is misleading, because the development did not involve rapid, electrifying discoveries but occurred over hundreds of years. The shift to farming eventually changed human life all over the world, setting the stage for everything that came later, including cities, states, social classes, and long-distance trade.

Environmental Change and the Roots of Agriculture

The first farmers did not see themselves as pioneers forging a new way of life. Even before farming began, some people were preparing themselves for permanent village life. Some, like the Abu Hureyra villagers, were settling alongside lakes or in valleys rich in easily collected wild grains. Around the world, archaeologists have discovered Neolithic period houses, baskets, pottery, pits for storing grain, and equipment for hunting, fishing, and grain preparation. However, documenting the steps to agriculture and settled life is not easy. Before 3500 B.C.E. we have no written sources. Many material artifacts still lie buried, while others have long since turned to dust.

Climate change helped trigger the shift to agriculture. After the last great Ice Age, the earth entered a long period of unusual warmth, which still persists. As they had for thousands of years, melting glaciers caused rising sea levels, covering about a fifth of previously available land. The spread of the Persian Gulf, the Black Sea, and the Mediterranean onto once occupied lowlands may have led to legends in the Middle East of a great flood and human expulsion from a "garden of Eden." Rising sea levels also covered many land links, including those connecting the British Isles to continental Europe and Japan to Asia. Another factor was probably population growth. Around 10,000 B.C.E., the world population had grown to perhaps 5 or 10 million, and in some regions hunting and gathering could no longer meet everyone's basic needs. Soon people gravitated to areas rich in wild grains and grazing animals, some of them abandoning their nomadic ways to live permanently near these rich food sources.

The Great Transition to Settled Agriculture

The environment continued to change, posing new challenges. The earth cooled again briefly about 9000 B.C.E., reducing food supplies, and a drought in the Middle East presented a crisis for some hunter-gatherer societies. Responding to the challenges, some began to store food and learn how to cultivate their own fields, even experimenting with cereal grains collected in a wild state. They pioneered **horticulture**

horticulture The growing of crops with simple methods and tools.

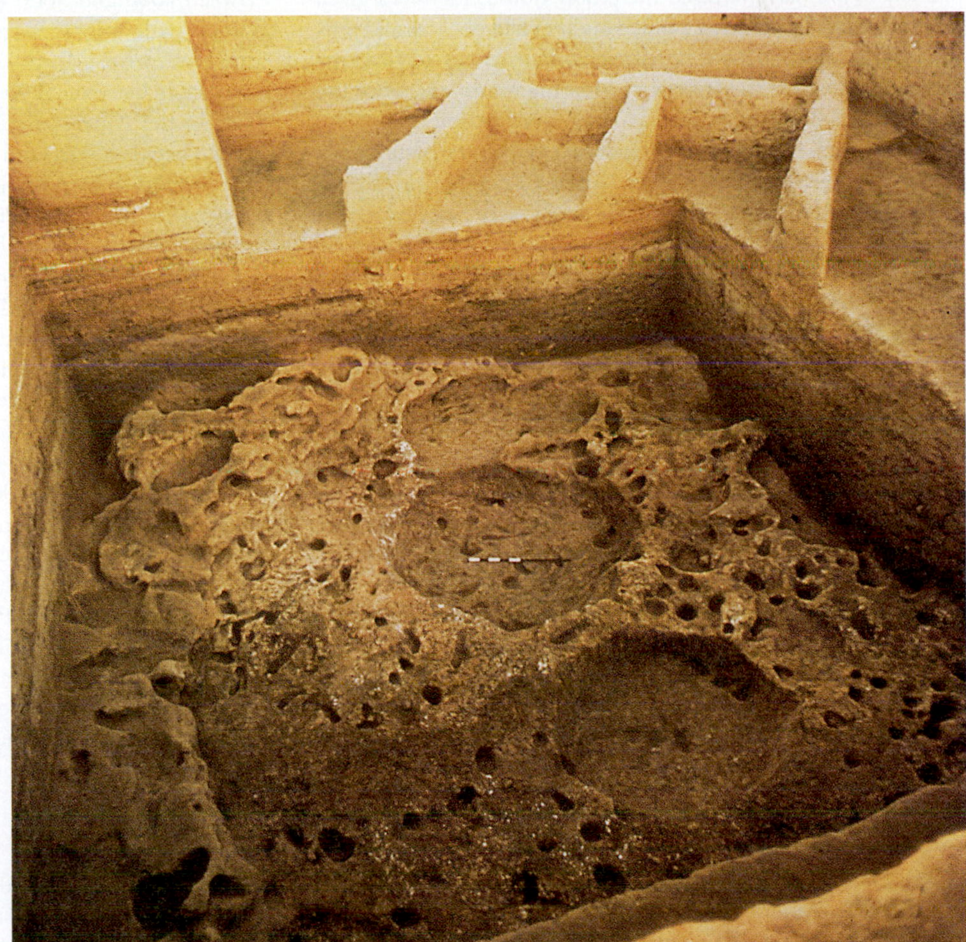

Andrew M.T. Moore

RUINS OF ABU HUREYRA The site of this ancient village overlooks the floodplain of the Euphrates River in northeastern Syria. The earliest settlement included intersecting pits that were turned into huts by roofs of reeds, branches, and poles.

(HORE-tee-kuhl-chur), the growing of crops with simple methods and tools, such as the hoe or digging stick, eventually spurring a profound reorganization of human society. Women may well have taken the lead in domesticating plants and some animals and in molding clay for storage and cooking pots. As the chief gatherers, women knew how plants grew and sprouted from seeds and the amount of water and sunshine needed to sustain plants. Women are generally the main food producers in horticultural societies today.

One major food-producing strategy was shifting cultivation, still used today by millions in Africa, Latin America, and southern Asia, especially in wooded areas. People cleared trees and underbrush by chopping and burning (hence the common term *slash and burn*). After clearing, people loosened the soil with digging sticks and scattered seeds around. Natural moisture such as rain helped the crops mature. But since the soil became eroded after a few years, shifting cultivators moved periodically to fresh land, returning to the original area only after the soil had recovered its fertility.

Farming promoted many radical changes in the way people lived and connected with their environments. Historians debate whether agriculture made life more secure, predictable, and healthy than hunting and gathering. But the domestication of plants and animals increased the production of food in a given amount of land, producing a much higher yield per acre and thus supporting much denser populations. Permanent settlements also made possible the storage of food for future use, since the pots and buildings did not have to be moved periodically.

However, since farmers depended on fewer plant foods than hunter-gatherers, they were more vulnerable to disaster from drought or other natural catastrophes. The earliest farmers could probably grow enough to feed themselves and their families with three or four hours of work a day. But requiring more food to feed growing populations forced them to exploit local resources more intensively and to work harder in their fields. Farmers also recognized that they had hard lives. An ancient Chinese song reflected this reality: "We clear the grasses and trees, We plow and plow the land, Two thousand men and women scrabbling weeds, Along the low wet lands, along the dike walls, The masters, the eldest sons, The laborers, the hired servants."[2] Agriculture eventually depended on peasants, mostly poor farmers who worked small plots of land that were often owned by others. Hard-working peasants were the backbone of most societies before the Industrial Revolution.

The Globalization and Diversity of Agriculture

The agricultural transformation eventually reached across the globe. Agriculture came first to Eurasia, where geography favored the movement of people to the east or west along the same general latitude, without abrupt climatic changes. By contrast, the Americas are constructed along a north-south axis, and northern and southern temperate regions are linked only through a huge tropical zone stretching from southern Mexico to northern and eastern South America. Some peoples, such as those in Australia and the Arctic, did not or could not make the transition from food gathering because of environmental and geographical constraints. Many societies contributed significantly to the discovery and production of the food resources we use today.

The dates for the beginning of agriculture vary considerably. The earliest known farming occurred in the area of southwestern Asia known as the "Fertile Crescent," encompassing what is today Iraq, Syria, central and eastern Turkey, and the Jordan River Valley, which had many fast-growing plants with high nutritional value, such as wheat, barley, chickpeas, and peas. The breakthrough came between 9500 and 8000 B.C.E. Food growing also began independently in several other parts of the world (see Map 1.2), although we still do not know precisely when because hot, humid climates are poor for preserving plant, animal, and human remains. In eastern Eurasia crop cultivation began around 7000 B.C.E. in China and New Guinea, 7000 or 6000 B.C.E. in India, 5000 or 4000 B.C.E. in Thailand, and 3000 B.C.E. in Island Southeast Asia.

In the Mediterranean region, farming began in the Nile Valley by at least 6000 B.C.E., if not earlier, and in Greece by 6500 B.C.E., reaching northward to Britain and Scandinavia between 4000 and 3000 B.C.E. Farming may have spread into Europe with migrants from western Asia who intermarried with local people. In Africa farming in the southeast Sahara may date to between 8000 and 6000 B.C.E. and Ethiopia to 4500 B.C.E. In the Americas cultivation apparently began in central Mexico between 7000 and 5500 B.C.E. and in the Andes (ANN-deez) highlands by 6000 B.C.E., if not earlier. Farming reached the Amazon Basin by 1500 B.C.E., Colorado by 1000 B.C.E., and the southeastern part of North America by 500 B.C.E.

The earliest crops grown varied by local environments and needs. Millet dominated in cold North China, rice in tropical Southeast Asia, wheat and barley in the dry Middle East, yams and sorghum in West Africa, corn in upland Mesoamerica, and potatoes in the high Andes. Some crops such as flax produced fiber to make clothing. Other plants had medicinal properties. Southwest Asians began making wine from grapes and beer from barley between 6000 and 3000 B.C.E. Over time farming became deeply ingrained in the psychology, social life, and traditions of many societies (see Witness to the Past: Food and Farming in Ancient Cultural Traditions). Farming technology gradually improved. People living in highlands with steep slopes, such as in Peru, Indonesia, China, or Greece, made fields on terraces, laborious to construct and maintain. Then, as more people moved from highlands into valleys, they used water from nearby marshes or wells or built large-scale water projects such as irrigation canals.

Animal Domestication

The domestication of animals for human use developed in close association with crop raising. Animals bred in captivity were gradually modified from their wild ancestors. Men may have looked after the larger animals such as oxen and cattle, while

[2]From Robert Payne, ed., *The White Pony: An Anthology of Chinese Poetry* (New York: Mentor, 1947), 39.

WITNESS TO THE PAST

Food and Farming in Ancient Cultural Traditions

As agriculture became an essential foundation for survival, it became increasingly important in the traditions and mindsets of societies around the world. The following excerpts show three examples of how food and farming were reflected in the cultural traditions of ancient societies. The first, an Andean ritual chant many centuries old, is a prayer for successful harvests addressed to an ancient deity. The second is from a farmer's almanac from eighteenth-century B.C.E. *Mesopotamia that offers guidance on cultivating a successful grain crop; this excerpt deals with preparing the field and seeding. The third reading, a song collected in China around 3,000 years ago, celebrates a successful harvest and explains how some of the bounty will be used.*

Andean Chant

Oh Viracocha, ancient Viracocha, skilled creator, who makes and establishes
"on the earth below may they eat, may they drink" you say;
for those you have established, those you have made
may food be plentiful.
"Potatoes, maize, all kinds of food may there be"

Excerpt from Farmer's Almanac

Keep a sharp eye on the openings of the dikes, ditches and mounds [so that] when you flood the field the water will not rise too high in it.... Let shod oxen trample it for you; after having its weeds ripped out [by them and] the field made level ground, dress it evenly with narrow axes weighing [no more than] two thirds of a pound each.... Keep your eye on the man who puts in the barley seed. Let him drop the grain uniformly two fingers deep.... If the barley seed does not sink in properly, change your share.... Harvest it at the moment [of its full strength].

Chinese Harvest Song

Rich is the year with much millet and rice;
And we have tall granaries
With hundreds and thousands and millions of sheaves.
We make wine and sweet spirits
And offer them to our ancestors, male and female;
Thus to fulfill all the rites And bring down blessings
in full.

THINKING ABOUT THE READING

1. Who did the Andeans believe determined the success of their harvest?
2. How did Mesopotamian farming depend on draft animals and cooperation?
3. How did ancient Chinese farmers use surplus grain and rice to fulfill obligations?

Sources: Brian M. Fagan, *Kingdoms of Gold, Kingdoms of Jade* (London: Thames and Hudson, 1991), 88; Samuel Noah Kramer, *Cradle of Civilization* (New York: Time-Life), 84; William Theodore De Bary, et al, eds., *Sources of Chinese Tradition*, Vol. 1 (New York: Columbia university Press, 1960), p. 13.

women took charge of smaller species such as sheep and pigs. Domesticated animals supplied meat and leather, aided in farming, produced fertilizer, or supplied transportation. For example, horses and camels made long-distance travel and communication easier, and plows became more efficient tools when pulled by oxen or cattle. One disadvantage was that domesticated animals passed on diseases to humans, although living with animals eventually led to immunities among peoples in Eurasia.

Much remains unclear about the chronology and location of animal domestication. For example, dogs may have been domesticated from gray wolves by at least 12,000 or perhaps 15,000 years ago in East Asia, Europe, or the Middle East. Dogs provided companionship, guarding, hunting assistance, and sometimes food. Chinese farmers kept tamed cats by 3000 B.C.E. Sheep, goats, pigs, chickens, and cattle were all domesticated in the Middle East and southern Asia between 9000 and 7000 B.C.E. Some contested evidence suggests early cattle domestication in East Africa and the Sahara region. The first domesticated horses and donkeys, which date back to around 4000 B.C.E., enabled the improved transportation that stimulated long-distance trade networks.

Zoological differences among the continents were crucial for advanced agriculture. Eurasia contained many species of large, plant-eating, herding mammals whose habits and mild dispositions made their domestication into draft animals possible. Outside Eurasia, the lack of draft animals hindered agricultural development. Africa (except for cattle) and Australia lacked such animals, and most of the candidates in the Americas, such as the horse and camel, were extinct by 10,000 B.C.E. The only American possibilities, the gentle llamas and alpacas of the South American highlands, were used as pack animals by 3500 B.C.E. but were not well suited for farming.

Agriculture and Its Environmental Consequences

The resulting population growth also contributed to environmental changes, some with negative consequences such as deforestation. Indeed, human activities have had an impact on environments since the time of *Homo habilis*. Stone Age hunters in both hemispheres may have contributed to the extinction of many animal species, but intensive agriculture more radically altered the ecology, especially as technology improved. Moreover, technological innovations solved some problems but did not always prove advantageous in the long run. For example, although the plow made it easier to loosen dirt and eliminate weeds to plant seeds deeper in nutrient-rich soil, it also exposed topsoils to water and wind erosion. Similarly, vast irrigation networks provided the economic foundations

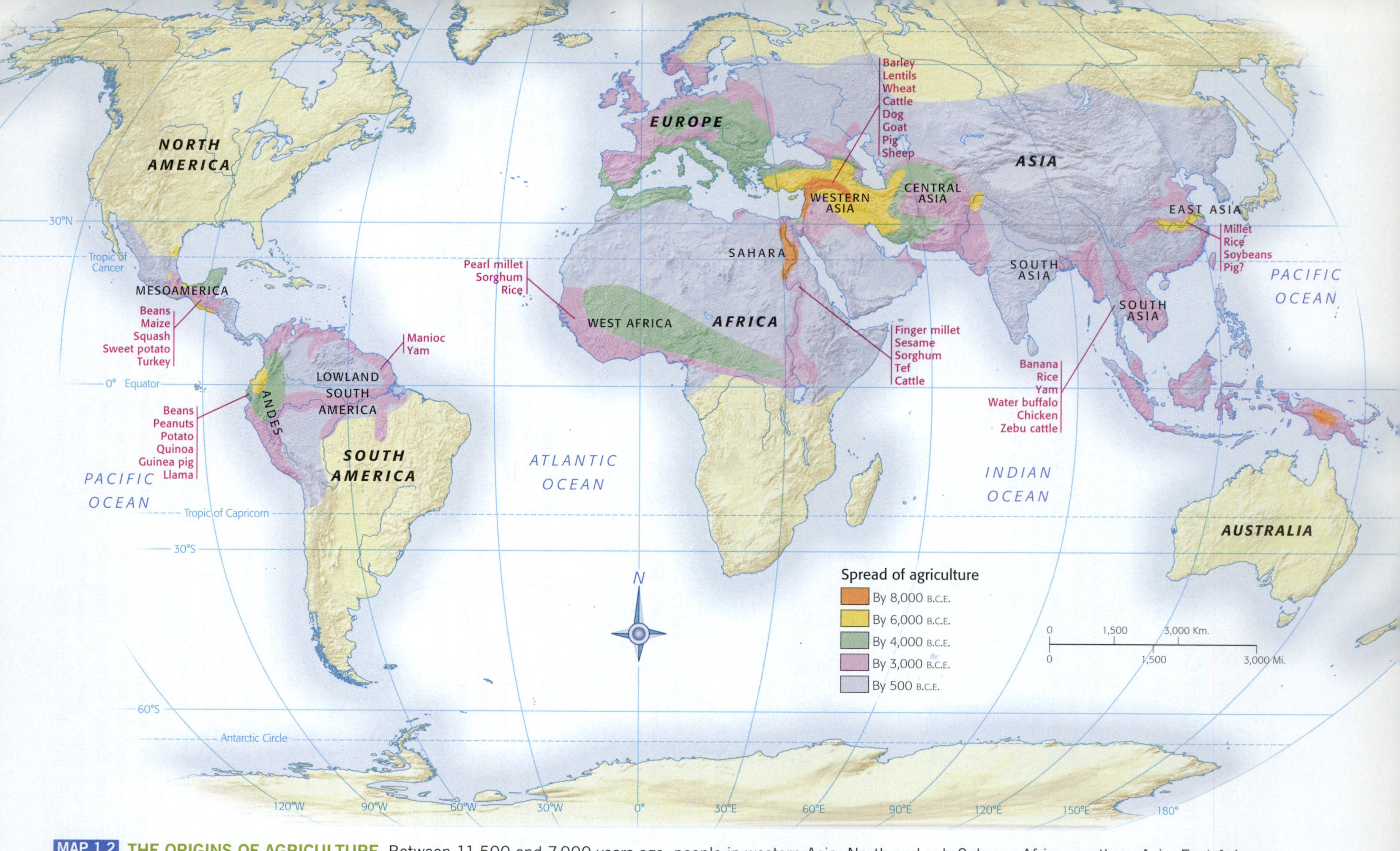

MAP 1.2 **THE ORIGINS OF AGRICULTURE** Between 11,500 and 7,000 years ago, people in western Asia, North and sub-Saharan Africa, southern Asia, East Asia, New Guinea, Mesoamerica, and South America developed agriculture independently and domesticated available animals. Later most of these crops and some of the animals spread into other regions.

for flourishing agriculture and denser settlement but required more labor than dry farming. They also tended to foster centralized governments that could allocate water resources among the people, placing more controls on people's behavior. Finally, adding water to poor soils can produce waterlogged land with a thick salt surface that ruins farming. In Mesopotamia and the Americas, irrigation ultimately created deserts, contributing to the rise and fall of societies.

Various activities fostered environmental destruction. Farming and animal raising placed demands on the land. Goats, for example, caused damage by browsing on shrubs, tree branches, and seedlings, preventing forest regeneration. Cattle required much pasture. People exploited nearby forests for lumber to build wagons, tools, houses, furniture, and boats. Contemporary observers were aware of the deforestation. For example, twenty-four centuries ago the philosopher Plato bemoaned the deforestation of the Greek mountains: "What remains is like the skeleton of a body emaciated by disease. All the rich soil has melted away, leaving a country of skin and bone."[3] Overgrazing and deforestation in the mountains feeding the main rivers produced silt that contained harmful salt and gypsum, which moved downstream to the sea, clogging canals and dams.

The changing human-environment relationship generated new religious ideas more complex than animism and polytheism in explaining humankind's relationship to broader forces. Early sacred and philosophical texts often justified human domination over nature. For example, the authors of the Hebrew book of Genesis believed God told humans to "be fruitful and multiply; fill the earth and subdue it; have dominion over the fish of the sea,…the birds of the air, and…every living thing that moves upon the earth."[4] Many ancient thinkers saw an ordered world in which every part had a role and purpose in a divine plan, with humans the ultimate beneficiaries.

DEA/M. SEEMULLER/De Agostini/Getty Images

SEATED GODDESS FROM WESTERN ASIA This baked-clay figure from one of the oldest towns in western Asia, ÇatalHüyük in Anatolia, shows an enthroned female, probably a goddess giving birth, guarded on both sides by catlike animals—perhaps leopards.

MAKE SURE YOU UNDERSTAND THESE KEY POINTS BEFORE MOVING ON

- **The shift from hunting and gathering to farming had tremendous consequences, but it occurred gradually, over hundreds of years.**
- **The end of the last great Ice Age and increased population density led people to shift from hunting and gathering to farming.**
- **Farming, which probably began in the area of Asia known as the "Fertile Crescent," could support much denser populations and allowed for food storage, but it also led to some new health problems.**
- **Irrigation and other technological advances led to larger crops but also caused great environmental damage.**

aplia™

The Emergence of Cities and States

How did farming and metallurgy establish the foundations for the rise of cities, states, and trade networks?

Farming generated more complex societies. Some western Asian people moved to fertile areas to farm, unloading their stone tools, clay pots, and plant seeds, and building mud and reed huts. Families formed small villages and had more children to help in the fields. Houses had a sleeping platform, bread oven, grain silo, and a corral for domesticated animals. Older women

[3]From Plato's *Critas*, quoted in L.S. Stavrianos, *Lifelines from Our Past: A New World History*, rev. ed.(Armonk, NY: M.E. Sharpe, 1997), 65.

[4]Genesis 1:28, *The Holy Bible*, New King James Version (Chicago: Thomas Nelson, 1983), 2.

served as religious specialists, acting as midwives, reciting myths, and composing verses. To honor a special deity the villagers built a temple. Eventually these villages with their temples grew into the first cities, establishing a foundation for the rise of states, trade networks, and writing.

ÇATALHÜYÜK A view of rooms and walls in one of the first known towns, ÇatalHüyük in eastern Turkey. The ruins contained many art objects, murals, wall sculpture, and woven cloth.

The Rise of New Technologies

Many times in history people came up against a serious resource problem, such as lack of food and water, and had to overcome the challenge or perish. Their efforts often led to some new technology with long-lasting value. One innovation, metalworking, made possible a new level of human control over resources supplied by the environment. The first metalworking was done with copper, and copper mining may have been the first real industry of the ancient world. Used in Europe for making weapons and tools as early as 7000 B.C.E. and in the Middle East by 4500 B.C.E., copper was traded over considerable distances and was perhaps the first major commodity to enjoy a world market. People also used gold. These two soft metals could be fairly easily cut and shaped with stones.

Soon specialist craftsmen were mining and working metals. By 3000 B.C.E. some specialists in western Asia had developed heating processes to blend copper together with either tin or arsenic to create bronze, and the bronze trade became a major spur to commerce in early Mesopotamia. By 1500 B.C.E. the technology for making usable iron had also been invented, although it took many centuries to perfect the new alloy for practical use. Bronze and iron made better, more durable tools (such as plows), but also more deadly weapons. Their use shaped many societies of the ancient and classical worlds.

Urbanization and the First Cities

Agriculture fostered population growth. By using cow's milk and grain meal for infant's food, women could now breastfeed for a shorter period and consequently bear children more frequently. In the Middle East the population grew from less than 100,000 in 8000 B.C.E. to over 3 million by 4000 B.C.E. Some farming villages grew into substantial prosperous towns. In one of the oldest, ÇatalHüyük(cha-TAHL hoo-YOOK) in central Turkey, roughly ten thousand residents lived in cramped mud-brick buildings with paintings décorating their walls. ÇatalHüyük and similar towns became centers of long-distance trade. By around 3700 B.C.E. another center, Tell Hamoukar (Tell HAM-oo-kar), had grown into a town enclosed by a defensive wall. It contained both a bakery and a brewery and seems to have had a growing bureaucracy, perhaps even a king. Road networks linked the various cities of the Tigris-Euphrates Basin.

With time permanent settlements became larger, dominating nearby villages and farms. They emerged where farmers produced a food surplus and could be taxed or coerced to share their excess crops to sustain people with no time or land for farming. Priests, scribes, carpenters, and merchants increasingly congregated in the growing settlements. Cities usually contained many shops, public markets, government buildings, and religious centers.

This urban revolution constituted a major achievement perhaps as significant as the agricultural transformation. In Southwest Asia governments led by new social hierarchies dominated the first small cities emerging between 3500 and 3200 B.C.E. Soon cities appeared elsewhere. Small shops and makeshift stalls selling foodstuffs, household items, or folk medicines lined many streets. Hawkers peddled their wares from door to door. Craftsmen in workshops fashioned the items used in daily life, such as pottery, tools, and jewelry. Some of the goods made, mined, or grown locally were traded by land or sea to distant cities. Thus the rise of cities reshaped societies and fostered networks of communication and exchange.

The Rise of States, Economies, and Recordkeeping

Food production and urbanization eventually led to the formation of states: formal governments that controlled a recognized territory and exercised power over both people and things.

The people within them, often from diverse ethnic and cultural backgrounds, did not necessarily share all the same values or allegiances. Complex urban societies organized into states developed at least 3,000 years ago on all the inhabited continents except Australia.

These urban societies relied on diversified economies that generated enough wealth to support a division of labor and social, cultural, and religious hierarchies. Farmers, laborers, craftsmen, merchants, priests, soldiers, bureaucrats, and scholars served specialized functions. The priests served the religious institutions that emerged as societies organized and standardized their beliefs. Some states constructed monumental architecture, such as large temples, palaces, and city walls. While men dominated most of the hierarchies and heavy labor, women also played key economic roles. They made the cloth: preparing the raw materials, spinning the yarn, weaving the yarn into fabrics, and fashioning and sewing the clothing, blankets, and other useful items, while passing along their knowledge from mother to daughter. Most urban societies were connected to elaborate trade networks extending well beyond the immediate region. By 4000 B.C.E. a network of merchant contacts linked India and Mesopotamia, 1,250 miles apart. Clay counting tokens used for trade had appeared by 3100 B.C.E., if not earlier. By 5000 B.C.E. the first seafaring vessels had been built around the Persian Gulf.

The early urban societies also introduced cultural innovations such as recordkeeping and literature. A system of recordkeeping could involve a written language, such as those developed by the Egyptians, Greeks, Chinese, and Maya, among others. Or records could be kept by a class of memory experts, such as the professional "rememberers" among many African and South American peoples. In most literate societies writing was usually reserved for the privileged few until recent centuries, so knowledge of literature was not widespread. But most societies created rich oral traditions of stories, legends, historical accounts, and poems that could be shared with all the people.

Some historians apply the term *civilization* to larger, more complex societies such as ancient Egypt and China that left an extensive record of bureaucratic governments, monumental architecture, writing, and influential thought, but this is a controversial concept that neglects societies with less known histories. Since ancient times some peoples have seen themselves as "civilized" and criticized other societies as "barbarians." *Civilization* could also refer to any large grouping of people with a common history and traditions, such as the Arabs, Maya, or French. Thus the term is too subjective to have much value in understanding world history. It is not used in this text.

The Rise of Pastoral Nomadism

Some societies adopted an alternative to agriculture and cities known as **pastoral nomadism**, an economy based on raising livestock. Both trade and conflict between pastoral nomads and settled farmers was a major theme in history. On land unsuitable for farming, some people began specializing in herding, moving their camps and animals seasonally in search of pasture and trading meat, hides, or livestock to nearby farmers for grain. Although pastoral nomadism involved dispersed rather than concentrated populations, some pastoral nomads exercised a strong influence on societies with much greater populations. Pastoral nomads mostly concentrated in grasslands and deserts. Grasslands covered much of central and western Asia from Mongolia to southern Russia, as well as large parts of eastern and southern Africa. By 2000 B.C.E., the Sahara region of northern Africa was part of a great inhospitable arid zone stretching from Africa's western tip eastward through Arabia into western Asia and then to the frontiers of China.

Pastoralists lived very differently than farmers. They domesticated horses in Central Asia around 4300 B.C.E. and camels in Arabia around 3000 or 2500 B.C.E. Although they had few material possessions, pastoralists often had humane values and a rich cultural life. Since they needed a large area to support each animal, herds had to be kept small to prevent overgrazing. Hence, herders lived in small, dispersed groups, generally organized by extended families that were often part of **tribes**, associations of clans tracing descent from a common ancestor. While some societies maintained egalitarian social structures, others were headed by chiefs. Among some Central Asians, women held a high status and even became warriors. Burial mounds in Turkestan contain the remains of what may be female warriors from 2,500 years ago, interred with daggers, swords, and bronze-tipped arrows. Some pastoralists became tough, martial peoples who were greatly feared by the farmers, and before modern times Central Asian pastoralists like the Huns and Mongols played a central role in world history.

Particularly influential in ancient world history were the tribes known collectively as the **Indo-Europeans** (IN-dough-YUR-uh-PEE-uns), so named because their original common tongue spawned the many related languages spoken today by these peoples' descendants. The original Indo-European homeland was probably located in Anatolia (modern Turkey), the nearby Caucasus Mountains, or the adjacent southern Russian/Ukrainian plains to the north. Eventually, because of the spread of these strongly patriarchal tribes, most people in Europe, Iran, and northern India came to speak Indo-European languages.

Indo-European expansion apparently occurred in several waves. Some Indo-Europeans may have moved into Europe and Central Asia as early as 6500 or 7000 B.C.E., carrying with them not only their language but also perhaps farming technology. The culturally mixed people who resulted may have been the ancestors of the Celts and Greeks. Between 3000 and 2000 B.C.E. many Indo-European pastoralists were driven from their western Asian homeland by some disaster, dispersing in

pastoral nomadism An economy based on breeding, rearing, and harvesting livestock.

tribes Associations of clans that traced descent from a common ancestor.

Indo-Europeans Various tribes who all spoke related languages deriving from some original common tongue and who eventually settled Europe, Iran, and northern India.

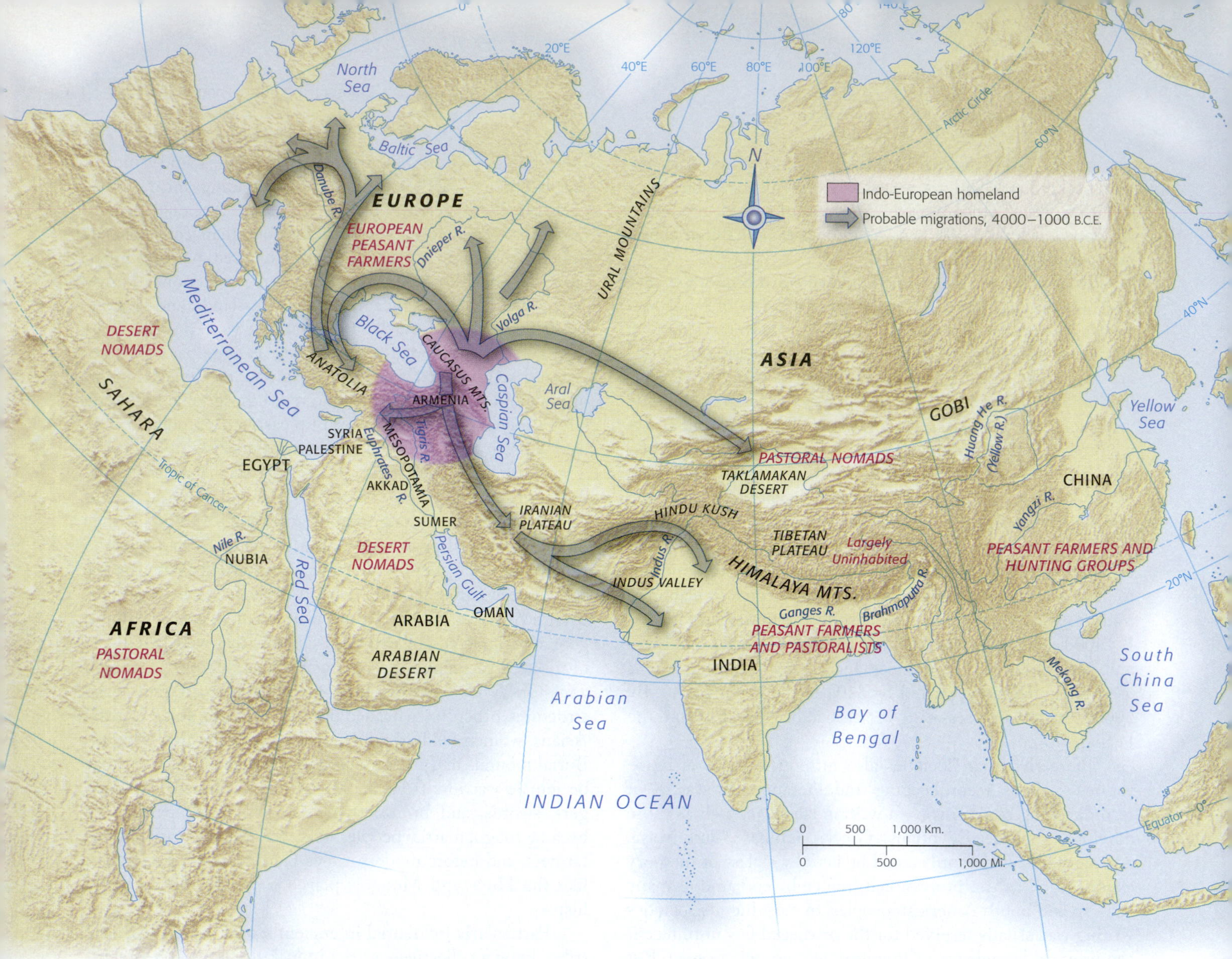

MAP 1.3 THE INDO-EUROPEAN MIGRATIONS AND EURASIAN PASTORALISM Some societies, especially in parts of Africa and Asia, adapted to environmental contexts by developing a pastoral, or animal herding, economy. One large pastoral group, the Indo-Europeans, eventually expanded from their home area into Europe, southwestern Asia, Central Asia, and India.

every direction, splitting up into smaller units, and driving their herds of cattle, sheep, goats, and horses with them. Encountering farming peoples, they turned to conquest (see Map 1.3).

This dispersal set the stage for profound changes across Eurasia. The Hittites gained dominance in Anatolia and then, around 2000 B.C.E., expanded their empire into Mesopotamia. Other tribes pushed on between 2500 and 1500 B.C.E., some to the west into Greece, some east as far as the western fringe of China, some south into Persia (Iran). From Persia some tribes moved southeast through mountain passes into northwestern India. Spreading their languages and imposing their military power, they eventually absorbed or subdued other peoples. Most eventually abandoned pastoral nomadism for farming, but their dispersal opened a new chapter in the history of Europe, the Middle East, and India.

MAKE SURE YOU UNDERSTAND THESE KEY POINTS BEFORE MOVING ON

- **Metals such as bronze and iron helped improve farming tools and weaponry.**
- **Highly productive farming allowed for the formation of the first cities, which became centers of trade.**
- **People in cities developed forms of recordkeeping and writing.**
- **Herders such as Indo-Europeans played an important role in spreading culture across Eurasia, though most eventually took up farming.**

CHAPTER SUMMARY

The story of humans and their societies constitutes only a tiny part of the broader 4.5-billion-year history of the earth. Some 4 million years ago our hominid ancestors emerged in Africa, learning to walk upright, to make and use tools, and to control fire. Eventually, evolution produced modern humans, who developed language and more complex social structures. During the long Paleolithic period, all humans, using simple technologies and living in small groups, hunted wild animals and gathered wild plants, maintaining a balance with their environment. While many such societies survived over the millennia, eventually environmental changes and other factors encouraged most peoples to adopt farming.

Beginning between 10,000 and 11,500 years ago, the climate warmed and populations increased. In a great transition, some people began to grow their own food and domesticate wild animals. Farming probably emerged first in southwestern Asia. By 2000 B.C.E. various peoples in Eurasia, Africa, and the Americas had adopted farming, a change that led to larger populations, altered people's relationship to the environment, and set the stage for cities, states, social classes, and recordkeeping in the Afro-Eurasian zone between 3500 and 3000 B.C.E. The first cities and states formed in sub-Saharan Africa and the Americas between 3000 and 1000 B.C.E. Some people living in the grasslands and deserts became nomadic pastoralists and interacted with settled farmers. The formation of distinctive societies and increased contact between peoples inaugurated a new era of human history.

KEY TERMS

hominids (p. 11)
australopithecines (p. 12)
Homo habilis (p. 12)
Homo erectus (p. 12)
Homo sapiens (p. 12)
Neanderthals (p. 13)
Denisovans (p. 15)
Cro-Magnons (p. 15)
Paleolithic (p. 15)
Mesolithic (p. 15)
Neolithic (p. 15)
matrilineal kinship (p. 16)
animism (p. 16)
polytheism (p. 16)
shamans (p. 16)
horticulture (p. 19)
pastoral nomadism (p. 25)
tribes (p. 25)
Indo-Europeans (p. 25)

2 Ancient Societies in Mesopotamia, India, and Central Asia, 5000–600 B.C.E.

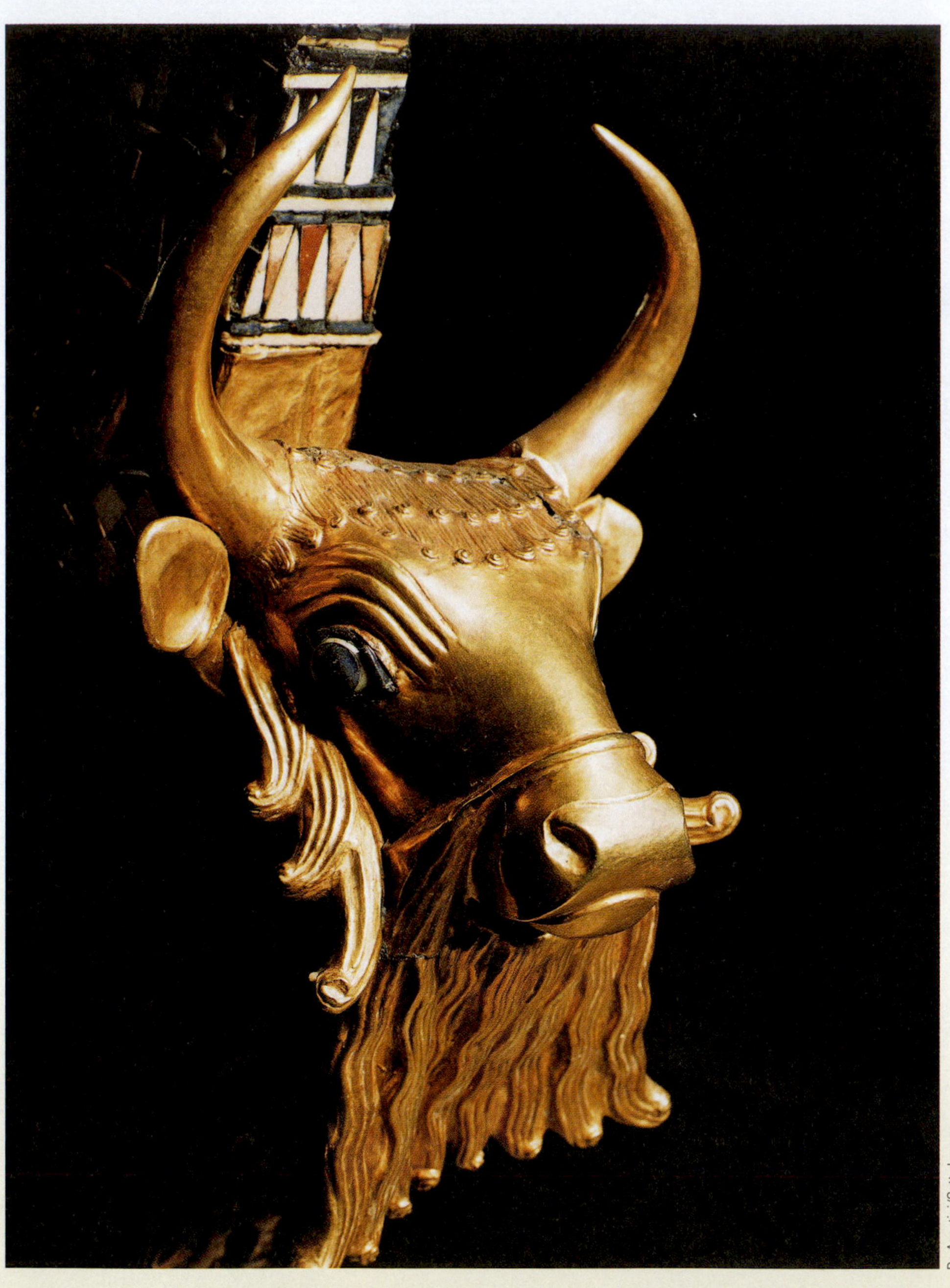

De Agostini/Getty Images

BULL'S HEAD FROM SUMERIAN LYRE This bull's head is part of the soundbox of a wooden harp. The harp, made in Sumeria around 2600 B.C.E., is covered with gold and lapis lazuli and reflects the popularity of music in Mesopotamian society.

Inanna filled Agade [a Mesopotamian city]... with gold. She filled the storerooms with barley, bronze, and lumps of lapis lazuli [a stone used in jewelry]. The ships at the wharves were an awesome sight. All the lands around rested in security.

—Poem praising the goddess of love and generosity, written in 2250 B.C.E.[1]

IN THIS CHAPTER

Some five thousand years ago in the Mesopotamian **(MESS-uh-puh-TAIM-ee-an)** city of Uruk **(OO-rook)**, an unknown artist carved a beautiful narrative relief on a large vase and donated it to the city's temple for the goddess of love, Inanna **(ih-NON-a)**, the first known goddess in recorded history. The scenes of domestic and religious life celebrate a festival honoring the goddess, while an agricultural scene shows sheep, barley, and water, the staples of the area's economy. A procession of men carry foodstuffs they will present as gifts of gratitude to Inanna, possibly the female figure with a tall horned headdress. The vase pictures for us the social order and rituals of one of the world's earliest cities.

Sometime after the people in Southwest Asia and India had become comfortable with farming technology, they began to make the next great transition by founding the first cities and states in the Indus Valley in northwestern India and all along the **Fertile Crescent**, a large semicircle of fertile land that included the valleys of the Tigris **(TIE-gris)** and Euphrates **(you-FRAY-teez)** Rivers stretching northwest from the Persian Gulf to the eastern shores of the Mediterranean Sea. The Mesopotamians divided their specialized workers into full-time farmers, professional soldiers, government officials, artisans, traders, and priests. Ancient Indians also established the foundations for several enduring religions.

The Mesopotamians and Indians were among various Afro-Eurasian peoples who built the foundations to sustain large populations. For at least three millennia a large majority of the world's population has lived in an arc stretching from Egypt and Mesopotamia eastward through India to China and Japan. The people of western Asia created the first systematic use of writing, bronze, large states, institutionalized religions to worship deities like Inanna, and networks to exchange products and information by land and sea. The city of Agade **(uh-GAH-duh)** was visited by traders from near and far, while Southwest Asia became a crossroads between Europe, Africa, and southern Asia and a great trade and communication hub.

Fertile Crescent A large semicircular fertile region that included the valleys of the Tigris and Euphrates Rivers stretching northwest from the Persian Gulf to the eastern shores of the Mediterranean Sea.

[1]The quote is from the Oriental Institute, the University of Chicago.

Early Mesopotamian Urbanized Societies, to 2000 B.C.E.

Why did farming, cities, and states develop first in the Fertile Crescent?

Around five thousand years ago, small city-states emerged in Mesopotamia, especially in the southern Tigris-Euphrates Valley. The connections between these diverse peoples helped their cultures change and grow. Over the centuries various peoples moved into the area, each adopting and building on the achievements of their predecessors. Their cities were dominated by religious temples, and their people were divided into elaborate social class structures. As conquerors combined city-states into empires, Mesopotamian societies were soon linked by trade to the Mediterranean and North Africa.

Western Asian Environments

Life in western Asia owed much to the geographic features that brought people together. Most early urban societies began first in wide river valleys such as the Tigris-Euphrates, Indus, and Nile because they provided life-giving irrigation for crops that supported larger populations. In Mesopotamia (the Greek word for the "land between the rivers"), the flooding of the Tigris and Euphrates Rivers, which stretch from the western edge of the Persian Gulf through today's Iraq into Syria and southeastern Turkey, made possible a flourishing society. The long river valley promoted interaction, both friendly and hostile, between peoples, as well as frequent invasions through mountain passes by people living to the north and east. To the northwest is the mountainous Anatolia **(ANN-uh-TOE-lee-uh)** Peninsula (modern Turkey), and to the east lies Iran (known through most of history as Persia), a land of mountains and deserts and the pathway to India and Central Asia. To the south the Arabian peninsula, largely desert, was characterized by oasis agriculture and nomadic pastoralism.

Ancient Mesopotamia had a climate similar to southern California today. Most rain fell in the winter, and summer temperatures in some places reached 120 degrees Fahrenheit. During the long, scorching summer, the land baked stone-hard, searing winds blew up a choking dust, and vegetation withered. The winter brought winds, clouds, and the occasional rains, while spring brought rains and melting snows from nearby mountains that swelled the rivers to flood level, sometimes submerging the plains. Still, the annual but unpredictable floods created natural levees that could be drained and planted, and the nearby swamps contained abundant fish and wildlife.

Many different peoples settled the region, some of them speaking Semitic languages, including Arabic and Hebrew, which are related to some African tongues. Speakers of Turkish and of Indo-European languages such as Persian, Armenian, and Kurdish arrived later. Europeans later referred to southwestern Asia as Asia Minor or the Near East, and to the region along the eastern Mediterranean coast as the Levant **(luh-VANT)** ("rising of the sun"). Geographers today use the label *Southwest Asia* and often lump the region together with Islamic North Africa under the broader concept of the "Middle East," midway between East Asia and Europe.

The Tigris and Euphrates Rivers fostered several Mesopotamian societies. The modern city of Baghdad is midway up the Tigris, and ancient Babylon was only a few miles away on the Euphrates. Such cities arose when the farmers and herders in the nearby hills needed more food. Possibly pushed by a cooler

	6,000 B.C.E.	5,500 B.C.E.	5,000 B.C.E.	4,500 B.C.E.	4,000 B.C.E.	3,500 B.C.E.
MESOPOTAMIA		5500 B.C.E. First Sumerian settlements				
INDIA AND CENTRAL ASIA						

climate, they left the hill country and created the first towns in the marshy areas near the head of the Persian Gulf, building elaborate irrigation canals to grow food after the annual floods. This irrigation had significant consequences, for it necessitated the cooperation that laid the foundations for organized societies and then cities. Yet irrigation also slowly degraded the soil, the salts it added eventually creating infertile desert.

The Pioneering Sumerians and Their Neighbors

Settling in southern Mesopotamia about 5500 B.C.E., the Sumerians built the first Mesopotamian cities and states (see Map 2.1). By 3500 B.C.E. Uruk in Sumer **(soo-MUHR)** had grown into a city, eventually reaching a population of fifty thousand. Other Mesopotamian peoples, such as those in the north at Tell Hamoukar (see Chapter 1), may have also forged early states. By 3000 B.C.E. Sumerians had created a network of city-states, urban centers surrounded by agricultural land that was controlled by the city and used to support its citizens. By 2500 B.C.E. these Sumerian societies had grown to several million people. Uruk was surrounded by 5 miles of fortified walls and had influence as far north as modern Turkey. An attack by Uruk on Tell Hamoukar is the world's oldest known example of large-scale organized warfare.

The Sumerians were clearly proud of their cities and felt that their city life made them superior to other peoples. A Sumerian myth begins with the lines "Behold the bond of Heaven and Earth, the city. Behold the kindly wall…its pure river, its quay where the boats stand…its pure canal."[2] The mud-baked brick houses of Sumerian cities were constructed around courtyards. The largest city building was the temple, or **ziggurat** **(ZIG-uh-rat)**, a stepped, pyramidal-shaped building (almost an artificial mountain) that was seen as the home of that city's chief god. One of these temples may have inspired the later Hebrew story of the tower of Babel **(BAY-buhl/BAH-buhl)**.

Sumerian Society and Economy

At first Sumerian cities were governed by assemblies composed of leading citizens. Whether these assemblies amounted to a kind of democratic government is a matter of scholarly debate. The assemblies seem to have appointed a city leader, sometimes a woman, with both secular and religious authority. However, the waging of wars led to more domination by rulers, priests, and nobles, and gradually women lost the right to be elected leader and serve in the assemblies. When war leaders became kings, or hereditary monarchs, the assemblies lost power.

The Sumerian nobility and priests controlled most of the land in and around the city, which was tilled by tenant farmers or slaves. A Sumerian proverb claimed that "the poor man is better dead than alive; if he has bread, he has no salt; if he has salt, he has no bread."[3] The many slaves, who included captives taken in battles and criminals, were treated as personal property but allowed to marry. Eventually royal officials, nobility, and priests controlled most of the economic life of the cities.

The Sumerians introduced **patriarchy**, a system in which men largely control women and children and also shape ideas about appropriate gender behavior. Sumerian women were generally subservient to

ziggurat A stepped, pyramidal-shaped temple building in Sumerian cities, seen as the home of the chief god of the city.

patriarchy A system in which men largely control women and children and shape ideas about appropriate gender behavior.

[2]The quote is from the Oriental Institute, the University of Chicago.

[3]Quoted in Frederick Gentels and Melvin Steinfield, *Hangups from Way Back: Historical Myths and Canons*, vol. 1, 2nd ed. (San Francisco: Canfield, 1974), p. 64.

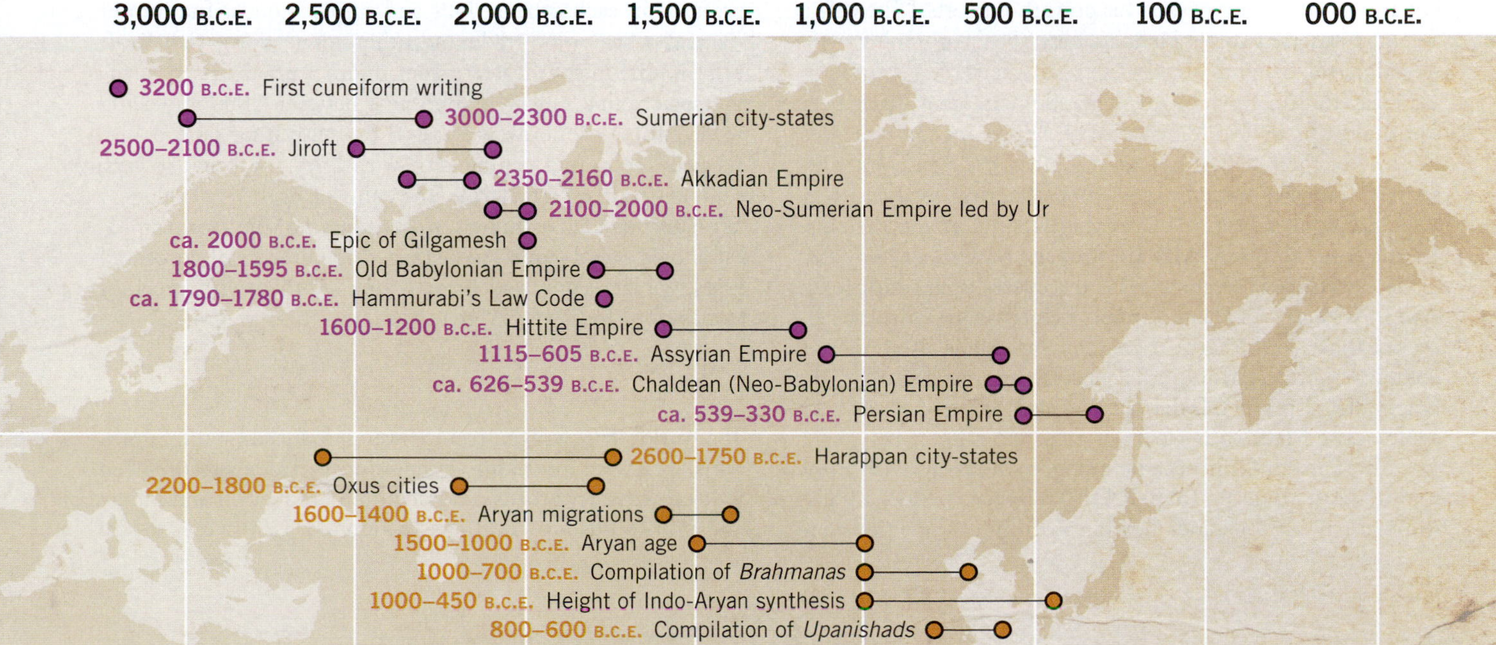

MAP 2.1 **ANCIENT MESOPOTAMIA** The people of Mesopotamia and the adjacent regions of the Fertile Crescent pioneered farming. The Mesopotamians also built the first cities and formed the first states. Sumerian cities dominated southern Mesopotamia for over a millennium, only to lose power to societies from northern Mesopotamia.

men, but they could inherit property, run their own businesses, and serve as witnesses in court. A queen enjoyed much respect as the wife of the king, and Sumerian religion allowed a woman to be the high priestess if the city divinity was female. Within family life, which was much treasured, women were important but also faced stereotypes, as this proverb suggests: "The wife is a man's future; the son is a man's refuge; the daughter is a man's salvation; the daughter-in-law is a man's devil."[4]

The trade networks involving Sumeria may have been some of the first in world history with significant consequences. Because of their lack of natural resources, the Sumerian cities formed extensive trade links with neighboring societies. They imported copper from the Caucasus Mountains and then discovered how to mix it with tin to make bronze, an alloy that made for stronger weapons. This discovery began the Bronze Age in western Asia; later bronze helped shape other societies in Eurasia and North Africa. The Sumerians also imported gold, ivory, obsidian, and other necessities from Anatolia, the Nile Valley, Ethiopia, India, the Caspian Sea, and the eastern shore of the Mediterranean.

The Persian Gulf became a major waterway, with many trading ports. Bahrain **(bah-RAIN)** Island served as a transshipment point for goods flowing in from all directions and as a hub where various traders and travelers met. Mesopotamian merchants traveled there carrying textiles, leather objects, wool, and olive oil and returned with copper bars, ivory, precious objects, and rare woods from various western Asian societies and India. Trade helped people learn and profit from each other's skills and surplus goods. The Sumerians also had some trade and other connections with Jiroft **(JEER-oft)** in southeastern Iran, another urban-based farming society that emerged sometime between 3000 and 2500 B.C.E. Jiroft's economy was based on cultivating date palms. Its gaily decorated capital city, with lofty red brick towers, supplied craftsmen to Uruk. The ruins of Jiroft city include a two-story citadel, a Sumerian-like ziggurat, the world's oldest known board games, and staggering numbers of decorated vases, goblets, cups, and boxes, often adorned with precious stones from India and Afghanistan.

Sumerian Writing and Technology

The world's first written records were produced by the Sumerians, who were innovators in many areas. Trade and the need to keep accurate records of agricultural production and public and private business dealings led around 3200 B.C.E. to the

[4]Quoted in William H. Stiebing, Jr., *Ancient Near Eastern History and Culture* (New York: Longman, 2003), p. 48.

Essam Al-Sudani/AFP/Getty Images

RUINS OF EARLY CITY OF URUK. Renowned for its walls, the Sumerian city was a rich source of art objects and fine architecture. Uruk's best-known king was the legendary Gilgamesh.

cuneiform (kyoo-NEE-uh-form) (Latin for "wedge-shaped") writing system. Temple recordkeepers, or scribes, made rough pictures (say, of an animal or fish) on soft clay with a stylus that made wedges in the clay and then baked the bricks on which these pictograms were scratched. Soon a stylized version of the pictogram stood for an idea, and eventually an even more abstract version with a phonetic sign described a speech sound.

Writing provided a way of communicating with people over long distances and allowed rulers to administer larger states. Those who controlled the written word, like those who master electronic communication in our day, had power, prestige, and a monopoly over a society's official history. Writing also gave temple scribes and religious leaders the power to determine how written texts attributed to the gods should be interpreted. Since writing required mastery of at least three hundred symbols, only a few people, mostly from the upper class, learned this skill. In part to produce scribes, the Sumerians created the world's first schools, where strict instructors beat students for misbehavior or sloppy work. A clay tablet describes the life of a pupil who spent twenty-four days a month in school and was frequently beaten: "My teacher said: 'Your hand [writing] is unsatisfactory.' [He] caned me. I [begin to hate] the scribal art."[5] However, because cuneiform eventually transformed pictures into phonetic sounds, it made the written word more accessible, even for people whose only goal was a good recipe for a meal of red broth and meat.

Writing became crucial in history by making it easier to express abstract ideas and create an intellectual life based on a body of literature. The oldest known signed poetry was composed by Enheduanna **(en-who-DWAHN-ah)**, a Sumerian priestess and princess living around 2300 B.C.E. Royal women were often authors. A written language based on clearly understood symbols also allowed communication among people who spoke different languages but understood the same written symbols. For example, the number 5 is understood today the same way by Spanish speakers, who pronounce it

cuneiform ("wedge-shaped") Latin term used to describe the writing system invented by the Sumerians.

[5]Quoted in Samuel Noah Kramer, *Cradle of Civilization* (New York: Time-Life Books, 1967), p. 122.

Eileen Tweedy / The Art Archive at Art Resource, NY

THE ROYAL STANDARD OF UR This mosaic from around 2500 B.C.E., made of inlaid shells and limestone, was found in a royal tomb. It depicts various aspects of life in the Mesopotamian city-state of Ur. The bottom panel shows a four-wheeled battle wagon drawn by a horselike animal. The middle panel features soldiers wearing armor and helmets. The top panel shows war prisoners being brought before the king.

"cinco," and German speakers, who say "funf." While giving a strong sense of identity to all who shared a language, writing also encouraged the spread of trade and culture, including religion, to other peoples.

Sumerians also pioneered the first use of the wheel, glass, and fertilizer, inventions that we still live with today; created some of the earliest calendars based on their observations of the movements of various celestial bodies; and introduced one of the first mathematical systems, based on the number 60. Remnants of this system can be seen today in our 60-minute hours and 60-second minutes. Many other peoples eventually adopted these innovations. Humanity also inherited from the Sumerians the division of night and day into twelve hours each.

Although they were not the first to convert barley into beer, the Sumerians, like us, enjoyed alcoholic beverages and designated a special goddess, called Ninkasi or "the lady who fills the mouth," to supervise beer production. The many taverns fostered early drinking songs: "I will summon brewers and cupbearers to serve us floods of beer and keep it passing round! Our hearts enchanted and our souls radiant."[6]

The Akkadian Empire and Its Rivals

For centuries each Sumerian city had its own king who ruled the people in the name of the city's god. This independence ended about 2350 B.C.E. when Sargon **(SAHR-gone)**, the ruler of Akkad **(AH-kahd)**, a region just north of Sumer whose capital was Agade, conquered Uruk and then united the other Sumerian cities under his family's rule. This was the world's first known empire, defined as a large state controlling other societies through conquest or domination. The Akkadians enslaved many people in Mesopotamia, and slaves constituted perhaps a third of the empire's population. Under Sargon trade between Mesopotamia and India reached a peak. Indeed, merchant ships from as far away as Oman **(O-mahn)** in eastern Arabia and even farther away, from India, docked at Agade's wharves, carrying copper and various exotic products.

Sargon's empire soon came into conflict with one created by another city, Ebla **(EBB-luh)** in northern Mesopotamia, whose large empire stretched from eastern Turkey to Mari **(MAH-ree)**, several hundred miles north of Akkad. By the twenty-first century B.C.E. the Akkadian Empire was destroyed, probably from a combination of internal conflicts, external attacks, and less rainfall due to a disastrous drought between 2200 and 1900 B.C.E. that affected much of Eurasia. Indeed, Mesopotamian societies were powerless against abrupt climate change, and Sumerian legends express dread of the periodic droughts: "The famine was severe, nothing was produced. The fields are not watered. In all the lands there was no vegetation [and] only weeds grew."[7] Irrigation canals silted up, and settlements became ghost towns as people migrated.

As the Akkadian Empire collapsed, a new Sumerian dynasty led by Ur took over much of the lower valley between 2100 and 2000 B.C.E., forming the neo-Sumerian Empire. Some Ur kings boasted of their commitment to art and intellectual life. But a coalition of enemies eventually sacked and burned Ur along with other Sumerian cities. Ur's temples were

[6]Quoted in Jean Bottero, *Everyday Life in Ancient Mesopotamia* (Baltimore: Johns Hopkins University Press, 2001), p. 71.
[7]Quoted in Brian Fagan, *The Long Summer: How Climate Changed Civilization* (New York: Basic Books, 2004), p. 138.

destroyed, its populations killed or enslaved, and its treasures plundered. A surviving lamentation describes the destruction: "Ur is destroyed, bitter is its lament. The country's blood now fills its holes like hot bronze in a mould. Our temple is destroyed, the gods have abandoned us, like migrating birds. Smoke lies on our city like a shroud."[8]

The Akkadians, Eblaites, and neo-Sumerians established the first empires in history, even though their creations were short-lived and not the large bureaucratic organizations we see in later empires. They were largely collections of city-states that acknowledged one city as overlord. It soon became clear that whoever had the best army would dominate Mesopotamia.

MAKE SURE YOU UNDERSTAND THESE KEY POINTS BEFORE MOVING ON

- **The first urban societies and states of Mesopotamia developed in the Tigris-Euphrates Basin.**
- **Sumerian society was hierarchical and patriarchal.**
- **The earliest writing system was probably the cuneiform system, developed by the Sumerians.**
- **The world's first empire, the Akkadian Empire, was founded by Sargon in an area just north of the Sumerians.**

Later Mesopotamian Societies and Their Legacies, 2000–600 B.C.E.

What were some of the main features of Mesopotamian societies?

The Sumerians and Akkadians established a pattern of city living, state building, and imperial expansion. From 2000 to 539 B.C.E. a series of peoples coming mainly from the north successively dominated Mesopotamia and created new empires, each contributing to the politics, laws, culture, and thought of the region. This pattern changed only when the entire area was incorporated into the Persian Empire.

The Babylonians and Hittites

Babylon was the first state to dominate Mesopotamia in this era. In 1800 B.C.E. the Amorites **(AM-uh-rites)** conquered Babylon, a city about 300 miles north of the Persian Gulf, and gradually extended their control. Babylon's most famous king, Hammurabi **(HAM-uh-rah-bee)**, who ruled from 1792 to 1750 B.C.E., had nearly three hundred laws collected to "make justice appear in the land, to destroy the evil and the wicked [so] that the strong might not oppress the weak."[9] His law of retaliation—an eye for an eye and a tooth for a tooth—remains famous today, and some of his principles appeared later in Hebrew laws.

By 1595 B.C.E. the Babylonian Empire had disintegrated from attacks by the Hittites **(HIT-ites)**, an Indo-European people from central Anatolia who expanded their power until they met the equally strong Egyptians in Syria and Palestine. The Hittite Empire dominated various parts of western Asia from 1600 to 1200 B.C.E. By sending plague victims into enemy lands, the Hittites pioneered the first biological weapons. Later they also developed iron weapons, which were superior to those made of bronze. They treated their subjects less harshly than the Babylonians and adopted many Mesopotamian gods, establishing a tradition of religious tolerance in the region.

The Assyrian Empire and Regional Supremacy

In 1115 B.C.E. the Assyrians **(uh-SEER-e-uhns)**—by creating a large, well-organized military; systematically using terror against enemies; and devising methods of bureaucratic organization that later empires imitated—began conquering an empire that was eventually larger than any before. One of their greatest kings, Tiglath-pileser **(TIG-lath-pih-LEE-zuhr)** III (745–727 B.C.E.), conquered the entire eastern Mediterranean shore, and later Assyrian rulers added Egypt to the empire. One Assyrian king described himself with some accuracy as "obedient to his gods and receiving the tribute of the four corners of the world."[10] Using iron weapons while their enemies still relied on softer bronze ones, the Assyrians launched armies of over fifty thousand men divided into a core of infantrymen aided by cavalry and horse-drawn chariots. They used battering rams and tunnels against the city walls of their enemies and employed guerrilla, or irregular hit-and-run tactics, when fighting in the forests or mountains.

Assyrian kings created a systematic bureaucracy to rule over several million people in the Tigris-Euphrates heartland and created an early version of the "pony express" that allowed them to send messages hundreds of miles within a week. Some kings were both brutal and learned. Ashurbanipal **(ah-shur-BAH-nugh-pahl)** (680–627 B.C.E.), who founded a great library to collect tablets from all over the country, boasted that, in school, he learned to solve complex mathematical problems and discovered the "hidden treasure" of writing.

Violence and the Fall of the Assyrians

The Assyrians were most remembered, and deplored, for their brutality, which ultimately contributed to their downfall.

[8]Quoted in Michael Wood, *Legacy: The Search for Ancient Cultures* (New York: Sterling, 1994), p. 34.

[9]Quoted in G. R. Driver and John C. Miles, eds., *The Babylonian Laws*, vol. II (Oxford: Clarendon Press), 1952, p. 7.

[10]Quoted in N. B. Jankowska, "Asshur, Mitanni, and Arrapkhe," in *Early Antiquity*, I. M. Diakonoff, ed. (Chicago: University of Chicago Press, 1991), p. 256.

Ashurbanipal bragged about mutilating and burning prisoners. After destroying the state of Elam in Iran, he boasted that "like the onset of a terrible hurricane I overwhelmed Elam. I cut off the head of…their braggart king. In countless numbers I killed his warriors." As to the capital city, "I destroyed it…[and] burned it with fire."[11] Soldiers routinely looted cities, destroyed crops, and impaled their enemies. To prevent revolts, the Assyrians often simply moved people to another part of the vast empire. For example, according to legends, inhabitants of one of the two Hebrew kingdoms were sent to Mesopotamia, where they disappeared from history (see Chapter 3). Yet the Assyrians also tolerated other religions, allowing the Hebrew faith to survive the conquest of their state.

Many hated Assyria's brutal rule. In 612 B.C.E., a coalition including the Chaldeans **(kal-DEE-uhns)** (also known as neo-Babylonians) captured the Assyrian capital at Nineveh **(NIN-uh-vuh)**. Their most memorable ruler, Nebuchadnezzar **(NAB-oo-kuhd-nez-uhr)** II (r. 605–562 B.C.E.), a brutal strongman, rebuilt Babylon and adorned it with magnificent palaces and elaborate terraced "hanging gardens." Built to please one of his wives, the gardens became famous throughout the ancient world. Nebuchadnezzar led the conquest of the remaining Hebrew kingdom in 586 B.C.E. The Chaldeans flourished from 626 B.C.E. until they were conquered by the much larger Persian Empire in 539 B.C.E.

Mesopotamian Law

Several documents tell us much about Mesopotamian life and beliefs. The eighteenth-century B.C.E. Law Code of Hammurabi reveals the social structures of this early urban society (see Profile: Hammurabi the Lawgiver). Hammurabi's Code makes clear both how people were valued and how they viewed laws, government, and social norms. In noting that families were responsible for the crimes of any of their members, the Code probably reflected a high crime rate, no doubt because of the tremendous gap between rich and poor. To keep lines of inheritance clear, Hammurabi prescribed harsh punishments for sexual infidelity and incest, as did many societies. Women who violated social norms generally suffered harsher punishments than men, just as the eyes and teeth of poor men or slaves were worth less than the same body parts among the upper classes. Each slave was branded with the owner's symbol, and some endured harsh lives of forced labor. Yet some slaves also owned their own assets, carried on business, and even acquired their own slaves.

The Code also addressed economic issues. In this class-conscious society, a surgeon could lose his hand if his patient was a free man who failed to survive the operation, certainly a disincentive to take up medicine. If the patient was a slave, however, the surgeon had only to replace him with another. If a house collapsed, killing its inhabitants, the builder could be executed. The high interest rates on loans confirmed a thriving commercial class. The Code's punishments tell us how precarious life must have been in this society, where a single small break in an irrigation canal wall could spell disaster.

Mesopotamian Religion and Literature

Like most early people, the Mesopotamians believed in a host of gods and goddesses, such as Inanna, later called Ishtar **(ISH-tar)**, the beautiful goddess of love who created desire. This polytheistic religion imposed no moral demands, but while the divinities came with human weaknesses, they were powerful enough to punish humans, who were created to serve them. People saw themselves as subject to the gods' whims and held ritual ceremonies in massive temples where the gods were housed. The Babylonians and later the Assyrians changed the names of some earlier gods but maintained the basic Sumerian view of the universe.

The *Epic of Gilgamesh* **(GILL-guh-mesh)**, first written down about 2000 B.C.E. but revised and retold by Mesopotamians for another 1,500 years, reveals some of their religious values and attitudes. Perhaps humanity's first epic adventure story, *Gilgamesh* echoes Hammurabi's view of the world as a dangerous place in which happiness is hard to find. Although only one part of a very rich legacy of literature and mythology, *Gilgamesh* had the most enduring and widespread influence, enriching the traditions of varied Eurasian societies.

In one version of the story, the hero, modeled after a real king in Uruk about 2750 B.C.E. and created to be two-thirds god and one-third man, engages in a series of adventures involving both the gods and men. With his friend Enkidu, Gilgamesh challenges and defeats the evil but divine giant who guards a mysterious cedar forest. Gilgamesh then rejects a proposal from Ishtar, telling her that she is fickle and recounting the disagreeable things she has done to her previous lovers, such as turning one of them into a wolf. In revenge, Ishtar causes the death of Enkidu. Reflecting on his friend's death, Gilgamesh searches for the key to eternal life, an ultimately futile quest involving many setbacks that reflects the general pessimism of Mesopotamian culture. A Uruk master scribe lamented: "Gilgamesh, what you seek you will never find. For when the Gods created Man they let death be his lot, eternal life they withheld. Let your every day be full of joy, love the child that holds your hand, let your wife delight in your embrace, for these alone are concerns of humanity."[12]

Scholars have noted the similarities between this story and stories found in the later Hebrew book of Genesis. In both there is a paradise: the garden of Eden for the Hebrews, Dilmun for the Mesopotamians. In both a great flood destroys humankind, a man challenges the god(s), and a serpent comes between a man and immortality. However, although the writer or writers of Genesis may have been influenced by *Gilgamesh*, there are some differences in tone and attitude between the Babylonian and Hebrew versions. In the Hebrew story, God sends a flood to punish humans for evil living. In more urban Mesopotamia, where floods were frequent and destructive, the

[11] Quoted in Kramer, *Cradle of Civilization*, p. 75.

[12] Quoted in Wood, *Legacy*, p. 32.

PROFILE

Hammurabi the Lawgiver

Hammurabi, a Babylonian king (r. 1792–1750 B.C.E.) who was also at times a diplomat, warrior, builder of temples, digger of canals, and, most famously, lawgiver, personified Mesopotamian society. Many surviving tablets, inscriptions, and letters made the king and his era the best documented in Mesopotamian history. He seems to have been a good administrator and able general who governed fairly and efficiently. Like other Mesopotamian kings, Hammurabi probably had a chief queen and various concubines, as well as several sons and daughters.

When Hammurabi became king, Babylon was an insignificant city-state. To expand its power, Hammurabi shrewdly allied with the powerful king of Ashur and allowed him to conquer some nearby cities. For some years Hammurabi's small domain remained one of many rival states. Like other kings, Hammurabi had intelligence agents in other cities keeping him abreast of important developments such as pending alliances and troop movements. A spy for another king wrote that "whenever Hammurabi is perturbed by some matter, he . . . tells me whatever is troubling him, and all of the important information I continually report to my lord." After his army repulsed an invasion by rivals, a confident Hammurabi engaged in a long series of wars that added all of southern Mesopotamia and then much of the north to his kingdom. Finally he conquered the strongest power, his former ally Ashur.

Kingship brought responsibilities. Hammurabi's letters reveal him sitting in his palace office and dictating to a secretary who recorded his orders or thoughts with a reed stylus on a clay tablet. Most letters conveyed commands to governors. His secretary also read aloud letters from officials. In his replies, Hammurabi tried to resolve problems, suggesting ways to clear a flooded shipping channel, warning delinquent tax collectors, punishing corrupt officials, or improving agricultural productivity. He also held daily audiences for petitioners seeking justice. Many decisions concerned temple property and administration, indicating the link between church and state.

Realizing the need to have uniform laws in his diverse country, Hammurabi compiled older laws, recent legal decisions, and social customs, arranged them systematically, and placed them on an 8-foot block of black basalt stone in the temple of Babylon's patron god, Marduk. At the top, an artist pictured Hammurabi receiving the symbols of kingship from Shamash, the sun-god and lawgiver. The Code of 282 laws informed citizens of their rights and demonstrated to both gods and people that the king was doing his job to uphold justice in a moral universe.

DeAgostini/Getty Images

HAMMURABI RECEIVING THE LAW CODE The top of this stela, which is 8 feet high, shows the powerful sun-god, Shamash, on his throne bestowing the famous Law Code to King Hammurabi.

For close to four millennia, we have been intrigued by the principles of this ancient Mesopotamian law code reflecting the harsh views of the era. It mandated two kinds of punishments, a monetary penalty and a retribution in kind, and the harshness of the punishment depended on the social class of the people involved: nobles and landowners, commoners, or slaves. Many laws discouraged burglary by prescribing instant death for those caught; mud-brick homes were not very secure. On the other hand, prostitution was legal. Some laws protected women and children from abuse and arbitrary treatment. For example, a husband who divorced his wife because she bore no sons had to return the dowry she brought into the marriage and forfeit the money he had given her parents for a bridal price. Since the Hebrews borrowed some of these laws, often in modified form, and passed them into Christian and Islamic traditions, Hammurabi's legacy remains influential today.

THINKING ABOUT THE PROFILE

1. How did Hammurabi increase the power of Babylon?
2. What were the purposes of his great Law Code?

Note: Quotation from William H. Stiebing, Jr., *Ancient Near Eastern History and Culture* (New York: Longman, 2003), 88–89.

gods "decide to exterminate mankind" because "the uproar of mankind is intolerable and sleep is no longer possible." But a dissenting god causes his favorite mortal to survive by building a boat and loading it with his family and "the seed of all living creatures, the game of the field, and all the craftsmen."[13]

The parallels between the Gilgamesh legend and Genesis remind us that the Gilgamesh story became widely known far beyond Mesopotamia. Some motifs can be found in Greek literature, such as the Homeric epics: reappear in the much later Islamic period, such as the stories of Aladdin and Sinbad; and are still found in the folk cultures of some villages. The Gilgamesh epic became one of the many unique traditions that shaped the societies of southwestern Asia and made them different from other early societies such as India and Egypt.

MAKE SURE YOU UNDERSTAND THESE KEY POINTS BEFORE MOVING ON

- **The Babylonians, Hittites, Assyrians, and Chaldeans created empires in Mesopotamia.**
- **The Babylonian king Hammurabi created a legal framework that included harsh punishments and reflected strict class divisions.**
- **The Assyrian Empire, known for its brutality, dominated a large region but was finally defeated by a coalition of enemies.**
- **The *Epic of Gilgamesh*, which shows parallels with the book of Genesis, reflects Mesopotamian values and perspectives, including a pessimistic view of life.**

The Earliest Indian and Central Asian Societies, 6000–1500 B.C.E.

What were some of the distinctive features of the Harappan cities?

India developed a society with cultural features vastly different from those of the Middle East, Europe, or China. Some Indians made the transition to farming very early, and the first cities east of Mesopotamia were founded around 2600 B.C.E. The city-states and the widespread Bronze Age culture they shared, often called **Harappan** **(HAR-up-un)**, were centered in the Indus **(IN-duhs)** River Valley and nearby rivers in what is now Pakistan and northwest India. Harappan culture eventually covered some 300,000 square miles, the largest in geographical extent of the ancient societies. Although the Harappans built no pyramids like the Egyptians or ziggurats like the Sumerians, they developed a remarkable society. To the north, an urban society also developed in Central Asia.

South Asian Environments and the Rise of Farming

River valley environments strongly shaped early Indian societies, just as they did Mesopotamia, Egypt, and China. The Indian subcontinent, about half the size of Europe, is rimmed by the Indian Ocean and the Himalayan Mountains, which boast the half dozen highest peaks in the world, including Mount Everest at nearly 30,000 feet. The Himalayas, which stretch some 1,500 miles east to west, inhibited regular communication between China and India. Just north of the Himalayas, the Tibetan Plateau is the source of great rivers, including the Indus and Ganges in India, the Yellow and Yangzi in China, and the Irrawaddy and Mekong in Southeast Asia, which eventually reach great plains and deltas. The highly fertile land fostered productive farming and dense settlement. Rice and wheat became the staple crops for most South and East Asians, and scavenging animals like chickens and pigs were more important food sources than beef cattle, which requires extensive pasture.

Harappan Name given to the city-states and the widespread Bronze Age culture they shared that were centered in the Indus River Valley and nearby rivers in northwest India.

India's distinctive features resulted in part from its physical environment and climate. The fertile north Indian plains, watered by the Indus and Ganges Rivers, are relatively flat and so encouraged cultural unity, cities, and kingdoms. By contrast, mountainous south India developed more cultural diversity with different languages from those of north India. Other culturally distinct regions include Bengal, framed by the delta of the Ganges River, and the fertile island of Sri Lanka (once known as Ceylon), just off India's southern tip.

The tropical climate affected Indian life. South and northeast India enjoy high rainfall, but today much of the northwest is desert. Although the annual rains sustain life, seasonal flooding poses a chronic problem. Water has been an especially sacred commodity in Indian life, thought, and literature. With many domesticated cattle, most Indians learned to consume dairy products, including yogurt, a local invention. By 7000–6000 B.C.E. many villages in the Indus region were pioneering productive farming. Thanks to surpluses of wheat and barley, by 3000 B.C.E. the population of the Indus Valley may have reached 1 million, and regional trading networks emerged, setting the stage for the emergence of cities.

[13] *The Epic of Gilgamesh*, trans. by N. K. Sandars (New York: Penguin Books, 1960), p. 108.

MAP 2.2 HARAPPAN CULTURE AND ARYAN MIGRATIONS The Harappan culture emerged in the city-states of the Indus River Basin. They had collapsed by around 1500 B.C.E., when the Aryan peoples from Iran began migrating into India and setting up states.

Harappan Cities

Around 2600 B.C.E., the first Indian urban society emerged from regional cultures in the semiarid Indus River Valley (see Map 2.2). Along the banks of the Indus, which later inspired the English term *India*, and nearby rivers such as the Saraswati, a vibrant urban-based culture thrived for hundreds of years and planted some seeds for the rich Indian culture that endures to the present. Silt spread by regular river floods served as a natural fertilizer, while nearby forests provided enough wood for baking the bricks used in building cities. Like the Nile, the flat, easily navigable Indus and its tributary rivers gave Harappan society considerable uniformity. Most of the Harappan cities were in the Punjab **(PUHN-jab)** and Sind provinces of modern Pakistan, a crossroads of major trading routes, but some were hundreds of miles to the west or east. Indeed, the Indus culture covered an area far larger than the Mesopotamian and Egyptian cultures combined. The two major Indus cities, called by archaeologists Harappa and Mohenjo-Daro **(moe-hen-joe-DAHR-oh)**, stood 400 miles apart. The 1,500 Harappan cities and towns contained a total population of perhaps 5 million people at their zenith.

All the cities shared many common features in construction, society, government, religion, and culture, revealing a society that valued order, organization, and cleanliness. Using the same pattern, administrators carefully laid out the cities using a north-south grid pattern with wide streets and large rectangular city blocks, separating residential and commercial districts from a smaller area for public affairs. Shops probably lined the main streets. The largest city, Harappa, some 3⅓ miles in circumference, contained perhaps eighty thousand people at its height. Massive brick ramparts 40 feet thick at their base partially protected it from the river waters and any potential human attackers. Large granaries provide evidence of wealth and stored voluminous supplies, perhaps of wheat for the local population, or export goods.

The Harappan people had exceptional housing for ancient times. Most buildings were made from bricks molded to a standardized size. More affluent residents lived in spacious homes constructed on strong brick foundations with interior courtyards that provided considerable privacy, but even the common people enjoyed well-built accommodations. The urban Harappans also enjoyed the ancient world's most advanced sanitation system. Most houses had a bathroom and drains to carry away the wastewater. Covered drains along city streets were more sanitary than those found in many modern cities. The close attention to providing and carrying away water and the huge public baths suggest an emphasis on washing and personal cleanliness for ritual purity, which later became important in Indian religion.

Scholars debate the identity of the Harappan people. Most scholars long believed that they spoke a **Dravidian (druh-VID-ee-uhn)** language, but some contemporary scholars consider this conclusion unsubstantiated.

Dravidian A language family whose speakers are the great majority of the population in southern India.

hotobank/Glow Images

RUINS OF MOHENJO-DARO This photo shows the great bath in the city. Like modern Indians, Harappans valued bathing for hygienic and possibly religious reasons.

Speakers of other languages may also have lived in these cities, which seem to have had cosmopolitan populations. Most modern Dravidian speakers live in southern India, where they are the great majority of the population.

Harappan Society and Its Beliefs

The Harappan governments, social system, and religious beliefs remain a puzzle. The available evidence for an organized monarchy is thin, as there are no elaborate palaces, temples, or monuments glorifying leaders. Each city was probably independent, perhaps governed by some powerful merchant guild or council of commercial, landowning, and religious leaders. The ruins contain few weapons, suggesting that, in contrast to Mesopotamia, war was uncommon. But only some people owned beautiful objects of personal adornment, such as necklaces and beads. The ruins also contain many toys made from clay or wood, indicating a prosperous society that valued leisure for children.

Harappan society had unusual gender relations for that era, different from the rigid patriarchies that characterized Mesopotamia or China as governments grew more powerful. Apparently Harappan husbands moved into their wives' households after marriage, suggesting a matrilineal system. Yet some customs harmed women. At least some Harappans may have practiced *sati* **(suh-TEE)**, the custom of a widow killing herself by jumping onto the funeral pyre as her dead husband is being cremated. A controversial recent study concludes that some female burials show sign of traumatic injuries from possible abuse.

Harappans mixed art with religion and even commerce. They made small, square, clay seals, possibly used by merchants for branding their wares. Some seals show farming activities; others contain portraits of domesticated animals, including bulls and water buffaloes, as well as the wild tigers, elephants, and rhinoceros that inhabited the nearby forests. Small bronze statues of dancers suggest that the Harappans enjoyed dance. Most scholars argue that they created a written language, although it seems more limited than Mesopotamian, Egyptian, and Chinese writing and remains undeciphered today. The seals, pottery, and various clay tablets contained some four hundred different signs that were completely unrelated to other scripts. Most likely many of the signs represent the names of merchants, businesses, or the commodities being sold.

Some Harappan religious notions contributed to Hinduism, a religion that developed after Harappan times. For example, one seal features a human figure with multiple faces, a regular feature of later Hindu icons, sitting in a yogalike position and surrounded by various animals. It may depict the great Hindu god **Shiva (SHEEV-uh)** in one of his major roles as "Lord of the Beasts." Harappans apparently already worshiped Shiva in his dual role as god of destruction and of fertility and the harvest. Possibly the later Hindu notions of reincarnation also derived from Harappan beliefs. Many small clay figurines with exaggerated breasts and hips suggest that mother-goddess worship was prominent in Harappan religious life, as it was in the Fertile Crescent and ancient Europe. Such artistic representations of voluptuous female deities remain common today in India, symbolizing earth and the life-bearing nature of women. Whereas a female orientation largely disappeared in the religions of many other societies, it remained prominent in Hinduism.

J. M. Kenoyer/Courtesy, Department of Archaeology and Museums, Government of Pakistan

HARAPPAN SEAL The seal from Mohenjo-Daro features a humped bull. The writing at the top has yet to be deciphered.

The Harappan Economy and the Wider World

The Harappan cities were hubs connected to southwestern and Central Asia through trade and transportation networks that fostered extensive contact. The diverse local economy flourished from cultivating barley and wheat with sophisticated irrigation techniques and from producing cotton and metal products, helping Harappan society remain stable and prosperous for hundreds of years. Like Indians today, the Harappans used spices in their cooking. They or their ancestors domesticated the camel, elephant, chicken, and, to aid farming, zebu (oxen) and water buffalo. These last two animals may have been worshiped, becoming the basis for the later respect accorded cows in Hinduism.

Harappans made other long-lasting contributions, among them cotton cloth and cotton textiles for clothing, one of ancient India's major gifts to the world. Skilled and aggressive Harappan traders traveled far and wide. Cotton was shipped in bulk to Mesopotamia, while metals, which were absent in the Indus Basin, were imported. A huge dock, massive granaries, and specialized factories at the coastal port of Lothal reflected a high-volume maritime trade. Many Harappan seals found at the Mesopotamian city of Ur suggest a steady trade between 2300 and 2000 B.C.E., with Bahrain Island in the Persian Gulf functioning as a major crossroads. Some Indian exports may even have reached Egypt and Crete. The Harappans exported surplus food, cotton, timber products, copper, and gold, as well as luxury items such as pearls, precious stone products, ivory combs, beads, spices, peacock feathers, and inlay goods made from shell or bone. They imported precious stones from southern India and silver, turquoise, and tin from Persia and Afghanistan.

The Decline and Collapse of Harappan Society

Eventually Harappan society declined, for reasons not altogether clear. Sometime between 1900 and 1750 B.C.E. a combination of factors disrupted the urban environment. By 1700 B.C.E. most of the Harappan cities had been destroyed or abandoned, although a considerable rural population remained. Seals and writing began to disappear. The careful grid pattern for city streets was abandoned, the drainage systems deteriorated, and even home sizes were reduced. Some evidence points to violence, plundering and banditry.

Harappan decline may have resulted from several factors. Perhaps the Harappans exhausted the land. Some evidence points to deforestation, increased flooding, excessive irrigation of marginal lands, soil deterioration, and especially drastic climate change. Apparently rainfall decreased significantly, and one major river, the Saraswati, dried up entirely. These catastrophes probably led to economic breakdown. The crop surpluses that had long sustained the cities disappeared, and people abandoned farms. Perhaps disease epidemics weakened the population.

The end of some of the Indus Valley cities may have been sudden, the result perhaps of an earthquake temporarily damming the rivers,

Shiva The Hindu god of destruction and of fertility and the harvest.

unleashing an awesome flood that quickly overwhelmed low-lying cities. Today as well, periodic Indus flooding remains a major problem; in 2010 massive floods in Pakistan destroyed many villages and towns, displacing hundreds of thousands. In the Harappan case, the hoards of jewelry, skeletons buried in debris, and cooking pots found strewn across kitchens indicate hastily abandoned homes. The rising floodwaters may have been accompanied by more earthquakes. Harappa, located on higher ground, and some other cities survived a while longer, although with much reduced populations.

The fate of the Harappan people and their cultures is also unclear. Some cities east of the Indus Valley remained populated for several more centuries, practicing modified forms of Harappan culture. Many Harappans may have migrated into central and southern India, mixing with local Dravidian populations and carrying with them a culture, technology, and agriculture that contributed to the Indian society to come. The calamities left the remaining Indus peoples weak and unable to resist later migrations of peoples from outside.

Central Asian Environments and Oxus Cities

Central Asia is the vast area of plains (**steppes**), deserts, and mountains that stretches from the Ural Mountains and Caspian Sea eastward to Tibet, western China, and Mongolia. Before modern times Central Asians played a role in history far greater than their relatively small populations would suggest, not only as invaders and sometimes conquerors but also as middlemen in the long-distance trade that developed between China, India, the Middle East, and Europe.

Much of Central Asia offered a harsh environment suitable mainly for pastoralists. It was inhabited by diverse peoples mostly speaking Ural-Altaic languages, including various Turkish and Mongol tongues. Large-scale population movements and frequent warfare between competing tribal confederations became common. Most of the steppe societies had skilled horsemen and were led by warrior chieftains. Some attacked and occasionally conquered northern China. Various Central Asian peoples also migrated through the mountain ranges into northwest India.

Although much of Central Asia was steppe lands, some areas supported city life, especially in Turkestan, the region from east of the Caspian Sea to Xinjiang **(SIN-john)** on China's western frontier. Archaeologists occasionally find important but previously unknown sites, including an early urban society in Central Asia that some call the Oxus **(OX-uhs)**, after the river that runs through the area. The Oxus society apparently thrived between 2200 and 1800 B.C.E., when the Harappan culture was also at its height, building walled cities with mud-brick buildings and carefully designed streets, drains, and temples around desert oases in what is now Uzbekistan and Turkmenistan. Enjoying a wetter climate than now, the people grew wheat and barley, forged bronze axes, carved figurines of women from stone and ivory, and decorated pottery. A tiny stamp seal with letter-like symbols dated to 2300 B.C.E. is evidence for writing, so far not linked to any other society. The Oxus cities, perhaps independent city-states, were situated along the later "Silk Road" trade routes between India and China, suggesting that this trade may be older than is often thought. They were closely linked to the Harappans and probably traded with China, Jiroft, and Mesopotamia. Eventually the cities were abandoned and, over the centuries, buried by sand.

MAKE SURE YOU UNDERSTAND THESE KEY POINTS BEFORE MOVING ON

- **The earliest Indian urban society, the Harappan, emerged in the Indus River Valley around 2600 B.C.E.**
- **The peaceful Harappans had well-planned cities with advanced sanitation, a culture that gave women high status, and a written language.**
- **The Harappans invented cotton cloth, and Harappan cities enjoyed extensive foreign trade with western and Central Asia.**
- **Harappan cities declined for unknown reasons, possibly due to environmental catastrophe.**
- **Many Central Asians practiced nomadic pastoralism but some built thriving cities in the Oxus region.**

The Aryans and a New Indian Society, 1500–600 B.C.E.

How did Indian society and the Hindu religion emerge from the mixing of Aryan and local cultures?

steppes The plains of Central Asia.

Aryans Indo-European-speaking nomadic pastoralists who migrated from Iran into northwest India.

Throughout India's long history, many people migrated from elsewhere into the subcontinent, some of them conquering parts of India. The assimilation of these various newcomers resulted in an increasingly diverse society. One such group, the **Aryans** **(AIR-ee-unzs)**, Indo-European-speaking nomadic pastoralists, migrated into northwest India, expanded across northern India, and introduced new cultures. The Aryan expansion between 1500 and 1000 B.C.E. built the foundation for a new society that mixed Aryan culture with the traditions of the indigenous peoples, including the Dravidians. Over many centuries a fusion of Aryan and Dravidian cultures, what historians label the **Indo-Aryan synthesis**, forged a new social system and Hinduism, a religion of diverse beliefs. But the Aryans had a greater impact in the north than in the mostly Dravidian south, which retained its own languages and writing systems. Despite regular contact with western, Central, and Southeast Asia, the patterns that developed were so distinctive and enduring that India even today is unlike any other society.

The Aryan Peoples and the Vedas

Most scholars agree that the Aryans began migrating by horse-drawn chariot from Iran (the Persian word for "Aryan") or Turkestan into northwestern India between 1600 and 1400 B.C.E., after the collapse of the Harappan cities, a time when rainfall in the Indus region was increasing again, improving economic conditions. Other Indo-Europeans had already settled in Iran, Mesopotamia, and parts of Central Asia. Aryans might have built the recently discovered four-thousand-year-old city ruins along today's Russia-Kazakhstan border, but the early migrants to India were probably pastoralists. Some historians and Hindu nationalists argue that Aryan settlement in India was far older and that the Harappans may have been Aryans. However, in the mainstream view, the Aryans arrived in small groups over several centuries, bringing with them a rich oral literature and unique ideas about government, society, and religion. As more arrived, the Aryans expanded throughout northern India. But archaeologists have found little material evidence, such as pots or weapons, that might reveal more of the process. Furthermore, unlike the Chinese and Greeks, ancient Indians never developed a tradition of historiography, the study and writing of history, perhaps because their conceptions of time emphasized the temporary nature of existence.

Much of what we know about the ancient Aryans comes from their literature, the **Vedas** **(VAY-duhs)** ("books of knowledge"). This vast collection of sacred hymns to the gods and thoughts about religion, philosophy, and magic was based on oral accounts carefully preserved by bards, the memory experts of each Indo-European tribe. The principal early source of Hindu religious belief, the Vedas reflected the world-view of the priestly class and were already old when written down centuries later. We can infer that the Aryans were organized into tribes that frequently moved their settlements. Their class system consisted of warriors, priests, and commoners. They were a cattle-raising people, as is reflected in one of the hymns: "A bard am I, my father a leech, And my mother a grinder of corn. Diverse in means, but all wishing wealth, Alike for cattle we strive."[14]

A militaristic people who harnessed horses to chariots and skillfully wielded bows and arrows and bronze axes, the Aryans had fought their way through blistering deserts and snowy mountains to reach India. Some Vedas celebrate Aryan victories against fortified settlements inhabited by peoples, probably including Dravidians, who had darker skins than the Aryans: "For fear of thee fled the dark-hued races, scattered abroad, deserting their possessions."[15] The various Aryan tribes could unite against a common enemy, but mostly they fought against each other.

The Aryans mixed their language with those of local people, creating **Sanskrit** **(SAN-skrit)**, the classical spoken language of north India, through which the Vedas were preserved through memorization and passed though generations. By the fourth century B.C.E., however, vernacular (everyday) Indo-European spoken languages were becoming more dominant in north India, and Sanskrit gradually became mostly a written language for religious and literary works. Since few Indians today learn to write or speak Sanskrit, some fear the language may eventually disappear. Some three-quarters of Indians today speak an Indo-European language.

Early Aryan Government, Society, and Religion

Persistent military conflict marked the early Aryan political and social structure. Each tribe's autocratic male ruler, known as a *raja*, sought as much power for himself and his group as possible. The Bharata **(BAA-ray-tuh)** was the most powerful tribe. Later, the ***Mahabharata*** **(MA-huh-BAA-ray-tuh)** ("Great Bharata"), the world's longest poem, probably composed in the eighth or ninth century but only written down around 400–500 B.C.E., spun a complex and entertaining tale of many cousins and their titanic battles for supremacy. Reflecting life around 1000 B.C.E., the *Mahabharata* is, like Homer's *Iliad*, drenched in the blood of endless struggles over succession and supremacy. The *Ramayana* **(ruh-MA-yawn-uh)** ("The Story of Rama"), another Aryan epic written down sometime after 500 B.C.E., may be based on the extension of Aryan power into southern India.

In the patriarchal Aryan family structure, the father dominated his wives and children. In the following centuries, both male supremacy and a hierarchy based on age became the standard Indian family pattern. The Aryans developed a living pattern known as the joint family, also common in China, in which the wives of all the sons moved into the larger patriarchal household, which included members from three or even four generations. The status of Aryan women changed with time. The early Aryans educated both daughters and sons in the Vedas. One Vedic hymn encouraged women to speak publicly, and women may have composed some of the hymns. Later women became more restricted and daughters less valued. They needed to obtain dowries (gifts for the prospective in-laws) in order to marry, could not participate in the sacrifices to gods, and did not inherit property.

The Vedas also reveal Aryan recreational interests such as horse-drawn chariot

Indo-Aryan synthesis The fusion of Aryan and Dravidian cultures in India over many centuries.

Vedas The Aryans' "books of knowledge," the principal source of religious belief for Hindus: a vast collection of sacred hymns to the gods and thoughts about religion, philosophy, and magic.

Sanskrit The classical spoken language of north India but now reserved mainly for religious and literary writing.

Mahabharata ("Great Bharata") An Aryan epic and the world's longest poem.

[14]Quoted in John Keay, *India: A History* (New York: Atlantic Monthly Press, 2000), p. 35.

[15]Quoted in Hermann Kulke and Dietmar Rothermund, *History of India*, 3rd ed. (New York: Routledge, 1998), p. 35.

racing and gambling. Indians invented both dice and chess. Indeed, gambling features prominently in the *Mahabharata;* one raja loses his kingdom through his fondness for games of chance. The Aryans were also fond of wine and music, using such instruments as lutes, flutes, and drums. Song and dance remain an integral component of Indian religious worship and ritual.

As sacred texts, the Vedas contained considerable information about Aryan religion, the significance of various gods, and the role of priests, confirming that the Aryans' religious views were similar to those of their Hittite cousins in western Asia. Each Aryan tribe boasted its own bards, poets who were also priests who presided over sacrifices and rituals because they alone had memorized the Vedic hymns. The oldest and most important Veda, the *Rig Veda* ("Verses of Knowledge"), probably composed by various poets between 1500 and 1000 B.C.E. but only written down by 500 B.C.E., contains over one thousand poems composed in Sanskrit, most of them soliciting the favor of Aryan gods.

Eliot Elisofon/Getty Images

ARYAN WARFARE Vedic stories remain popular in modern India. This scene from an old temple wall of Aryan warfare depicts embattled gods and demons from the *Mahabharata.*

The Aryans worshiped a pantheon of nature gods, to whom they offered sacrifices. The *Rig Veda* describes some thirty-three deities led by the thunderbolt-wielding war-god Indra **(INN-druh)**, ever youthful, heroic, and victorious. Many poems celebrate the awesome power of the deities, as in the following tribute to the storm-gods: "You are terrible and powerful, O storm gods. You bring everlasting rain in the desert. Dark rain clouds shroud the sky, Turning day into night, drenching the earth."[16] The Rig Veda reflects an open-minded intellectual pluralism and tolerance, one poem even defending heretics and atheists. Aryan religion also included speculations on the deepest mysteries of existence. One poem, the "Hymn of Creation," is one of the most ancient expressions of questions about the creation of the universe: "Who really knows? Who will here proclaim it? Whence was this creation? The gods came afterwards, with the creation of the universe. Who then really knows whence it has arisen?"[17] This hymn also suggests a time before time when there was no space or sky, night or day, life or death. Then, in a kind of Big Bang, the cosmos was created by the power of heat (see Chapter 1).

brahmans The priests, the highest-ranking caste in Hindu society.

kshatriyas Warriors and landowners headed by the rajas in the Hindu caste system.

vaisyas The merchants and artisans in the Hindu caste system.

sudras The poorer farmers, farm workers, and menial laborers in the Hindu caste system.

Aryan Expansion and State Building in North India

Many Aryans eventually moved eastward into the Ganges **(GAN-geez)** Valley between 1000 and 450 B.C.E., building kingdoms and mixing with local peoples. During this time they changed through conflict, cooperation, and assimilation with the peoples they encountered, eventually adopting systems of farming, village structure, and some religious concepts from local peoples, but also contributing their language, social system, and many religious beliefs to the mix.

Throughout north India, city development and economic growth encouraged political consolidation into kingdoms. By the sixth century B.C.E. sixteen major Aryan kingdoms stretched from Bengal westward to the fringes of Afghanistan, most of them in the central Ganges region. However, kings did not have unlimited power; they were still advised by councils of warriors. Thus no kingdom was yet strong enough to conquer all the others and create a unified government for all north India until the establishment of the Mauryan Empire in 321 B.C.E. (see Chapter 5).

The Roots of the Caste System

The Indo-Aryan synthesis modified the social structure. Perhaps incorporating some Harappan traditions, a four-tiered class division emerged that comprised the **brahmans (BRAH-munz)**, or priests; the **kshatriyas (kuh-SHOT-ree-uhs)**, the warriors and landowners; the **vaisyas (VIGH-shuhs)**, or merchants and artisans; and the **sudras (SOO-druhs)**, mostly poorer farmers, farm workers, and menial laborers. The priests enjoyed many special privileges as guardians and interpreters of sacred knowledge. Over time the sudras, mostly of non-Aryan

[16] William McNaughton, ed., *Light from the East* (New York: Laurel, 1978), p. 398.
[17] Quoted in Burton Stein, *A History of India* (Malden, MA.: Blackwell, 1998), p. 53.

WITNESS TO THE PAST

Hindu Values in the *Bhagavad Gita*

The Bhagavad Gita, *a philosophical poem in the* Mahabharata, *helped shape India's ethical traditions while providing Hindus with a practical guide to everyday life. The following excerpt is part of a dialogue between the god Krishna (Vishnu) and the poem's conflicted hero, the warrior Arjuna* **(are-JUNE-ah)**, *on the eve of a great battle in which Arjuna will slaughter his uncles, cousins, teachers, and friends. The reading summarizes some of Krishna's advice in justifying the battle. Krishna suggests that Arjuna must follow his destiny, for while the physical body is impermanent, the soul is eternal. The slain will be reborn. Furthermore, humans are responsible for their own destiny through their behavior and mental discipline. They also, like Arjuna, need to fulfill their obligations to society.*

The wise grieve neither for the living nor for the dead. There has never been a time when you and I and the kings gathered here have not existed, nor will there ever be a time when we will cease to exist. As the same person inhabits the body through childhood, youth, and old age, so too at the time of death he attains another body. The wise are not deluded by these changes.

When the senses contact sense objects, a person experiences cold or heat, pleasure or pain. These experiences are fleeting; they come and go. Bear them patiently. . . . Those who are not affected by these changes, who are the same in pleasure and pain, are truly wise and fit for immortality. Assert your strength and realize this!

The impermanent has no reality; reality lies in the eternal. Those who have seen the boundary between these two have attained the end of all knowledge. Realize that which pervades the universe and is indestructible; no power can affect this unchanging, imperishable reality. The body is mortal but he who dwells in the body is immortal and immeasurable. . . . As a man abandons worn-out clothes and acquires new ones, so when the body is worn out a new one is acquired by the Self, who lives within. . . . Death is inevitable for the living; birth is inevitable for the dead. Since these are unavoidable, you should not sorrow. . . .

Now listen to the principles of yoga [mental and physical discipline to free the soul]. By practicing these you can break through the bonds of karma. On this path effort never goes to waste, and there is no failure. . . . When you keep thinking about sense objects, attachment comes. Attachment breeds desire, the lust of possession that burns to anger. . . .

They are forever free who renounce all selfish desires and break free from the ego-cage of "I," "me," and "mine" to be united with the Lord. This is the supreme state. Attain to this, and pass from death to immortality. . . . Strive constantly to serve the welfare of the world; by devotion to selfless work one attains the supreme goal of life. Do your work with the welfare of others always in mind.

THINKING ABOUT THE READING

1. What key aspects of Hindu thought are revealed in the poem?
2. How do the attitudes toward life, death, and desire influence the behavior of individuals?
3. What are some of the viewpoints in this ancient poem that might be considered universal in their appeal?

Source: From *The Bhagavad Gita,* trans. by Eknath Easwaran, founder of the Blue Mountain Center of Meditation, copyright 1985. Reprinted by permission of the Nilgiri Press, P.O. Box 256, Tomales, CA 94971, www.easwaran.org.

origins, were locked into a permanent low status and were prohibited from studying the magically potent Vedic hymns.

The Sanskrit term for a class division or ritual status—*varna* **(VARN-uh)**—meant "[skin] color," suggesting that the lighter-skinned Aryans wanted to maintain their domination over, and purity from "pollution" by, the darker-skinned indigenous people. Many centuries later, Portuguese visitors referred to the system as *castas* ("pure"), the origin of the Western term *caste.* Aryans used religion to justify this class system. One *Rig Veda* hymn attributed the classes to the Lord of Beings, the originator of the universe: "When they divided the Man, into how many parts did they divide him? . . . The brahman was his mouth, of his arms was made the kshatriya. His thighs became the vaisya, of his feet were born the sudra."[18]

Over many centuries, this four-tiered class hierarchy evolved into the immensely complex **caste system**. Each hereditary social class was restricted to certain occupations, and its members were restricted in their relations with members of other castes. For example, only members of closely allied groups could intermarry. Below the caste system were a large group of outcasts (**pariahs**) or untouchables, labeled such because the higher castes considered their touch defiling. The pariahs performed tasks considered "unclean," such as tanning animal hides and removing manure. This system, probably in place in some form by 500 B.C.E., differed in many respects from the modern caste system. Although it was never rigid and changed over time, it provided the basic structure of Hindu society for several millennia.

caste system The four-tiered Hindu social system comprising hereditary social classes that restrict the occupation of members and their relations with members of other castes.

pariahs The large group of outcasts or untouchables below the official Hindu castes.

Indo-Aryan Society and Economy

The Vedas and other early literature reveal some of the expectations and attitudes of ancient

[18]Quoted in A. L. Basham, *The Wonder That Was India* (New York: Grove Press, 1959), p. 241.

Indian society. For example, contained within the *Mahabharata* is a philosophical poem, the ***Bhagavad Gita*** **(BAA-guh-vad GEE-tuh)** ("Lord's Song"), the most treasured piece of ancient Hindu literature (see Witness to the Past: Hindu Values in the *Bhagavad Gita*). It encourages people to do their duty to their superiors and kinsmen resolutely and unselfishly. It also explains that death is not a time of grief because the soul is indestructible. The other great ancient epic, the *Ramayana*, resembles the *Odyssey* of the Greek Homer in that it tells of endless court intrigues and a hero's wanderings while his wife remains chaste and loyal.

The *Ramayana* illustrates the early Hindu notion of perfect manhood and womanhood through the main characters: Rama, the husband, and Sita **(SEE-tuh)**, his wife, who demonstrate mutual loyalty, devotion, and self-sacrifice. But Sita is also faithful in supporting her husband and family, strongly influencing cultural expectations of womanhood, especially in north India. Women enjoyed a higher status in south India, where both matriarchal and matrilineal traditions persisted for centuries, and goddesses remained especially central to religious life.

Indo-Aryan technology derived from both foreign and local developments. The Aryans used iron, especially once they reached iron-rich districts in the Ganges region around 1000 B.C.E. Soon they made the transition from a pastoral economy to a combination of pastoral and agricultural pursuits that emphasized grains like barley and wheat. One Veda prays: "Successfully let the good ploughshares' thrust part the earth, successfully let the ploughman follow the beasts of draft."[19] The use of plows and the expansion of irrigated agriculture greatly increased the available food supply and thus fostered population growth. India's population in 500 B.C.E. has been estimated at 25 million, including 15 million in the Ganges Valley.

Hinduism: A New Religion of Diverse Roots

Although Indian religion has changed much since the Harappans, it has remained unique. Nothing in the Middle East or Europe remotely resembles basic bedrock Indian beliefs such as reincarnation. What modern Indians would clearly recognize as Hinduism had probably not fully formed until the beginning of the Common Era. The term *Hinduism* was not applied to these traditions until recent centuries, but the foundations were clearly established in ancient times. Hinduism can be seen historically as a synthesis of Aryan beliefs with Harappan and other indigenous traditions that developed over many centuries. At the most basic level, Hindus respect the authority of the Vedas and accept one of the main Hindu gods as their principle deity. As the religion became more complex, it probed ever more deeply into cosmic mysteries, resulting in ferment and questioning.

Bhagavad Gita ("Lord's Song") A poem in the *Mahabharata* that is the most treasured piece of ancient Hindu literature.

Brahmanas Commentaries on the Vedas that emphasize the role of priests (brahmans).

Upanishads Ancient Indian philosophical writings that speculated on the ultimate truth about the creation of life.

The Hindu religious system became one of the richest and most complex in the world, with gods, devotions, and celebrations drawn from various regional cultures. The Aryans gradually turned from their old tribal gods to deities of Harappan origin such as Shiva. Hence the rise of the great gods of Hinduism: *Brahma* **(BRA-ma)** (the Creator of life); *Vishnu* **(VISH-noo)** (the Preserver of life); and *Shiva* (among other functions, the Destroyer of life). Vishnu is a benevolent deity who works continually for the welfare of the world. Shiva personifies the life force and embodies both constructive and destructive power. In popular worship Vishnu and Shiva had the most devotees. Hinduism never developed a rigid core of beliefs uniting all followers; instead, it loosely linked together diverse practices and cults that shared a reverence for the Vedas. The Vedic thinkers were influenced by pre-Aryan meditation techniques and mystical practices, such as those that were later known as *yoga*. The Hindus came to believe that everyone must behave properly so that the universe can function in an orderly manner. They came to see human existence as temporary and fleeting and only the realm of the gods as eternal.

The Vedas underwent three major stages of development to become accepted as revealed literature. The earliest stage included the poems and hymns in the *Rig Veda* and several other collections. From around 1000 to 700 B.C.E. a series of prose commentaries on the earlier Vedas appeared that also prescribed proper procedures for worshiping the gods. These commentaries, the ***Brahmanas*** **(BRA-ma-nus)**, emphasize the central role of the priests, or brahmans. At this time, the prevailing religion can be termed Brahmanism. Later still, between 800 and 600 B.C.E., a third group of more philosophical ideas appeared, poetic dialogues known as the ***Upanishads*** **(oo-PAHN-ih-shahds)** ("sitting around a teacher"). These oral and later written compositions, which speculated on the ultimate truth about the creation of life, offered a striking contrast to the emphasis on ritual, devotion, and ethics in the older works because they came from an atmosphere of questioning and rebellion against priestly power. They also gave women more importance; the dialogues include the story of an exceptionally learned female.

The religious atmosphere of ancient India was dynamic, with growing tensions between competing ideas about the nature of existence and appropriate human behavior. For example, the *Ramayana* contrasts the luxury-filled decadence of the royal courts with the austere existence of hermit-sages dwelling in the forest and practicing forms of meditation and mysticism. The movements that developed out of this ferment in the first millennium B.C.E. transformed the framework of Indian religion, fostering both Buddhism and the modified form of Brahmanism known today as Hinduism, as we shall see in Chapter 5.

[19]Quoted in Romila Thapar, *Early India from the Origins to AD 1300* (Berkeley: University of California Press, 2002), p. 116.

MAKE SURE YOU UNDERSTAND THESE KEY POINTS BEFORE MOVING ON

- **The Indo-European Aryans, a cattle-raising tribal people, migrated into north India 3,500 years ago, mixing with local peoples.**
- **The Vedas, written in Sanskrit, are religious writings that reveal information on the Aryan religion and their patriarchal culture.**
- **The *Bhagavad Gita*, which emphasizes one's earthly duty and the soul's immortality, became the most treasured piece of Indian literature.**
- **Hinduism developed over many centuries but never became a rigid belief structure.**

CHAPTER SUMMARY

Mesopotamian society and early Indian society were two of humankind's first experiments with farming, cities, and states, both using technologies that were unheard of in Neolithic times. These ancient societies also developed different religious notions, social systems, and political structures. They were shaped by the challenges and opportunities of flood-prone river valleys: Mesopotamian society arose between the Tigris and Euphrates Rivers, and Harappan society arose in the Indus River Valley. Mesopotamians introduced the first cities and states, the cuneiform system of writing, bronze metalworking, mathematics, and science. Their many kingdoms were united under several different empires. Mesopotamia was also part of the early trade networks linking the Mediterranean Basin with India. Such connections among societies were a crucial and continuing part of history. In northwest India the Harappans built peaceful, bustling, and well-planned cities, produced cotton products, developed sophisticated sanitation systems, and participated in a trading network that reached into the Fertile Crescent and Central Asia. After the Harappan collapse, Aryan migrants established political control. The mixing of Harappan and Aryan cultures shaped a new Indian society, establishing the foundation for a caste system and the religion of Hinduism.

KEY TERMS

Fertile Crescent (p. 29)
ziggurat (p. 31)
patriarchy (p. 31)
cuneiform (p. 33)
Harappan (p. 38)
Dravidian (p. 40)
Shiva (p. 41)
steppes (p. 42)
Aryans (p. 42)
Indo-Aryan synthesis (p. 43)
Vedas (p. 43)
Sanskrit (p. 43)
Mahabharata (p. 43)
brahmans (p. 44)
kshatriyas (p. 44)
vaisyas (p. 44)
sudras (p. 44)
caste system (p. 45)
pariahs (p. 45)
Bhagavad Gita (p. 46)
Brahmanas (p. 46)
Upanishads (p. 46)

3 Ancient Societies in Africa and the Mediterranean, 5000–600 B.C.E.

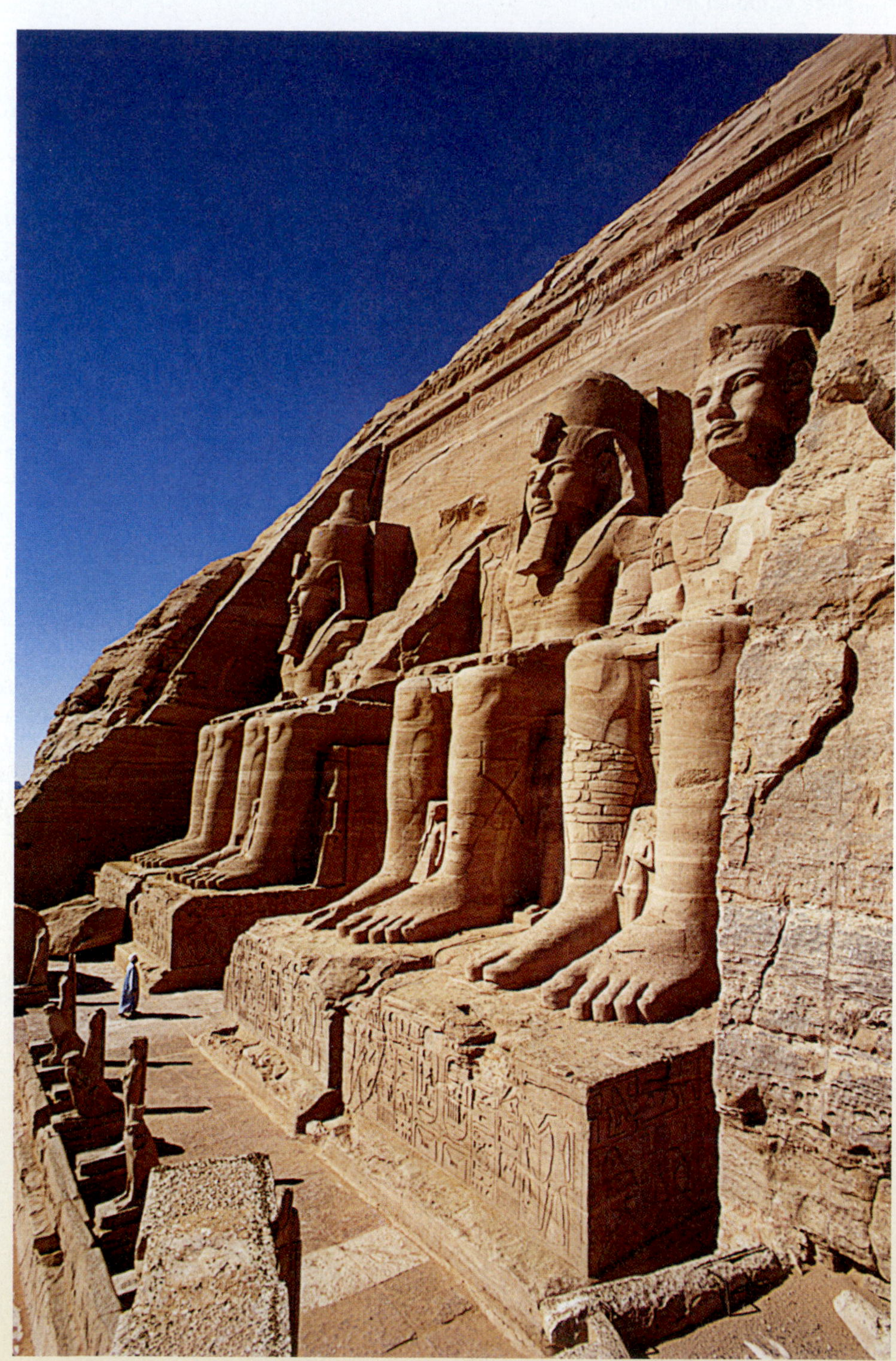

George Holton/Science Source

ABU SIMBEL The great temple with its colossal statues at Abu Simbel overlooking the Nile River in Egypt was built as a monument to honor the powerful thirteenth-century B.C.E. pharaoh Rameses the Great, who presided over empire building and economic prosperity.

Behold, the heart of his majesty was satisfied with making a very great monument; never has happened the like since the beginning. He made it as an everlasting fortress. It is wrought with gold and many costly stones.

—Temple inscription at Thebes, Egypt, fourteenth century, B.C.E.[1]

IN THIS CHAPTER

Around 1460 B.C.E. Queen Hatshepsut **(hat-SHEP-soot)**, Egypt's powerful ruler, ordered a temple built on the banks of the Nile River for the glory of the highest god, Amon-Re **(AH-muhn-RAY)**, with terraced gardens planted with fragrant myrrh. To obtain the myrrh, Hatshepsut ordered an expedition down the Red Sea to a place previously visited by Egyptians: Punt **(poont)** on the northeast African coast, probably modern Somalia **(so-MAH-lee-uh)**. The new expedition returned with myrrh trees, jewels, incense, and other treasures. Like other Egyptian rulers, Hatshepsut commemorated these results on her magnificent new temple's walls with inscriptions and pictures: "The loading of the cargo-boats with great marvels of Punt...good woods, ebony, pure ivory, gold, monkeys....Never were brought such things to any king, since the world was."[2] To obtain such luxury products, Egyptians had become shipbuilders and sailors, connecting to a wider world. Indeed, foreign trade had made Egypt the ancient world's wealthiest society.

Among the Egyptians and some other African and eastern Mediterranean societies—including Hebrews, Minoans **(mih-NO-uhns)**, Mycenaeans **(my-suh-NEE-uhns)**, Phoenicians **(fo-NEE-shuhns)**, and early Greeks—urban life was fostered by dramatic changes resulting from contact among different peoples. Interaction between Egypt and neighboring peoples promoted cultural development in the Nile Valley and the Mediterranean. Like the Tigris-Euphrates and Indus Valleys, the Nile Valley fostered population growth, social organization, large state structures, and elaborate religious systems.

Ancient peoples also created unique societies elsewhere in Africa and the eastern Mediterranean. Diverse sub-Saharan African societies developed or borrowed farming and metal technologies, and some built cities. However, unlike Egypt's spectacular pyramids, many of the sub-Saharan people's monuments and buildings were later covered by rain forest, blowing sand, or wayward rivers. Meanwhile, on eastern Mediterranean islands and shores, various peoples traded widely, built cities, and developed religious concepts that endure to this day.

[1]Quoted in Lionel Casson, *Ancient Egypt* (New York: Time Incorporated, 1965), 120.
[2]Quoted in David Phillipson, *African Archaeology*, 2nd ed. (Cambridge: Cambridge University Press, 1993), 152.

The Rise of Egyptian Society

How did the environment shape ancient Egypt?

The mixing of several different peoples in the Nile River Valley in North Africa around 3000 B.C.E. created an Egyptian society so successful that it survived in more or less its basic form for nearly two thousand years. The river valley's location allowed the Egyptians to develop many traditions and ideas completely different from those in nearby Mesopotamia, Palestine, and Crete. Reflecting the importance of this river, the classical Greek historian Herodotus **(heh-ROD-uh-tuhs)** called Egypt the "gift of the Nile."

North African Environments

Egypt was shaped by the environmental features of North Africa, a region stretching from Morocco to the Red Sea. To the north the Mediterranean Sea's maritime routes enabled the spread of products, ideas, technologies, and peoples, while the Red Sea connected Egypt to Northeast Africa, Arabia, and India. In Egypt itself, agriculture flourished only in the narrow Nile Valley; west of the Nile the vast Sahara Desert stretched all the way to Africa's western coast. In northwestern Africa (today's Tunisia, Algeria, and Morocco), mountain ranges separated the desert from the Mediterranean and Atlantic coastal plains, where farming was also possible.

The Nile River was the key to the formation of Egyptian society (see Map 3.1). By the fourth millennium B.C.E. the grasslands and forests of earlier times had turned to desert and the silt deposited by the fall flooding had made the Nile Valley fertile. Thanks to the inhospitable deserts on both sides, the northern Nile Valley enjoyed many centuries of uninterrupted development, allowing Egypt to thrive for centuries without significant outside challenges. On the navigable and slow-moving Nile, boats drifted northward with the current and used southerly winds to move south; thus the river proved a great highway promoting political stability and uniformity.

Foundations of Egyptian Society

Arising in 3100 or 3000 B.C.E., Egypt's urban society developed a few centuries later than the societies in Mesopotamia. With little rainfall, Egypt required irrigation works to take advantage of the rich silt. Unlike the wide Tigris-Euphrates Valley, the Nile Valley was only 10 miles wide, so the population was more concentrated, and new peoples continually arrived in this area. The once fertile Sahara region began drying out by 5000–4000 B.C.E., forcing the Sahara peoples to move to western Africa grasslands, the northern coast, or into the Nile Valley. Other early migrants came from western Asia and from the Horn of Africa, southeast of Egypt. The Egyptian population eventually included peoples of Semitic, Berber **(BUHR-bur)**, Ethiopian, Somali, black African, and, later, Greek origins. Egypt also

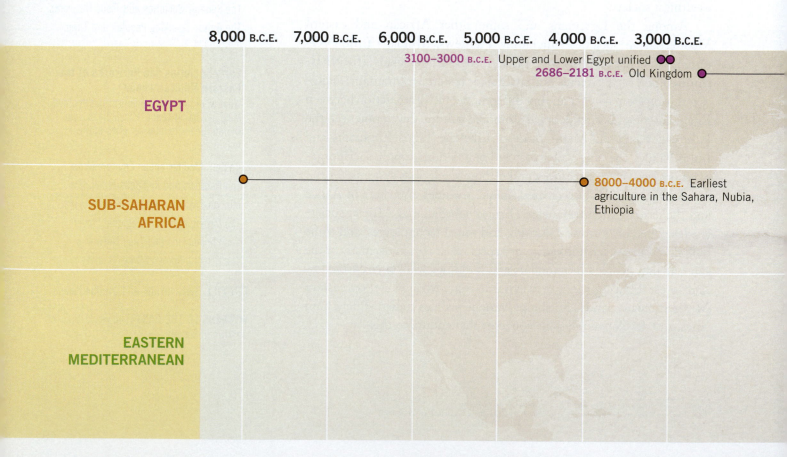

8,000 B.C.E. | 7,000 B.C.E. | 6,000 B.C.E. | 5,000 B.C.E. | 4,000 B.C.E. | 3,000 B.C.E.

EGYPT

3100–3000 B.C.E. Upper and Lower Egypt unified

2686–2181 B.C.E. Old Kingdom

SUB-SAHARAN AFRICA

8000–4000 B.C.E. Earliest agriculture in the Sahara, Nubia, Ethiopia

EASTERN MEDITERRANEAN

enjoyed close relationships with the Nubians, black African peoples living in what is today southern Egypt and northern Sudan. Berbers dominated northwest Africa. The ancient Egyptian language belonged to the Afro-Asiatic family, which included Semitic and Berber languages and many African tongues.

Unlike the Mesopotamia floods, Nile flooding came on an exact schedule. A central government organized people to prepare the cropland for the flooding, such as by building dikes to contain the floodwater used in irrigation. The backbreaking work required to maintain the irrigation canals reminds us that, for peasants at least, a complex society was a mixed blessing. If the floodwaters were not carefully channeled, little would grow. When weak governments left the dikes untended, the desert spread and famine struck the land. But with political order and dike maintenance, the valley supported a high population. By 1000 B.C.E., Egypt's population had reached 3 or 4 million. Given their general good fortune, it is not surprising that Egyptians saw themselves as the center of the world. As far as they knew for many centuries, they were.

In earliest times, the 100-mile-long area from the modern city of Cairo down the Nile to the fertile Nile Delta and sea was considered Lower Egypt or the northern kingdom (see Map 3.1). The area from Cairo to Aswan **(AS-wahn)**, some 650 miles south, was Upper Egypt or the southern kingdom. The legendary Upper Egyptian King Menes **(MEH-neez)** united these two states about 3100–3000 B.C.E., setting the stage for three successive eras: the Old Kingdom (2686–2181 B.C.E.), the Middle Kingdom (2040–1786 B.C.E.), and the New Kingdom (1550–1064 B.C.E.). During each period various dynasties ruled Egypt, while the intermediate periods were marked by disorder or foreign conquest. After 1075 B.C.E. Egypt increasingly fell victim to the empire building of western Asian, Mediterranean, and other African peoples.

The Old Kingdom: Egypt's Golden Age

Most of us can picture the Old Kingdom because of the pyramids built in this splendid era, which have awed visitors for thousands of years and illustrate Egyptian self-confidence. Perhaps the greatest and most enduring of the ancient world's construction projects, they reflected a powerful government, unsurpassed organizing talent, a prosperous society, and unique values and beliefs. The largest pyramid, that of the twenty-fifth-century pharaoh Cheops at Giza, is nearly 500 feet high, covers an area of nearly 200 square yards, and remained the tallest building in the world until the twentieth century. Tens of thousands of workers moved the nearly 6 million tons of limestone into place on ramps and wooden rollers without the benefit of winches, pulleys, or scaffolds. The builders of the great pyramid of Pharaoh Khufu probably had to set a block of stone in place every two minutes over a ten-hour workday for some two decades. Most of the workers were not slaves, and many were highly skilled artisans. Workers and their families lived in villages with ample food and good housing supplied by the government. This did not prevent complaints. One disgruntled draftsman wrote to his superior: "If there is some beer, you do not look for me, but if there is work, you do look for me. I am

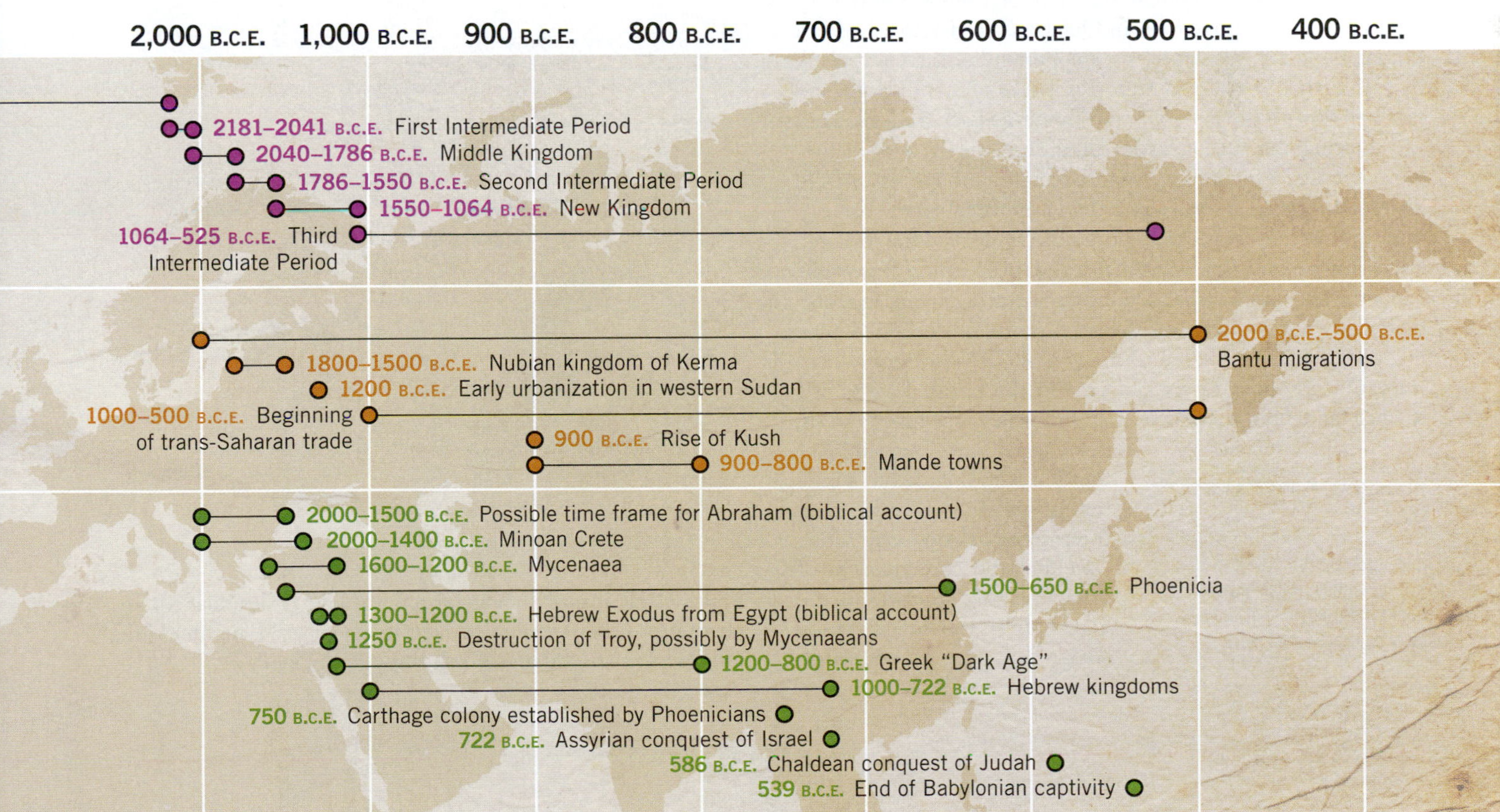

a man who has no beer in his house."[3] Indeed, some studies suggest that worker strikes and social unrest occurred even as the rulers used propaganda campaigns to encourage acceptance of government power.

The rulers of Egypt, known as **pharaohs (FAIR-os)** (from per-o or "great house"), had immense power to order such projects because their subjects believed them to be the divine offspring of the sun-god Re, the creator of heaven, earth, and humans. Pharaohs also had soldiers and the authority of priests and religion to support their rule. Writing, invented by 3000 B.C.E., enabled smooth functioning administration. The Egyptian writing system of **hieroglyphics (hi-ruh-GLIF-iks)**, like Sumerian cuneiform, evolved from pictograms into stylized pictures expressing ideas. The pharaohs, considered the owners of all the land and people, governed a highly centralized state from the city of Memphis, strategically located where the Nile Valley met the delta. A chief minister supervised the administrative structure, including tax collection, grain storage in government warehouses, and salaries for government officials. Most ministers came from noble families, but occasionally pharaohs recruited for talent. One advised his son: "Do not distinguish the son of a noble man from a poor man, but take to thyself a man because of the work of his hands."[4]

The royal government expanded trade, dispatching expeditions east to Arabia, south to Nubia **(NOO-bee-ah)**, and northeast to Lebanon, Syria, and Anatolia. Hence, around 2600 B.C.E. forty ships brought cedar logs, probably from today's Lebanon, to make the cedar wood doors of the royal palace. Requiring huge efforts and expense, sailing expeditions to Punt to obtain exotic raw materials were less frequent, maybe fifteen or twenty over 400 years. For these expeditions, several thousand workers had to move construction materials and their supplies by donkey across 100 miles of desert from Qena, a Nile city, to a Red Sea harbor, build the 100-foot-long ship, then disassemble it plank by plank when it returned from Punt several months later, and finally trek with the materials and the cargo back to Qena.

During the final decades of the twenty-second century B.C.E. the Old Kingdom went into decline, perhaps because the expense of the great royal tombs had impoverished the country, The royal governors became more independent of the pharaoh, and many peasants reasoned that if the ruler's power was weakened, the gods were displeased. Environmental change may also have undermined the government. A dramatic decline in rainfall around 2200 B.C.E. led to many years of poor harvests and starvation in upper Egypt, as some of the fertile delta turned to dust and fires swept through the valley, destroying crops, trees, and homes. The demise of the Old Kingdom led to a century of social disorder, the First Intermediate Period. One scribe lamented the consequences of this upheaval: "The son of the high-born is no longer to be recognized. Men do not sail to Byblos **(BIB-loss)** [Phoenicia] today. Gold is diminished. To what purpose is a treasure without its revenues? Laughter hath perished. It is grief that walketh through the land."[5]

pharaohs Rulers of ancient Egypt.

hieroglyphics The Egyptian writing system, which evolved from pictograms into stylized pictures expressing ideas.

MAP 3.1 ANCIENT EGYPT AND NUBIA The Egyptian and Nubian societies developed along the Nile River. Egypt traded with, and sometimes controlled, the peoples of the Levant on the eastern Mediterranean coast.

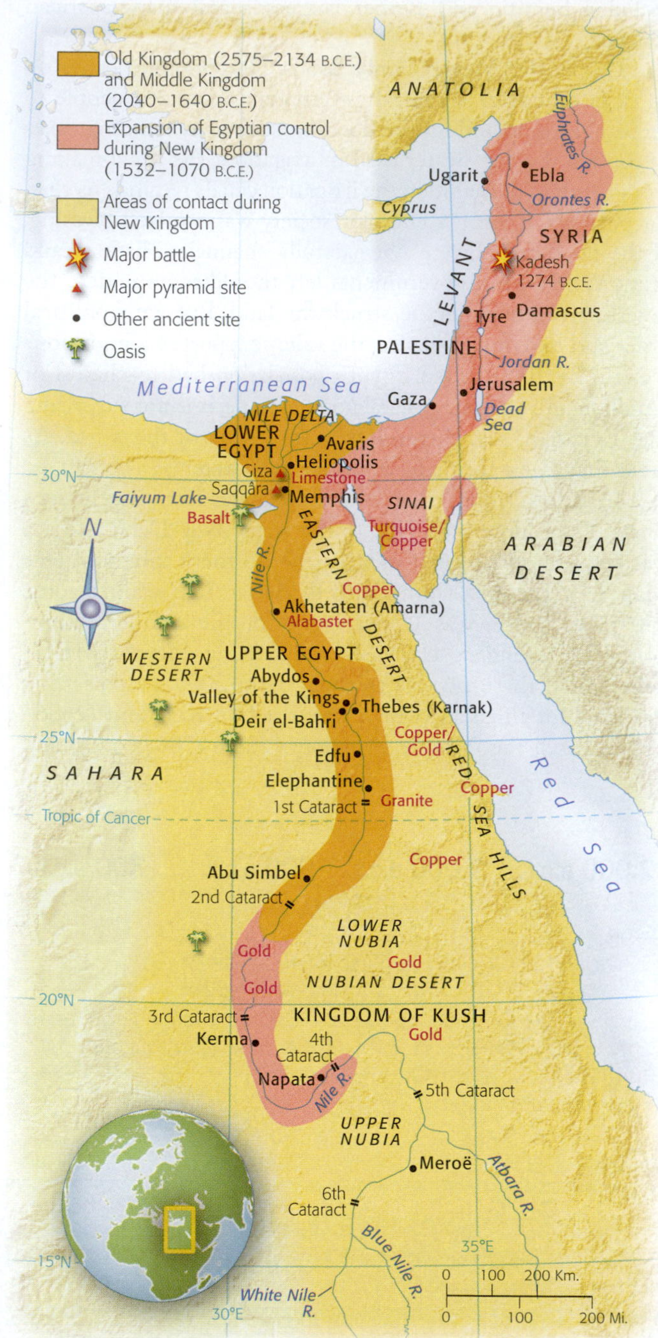

[3]Quoted in *Egypt: Land of the Pharaohs* (Alexandria, VA: Time-Life Books, 1992), 142.
[4]Quoted in Casson, *Ancient Egypt*, 95.
[5]Quoted in Carl Roebuck, *The World of Ancient Times* (New York: Charles Scribner's Sons, 1966), 72.

The Middle Kingdom and Foreign Conquest

Eventually the pharaohs of a new dynasty restored strong government, moving the capital to Thebes in the south and establishing stronger control over the governors. This Middle Kingdom lasted for four hundred years and saw Egyptian influence extend to Palestine and, briefly, to Nubia. Amon-Re, a fusion of two great gods, now became Egypt's chief god, proclaimed the ancestor of the divine pharaoh.

However, foreign conquest and domestic disorder brought an end to the Middle Kingdom, launching the Second Intermediate Period. The Hyksos **(HICK-soes)**, an iron-using Semitic people from Syria and Palestine, conquered some of Lower Egypt. Hyksos rule led to further divisions: an Egyptian dynasty ruled Upper Egypt from Thebes, and the Nubians established yet a third state. The Hyksos adopted Egyptian customs and brought several improvements to Egypt, including increased trade with the eastern Mediterranean and Mesopotamia, and military innovations, such as iron, smaller shields, body armor, powerful bows, and, especially, horse-drawn chariots.

© WitR/Shutterstock.com

GREAT PYRAMID AT GIZA Three Egyptian pharaohs from the twenty-sixth century B.C.E. were buried in these magnificent pyramids, which symbolized the power of Old Kingdom Egypt. The rearmost pyramid, built for Pharaoh Cheops, remains the largest all-stone building ever constructed.

The New Kingdom and Egyptian Expansion

In the mid-1500s B.C.E. dynamic new rulers reestablished Egypt's regional power and fostered social and religious changes. Using the new military technology, these pharaohs began the most expansionist period of ancient Egyptian history. During the New Kingdom, Egypt became more active in the western Asian and Mediterranean worlds, sending armies on repeated campaigns into Palestine, Syria, the Euphrates River, and Nubia. Foreigners from as far away as Babylon served in the Egyptian court. This power derived partly from Egypt's position as the major regional supplier of gold, which it obtained mostly from Nubia and Punt.

For a few years Egypt was ruled by a female pharaoh, Hatshepsut (r. ca. 1479–1458), the daughter and wife of pharaohs. To ensure that she looked like a proper pharaoh, Hatshepsut apparently wore male clothing and the headdress and false beard that were symbols of royalty. Hatshepsut supervised military campaigns in both the north and south.

Another New Kingdom pharaoh, Amenophis **(AH-men-o-fis)** IV (r. 1353–1333), rebelled against the priests of Amon-Re and promoted the worship of a new sun-god, Aten, who he claimed was the only god (other than the pharaoh himself). Amenophis changed his name to Akhenaten **(AH-ke-NAH-tin)** ("servant of Aten") and wrote a famous hymn to Aten: "Beginner of Life. How manifold are thy works? They are hidden from the sight of men, O Sole God. Thou didst fashion the earth according to thy desire."[6] This experiment with **monotheism**, the belief in a single, all-powerful god, intrigues historians because it occurred at roughly the same time that the Hebrews were developing a similar belief. Some scholars see cross-cultural influences at work, and some Hebrew psalms and proverbs are clearly derived from Egyptian writings. At Akhenaten's death, however, the priests successfully pressured his successor to return to Amon-Re worship.

The high point of Egyptian empire building was reached when Pharaoh Rameses **(ram-ih-SEEZ)** II (r. 1290–1224) signed a treaty with the Hittites dividing Syria and Palestine between them. In 1208 Libyan tribes invaded the Nile Delta. Although they were pushed out. Egypt began its long decline as a regional power. From about 750 to 650 B.C.E., a dynasty from the Kush kingdom in Nubia ruled Egypt, adopting Egyptian customs and hieroglyphics. Finally, Egypt was conquered by the Assyrians in the seventh century, followed by the Persians in the late sixth century B.C.E.

monotheism The belief in a single, all-powerful god.

[6]Quoted in *Egypt: Land of Pharaohs*, 89.

MAKE SURE YOU UNDERSTAND THESE KEY POINTS BEFORE MOVING ON

- **The regular flooding of the Nile River provided the ancient Egyptians with a highly fertile valley and a dependable growing season.**
- **A strong central government allowed the Egyptians to make the most of their agricultural system.**
- **The pyramids were built by the Egyptian pharaohs of the Old Kingdom, thought to be descendants of the sun-god.**
- **The New Kingdom was a time of Egyptian expansion into western Asia and the Mediterranean, but it ended with the decline of Egyptian dominance.**

Egyptian Society, Economy, and Culture

What were some unique features of Egyptian society?

Like other ancient societies, the Egyptians had many distinctive customs, technologies, and beliefs. All social classes, blessed with many centuries of good crops, seemed to mostly view themselves as favored. One writer celebrated the Nile Delta as "full of everything good—its ponds with fish and its lakes with birds. Its meadows are verdant, its melons abundant. Its granaries are so full of barley that they come near to the sky."[7] Although peasants and workers labored hard and had fewer comforts than the upper classes, they at least had a secure life and predictable routine. Women enjoyed considerable freedom. Finally, Egyptian cities grew rich by trading with distant suppliers and markets.

Society

Like other urban societies, Egypt was divided into social classes with different responsibilities and roles. The pharaoh theoretically owned everything in the kingdom, and the pharaoh, priests, and nobles owned 80 to 90 percent of all the usable land (see Profile: Hekanakhte, an Egyptian Priest). The scribe, or "writing man," held an honored upper-class occupation. "Be a scribe," a young man was advised in one source. "Your limbs will be sleek. Your hands will grow soft. You will go forth in white clothes with courtiers saluting you."[8] Peasants maintained the irrigation works and paid high taxes. Perhaps 10 or 15 percent of the population, slaves were mostly prisoners of war and foreigners, including Nubians and people from Palestine, among them some Hebrews. Most worked in wealthy homes, palaces, or temple estates, and some built pyramids and monuments.

Egyptians valued security and regularity more than social equality. Since planting was relatively easy in the soft soil, they did not need heavy plows. Despite occasional grueling labor on construction projects, peasants showed little sustained discontent except during the troubled intermediate periods. Although the rich ate meat and the poor had beer, bread, and beans ("beer and bread" was an ancient Egyptian greeting, much like "have a good day"), most people thought themselves lucky. Their massive tombs and mummies may seem gloomy, but their temples were once bright with paint and gold. Egyptians told bawdy and often irreverent stories, played musical instruments such as flutes, pipes, and harps, and got drunk. Both men and women used cosmetics such as eyeliner to enhance their physical attractions. In seeking beauty aids, Egyptians became the world's first chemists. Young people wrote sentimental poems to sweethearts. One love poem by a girl reported on a swim with her lover:

Diving and swimming with you here,
Gives me the chance I've been waiting for,
To show my looks,
Before an appreciative eye.
My bathing suit of the best material.
Nothing can keep me from my love,
Standing on the other shore.[9]

With flexible gender roles, women enjoyed more independence and legal rights than women in other ancient societies. Hatshepsut was the most famous of at least four women pharaohs. Legal distinctions also seemed to be based more on class than on gender. A woman could inherit, bequeath, and administer property, conclude legal settlements, take cases to court, initiate divorce, and testify. Some women could probably read and write, and many were involved in well-paying economic activities. Women weavers produced some of the finest cloth in world history. Wives also enjoyed rough equality with husbands and assumed the public and family responsibilities of their deceased spouses. They served as doctors and priestesses, and a few women even held administrative positions. Yet, public duties were normally reserved for men. An Old Kingdom sage advised men to "love your wife at home, as is proper. Fill her belly and clothe her back. Make her heart glad as long as you live. You should not judge her, or let her gain control."[10]

Cities, Trade, and Technology

Whereas Mesopotamian cities had long been trading centers, Egyptian cities were largely administrative centers to house tax collectors, artisans in government workshops, shopkeepers, and

[7]Quoted in Felipe Fernandez-Armesto, *Civilizations: Culture, Ambition, and the Transformation of Nature* (New York: Simon and Schuster, 2001), 195.
[8]Quoted in Brian M. Fagan, *People of the Earth: An Introduction to World Prehistory*, 9th ed. (New York: Longmans, 1998), 407.
[9]Quoted in Ezra Pound and Noel Stock, *Love Poems of Ancient Egypt* (Norfolk, CT: New Directions, 1962).
[10]Quoted in Barbara Mertz, *Red Land, Black Land: Daily Life in Ancient Egypt*, rev. ed. (New York: Dodd, Mead and Company, 1978), 56.

PROFILE

Hekanakhte, An Egyptian Priest

Hekanakhte **(heh-KHAN-akt)**, who lived about 2000 B.C.E., was the ka-priest of a deceased chief government minister, Ipi. His duty was to tend the tomb of his patron, near the city of Thebes, to protect the deceased individual's guardian spirit or soul (ka). Wealthy individuals like Ipi left money or other resources to support a priest to perform these duties. If the ka were not honored with these ceremonial offerings, Egyptians feared that it would die a "second death" or be annihilated.

Stefano Ravera/Alamy

MEASURING AND RECORDING THE EGYPTIAN HARVEST This wall painting from a tomb in the city of Thebes shows officials and peasants figuring the size of the annual harvest.

In addition to a large estate Ipi left to support Hekanakhte and his family, Hekanakhte also supervised other properties left to his care, visiting them much of the year. During his absences he wrote many letters to his eldest son, Mersu, who read them and then discarded them in a local tomb. The dry desert climate preserved them until they were discovered by an archaeologist in 1922. These letters reveal family life in the Middle Kingdom. Hekanakhte had a large family, including five sons, two of them married, and all of them living at home. He also supported his mother, a poor female relative, and a widowed daughter.

Hekanakhte's letters give advice on cultivating and tending the grain crops. Some were written during a bad year, when inadequate Nile flooding rendered harvests slim. The priest tells his son that he is sending some food and carefully lists what each family member is to receive. He reminds family members not to complain, since "half life is better than dying together." Hekanakhte orders that only those who work should get food and urges Mersu to "make the most of my land . . . dig the ground deep with your noses." He also tells his son what seeds to plant and where to plant them. And he warns his son not to overpay the help or his own personal funds will be reduced. Trust between father and son seems to have been in short supply.

Hekanakhte frequently addressed family disputes. Apparently he spoiled Mersu's younger brother, Snerfu, constantly reminding Mersu to give this youngest son things he wanted. Hekanakhte decided late in life, after his wife died, to take a young concubine, Iutenhab **(YOU-ten-hob)**, who disrupted the household with her many requests. The priest tells his son to fire a maid who had offended Iutenhab. Given the nagging tone of many of Hekanakhte's letters to his long-suffering son, it may not surprise us that one of the letters had been left unopened.

THINKING ABOUT THE PROFILE

1. What were the duties of a ka-priest?
2. What do these letters tell us about family relationships in this social class?

Note: Quotations from Barbara Mertz, *Red Land, Black Land: Daily Life in Ancient Egypt* (New York: Dodd, Mead, 1978), 127.

the priests who cared for the local temple. Unlike their Mesopotamian counterparts, Egyptian city dwellers did not think of themselves as attached to the city but were subjects of the pharaoh, and most lived in villages.

Most of the Egyptians' wide-ranging trade involved the import of luxury goods by the wealthy. Egyptians traded with sub-Saharan Africans as far south as the Congo River Basin, with the Berber peoples of Libya and Algeria to the west, with the societies along the Red Sea to the east, with Palestine, Phoenicia, and Mesopotamia to the northeast, and with southeastern Europe. Gold, semiprecious stones, and such exotic things as frankincense, myrrh, ivory, ostrich feathers, and monkeys came from sub-Saharan Africa through Nubia or via the Red Sea and were exchanged for furniture, silver, tools, paper, and linen. Egyptians mined copper in the nearby Sinai **(SIGH-nigh)** Peninsula, while the Nile Delta provided papyrus and waterfowl.

The Egyptians understood enough mathematics and physics to make the pyramids perfectly level and to match the corners of each pyramid with the four points of the compass. They also used a solar calendar that divided the year into 365 days and twelve months. In arithmetic, the Egyptians understood fractions but had no concept of zero. In medicine, Egyptians used both surgery and herbal remedies to treat illnesses. They recognized that the heart was a pump, were able to cure some eye diseases, and did some dental work. Modern observers still admire Egyptian technical skill in treating the dead, reflected in the mummies held in museums worldwide. Using a form of salt and the extremely dry climate, Egyptian morticians preserved human tissue well enough that the distinct features of individuals can be seen four thousand years later.

Religion

Egyptian religious and moral beliefs included many myths, unique views of death, and some two thousand gods and goddesses, most of them benevolent. Like their Mesopotamian counterparts, the Egyptian gods explained nature but were also made in the image of humans and shared human weaknesses. The emphasis on preserving bodies indicates a chief feature of Egyptian religion, the belief that a person's soul could be united with his or her body after death, but only if the body was properly preserved. Initially only pharaohs could expect this afterlife, which mirrored life on earth. By the Middle Kingdom, all who could afford some form of mummification and whose souls passed a final moral judgment after death were candidates for immortality. People devoted vast resources to this quest.

The most dramatic and long-lived of the Egyptian myths concern Osiris **(oh-SIGH-ris)**, a god-king, and his wife Isis **(EYE-sis)**. Murdered by his brother, Osiris descended to the underworld, where he established justice there as he had done on earth. A famous Egyptian drawing from the Book of the Dead, which depicts the afterlife, shows Osiris weighing the heart of a dead princess against the symbol of justice and truth. The Book of the Dead describes a confession that the dead person is to repeat as part of this judgment by Osiris indicating that he or she has not murdered or cheated anyone.

Because of the Book of the Dead, the pyramids, and the mummified remains, some scholars have viewed ancient Egyptians as preoccupied with death and the afterlife. But the Egyptians were probably not as preoccupied with death as the physical remains suggest, doubtless enjoying life as much or more than other people. Many wall paintings imply that even the lower classes accepted their lot and found ways to cope. They show farmers and herders telling jokes, women bringing them their lunches, children squabbling, and shepherds asleep under a tree, a dog or flask of beer beside them. They could find solace in religion and were in awe of the pharaoh who sat, as the gods ordained, at the apex of the social pyramid.

MAKE SURE YOU UNDERSTAND THESE KEY POINTS BEFORE MOVING ON

- **Though Egyptian society was divided into classes, with the rich enjoying lavish lifestyles, even the poor were relatively comfortable.**
- **Women had greater independence and rights in Egypt than in any other ancient society, but their roles were still quite limited.**
- **Ancient Egyptians had great technical skill in architecture, medicine, and preserving the dead.**
- **Ancient Egyptians believed they could obtain immortality if their bodies were mummified and if they passed a moral judgment after death.**

aplia

Ancient Sub-Saharan African Societies

What were some achievements of the ancient Nubian, Sudanic, and Bantu peoples?

Africa is the original homeland for all of humanity, and Egypt was only the best known of the early farming societies and states that emerged on the continent. Various African societies became linked to each other and the wider world through growing networks. Like the annual Nile floods for Egypt, the environment also influenced sub-Saharan African farming and technology. While historians tend to emphasize state building and monarchs, many Africans rejected political centralization, choosing public participation rather than kings and bureaucracies. However, strong states emerged in Nubia and the Sudan.

Meanwhile, migrating **Bantu (BAN-too)** peoples spread farming, iron metallurgy, and their languages widely in the southern half of the continent.

Sub-Saharan African Environments

Geography and climate have shaped African history. With one-fifth of the earth's landmass, Africa is the second largest continent after Eurasia and occupies more land than the United States, Europe (excluding Russia), China, and India combined. The equator bisects Africa, giving most of the continent a tropical climate. Lush rain forests have flourished along West Africa's Guinea coast and in the vast Congo River Basin in the heart of the continent. These equatorial regions are home to many insects, parasites, and bacteria that cause debilitating diseases like malaria, yellow fever, and sleeping sickness. Since the last is deadly to cattle and horses, the plow or wheel became impractical in Africa. Most of the continent, however, is parched desert or savannah grasslands. African weather can be erratic, with fluctuating, often unpredictable rains. Rain diminishes north and south of the equator, producing a huge dry zone that is home to pastoral societies and herds of large wild animals and that receives less than 10 inches of rain a year. In some regions the poor-quality soil has been easily eroded, fostering low agricultural productivity. Nonetheless, early farmers cultivated the grassland-covered region known as the **Sudan (soo-DAN)**, stretching along the southern fringe of the Sahara Desert from Africa's western tip to the Nile Basin.

Geography often hindered communication. Africa's eastern third includes extensive mountains and plateaus where great lakes and volcanic soils permitted denser populations. The eastern highlands also produced great river systems, including the Nile, Congo, and, in the south, the Zambezi **(zam-BEE-zee)**, but all these rivers have numerous rapids and waterfalls that limited boat travel. Only the Niger **(NIGH-jer)** River, which flows through West African plains, is navigable over large distances. Much of the African coast has sandbars that create great swells, making landing a boat difficult. Furthermore, there are few bays, gulfs, inland seas, or natural harbors to serve as maritime hubs. Only along the eastern, Red Sea, and Mediterranean coasts did a few protected bays and prevailing winds favor seagoing trade.

The catastrophic climatic change that created and expanded the Sahara Desert strongly shaped early African societies. In 3500 B.C.E. the Sahara region was relatively wet, a rich grazing land with lakes and rivers occupied by hunting, gathering, fishing, and some farming societies. Ancient rock art portrays people dancing, worshiping, riding chariots, and tending horses and cattle. The paintings endow women with dignity as they raise children, gather plants, and make baskets, pottery, and jewelry. Then, as rain patterns shifted southward, **desertification** began, the process by which productive land is transformed into mostly useless desert. By 2000 B.C.E. the Sahara region was harsh desert. People contributed by overgrazing marginal lands and burning forests to create grasslands. The same desertification processes continue today on the Sahara's southern fringe. As most inhabitants migrated elsewhere, the Sahara was left largely to nomadic herders of cattle, goats, and camels. Eventually it marked a general boundary between the Berber and Semitic peoples along the southern Mediterranean coast and the darker-skinned peoples in the rest of Africa. But the desert barrier did not prevent considerable social, cultural, and genetic intermixing and exchange.

The Origins of African Agriculture

Geographical challenges did not prevent agriculture from developing early from both local and imported discoveries. Some 12,000 or 13,000 years ago, people in the eastern Sahara made pottery, probably for storing food and water, two centuries earlier than Middle Eastern people. Between 8000 and 5000 B.C.E., people in Nubia and the Sahara became farmers, followed by Ethiopians. By 2500 B.C.E. farming was widespread in West, Central, and East Africa. In West Africa almost all food crops developed from local wild African plants like sorghum, millet, yams, and African rice. Rice became a major crop in the rain forest zone. Saharans also domesticated cotton and worked it into fabrics using spindles of baked clay, perhaps by 5000 B.C.E. Other crops came later from outside Africa, including wheat, barley, and chickpeas from the Middle East and bananas from Southeast Asia. But the movement went in both directions. Crops domesticated in West Africa such as sorghum and sesame reached India and China well before 2000 B.C.E.

Animal domestication presented a greater challenge. Cattle were probably domesticated very early from local sources in the southern Sahara and East Africa. But no other African animals were suitable for domestication, and some were dangerous predators. Rock art reveals possible attempts to domesticate giraffes, antelopes, and elephants, but most draft animals had to come from North Africa and Eurasia. Goats and sheep were brought in from the Middle East.

African peoples overcame geographical barriers in many ways. The major response to difficult climate and soils was a subsistence economy rather than the high-productivity agriculture possible in Egypt, China, India, Southeast Asia, or southern Europe. Many chose farming by shifting cultivation, moving their fields around every few years and letting recently used land lie fallow for a while to regain its nutrients. If not abused, this system worked well for centuries. Only in a few fertile areas was intensive sedentary agriculture possible. Pastoral nomadism became the specialty of some groups in dry regions.

Ancient African Metallurgy

Most sub-Saharan peoples learned to make metal tools and weapons. Copper may have been mined in the Sahara by 1500 B.C.E. There was no pronounced bronze age, and generally the use of bronze came around the

Bantu Sub-Saharan peoples who developed a cultural tradition based on farming and iron metallurgy, which they spread widely through great migrations.

Sudan A grassland region stretching along the southern fringe of the Sahara Desert from the western tip of Africa to the Nile Valley.

desertification The process by which productive land is transformed into mostly useless desert.

same time as or later than iron. Sub-Saharan Africans were among the world's earliest ironworkers, probably making iron by at least 1000 B.C.E. on the northern fringe of the Congo Basin. Iron smelters were built around 900 B.C.E. in the Great Lakes region, and between 600 and 300 B.C.E. iron was being mined, smelted, and forged widely in West and East Africa, with West Africans possibly influenced by iron and bronze metallurgy established on the North African coast. Since major iron ore deposits were rare, ore and iron artifacts had to be transported over long distances. Mining and working iron were both difficult operations, and those who did them occupied a special position in the community. Among the Haya **(HI-uh)** people in Tanzania **(TAN-zeh-NEE-uh)**, when a new king was installed on the throne, he made a ritual visit to the blacksmith's hut, symbolizing the special relationship between the king and the ironworkers.

Iron technology gradually improved. In many places miners had to dig open pits or vertical shafts to reach ore deposits deep underground. Furnaces for smelting ranged from simple open holes in the ground to elaborate clay structures 6 or 8 feet high with blower systems. The craftsmen made spear blades and arrowheads for warriors and hunters; hoes, axes, machetes, and knives for farmers and traders; bangles and rings for jewelry; gongs to produce music; hammers, hinges, and nails for household use; and iron bells for ceremonies and rituals.

Agriculture and metallurgy came to various African regions at different times, depending on circumstances, spreading to the southern half of the continent last. Originally much of this region was inhabited by expert hunter-gatherers such as the !Kung (see Chapter 1), successful adapters to their environment who had little incentive to develop agriculture or ironworking. Gradually most of these groups were assimilated by or pushed farther south by iron-using farmers.

Early Urban Societies in Nubia

The first known urban African state after Egypt emerged in Nubia (see Map 3.1), today the northern half of the country of Sudan and far southern Egypt. Like Egyptians, Nubians turned to the Nile for survival. The region is mostly desert, but a thin area along the Nile was fertile; copper and gold could be mined nearby. The first Nubian kingdom may have formed as early as 3100 B.C.E. Egypt dominated the region for many centuries, occasionally through military occupations, and exchanged pottery and copper items for Nubian ivory, ebony, ostrich feathers, and slaves. An independent Nubian kingdom, Kerma **(CARE-ma)**, appeared between 1800 and 1600 B.C.E. Extensive ruins of stone and mud-brick buildings, massive cemeteries, large towers, painted pottery, and copper vessels and weapons confirm a prosperous, well-organized society. Around 1500 B.C.E. Egyptian forces occupied Nubia and destroyed the Kerma state.

When Egyptian power declined around 900 B.C.E., a larger Nubian state, Kush **(koosh)**, emerged, launching a golden age of trade, culture, and metallurgy. The Kushites conquered Egypt in the eighth century B.C.E. but were pushed out by the Assyrians after a century of occupation. As a major regional trading hub, Kush was linked by overland caravan routes with the Niger and Congo Basins and with the Ethiopian highlands. It provided central and southern African goods to the Mediterranean and Red Sea regions and to markets as distant as India and China, importing Roman goblets and Chinese copper vessels.

Kush clearly benefited from its foreign contacts, adding imported ideas to Nubian traditions. For example, Egyptian and western Asian irrigation technology made farming possible in this barren area. Kushites worshiped both Egyptian and local gods and buried their kings in Egyptian-style pyramids. A sixth-century B.C.E. inscription tells us that King Aspelta **(as-PELL-ta)**, the son of the Egyptian sun-god, built a pyramid of white stone. However, while Kushite art reflected Egyptian and sometimes Greek influence, the overall effect remained distinctively Nubian. Kushite society may have also been matrilineal; some women held key political positions, including that of queen, and kings sometimes traced their descent through female ancestors.

Kush linked Africa and Mediterranean societies. By 600 B.C.E. it was the major African producer of iron, giving it an even more crucial economic influence on the ancient world. The ancient Greek poet Homer described Kushites as "the most

Aspelta (after Budge) From Derek A. Welsby, The Kingdom of Kush (British Museum Press).

CORONATION STELA OF KUSHITE KING ASPELTA (CA. 600 B.C.E.) The stela and inscription celebrate the coronation of King Aspelta. Related to the royal line through his mother, he was chosen from among many candidates by high priests acting in the name of the gods.

[11]Quoted in *Africa's Glorious Legacy* (Alexandria, VA: Time-Life Books, 1996), 18.

just of men; the favorites of the gods. The lofty inhabitants of Olympus **(oh-LIM-pus)** (home of Greek gods) journey to them, and take part in their feasts."[11]

The Sudanic Societies and Trade Networks

In ancient times peoples in the Sudan grasslands of West Africa also developed towns, perhaps a few small kingdoms, and long-distance trade routes including to Nubia and Egypt. By 1200 B.C.E. farmers in Mauritania **(MORE-ee-TAIN-ee-uh)** had built over two hundred stone villages and towns in what is now mostly uninhabited desert. They may have been the ancestors of the Mande **(MAN-da)** peoples, who now occupy a large area of the western Sudan. By 900 or 800 B.C.E. population increase had transformed walled villages into large, well-constructed towns. Eventually the expanding Sahara swallowed this society and the people probably moved south.

Long-distance trade, especially the caravan routes crossing the Sahara Desert, greatly aided the growth of Sudanic societies. The earliest caravan activity dates back to 1000 or 500 B.C.E. Some groups took up commerce as their primary activity, and this trans-Saharan trade depended on pack animals introduced by Berbers, initially mules and horses and later camels. First domesticated in parched Arabia, camels could endure many days of caravan travel without water. Eventually a large trade system linked the Sudanic towns with the southern Mediterranean coast and the forest zone to the south.

While each society developed distinctive notions of the cosmic order and their place within it, there were common patterns (see Witness to the Past: The World-View of an African Society). Many peoples, like the Mande and Igbo **(EE-boh)**, believed in one divine force or supreme being, either male or female, who created the cosmos, earth, and life and then remained remote from human affairs. Africans needing immediate spiritual help appealed to secondary gods and spirits. Thus sub-Saharan African religion became a mix of monotheism, polytheism, and animism.

African societies shaped these beliefs into complex and enduring artistic traditions. For example, in what is now central Nigeria, the Nok people, mostly farmers and herders, worked iron by 500 B.C.E.. Nok artists also fashioned exquisite terracotta pottery and sculpture, including life-size and realistic human heads. These creations influenced the later art of several Nigerian societies.

Werner Forman/Art Resource, NY

NOK TERRACOTTA SCULPTURE OF HEAD Elaborate, life-size, technically complex sculptures reveal something of Nok material life in ancient Nigeria. Some figures sit on stools, carry an axe, or wear beads.

The Bantu-Speaking Peoples and Their Migrations

Today people who speak closely related Bantu languages occupy most of Africa south of a line stretching from today's Kenya in the east to Cameroon in West-Central Africa. All of these societies can trace their distant ancestry back to the same location in West-Central Africa (see Map 3.2). In their migrations, the Bantu incorporated many of the peoples they encountered and modified their own cultures to suit local conditions. Recent scholarship suggests that the diffusion of Bantu technologies and languages, which local peoples adopted, was as important as actual human movement in expanding Bantu culture. The Bantu occupation of central, eastern, and southern Africa constitutes one of the great population movements in world history, a saga similar to the settlement of the Pacific islands and the Indo-European migration into western and southern Eurasia. As the Bantu spread out, they gradually divided into over four hundred different ethnic groups.

The Bantu originated along the Benue **(BAIN-way)** River in eastern Nigeria and western Cameroon **(KAM-uh-roon)**. But agriculture fostered overcrowding by 2000 B.C.E., spurring some to migrate eastward into the lands just north of the Congo River Basin. Bantu settled the Great Lakes region of East Africa between 1000 B.C.E. and 500 B.C.E., and some also began moving south into the Congo River Basin. They mixed with the local peoples, exchanging technologies and cultural patterns.

The Bantu benefited from iron metallurgy and agricultural technologies, using iron tools and weapons to open new land and subdue the small existing populations. Some also adopted cattle and goat raising. By 2,000 years ago some Bantu living in northeast Africa had also learned to grow domesticated bananas and plantains (large bananas) imported from Southeast Asia, as well as sorghum **(SOAR-gum)** from the Nile Valley. These high-yielding crops provided a spur to population growth, encouraging new migration into southern Africa.

WITNESS TO THE PAST

The World-View of an African Society

While few primary sources survive for the ancient period in sub-Saharan Africa, contemporary oral traditions may offer some insight into ancient understandings of the natural and spiritual realms. This excerpt on the world-view of the Igbo people in southeastern Nigeria was compiled by an Igbo anthropologist. Many Igbo perspectives may derive from the Nok and Bantu cultures, whose ancestral homelands are near the region where the Igbo live today.

There is the world of . . . all created beings and things, both animate and inanimate. The spirit world is the abode of the creator, the deities, the disembodied and malignant spirits, and the ancestral spirits. It is the future abode of the living after their death. . . . Existence or the Igbo . . . involves the interaction between the material and . . . spiritual, the visible and . . . invisible, the good and . . . bad, the living and . . . dead. . . . The world of the "dead" is . . . full of activities. . . . The principle of seniority makes the ancestors [in the world of the "dead"] the head of the [extended kinship system in the world of man]. . . .

The world as a natural order which inexorably goes on its ordained way . . . is foreign to Igbo conceptions. Rather, their world is a dynamic one—. . . of moving equilibrium . . . that is constantly threatened, and sometimes actually disturbed by natural and social calamities. . . . But the Igbo believe that these social calamities and cosmic forces which disturb their world are controllable and should be "manipulated" by them for their own purpose . . . [to maintain] . . . social and cosmological balance in the world. . . . They achieve this balance . . . through divination, sacrifice, and appeal to the countervailing forces of their ancestors . . . against the powers of the malignant spirits. . . . The Igbo world is not only a world in which people strive for equality; it is one in which change is constantly expected. . . . Life on earth is a link in the chain of status hierarchy which culminates in . . . ancestral honor in the world of the dead. . . .

They believe in a supreme god, a high god, who is all good [but a] . . . withdrawn god . . . who has finished all active works of creation and keeps watch over his creatures from a distance. . . . Although the Igbo feel psychologically separated from their high god, he is not too far away, he can be reached, but not as quickly as can other deities who must render their services to man to justify their demand for sacrifices. . . . Minor gods [can] be controlled, manipulated, and used to further human interests. . . . Given effective protection, the Igbo are very faithful to their gods.

THINKING ABOUT THE READING

1. How do the Igbo understand the relationship between the human and spiritual worlds?
2. What is the role of the supreme god in their polytheistic theology?
3. How might their beliefs about the relationship of the human and spiritual realms shape Igbo society?

Source: From Victor Uchendu, *the igbo of Southeast Nigeria,* 1E © 1965 Wadsworth, a part of Cengage Learning, Inc. Reproduced by permission.

MAKE SURE YOU UNDERSTAND THESE KEY POINTS BEFORE MOVING ON

- **Small-scale agriculture flourished in Africa, though widespread disease made it difficult to domesticate animals.**
- **The Nubian kingdom of Kush increased in power as Egypt declined and became a major trading hub linking the peoples of Africa to the Mediterranean.**
- **Caravan routes through the Sahara allowed for trade and for links among widely separated African peoples.**
- **The Bantu spread widely throughout Africa, mixing their culture and traditions with those of local peoples.**

Early Societies and Networks of the Eastern Mediterranean

What were the contributions of the Hebrews, Minoans, Mycenaeans, Phoenicians, and Dorian Greeks to later societies in the region?

During the second millennium B.C.E. smaller bronze- and then iron-using societies in the eastern half of the Mediterranean Basin were developing influential ideas or establishing cities and states. The Hebrews created the foundation for three major religions, the Minoans became an economic bridge between western Asia and southeastern Europe, and the warlike Mycenaeans built the first cities in Greece. The Phoenicians created a new alphabet, established colonies in the western Mediterranean, and fostered networks connecting many ancient societies. Greek migrants built an influential society.

MAP 3.2 BANTU MIGRATIONS AND EARLY AFRICA The Bantu-speaking peoples spread over several millennia throughout the southern half of Africa. Various societies, cities, and states emerged in West and North Africa.

Eastern Mediterranean Environments

The history and diet of eastern Mediterranean peoples were influenced by the regional climate, with its cool, rainy winters and hot, dry summers. On the northern shores, people grew grain, made bread, and planted olive trees and grape vines, and both olive oil and wine became export crops. Pastoralism was common in the drier lands of Lebanon and Palestine. Finally, the Mediterranean Sea, a mostly placid body of water, fostered boat building, maritime trade, and other contacts between diverse societies (see Map 3.3).

One of the densest populations emerged in Greece, located across the Aegean **(ah-JEE-uhn)** Sea from Anatolia. Unlike Mesopotamia and Egypt, where river valleys invited the creation of large political units, Greece consists of small valleys separated by mountains and has an extensive coastline with many good harbors. This geography encouraged political fragmentation and intellectual diversity. Destined to live in small,

MAP 3.3 THE ANCIENT EASTERN MEDITERRANEAN The Hebrew, Minoan, Mycenaean, Phoenician, and Greek societies developed along the eastern shores of the Mediterranean Sea, exchanging goods and ideas with each other and with other western Asians and the Egyptians.

independent city-states, the Greeks also became a seafaring, trading people who could travel by sea east to Ionia (today western Turkey), south to Crete, or west to southern Italy more easily than they could establish connections with nearby inland towns. Thus the Mediterranean linked the Greeks to other peoples such as the Minoans, Egyptians, and Phoenicians.

The Hebrews and Religious Innovation

The Hebrews, a Semitic people, were one of many groups of pastoral nomads led by powerful men known as patriarchs (from the Greek word for "rule by the father"). Their population was small, their economic and technological developments unimpressive, and their political achievements short-lived. The united Hebrew monarchy lasted less than a century. Yet the Hebrew contribution to religious history, especially to Christian and Islamic traditions, exceeds that of either the Mesopotamians or Egyptians.

The Hebrews trace their ancestry back to Abraham, a patriarch who supposedly lived in Mesopotamia sometime between 2000 and 1500 B.C.E. Abraham and his two sons, Isaac and Ishmael, are considered the spiritual ancestors of three monotheistic religions—Judaism, Christianity, and Islam—often called the Abrahamic faiths and collectively having some 3 billion followers today. The books of the Hebrew Bible contain the Hebrews' basic laws and provide the main source for their early history.

Modern Israeli and Western historians and archaeologists heatedly debate the historical reliability and antiquity of the Bible, which was probably based in part on oral traditions, and even whether key figures such as Abraham, Moses, and King David were real or mythical. As archaeology cannot confirm very much of the earliest history, every newly discovered artifact is subject to controversy. Some scholars think the biblical books are quite old, others that most or all of the books were composed after 700 B.C.E. to support rival Hebrew factions. Some Bible stories seem based on Mesopotamian and Egyptian traditions, such as the great flood in the Epic of Gilgamesh. For example, some of the advice in the Hebrew Book of Proverbs echoes ideas in more ancient Egyptian writings. These ongoing controversies underline the importance of Hebrew religion to later history.

In the biblical account, Abraham led a few followers on a migration from southern Mesopotamia to Palestine. Although born into a polytheistic world, Abraham recognized one supreme god. Peoples from Palestine had long migrated, either voluntarily or as slaves, to Egypt. A group of Hebrews who had gone to Egypt and been enslaved were freed and left Egypt, probably in the thirteenth century. This "Exodus" from Egypt and eventual return to Palestine was led by Moses, whom the later Hebrews acclaimed their religion's founder. Moses gave his name to a code of laws, including the Ten Commandments.

Around 1000 B.C.E. the Hebrews had enough unity to establish a monarchy centered in the small city of Jerusalem. But Hebrew unity proved short-lived. After the death of King Solomon in 922 B.C.E., the monarchy split into two kingdoms, Israel and Judah. In 722 the Assyrians conquered Israel and resettled its inhabitants elsewhere in their empire. When Assyria fell, the Hebrew prophet Nahum **(NAY-hum)** expressed joy: "Nineveh [the Assyrian capital] is laid waste; who will bemoan her? All who hear the news of you will clap their hands over you."[12] In 586 the Chaldeans conquered Judah and moved its leaders to Babylon. The bitterness of the "Babylonian Captivity" was reflected in a Hebrew psalm: "By the rivers of Babylon, there we sat down, yea, we wept when we remembered Zion."[13] This exile ended in 539 when the Persians conquered the Chaldeans and allowed the Hebrews to return to Palestine, which later became part of the Roman Empire. The Jews were again dispersed after a revolt against Roman rule in 70 C.E., and from that time until the establishment of modern Israel in 1948 C.E., there was no Jewish state.

The Hebrews' religious history, especially their ethical code, makes them memorable in world history. Four religious concepts later influenced the Western and Islamic traditions: monotheism, morality, messianism, and meaning in history. Many Hebrews worshiped a single god, Yahweh **(YA-way)**, who, they believed, had made a covenant with their earliest patriarchs and reinforced it when Moses received the Ten Commandments. If they would obey him, he would protect them. Gradually the Hebrews reshaped monotheism, asserting that there is only one God, Yahweh, for all peoples, as the prophet Isaiah proclaimed: "There is no other God besides Me, a just God. Look to Me, and be saved, all you ends of the earth!"[14]

Hebrew holy men known as prophets refined two other Hebrew religious concepts, morality and messianism, emphasizing that following Yahweh also meant leading a moral life, refraining from lying, stealing, adultery, and persecution of the poor and oppressed. Unlike Hammurabi's Code, the law of Moses also emphasized compassion for the poor and mercy. Also, Hebrew law required punishing only the wrongdoer, not members of his or her family. Another major concept, **messianism**, asserted that God had given the Hebrews a special mission in the world. As the Hebrews faced their time of troubles after the division of Solomon's kingdom and the fall of Judah, messianism acquired a broad spiritual meaning of bringing proper ethical behavior and moral truth to all peoples. The book of Isaiah contends: "I will give you as a covenant to the people, as a light to the [nations]. To open blind eyes, to bring out prisoners from the prison, those who sit in darkness."[15] This idea later inspired Christian missionary work.

The final contribution is the idea that history itself has meaning and moves forward in a progressive, linear fashion, meaning that this earthly world was where human beings worked out their salvation by choosing good over evil. This belief gave birth later to the idea of progress, the notion that the future will be better than the past. It stood in contrast to Hindu ideas that the material world is illusory and time is cyclical.

Minoan Crete and Regional Trade

Between about 2000 and 1400 B.C.E. an influential urban society and network hub, now called Minoan **(mi-NO-an)**, thrived on the island of Crete **(kreet)**, which lies just south of the Greek peninsula. Crete's strategic location made it a center for sea trade between Egypt, western Asia, and southeastern Europe, and its achievements intrigue historians. Like Harappan cities, some Minoan cities had indoor plumbing and streets with drains and sewers. Paintings and sculptures show some Mesopotamian and Egyptian influences, but they also differ in style. Minoans apparently worshiped many female deities, including a mother goddess. The absence of fortresses or defensive walls suggests that they relied on their fleet to protect them. Yet, while many accounts portray Minoans as largely peace-loving, some recent studies find more evidence of violence, martial traditions, and warfare. Around 1630 B.C.E. many cities were destroyed, perhaps from earthquakes following a massive volcanic explosion that blew apart the nearby island of Thera **(THER-uh)** (today's Santorini). The sinking of most of Thera and the dispersal of the survivors may have led to the legend of a lost continent, Atlantis.

The Minoans were innovators who pioneered a mixed agriculture well suited to the region's sunny, dry climate. The first great Mediterranean sea power, they traded extensively with Sicily, Greece, and the Aegean islands and sent wine, olives, and wool to Egypt and southwest Asia. Crete also served as a meeting

messianism The Hebrew belief that their God, Yahweh, had given them a special mission in the world.

[12]Nahum 3:7, 19, *The Holy Bible*, New King James Version (Chicago: Thomas Nelson, 1983), 908.
[13]Psalm 137:1, *Holy Bible*, 639.
[14]Isaiah 45:21–22, *Holy Bible*, 721.
[15]Isaiah 42:6–7, *Holy Bible*, 717.

Erich Lessing / Art Resource, NY

THE CAPTIVITY OF ISRAELI WOMEN AT NINEVEH This relief comes from the palace of the Chaldean king Sennacherib in Nineveh. It was probably carved at the beginning of the seventh century B.C.E.

place connecting, through trade, western Asians and North Africans with various European societies. The Minoans possessed two writing scripts, one of possibly Mesopotamian origin and the other related to early Greek. Scholars have now learned to read some of it, including accounts of goods manufactured, crops harvested, religious festivals, and war preparations.

The Mycenaeans and Regional Power

The Mycenaeans, Indo-Europeans named after the city of Mycenae **(my-SEE-nee)** in southern Greece, also became an important power between 1600 and 1200 B.C.E. after migrating into the Greek peninsula. Bronze swords and armor in their graves indicate that they were a warrior society whose economy was tightly controlled by the king and his scribes. Eventually the Mycenaeans conquered Crete (whose Minoan society had already collapsed), all of southern Greece, and the Aegean islands, forming an empire from which they collected taxes and tribute. They dispatched ships to Sicily, Italy, and Spain and into the Black Sea and engaged in war with rivals, operating out of strong fortresses. According to legends, around 1250 the Mycenaeans conquered Troy, a prosperous Hittite trading port along the northwestern coast of Anatolia, inspiring Homer's epic story, the *Iliad*, some 500 years later. Scholars debate whether an actual Trojan War occurred, some suspecting that the Homeric stories combine oral accounts of various conflicts, but the stories strongly influenced the later Greeks and Romans.

By 1200, however, the Mycenaeans themselves faced collapse, perhaps from prolonged drought resulting from climate change, a possible series of earthquakes, or civil wars and attacks by warlike Indo-Europeans known as the Dorian Greeks, who were migrating into the peninsula. After 1200 various groups known as "Sea Peoples" pillaged and disrupted trade throughout the Aegean and eastern Mediterranean. But eventually a creative society emerged in Greece that incorporated many influences from the Dorian Greeks, Mycenaeans, Phoenicians, and Egyptians.

The Phoenicians and Their Networks

The Phoenicians linked Mediterranean and Southwest Asian peoples by trade networks. Between 1500 and 1000 B.C.E. this Semitic people, known to the Hebrews as the Canaanites **(KAY-nan-ites)**, established themselves along the narrow coastal strip west of the Lebanon mountains, building the great trading cities of Tyre **(tire)**, Sidon **(SIDE-en)**, and Byblos **(BIB-los)**. Tyre offered luxury goods from many societies and attracted the finest artists and craftsmen. The Hebrew prophet

John Elk/Lonely Planet Images/Getty Images

WALL PAINTING FROM THERA, CRETE The paintings in palaces and homes show slices of Minoan life. This portrays female boxers, hinting that women played many roles in Minoan society.

Ezekial denounced the rich, vibrant city and its extraordinary network of mercantile connections: "Your borders are in the midst of the seas. All the ships of the sea were in you to market your merchandise."[16]

Although sometimes dominated by Egypt, Phoenician cities were fiercely competitive and independent states headed by kings. While the Phoenicians spoke a common language and worshiped the same gods, they never united. Their most famous cultural achievement, the simplification of Mesopotamian cuneiform writing into a phonetic alphabet of twenty-two characters, helped spread their influence in the Mediterranean and became the basis of later European alphabets.

Only a few tablets containing information on Phoenician government, society, and religion survive. Most of what we know comes from writings by Egyptians, Greeks, and Hebrews, peoples who admired the Phoenicians' skills as scribes, seafarers, engineers, and artisans but also denounced them as immoral profiteers and cheaters. Deserved or not, the Phoenician image as schemers survives into modern times. Our term for a shameless woman, *Jezebel*, is derived from a princess of Tyre.

Between 1000 and 800 B.C.E., the seafaring Phoenicians replaced the declining Mycenaeans as the leaders in Mediterranean trade with western Asia, becoming experts in new methods of dyeing cloth. They may also have traveled as far as England to get supplies of tin. Phoenicians established colonies or trading posts in Sicily, Italy, Spain, and beyond the Strait of Gibraltar in Morocco. Some historians think they may have reached the Canary Islands and Madeira in the Atlantic Ocean. Thus the Phoenicians became the ancient Mediterranean's greatest mariners.

Between 1000 and 500 B.C.E., the Mediterranean Sea became a major source of goods and wealth. Solid bars of precious metals served as currency. Using their colonies for resupply and repair, the Phoenicians traveled long distances to secure iron, silver, timber, copper, gold, and tin, all valuable commodities in western Asia and Egypt. Legends suggest that around 600 B.C.E., under the sponsorship of the Egyptian king, a Phoenician fleet may even have sailed around Africa in a

[16]Ezekiel 27:3–4, 9, *Holy Bible*, 835.

three-year expedition, but these journeys cannot be substantiated. In 650 B.C.E. the Assyrians conquered the Phoenician home cities and brought an end to their dynamic power, but some Phoenician colonies lived on, most famously Carthage in North Africa near what is today Tunis. Carthage became the capital of a major trading empire and the chief competitor to the Romans in the western Mediterranean by the third century B.C.E. Carthaginian sailors later explored far down the coast of West Africa.

The Eclectic Roots of Greek Society

The fall of the Mycenaeans and the Phoenicians set the stage for another seafaring people, the Greeks, to found an influential urban society. During the four centuries after the destruction of Mycenae, called the Greek "Dark Age" (1200–800 B.C.E.), organized states and writing disappeared, and the economic and social environment changed considerably. Dorian Greeks settled much of the Greek peninsula, and many Mycenaeans dispersed, some settling the offshore islands and others crossing the Aegean Sea to Ionia, where they established cities. The Greek world, scattered, as the philosopher Plato later put it, like frogs around a pond, became a mix of Mycenaean and Dorian peoples and traditions.

The Greeks were famous as both maritime traders and warriors, their respect for military strength reflected in the works of Homer, oral epics written down between the eleventh and the eighth centuries B.C.E. that became an integral part of the Greek tradition. Whether Homer was an actual person or the collective name for several authors who compiled these epic poems into a narrative remains debated. Many themes in the epics may reflect influences from Mesopotamian literature such as the Epic of Gilgamesh, indicating the spread of ideas around the eastern Mediterranean world.

The first Homeric epic, the *Iliad*, set during an attack on Troy by some Greek cities led by their king Agamemnon **(ag-uh-MEM-non)**, emphasizes valor in war but also warns its readers against excessive pride. Arrogance leads the Greeks to make some nearly fatal mistakes. For example, after a quarrel with Agamemnon the Greek hero Achilles **(uh-KIL-eez)** refuses to fight. When Achilles' friend Patroclus **(puh-TROW-klus)** takes Achilles' place in the battle and is killed by Hector, the Trojan leader, a remorseful Achilles then kills Hector. The poem ends when Hector's father, Priam, comes to ask Achilles for his son's body. Achilles is moved by Priam's courage, and both men share their grief. This poem and Homer's second epic, the *Odyssey*, a story of the adventures of Odysseus **(oh-DIS-ee-us)**, or Ulysses, as he returns home after the Trojan War, portrayed the Greek gods as superheroes who intervened to help their human friends and hinder their enemies. The Homeric world measured virtue by success in combat rather than justice or mercy. Yet these great epics continue to be read, not only because of their dramatic and often brutal war scenes, but also because they tell us something about the tragedy of human life. This emphasis on both human power and suffering remained a part of Greek literature throughout the following centuries.

The Homeric epics and belief in their gods greatly influenced the emerging Greek society. The Greeks also borrowed ideas from the Egyptians and western Asians, although the degree of outside influence on early Greek culture is debated (see the Historical Controversy for Part A). The Mediterranean provided a zone of interaction for peoples living around its rim. Phoenician ships, which had avoided a turbulent Greece for several hundred years, began to show up again, restoring Greek contact with the eastern Mediterranean and its regional trade networks. Soon the Greeks adopted and modified the Phoenician alphabet. These centuries built a foundation for a dynamic Greek society in the Classical period.

MAKE SURE YOU UNDERSTAND THESE KEY POINTS BEFORE MOVING ON

- **The Hebrews were politically fragmented, but their religious writings, with their emphasis on monotheism, morality, messianism, and meaning in history, have had a tremendous impact on religious history.**
- **Around 1250 B.C.E., the Mycenaeans possibly conquered Troy; this event later inspired Homer's epic, the *Iliad*.**
- **The Phoenicians, the region's greatest maritime traders, simplified the Mesopotamian cuneiform writing into an alphabet, which served as the basis for later European alphabets.**
- **The Homeric epics, the *Iliad* and the *Odyessy*, greatly influenced the emerging Greek society, which was a synthesis of Mycenaean and Dorian Greek peoples.**

CHAPTER SUMMARY

Egypt is often called "the gift of the Nile" because it arose in the flood-prone Nile River Valley. The Egyptian system, led by kings, lasted for several thousand years in its basic form. In their stable and predictable environment, the Egyptians invented the hieroglyphics writing system and developed a more optimistic world-view and culture than the Mesopotamians. Egyptians also participated in trade networks linking western Asia and the Mediterranean Basin with sub-Saharan Africa and India.

Many sub-Saharan African peoples also invented or adopted agriculture and metallurgy, building the framework for cities and states. An environment of grasslands, forests, and the expanding Sahara Desert shaped their history, and the gradual drying out of the Sahara region forced many people to migrate. Cities arose early in Nubia (along the central Nile), probably stimulated by long-distance trade and contacts with Egypt. The Sudan fostered distinctive cultures. The Bantu peoples, in one of the greatest migrations in history, spread their farming and iron-based culture and languages widely in the southern half of Africa.

The Mediterranean societies also benefited from regional connections. The trade routes of the seafaring Minoans, Mycenaeans, and Phoenicians enriched the peoples of western Asia and the Mediterranean Basin by bringing them material goods, markets, cultural contacts, and a practical new alphabet. Contact with Egyptians and Mesopotamians influenced the Hebrews' evolving understanding of their mission, and of Yahweh. Some of these contributions, such as the Phoenician alphabet and Hebrew religious and ethical concepts, have influenced many peoples down to the present day. Greece arose from interaction among several Mediterranean societies in a turbulent period during which Homer wrote his great epics.

KEY TERMS

pharaohs (p. 52)
hieroglyphics (p. 52)
monotheism (p. 53)
Bantu (p. 57)
Sudan (p. 57)
desertification (p. 57)
messianism (p. 63)

4 Around the Pacific Rim: Eastern Eurasia and the Americas, 5000–600 B.C.E.

Je Agostini/Getty Images

SHANG BRONZE VASE The Shang made some of the ancient world's finest bronze tools and vessels. This ritual vase has an animal motif.

He encouraged the people and settled them. He called his superintendent of works [and] minister of instruction, and charged them with the building of the houses. Crowds brought the earth in baskets. The roll of the great drum did not overpower [the noise of the builders].

—Chinese poem from the second millennium B.C.E.[1]

According to Chinese tradition, around 1400 B.C.E. a ruler named Pan Keng ordered a new capital city, Anyang **(ahn-yahng)**, to be built alongside the Huan River. The king and his officials supervised the citizens as they worked to the beat of a drum. The king had high expectations for his new capital. The rich soil fostered productive farms, while the river supplied water and aided in defense. People could find timber, hunt, or seek relief from the summer heat in nearby mountains. Probably China's first planned city, Anyang was surrounded by four walls facing the points of the compass, reflecting the ancient adage that without harmony nothing lasts. Three and a half millennia later archaeologists found exquisite ritual bronzes and "dragon bones," animal bones carved with some of the earliest Chinese writing. For hundreds of years, local chemists, not knowing their priceless historical value, had been grinding up these bones to make folk medicine. But they showed that ancient China, like Mesopotamia and Egypt, had both cities and a writing system. Although Anyang's buildings crumbled with time, these ancient Chinese established a society that still retains many of its original ideas and customs.

People in China and Korea were among the earliest people to develop farming and metalworking, while Southeast Asians pioneered in maritime technology. Despite formidable geographical barriers, very early trade networks connected China and Southeast Asia to other parts of Eurasia. The same process took place on the other side of the Pacific Ocean. In the Americas, too, many people underwent the great transitions to farming, cities, regional networks of exchange, and complex social structures, although mountains, deserts, and forest barriers tended to isolate North, Central, and South American societies from each other.

[1]From the ancient Chinese *Book of Songs*, quoted in Herlee Glessner Creel, *The Birth of China: A Survey of the Formative Period of Chinese Civilization* (New York: Frederick Unger, 1937), 64.

IN THIS CHAPTER

The Formation of Chinese Society, 6000–1750 B.C.E.

How did an expanding Chinese society arise from diverse local traditions?

Societies change in part through contact with each other; while forbidding desert and mountain barriers complicated contact with China, they did not prevent some influences from crossing borders. Nevertheless, China joined Harappa, Mesopotamia, Egypt, and Minoan Crete in pioneering distinctive ways of life. Productive farming, creative cultures, and the rise of states laid the framework for a society now at least four thousand years old.

China and Its Regional Environments

The Chinese faced many challenges in communicating both with each other and with distant peoples. China's vast size, combined with a difficult topography, made transportation difficult while encouraging regional cultural and political loyalties. The early Chinese were sometimes divided into competing states, and governments struggled to enforce centralizing policies. The Himalayas **(him-uh-LAY-uhs)**, the high Tibetan **(tuh-BET-en)** Plateau, and great deserts inhibited contact with South and West Asia. However, the Chinese did have regular trade and conflict with Central Asians, North Asians, Southeast Asians, and Tibetans, whose cultures, languages, and ways of life were very different from the Chinese. The Chinese sometimes extended political control over these peoples and sometimes were invaded and even conquered by them.

Modern China covers as much land as western and eastern Europe combined. Because most people in ancient China lived in the eastern river valleys and plains rather than along the coast, maritime commerce did not develop until around 1000 C.E. The large land area and China's three major river systems helped shape Chinese regionalism. The Yellow, or Huang He **(hwang ho)**, River; the Yangzi **(yahng-zeh)**, or Yangtze, River; and the West, or Xijiang **(SHEE JYAHNG)**, River all flow from west to east and hence do not link the northern, central, and southern parts of China. The Yellow River, sometimes termed "China's sorrow" because of its many destructive floods, flows some 3,000 miles through north China to the Yellow Sea, but it is easily navigable only in some sections. The more

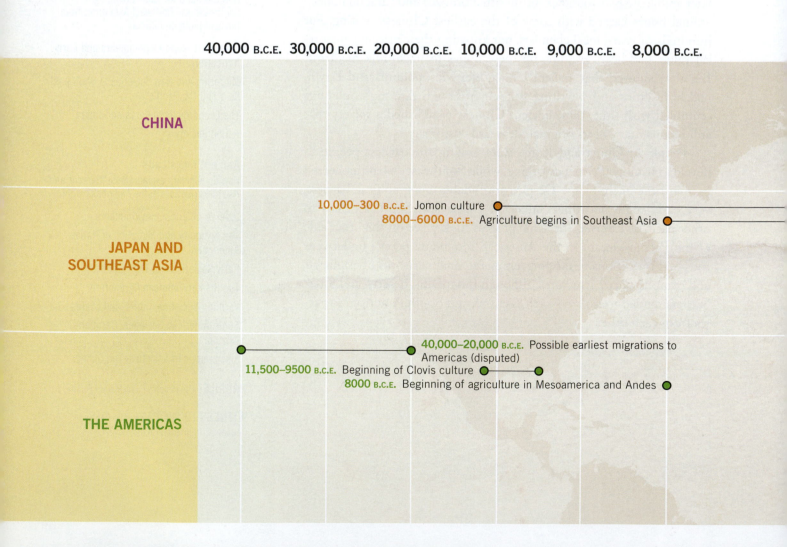

40,000 B.C.E. 30,000 B.C.E. 20,000 B.C.E. 10,000 B.C.E. 9,000 B.C.E. 8,000 B.C.E.

CHINA

JAPAN AND SOUTHEAST ASIA

10,000–300 B.C.E. Jomon culture

8000–6000 B.C.E. Agriculture begins in Southeast Asia

THE AMERICAS

40,000–20,000 B.C.E. Possible earliest migrations to Americas (disputed)

11,500–9500 B.C.E. Beginning of Clovis culture

8000 B.C.E. Beginning of agriculture in Mesoamerica and Andes navigable but also flood-prone Yangzi, the world's fourth-longest river, flows through central China, a region of moderate climate and the densest population. The shorter West River system helps define mountainous, subtropical south China.

China's neighboring regions had diverse environments and distinctive cultures. Central Asia's deserts and grasslands, with their blazing hot summers and long, cold winters, were mostly unpromising for intensive agriculture. The rugged, pastoralist Central Asian societies who lived in these areas traded with, warred against, and sometimes conquered the settled farmers of China, Korea, and India. Those who most affected Chinese history included diverse Turkish-speaking peoples, some from the dry Xinjiang **(SHIN-jee-yahng)** region of far western China. In contrast, the Tibetans were subsistence farmers and herders. The ancient Chinese also forged occasional relations with people in mainland Southeast Asia, Manchuria, and Korea.

Early Chinese Agriculture

Agriculture in China began around 7000 B.C.E., perhaps 1,000 years later than in Mesopotamia. Neolithic settlements existed all over China, suggesting Chinese society's diverse roots. The Yellow and Wei River Valleys in north China fostered early farming, with the modest annual rainfall and frequent flooding making the region somewhat similar to the Nile, Tigris-Euphrates, and Indus Basins. Winds blowing in from the Gobi Desert of Mongolia to the northwest deposited massive amounts of dust that enriched north China soils. Initially the wheatlike, highly drought-resistant millet and later, wheat, likely imported from India or Mesopotamia, became northern China's main cereal grain. Ancient songs tell us something about the farming routine:

> They clear away the grass, the trees; Their ploughs open up the ground. In a thousand pairs they tug at weeds and roots, Along the low grounds, along the ridges. They sow the many sorts of grain, The seeds that hold moist life. How that blade shoots up, How sleek, the grown plant.[2]

Farther south, the Chinese in the Yangzi River Basin began cultivating rice by 5000 B.C.E. Thus very early two

[2] *The Book of Songs*, translated by Arthur Waley (London: George Unwin, 1954), 162.

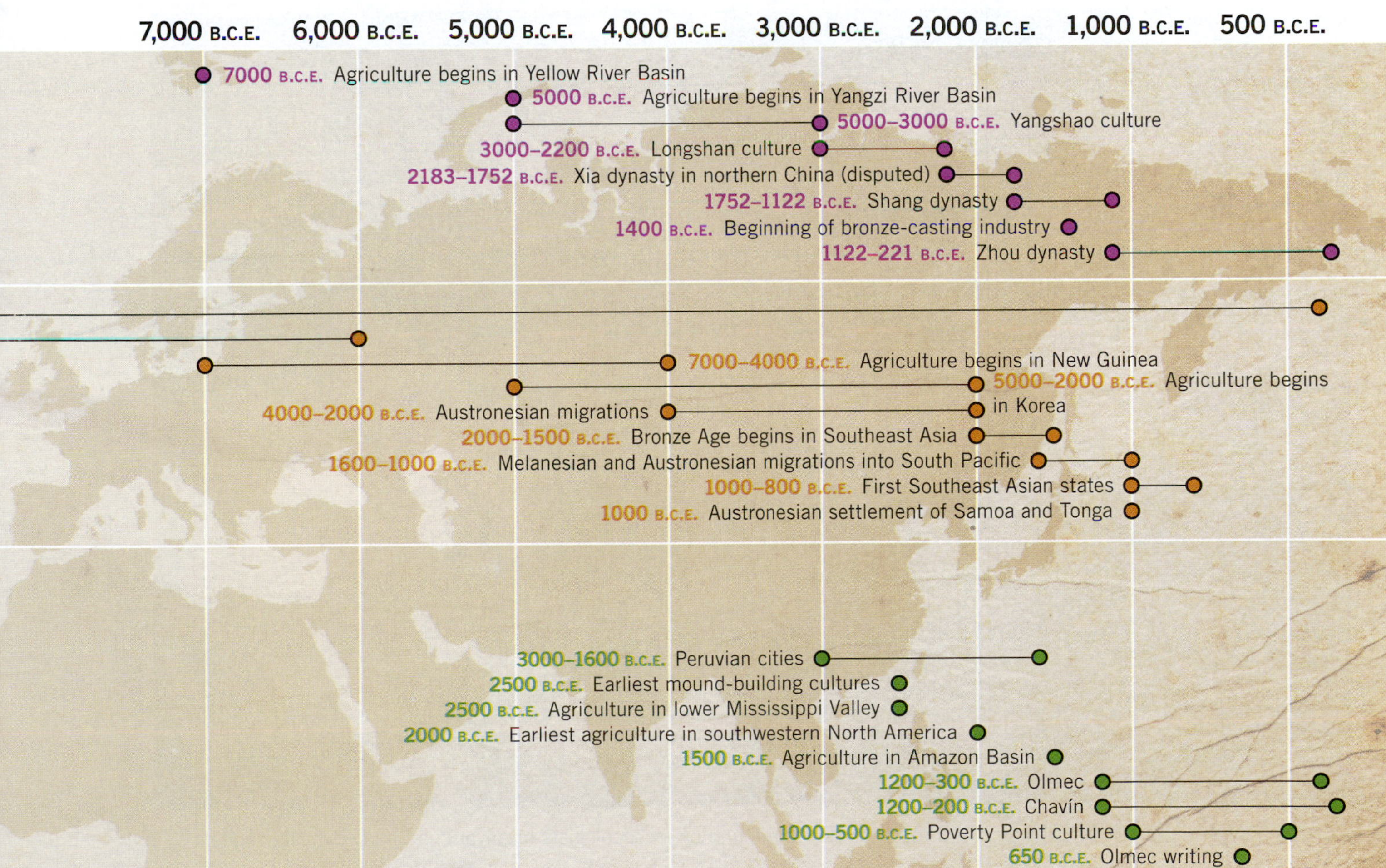

distinct agricultural traditions emerged. In the cooler, drier north, drought-tolerant crops like wheat, millet, pears, and apricots were mainstays. In the wetter, warmer southern half of China, irrigated rice predominated. But rice became so important that for several thousand years Chinese have greeted each other by asking, "Have you eaten rice yet?" and have described losing a job as breaking one's rice bowl.

Highly productive agriculture promoted China's success. Despite sporadic famine, the Chinese people were basically well fed and well housed throughout much of history. Productive farming also promoted population growth: China contained between 2 and 4 million people by 3000 B.C.E. Using chopsticks, the Chinese ate well enough that they came to perceive food as more than simple fuel. Cooking became an art form and an essential component of social life, and folk religion included a God of the Kitchen. Many regional cooking variations developed, represented by the Cantonese, Hunanese **(hoon-ahn-eez)**, Mandarin, and Sichuanese **(SUH-chwahn-eez)** restaurants in large cities around the world.

The Growth and Spread of Chinese Culture

Neolithic China had several distinctive traditions. The Yangshao **(YANG-shao)** ("painted pottery") culture, which emerged in the middle Yellow River region around 5000 B.C.E., covered an area of north China larger than Mesopotamia or Egypt. Yangshao people made fine painted pottery, used kilns, bred pigs and dogs, weaved thread, and buried their dead in cemeteries, suggesting belief in an afterlife. Houses were mostly round or square with thatched roofs arranged around a central square. Village graves suggest that some 20 percent of those buried were under fifteen years of age and that only a small minority lived past forty. Chinese also raised silkworms and fashioned the silk into clothes, and silk making became a unique Chinese activity, often handled chiefly by women, with Chinese silk exported all over Eurasia. Other traditions have ancient roots as well. A 7,000-year-old seven-holed flute is the oldest still playable musical instrument ever found in the world, and evidence for jade carving, for which Chinese later became famous, has been found in several regions. Since floods and earthquakes were common, the early Chinese also experimented with techniques to predict the future so they could avoid disaster.

About 3000 B.C.E., when the Sumerians were building their cities, an expansive Chinese culture was coalescing out of various regional traditions. As late as 2000 B.C.E. many different cultures remained in China, and the peoples in southern China may have been more closely related to those people settling Southeast Asia than to the Chinese of the Yellow

Keren Su/China Span/Getty Images

SHANG ERA CHARIOTS The remains of these chariots were found by archaeologists in Anyang, a Shang dynasty capital.

River Basin. But gradually northern and central Chinese societies merged their traditions into a common cultural zone, with the Yellow River Basin remaining a major core of creativity. The Longshan **(LUNG-shahn)** ("black pottery") culture (3000–2200 B.C.E.) fostered a division of labor and social classes, built strong houses and walled villages and towns, and developed weapons. They also made pottery almost as hard as metal, carved high-quality jade, and created a simple pictographic writing. Millennia before any other society, the Chinese also used industrial diamonds to polish ceremonial ruby and sapphire axes, giving them a fine sheen. Meanwhile, in the Yangzi Basin, people produced distinctive traditions of agriculture, animal domestication, town building, and bronze metallurgy that were at least as old, if not older, than those of north China.

During the first millennium B.C.E., Chinese identity, customs, and migrants gradually expanded into south China, displacing or absorbing most of the indigenous **(in-DIJ-uh-nuhs)** peoples (the original inhabitants) in the south, although many ethnic minorities still live there. This mixing of different peoples produced a Chinese culture that encompassed many regional traditions and, at times, different states, held together by common customs and a standardized written language. Political unity helped but was not essential to this common cultural identity.

Population growth and shared culture made possible the first state. Chinese historians labeled this state the Xia **(shya) (Hsia)** dynasty (2183–1752 B.C.E.), but its existence is still debated. A city, Erlitou, built around 2000 B.C.E. near the Yellow River, shows evidence of royal palaces and bronze casting and was perhaps the Xia capital. The Xia may have presided over an occupationally diverse society including scribes, metallurgists, artisans, and bureaucrats. Some influences also filtered in from Central Asia, including the horse and chariot and ironworking, but in general, the Chinese themselves developed the ideas and institutions that gave their society the ability to expand, grow, adapt, and coordinate large populations.

MAKE SURE YOU UNDERSTAND THESE KEY POINTS BEFORE MOVING ON

- Early Chinese society was concentrated inland from the sea and was frequently fragmented into various states.
- In the cold, dry Chinese north, crops such as wheat and millet were grown, while in the wetter, warmer south, rice was dominant.
- Members of the Yangshao ("painted pottery") society were skilled craftspeople who excelled at carving, weaving, and village design.
- As time passed, the widely diverse Chinese people began to knit themselves together in one broad society with traditions that persist to this day.

The Reshaping of Ancient Chinese Society, 1750–600 B.C.E.

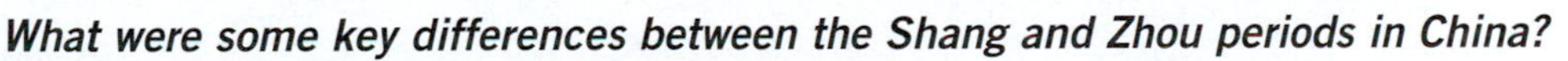

What were some key differences between the Shang and Zhou periods in China?

The Shang **(shahng)** dynasty established China's first powerful state and an expanding culture based on bronze technology. Under the Shang's successor, the more decentralized, iron-using Zhou **(joe)** dynasty, the Chinese improved writing and developed literature. Some enduring religious notions also appeared in these centuries. Isolation from other Eurasian states fostered a feeling of cultural superiority. The Chinese perceived themselves surrounded by less developed neighbors who either adopted Chinese customs or invaded China to enjoy its riches. Strong governments, technological developments, and writing helped make China the most influential East Asian society.

The Shang Dynasty Reshapes Northern China

The Shang (1752–1122 B.C.E.), China's first well-documented dynasty, began around the same time that Hammurabi ruled in Babylon and the Harappan society collapsed. A people from China's western fringe, the Shang, like the Aryan migrants into India, had adopted from Central Asians horse-drawn chariots for warfare. Conquering the eastern Yellow River Basin and imposing a hierarchy dominated by landowning aristocrats (see Map 4.1), they presided over a growing economy and built more cities. However, many Chinese outside Shang control maintained their own states and unique customs.

The Shang established an authoritarian state to coordinate irrigation and dam building. Shang kingship was passed on to a monarch's brother or son. Kings presented themselves as heading the country as a father did a family, claiming both political and spiritual leadership. Shang kings usually had dozens of wives, many of them probably the daughters of regional leaders allied to the monarchy. Like the Aryans, they emphasized military techniques, using a lethal combination of archers, spearmen, and charioteers. Throughout Chinese history, much of this military power was used to defend their northern borders against pastoral nomads, who were often tempted to invade the Yellow River Valley because of the relative prosperity of China in comparison to the marginal existence possible in the grasslands and deserts beyond the frontiers.

The Shang flourished economically and technologically, building many administrative and commercial cities. Anyang, the ruler Pan Keng's capital city, was surrounded by a wall 30 feet high and 60 feet wide; the city and its suburbs spread out over some 10 square miles. Some ten thousand workers spent eighteen years building Anyang, a feat that reflected considerable political and social organization. Technology improved with bronze, which was introduced in 1400 B.C.E. Considered the most skilled bronze casters in the ancient world, the Shang produced flawless bronze arrows, spears, sculpture, pots, and especially ritual vessels for drinking wine. They also made the glazed pottery that was the forerunner of the porcelain ("china") for which the Chinese would later become so famous.

Landowning aristocrats, many of them government officials, dominated the Shang hierarchy, enjoying luxurious surroundings and residences built on cement-like foundations. Aristocratic women held a high status. For example, Fuhao **(foo-HOW)**, the wife of a Shang king who seems to have been charged with protecting the borders of the Shang state, governed her own territory and led military campaigns. Leaders like Fuhao and their families were buried in elaborate royal tombs with great quantities of valuable objects. Among the vast treasure trove buried with Fuhao were 7 human sacrifices and 7 dogs, 564 objects of carved bone, 110 marble objects, 3 ivory carvings, 500 bone hairpins, 755 jades, some 7,000 cowry shells (used as money), and 3,500 pounds of bronze tools, mirrors, bells, and weapons (including 2 large battle-axes that honor her military exploits).

Commoners included skilled artisans, scribes, and merchants. The lower classes of farmers and laborers, including many slaves, were often mobilized by the powerful state for major building projects. The Shang were harsh masters, practicing human and animal sacrifice as part of their religious observances, often using slaves as victims.

The Shang's momentous contribution was an elaborate writing system. Hoping to predict the future, influential people

MAP 4.1 SHANG AND ZHOU CHINA The earliest Chinese states arose in north China along the Yellow River and its tributaries. The bronze-using Shang dynasty presided over the first documented state and were succeeded by the iron-using Zhou, who governed much of north and central China.

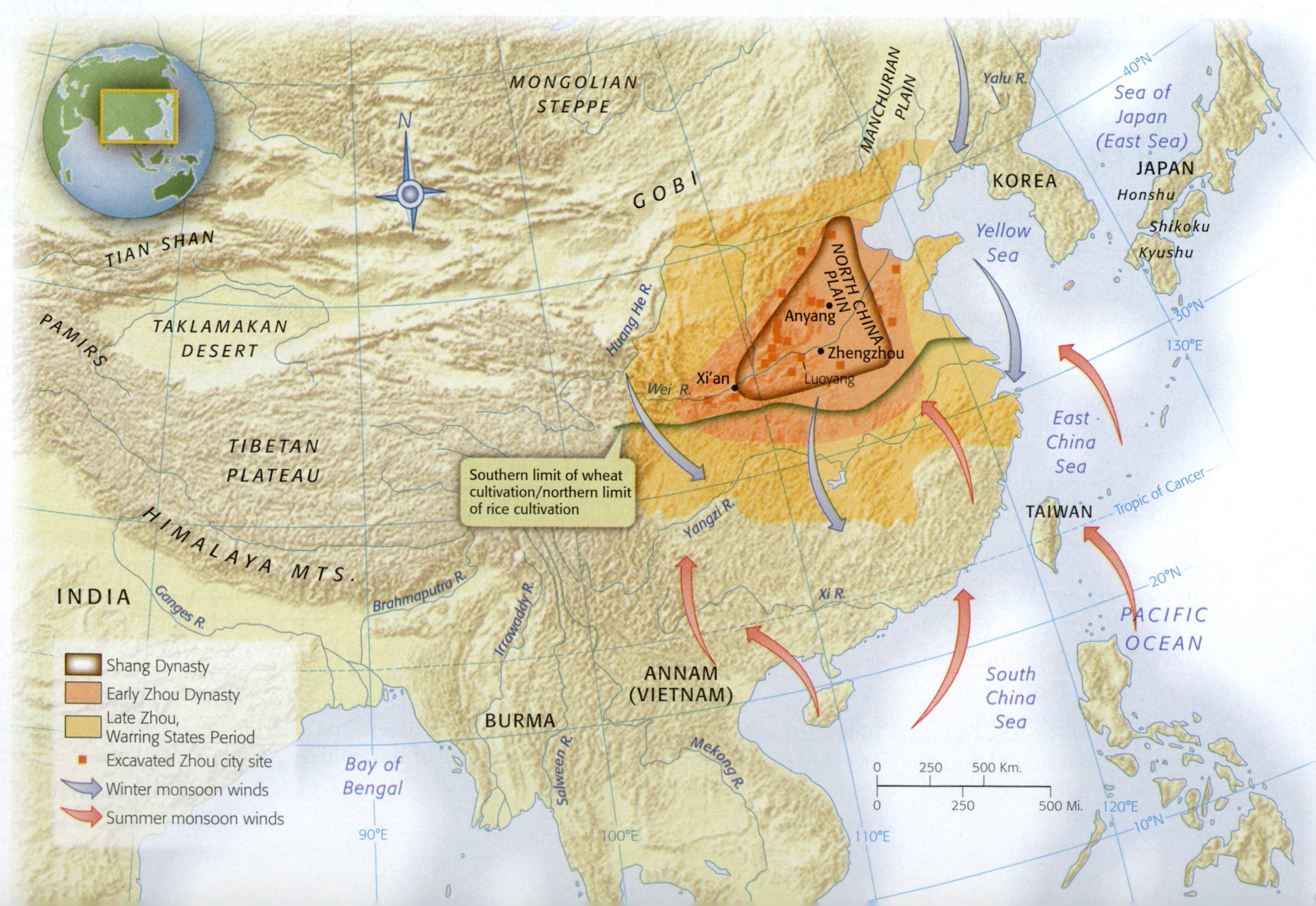

DEA PICTURE LIBRARY/De Agostini Picture Library/Getty Images

SHANG BRONZE PITCHER This type of pitcher, decorated with one of several distinctive Shang designs, was used for wine.

wrote questions addressed to the gods on animal bones and tortoise shells, inquiring about the abundance of the next harvest, the outcome of a battle, the weather, or the birth of an heir. For example, one inquired whether "if the king hunted, whether the chase would be without mishap."[3] Some prestigious officials were experts in interpreting the future with these bones. The writing found on oracle bones was clearly the forerunner of today's Chinese writing.

The Early Zhou and Their Government

As Shang power faded, a state on the western fringe of China invaded and overthrew the Shang, forming a new dynasty, the Zhou (1122–221 B.C.E.), and a decentralized type of government differing considerably from the Shang approach. The Duke of Zhou supposedly urged that "we must go on, abjuring all idleness, until our reign is universal and there shall not be one who is disobedient to our rule."[4]

The Zhou's relatively weak central government ruled over small states that had considerable autonomy but owed service obligations to the king. This decentralization reflected Zhou realism. Despite their impressive military technology, the Chinese had spread too far to administer their society effectively. The royal family directly ruled the area around their capital but parceled out the rest to followers and relatives who became local lords with much local power. Hence the Zhou kings presided, however symbolically, over a much larger land area than did the Shang, from southern Manchuria to the Yangzi Basin (see Map 4.1). They also began to call their country Zhongguo ("Middle Kingdom"), which endures today as the name used by the Chinese for their country.

To solidify their position, the Zhou justified their triumph over the Shang with a new concept: the **Mandate of Heaven**. According to this belief, rulers had the support of the gods ("Heaven") so long as conditions were good. However, when there was war, famine, or other hardships, Heaven withdrew its sanction and rebellion was permissible. The decadent and cruel Shang, the Duke of Zhou argued, lost their right to rule. Ever since the Chinese have invoked the Mandate of Heaven to justify the demise of a discredited government, and over time this radical new concept was used against the Zhou and all later dynasties as well. Monarchs lost their legitimacy if their misrule led to a crisis.

Furthermore, Chinese scholars began to view their political history in terms of the **dynastic cycle**. Instead of seeing a straight line of progress in history, as the Hebrews did, the Chinese focused on dynasties of ruling families who followed the same general pattern as their predecessors. A new dynasty brought peace and prosperity. Then overexpansion and corruption led to costly government, bankruptcy, social decay, and rebellions, eventually resulting in a new dynasty. This concept shaped Chinese thinking for the next twenty-five hundred years.

The Zhou system was unstable, plagued by chronic warfare between the various substates, with larger substates conquering smaller ones. As a result, by 400 B.C.E. the 1,700 substates of the early Zhou years were reduced to 7 that had considerable power in counteracting the weakening Zhou kings. Furthermore, Central Asians were obtaining faster ponies, forcing the Chinese to erect better defenses against their relentless pressure.

Early Zhou Society and Economy

Zhou government also fostered a rigid society clearly divided into aristocrats, commoners, and slaves. The nobility, owing allegiance to the king as vassals but governing their own realms, owned large estates defended by private armies and worked by slaves. The merchants enjoyed considerable freedom of action and often became rich. The majority of slaves were criminals and soldiers from rival ministates captured in the frequent wars. Peasants were mostly bound to the soil on land owned by aristocrats (see Witness to the Past: The Poetry of Peasant Life in Zhou China); they were assigned work and punished if it was not done. Their songs reflected resignation: "We rise at sunrise, We rest at sunset. Dig

Mandate of Heaven A Chinese belief that rulers had the support of the supernatural realm as long as conditions were good, but rebellion was justified when they were not.

dynastic cycle The Chinese view of their political history, which focuses on dynasties of ruling families.

[3]From John Minford and Joseph S. M. Lau, eds., *Classical Chinese Literature: An Anthology of Translations*, vol. 1 (New York: Columbia University Press, 2000), 16.
[4]Quoted in Creel, *Birth of China*, pp. 228–229.

WITNESS TO THE PAST

The Poetry of Peasant Life in Zhou China

We can learn something of Zhou common folk, especially the peasants who worked the land, from The Book of Songs, *a collection of 305 poems, hymns, and folk songs compiled between 1000 and 600 B.C.E.*

Some songs address ordinary people at their labor. Men weed the fields, plant, plow, and harvest. Women and girls gather mulberry leaves for silkworms, carry hampers of food to the men in the fields for lunch, and make thread:

The girls take their deep baskets, And follow the path under the wall, to gather the soft mulberry-leaves.

Some of the songs deal with courtship and love, sometimes revealing strong emotion, as in this song by a girl about a prospective sweetheart:

That the mere glimpse of a plain cap, Could harry me with such longing, Cause me pain so dire.... Enough! Take me with you to your house.... Let us two be one.

Within the family, the father had nearly absolute authority over his wife and children. When the family patriarch died, his wife became the family head. Children were expected to obey their parents, but some songs reveal that mutual affection and gratitude were common:

My father begot me. My mother fed me, Led me, bred me, Brought me up, reared me, Kept her eye on me, tended me, At every turn aided me. Their good deeds I would requite.

Peasant lives were filled with toil and hardship, but they could find some relief from drudgery in friendship and kinship. Entertaining relatives and friends was a major leisure activity:

And shall a man not seek to have his friends? He shall have harmony and peace. I have strained off my liquor in abundance, the dishes stand in rows, and none of my brethren are absent. Whenever we have leisure, let us drink the sparkling liquor.

Peasants faced many demands on their time and labor. Songs complain and even protest about an uncaring government and its rapacious tax collectors:

Big rat, big rat, Do not gobble our millet! Three years we have slaved for you. Yet you took no notice of us. At last we are going to leave you, And go to the happy land... where no sad songs are sung.

Some songs record abject poverty and misery:

Deep is my grief. I am utterly poverty-stricken and destitute. Yet no one heeds my misfortunes. Well, all is over now. No doubt it was Heaven's [the supernatural realm's] doing. So what's the good of talking about it!

Zhou peasants needed all the help they could get, and some songs seem to be prayers to Heaven to bless their lives:

Good people, gentle folk—Their ways are righteous.... Their thoughts constrained.... Good people, gentle folk—Shape the people of this land.... And may they do so for ten thousand years!

THINKING ABOUT THE READING

1. What do the songs tell us about the importance of families and friends to the Zhou Chinese?
2. What did peasants think about those who ruled them? Can you say why?

Source: The Book of Songs, translated by Arthur Waley (London: George Allen and Unwin, 1954) © copyright by permission of The Arthur Waley Estate.

wells and drink, Till our field and eat—What is the strength of the emperor to us?"[5] Yet there were some checks on landowner power. The workers and slaves of the more repressive and exploitive lords migrated or absconded, depopulating the land and ruining their landlord.

Patriarchal society imposed rigid gender roles. Parents arranged all marriages. A song from this period states: "How does one take a wife? Without a matchmaker she cannot be got." Before or after marriage most women worked hard, mostly in the home preparing food, doing housekeeping, and making clothes. Society expected women at all levels to be submissive, enjoying no official role in public affairs. While many elite women were literate, few peasant women or men enjoyed opportunities to learn reading and writing. Both genders valued friendship and kinship, as another song illustrates: "Of men that are now, None equals a brother. When death and mourning affright us, Brothers are very dear."[6]

Zhou China nurtured many significant technological and economic developments. Ironworking reached China from Central Asia by around 700 B.C.E., providing better plows and tools than bronze but also improving weaponry. Newly introduced soybeans provided a rich protein source that enriched the soil, and by 600 B.C.E. agricultural surpluses had spurred population growth to around 20 million. Trade grew, merchants became more prominent, and China developed a cash economy with copper coins.

Zhou social life often revolved around food. The ruler's Chief Cook held a high state office, and lavish feasts

[5] From Minford and Lau, *Classical Chinese Literature*, 150.

[6] The two songs are from Waley, *Book of Songs*, 68, 203.

cemented social ties. Indeed, the banquet was a chief diplomatic tool at all levels of society, often lubricated by wine: "When we have got wine, we strain it; When we have got none, we buy it!"[7] However, the costly and complicated ceremonies enjoyed by the rich did not extend down to peasants, who had little money for anything more than basic hospitality.

The Evolution of Chinese Writing and Religion

A distinctive Chinese writing system arose to solve the special problems posed by the many, often mutually unintelligible spoken languages. Some six hundred dialects of Chinese are still spoken today, a heritage of many local cultures. Most of the Chinese north of the Yangzi River speak closely related Northern Mandarin dialects, but other Chinese, especially in the southern half of China, have vastly different dialects. Chinese from Guangzhou **(GWAHN-cho)** and Beijing **(bay-JING)** would not understand each other if they only spoke their local dialects. Another difficulty is that the monosyllabic Chinese languages are tonal: the stress placed on a sound changes its meaning. For example, depending on the tone employed by the speaker, in Mandarin the sound ma can mean "mother," "hemp," "horse," or "to curse," or indicate a question. To overcome these problems, the Chinese developed one written language based not on sound but on characters. The early Shang pictographs resemble crude pictures of an object, such as a man or bird. Later they evolved into complex ideographs, characters standing for ideas and concepts. Some fifty thousand new characters have been created since the Shang (see Figure 4.1). The system's practicality became apparent when modern Chinese linguists faced great difficulty converting tonal words into a Western-type alphabet.

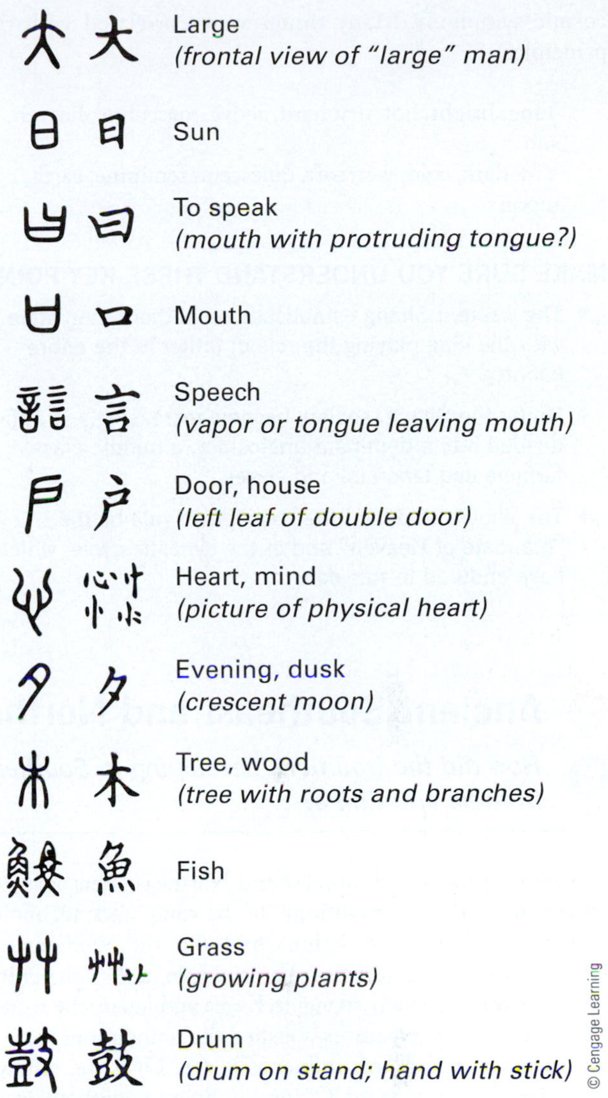

As in Mesopotamia and Egypt, writing promoted political and cultural unity by making possible communication between people speaking different dialects. Otherwise the Chinese might have split into many small countries, as occurred in India and Europe for much of history. Thus writing helped to create the world's largest society on earth, unifying rather than dividing peoples of diverse ancestries, regions, and languages. The written language also gave prestige to those who mastered it. As the writing brush became the main writing instrument, writing became an art form, and every literate Chinese something of an artist. Yet the difficulty of memorizing thousands of characters limited literacy mostly to the upper classes with the time and money to study. Education, scholarship, and literature became valued commodities.

Chinese ideas on the mysteries of life and the cosmic order also developed. Shang religion emphasized ancestor worship, magic, mythology, agricultural deities, and local spirits. These ideas evolved by later Zhou times into distinctive ideas, including the notion of a generalized supernatural force the Chinese called *tian* **(tee-an)**, which governed the universe. The **Yijing** **(yee-CHING)** (Book of Changes), a collection of sixty-four mystic hexagrams and commentaries to predict future events, later became influential throughout East Asia. Its main theme was that heaven and earth are in a state of continual change.

Modern form	Meaning
大	Large *(frontal view of "large" man)*
日	Sun
曰	To speak *(mouth with protruding tongue?)*
口	Mouth
言	Speech *(vapor or tongue leaving mouth)*
户	Door, house *(left leaf of double door)*
心	Heart, mind *(picture of physical heart)*
夕	Evening, dusk *(crescent moon)*
木	Tree, wood *(tree with roots and branches)*
魚	Fish
艸	Grass *(growing plants)*
鼓	Drum *(drum on stand; hand with stick)*

FIGURE 4.1 EVOLUTION OF CHINESE WRITING This chart shows early and modern forms of Chinese characters, revealing how pictographs, often recognizable, matured into increasingly abstract ideographs.

The *Yijing* was closely related to Chinese cosmological thinking, the theory of *yin* and *yang*, which had appeared in simple form by the Shang. Yin and yang, the two primary cosmic forces, power the universe through their interaction. Neither one permanently triumphs; rather, they are balanced, in conflict and yet complementary in a kind of

Yijing (Book of Changes) An ancient Chinese collection of sixty-four mystic hexagrams and commentaries upon them that was used to predict future events.

[7]Waley, *Book of Songs*, 205.

cosmic symphony. Many things were correlated with these principles:

> Yang: bright, hot, dry, hard, active, masculine, heaven, sun
> Yin: dark, cold, wet, soft, quiescent, feminine, earth, moon

Given the Chinese preference for hierarchy, yang was superior to yin, and male superior to female, justifying inequalities in society. Yin-yang dualism remains important throughout East Asia. The Chinese strongly influenced their neighbors in Korea, Vietnam, and Japan, and over the centuries many Chinese ideas and institutions diffused to the peoples on their fringe.

MAKE SURE YOU UNDERSTAND THESE KEY POINTS BEFORE MOVING ON

- **The western Shang established an authoritarian state, with the king playing the role of father to the entire country.**
- **Under the Shang, society became increasingly stratified, divided into a dominant aristocracy, a middle class, farmers and laborers, and slaves.**
- **The Zhou introduced the concepts of rule by the "Mandate of Heaven" and of the dynastic cycle, which have endured to this day.**
- **A common written language provided a unifying link for the Chinese, who spoke hundreds of different dialects (many of which are still spoken today).**

Ancient Southeast and Northeast Asians

How did the traditions developing in Southeast and Northeast Asia differ from those in India and China?

China's neighbors in Southeast and Northeast Asia also made important early contributions in farming and technology. Although influenced by China or India, they demonstrated many unique characteristics. For example, although Chinese influence was especially strong in Korea and Japan, the Koreans and Japanese had already established the foundations for complex societies before this influence began. Over the following centuries they integrated Chinese influences with their own ideas and customs, maintaining separate ethnic identities.

Southeast Asian Environments and Early Agriculture

While historically linked to China and India, Southeast Asian peoples, shaped in part by geography and climate, developed in distinctive ways. Separated from the Eurasian landmass by mountain and water barriers, Southeast Asia stretches from modern Burma (or Myanmar) eastward to Vietnam and the Philippines and southward through the Indonesian archipelago. The region's tropical climate, with long rainy seasons, fostered rain forests over much of the land. But the great rivers that flow through mainland Southeast Asia, such as the Mekong **(MAY-kawng)**, Red, and Irrawaddy **(ir-uh-WAHD-ee)** Rivers, also carved out broad, fertile plains and deltas that could support dense human settlement.

The topography both helped and hindered communication. The shallow seas fostered maritime trade, seafaring, and fishing and linked the large islands such as Sumatra **(soo-MAH-truh)**, Java **(JA-veh)**, and Borneo (Kalimantan) to their neighbors. In contrast, the heavily forested highlands inhibited overland travel and encouraged diverse religions, languages, and states. An Indonesian proverb well describes the mosaic of cultures that resulted: "different fields, different grasshoppers; different pools, different fish."

Some scholars think that the transition to food growing began in Thailand and Vietnam by 8000 or 9000 B.C.E., but most doubt that it commenced earlier than 6000 B.C.E. Rice was probably domesticated in south or central China first and then spread into Southeast Asia, becoming a major crop by 3000 B.C.E. The two regions were closely linked in Neolithic times, and the people then living in southern China were probably more closely related to the modern Thai and Vietnamese than to modern Chinese. Southeast Asians may have been the first to cultivate bananas, yams, and taro and domesticated chickens, pigs, and perhaps even cattle.

Southeast Asians also developed or improved technologies originally from India, Mesopotamia, and China. By 1500 B.C.E. fine bronze was being produced in Thailand, where people lived in houses perched on poles above the ground, still a common pattern in Southeast Asia, and women made beautiful hand-painted and durable pottery. Village artists fashioned bronze and ivory jewelry and household items. Whereas elsewhere in Eurasia the Bronze Age was synonymous with cities, kings, armies, huge temples, and defensive walls, in Southeast Asia bronze metallurgy derived from villages. For example, in Dong Son village, Vietnam, people made huge bronze drums that were traded all over Southeast Asia. Tin mined in Southeast Asia

DONG SON BRONZE DRUM These huge Dong Son bronze drums, named for a village site in Vietnam, were produced widely in ancient Southeast Asia and confirm the extensive long-distance trade networks.

may have reached the Indus cities, and iron was being worked by 500 B.C.E., several centuries later than in northern China.

Migration and New Societies in Southeast Asia and the Pacific

Gradually new societies formed from local and migrant roots. The early Southeast Asians probably included the Vietnamese, Papuans **(PAH-poo-enz)**, Melanesians **(mel-uh-NEE-zhuhns)**, and Negritos **(ne-GREE-tos)**. Migrants came into Southeast Asia from China sometime before the Common Era, assimilating local peoples or prompting them to migrate eastward through the islands. Today Papuans and Melanesians are found mostly in New Guinea and the western Pacific islands, while the remaining small-statured, dark-skinned Negritos mostly live in remote mountains and islands. The newcomers probably mixed their cultures and languages with those of the remaining indigenous inhabitants, producing new peoples such as the Khmers **(kuh-MARE)** (Cambodians), who later established states in the Mekong River Basin.

Over the course of several millennia, peoples speaking Austronesian **(AW-stroh-NEE-zhuhn)** languages and possessing advanced agriculture entered island Southeast Asia from the large island of Taiwan, just east of China. Beginning around 4000 B.C.E., Austronesians began moving south into the Philippine Islands, and by 2000 B.C.E. into the Indonesian archipelago (see Map 4.2), settling Borneo, Java, Sumatra, and other islands. Austronesian languages became dominant in the Philippines, Indonesia, the Malay Peninsula, and the central Vietnam coast. The Austronesians brought with them domesticated pigs and dogs, grew rice and millet, and possessed a knowledge of tatooing, which became a common practice. Some early Austronesians built sophisticated oceangoing sailing vessels with multilayered hulls and maneuverable square sails. Indonesian islanders were the major seafaring traders of eastern Eurasia before the Common Era, the counterparts to the Phoenicians in the Mediterranean Basin.

The Austronesian migrations affected other regions as well. Melanesians migrated eastward into the western Pacific islands beginning around 1500 or 1600 B.C.E., carrying Southeast Asian crops, animals, and house styles as far east as Fiji. Traveling in outrigger canoes and, later, in large double-hulled canoes, some Austronesians also sailed into the Pacific, mixing their cultures, languages, and genes with those of the Melanesians. By around 1000 B.C.E. Austronesian settlers had reached Samoa and Tonga. These voyages were intentional efforts at discovery and colonization by fearless mariners who developed remarkable navigation skills, reading the stars and the swells.

In Samoa and Tonga, Polynesian culture emerged from Austronesian roots. The ancient western Pacific culture known as **Lapita**, stretching some 2,500 miles from northeast of New Guinea to Samoa, was marked by distinctive pottery and a vast trading network. Some Polynesians eventually reached as far east as Tahiti and Hawaii, both 2,500 miles from Tonga.

The Austronesians, Khmer, Vietnamese, and others established societies based on intensive agriculture, fishing, and interregional commerce. By 1000 B.C.E. Austronesian trade networks stretched over 5,000 miles, from western Indonesia to the central Pacific. Using advanced boats, they were carrying out maritime trade with India by 500 B.C.E. Indonesian cinnamon even reached Egypt. Ancient Southeast Asia was also a world of spirits identified with locations (mountains, streams, trees, fields, stones) and ancestors. This animist heritage has by no means passed from the contemporary scene, where many people mix respect for spirits with a universal religion like Buddhism, Islam, or Christianity. The Vietnamese, who created the first known Southeast Asian states between 1000 and 800 B.C.E., believed in a god that "creates the elephants [and] the grass, is omnipresent, and has [all-seeing] eyes."[8]

The Foundations of Korea and Japan

Korea and Japan, though neighbors, were shaped by different environments (see Map 4.1). The 110 miles of stormy seas that separate them at their closest point did not prevent contact but made it sporadic. Korea occupies a mountainous peninsula 600 miles long and 150 miles wide. Japan's 3,400 islands stretched across several climatic zones, with over 90 percent of the land on three

Lapita The ancient western Pacific culture that stretched some 2,500 miles from just northeast of New Guinea to Samoa.

[8]Quoted in Nguyen Ngoc Bich, "The Power and Relevance of Vietnamese Myths," in *Vietnam: Essays on History, Culture and Society*, ed. David P. Elliott et al. (New York: Asia Society, 1985), 62.

MAP 4.2 THE AUSTRONESIAN DIASPORA Austronesians migrated from Taiwan into Southeast Asia, settling the islands. Later some of these skilled mariners moved east into the western Pacific, settling Melanesia. Eventually some of their ancestors settled Polynesia and Micronesia.

islands: densely populated Honshu **(hahn-shoo)**, frigid Hokkaido **(haw-KAI-dow)** in the north, and subtropical Kyushu **(KYOO-shoo)** in the south. Thanks to mountains, only a sixth of Japan's land is suitable for intensive agriculture. The archipelago lacks most metals.

Koreans began farming between 5000 and 2000 B.C.E., by which time they were building over 100,000 large stone monuments reminiscent of the famous Stonehenge in England. Later they creatively adapted rice growing, which originated in warm southern lands, to their cool climate. As agriculture became more productive, the population grew rapidly, generating a persistent migration of Koreans across the straits to Japan. Small states based on clans emerged. In a pattern still common today, female shamans led the animistic religion. Despite centuries of contact, the neighboring Chinese never assimilated the Koreans, in part because the nontonal Korean and tonal Chinese spoken languages were very different.

Koreans imported bronze and then ironworking, probably from China and Central Asia. Shang refugees brought more Chinese culture and technology, but Koreans also created their own useful products, including fine pottery. Facing frigid winters, Koreans invented an ingenious method of radiant floor heating, still widely used today, that circulates heat through chambers in a stone floor. Much later, Chinese and Romans devised similar schemes.

The Japanese were more isolated than the Koreans from China and no less creative, producing some of the world's oldest pottery. Human settlement began perhaps 40,000 years ago, before rising sea levels separated Japan from the mainland. These early settlers were probably the ancestors of the Ainu **(I-noo)**, who are genetically close to other East Asians despite their unusually light skin and extensive body hair. The ancestral Ainu built seaworthy boats, for they settled the Kurile **(KOO-reel)** Islands north of Japan and the Ryukyus to the south while trading with eastern Siberia. Ainu relics have also been found in the Aleutian **(ah-LOO-shan)** Islands off Alaska, suggesting some connection there in ancient times. Today the remaining few thousand Ainu, who mostly live on Hokkaido and Sakhalin Islands, face cultural extinction.

When the non-Ainu ancestors of today's Japanese arrived in the islands remains unclear. Some may have come from Korea beginning 3,000 or 4,000 years ago. Ainu and newcomers mixed over the millennia. Genetic studies link modern Japanese to the Ainu, Siberians, and especially Koreans.

DOGU FIGURINE Jomon fired-clay figures, like this one, typically portray women and may have been used in fertility rites. Many have a heart-shaped face and an elaborate hairstyle.

Jomon Society

The best-documented Japanese early society, called **Jomon** **(JOE-mon)** ("rope pattern") because of the ropelike designs on their pottery, began around 10,000 B.C.E. and endured until 300 B.C.E. Probably an Ainu culture, Jomon were divided by various languages and regional customs, a diversity perhaps reflecting the arrival of Korean migrants. Some Jomon customs, such as tatooing the body and building houses elevated above the ground on posts, hint that some migrants, perhaps Austronesians, may have arrived from the south. However, the major migrations, which brought iron-using Korean settlers, came later, between 500 and 700 B.C.E. The Jomon traded with Korea and Siberia.

Living primarily from hunting, gathering, and fishing, by 5000 B.C.E. the Jomon lived in wooden houses containing elaborate hearths, probably centers for family gatherings. Diverse foods made up their well-balanced, nutritious diet, including shellfish, fish, seals, deer, wild boar, and yams. No evidence exists for complex agriculture until around 500 B.C.E.

A very different spoken language helped preserve cultural distinctiveness despite much Chinese cultural influence. Whether the Japanese language, distantly related to modern Korean, was spoken by Jomon or brought by later immigrants remains uncertain. Probably between 500 B.C.E. and 500 C.E., most of the Ainu languages were overwhelmed by a Japanese language possibly based on a Korean dialect. Perhaps in response to increasingly crowded conditions, the

Jomon The earliest documented culture in Japan, known for the ropelike design on its pottery.

Japanese language promoted tact and vagueness, and the Japanese became adept at nonverbal understanding. These tendencies, which are useful in discouraging social conflict, remain part of Japan's unique heritage.

MAKE SURE YOU UNDERSTAND THESE KEY POINTS BEFORE MOVING ON

- **The peoples of Southeast Asia established early maritime trading networks, while inland geographical boundaries led to the development of extremely diverse cultures.**
- **Korea and Japan, while being strongly influenced by the Chinese, were shaped by different environments and created unique cultures and societies.**
- **Partly because of its distinct language, Korea was never assimilated into China and developed special technologies, such as radiant floor heating, to meet its needs.**
- **Japan's language promoted tact and vagueness, probably to prevent social conflict in an increasingly populated area.**

Ancient Americans

How do scholars explain the settlement and rise of agriculture in the Americas?

After the migrations of humans from Eurasia to the Americas thousands of years ago, American societies developed in isolation from those in the Eastern Hemisphere. Diverse cultures often flourished from hunting and gathering, and later some regions pioneered agriculture and, in Mexico and the Andes, created urban societies and states. Population movement and adaptations to differing environments shaped these varied people's most ancient history, but Americans also shared some common ideas.

Diverse American Environments

Most land in the Western Hemisphere land is found on two continents, North and South America, that are linked by the long, thin strand of Central America. A string of fertile islands also rings the Caribbean Sea from Florida to Venezuela. Whereas Eurasia lies on an east-west axis, the Americas lie on a north-south axis, with a large forest-covered tropical zone separating more temperate regions. Migrating peoples or long-distance travelers encountered very different environments.

Despite its smaller land area, the Western Hemisphere contains as much diversity of landforms and climate as the Eastern Hemisphere. Extensive tropical rain forests originally covered much of Central America, the Caribbean islands, and the vast Amazon and Orinoco **(or-uh-NO-ko)** River Basins of South America, making intensive farming difficult, although some people developed simple farming. Rain-drenched forests also once covered the northern Pacific coast, while southeastern North America had more temperate woodlands. The long winters in much of North America made hunting and gathering the most practical subsistence option. Like the Himalayas in Asia, the high Andes, which stretch nearly 5,000 miles down the western side of South America, limited travel and communication, while in North America the Rocky Mountains provided an east-west barrier. Coastal mountains running along the northern Pacific coast trap rain clouds, creating huge deserts in western North America. Both continents also have extensive grasslands. Some of the great river systems, such as the Mississippi, fostered long-distance trade.

The Antiquity and Migration of Native Americans

Native Americans' ancestry and antiquity generate heated scholarly debate. Most anthropologists agree that modern Native Americans are descended from stone tool–using Asians who crossed the Bering Strait from Siberia to Alaska, probably when Ice Age conditions lowered ocean levels and created a wide land bridge. Some may have skirted coasts by boat. Seeking game like bison, caribou, and mammoths, migrants could have moved south through ice-free corridors or by boat along the Pacific coast and gradually dispersed throughout the hemisphere. Several waves of migrants, probably in small numbers, from different cultural backgrounds in Asia might account for the over two thousand languages among Native Americans.

The traditions of many Native American peoples place their origins in the areas where they lived 500 years ago, but some may have lived in these places for many centuries before that. While their origin stories, rich in spiritual meaning, deserve respect, much evidence supports the notion wof ancient migration from Asia. No remains of any hominids earlier than modern humans have been found in the Americas. Furthermore, the common ancestry of modern Native Americans is clear from the remarkable uniformity of DNA, blood, virus, and teeth types, which all connect them to peoples in northern Mongolia and central and eastern Siberia. Several scholars have also suggested that some tool cultures in eastern North America are similar to those of Stone Age peoples who lived in Spain and France several millennia earlier. But the evidence for possible European or perhaps Southeast Asian ancestry is sparse. If such migrants did once settle in the Americas, they likely died out or were absorbed by the peoples of Northeast Asian ancestry.

The question of when the first migrants arrived in the Americas perplexes archaeologists. Traditionally most trace the migration back to the **Clovis** culture some 11,500 to 13,500 years ago, named after spear points discovered at Clovis, New Mexico, but widespread in North and Central America. However, a different projectile point culture existed in Oregon during or even before Clovis times, and recent skeleton and artifact discoveries in North and South America are much older. Monte Verde **(MAWN-tee VAIR-dee)**, a campsite in southern Chile that is over 10,000 miles from the Bering Strait, may be at least 12,500 years old and perhaps much more ancient. Monte Verde people lived in rectangular houses with log foundations and exploited a wide variety of vegetable and animal foods. Various other sites in North America, Mexico, and Brazil challenge the Clovis-first theory, but none offers conclusive evidence that convinces all skeptics. For example, sites in Pennsylvania, South Carolina, Texas, and Virginia may place people in eastern North America between 17,000 and 19,000 years ago. These scattered discoveries suggest but do not yet prove an ancient migration perhaps 20,000 years ago or more.

The earliest Americans, or Paleo-Indians, survived by hunting, fishing, and gathering while adapting to varied environments. Skilled hunters and armed with spears, they may have contributed to the extinction of large herbivore animals such as horses, mammoths, and camels, which disappeared from the Western Hemisphere between 9000 and 7000 B.C.E. A similar die-off in Eurasia at the end of the Ice Age suggests that climate change was a factor. The extinctions in both hemispheres likely resulted from some combination of overhunting, environmental change, and perhaps an apocalyptic disease affecting large mammals. But on the North American Great Plains, many people still hunted bison on foot.

Some peoples flourished from hunting, fishing, and gathering for many millennia. In the Pacific Northwest, coastal peoples built oceangoing boats and sturdy wood houses, while along the Peruvian coast deep-sea fishermen exploited the rich marine environment. In southern California the Chumash **(CHOO-mash)** society, like Japan's Jomon culture, lived well from a vegetation and meat diet including large marine mammals such as seals. The Chumash built large, permanent villages headed by powerful chiefs. Yet Pacific coast peoples such as the Chumash were also subject to climate change, which periodically brought drought by altering plant and animal environments.

By In North America by 4000 B.C.E. extensive long-distance trade networks linked people over several thousand miles from the Atlantic and Gulf coasts to the Great Plains and Great Lakes. Dugout canoes moved copper and red ocher from Lake Superior, jasper (quartz) from Pennsylvania, obsidian from the Rocky Mountains, and seashells from both the Gulf and East Coasts. Great Lakes copper was traded as far away as Mexico, New England, and Florida.

Early Societies and Their Cultures

Over many millennia Americans developed distinctive social and cultural patterns emphasizing cooperation within families, animistic religion, and ceremonies for such events as initiations into adult life and courtship. Most people lived in egalitarian bands linked by kinship and marriage. Men often sought a personal guardian spirit through a visionary experience induced by fasting, enduring physical pain, or taking hallucinogenic drugs. Shamans claiming command over spirits or animal souls connected the human and spirit worlds. Most Americans revered the food-producing earth as sacred. Some also adopted creation stories widely shared with other peoples.

Some Americans organized communities around **mound building**, the construction of huge earthen mounds, often with temples on top. The oldest mound so far discovered, in Louisiana, dates to 2500 B.C.E. Beginning around 1600 B.C.E., some other hunter-gatherers in North America's eastern woodlands and Gulf Coast became mound builders. One major site, Poverty Point in northeastern Louisiana, was occupied between 1000 and 500 B.C.E. (see Profile: The Poverty Point Mound Builders). At its height it was about 3 square miles in area and home to perhaps five thousand people. Its largest mound, an effigy of a bird that can only be seen from the air, was 70 feet high, comparable to an eight-story apartment building, and 700 feet long and apparently built in several months. Poverty Point served as the hub of a trading system, importing goods from as far away as the Ohio and upper Mississippi River Valleys and exporting stone and clay products such as pendants and bowls to Florida, Missouri, Oklahoma, and Tennessee.

The Rise of American Agriculture

Americans were some of the earliest farmers, but they developed very different crops than the peoples of Afro-Eurasia. Population growth, long-distance trade, and changing weather conditions helped spark this great transition. Hunter-gatherers were vulnerable to devastating droughts in years when the periodic weather change known today as *El Niño* **(EL NEE-nyo)** shifted both rainfall patterns and the marine environment, perhaps prompting experiments with growing food. Some of the chief crops, such as maize (corn), were much more difficult to master than the big-seeded grains of the Fertile Crescent. Furthermore, with no potential draft animals, farmers needed to be creative in growing and transporting food.

Some Americans made the transition not long after Southwest Asians. In Mesoamerica (the region from Mexico through northern Central America), bottle gourds and pumpkins may have been raised by 8500 or 8000 B.C.E. and maize, sweet potatoes, and beans by 3500 B.C.E. Andes people cultivated chili peppers and kidney beans by about 8000 B.C.E. and later cultivated potatoes. Some Andeans, like early Eurasian farmers, built elaborate irrigation canals that created artificial garden plots. By 3000 or 2500 B.C.E., Peruvian coastal peoples raised cotton, squash, sweet potatoes, and maize. By 1500 B.C.E. farming had spread to the Amazon Basin. In North America the southwestern peoples ingeniously adapted farming to their poor soils and desert conditions, growing maize, squash, beans, and corn. Eventually maize, beans, and squash became mainstays

Clovis A Native American culture dating back some 11,500 to 13,500 years.

mound building The construction of huge earthen mounds, often with temples on top, by some ancient peoples in the Americas.

PROFILE

The Poverty Point Mound Builders

While the spectacular mounds at Poverty Point are the site's most striking legacy, the archaeological research has also revealed a remarkable community. The inhabitants did not need farming because their location, in a fertile valley nourished by annual Mississippi River floods, offered a benign hunting and gathering environment and a gentle climate. The people enjoyed a rich and varied diet. Men used spears, spear throwers, darts, and knives to hunt turkey, duck, deer, and rabbit and caught bass, catfish, alligator, and clams in the rivers. Women collected acorns, hickory nuts, walnuts, wild grapes, persimmons, sunflower seeds, squash, and gourds.

Probably governed by chiefs, the people lived in wood houses around a central plaza and six mounds. Men and women crafted many tools and art objects, trading some hundreds of miles away, and heated small decorated baked-clay balls, found by the thousands in the ruins, for cooking or boiling water. Since cooking was women's work, women probably made these clay balls, perhaps helped by their children. Each woman had her own preference for design and shape. Stoneworkers ground and polished hard stones into ornaments and useful artifacts, chipping various stones into points, blades, and cutting tools. Solid-clay female figurines, sometimes pregnant, possibly served as fertility symbols. Using red jasper, people also fashioned beautiful bead necklaces, bird-head pendants, and human effigies.

Located at the intersection of important waterways, Poverty Point was linked to trade networks that brought in Appalachian metal for bowls and platters, stone from the Ozarks and Oklahoma, and flint from as far away as Illinois and Ohio. The finely crafted red jasper items, often shaped like animals such as owls, have been found in distant settlements. Some of the Poverty Point men may have ventured out on trading expeditions or to bring home valuable stones from as far away as Missouri. Men and perhaps women undoubtedly arrived regularly in canoes full of trade goods to exchange.

At times the people were mobilized to build new mounds or rebuild old eroding ones. The complete earthworks contain an immense 1 million cubic yards of soil; to make them, the people probably had to transport 35 to 40 million 50-pound basket loads to the site. Several thousand people may have participated in the construction, which was carefully planned and directed so that it followed a geometric design. The mounds perhaps aided astronomical observations as a solar calendar, or perhaps served as a regional ceremonial center for social, political, or religious purposes. Some priestly or ruling class may have lived atop the mounds, as was common in some mound-building societies around the hemisphere. At least 150 smaller satellite sites, scattered along the Mississippi for several hundred miles, all contain similar artifacts, suggesting that Poverty Point was the center of both an economic and a political network.

The culture disappeared by 500 B.C.E., the people having dispersed to smaller settlements. There are no signs of war or major environmental change. Perhaps some political or religious crisis disrupted society. Whatever the case, the Poverty Point people and their culture were lost to history, leaving only the badly eroded but still impressive ruins of today.

Gilcrease Museum/Tulsa/Oklahoma

POVERTY POINT JASPER BEAD Trade goods, such as this red jasper bead shaped like a locust, were produced at Poverty Point in Louisiana and traded over many hundreds of miles in eastern and central North America.

THINKING ABOUT THE PROFILE

1. What sort of life did the Poverty Point people experience?
2. What role did Poverty Point play in the region?

from the Southwest to the northeastern woodlands, providing a nutritionally balanced diet.

Three basic farming patterns eventually shaped American societies. Mesoamerican highland and valley people relied on maize, beans, and squash. Societies in the high Andes emphasized potatoes and other frost-resistant tubers. South America's topical forest societies grew manioc, sweet potatoes, and root crops. These differing farming patterns proved significant for later world history because the great diversity later enriched modern food supplies. Americans domesticated more different plants than had all the Eastern Hemisphere peoples combined, including three thousand varieties of potatoes, as well as chocolate, quinine, and tobacco.

However, because they lacked draft animals, the Americans practiced less intensive agriculture than Eastern Hemisphere people. The only large herd animals available for domestication, the llama and alpaca of the Andes, were tamed by 3500 B.C.E., mostly for use as pack animals and wool sources. Although Americans domesticated turkeys and guinea pigs for eating, there were no surviving counterparts to horses, cattle, and oxen. With no animals to pull, plows or wheels were useless. People innovated by creating irrigation schemes such as terraced hillsides and the floating gardens in Central Mexico, which turned swamps into productive fields, but the intensive farming that supported huge populations in China or India was impossible in the Americas.

The lack of draft animals also meant that Americans were exposed to fewer infectious diseases and epidemics. In the Eastern Hemisphere, domesticated animals passed diseases such as measles and smallpox to humans through germs and parasites, precipitating deadly outbreaks. Historians disagree over whether Americans may have been healthier than people across the oceans. Although many enjoyed long lives, many also suffered from various ailments. Furthermore, isolation from the Eastern Hemisphere left Native Americans vulnerable to the diseases brought by Europeans and Africans beginning in 1492 C.E., for which they had no immunity. These diseases eventually killed the great majority of Native Americans.

Farming Societies, Cities, and States

Communal activity was essential in early villages as people cooperated for survival. In the northern Andes, people fashioned ceramics between 3000 and 2500 B.C.E. Institutionalized religions took shape, led by a priestly caste, and human sacrifice became common in both Mesoamerica and the Andes to honor the gods and keep the cosmos in balance. Far earlier than the more famous Egyptian mummies, some South American and North American societies developed processes for mummifying the bodies of the deceased through drying, perhaps because of religious beliefs about death and the afterlife. Some Andean and Mesoamerican societies also began building permanent structures for religious, governmental, or recreational purposes. Pacific coast and Andean cultures in South America constructed monumental architecture, including stepped pyramids, by the third millennium B.C.E., about the same time as Egypt, India, and China. By 5000 B.C.E. a southern Mexico site contained a dance ground or ball court, and ceremonial ballgames involving teams of players attempting to knock a rubber ball through a high stone hoop became a fixture of Mesoamerican life for millennia.

Agriculture, monumental construction, population growth, and long-distance trade provided a foundation for the first cities and states in the Andes and Mesoamerica between 3000 and 1000 B.C.E. (see Map 4.3). People worked copper, gold, and silver to create tools, weapons, and jewelry, and growing towns with public buildings became centers of political, economic, and religious activities. Massive ceremonial centers hundreds of feet long were constructed along the Peruvian coast, and elsewhere huge mounds laid the foundation for great pyramids. Between 4000 and 1 B.C.E. the population of the Americas grew from 1 or 2 million to around 15 million, over two-thirds concentrated in Mesoamerica and western South America. Long-distance trade routes also became more common, moving commodities such as obsidian, mirrors, seashells, and ceramics.

Nathaniel Tarn/Science Source

OLMEC HEAD This massive head from San Lorenzo is nearly 10 feet high. The significance of such heads (and the helmets they wear) remains unclear, but they might represent chiefs, warriors, or gods.

MAP 4.3 OLMEC AND CHAVÍN SOCIETIES The earliest known American states arose in Mesoamerica and the Andes. The Olmec and Chavín both endured for a millennium.

South American Societies: Caral and Chavín

About the same time as the Harappan cities and the Egyptian pyramids, the first large settlements built around massive stone structures emerged around 3100 B.C.E. in the Norte Chico region between the Andes and the Pacific coast in north-central Peru. The largest of these settlements and America's first known city, Caral, had some three thousand residents living in a 150-acre complex of plazas, pyramids, and residential buildings. The major pyramid, 60 feet tall and covering the equivalent of four football fields, contained an amphitheater capable of seating hundreds of spectators for civic or religious events. An elite group of priests and planners lived in large, well-kept rooms atop the pyramids. Eventually some twenty pyramid complexes occupied land for many miles around.

The Norte Chico economy was based on marine resources such as fish and on growing squash, sweet potatoes, fruits, beans, cotton, and possibly maize. The people do not seem to have made ceramics or enjoyed many arts and crafts. However, Caral was a major hub for trade routes from the Pacific coast through the Andes to the Amazonian rain forest. There is evidence for human sacrifice. The people evidently enjoyed music, using animal bone flutes. But Caral collapsed for unknown reasons around 1600 B.C.E.

Chavín The first major urban civilization in South America (900–250 B.C.E.).

Chavín (cha-VEEN), situated 10,000 feet above sea level in northwestern Peru, emerged the same time as the Olmec (discussed below), around 1200 or 1000 B.C.E., and collapsed by 200 B.C.E. The Chavín people created flamboyant sculpture and monumental architecture, developed a highly original art focusing on real or mythical animals, and worked gold and silver. At its height, the main city probably had some three thousand inhabitants. Chavín became a major regional power, trading widely with the coast and spreading its religious cult to distant peoples. The people worshiped two main deities, and their ceremonial center became a site of pilgrimage for the faithful from a wide area. Chavín also perpetuated some of the architectural and religious patterns that became common in the Andes. It became politically and economically dominant in a densely populated region that included two distinct ecological zones, the Peruvian coastal plain and the Andean foothills.

Mesoamerican Societies: The Olmec

The **Olmec (OHL-meck)**, a people who lived along Mexico's Gulf coast, formed the earliest known urban society in Mesoamerica by 1200 or 1000 B.C.E., flourishing until 300 B.C.E. (see Map 4.3). A powerful chieftain probably ruled each Olmec city. The earliest city, known today as San Lorenzo, was built on an artificial dirt platform three-quarters of a mile long, half a mile wide, and 150 feet high. Home to some twenty-five hundred people, San Lorenzo was situated above fertile but frequently flooded plains. Another Olmec city, La Venta, included huge earth mounds that required massive labor to build. The stones for Olmec sculptures and temples had to be brought from 60 miles away, and some of the blocks weigh more than 40 tons. The Olmec studied astronomy to correctly orient their cities and monuments with the stars.

The Olmec created remarkable architecture, art, and a writing system. The purpose of the huge sculptured stone heads they erected is unknown, but they might represent rulers. The Olmec built temples and pyramids in ceremonial centers and palace complexes, and their artists carved human and animal figures as well as supernatural beings in sculpture and relief. By around 650 B.C.E. the Olmec had also developed perhaps the first simple hieroglyphic writing in the Americas, which influenced other Mesoamerican peoples, especially the Maya. Mesoamerican writing kept records of kings, rituals, and the calendar, much as writing did in Egypt.

Commerce and the networks it created were a key to Olmec influence. The Olmec traded with Mexico's west coast and Central America, importing basalt, obsidian, iron ore, and jade, which they fashioned into ceremonial objects, masks, and jewelry. They may also have exploited cocoa trees for chocolate. Extensive communication between the Olmec and neighboring peoples contributed to some cultural homogeneity in Mesoamerica, especially in religion. Olmec religious symbols and myths emphasized fearsome half-human, half-animal supernatural beings, the prototypes of later Mesoamerican deities. Religious ceremonies requiring precise measurement of calendar years and time cycles fostered mathematics and writing. Although their society eventually disappeared, the Olmec established enduring patterns of life, thought, and kingship in Mesoamerica that influenced later peoples like the Maya (see Chapter 9).

Olmec The earliest urban society in Mesoamerica.

MAKE SURE YOU UNDERSTAND THESE KEY POINTS BEFORE MOVING ON

- **Early American peoples survived primarily by hunting, gathering, and fishing, as well as by trading over large distances.**
- **Mutual cooperation, earth worship, personal connections with guardian spirits, and shamanism were prominent features of early American cultural and spiritual life.**
- **In response to the challenges posed by different climates, American peoples domesticated more different plants than all the peoples of the Eastern Hemisphere.**
- **Lacking draft animals, Americans came up with ingenious approaches to farming.**
- **Various technological breakthroughs led to the development of urban societies in Mesoamerica and the Andes.**

CHAPTER SUMMARY

The Chinese made the transition to agriculture, cities, and states in river valleys. The Himalayan Mountains, the Tibetan Plateau, and vast deserts allowed only sporadic contact between China and most other societies. Gradually an expanding Chinese society incorporated many local traditions. The Shang built a powerful state while developing bronze technology and a unique writing system. The Zhou replaced the Shang and presided over a more decentralized system that saw further technological and cultural development, including more advanced writing and literature. China's neighbors in Southeast Asia, Korea, and Japan were also creative in farming and technology, forming unique cultural identities and traditions. Austronesians migrating into Southeast Asia were skilled mariners, and some of them settled the Pacific islands.

Scholars still debate the origin and antiquity of settlement in the Americas, but most conclude that migrants moved from eastern Eurasia by land or boat many millennia ago. For centuries, hunting, fishing, and gathering supported a viable way of life. The Americans did not have the rich farmland and draft animals common in Eurasia. Nonetheless, farming appeared nearly as early as in the Eastern Hemisphere, a result of population growth, climate change, and technological development. Americans domesticated a wide variety of crops and also forged long-distance trade networks, religious institutions, cities, and states.

KEY TERMS

Mandate of Heaven (p. 75)
dynastic cycle (p. 75)
Yijing (Book of Changes) (p. 78)
Lapita (p. 79)
Jomon (p. 81)
Clovis (p. 83)
mound building (p. 83)
Chavín (p. 86)
Olmec (p. 87)

Patriarchy and Matriarchy in the Ancient World

Today, as in the past, men generally hold political, economic, and religious power in most societies thanks to patriarchy, a system whereby men largely control women and children, shape ideas about appropriate gender behavior, and generally dominate society. Many people assume that patriarchal social organization springs from some innate human characteristic, symbolized by the common expression that this is a "man's world." But the situation is more complex historically.

The Problem

The prevalence of patriarchy raises three important questions. First, was there ever a time when women held equal power and status to men? Second, was matriarchy, in which women enjoy social and political dominance, complete equality with men, or strong influence, ever common? And third, can we identify a particular period when patriarchy triumphed? These questions spark heated scholarly debates.

The Debate

The first question is the easiest to answer. Historians are reasonably sure that, among many peoples, women had greater equality with men during the Stone Age than in later eras. These small, closely knit hunter-gatherer societies, like the !Kung of southern Africa today, were often egalitarian, had weak leaders, and owned little private property to fight over. But, despite a rough equality due to women's ability, essential for a society's survival, to gather food and medicinal herbs, evidence that very many prefarming societies allowed women more publicly recognized authority than men remains limited. Some peoples who practiced simple farming, such as the Iroquois, Cherokee, Hopi, and Zuni in North America, accorded women considerable influence within a matrilineal culture, even if men usually had ultimate decision-making power.

In response to the second question, some scholars have argued that a "golden age of matriarchy" existed before the rise of urban societies and states in Europe and the Middle East, and perhaps also in India, Japan, Southeast Asia, and the Americas. They point to the many figurines of females, many perhaps of goddesses, unearthed at archaeological sites worldwide. Goddess worship, they believe, correlated with high female status; women were cherished for giving birth and nurturing the young, giving them a connection to the earth and spirits. Patricia Monaghan identifies more than 1,500 different goddesses worldwide, representing everything from mother to warrior.

Perhaps the most debated recent studies are by Lithuanian archaeologist Marija Gimbutas, whose writings, based on discoveries at sites such as Çatal Hüyük in Turkey, the Minoan palace at Knossos, and Stonehenge, portray ancient people in Europe and Anatolia as egalitarian and peaceful farmers led by influential women. These female-oriented societies, she says, were destroyed around 3500 B.C.E. by more violent Indo-European nomads from Central Asia, who brought patriarchy with them. From then on, patriarchy spread across Europe. Similarly, Riane Eisler, Judith Lorber, and Heidi Goettner-Abendroth describe ancient, goddess-worshiping farming cultures in eastern and southern Europe, where men and women ruled equally, with no war or inequalities of wealth. Few propose complete female control of ancient governments; Goettner-Abendroth defines matriarchy as gender-egalitarian societies or "nonpatriarchy." Like Gimbutas, most contend that Indo-European newcomers imposed male governments on these earlier societies.

However, many scholars dispute these authors' claims about ancient matriarchies with nonviolent social orders and equal status for each gender. For example, Lotte Motz, Lucy Godison, and Christine Morris argue that goddess worship theories are unproven. Motz claims that female images are no more common in early Europe than those of men and animals. Furthermore, the figurines may have been used in fertility rites rather than revered as spiritual forces. Motz and Cynthia Eller also suggest that mother goddess theories reflect not ancient realities of polytheistic religions but modern political and cultural attitudes, including a feminism that challenges patriarchy and biases about women's roles. Critics accuse Eller of misrepresenting matriarchal concepts. Nor can we assume that worshiping female deities actually gave real power to women. After all, the patriarchal ancient Mesopotamians and Greeks worshiped various female deities, including a goddess of love, and many modern patriarchal cultures, such as the Chinese, Japanese, Hindu Indian, and Yoruba, include female deities in their pantheons. And although many Europeans have revered the Virgin Mary over the past two millennia, men still dominate European society and the Catholic Church.

If the notion of ancient matriarchies transformed by force into patriarchies remains debatable and has been disputed by some recent historical scholarship, we are still left with the third question, how and when did patriarchy emerge? Anthropologist Sherry Ortner argues for a slow but inevitable transition from the egalitarianism of food collecting to male domination in the early cities and states. To Ortner, patriarchy derived from technological and social upheavals rather than a will to power by aggressive men. Childbearing played a role because, while women stayed home having and raising children, men could travel and engage in more paid work, warfare, and governmental, leisure, and religious activities. That development led to

Erich Lessing/Art Resource, NY

GODDESS FIGURE This female figure found in France, probably a mother-goddess, was probably used in fertility rights. Such figures have been found in many ancient societies studied by archaeologists.

gender stereotypes of women in unpaid work at home and men at paid work elsewhere. Also arguing for a gradual change, anthropologist Elizabeth Barber contends that farming people needed products, such as metal ores, that had to be gained through long-distance trade. This gave power to the more mobile and physically stronger men, who could travel to distant places and transport the heavy cargoes home. To be sure, knowledge of cloth making and the fiber arts gave women importance in ancient societies, since men also used products such as clothing and blankets; nevertheless, patriarchy, they argue, emerged gradually as society slowly changed and began to reward strength and mobility.

There is considerable evidence that men increased their power over women in many early urban societies. Historian Gerda Lerner analyzed male power in the Mesopotamian city-states, where kings or male assemblies ruled. Law codes such as Hammurabi's favored men; only women could be divorced or sold into slavery for adultery. Laws also restricted women's freedom of movement and treated them as private property. By this time, Lerner argues, gods had become more important than goddesses, and male power was legally recognized and sanctioned by religion.

Evaluating the Debate

Until recently historians and archaeologists have neglected the role of women. When we study ancient societies, we may unknowingly be influenced by modern attitudes. We are more likely to study kings and wars than the beginnings of herbal medicine, cloth production, and the role of women as negotiators in community disputes. We have not heard the last word from scholars on the question of ancient matriarchies and patriarchies, but their disputes have made us more aware of the role of women in history.

THINKING ABOUT THE CONTROVERSY

1. Why can worship of a mother-goddess be understood in different ways?
2. What are the main arguments for and against the ancient matriarchies thesis?

(Continued)

3. Why do we need to understand patriarchy to comprehend world history?

Exploring The Controversy

Some major works supporting the ancient goddess and matriarchy thesis include Marija Gimbutas, *Goddesses and Gods in Old Europe, 6500–500* B.C.*: Myths and Cult Images* (Berkeley: University of California Press, 1982); Gimbutas, *The Language of the Goddess: Unearthing the Hidden Symbols of Western Civilization* (New York: Harper and Row, 1989); Gimbutas, *The Living Goddesses* (Berkeley: University of California Press, 1999); Riane Eisler, *The Chalice and the Blade: Our History, Our Future* (San Francisco: Harper and Row, 1995); Heidi Goettner-Abendroth, *Matriarchal Societies* (London: Peter Lang, 2012); and Goettner-Abendroth, ed., *Societies of Peace: Matriarchies Past Present and Future* (London: Inanna Publications, 2009). Judith Lorber challenges basic assumptions about gender in *Paradoxes of Gender* (New Haven: Yale University Press, 1994). Patricia Monaghan, *The New Book of Goddesses and Heroines* (New York: Llewellyn Publications, 1997), provides a useful reference on mythological and legendary female deities from many lands and eras.

Strong criticism of the ancient matriarchy thesis can be found in Lucy Godison and Christine Morris, eds., *Ancient Goddesses: The Myths and the Evidence* (Madison: University of Wisconsin Press, 1999); Lotte Motz, *The Faces of the Goddess* (New York: Oxford University Press, 1997); and Cynthia Eller, *The Myth of Matriarchal Prehistory: Why an Invented Past Won't Give Women a Future* (Boston: Beacon Press, 2001). Among major books on the making of patriarchy and gender roles are Elizabeth Barber, *Woman's Work: The First 20,000 Years: Women, Cloth, and Society in Early Times* (New York: W.W. Norton, 1994); Gerda Lerner, *The Creation of Patriarchy* (New York: Oxford University Press, 1986); and Sherry Ortner, *Making Gender: The Politics and Erotics of Culture* (Boston: Beacon Press, 1997).

SOCIETIES NETWORKS TRANSITIONS

PART II

The Classical Societies and Their Legacies, ca. 600 B.C.E.– ca. 600 C.E.

CHAPTER OUTLINE

The Classical period, roughly the centuries between 600 B.C.E. and 600 C.E., was a formative era that saw a flourishing of societies and networks in nearly every inhabited part of the globe. In the second century B.C.E. a Greek historian, Polybius, recognized the expanding horizons of his time and concluded that "the world's history has been a series of unrelated episodes, but from now on history becomes an organic whole. The affairs of Europe and Africa are connected with those of Asia and all events bear a relationship and contribute to a single end."[1] In his perception of increasing connections across cultures, Polybius identified a crucial transition. During the Classical period a vast exchange of ideas, cultures, and products grew in the Afro-Eurasian zone, while creative philosophies established new value systems or reinforced existing ones in the Mediterranean world and Asia. The Chinese sent missions into western Asia, where they met Persians and Greeks.

The commercial exchanges that were carried out along the trade routes represented the first glimmerings of a world economy centered on Asia. Greek merchants traveled as far as south India. Goods from Persia and Rome reached Southeast Asia, while Romans craved Chinese silk, Arabian incense, and Indian spices. Between 350 B.C.E. and 200 C.E. the Afro-Eurasian world was also transformed by large regional empires. In the wake of these empires, universal religions such as Buddhism and Christianity crossed cultural boundaries, becoming permanent fixtures of world history. Economic and social patterns changed as each society, while having its own dynamics, was also altered by contact with others.

Transitions
The Axial Age of Philosophical Speculation

Between around 600 and 400 B.C.E., several societies of Eurasia faced a remarkably similar set of crises. People in China, India, Persia, Israel, and Greece were all beset by chronic warfare, population movement, political disruption, and the breakdown of traditional values. Improved ironworking technology produced better tools but also more effective weapons. Political instability was common, as rival states competed with each other for power in China, India, the Middle East, and Greece. These troubled conditions led to a climate of spiritual and intellectual restlessness, provoking a questioning of the old order. Because of the many influential and creative thinkers of this age, some scholars have called this an "axial period" or turning point, a crucial transition in history. Other scholars doubt the utility of this concept in explaining early Classical era thought.

Many of the great Axial Age thinkers lived at roughly the same time, between 600 and 350 B.C.E. Laozi (credited by tradition as the inspiration for Daoism) and Confucius in China lived and taught in the sixth century around the same time as Buddha and Mahavira (the founder of the Jain faith) in India and the Greek thinkers Thales and Heraclitus. Other major Axial Age thinkers included the Hebrew prophets Jeremiah, Ezekiel, and the second Isaiah, as well as Socrates, Plato, and Aristotle in Greece. Although he may have lived much earlier, the teachings of the Persian Zoroaster also became more prominent in this era. The Axial Age intellectuals produced enduring philosophical, religious, and scientific ideas that became the intellectual underpinning of many cultural traditions and fostered new ways of thinking.

Several common philosophical themes can be identified in Axial Age thinking. First, especially in China and

[1]Quoted in Michael Wood, *Legacy: The Search for Ancient Cultures* (New York: Sterling, 1994), 192.

Greece, thinkers questioned the accepted myths and gods and promoted a humanistic view of life, one more concerned with the social and natural order than the supernatural order. Second, most thinkers stressed moral conduct and values, a vision that often rejected the violent, selfish pursuit of material power they saw around them. Some, like the Buddha, Mahavira, and Laozi, were pacifists who denounced all violence. Third, Confucius, the Hebrew prophets, and several Greeks were also among the first people to think about history and its lessons for societies. Fourth, while few of these thinkers favored social equality, many argued that rulers should govern with a sense of obligation to the powerless and less fortunate. Finally, all the Axial Age thinkers believed that the world could be improved, either by the actions of ethical individuals or by the creation of an ideal social order, or both. Many people today are still influenced by Laozi's advice to live in accordance with nature, the Confucian dream of an ordered society based on proper ethical conduct, the Buddha's rules for ending human suffering, Mahavira's belief in absolute nonviolence, the prophetic Hebrew vision of universal justice and monotheism, the Greek emphasis on rational analysis, and the Zoroastrian notion of opposing forces of darkness and light.

CONFUCIUS AND LAOZI IN CONVERSATION This picture engraved on a stone tablet in an old Confucian temple shows Confucius visiting Laozi in the city of Loyang and amiably discussing with him views on ritual and music.

Snark / Art Resource, NY

The consequences of the Axial Age were not only philosophical and religious but also scientific and political. Across Eurasia people raised fundamental questions about many phenomena and answered them by systematic investigation. Greek thinkers such as Aristotle influenced European and Middle Eastern science, and their ideas later inspired new discoveries by Roman and Islamic scientists. Chinese influenced by Confucianism and Daoism also created another rich scientific tradition. Indians became some of the classical world's greatest mathematicians and astronomers. Together, the classical Greeks, Chinese, Indians, and the ancient Mesopotamians and Egyptians built the foundations for modern science. Axial Age ideas also became the basis for new political ideologies for building stronger states. As a result of strengthening state institutions and leaders, in China, India, Persia, and Greece the Axial Age ended in mighty empires that reflected a new order of technological and organizational planning.

Transitions
The Age of Regional Empires

The empires that arose in much of Eurasia during or at the end of the Axial Age were greater in size and impact than those that had flourished in ancient times. The Persian Empire set the stage, thriving for nearly three centuries. More regional empires appeared between 350 B.C.E. and 250 C.E., from China in the East to Rome in the West, that were much grander in scale than earlier empires. The Romans conquered the Mediterranean Basin, the Parthians and then the Sasanid Persians some of western and Central Asia, the Chinese Han Empire much of East and Central Asia, and the Mauryan state much of the Indian subcontinent. Most of the empires built on the ideas of classical sages and religious leaders in organizing society. In so doing they helped resolve the crises, such as political instability, that had sparked the rise of the Axial Age reformers. Empires also appeared in sub-Saharan Africa and the Americas, but on a smaller scale than in Eurasia.

The Rise of Empires

The first great regional empires in the Eastern Hemisphere developed during the Axial Age. The Achaemenid Empire of Persia (550–334 B.C.E.) dwarfed its Middle Eastern predecessors and was the first large empire that ruled so many diverse societies, from Egypt and northern Greece to Central Asia. Persian kings had reason to brag that they were kings of lands containing many people, of the great earth far and wide. The Hellenistic Empire created by Alexander and the Macedonian Greeks built directly on the experiences of Persian imperial rule.

By the end of the Axial Age, in the third and fourth centuries, new empires arose in Eurasia in part as a result of increased warfare, such as fighting between warring states in India, China, and the western Mediterranean. In each region one state eventually subdued its rivals. Changing social and economic conditions also helped spur the

GREAT EMPIRES AND TRADE ROUTES During the Classical period, great empires often dominated East Asia, India, western Asia, North Africa, and southern Europe. Extensive land and maritime trade routes linked East Asia with western Eurasia, West Africa with the Mediterranean, and East Africa with southern Asia.

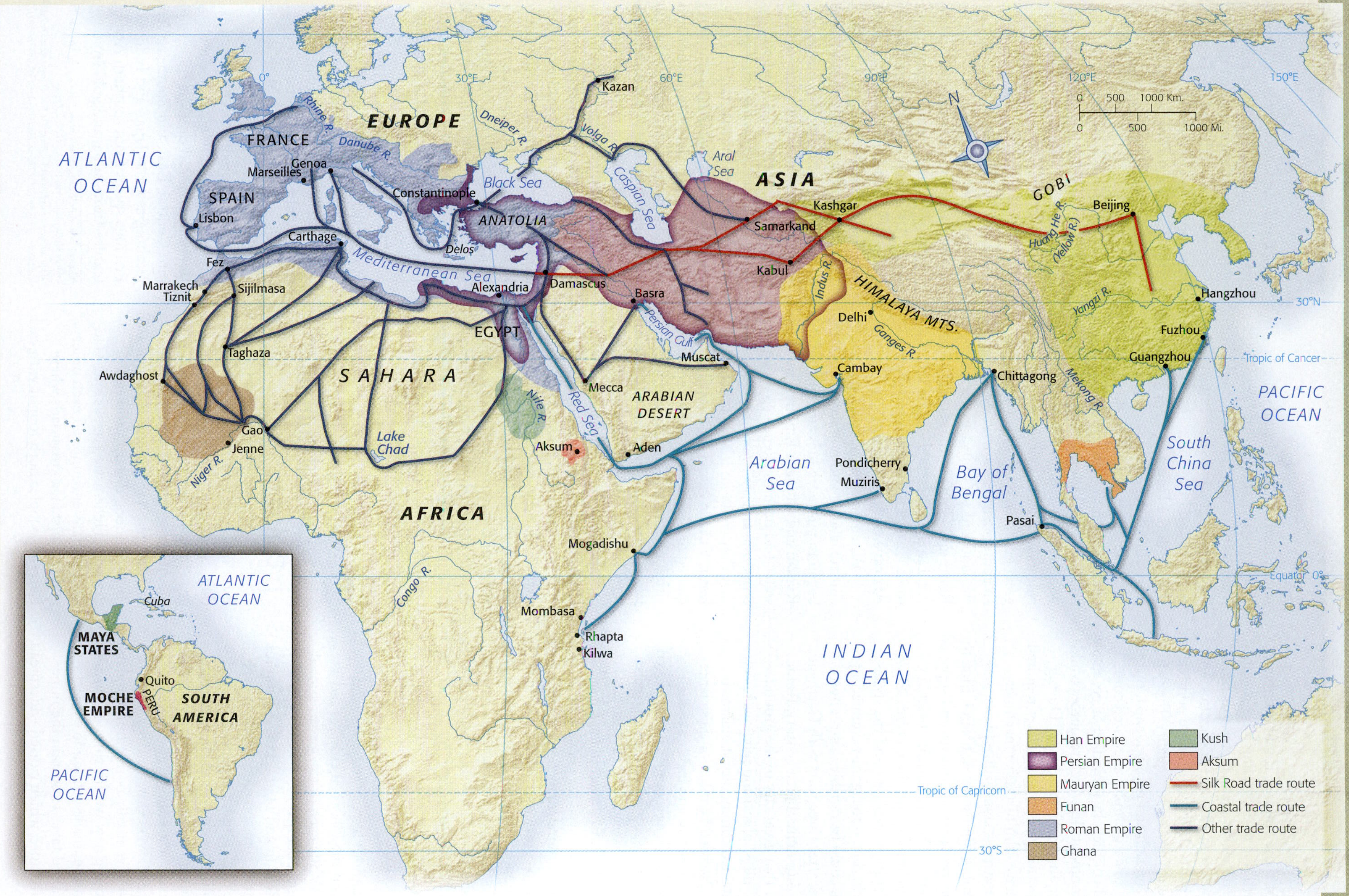

rise of these empires. Rapid economic growth due to expanding long-distance trade networks made merchants more important in all of these societies, and merchants then sought more political influence and social equality. The gap between rich and poor widened. But the move toward empire alleviated some social conflicts by providing large, stable environments in which resources could be acquired and distributed. During this period, the growing states required extensive administrative machinery, larger armies, standardized laws, and governing philosophies. From China to Rome, provinces paid taxes and supplied soldiers to the large armies needed to sustain and expand the empires. Since everything was bigger and the stakes were higher, wars against competing states could be terribly destructive: hence, after three wars with Carthage spanning more than a century, Rome razed that great city to the ground.

Philosophical and religious beliefs maintained community standards but were also used by rulers of these large states to sustain and legitimize their power. In China Confucian ideas urged people to respect leaders, and Legalist thinkers told leaders to exercise power ruthlessly. In Mauryan India, King Ashoka enhanced his position by using Buddhist moral injunctions emphasizing peace, tolerance, and welfare to win popular support: "All men are my children, and just as I desire for my children that they should obtain welfare and happiness, so do I desire [the same] for all men."[2]

The Decline of Empires

Throughout history states rise and fall, and the Classical empires did as well. While each of the great regional empires declined for different reasons, the Roman and Han Chinese Empires suffered from some of the same problems. Each empire expanded beyond its ability to support itself, weakening administrative structures and finances. Both of these empires also suffered from civil wars and growing domestic unrest. Eventually both empires, unable to acquire new wealth through further expansion, made economic cutbacks and raised taxes to sustain the imperial structure, which caused widespread resentment. A third-century C.E. Roman writer argued that "the World itself testifies to its own decline.... The loss of strength and stature must end...in annihilation."[3]

Both the Han and Roman Empires were also plagued by environmental problems. They flourished during the peak of warmth between 200 B.C.E. and 200 C.E. With the return of colder weather after 200 C.E., however, agricultural production declined and the great empires collapsed or weakened. In addition, diseases traveled along the land and sea routes, undermining Rome and China in the second century C.E. Later, in the 590s, plague killed some 25 million West Asians, North Africans, and Europeans.

When pastoral nomads, pushed by climate change and population growth, began to put more pressure on the Roman and Chinese Empires, these states had been weakened so much by economic and environmental problems that they could no longer effectively resist. Various peoples eventually conquered or displaced the great empires, although they also usually adopted Roman, Indian, Persian, or Chinese culture. But the imperial idea never died, especially in China. Hence, the imperial China of the eighteenth century C.E., which incorporated many non-Chinese societies, clearly descended in recognizable form from the Han of 150 B.C.E. Western Europeans never succeeded in reviving the Roman Empire, even though some Christian German kings centuries later claimed the title of "Holy Roman Emperor."

Networks
Trade and Cultural Contact

By stimulating commerce, communication, and unprecedented population growth, the Classical empires fostered the spread of ideas and technologies into neighboring societies and increased contact among distant peoples. For example, Hellenistic Greeks and Mauryan Indians encountered each other in Afghanistan, a crossroads where Eurasian peoples both fought with each other and exchanged ideas. Spurred by imperial expansion, Roman culture and then Christianity permeated the Mediterranean Basin, Hellenistic Greek culture spread in western Asia and North Africa, and China influenced Japan, Korea, Vietnam, and Central Asia.

The Diffusion of Trade, People, Ideas, and Diseases

In Eurasia trade routes grew out of transportation systems constructed to channel resources to imperial capitals. China built canals unprecedented in scale, Achaemenid Persia and Mauryan India constructed east-west highways, and the Romans developed 150,000 miles of paved roads. These roads and canals, along with seaports, became linked to long-distance trade networks, which brought many societies into closer contact with major empires.

Population growth, largely facilitated by the successful agricultural systems that these vast empires supported, also led to increased movement, as people sought open lands and better opportunities. Responding to population pressures, Chinese migrants moved into central and southern China; Germanic and Turkish peoples spread into central Europe and western Asia, respectively; Bantu-speaking peoples occupied the southern half of Africa; and Austronesians settled remote Pacific islands. As groups migrated, they assimilated local peoples and cultures and adapted their lives to new surroundings.

The networks of trade, like those of imperial expansion and missionary activity, linked distant peoples while spreading the influence of cultures more widely. The Greeks picked up scientific and mathematical knowledge as well as some religious notions from the Egyptians and Phoenicians. Indian cultural influences, including Buddhism, spread over the trade routes into Central, East, and Southeast Asia, reaching as far as Japan and Indonesia. Precious spices from southern Arabia, textiles from India, and gold from

[2]Quoted in Romila Thapar, *Asoka and the Decline of the Mauryas* (Delhi: Oxford University Press, 1997), 147.

[3]Cyprian, quoted in Robert P. Clark, *The Global Imperative: An Interpretive History of the Spread of Humankind* (Boulder: Westview, 1997), 3.

Malaya and West Africa found their way to the Mediterranean societies.

Trade also connected Mesoamerica with neighboring regions and fostered networks of exchange in both North America and South America. For example, copper from the North American Great Lakes reached the Gulf Coast, and Mesoamerican ball games spread far and wide. Crops like corn and tomatoes also traveled American trade routes.

Diseases began to limit population growth in the later Classical period. Networks of communication were often networks of contagion, port cities being the major hubs of transmission. Epidemics of smallpox and plague resulted from travelers unknowingly spreading new diseases into areas where people had not yet built up immunities to them. Epidemic diseases may have killed as much as 25 percent of the population of China and the Roman Empire during the second and third centuries C.E. As a result of the various disease outbreaks, by 600 B.C.E. the world population remained between 200 and 240 million, similar to what it had been six centuries earlier, with the great majority concentrated in Asia, especially China.

CROSSING THE PAMIR MOUNTAINS The Pamir Mountains, separating the deserts of what is now western China from the deserts and grasslands of Turkestan and Afghanistan, were one of the more formidable barriers faced by camel caravans traveling the Silk Road. To avoid the blistering summer heat of the desert, the caravans often traveled in winter and thus had to maneuver through mountain snows.

Michael Fairchild/Peter Arnold/Getty Images

The Silk Road Network

As overland trade expanded over wider areas, the Silk Road, which linked China via Central Asia to the Middle East and Europe, became and remained a major long-distance network of exchange—in effect the first transcontinental highway, allowing people, goods, and ideas to travel thousands of miles. The huge amounts of gold and silver exported by Rome to pay for the Chinese silk and porcelain and Indian spices that traveled the route did some damage to the Roman economy. Overland trade expanded with the growing use of camels. After the invention of an efficient saddle allowed this pack animal to be used for longer journeys across the deserts and plains of Asia and Africa, camels became the trucks of the premodern Afro-Eurasian zone. And the merchants who used the camels carried not only bullion and products but also religions, especially Buddhism, which spread along the Silk Road into Central Asia and China.

Cities grew up along the Silk Road across Central and western Asia to serve as suppliers and middlemen to the merchants. These cities, such as Kashgar in Xinjiang and Samarkand in Turkestan, became part of a contact zone linking many societies. Hubs at the eastern end of the Mediterranean served as transshipment points for goods traveling between China and Rome. This trade aided some societies. For example, the Persian-speaking Sogdians dominated Central Asian trading cities. Chinese sources described the Sogdians as trained for trade: "At birth honey was put in their mouths and gum on their hands. They learned the trade from the age of five. On reaching twelve they were sent to do business in a neighboring state."[4]

Maritime Networks

Maritime trade also flourished during this period, enriching various ports. Hence, both trade goods and cultural influences were carried by sea between eastern and western Asia. Eventually a vast maritime Silk Road linked China and Southeast Asia to India and Sri Lanka, and then stretched westward to Persia, Arabia, the East African coast, and beyond to Europe and North Africa. Some cities flourished as hubs for this maritime trade. For instance, between 100 and 500 C.E. the Egyptian port of Berenike on the Red Sea was regularly visited by ships from India. Products from as far away as Java and Cambodia reached the markets of Berenike, and eleven different written languages, including Greek and Sanskrit, were used there. Berenike was also linked through Alexandria to the Mediterranean societies.

Sailing networks also connected the entire Mediterranean Basin. For several centuries one key network hub was the tiny Greek island of Delos **(DEH-los)** in the Aegean Sea, of which it was said, "Merchant, sail in and unload! Everything is as good as sold."[5] Merchants from all over, including Greeks from around the Mediterranean, Romans, Syrians, Jews, Phoenicians, and Arabs, flocked to

[4]Quoted in Frances Wood, *The Silk Road: Two Thousand Years in the Heart of Asia* (Berkeley: University of California Press, 2001), 66.

[5]Quoted in Lionel Casson, *The Ancient Mariners: Seafarers and Sea Fighters of the Mediterranean in Ancient Times*, 2nd ed. (Princeton: Princeton University Press, 1991), 166.

Delos to trade. Some merchants developed temporary or permanent communities far from home. For example, Jews sunk roots in southwest India, Indian merchants in Southeast Asia, Indonesians and Arabs in East Africa, and Greeks all over the Mediterranean and Black Sea Basins.

In some places maritime commerce faced serious limitations. Because of formidable currents, only the strongest oars would allow a boat to pass through the Strait of Gibraltar separating Spain from North Africa. This problem inhibited trade between Mediterranean and Atlantic societies for many centuries. In the Americas some people, using balsa rafts, traded along the Pacific coast of South and Central America, while others used canoes to travel between Caribbean islands.

Transitions
The Rise of World Religions

Filling a vacuum created by imperial decay, political instability, and cultural decline, universal religions—Christianity, Buddhism, Hinduism, and Zoroastrianism— became more prominent in Afro-Eurasia during the later centuries of the Classical period, marking another great transition that reshaped societies. Instead of the gods of the ancient world, which were local and identified with particular cities or cultures, these new religions were portable and appealed across cultural boundaries. They could be carried along trade routes, attracting believers far from their lands of birth.

Religions spread along land and sea trade routes, as missionaries accompanied or were themselves traders. About six centuries after its founding in India, Buddhism reached China via the Silk Road and Southeast Asia over the maritime trade routes. Christianity, with roots in the eastern Mediterranean, spread to Rome and then permeated northern Europe while also establishing roots in western Asia and North and Northeast Africa. Other faiths also established a presence. Manichaeism, a mix of Christian and Zoroastrian influences, attracted believers from North Africa to China. Judaism also gained some converts in Arabia, the Caucasus, and Ethiopia. By 500 or 600 C.E. small Christian and Jewish communities had even been established in Central Asia, western India, and northern China.

The universal religions gave people hope in the face of the political and social crises that marked the decline of the great regional empires. Sometimes these new religions merged with or incorporated existing beliefs. In East Asia, for example, Buddhism gradually blended with or accommodated Confucianism, Daoism, and Shinto, and, in northern Europe, Christianity acquired a Germanic or Celtic flavor over the centuries.

In sub-Saharan Africa and the Americas, some religious beliefs reached across many societies, becoming the counterparts to the organized Eurasian religions. The polytheistic beliefs of Sudanic peoples gradually spread to central, eastern, and southern Africa, while in the Americas the Olmec introduced gods and views of the universe that contributed to the later religious beliefs of the Maya. Some American peoples practiced human sacrifice as offerings to the gods, as did some Afro-Eurasian societies, among them the Celts, Minoan Crete, early ancient Egypt, and Shang China.

Societies
Religion and Culture

Though only a part of life and changing over time, the universal religions became a major force in shaping the societies and regions in which they became dominant, eventually creating, for example, a largely Hindu India, a Buddhist Sri Lanka, and a Christian Europe. After the regional empires collapsed into many rival states in the Mediterranean, India, and China, religious institutions transcended political divisions, fostering cultural unity across borders. Hindus, Buddhists, and Christians often saw themselves as part of larger faith communities. As a result, Chinese Buddhist pilgrims made the long and arduous journey to India to study with Indian Buddhists, and many Christians looked to the bishops in faraway cities such as Rome for guidance. Spirituality permeated the lives of people all over the world. Religion also offered the poor the hope that they might end their suffering and low status, if not in this life then through reincarnation or in some form of heaven.

All the universal religions, as well as the religions of urban American societies, had certain features, practices, and beliefs in common. They had sacred scriptures (written or oral), such as the Hindu Vedas and Christian Bible, strict moral codes, organized priesthoods, theologies laying out core beliefs, and some concept of existence after death. Most faiths also encouraged followers to treat others as they wanted to be treated themselves. As the devout shared a belief in the universal truth of their religion, the faiths became important forces of social control. For example, Hindu ideas of reincarnation and karma underpinned the Indian caste system, encouraging people to accept their status. Christians focused on attaining Heaven and were warned that questioning religious authority and beliefs might prevent salvation. Some of the religious establishments grew intolerant of dissent. For this reason, Christian bishops established a consensus on doctrine, excluding ideas considered to be heresy. Those who disagreed with orthodoxy might be banned or punished, and they were expected to face retribution after death in Hell, the abode of evil, an underworld for wicked people and disbelievers. All the religions were patriarchal to one degree or another, adding religious sanction to the growing suppression of women.

Buddhism spawned a new social and spiritual movement, monasticism, that also became a growing component of organized Christianity by the third century C.E. Whether Christian or Buddhist, monasteries provided educational and charitable services while providing a focus for community religious life. In societies as far removed as England, Nubia, Sri Lanka, and China, a substantial number of men (and some women) joined monastic orders, abandoning the humdrum existence of everyday life for a focus on prayer and meditation and usually bound by a rigid code of celibacy and poverty.

For centuries artists in the Christian Ethiopian kingdom, in the highlands of Northeast Africa, painted biblical figures on the pages of religious manuscripts. The artists often used Ethiopian motifs, and this painting of the Hebrew king David, adorned in rich robes and crown and playing a harp-type instrument, resembles that of an Ethiopian king.

Societies
Social Systems and Attitudes

The social systems and attitudes of the Classical period set the patterns for centuries to come. In many places gender roles hardened. Because the great empires were made through military conquest, they were very masculine in nature. Some of the new philosophies and religions gave power to older men and generally urged women to stay in the background. In addition, the faiths that replaced Greek and Roman religions removed goddesses as objects of worship in the Mediterranean world, although in southern Asia many Hindus continued to revere female deities. Although women had some legal protections in Greece and Rome, many also lived generally domestic and often secluded lives. Women faced increasing restrictions in China and northern India, where they were expected to be obedient to men. Patriarchy was also common in Africa, the Americas, and the Pacific islands. But wherever they lived, women had varied experiences. Some were treated as property, assigned by their fathers to husbands, and many faced permanent dependency on fathers, husbands, and sons. Only a small minority of women anywhere were educated. However, a few attained great power as queens.

Homosexuality existed in all classical societies and was generally tolerated in some, especially in Greece and Rome. Chinese historians reported that many emperors of the era had male lovers in addition to their wives and concubines. Chinese also tolerated lesbian relationships among women in polygamous households. But in many places official attitudes concerning gender roles and sexual behaviors became more rigid over time, pushing homosexuals to the margins of society.

Another form of repression, slavery, was practiced in many classical societies around the world. Most people saw slavery as a part of the natural order of things and essential to economic life. Slaves everywhere were bought and sold at the whim of the owner, and their lives and labor were controlled. Most slaves were poor, although some Greek and Roman slaves held high positions in society or were attached to prosperous families. In societies such as Han China, Mauryan India, and the Maya society, slaves were only one segment of the lower class, whereas in Greece and Rome they constituted a large part of the population and were used in every area of the economy, from mining and construction to prostitution and domestic work. Slavery mostly died out in China and India during the first millennium C.E. and became less important in Europe after the collapse of the Roman Empire, showing that societies do change, often dramatically, over time.

5 Classical Societies in Southern and Central Asia, 600 B.C.E.–600 C.E.

Ancient Art & Architecture / DanitaDelimont.com

GOLD COIN This gold coin, showing a horseman, was made in India during the reign of King Chandragupta II, who presided over a great and prosperous Indian empire, with a dynamic economy, between 380 and 415 C.E.

The merchants used to move about in the rivers as they wished, in the forests as if in gardens and on mountains as if in their own houses. As [the King] used to protect the earth so it too gave him gems out of mines, corns from the fields, and elephants from forests.

Indian writer Kalidasa (kahl-I-Dahss-uh), fifth century C.E.[1]

Sometime around 80 C.E. an unknown Greek boarded an India-bound trading ship that left the Egyptian port of Berenike **(BER-eh-nick-y)**. After braving the dangers from pirates in the Red Sea and along the Arabian coast, the ship reached the Indus River, where the merchants exchanged clothing, silverware, and glassware for semiprecious stones from Afghanistan, Chinese silks, and Indian textiles. Along India's west coast, they stopped near present-day Bombay, trading silverware and Italian wine for pepper. Upon reaching the great port of Muziris **(MOO-zir-us)** in southwest India, the sailors probably haunted the waterfront dives. An Indian poet recorded the arrival of ships like this at Muziris: "The beautiful vessels stir white foam on the river, arriving with gold and departing with pepper."[2] The ship then sailed around the southern tip of India and up the east coast, stopping to collect pearls, textiles, spices, and gems. Finally it returned to Egypt, the merchants aboard hoping to make a fortune from their cargo.

From Egypt, western Asia, and East Africa ships arrived annually at Indian seaports to trade, collecting fabulous trade goods, such as pepper, cinnamon, cotton, and gems, for sale in distant markets. India also attracted sojourners and permanent settlers arriving by sea or overland. Those who arrived over the mountains from windswept Central Asia found the Indian sun a blazing fury and the drenching summer rains a shock. For newcomers, the Indian culture and religion seemed more unusual than the climate. But Indian society was adaptable and accommodating. Most immigrants found themselves gradually enfolded into Indian religions, which allowed for many paths to understanding. Resilient Hinduism bent to meet the varying needs of dissimilar people. This adaptability also helped Indian culture spread into Southeast Asia.

During this era Classical South and Southeast Asia flowered in state building, new trade networks, and religious thought, establishing many patterns that endured into modern times. Several South Asian empires forged political unity and made India a leading world power. Hinduism developed new schools of thought, while Buddhism **(BOO-diz-uhm)** arose to become a major faith in many parts of Asia. Meanwhile, various Central and Southeast Asian societies established states and social systems that differed greatly from those in India and China while becoming major participants in international trade.

[1]Quoted in Jeannine Auboyer, *Daily Life in Ancient India: From 200 B.C. to 700 A.D.* (London: Phoenix, 2002), 62.
[2]Quoted in Lionel Casson, *The Ancient Mariners: Seafarers and Sea Fighters of the Mediterranean in Ancient Times*, 2nd ed. (Princeton: Princeton University Press, 1991), 202.

IN THIS CHAPTER

The Transformation of Indian Society, Religion, and Politics

How did Buddhism and the Mauryas shape Indian society?

The forging of a new society from Aryan and local traditions continued for centuries, affecting life and thought. The distinctive caste system became a key structure, and Hinduism grew more diverse and complex. Jainism and Buddhism sprouted from Axial Age religious ferment, Classical Eurasia's great philosophical awakening that spawned new ways of thinking from Greece to China. India's first large centralized state, the Mauryan **(MORE-yuhn)** Empire, emerged in part from contact with peoples to the west.

Caste and Indian Society

The social configuration we know today as the caste system took shape in the Classical period. Caste members often practiced a common occupation as priests, warriors, merchants, artisans, or farmers, while still others performed more menial tasks. Hindu values supported caste membership, including beliefs in reincarnation. But although social and religious practices became similar throughout India, the caste system was never uniform and unchanging.

Over time the caste system became more fully developed and hereditary. The Code of Manu **(MAN-oo)**, a political and legal document with advice for a Hindu king, formalized rules regarding caste relations. Gradually the four main castes (varna) subdivided into thousands of subcastes known as jati ("birth groups"), each with its own rules and, frequently, occupational specialization. Each person was born into a caste that maintained a moral code stipulating such duties as family maintenance and specifying which jatis could supply marriage partners. Regulations prescribed the types of food that caste members could consume, who could cook and serve the food, and who could accompany the diner. Vegetarianism became more common among the higher castes, with cows being protected. By 500 C.E. pious Hindus avoided eating beef because the cow was now considered sacred, the symbol of life and motherhood because it gave dung for fuel and fertilizer and milk for food. Cows wandered at will, eating whatever grain they found. Scholars debate whether cows spreading disease and consuming scarce food resources outweighs their gifts to people.

Hindu ideas sanctioned the emerging caste system. The doctrine of karma held that one's status in the present life was

VILLAGE SCENE In classical times most Indians lived in villages. This modern painting portrays an Indian house and villagers working, some as farmers, while the Hindu god Shiva watching over and blessing the village.

	600 B.C.E.	500 B.C.E.	400 B.C.E.	300 B.C.E.	200 B.C.E.	100 B.C.E.
INDIA	563–483 B.C.E. Life of the Buddha 326 B.C.E. Alexander the Great's army reaches western India 322–185 B.C.E. Mauryan Empire 269–232 B.C.E. Reign of Ashoka 200 B.C.E.–150 C.E. Division of Buddhism into Theravada and Mahayana schools					
SOUTHEAST ASIA	111 B.C.E.–939 C.E. Chinese colonization of Vietnam					

determined by deeds in past lives. Every action had repercussions, the sum of one's karma in past lives determining one's fate in this life. Hindus considered the three top caste groupings further along the path of reincarnation, holding low-caste Indians responsible for their status because of their presumed past sins. Their only hope lay in dutifully performing their present duties and obligations. Below the formal caste system were the untouchables, or pariahs **(puh-RYE-uhz)**, some 10 percent of the population who lived largely in their own neighborhoods and were generally condemned to trades and crafts regarded as undesirable (such as carrying water to village houses) or unclean because their function involved being polluted by filth or the taking of animal life. They worked as sweepers of village streets, fishermen, butchers, gravediggers, tanners, leatherworkers, and scavengers.

The caste system has functioned for the past twenty-five hundred years, providing stability, security, long-term continuity to society, and meaning and direction to Indians' lives. It has promoted mutual aid within each caste and regulated village life, as subcastes exchange goods or services with other subcastes in the village. Regional variations also developed; for example, in south India, Bengal, and northwestern India, the caste system remained less complex. Caste, village, and family became the pillars of society, contributing to a group orientation and an acceptance of authority. Although strong in many villages, however, the system has been breaking down in the larger cities. It is difficult to avoid close contact with members of other castes while eating in a restaurant, being confined in a hospital, or working in an office or factory.

The Shaping of Hinduism

The religion known today as Hinduism faced increasing dissent during the Classical period, fostering new thinking. Some historians argue that Hinduism as a coherent religion with sacred writings and a common identity only emerged in the past few centuries and that, for much of history, Hinduism remained a loose collection of varied beliefs, rituals, legends, practices, festivals, and shrines, with no centralized religious authority and deep knowledge of the Vedas restricted to the priestly class, the brahmans. They alone had mastered the scriptures and hymns for worship, and they alone presided over rituals. Enriched by gifts from the devout, many priests became wealthy landowners. Eventually, however, some Indians who resented priestly wealth and corruption debated the accepted wisdom. Like the Chinese and Greek philosophers, they spawned movements emphasizing new approaches to worship and spiritual fulfillment, especially meditation. Some reformist writings were collected in the Upanishads, the final portion of the vast Hindu scriptures.

Thanks to this new spirituality, Hinduism's highest ideal became escape from sensual pleasures and the material world (seen as an "illusion") and the joining of one's individual soul with **Brahman**, the Universal Soul, or Absolute Reality, that fills all space and time. Some seekers rejected society, seeking mystical unity with the divine. Hindu holy men, greatly admired, abandoned worldly pleasures through such practices as yoga **(YOH-guh)** ("yoke" or "union"), a system of physical and mental exercises emphasizing breath control to promote mental concentration, calmness, and a trancelike state that produced a mystical awareness of a universal soul. Union with the universal soul meant ending the cycle of reincarnation through devotion to God, selfless action, and knowledge achieved through intense meditation. Only by escaping from one's ego by abandoning the desires and actions that prevent release from earthly lives could a person end the round of reincarnation and finally achieve the ultimate bliss of merging with Brahman, described in the Upanishads as a deep, dreamless sleep. "In thinking 'This is I' and 'That is mine,'" warns the Upanishads, "one binds himself to himself, as does a bird with a snare!"[3]

Brahman The Universal Soul, or Absolute Reality, that Hindus believe fills all space and time.

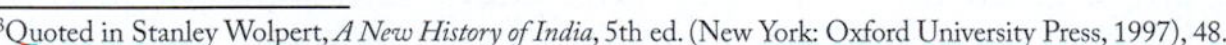

[3]Quoted in Stanley Wolpert, *A New History of India*, 5th ed. (New York: Oxford University Press, 1997), 48.

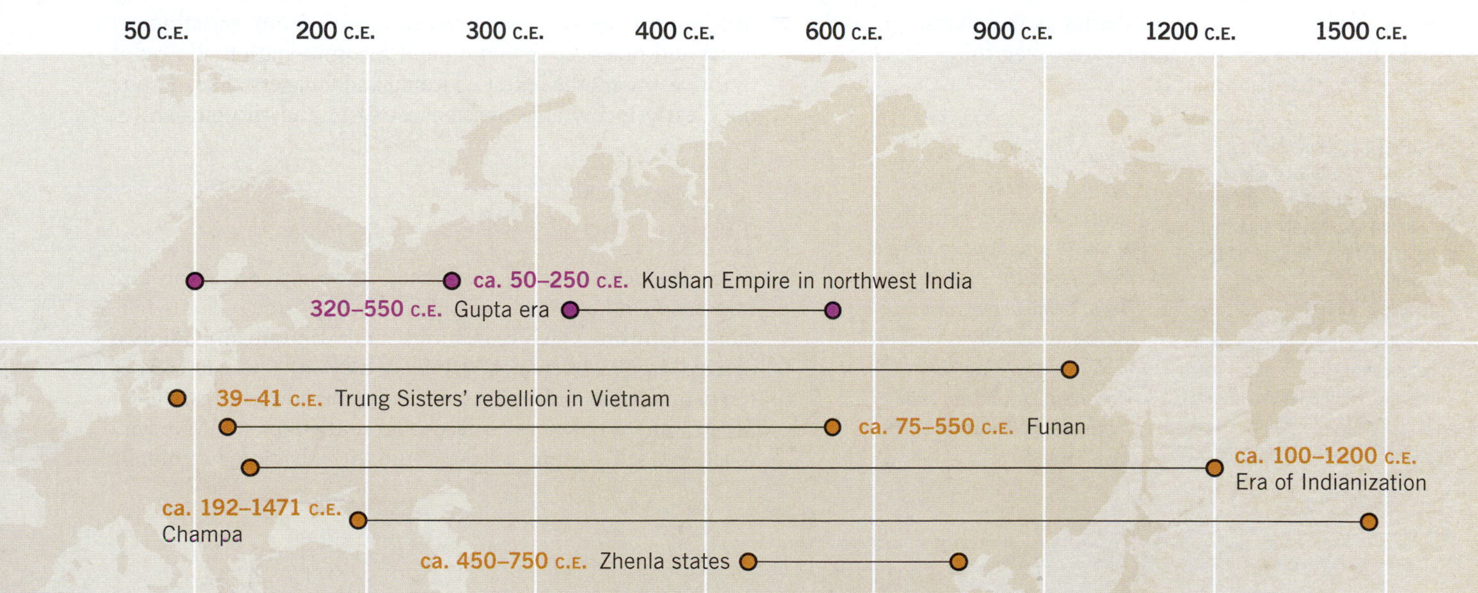

akg-images / Jean-Louis Nou

WORSHIP OF BUDDHIST RELICS In the first century C.E. Buddhists erected a pillar containing this frieze of a stupa housing relics of the Buddha. The stupa is surrounded by throngs of worshipers and pilgrims making music and bringing offerings to honor the Buddha.

New forms of worship also stressed devotion or prayer focused on specific gods such as Vishnu or Shiva. Every home had a shrine to worship such deities, and great throngs made annual pilgrimages to sacred places such as the Ganges River. Eventually the spiritual quest led to new schools of thought such as **Vedanta** **(vay-DAHNT-uh)**, meaning "completion" of the Vedas. Vedanta offered mystical experience, belief in the underlying unity of all reality, and sophisticated interpretations of the countless gods found in popular Hinduism, a diversity often summed up by the phrase "33,000 gods." Rejecting polytheism, Vedanta viewed these deities as manifestations of the single Absolute Reality that pervades everything. The Upanishads states that Brahman is

Vedanta ("Completion of the Vedas") A school of classical Indian thought that offered Hindus mystical experience and a belief in the underlying unity of all reality.

Jainism An Indian religion that believes that life in all forms must be protected because everything, including animals, insects, plants, sticks, and stones, has a separate soul and is alive.

God, all gods, the five elements—earth, air, fire, water, ether; all beings, great or small, born of eggs, born from the womb, born from heat, born from soil; horses, cows, men, elephants, birds; everything that breathes, the beings that walk and the beings that walk not.[4]

Hinduism developed a tolerant approach to religious differences. As many invaders swept into India, most of them found a place in Hinduism, which incorporated diverse beliefs, even integrating some non-Hindu figures into devotional cults. Indians worshiped God in many forms. As an old Indian folk song puts it: "Into the bosom of the great sea, flow streams that come from hills on every side. Their names are various as their springs. And thus in every land do men bow down, To one great God, though known by many names."[5] Rather than a centralized church and rigidly defined theology, Hinduism developed as loosely connected sects with many variations of belief and practice. Toleration and accommodation allowed it to thrive among the better educated and villagers alike, despite the clearly inequitable divisions of caste and the burdens of karma.

Jainism and Buddhism

Two dissident ascetics eventually gave up on reforming Hinduism and founded movements that became separate religions, Jainism **(JANE-iz-uhm)** and Buddhism. **Jainism** derived from Mahavira **(MA-ha-VEER-a)** ("Great Hero"), the pampered son of a tribal chief who abandoned his affluent life to wander naked as an ascetic around 500 B.C.E. Mahavira practiced self-torture as the route to salvation, eventually

[4]From Swami Prabhavananda and Frederick Manchester, eds., *The Upanishads: Breath of the Eternal* (New York: Mentor, 1957), 62.
[5]C. E. Gover, *The Folk-Songs of Southern India* (London: Trubner and Co., 1872), 165.

WITNESS TO THE PAST

Basic Doctrines in the Buddha's First Sermon

Buddhist tradition holds that, after achieving enlightenment, the Buddha preached his first sermon in a deer park in the Ganges city of Varanasi (Benares) around 527 B.C.E. One of the most important sources of belief for all Buddhists, the sermon laid out the framework of Buddha's moral message, including the Middle Way between asceticism and worldly life, the Noble Eightfold Path, and the Four Noble Truths. These are the most important concepts in all branches of Buddhism.

There are two ends not to be served by a wanderer.... The pursuit of desires and of pleasure which springs from desire, which is base, common, leading to rebirth, ignoble and unprofitable; and the pursuit of pain and hardship [asceticism], which is grievous, ignoble, and unprofitable. The Middle Way of the [Buddha] avoids both of these ends. It is enlightened, it brings clear vision, it makes for wisdom, and leads to peace, insight, enlightenment, and Nirvana. What is the Middle Way? It is the Noble Eightfold path—Right Views, Right Resolve, Right Speech, Right Conduct, Right Livelihood, Right Effort, Right Mindfulness, and Right Concentration....

And this is the Noble Truth of Sorrow. Birth is sorrow, age is sorrow, disease is sorrow, death is sorrow; contact with the unpleasant is sorrow, separation from the pleasant is sorrow, every wish unfulfilled is sorrow—in short, all of the five components of individuality are sorrow.

And this is the Noble Truth of the Arising of Sorrow. It arises from craving, which leads to rebirth, which brings delight and passion, and seeks pleasure from here, now there—the craving for sensual pleasure, the craving for continued life, the craving for power.

And this is the Noble Truth of the Stopping of Sorrow. It is the complete stopping of the craving, so that no passion remains, leaving it, being emancipated from it, being released from it, giving no place to it.

And this is the Noble Truth of the Way which Leads to the Stopping of Sorrow. It is the Noble Eightfold Path....

THINKING ABOUT THE READING

1. What does the Buddha mean by the Middle Way?
2. What causes suffering, and how can people stop it?
3. What conduct do these ideas promote?

Source: From *Sources of Indian Tradition*, Vol. 1 by William Theodore de Bary et al., eds.

starving himself to death. Jains believed that life in all forms must be protected because everything—animals, insects, plants has a living soul. Jain monks and nuns sweep the ground to avoid stepping on insects and some wear a cloth over the mouth to prevent inhaling them. In Mahavira's words, "All things living, all beings whatever, should not be slain, or treated with violence."[6] Most Jains became merchants and bankers, and they are prominent today in India's economic elite. Given the emphasis on austere behavior and a spartan vegetarian diet, the sect never became very large; perhaps 4.5 million Jains live in the world today. But Jainism influenced Hindu ideas of nonviolence. Twenty-five centuries after Mahavira, Mohandas Gandhi, a devout Hindu, utilized Jain ideas in developing his philosophy of nonviolence and passive resistance to oppressive rule.

More important in the long run, **Buddhism**, based on the teachings of a major Axial Age thinker, eventually spread out of India to become a major faith in Central, East, and Southeast Asia and Sri Lanka. The religion's founder, Siddartha Gautama **(si-DAHR-tuh GAUT-uh-muh)** (563–483 B.C.E.), was a prince of a small kingdom in what is now Nepal and a contemporary of Confucius, Mahavira, and several other Axial Age thinkers. As with Jesus of Nazareth and Confucius, his life and thought are known largely through his followers' written accounts. Siddartha led a privileged, self-indulgent life and was shocked when he ventured from the palace and encountered the miseries experienced by common people. He then abandoned his royal life, wife, and family to search for truth as a wandering holy man, living in the forest, practicing yoga, meditating, begging for his food, and nearly dying from fasting. He met skeptics who argued that there is no afterlife or god. Eventually Siddartha believed he understood cosmic truths and began teaching his new religion, attracting many disciples, who called him the Buddha ("The Enlightened One"). He also rejected the caste system as immoral.

Buddha emphasized the Four Noble Truths (see Witness to the Past: Basic Doctrines in the Buddha's First Sermon): (1) this life is one of suffering and ignorance; (2) suffering stems from desiring what one does not have and clinging to what one already has for fear of losing it; (3) to stop suffering, one must stop all desire; and (4) one does this by following the Noble Eightfold Path of correct views, intent, speech, actions, trade (or profession), effort, mindfulness, and concentration. Following this path means leading a good life that does no harm to others. To Buddhists, the world is in a constant state of flux; when mortals try in vain to stop the flow of events, they suffer. Buddhism is neither monotheistic nor polytheistic, and the Buddha was ambivalent as to whether a god or gods existed. Buddhists were encouraged to follow "the Middle Way," a

Buddhism A major world religion based on the teachings of the Buddha that emphasized putting an end to desire and being compassionate to all creatures.

[6]Quoted in Wolpert, *New History*, 54.

lifestyle midway between austere asceticism and the real world of society. This meant living morally, nonviolently, and moderately and considering the needs of others. For example, men were urged to treat their wives with respect. Asked to summarize his beliefs, the Buddha replied: "Avoid doing evil deeds, cultivate doing good deeds, and purify the mind."[7] The Buddha did not oppose acquiring wealth but believed that wealth alone did not bring happiness. He also condemned the irresponsible use of wealth, such as wasting it on drinking, gambling, and laziness rather than saving some for emergencies and donating some to worthy causes.

Although rejecting priestly power and the caste system and the Vedas as religious truth, Buddha adopted and modified many Hindu ideas. To be released from the chronic cycle of birth and rebirth, Buddhists were urged, like Hindus, to abandon all sense of self but with the goal of **nirvana** **(neer-VAHN-uh)** (literally, "the blowing out"), an advanced consciousness bringing everlasting peace or end of suffering through perfection of wisdom and compassion. Buddhists also avoided taking animal life if possible, many becoming vegetarians. Like Mahavira, Buddha promoted a major innovation, **monasticism** **(muh-NAS-tuh-siz-uhm)**, a life of penance, prayer, and meditation. Eventually joining together in communities of other seekers, monks and nuns adopted chastity, poverty, and nonviolence, suspended family ties, followed rules of proper conduct, and practiced yoga for concentration, meditation, and self-discipline. They begged for their food, thus affirming their humility and allowing believers to gain merit by giving them food and other necessities. Eventually Buddhism became a major influence on the first great Indian imperial state, the Mauryan Empire.

Foreign Encounters and the Rise of the Mauryas

For several centuries, northwest India remained in close communication with Persia and then Hellenistic Greece. The Persians conquered much of the Indus River Valley in 518 B.C.E., bringing India to the attention of the Greek historian Herodotus, whose fabulous stories tantalized the young Macedonian ruler, Alexander the Great, who conquered the Greeks and then a great empire in western Asia and North Africa (see Chapter 7). By 326 B.C.E. Alexander's forces had reached the Indus River and soon subdued several small Aryan kingdoms east of the Indus. Impressed with the country's wealth, the Macedonian conqueror discussed religion and philosophy with Indian scholars and apparently dispatched his notes back to his own teacher, Aristotle, making some Greek thinkers aware of Buddhist and Hindu ideas. A few Indian thinkers may even have visited Athens and Alexandria. With his homesick soldiers rebellious, however, Alexander returned to Persia, where he died. His legacy endured in northwest India, and Greek artistic styles helped to shape Buddhist art. Furthermore, the Greek imperialists set up a powerful state in northern Afghanistan known as Bactria **(BAK-tree-uh)**, and some Greeks also remained behind in northwest India, intermarrying with local women.

nirvana ("the blowing out") For Buddhists a kind of everlasting peace or end of suffering achieved through perfection of wisdom and compassion.

monasticism The pursuit of a life of penance, prayer, and meditation, either alone or in a community of other seekers.

Alexander's invasion created a political vacuum filled by the military forces of Chandragupta **(CHUHN-druh-GOOP-tuh)** Maurya, who established the first imperial Indian state, the Mauryan Empire (322–185 B.C.E.). Perhaps inspired by Alexander, Chandragupta transformed himself from the ruler of a Ganges state, Magadha **(MAH-guh-duh)**, into the monarch of half the subcontinent (see Map 5.1). Eventually the Mauryan Empire included eastern Afghanistan, most of north and central India, and parts of south India. The Mauryas maintained diplomatic relations with many societies, including Greece, Syria, and Egypt. Chandragupta, a cynical political realist skilled in manipulating power, was influenced by his chief adviser, Kautilya **(cow-TILL-ya)**, who favored political centralization and compiled the initial draft of a manual for rulers on obtaining and holding power.

The Classical world's most efficient government ruled the empire. A large army and secret police maintained order, with spies keeping government officials under constant surveillance. An ambassador from Greece particularly admired the conscientious justice system, in which the king presided personally over court sessions and settled disputes. To maintain the expensive government, the state heavily taxed agriculture, trade, mining, herding, and other economic activities. Village councils composed of older men from leading families enjoyed considerable local autonomy, a pattern that became entrenched over the centuries. The Mauryan monarch lived in great splendor, often in seclusion and surrounded by women who cooked his food, served his wine, and in the evening carried him to his apartment, where they lulled him to sleep with music. To discourage opposition, Indian rulers had long claimed to be blessed by the gods and endowed with supernatural and magical powers. Yet the realization that excessive taxes and forced labor might drive the people into rebellion provided checks on autocratic power.

Mauryan Life, Institutions, and Networks

Many of Mauryan India's 50 to 100 million people lived in cities, the centers for a prosperous economy. With 500,000 residents, the capital, Patna **(PUHT-nuh)** (then called Pataliputra) on the Ganges River, was the world's largest city and widely celebrated for its parks, public buildings, libraries, and a great university that attracted many foreign students. The fortified timber wall around the city, which had 570 towers, was roughly 21 miles long, suggesting that Patna was about twice as large as Rome several centuries later.

Mauryan prosperity depended on the world's most advanced trading system and craft industries, including many skilled woodworkers, ivory carvers, stonecutters, and producers of fine

[7]Quoted in Roy C. Amore and Julia Ching, "The Buddhist Tradition," in *World Religions: Eastern Traditions*, ed. Willard G. Oxtoby (New York: Oxford University Press, 1996), 230.

MAP 5.1 THE MAURYAN EMPIRE, 322–185 B.C.E. During the Classical period major states arose in north India, most notably the Mauryan, Kushan, and Gupta Empires. The brief encounter with the Greek forces led by Alexander the Great, which reached the Indus River Valley in 326 B.C.E., may have stimulated the Mauryas to build India's first empire.

cotton fabrics. Products and merchants moved along the major east-west highway stretching from near present-day Calcutta **(kal-KUHT-uh)** through the Ganges and Indus Valleys to Afghanistan. Many resident foreign merchants fostered an active trade with China, Arabia, and the Middle East. Artisan and merchant guilds supervised the private sector, while the government owned mines and forests and engaged in shipbuilding, arms manufacture, and textile production. Public granaries stored surplus food.

Ashoka and Buddhist Monarchy

The Mauryas reached their height under Chandragupta's grandson, the enlightened king Ashoka **(uh-SHOH-kuh)** (whose name means "Sorrowless"), a major political and religious figure in world history. The ambitious Ashoka (r. 269–232 B.C.E.) rose to power through bloody campaigns of eliminating rivals and expanding into frontier lands. His early edicts, many of them carved in rocks and sandstone pillars, boast of many enemies slain and captured. Then, at some point, he experienced a spiritual conversion and became a devout Buddhist, proclaiming his remorse at past atrocities and his commitment to nonviolence. One edict noted that Ashoka "began to follow righteousness, to love righteousness. The greatest of all victories is the victory of righteousness."[8]

Ashoka spent his remaining years promoting the Buddha's pacifist teachings, pledging to bear wrong without violent retribution, look kindly on all his subjects, and ensure the safety, happiness, and peace of mind of all living beings. He designed laws to encourage compassion, mutual tolerance, vegetarianism, and respect for all forms of life. He also sponsored hospitals and medical care paid for by the state. Although Ashoka dispatched Buddhist missions to spread the religion into Sri Lanka, Southeast Asia, and Afghanistan, he neither made Buddhism the state religion nor persecuted other faiths. While he financed the building of Buddhist temples and stupas **(STOOP-uhz)** (domed shrines), government aid was distributed to all religious groups. The king argued that "all sects deserve reverence. By thus acting a man exalts his own sect and at the same time does service to the sects of other people."[9] Ashoka styled himself "Beloved of the Gods," a semideity. The Mauryas created a political legacy of the universal emperor, a divinely sanctioned leader with a special role in the cosmic scheme of things.

Ashoka's successors were less able, and a half century after his death, the Mauryan Empire collapsed, the mounting costs of governing a large empire through a centralized bureaucracy having drained the treasury. The Mauryan Empire's demise set a political pattern different from China, where long periods of unity were the norm. In India, periods of unity were relatively brief, followed by prolonged fragmentation. But Indians possessed a strong sense of cultural unity and loyalty to the social order, including the family and caste, rather than to the state.

[8] Quoted in Rhoads Murphy, *A History of Asia*, 4th ed. (New York: HarperCollins, 2003), 74.
[9] Quoted in Lucille Schulberg, *Historic India* (New York: Time-Life Books, 1968), 80.

Borromeo/Art Resource, NY

ASHOKA COLUMN This 32-foot-tall sandstone column, erected in northeast India around 240 B.C.E., weighs 50 tons. The inscriptions on the pillar outline Ashoka's achievements and offer advice on how citizens of the empire should behave.

MAKE SURE YOU UNDERSTAND THESE KEY POINTS BEFORE MOVING ON

- New spiritual movements within Hinduism, such as yoga and Vedanta, challenged priestly control and emphasized the goal of escaping the ego.
- Jainism and Buddhism split off from Hinduism, but only Buddhism, which offered guidelines for achieving nirvana, gained wide appeal.
- After Alexander's retreat, Chandragupta established the first imperial Indian state, the centralized, autocratic Mauryan Empire, which included the Indus and Ganges Basins.
- King Ashoka, Chandragupta's grandson, became a pacifist convert to Buddhism, which he helped to spread to Sri Lanka, Southeast Asia, and Afghanistan.

South and Central Asia After the Mauryas

What were some of the ways in which Classical India connected with and influenced the world beyond South Asia?

The Maurya collapse in the early second century B.C.E. launched five hundred years of political fragmentation before the rise of the next empire, that of the Guptas. These centuries saw increasing contact between India and the outside world, with Indian cultural influence, especially Buddhism, spreading into Central Asia. Various Central and West Asian peoples swept into northwestern India, conquering the Indus Valley and mixing with local peoples, who eventually absorbed the invaders and their ways. Substantial foreign trade and Buddhist missions to neighboring societies also occurred.

Indians and Central Asians

India maintained constant relations with Central Asia, the area stretching from Russia eastward to China's borders. The Turkestan region north of India, where many people spoke Turkish languages, served as a key contact zone for networks stretching east to China, south to India, and west to Persia and Russia. As trade between China and western Asia increased, cities sprouted along the overland route (known as the Silk Road) through Turkestan, whose commerce was dominated by Sogdians **(SAHG-dee-uhns)**, Persian-speaking Zoroastrians or Buddhists with a written language and literature. A Chinese traveler described the major Sogdian city, Samarkand **(SAM-uhr-kand)**, as "a great commercial entrepot, very fertile, abounding in trees and flowers, Its inhabitants skilled craftsmen, smart and energetic."[10]

Various Central Asian pastoralists, unable to penetrate China's defenses or pressured by Chinese expansion, moved westward, including the Huns, who developed the most effective weapon of the day, a reflex bow. Attacks by horseback-riding Huns pushed various peoples into Europe. Some Huns followed into southern Russia and Hungary and in the fourth and fifth centuries C.E. Huns invaded the weakened Roman Empire (see Chapter 8).

Diverse Central and West Asian peoples migrated through the mountain ranges into northwest India, introducing new cultural influences. Hellenistic Bactria in Afghanistan was a crossroads where Greek, Persian, and Indian cultures met and mixed; Bactrian invaders reintroduced Greek influence to the Indus Basin, inspiring a Greek- and Roman-influenced form of Buddhist painting and sculpture. Eventually they became absorbed into the broad fold of Indian society.

In 50 C.E. the **Kushans (KOO-shans)** from Central Asia conquered much of northwest India while constructing an empire also encompassing Afghanistan and many Silk Road cities. They promoted extensive trade between India and China, the Middle East, and the eastern Mediterranean and encouraged the mix of Indian and Greco-Roman culture. Some Kushan leaders embraced Buddhism and spread the religion into Central Asia, from which it then diffused to China. The Kushan king Kanishka **(ka-NISH-ka)** (r. 78–144 C.E.) patronized artists, writers, poets, and musicians and tolerated all religions. Like invaders before them, the Kushans intermarried with local people, enhancing the hybrid character of northwestern India's culture. When Kushan rule ended in 250, a patchwork of competing states emerged in north India.

South India and Sri Lanka

Northwestern India's political instability was duplicated elsewhere, with frequent warfare between competing states. Some southern states flourished from maritime trade linking China to the Persian Gulf, and south India gained renown as far west as Greece and Rome for products such as gold. Both south India and the large island of Sri Lanka saw considerable political and cultural development. North Indian culture, including Aryan myths, values, rituals, and divine kingship, appealed to south Indian rulers. South Indians also adopted the caste system, although less rigidly than northerners.

Yet Aryan ideas did not destroy southern regional traditions. For example, the Dravidian-speaking Tamils, who inhabit India's southeastern corner, developed a vigorous cultural tradition esteeming poetry. Their temple-filled mountain city of Madurai **(made-uh-RYE)** had several colleges and became a major center of Hinduism, literature, and education. A second century C.E. Tamil poem describes Madurai's religious function and devout people:

> *The great and famous city of Madurai, Is like the lotus flower of God Vishnu. Its streets are the petals of the flower. God Shiva's temple is the center. The citizens are the plentiful pollen; The poor, the crowding beetles. And in Madurai, we wake to the chanting of the four Vedas, Sacred sculptures from the tongue of Brahma, born of the lotus flower.*[11]

Just south of India, on Sri Lanka (Ceylon), a very different society emerged. As Indian migrants intermarried with local people, they formed kingdoms and eventually produced the Sinhalese **(sin-huh-LEEZ)** society. Sri Lanka became a trading hub between Southeast Asia and the Middle East. In the first century B.C.E. the Sinhalese, to improve their rice growing, also began constructing one of world history's most

Kushans An Indo-European people from Central Asia who conquered much of northwest India and western parts of the Ganges Basin, constructing an empire that also encompassed Afghanistan and parts of Central Asia.

[10]Xuan Zang, quoted in David Christian, *A History of Russia, Central Asia, and Mongolia*, vol. 1 (Malden, MA: Blackwell, 1998), 254.
[11]From McNaughton, *Light from East*, 377.

intricate irrigation systems, building canals dozens of miles long and artificial lakes covering thousands of acres, a water control engineering feat requiring complex hydraulic technology and comparable to that of ancient China and Mesopotamia. During Ashoka's reign, Buddhist missionaries converted most Sri Lankans, and the Sinhalese came to view themselves as protectors of Buddhism. Hindu Tamils also crossed the narrow straits and settled the northern part of the island. For the next two millennia, Sri Lanka's Sinhalese Buddhist and Tamil Hindu societies coexisted, sometimes uneasily.

Indian Encounters with the Afro-Eurasian World

The post-Maurya era stands out for its unprecedented communication with other societies and connection to exchange networks. Indeed, India became a central hub in a vast maritime trade system stretching from the Roman-dominated Mediterranean Basin through Egypt and the Red Sea to southern Asia, Southeast Asia, and southern China. Even Mediterranean merchants visited India. India dispatched spices, cloth, silks, ivory, sandalwood, furniture, and art works to the Roman Empire for gold coins, silver, copper, tin, lead, and wine. The Roman writer Pliny **(PLIN-ee)** claimed that importing Indian goods cost the Roman treasury dearly. Around 80 C.E. a Greek handbook for merchants interested in trade with India described sailing routes and India's products and culture. The author recommended a south Indian port offering a large quantity of cinnamon and pepper as well as multicolored textiles, tin, copper, gems, diamonds, sapphires, fine-quality pearls, ivory, and Chinese silk. Various Indian words were incorporated into the Greek language, especially for spices such as ginger and foods like rice.

China-India trade continued along the Silk Road, while many Indian traders traveled to Southeast Asia. Expanding foreign and domestic trade brought much wealth to India's commercial and artisan castes, and gold coins fostered banking and financial houses. But this commercial dynamism mostly occurred in cities. Foreign products did not often reach villages, where the bartering of services between farmers, craftsmen, and servants defined social and economic relations.

Theravada ("Teachings of the Elders") One of the two main branches of Buddhism, the other being Mahayana, that arose just before the Common Era. Theravada remained closer to the Buddha's original vision.

Mahayana ("the Greater Vehicle" to salvation) One of the two main branches of Buddhism; a more popularized form of Buddhist belief and practice than Theravada. Mahayana Buddhism tended to make Buddha into a god and also developed the notion of the bodhisattva.

bodhisattva ("one who has the essence of Buddhahood") A loving and ever compassionate "saint" who has postponed his or her own attainment of nirvana to help others find salvation through liberation from birth and rebirth.

Indian philosophy and religious ideas reached foreign audiences. Some Indian philosophers may have visited western Asia, where their ideas may have influenced some religious movements. The Buddhist idea of monasticism also expanded from India to western Asia, perhaps inspiring the rise of Christian monasticism. Buddhist ideas and art also spread into Central Asia's Silk Road cities. Buddhist converts, such as the Chinese monk Faxian **(fah-shee-en) (Fa-hsien)**, ventured to India to study Buddhism. Thus, like Hellenistic Greek culture throughout the eastern Mediterranean and western Asia, Indian cultural influence flowed out to the world.

Religious Changes in South Asia

During the post-Mauryan centuries in India, Buddhism divided and declined, Hinduism resurged, and both Christianity and Judaism arrived. Increasingly two major schools with competing visions split Buddhism in the two centuries preceding the Common Era. Some reformers criticized the religion as being remote from the real world, atheistic in its rejection of a god, excessively individualistic, requiring too much self-discipline, and denying any afterlife. During the Kushan domination of northern India, the division into two schools, the mainstream Theravada **(TEAR-eh-vah-duh)** and the reformist Mahayana **(MAH-HAH-YAH-nah)**, became complete.

Theravada ("Teachings of the Elders") remained closer to Buddha's original vision and clearly descended from Ashoka's Buddhism. To its followers the Buddha was not a god but rather a human teacher. Since the ever-changing universe had no supreme being or gods, people could only take refuge in the wise and compassionate Buddha, his teachings, and the community of monks who maintained them. Each believer was responsible for acquiring merit through devotion, meditation, and good works, such as feeding monks or supporting a temple. The only sure way to end rebirth and reach nirvana was to become a monk and abide by strict monastic rules, and many men did so for at least a few years.

The other school, **Mahayana** ("the Greater Vehicle" to salvation), was a more popularized and less demanding form of belief and practice. Mahayana developed many sects, most considering the Buddha a god. Mahayana followers found comfort in devotion to a loving deity (Buddha) and stressed charity and good works as paths toward salvation. A central concept is the **bodhisattva** **(boe-dih-SUT-vuh)** ("one who has the essence of Buddhahood"), a loving and compassionate "saint" who has died but has postponed his or her own attainment of nirvana to help others find salvation. In China, Mahayanists converted nirvana into an appealing heaven, with the wicked assigned to a terrifying hell. Perhaps Mahayana ideas about achieving salvation with the help of a saint contributed to Hebrew concepts of a messiah, or the reverse. Perhaps Persian Zoroastrianism influenced both Mahayana Buddhism and Christianity.

Although several Buddhist monastic orders and some believers remained, Indian Buddhism gradually assimilated into Hinduism. Perhaps Buddhism was too pessimistic, portraying life as suffering in contrast to many life-affirming Hindu gods. But Buddhism flourished abroad by providing spiritual support in times of rapid political change or instability.

MAP 5.2 THE SPREAD OF BUDDHISM IN ASIA, 100–800 C.E. Buddhism originated in what is today Nepal and became a major religion in India during the Classical period. From India it spread into Central Asia, China, Korea, Japan, and Southeast Asia as far east as Java.

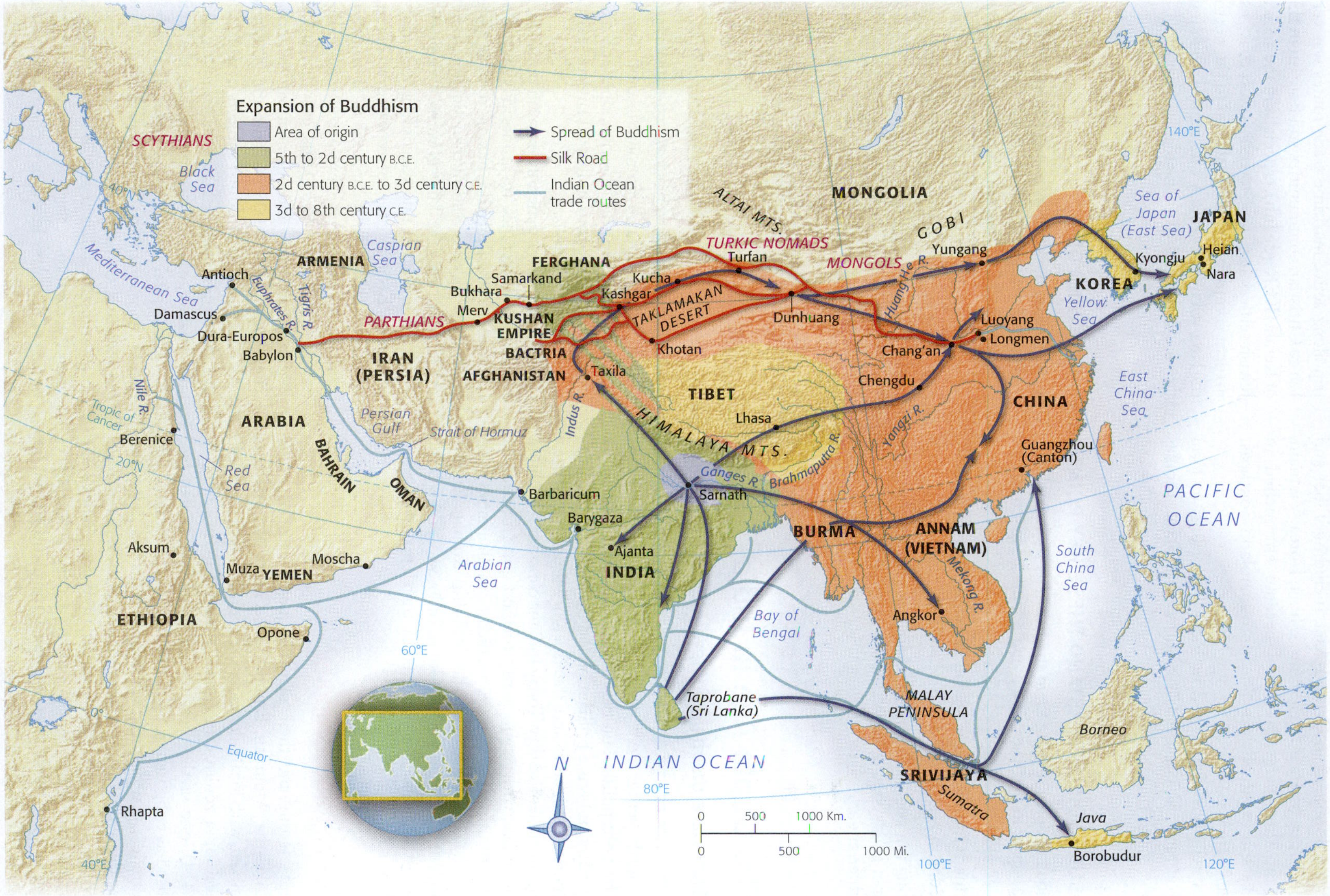

It spread along the trade routes, accommodating itself to local traditions and faiths. The Mahayana school eventually became dominant in Central Asia, including Tibet and Mongolia, from where it filtered into China, Korea, Vietnam, and Japan. The Theravada school became entrenched in Sri Lanka and eventually expanded into mainland Southeast Asia (see Map 5.2).

New religions also arrived in India. According to local legends, around 52 C.E. the Christian apostle Saint Thomas established Christian churches and attracted followers along southwestern India's Malabar **(MAL-uh-bahr)** coast. Such a trip along active maritime trade routes was certainly possible. Large Christian communities still flourish in the Malabar state of Kerala **(KER-uh-luh)**, especially in the ancient coastal ports. Jewish settlers also came to India's west coast, establishing permanent communities in Kerala and to the north at Bombay. In the later twentieth century C.E., many Indian Jews emigrated to the new Jewish state of Israel.

MAKE SURE YOU UNDERSTAND THESE KEY POINTS BEFORE MOVING ON

- **Various peoples, among them the Kushans from Central Asia, invaded northwest India and adopted aspects of Indian culture.**
- **Northern Indian culture spread to the south, and Buddhism was adopted in Sri Lanka.**
- **During the post-Mauryan era, there was great demand for Indian goods among traders from western Asia and the Mediterranean.**
- **Buddhism declined in popularity in India as Hinduism adopted many of its ideas, but it spread to Central Asia, China, and Southeast Asia, where it flourished.**

The Gupta Age in India

What were the main achievements of the Gupta era?

In the fourth century C.E. the great Gupta **(GOOP-tuh)** Empire brought political unity to India once again. The Gupta era (320–550 C.E.) was a brilliant period that saw the assimilation of both immigrants and the foreign cultural influences, reshaping an ancient society. Today Indians consider the Gupta their golden age, with its prosperity, tolerant government, and major contributions in science, medicine, mathematics, and literature. In comparison with the declining Roman Empire and turbulent post-Han China, Gupta India was perhaps the world's most dynamic society, visited by travelers and pilgrims from all over Asia.

Government and Economy

The Gupta family and their allies conquered most of north India. Like the Mauryan Empire, the Gupta Empire was decentralized, with local rulers acknowledging Gupta overlordship. The Gupta zenith came under King Chandra Gupta II (r. 375–414), one of the most revered figures in Indian history, praised as enlightened, bold, and resourceful. Internal and external trade, the widespread use of gold and silver coins, and highly productive agriculture fostered prosperity. India increasingly became the world's textile center, producing fabrics like linen, wool, and cotton; it also produced pepper and spices for export to the Middle East, Europe, China, and Indonesia. Although the Gupta government favored merchants and farmers, the rulers, like the Mauryas, operated all metal and salt mines as well as various industrial enterprises such as arms factories and textile mills.

Gupta Indians generally enjoyed domestic peace, personal freedom, and tolerance for minority views. One fifth-century Chinese Buddhist pilgrim, Faxian, was impressed by the prosperity, state services, and humane justice system: "The people are very well off. The king governs without corporal punishment. Criminals are fined according to circumstances, lightly or heavily. Even in cases of repeated rebellion, they only cut off the right hand. The people kill no living thing."[12] The rulers promoted a Hindu revival but permitted no official discrimination against Buddhists or Jains, even helping to build a great Buddhist monastery and university at Nalanda **(na-LAN-da)**, where more than 10,000 students and 2000 teachers from all over Asia explored Buddhist subjects as well as logic, medicine, and Hindu philosophy. However, tolerance did not extend to untouchables, who still occupied a degraded status.

The capital city, Patna, boasted hospitals providing free care to the poor and handicapped. A great university attracted ten thousand students, many from other Asian societies. One observer reported that he saw in Patna "the workshops thriving along the royal road, the river furrowed by boats, and maidens flirting with youths in the parks on the outskirts of town."[13]

[12]Quoted in John Keay, *India: A History* (New York: Atlantic Monthly Press, 2000), 145.

[13]Kalidasa, quoted in Auboyer, *Daily Life*, 117.

Gupta Society

Indian social patterns were never stagnant. As male authority became more dominant over time, women's status gradually declined throughout northern India. By Mauryan times women enjoyed fewer opportunities to pursue intellectual or religious leadership. The Mahabharata warned men not to put "confidence in a woman or a coward, a lazybones, a violent man, a self-promoter, a thief, much less an atheist."[14] However, patriarchy remained weaker in south India. Matrilineal kinship systems remain common in Kerala, and southern women often enjoyed more freedom than northern women. Hinduism in south India placed more emphasis than the north on goddess worship, perhaps giving women higher status. The *Kama Sutra*, a detailed sexual handbook written in the third century C.E., offered ideas about gender that seem almost modern, including a liberal approach to sexual freedom and a somewhat understanding approach to homosexuality.

However, in general the Gupta age was not golden for women. Brahmans imposed their rigid views on gender relations. The Code of Manu tied women to the patriarchal family, urging that "in childhood a female must be subject to her father, in youth to her husband, and when her lord is dead, to her sons; a woman must never be independent."[15] The code restricted women's property rights and recommended early marriage to preserve chastity. Girls commonly married well before puberty, after negotiations between the senior men of the two families involved. Widows could no longer remarry, and the ancient custom of sati **(suh-TEE)**, of wives joining their late husbands on the funeral pyre, became more widespread. Many Indian writers denounced it, since families often forced an unwilling wife to agree.

Gupta Science, Mathematics, and Culture

Intellectual and cultural pursuits flourished. Gupta India became the world's leading producer of scientific knowledge, planting some of the roots of modern science. The Guptas boasted of India's "nine gems," a group of knowledge producers that included one of the world's major astronomers, mathematicians, and physicists, Aryabhata **(AR-ya-BAH-ta)** (ca. 476–550), who taught that the earth was round, rotated on its own axis, and revolved around the sun as one of a family of planets. He also correctly analyzed lunar eclipses, calculated the moon's diameter and the earth's circumference, and precisely determined the solar year at 365.36 days. In verse, Aryabhata discussed physics, including the earth's rotation and the nature of gravity. Many of these insights did not spread outside India until centuries later.

Gupta innovations in mathematics compare to the invention in western Asia of the wheel and alphabet: all pathbreaking and revolutionary in their consequences. Aryabhata analyzed quadratic equations and the value of pi. The greatest Gupta

Werli Francois/Alamy

MOURNING THE BUDDHA'S DEATH This painting from a Nepal monastery presents the final moments of the Buddha's life.

[14]Quoted in Stephanie W. Jamison, *Sacrificed Wife/Sacrificer's Wife: Women, Ritual, and Hospitality in Ancient India* (New York: Oxford University Press, 1996), 13.

[15]Quoted in Barbara N. Ramusack, "Women in South and Southeast Asia," in *Restoring Women to History* (Bloomington, IN: Organization of American Historians, 1988), 9.

achievements were the concept of zero and the decimal system. Indians probably chose 10 as a base number because it corresponded to the number of fingers. Now individual numbers were needed only for 0 through 9. By contrast, for the ancient Greeks each 8 in 888 was different. And for the Romans, 888 was written as DCCCLXXXVIII, complicating multiplication and division. The simple and logical Indian numbering system eventually reached the Middle East and later, through the Arabs, Europe. Only in the fifteenth century, a thousand years after Gupta times, did European scientists and mathematicians adopt "Arabic" numerals, opening the door to modern science and mathematics.

Remarkably creative in industrial chemistry, Gupta Indians made soap and cement, produced the world's finest tempered steel, and transformed sugar-cane juice into granulated crystals for easy storing or shipping. Europeans later adopted India's fine dyes and fabrics; cotton, calico, and cashmere are all Indian words. Indians also enjoyed a long tradition of medicine. Yoga practitioners promoted mental and spiritual discipline, studying posture, breath control, and pulse regulation, and Gupta physicians discovered the spinal cord's function, sketched out the nervous system structure, and expanded knowledge of physiology and herbal medicines. Gupta India had the world's best medical system, drugs, and therapeutic methods. Doctors sterilized wounds, did Caesarian deliveries, developed plastic surgery, and vaccinated patients against smallpox.

Gupta literature and performing arts flourished. Writing mostly in Sanskrit, writers produced religious works, poetry, and prose. The most popular writer, Kalidasa **(kahl-i-DACE-uh)** (ca. 400–455), rendered ancient legends and popular tales into drama and lyrics. Kalidasa's famous poem, "The Cloud Messengers," uses a passing cloud surveying the panoramic landscape to capture the heartache of lovers separated by a vast distance: "I see your body in the sinuous creeper, your gaze in the startled eyes of deer, your cheek in the moon, your hair in the plumage of peacocks, and in the tiny ripples of the river I see your sidelong glances."[16] Theater, music, and dance established the basis for the Indian performing arts of today. Imported from western Asia, instruments such as the lute, or vina **(VEE-nuh)**, and zither, or sitar **(si-TAHR)**, became popular. Improvisational instrumental pieces known as ragas **(RAHG-uhz)** inspired religious and philosophical contemplation. Gupta artists also produced religious sculptures and paintings, especially on cave or temple walls.

Decline of the Guptas

Central Asian invaders ended Gupta rule. In the fifth century C.E. Huns conquered part of northwestern India. Gupta power held them off, but the effort depleted the treasury, and other Central Asians followed the Huns into north India. When the Guptas collapsed, the varied Hindu states could not unite, and India entered a period of fragmentation, political instability, and frequent warfare that persisted for several centuries and left Indians open to conquest by Muslim peoples.

Yet India remained part of the wider world. Seafarers from the southeastern coast made piratical raids deep into Southeast Asia, while the maritime trade linking southern India with Southeast Asia and China intensified dramatically. Cargo-laden Indian fleets sailed with the monsoon winds far to the east.

MAKE SURE YOU UNDERSTAND THESE KEY POINTS BEFORE MOVING ON

- **Under the decentralized Gupta Empire, based in northern India, the government attained prosperity while pursuing religious tolerance.**
- **During the Gupta era, science, mathematics, literature, and the arts all thrived.**
- **The Guptas formulated the concept of zero, which made the decimal system possible and made mathematical computation infinitely more powerful.**
- **The Gupta Empire was greatly weakened by Hun invasion, and soon thereafter it collapsed and other Central Asian groups invaded India.**

The Development of Southeast Asian Societies

How did Southeast Asians blend indigenous and foreign influences to create unique societies?

In the tropical lands east of India and south of China, many societies borrowed political, religious, and cultural ideas from the two neighboring regions, although the impact of these ideas varied greatly. Southeast Asian states were products of indigenous as well as outside forces. Most of the early Southeast Asian societies were centered on coastal plains and in river valleys, where they flourished from both productive agriculture and extensive foreign trade and established enduring patterns in government, religion, and economics.

[16]Quoted in A. L. Basham, *The Wonder That Was India: A Survey of the History and Culture of the Indian Sub-continent Before the Coming of the Muslims*, 3rd. rev. ed. (New Delhi: Rupa and Company, 1967), 420.

Austronesian Seafaring, Trade, and Migrations

Seafaring and maritime trade were major forces in the development of some Southeast Asian societies. One group of Austronesians **(AW-stroh-NEE-zhuhns)**, the Malays **(muh-LAYZ)**, enjoyed a strategic position for maritime commerce and cultural mixing. The Straits of Melaka **(muh-LAK-uh)**, between Sumatra **(soo-MAH-tra)** and Malaya **(muh-LAY-a)**, was a crossroads through which peoples, cultures, and trade passed, some taking root. These lands also provided gold, tin, spices, and forest products, some traded as far west as Rome. The prevailing climatic patterns in the South China Sea and Indian Ocean allowed ships sailing southwest and southeast to meet in the straits, where their goods could be exchanged.

Early in the Common Era small Malay trading states in the Malay Peninsula and Sumatra prospered, like the Phoenicians and Greeks, from maritime trade to distant shores. In the third century B.C.E., Malay ships visited China using a sail that may have inspired the revolutionary four-sided lateen **(luh-TEEN)** sail used later by Arabs and Polynesians, allowing ships to sail directly into the wind. Malays opened the maritime trade between China and India by carrying cinnamon grown on the China coast across the Indian Ocean to India and Sri Lanka. Some Austronesian sailors returned with Indian ideas about government and religion. Indonesians also introduced Southeast Asian foods (especially bananas and rice), outrigger canoes, and musical instruments (including the xylophone) to East Africa.

Between the fourth and sixth centuries C.E., instability in Central Asia disrupted the overland Silk Road, making the Indian Ocean connection linking China, India, and the Middle East more crucial. While this change benefited some Southeast Asians, the voyages held many dangers. The Chinese Buddhist pilgrim Faxian, sailing from Sri Lanka to Sumatra in 414 C.E., reported that he "set sail on a large merchant ship which carried about two hundred passengers. A small boat trailed behind, for use in case the large vessel should be wrecked, as sailing on this sea was most hazardous. [We] were caught up in a typhoon [which] lasted for thirteen days. That sea is [also] infested with pirates."[17]

Austronesian seafaring also led to migration. Between 100 and 700 C.E. some Indonesians migrated across the Indian Ocean to settle on the large island of Madagascar **(mad-uh-GAS-kuhr)**, off Africa's southeast coast. Today their descendants account for the majority of the island's population and speak Austronesian languages. Beginning in ancient times, other Austronesians moved from Southeast Asia into the western Pacific. Their descendants, the Polynesians **(pahl-uh-NEE-zhuhns)** and Micronesians **(my-kruh-NEE-zhuhns)**, settled the central and eastern Pacific islands (see Chapter 9). The Marianas **(MAR-ee-AN-uhz)**, including the islands of Guam and Saipan, may have been settled directly by Austronesians sailing east from the Philippines and possibly Taiwan between 1500 and 1000 B.C.E. As a result of these movements, Austronesian-speaking societies stretched thousands of miles from Madagascar eastward through Indonesia and the Philippines to Hawaii and Easter Island in eastern Polynesia.

Indianization and Early Mainland States

Various states developed on the Southeast Asian mainland. The most populous societies emerged along the fertile coastal plains or in the great river valleys like the Mekong and Red, where irrigated rice cultivation was possible, providing a highly productive and labor-intensive economic mainstay that was sustainable for generations. By promoting cooperation, this economy fostered centralized kingdoms such as Van Lang in northern Vietnam, which was ruled through a landed aristocracy who controlled rice-growing estates worked by peasants. By 500 B.C.E. a few small bronze- and iron-using states emerged, and during the third century B.C.E. the earliest cities

Kimberley Coole/Getty Images

RELIEF OF INDONESIAN SHIP The Indonesians were skilled mariners. This rock carving, from a Buddhist temple in central Java, depicts a sailing vessel of the type commonly used by Indonesian traders in the Indian Ocean and South China Sea in this era. These ships also carried Indonesian colonists to East Africa and Madagascar.

[17]From Harry J. Benda and John A. Larkin, eds., *The World of Southeast Asia: Selected Historical Readings* (New York: Harper and Row, 1967), 3–4.

with monumental architecture appeared. At Co Loa, near modern Hanoi, King An Duong built a huge citadel surrounded by a wall 5 miles long and 10 yards wide. Urban societies also emerged among peoples such as the Khmers **(kuh-MEERZ)** (Cambodians).

Influences from China and India also generated change. Han China conquered northern Vietnam, imposing a colonial rule that endured for a millennium (111 B.C.E.–939 C.E.) and spreading many Chinese cultural patterns. Chinese traders visited many Southeast Asian societies over the centuries. Elsewhere Indian influence fostered a very different society. Around two millennia ago, Indian traders and brahman priests began traveling the oceanic trade routes. They brought with them Indian concepts of religion, government, and the arts and settled in some states, marrying into or becoming advisors to influential families. Furthermore, Southeast Asian merchants and sailors visiting India returned with Indian ideas.

Indianization, a mixing of Indian with indigenous ideas, influenced many Southeast Asian societies about the same time as Classical Greco-Roman culture spread around the Mediterranean. For a millennium, Southeast Asian peoples such as the Khmers in the Mekong Basin, the Chams along Vietnam's central coast, and the Javanese **(JAH-vuh-NEEZ)** on the fertile island of Java remained connected to India, adapting Indian writing systems to local spoken languages. Mahayana Buddhism and Hinduism became popular, especially among the upper classes, fusing with indigenous animisms that emphasized communicating with spiritual forces. Many Southeast Asians blended outside and local religions rather than following one exclusively. In politics, Southeast Asian rulers became powerful kings claiming to possess supernatural powers and religious sanction, which made their positions difficult to challenge.

However, although borrowing helped shape Southeast Asians, they also took outside ideas that they wanted and adapted them to their own cultures, creating a distinctive synthesis. In this they followed a similar pattern as the Japanese and western Europeans. For example, the Hindu and Buddhist architecture and temples of Burma, Cambodia, or Java differed substantially from the South Asian models as well as from each other.

Funan, Zhenla, and Champa

Over time productive agriculture, maritime commerce, and Indianization fostered stronger mainland states. Between 75 and 550 C.E. Funan **(FOO-nan)**, populated by Khmer and some Austronesians, flourished in the fertile Mekong Delta of southern Vietnam. Funan traded with China, valued literacy, built complex irrigation systems to turn swamps into productive agricultural land, and apparently had some authority over Cambodia and southern Thailand (see Map 5.3). A Chinese envoy in the third century reported that the Funan king "gave three or four audiences [each day]. Foreigners and subjects offered him presents of bananas, sugar cane, turtles, and birds.... The king, when he travels rides an elephant."[18] Trade goods from as far away as Rome, Arabia, Central Asia, and perhaps East Africa have been found in Funan's ruins, and merchants from various countries (including India and China) lived in the major port city. Another Khmer state, Zhenla, in the middle Mekong Basin, became prominent in the fifth century when Funan declined.

Indianization The process by which Indian ideas spread into and influenced many Southeast Asian societies; a mixing of Indian with indigenous ideas.

MAP 5.3 FUNAN AND ITS NEIGHBORS The first large mainland Southeast Asian states emerged during the Classical period. The major states included Vietnam, which became a Chinese colony in the second century B.C.E., Funan, Zhenla, and Champa.

Meanwhile, the coastal, Austronesian-speaking Cham people of central Vietnam formed several Indianized states known collectively as Champa **(CHAM-pa)**, which tried to control the coastal commerce between China and Southeast Asia. The strongly Hindu Chams gained renown as sailors, merchants, and sometimes pirates, frequently fighting the Vietnamese pushing southward. The Vietnamese finally conquered much of Champa in 1471.

Vietnam and Chinese Colonization

China's final conquest and annexation of Vietnam in 111 B.C.E. ended the kingdom's independence. The Chinese policy was to assimilate the Vietnamese and implant Chinese values,

[18]Quoted in Lawrence Palmer Briggs, *The Ancient Khmer Empire* (Philadelphia: American Philosophical Society, 1951), 22, 29.

PROFILE

The Trung Sisters, Vietnamese Rebels

Some of the major anti-Chinese rebellions in Vietnam were led by women such as the Trung Sisters in 39 C.E. Even after two thousand years, the Vietnamese honor the two sisters and their martyrdom with annual ceremonies at cult shrines dedicated to their memory. Their revolt was prompted by Chinese attempts to raise taxes and consolidate their control over the indigenous landed aristocracy. However, our knowledge of the two sisters is limited. Some historians consider them semimythical rather than flesh and blood. The Trung Sisters became enshrined in images of brave and beautiful sword-bearing women mounted on elephants, leading their troops against the Chinese.

The sisters are believed to have been daughters of a prominent landowning family from near Hanoi. The older sister, Trung Trac, had married a member of another aristocratic family. When her husband protested an increase in taxes, he was apparently executed. The spirited sisters then sparked a rebellion that rapidly spread throughout the country and involved both the elite and the peasantry. With local Chinese officials in retreat, her followers declared Trung Trac queen of a newly independent country. The sisters abolished taxes, but, as traditionalists, they also sought to restore the pre-Chinese order dominated by landed aristocrats and protect local autonomy. Despite their aristocratic agenda, the common people joined the revolt because of their hostility to the authoritarian rule of the Chinese governors.

THE TRUNG SISTERS This painting by a Vietnamese artist shows the Trung Sisters riding into battle on war elephants against the Chinese.

Han dynasty rulers, unwilling to see this valuable part of their empire secede, dispatched their most able general and his army to destroy the rebellion. As the fighting and repression grew, most of the sisters' upper-class supporters abandoned their cause. Eventually their remaining forces were defeated in 41 C.E., and the sisters either committed suicide or were captured and executed. China now intensified its direct control of Vietnam and launched a more deliberate assimilation policy to integrate Vietnam politically into China proper.

Although their revolt failed, the Trung Sisters established a model for later rebels, some of them also women. Another famous anticolonial leader, the nineteen-year-old Lady Trieu in the third century C.E., demonstrated a similar commitment. When advised to marry rather than fight, she replied: "I want to ride the storm, tread the dangerous waves, win back the fatherland and destroy the yoke of slavery. I don't want to bow down my head working as a simple housewife." The Lady Trieu seems an almost modern figure in her patriotic and social defiance. In the nineteenth and twentieth centuries, Vietnamese women inspired by the Trung Sisters and Lady Trieu took up arms alongside men to fight oppressive governments and invading forces, including the French and later Americans.

THINKING ABOUT THE PROFILE

1. What sparked the rebellion led by the Trung Sisters?
2. What does the experience of the Trung Sisters tell us about Vietnamese society under Chinese rule and the role of women in that society?

Note: Quotation is from Thomas Hodgkin, *Vietnam: The Revolutionary Path* (New York: St. Martin's, 1981), 22.

customs, and institutions, with the result that China's patriarchal family system, written language, and political ideas sank deep roots. At the same time, most Vietnamese adopted Chinese philosophies and religions like Confucianism, Daoism, and Mahayana Buddhism but mixed them with earlier ancestor and spirit worship.

While the Vietnamese adopted many Chinese patterns, they resisted cultural assimilation and sustained a hatred of Chinese rule. The survival of Vietnamese identity, language, and many customs during a millennium of colonialism constituted an unparalleled display of national determination. Many revolts, some led by women, punctuated the colonial period, all of them well remembered today as symbols of patriotism (see Profile: The Trung Sisters, Vietnamese Rebels). Chinese officials harshly retaliated: "At every stream, cave, marketplace, everywhere there is stubbornness. Repression is necessary."[19] A long history of resistance to the Chinese, a sense of nationhood, and a desire for independence also helped the Vietnamese resist assimilation. Chinese and later foreign conquerors such as the French in the modern era found that they had to conquer each village, one by one. This history of resistance to foreign invaders meant frequent warfare. A Vietnamese Buddhist poet described the results: "War, no end to it, people scattered in all directions. How can a man keep his mind off it? The winds dark, the rains violent year after year, laying waste the land, over and over."[20] The Vietnamese eventually regained independence from China in the tenth century.

Economies, Societies, and Cultures

Despite the great differences between Southeast Asian societies, there were many commonalities. Most of the larger states had multiethnic populations, including foreign merchants. Chinese envoys described Funan's walled cities, palaces, and people who ate with silver utensils; paid their taxes with gold, silver, perfumes, and pearls; had many books and maintained well-kept archives; and used an Indian writing system. But although commerce was common, most Southeast Asians were farmers and fishermen living in self-sufficient villages held together by kinship and cooperation for mutual survival.

Many Southeast Asian family systems contrasted with those in China or India. While the Vietnamese followed a patriarchal pattern like China, others developed flexible systems incorporating both paternal and maternal kin. The Chams were matrilineal, and both men and women could have more than one spouse. In Southeast Asia women generally enjoyed a higher status and played a more active public role than they did in China, India, the Middle East, and Europe, dominating most village markets. The Southeast Asian pattern of blending religions and cultures, along with extensive trade, made Southeast Asian societies distinctive.

MAKE SURE YOU UNDERSTAND THESE KEY POINTS BEFORE MOVING ON

- **The lands bordering the Straits of Melaka were rich in natural resources, and their peoples engaged in wide-ranging maritime trade.**
- **Austronesians settled over a wide area, from Madagascar, off the coast of Africa, to the Pacific islands of Polynesia.**
- **Southeast Asians were influenced by both Chinese and Indian culture, but they retained distinct aspects of their native cultures.**
- **Though different from each other, Southeast Asian societies tended to be multiethnic and able to blend diverse elements into cultural unity.**

[19]Quoted in Keith Taylor, "The Rise of Dai Viet and the Establishment of Thanglong," in *Explorations in Early Southeast Asian History: The Origins of Southeast Asian Statecraft*, ed. Kenneth R. Hall and John K. Whitmore (Ann Arbor: University of Michigan Center for South and Southeast Asian Studies, 1976), 153.

[20]From Nguyen Ngoc Bich, ed., *A Thousand Years of Vietnamese Poetry* (New York: Knopf, 1975), 89.

CHAPTER SUMMARY

The Classical period saw dramatic changes in India and Southeast Asia, some generated by outside influences such as migration and long-distance trade. India developed unique social systems and religious ideas. For example, the caste system divided the population into categories based on descent, and Hinduism flowered into various schools of speculative thought. Buddhism challenged both Hinduism and the caste system in the first millennium B.C.E. Hinduism and Buddhism shared many beliefs, such as reincarnation and karma, but differed in their conception of gods and the path to ending reincarnation.

India's political, economic, and intellectual life also changed. The Mauryan Empire united India, and under Ashoka the empire reflected humane and peaceful Buddhist values. The Classical period also saw the forging of deeper cultural and trade connections between India and other regions, and many peoples migrated into the country from Central Asia.

Buddhism spread into both Central and Southeast Asia, becoming a major world religion. During the Gupta golden age, Indians achieved new knowledge in science and mathematics that later influenced the Middle East and Europe.

The states that emerged in Southeast Asia were based on maritime trade, rice agriculture, and the blending of local and foreign influences. The Austronesian sailors fostered trade networks over vast distances, and kingdoms arose in Cambodia and Vietnam. Indian religious, political, and cultural ideas had a great impact in many parts of the region, and China's conquest of Vietnam spread Chinese influence.

KEY TERMS

Brahman (p. 101)
Vedanta (p. 102)
Jainism (p. 102)
Buddhism (p. 103)
nirvana (p. 104)
monasticism (p. 104)
Kushans (p. 107)
Theravada (p. 108)
Mahayana (p. 108)
bodhisattva (p. 108)
Indianization (p. 114)

6 Eurasian Connections and New Traditions in East Asia, 600 B.C.E.–600 C.E.

Giorgio Lotti/Mondadori Portfolio via Getty Images

FRESCO FROM MOGAO CAVES The Mogao Caves, situated along the Silk Road in western China, contain many frescoes reflecting Silk Road life and the spread of Buddhism into the region. This fresco, painted in the third century C.E., shows the Buddha meditating, flanked by two bodhisattvas holding lotus flowers and other goods.

After the Han had sent its envoys to open up communications with the state of Da Xia [in today's Afghanistan], all the barbarians of the distant west craned their necks to the east and longed to catch a glimpse of China.

—Chinese diplomat Zhang Qian, reported by historian Sima Qian, CA. 100 B.C.E.[1]

In 138 B.C.E. the Chinese emperor, Wu Di **(woo tee)**, sought contact with a Central Asian group, the Yuezhi **(yueh-chih)**, to forge an alliance against their mutual enemy, the Xiongnu **(SHE-OONG-noo)**, Central Asians threatening China. An imperial court attendant, Zhang Qian **(jahng chee-YEN)**, volunteered to undertake the dangerous diplomatic mission. A strong man known for his generosity and ability to make friends with non-Chinese, Zhang commenced the journey west with only a small escort. He was captured by the Xiongnu and held prisoner for ten years but finally escaped. He and his party continued west, following a route later known as one of the world's great trade networks: the Silk Road. Zhang crossed the Pamir **(pah-MEER)** Mountains, visiting lands in Afghanistan and Turkestan, whose people already avidly imported Chinese silk (hence the name Silk Road). Although his diplomatic mission failed, after twelve years away Zhang brought back useful products, including the grape, and informed Wu Di about the lands to the west.

For over a millennium after Zhang's journey, China connected with the lands much farther west through overland trade and travel through Central Asia. Every year merchants gathered just outside the walls of the Chinese city and often capital, Chang'an **(CHAHNG-ahn)** (today's Xian **[SEE-ahn]**), to form a caravan, loading metals, ceramics, spices, scrolls of paintings, seeds, and above all piles of silk on their horses and donkeys. These veteran Chinese and Central Asian travelers understood the dangers ahead, including blinding sandstorms and ruthless bandits, but also the fabulous profits to be made. After traveling west for weeks, skirting the Great Wall, at the last Chinese outpost, the Jade Gate, they exchanged horses and donkeys for camels, better suited to journeys through harsh deserts. After weeks of travel across waterless wastes, the caravan crossed the snow-covered Pamir Mountains. Finally, several thousand miles from Chang'an, the travelers arrived at Turkestan cities to trade or sell their precious commodities. Much of this cargo was then sent on to India, western Asia, and southern Europe. In spite of great distances and immense geographical barriers, this vast network tied China to the world beyond and made peoples as far west as Rome aware of China.

China and its neighbors, Korea and Japan, being a great distance from the Middle East, India, and Europe, fostered unique technologies, governments, religions, and philosophies. But peoples, ideas, and commercial goods traveling the trade networks from Central Asia and India also influenced East Asians. The classical blossoming of East Asian cultures established frameworks for these societies in the following centuries.

[1]*Records of the Historian: Chapters from the Shih Chi of Ssu-ma Ch'ien*, translated by Burton Watson (New York: Columbia University Press, 1969), 274.

IN THIS CHAPTER

Changing China and Axial Age Thought, 600–221 B.C.E.

What were the distinctive features of Chinese philosophies that emerged during the late Zhou period?

Although Chinese technology, science, and philosophy developed largely independently from outside influences, the Chinese also responded to many of the same challenges faced by other societies. For example, they needed ideas to explain the universe and bring order to their lives. During the late Zhou period, when changes in society and politics produced unsettled conditions, Chinese philosophers seeking to restore order spawned schools of thought that endured for several millennia.

Late Zhou Conflicts

The Zhou dynasty endured for nearly 900 years (1122–221 B.C.E.), but after 500 B.C.E. it experienced rapid social and economic change and chronic warfare, known as the "Warring States Period," that was worsened through advances in iron weapons (see Map 6.1). Local lords did not challenge the Zhou king directly but increasingly ignored him, fighting instead among themselves for supremacy. This prolonged crisis fostered changes in many areas of Chinese life. For example, despite the fighting, by 250 B.C.E. China had become the earth's most populous society, with 20 to 40 million people. Improving technology and communications fostered commerce and cities. Political and economic power gradually shifted to the eastern Yellow River Basin, while Chinese culture expanded south of the Yangzi River Basin, which became the major agricultural region because of fertility and favorable climate. Social mobility increased, as many peasants and slaves abandoned their homes and moved to open land or to the cities. The growing merchant class also gained influence. A Chinese historian recorded the situation: "The law honors farmers, yet farmers have become poorer; the law degrades merchants, yet merchants have become richer."[2]

Late Zhou Technology and Science

The late Zhou age saw many advances in Chinese technology and science. In the sixth century B.C.E., knowledge of ironworking filtered in from Central Asia led to the creation of iron-tipped ox-drawn plows, which improved agricultural productivity. Zhou Chinese also became the first people to manufacture cast iron, which was much easier to shape into products such as superior axes, hoes, ploughshares, picks, swords, and chariots. Chinese iron plows were the world's most efficient farm tools before the second millennium C.E. In thus joining the Iron Age, China achieved equal technological footing with western Asia. The Chinese also improved water control and conservation. In 250 B.C.E., for example, to control the fickle upper Yangzi River, they constructed a vast complex of dikes, canals, and dams that is still used today. They also grew soybeans, which provided a rich protein source and enriched the soil. Late Zhou Chinese also invented the first compasses and improved mathematics, amending the Shang decimal system by adding a place for the zero in equations. While they had long produced silk from strands made by a caterpillar that fed on mulberry trees, in Zhou times the Chinese developed better methods of weaving the silk.

One Hundred Philosophical Schools

The later Zhou era was highly creative, producing so many competing philosophies that historians refer to the "hundred schools of thought." Part of the widespread intellectual creativity in Eurasia during the Axial Age, this creativity fostered intellectual traditions that endured through the centuries. The hundred schools resulted partly from the Warring States

[2]Quoted in Arthur Cotterell and David Morgan, *China's Civilization: A Survey of Its History, Arts, and Technology* (New York: Praeger, 1975), 58.

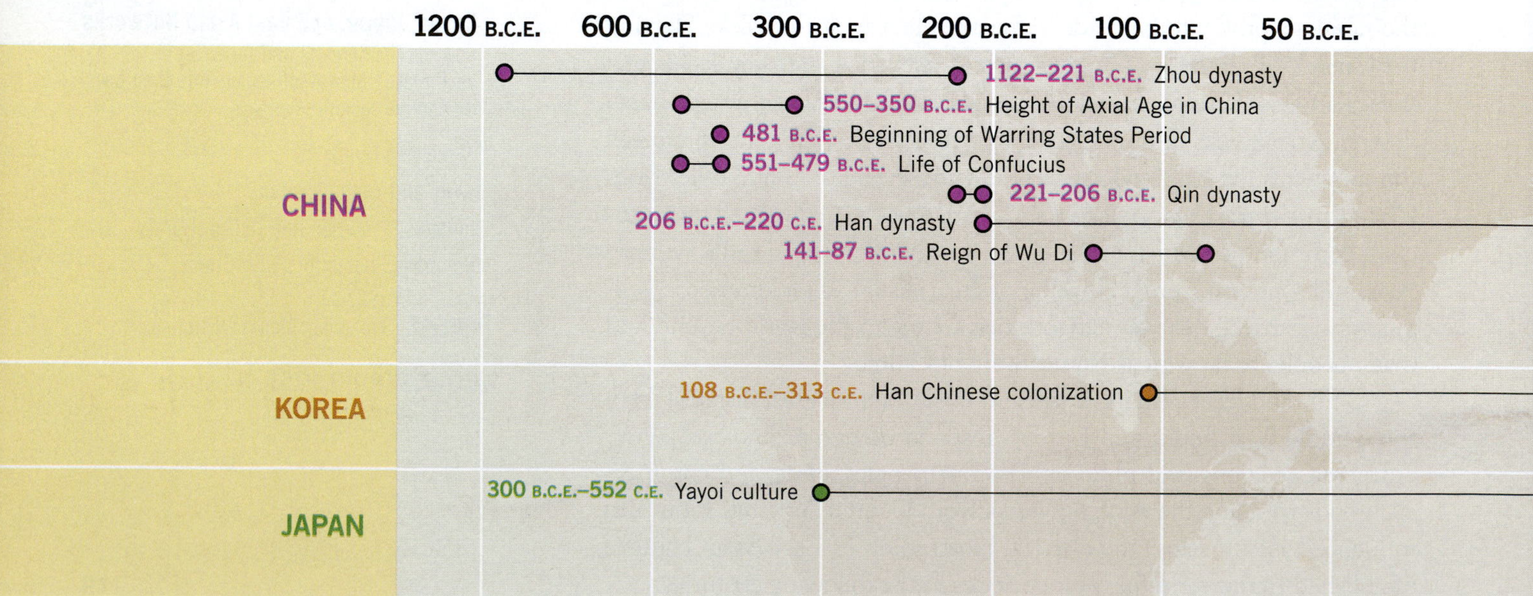

MAP 6.1 CHINA IN THE SIXTH CENTURY B.C.E. During the late Zhou era China was divided into competing, often warring, states, only loosely ruled by the Zhou kings. Some, such as Ch'u and Wu, were large. In the third century B.C.E. the westernmost state, Qin, conquered the others and formed a unified empire.

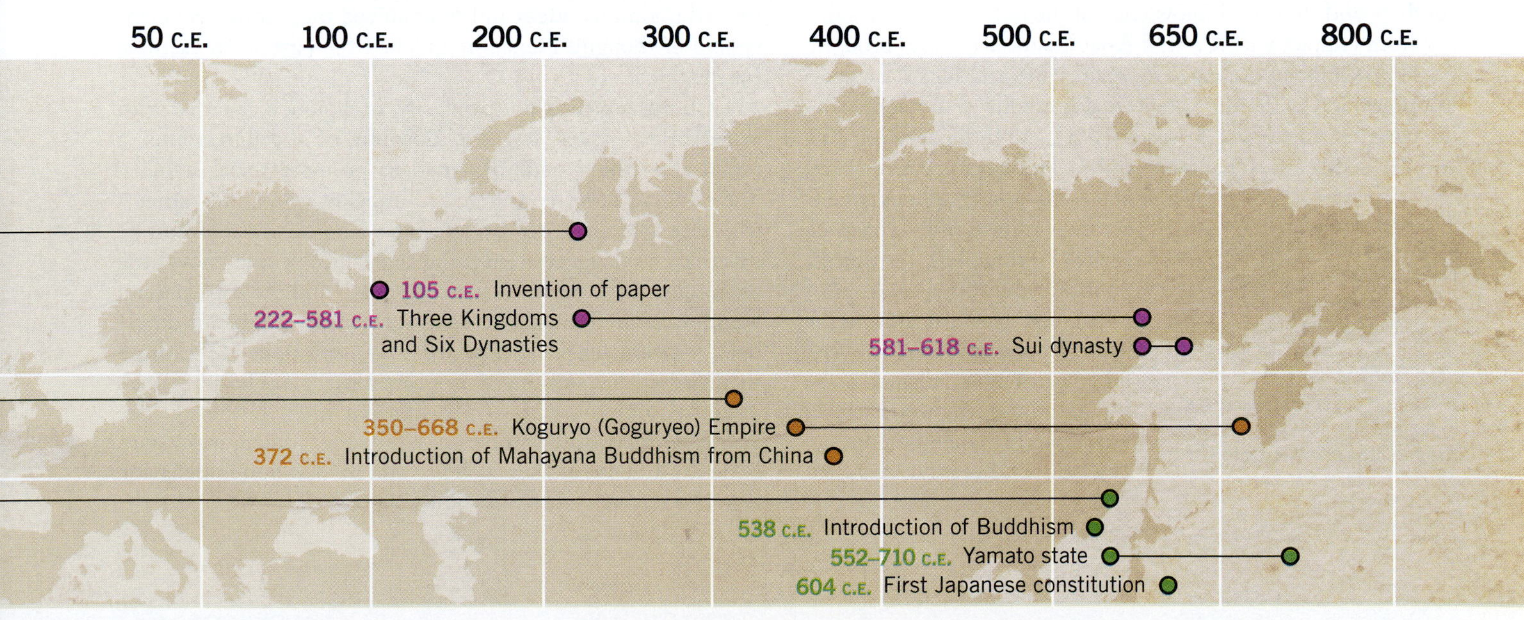

Keren Su/Lonely Planet Images/Getty Images

CONFUCIUS Stone rubbing of a portrait of Confucius from an ancient temple. For twenty-five hundred years Confucius was the most honored and influential Chinese thinker, remembered in countless paintings, woodblock cuts, and carvings on walls.

conflicts and increased knowledge of the outside world resulting from contact with Central Asian pastoralists, who brought horses to China in exchange for grain, wine, and silks. New philosophies and widening intellectual horizons also emerged in the Mediterranean world, western Asia, and India between 600 and 250 B.C.E. (see Chapters 5 and 7). Hoping to restore peace and harmony, philosophers across Eurasia emphasized ethical principles, criticized political conditions, and proposed new political and social ideas. At the era's end, powerful empires emerged in China, India, and the Mediterranean.

Confucianism A Chinese philosophy based on the ideas of Confucius emphasizing the relations among people.

The Analects The book of the sayings of Confucius collected by his disciples and published a century or two after his death.

From the late Zhou period onward, Chinese thought differed dramatically from that of other societies. The Chinese viewed people as social and political creatures within communities and, unlike India, placed less emphasis on an afterlife and powerful gods. While Chinese thinkers did not ignore the supernatural, their main focus remained humanistic. This approach reflected the philosophers' position in society as pragmatic men who often served in government. Some also wandered from one Zhou state to another offering their services and became teachers. Their disciples collected their sayings or thoughts into the classic texts venerated by later generations, creating Confucianism, Daoism, and Legalism, all philosophies that ultimately stood the test of time and influenced China for the next two millennia. The divisions between and within the various schools were never rigid, but each had certain core ideas.

Confucius and His Legacy

The most influential new philosophy, **Confucianism** **(kun-FYOO-shu-NIZ-um)**, based on the ideas of Confucius, emphasized relations among people. Kong Fuzi **(kong foo-dzu)** ("Master Kung"), better known in the West as Confucius, probably lived from 551 to 479 B.C.E. As with the Buddha in India or Jesus of Nazareth, we know of his life and ideas through the writings of his followers. Confucius left no direct writings, but his sayings were collected and published a century or two after his death in a book called ***The Analects*** (see Witness to the Past: *The Analects* and Correct Confucian Behavior). Born into a modest but aristocratic family, Confucius attempted unsuccessfully to gain a government position in various states and then spent years as a teacher of dazzling ability, attracting over his career some three thousand students from all social classes. The sage claimed that he had "never refused to teach anyone, even though he came to me on foot, with nothing more to offer as tuition than a package of dried meat."[3] Maintaining that education was the key to promoting morality, Confucius stressed the study of history, philosophy, literature, poetry, and music. Considering himself not a creator of new ideas but rather a transmitter of ancient wisdom, he revived traditional ideas and reorganized them into a coherent system of thought. Hence he extolled the past as an example for the future.

Confucianism is not primarily a religion, concerned with otherworldly issues, but a philosophy of social relations, a moral and ethical code designed to promote social stability. The Chinese never considered Confucius a god, but rather a wise sage to be honored by offerings. Confucius could best be described as an agnostic, arguing that, since people know little about life, they cannot know about death and the supernatural world. Like the Ionian Greeks a world away, Confucius developed a rationalist view opposed to superstition. He asserted that wisdom was working to improve society and keeping one's distance from the gods while showing them reverence. The answer to the world's problems, Confucius argued, was virtue, ethics, and, above all, benevolence and moderation in behavior.

[3]Quoted in H. G. Creel, *Chinese Thought from Confucius to Mao Tse-Tung* (New York: Mentor, 1953), 32.

WITNESS TO THE PAST

The Analects and Correct Confucian Behavior

The Analects *is the main record of Confucius and his thought that survived the Warring States Period and the book burnings of the next dynasty. Compiled by his disciples many years after his death, it is presented largely in the form of questions from his followers and answers, short aphorisms, or long discourses by the sage. Divided into twenty chapters, the book covers many topics, mostly peoples' conduct and aspirations. It became the most important book in China from the Han dynasty down to modern times. These fragments present a few of Confucius's thoughts about the correct behavior of gentlemen (the rulers and other leaders), sons and daughters, and people in general.*

[About the gentleman], Confucius said, "The gentleman concerns himself with the Way [the natural order that is also a moral order]; he does not worry about his salary. Hunger may be found in plowing; wealth may be found in studying. The gentleman worries about the Way, not about poverty.... The gentleman reveres three things. He reveres the mandate of Heaven; he reveres great people; and he reveres the words of the sages. Petty people...are disrespectful of great people and they ridicule the words of the sage. The gentleman aspires to things lofty; the petty person aspires to things base. The gentleman looks to himself; the petty person looks to other people. The gentleman feels bad when his capabilities fall short of some task. He does not feel bad if people fail to recognize him...."

[About filial piety or respect for parents], Confucius said, "Nowadays, filial piety is considered to be the ability to nourish one's parents. But this obligation to nourish even extends down to the dogs and horses. Unless we have reverence for our parents, what makes us any different? Do not offend your parents.... When your parents are alive, serve them according to the rules of ritual and decorum. When they are deceased, give them a funeral and offer sacrifices to them according to the rules of ritual and decorum.... It is unacceptable not to be aware of your parents' ages. Their advancing years are a cause for joy and at the same time a cause for sorrow...."

[About humanity], Confucius said, "If an individual can practice five things anywhere in the world, he is a man of humanity.... [These are] Reverence, generosity, truthfulness, diligence, and kindness. If a person acts with reverence, he will not be insulted. If he is generous, he will win over the people. If he is truthful, he will be trusted by the people. If he is diligent, he will have great achievements. If he is kind, he will be able to influence others.... When you go out, treat everyone as if you were welcoming a great guest. Employ people as if you were conducting a great sacrifice."

THINKING ABOUT THE READING

1. What are some of the main qualities expected of a gentleman?
2. How might Confucian views on respect for parents have influenced the family system?
3. How did the advice reflect Confucius's humanistic emphasis?

Source: Adapted from The Free Press, a Division of Simon & Schuster Inc. from CHINESE CIVILIZATION AND SOCIETY, A Sourcebook, Second Revised & Expanded Edition by Patricia Buckley Ebrey.

Confucius also advised people to think about the future; if they do not think about problems that are still distant, they will have to worry about them later.

Confucius advocated an autocratic but paternalistic government in which the ruler held responsibility for the people's welfare. Even distribution of goods, he argued, eliminates poverty and promotes harmony, hence ensuring stability. The family constituted the model for the state. Just as children should respect and obey their parents, a custom known as **filial piety (FILL-eal PIE-uh-ty)**, so citizens should obey a fair government and play their assigned roles in a society defined by order and hierarchy: "Let the ruler be ruler, and the minister minister; let the father be father, and the son son."[4] Confucius advocated duty and obedience of inferiors to superiors: of wife to husband, son to father, younger to older, and citizen to king; but authority must be wielded justly and wisely. Government was fundamentally a matter of ethics: abusive power became illegitimate. When asked what thought should guide the conduct of both leaders and citizens, Confucius replied: "Do not do to others what you yourself do not desire."[5]

Confucian teachings have had a more enduring influence on East Asia than those of any other thinker, becoming in some form or another the official doctrine in China, Korea, Vietnam, and Japan and helping set a common pattern of compromise. As a Chinese proverb advised, people should "bend like bamboo" to avoid conflict with others. To promote harmony, Confucianism stressed rules of courtesy. For example, a late Zhou book of etiquette advised men on how to behave when visiting another man of equal status: if the host should "yawn, stretch himself, ask the time of day, order his dinner, or change his position, then [the guest] must ask permission to [leave]."[6] Ritual and etiquette maintained stability and discipline.

filial piety The Confucian rule that children should respect and obey their parents.

[4]Quoted in Ch'u Chai and Winberg Chai, *Confucianism* (Woodbury, NY: Barron's, 1973), 45.
[5]Quoted in Dun J. Li, ed., *The Essence of Chinese Civilization* (Princeton: D. Van Nostrand, 1967), 6.
[6]From Patricia Buckley Ebrey, ed., *Chinese Civilization: A Sourcebook*, 2nd ed., revised and expanded (New York: Free Press, 1993), 43–44.

Confucian ideas promoted social order and continuity across generations for centuries.

However, Confucian ideas, revised to some extent by followers, became increasingly rigid in application over the centuries, leading to a conservatism and inflexibility that Confucius might have condemned. Two of the sage's main followers, who lived one and a half centuries later, represented opposing schools of interpretation. Mengzi **(MUNG-dze)** (Mencius) (372–289 B.C.E.) advocated a liberal, even permissive government, the ruler embracing benevolence and righteousness as his main goals. Believing human nature was essentially good, Mengzi was extremely optimistic about society's prospects. Xunzi **(SHOON-dze)** (Hsun Tzu) (310–220 B.C.E.) disagreed, viewing human nature as essentially bad. Hence, the state must enforce goodness and morality. Xunzi's belief that Confucian writings were the source of all wisdom fostered dogmatism.

Daoism and Chinese Mysticism

The second major philosophy, **Daoism (DOW-iz-um)**, taught that people should adapt to nature. Legends attributed Daoism's main ideas to Laozi **(lou-zoe)** (Lao Tzu or "Old Master"), an older contemporary of Confucius and a disillusioned bureaucrat who became a wandering teacher. If such a man ever lived, he probably did not write the two main Daoist texts, which were most likely composed or compiled during the third century B.C.E.

Daoism was a philosophy of withdrawal for people appalled by warfare. Daoist thinkers advised people to follow the "way of the universe," or *dao*, described as "unfathomable, the ancestral progenitor of all things, everlasting. All pervading, dao lies hidden and cannot be named. It produces all things. He who acts in accordance with dao becomes one with dao."[7] Convinced that people could never dominate their environment, Daoists urged allying with it, becoming simple, without desire and striving, and content with what is. A Daoist text expressed disgust with everyday life: "To labor away one's whole lifetime but never see the result, and to be utterly worn out with toil but have no idea where it is leading, is this not lamentable?"[8] Unlike Confucians, Daoists encouraged the Chinese to conform to the natural world rather than to social expectations and corrupt, oppressive governments, believing that rulers who promoted rigid, violent, aggressive, warlike, and authoritarian policies violated the natural order. One main text contended that the wise person prefers fishing on a remote stream to serving as emperor. Mystical and romantic, Daoism fostered an awareness of nature and its beauties that were reflected in Chinese poetry and landscape painting, which often recorded towering mountains, roaring waterfalls, and placid lakes.

Daoism A Chinese philosophy that emphasized adaptation to nature.

Legalism A Chinese philosophy that advocated harsh control of people by the state.

Daoism later fragmented into several traditions. Popular Daoism became a religion of countless deities and magic, with some followers seeking an elixir of immortality, often experimenting with a wide variety of foods. By contrast, philosophical Daoism appealed to the better educated, urging individuals to turn inward and experience oneness with the universe. Daoist writers found it difficult to express their basic ideas, one claiming that "those who know do not speak; those who speak do not know."[9] Some Daoist writings contained stories filled with mysticism, unity with nature, and a humbling relativism:

> *One time, Chuang-tzu dreamed he was a butterfly, flitting around, enjoying what butterflies enjoy. The butterfly did not know that it was Chuang-tzu. Then Chuang-tzu started, and woke up, and he was Chuang-tzu again. And he began to wonder whether he was Chuang-tzu who had dreamed he was a butterfly dreaming that he was Chuang-tzu.*[10]

Daoists advised Confucianists to flow with the heart rather than struggle with the intellect. The active Confucian bureaucrat of the morning became the dreamy Daoist poet or nature lover of the evening. Daoism complemented Confucianism by enabling the Chinese to balance the conflicting needs for social order and personal autonomy, adding enjoyment, reflection, and a sense of freedom.

Legalism and the Chinese State

Among the dozens of other competing philosophies, **Legalism**, which advocated that the state maintain harsh control of people, also had an enduring influence. Influenced by the Confucian Xunzi, Legalists emphasized unrestrained state power, an authoritarian government that secured prosperity, order, and stability by controlling all economic resources and instilling discipline through compulsory military duty and harsh laws. The ruler needed to be strong and disregard peoples' rights or desires. Ridiculing Confucian humanism, Legalists favored controlling people through punishments and rewards, commands and prohibitions, and they ridiculed Confucian humanism.

Although Legalism influenced politics, Chinese always balanced it with the more humane ideas of Confucius and Mengzi, who stressed moral persuasion rather than coercion. Hence, many Chinese did not follow one philosophy to the exclusion of others. Despite sometimes severe laws, local officials had flexibility in implementing them, taking into account the social context.

[7]The quotes are from Lionel Giles, *The Sayings of Lao Tzu* (New York: E.P. Dutton, 1908), 19, 22, 25.

[8]Quoted in Creel, *Chinese Thought*, 85.

[9]Quoted in Arthur Waley, *The Way and Its Power: A Study of the Tao Te Ching and Its Place in Chinese Thought* (New York: Grove Press, 1958), 210.

[10]From William McNaughton, ed., *Light from the East: An Anthology of Asian Literature* (New York: Laurel, 1978), 132.

MAKE SURE YOU UNDERSTAND THESE KEY POINTS BEFORE MOVING ON

- **Despite chronic civil warfare, China became the most populous society on earth; iron technologies and other breakthroughs made China competitive with western Asia.**
- **Instability resulting from military conflict led intellectuals to question basic tenets of society and government, thus creating the "hundred schools of thought."**
- **Three enduring Chinese philosophies from this period—Confucianism, Daoism, and Legalism—have influenced Chinese state and culture through two millennia.**
- **Chinese philosophies emphasized humanism rather than the supernatural or gods.**

aplia

Chinese Imperial Systems and the World

What developments during the Han dynasty linked China to the rest of Eurasia?

More than Indian, Middle Eastern, or European societies, China has experienced cohesion, continuity, and blending of diverse influences throughout much of its history. For example, although Central Asians often attacked and even occasionally conquered China, the invaders maintained continuity by adopting Chinese culture, a process known as **Sinicization** **(SIN-uh-sigh-ZAY-tion)**. But one major transition quickly changed the face of China: replacing the multistate Zhou system with a centralized empire. The new imperial China was forged by the harsh rulers of Qin **(chin)** and by the Han dynasty, which conquered a large empire, fostered foreign trade, and established enduring political patterns. Hence, China after 221 B.C.E. set a new pattern for the centuries to follow.

Sinicization The process by which Central Asian invaders maintained continuity with China's past by adopting Chinese culture.

Georg Gerster/Science Source

THE GREAT WALL This panorama from the region just north of Beijing shows a portion of the wall reconstructed in the fifteenth century C.E. The wall was an attempt to mark the northern boundary of China and keep out nomadic invaders.

During these years the Chinese family matured into its basic form, dramatic economic growth affected peasant life, the Chinese examined their own history for lessons, and technology and science advanced, improving mathematics and health.

The Qin Dynasty

Late Zhou political turmoil ended when the Qin dynasty (221–206 B.C.E.) conquered the other states and implemented repressive Legalist ideas, transforming the China of many states into an empire with an authoritarian central government. Advised by Legalist thinkers, Qin rulers had made their state the strongest within the Zhou system by enforcing government monopolies over many trade goods. Like Sparta in Greece, Qin's population was militarized, with men serving as citizen-warriors. The Qin began conquering other Zhou states, with the brutal Legalist prime minister, Li Si **(lee SHE)** (Li Ssu), the chief deputy to the eventual first emperor of all China, arguing that those who used the past to oppose the present, meaning the Confucians, had to be exterminated.

In 221 B.C.E. the Qin, after finally defeating all the remaining Zhou states, established a new government that ruled most of the Chinese people. The first Qin ruler assumed the new and imposing title of Shi Huangdi **(SHE hwang-dee)** ("first emperor"), surrounding himself with mystery and pomp to enhance his prestige while concealing himself from the consequences of his decrees. The autocrat lived in carefully guarded privacy, moving secretly from one apartment to another in his vast palaces. To reveal his movements was a crime instantly punished with death. Mandating a total reordering of China along Legalist lines, the emperor constructed a monolithic and united state that sought to control all aspects of Chinese life. The Qin sent armies to incorporate much of southern China and, for a while, Vietnam into the empire. Chinese society eventually assimilated many southerners. Given this unification, the name *Qin* is fittingly the origin of the Western name for China.

Later Chinese historians viewed the Qin era as one of the country's most terrible periods. Common people hated the forced labor, strict laws, spies, general surveillance, and thought control that were paramount in the police state. Intellectuals despised the Qin for purging non-Legalist thought, including Confucianism, as subversive doctrines. The Qin burned thousands of books and executed many scholars, often burying them alive, ending the intellectual creativity of the hundred schools.

Despite the repression, Shi Huangdi's policies fostered public works projects, economic growth, and social change. The Qin standardized weights and measures, unified agricultural practices, codified laws, built roads, bridges, dams, and canals, and standardized the written language so that all literate Chinese could communicate easily. To foster economic growth, the Qin established state monopolies over essential commodities like salt, raised taxes, and required forced labor on government projects. Ever since the Chinese have accepted a strong government role in economic matters. The harsh Qin laws also ended crime, as a later Chinese scholar conceded: "Nothing lost on the road was picked up and pocketed, the hills were free of bandits, men avoided quarrels at home."[11] Qin land reform also undermined the old aristocracy's power, a mighty blow to the Zhou social structure.

The most famous Qin public works project was constructing an early and limited version of a Great Wall along China's northern borders as a barrier against encroachment by Central Asian warriors. The Chinese traded with Central Asians but also fought with and feared them. A few partial earthen walls had already been built in Zhou times, but the Qin consolidated these into a more formidable structure, later known as the Great Wall. Vast numbers of conscripted laborers built the Great Wall, one of the ancient world's greatest architectural achievements. Later dynasties periodically rebuilt and added to the wall. The present brick and stone wall that so astounds tourists derives mostly from reconstruction and expansion work six centuries ago, after which the wall stretched over 1,400 miles across north China. Properly manned, it could be an effective defense, but only the wealthiest emperors could afford that expense. Although seldom successful in curbing invaders, the wall symbolically affirmed the empire's territorial limits.

But the Qin dynasty itself proved short-lived. Many hated Shi Huangdi, and his expansionist policies provoked conflict with neighboring peoples. Fearing general revolt, his inner circle kept the first emperor's death in 210 B.C.E. secret. He was buried in a huge underground mausoleum together with seven thousand realistic life-size terracotta horses and warriors, each with individual facial features and clothing, brandishing bronze weapons. It took 700,000 laborers to construct the final resting place and its contents. When news finally spread of Shi Huangdi's death, peasant revolts broke out. In 206 B.C.E. a rebel alliance defeated the Qin forces. As various rebel groups vied for power, a former peasant led his forces to victory, establishing a new dynasty, the Han **(HAHN)**.

The Han Empire

The Han dynasty (206 B.C.E.–220 C.E.) made China a major force in Eurasian trade, diplomacy, and imperialism. The Han built a huge empire stretching far into Central Asia (see Map 6.2); trade across this area allowed greater contact with people to the west. While building a strong state, they also modified the Qin's harsh Legalist structure. The brilliance of Han rule and the expansion of Chinese society southward set the pattern for later dynasties, leading Chinese to call themselves the Sons of Han.

The middle Classical period was the age of empires, with large segments of Eurasia and North Africa dominated by large imperial structures like the Han. Built on Axial Age ideas, these empires resolved the crises that had sparked their rise. But they eventually declined as their structures and finances weakened, the conquered populations revolted, and nomadic peoples invaded the imperial heartlands. The Han and Roman Empires

[11]Sima Qian quoted in Arthur Cotterell, *The First Emperor of China* (New York: Penguin, 1988), 106.

[12]Quoted in Frances Wood, *The Silk Road: Two Thousand Years in the Heart of Asia* (Berkeley: University of California Press, 2002), 55.

reached their zenith around the same time and resembled each other in population, although Rome's empire was larger in territorial size. In 2 C.E. the Han Empire contained at least 60 million people, most of them in China proper, and the Roman Empire ruled some 55 million, most of them outside Italy.

The pinnacle of Han imperial power came under the emperor Wu Di, who ruled for over half a century (141–87 B.C.E.). After establishing control at home, Wu Di, a firm believer that the best defense is a good offense, launched bloody campaigns to counteract the encroaching pastoral nomads, especially the branch of Huns the Chinese called Xiongnu, a large tribal confederation that had constantly threatened China. As a result, some nomad groups were deflected to the west.

Empire building and diplomacy soon linked China to western Eurasia, Northeast Asia, and Southeast Asia. The Han sent ambassadors such as Zhang Qian to distant Central Asians seeking allies against common enemies. Wu Di also dispatched great armies, some numbering as many as 150,000 men, to conquer southwestern China, northern Korea, Vietnam, the Xinjiang **(shinjee-yahng)** region on China's western borders, Mongolia, and parts of Turkestan. Wu Di wrote a poem about a successful military campaign that brought many horses as tribute: "The heavenly horses are coming from the Far West. They crossed the Flowing Sands, for the barbarians are conquered."[12] China ruled Korea for four centuries and Vietnam for one thousand years. Soon Chinese power extended even further, as states in Afghanistan sent tribute to Han emperors. One disgruntled Han soldier wrote a protest: "In the wilderness we dead lie unburied, fodder for crows. Tell the crows for us, 'We've always been brave men.'"[13] A Chinese army of ninety thousand men reached as far as the Caspian Sea, and a small force led by a General Gan Ying apparently traveled through Parthia to the Persian Gulf in 97 C.E., the first Chinese known to reach there. On his return General Gan reported on the customs and topography of these western states, as well as on the vast Roman Empire.

[13] From John Minford and Joseph S. M. Lau, eds., *Classical Chinese Literature: An Anthology of Translations*, vol. 1 (New York: Columbia University Press, 2000), 387.

MAP 6.2 THE HAN EMPIRE The Han Empire fluctuated in size but at its height controlled most of today's China, Korea, northern Vietnam, and a long corridor through Central Asia to Turkestan.

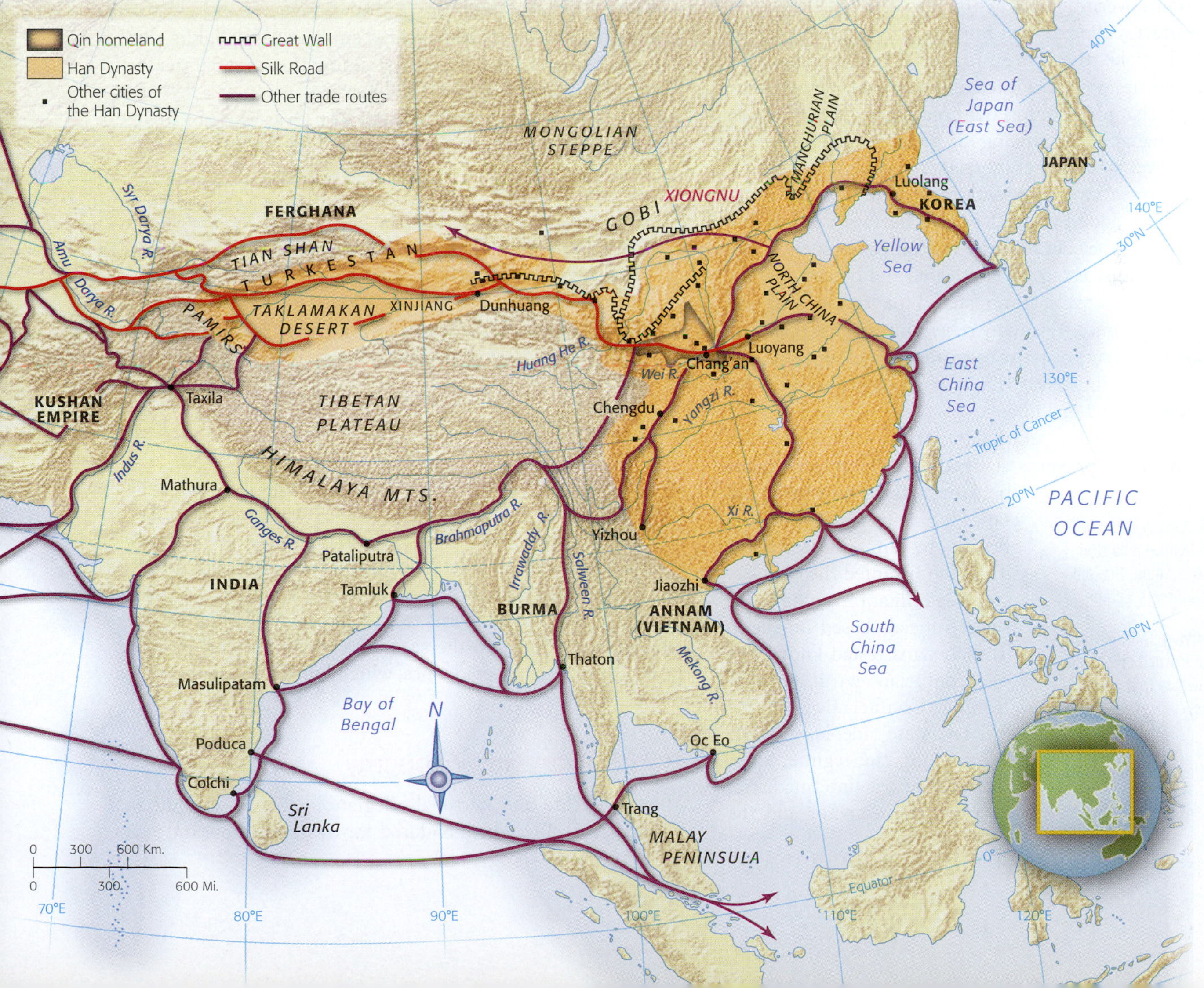

The Silk Road and Eurasian Trade

The Han presence in Central Asia fostered a lively overland caravan route, the **Silk Road**, linking China with India, the Middle East, and southern Europe. Central Asian cities such as Kashgar **(kahsh-gar)** and Samarkand **(SAM-mar-kahnd)** serviced the trade and its merchants, forming an important contact zone between East and West. Chinese silk, porcelain, and bamboo moved west across the deserts and mountains to Baghdad and eastern Mediterranean ports, some eventually reaching Rome. Each westbound caravan carried lightweight, easily packed silk and then returned with horses and luxury goods such as Egyptian glass beads, Red Sea pearls, and Baltic amber.

The Silk Road greatly influenced participating people. To pay for Chinese luxuries, the Romans dispatched silver to China, causing a serious trade imbalance that contributed to the decline of the Western Roman Empire. Thus the Han Empire ultimately affected distant Europe politically and economically. Chinese adopted some Central and West Asian products, such as stringed musical instruments and new foods. Imperial power and foreign trade generated an economic boom and commercial growth.

Han Government and Politics

The basic Han government structure survived until the early twentieth century. Whereas the Qin sought to transform China in one brutal stroke, the more pragmatic and cautious Han softened Legalism with Confucian humanism, demonstrating that Confucian philosophy could maintain stability amidst momentous change. This mixing of Legalism with Confucianism, of power with ethics, characterized China's political system for the next two thousand years. During Han times the civil service included about 1 person for every 400 to 500 people, a small number because the central government had a restricted role, mainly ensuring law, order, and border defense. Bureaucrats collected taxes, administered the legal system, and officered military forces. Yet many rebellions suggest that high taxes and demands that peasants provide military or labor service, such as rebuilding river dikes or repairing washed-out roads, generated occasional unrest.

Educated men (later called **mandarins**) staffed the Han bureaucracy. Chinese proverbs claimed that the country might be won by the sword but could be ruled only by the writing brush—by an educated elite. The Han invented the civil service examination system to select officials based on merit. These exams tested knowledge of Confucian writings, confirming Confucianism as the official state ideology while legitimizing the regime. Since they served as intermediaries between the emperor and the people, the mandarins' prestige moderated the tendency toward despotism. The emerging Han bureaucracy marked the rise of the **scholar-gentry**, a social class based on learning, officeholding, and landowning; many mandarins came from wealthy landowning families. Still, scholar-officials could not guarantee their sons' competence, and some poor men did rise by passing the civil service exams.

Silk Road A lively caravan route through Central Asia that linked China with India, the Middle East, and southern Europe.

scholar-gentry A Chinese social class of learned officeholders and landowners that arose in the Han dynasty.

mandarins Educated men who staffed the Chinese bureaucracy.

During the Han the concepts of the Mandate of Heaven and the dynastic cycle became ingrained in Chinese historical thinking (see Chapter 4). Premodern Chinese scholars believed that emperors ruled as deputies of the cosmic forces, but only so long as they possessed justice, benevolence, and sincerity. In each dynasty, able early rulers were succeeded by debauched weaklings indulging their pleasures, keeping harems of wives, concubines, and sometimes boys. Such imperial misrule justified rebellion. Dynastic rise and fall also correlated with economic trends: a strong new dynasty generated prosperity, luring ambitious emperors into overextending imperial power and squandering human and financial resources. The Han elite lived and died lavishly; the tomb of one princess contained a 2,000-piece jade suit sown with gold wire.

Wasteful expenditures created financial difficulties. Governments could no longer fund the large military commitment to protect the country, and some bureaucrats became corrupt. Growing deficits led to higher taxes, forcing many poorer peasants to sell their land to influential landlords, who evaded taxes. This pattern was illustrated by Han emperor Wu Di. His glorious empire came at a huge cost, straining the imperial treasury. Some Han scholars opposed military expansion as a senseless waste of lives and tax revenues, and Wu Di's successor invited some of them to make their case before him. They did so, arguing that,

> *at present, morality is discarded and reliance is placed on military force. Troops are raised for campaigns and garrisons are stationed for defense. It is the long-drawn-out campaigns and the ceaseless transportation of provisions that burden our people at home and cause our frontier soldiers to suffer from hunger and cold.*[14]

But higher officials responded that the spending was necessary to protect the country.

The Han dynasty finally collapsed in 220 C.E., not unlike the fall of Rome several centuries later. Critical factors for both empires included inadequate revenues, peasant revolts, powerful landed families contending for power, and raids by pastoralists. Across Eurasia unusually warm conditions between 200 B.C.E. and 200 C.E. came to an end, and the colder weather affected agriculture. In the second century C.E. both empires were also ravaged by epidemics, which killed millions and thus reduced tax revenues.

Han Society and Economy

Han social life and personal allegiance revolved around the Confucian family, which endured for over two thousand years

[14]Ebrey, *Chinese Civilization*, 61–62.

because it provided great psychological and economic security. Each person belonged to a large family transcending time. The Chinese honored their ancestors while also considering the welfare of future generations. They idealized the joint family, three or four generations living together under one roof. But only wealthy families could support the large houses and private courtyards that made the joint family possible. Families were led by an autocratic patriarch, or senior male, who commanded respect, and the Chinese traced descent exclusively through the male line. Children were expected to respect both parents and venerate their elders, with family interests always taking precedence over individual ones. Laws held the family accountable for the actions of its members, discouraging disgraceful behavior by individuals.

This family system disadvantaged most women, requiring them to be devoted to their parents, then to their husband and sons; care of the family and children was their central preoccupation. Parents arranged marriages with the goal of linking families, and a young wife joined her husband's family and was subject to his parents' authority. Ban Zhao **(ban chao)**, an accomplished historian, astronomer, and mathematician, wrote an influential book on women's place in society in which she stressed Confucian obligations of selfless behavior, devotion, and obedience. But although many marriages were happy, the sorrows of unhappy women became a common literary theme. Many Chinese novels and plays concerned unrequited love or lovers forced to marry others. Although gender roles became more rigid than in earlier times, besides doing housework and caring for children many women engaged in small-scale trade, worked long hours in the fields, and formed groups to spin or weave together. Yet, as a Han proverb noted, "To prick embroidery does not pay as much as leaning upon a market door."[15]

Women's experiences were never standardized, and their independence and influence depended on age, social class, and local practices. A few women like Ban Zhao achieved wide acclaim, and some elite women gained an education, a handful becoming celebrated poets. The mother of the Confucian thinker Mengzi won esteem as a model of astuteness and assertiveness, yet she was reported to have said that a "woman's duties are to cook the five grains, heat the wine, look after her parents-in-law, make clothes, and that is all!"[16] In contrast, some peasant women, who worked in the fields alongside their men, were strong-willed and exercised influence in their families and villages.

Intensive farming, especially the growing of cereal crops by peasants, dominated China's economy from the Han dynasty onward. Landowning became the major goal of economic endeavor and investment, and peasants had to produce a food surplus for the 20 percent of the people living in towns and cities. Working fertile land, peasants achieved high yields, becoming some of the world's most efficient farmers through hard physical labor, especially in growing rice. Peasants did not lead easy lives. Fields had to be flooded with irrigation water and drained, and the rice had to be sown, transplanted, and harvested, all by hand. Peasants divided family land and movable property equally among sons, leaving some with too little land to live on. Hence, many peasants were forced into tenancy to landlords. However, slavery, an important feature of Shang and Zhou society, became less common during the Han.

Population pressure and peasant land shortage also fostered political stability. By the second century B.C.E., farmers had used practically all the good agricultural land in northern China. The economy's labor-intensive nature was also apparent outside agriculture. Transportation meant porters with

DEA/G. DAGLI ORTI/De Agostini Picture Library/Getty Images

HAN ERA VILLAGE HOUSE This terra cotta model made during the Han dynasty illustrates a fortified village house with a courtyard.

[15]Quoted in Brett Hinsch, *Women in Early Imperial China* (Lanham, MD: Rowman and Littlefield, 2002), 72.
[16]Quoted in Ebrey, *Chinese Civilization*, 73.

PROFILE

Sima Qian, Chinese Historian

Perhaps the greatest Han dynasty historian was Sima Qian (ca. 145–90 B.C.E.). His dying father, a high court official and historian, begged his son on his deathbed to continue compiling a history of China and its neighbors from earliest times. "I have failed to set forth a record of all the enlightened rulers and wise lords, the faithful ministers and gentlemen who were ready to die for duty," he conceded. His dutiful son replied, "I shall not dare to be remiss," and made the project his life's work. At twenty, Sima Qian began a grand tour of the empire, examining historical sites, such as the tomb and family home of Confucius.

After receiving an official appointment, the young scholar was sent to newly conquered territories in the southwest and then far northwestern outposts, including Mongolia; he also traveled extensively with Emperor Wu Di. Like his father, Sima Qian was appointed Grand Astrologer, a post dealing with time and the heavens, and helped reform the calendar. But, being an honest man who spoke his mind, he alienated the emperor by defending a respected general whose brave attack against the Huns had failed for lack of support. As punishment Sima Qian was castrated.

Using his immense learning, combined with access to the vast imperial library containing the public records, Sima Qian produced his major book, *Records of the Grand Historian*, which covered two thousand years of history in 130 chapters, roughly 10,000 pages of text. This monumental history ranges across many topics, including astronomy, astrology, science, music, religious sacrifices, and economic patterns. It offers sketches of famous men from many walks of life, including political and military leaders, merchants, philosophers, scholars, comedians, assassins, rebels, bandits, and poets. *Records* describes foreign peoples and lands well known to the Chinese, from Korea to Afghanistan. Because it also covers rivers and canals, we know much of Wu Di's ambitious conservation and irrigation schemes. In addition, Sima Qian was the first historian to offer a comparative appraisal of China's various philosophical traditions, in which he showed particular sympathy to Daoism.

The book is strongest on the history of his times. Because Sima Qian's castration had embittered him toward Wu Di, some chapters are filled with covert satires on the emperor and warnings about his increasing power. His most original writing came in the chapters on people and contemporary affairs. Consider this criticism of those abusing their power:

> *We see that men whose deeds are immoral and who constantly violate the laws end their lives in luxury and wealth and their blessings pass down to their heirs with-out end. And there are others who expend anger on what is not upright and just, and yet, in numbers too great to be reckoned, they meet with misfortune and disaster. I find myself in much perplexity.*

Landov

SIMA QIAN This modern painting, by an unknown artist, imagines what Han China's great historian, Sima Qian, might have looked like.

Sima Qian's vital narrative and lively prose made his book popular reading among Chinese scholars for many centuries. Concerned with both his literary and his moral legacy, Sima Qian concluded, in words that still stir historians: "I have assembled and arranged the ancient traditions, and if they may be handed down and communicated surely I would have no regrets," and, "those who do not forget the past are masters of the future." Sima Qian set the standard to be followed by later historians in China.

THINKING ABOUT THE PROFILE

1. How did Sima Qian become a historian?
2. What does his life tell us about the pleasures and hazards of being a high official in Han China?
3. What made his historical writing so valuable to later readers?

Note: Quotations from Ben-Ami Scharfstein, *The Mind of China: The Culture, Customs, and Beliefs of Traditional China* (New York: Dell, 1974), 89–91; and Sima Qian, *Historical Records*, translated by Raymond Dawson (Oxford: Oxford University Press, 1994), 177.

carrying poles, men pushing wheelbarrows, and men bearing the sedan chairs of the elite. Men also walked along narrow paths pulling boats upriver through the narrow gorges of the Yangzi River. While the famous sericulture (silk-making) industry produced silks and brocades of the finest weave, producing 150 pounds of silk required feeding and keeping clean the trays of 700,000 worms.

Chinese Historiography

The Chinese developed one of the greatest traditions of studying and writing about history, or historiography. Recording history was probably inevitable among a people who looked to the past for guidance in the present. Chinese history writing goes back to the Zhou dynasty, when a largely factual and chronological political history of the state of Lu, known as *The Spring and Autumn Annals*, was compiled. Confucians read into the prose a moral assessment of history. Beginning with the Han, most dynasties employed professional historians, such as the Han era's Sima Qian **(SI-mu tshen)** (see Profile: Sima Qian, Chinese Historian). Later Chinese historians adopted Sima Qian's belief that past events, if not forgotten, also taught about the future. They tended to favor political history, concentrating on personalities, stories, wars, and the doings of emperors while neglecting long-term social and economic trends.

The greatest Chinese historians wrote monumental works and had much in common with each other. They aimed for objectivity, carefully separating their editorial comments from the narrative text. Like all historians, they had to decide what to include and omit, focusing more on people and their foibles than on supernatural intervention. Historical literature also served as a manual for government, discussing the success and failure of past policies to achieve wisdom and promote morality.

MAKE SURE YOU UNDERSTAND THESE KEY POINTS BEFORE MOVING ON

- **Legalism, with its strict authoritarianism and negative view of human nature, was the dominant philosophy of the Qin rulers.**
- **The diplomatic and military expansion under the Han rulers set the stage for expanded trade, including the development of the Silk Road linking China to western Asia and Europe.**
- **The structure of government established during the Han, characterized by a blending of central and local authority and a softening of Legalism with Confucian humanism, endured until the early twentieth century.**
- **The family structure became the central social institution; its patriarchal hierarchy, codified in law, put the needs of the group above the needs of the individual.**

China After the Han Empire: Continuity and Change

What outside influences helped shape China after the fall of the Han?

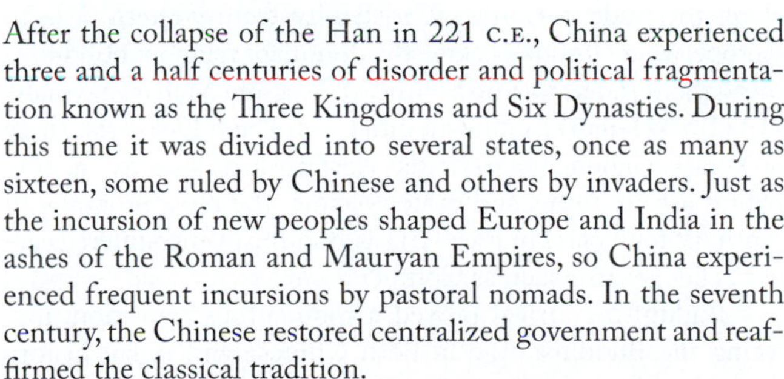

After the collapse of the Han in 221 C.E., China experienced three and a half centuries of disorder and political fragmentation known as the Three Kingdoms and Six Dynasties. During this time it was divided into several states, once as many as sixteen, some ruled by Chinese and others by invaders. Just as the incursion of new peoples shaped Europe and India in the ashes of the Roman and Mauryan Empires, so China experienced frequent incursions by pastoral nomads. In the seventh century, the Chinese restored centralized government and reaffirmed the classical tradition.

Disunity, Invasion, and Cultural Mixing

During the troubled post-Han period, pastoral nomads attacked north China. Although chiefly livestock herders, most used bronze and iron. Brutal winters and keen competition for good grazing land made these martial peoples scornful of but also attracted to China's richer life. Skilled in horseback warfare, sometimes they breached the Great Wall, especially when they united in confederations under strong chiefs. These invasions produced what historians term the "Great Wall Complex": a natural Chinese paranoia about border security and perpetual fear of aggressive outsiders. In this mindset, all non-Chinese were barbarians hoping to share in China's cultural glory and material wealth. These invasions also prompted many Chinese to move south, solidifying the Chinese character of the region.

A much loved fifth-century ballad, perhaps based on an actual person, recalls a young woman warrior, Mulan, who disguises herself as a man to fight invading Central Asians. Only after she distinguishes herself in battle do her comrades discover her gender. The ballad makes a case for gender equality: "For the male hare has a lilting, lolloping gait, and the female hare has a wild and roving eye; But set them both scampering side by side, And who so wise could tell you 'This is he?'"[17]

Chinese learned to endure both division and invasion by outsiders, developing a remarkable defense mechanism: assimilation. Most of the conquerors eventually ruled in a Chinese way, using the Confucian bureaucracy while adapting much

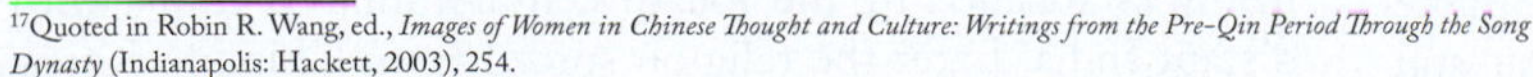

[17]Quoted in Robin R. Wang, ed., *Images of Women in Chinese Thought and Culture: Writings from the Pre-Qin Period Through the Song Dynasty* (Indianapolis: Hackett, 2003), 254.

Werner Forman / Art Resource, NY

BUDDHA STATUE AT YUNGANG This huge statue of the Buddha, created around 290 C.E., is 45 feet tall. It is one of thousands found along cliffs in western China and elsewhere along the Silk Road.

Chinese culture, while the Chinese tolerated rule by foreigners who respected and protected their culture. Hence social institutions and economic patterns proved able to survive conquest. But the Chinese also learned from the invaders. This merging of cultures provided a foundation for the later rejuvenation of a China that would be greater than the empires of Qin and Han.

After the Han, China became even more connected to the world, fostering a vital, cosmopolitan culture. One fifth-century emperor loved everything foreign: dress, art works, food, beds, chairs, harps, dances. Ideas and products traveled both directions along the Silk Road and by land and sea between China and Southeast Asia, and Chinese objects from this era often showed Indian, Persian, Mesopotamian, Greek, or Roman influences. The graves of wealthy Chinese frequently contained Roman glass, Persian silver vessels, images of Greek gods, and cups made from Indonesian shells. China's openness to ideas from outside also led many Chinese to embrace an Indian religion, Buddhism.

Buddhism and China's Eclectic Religious Tradition

During the later Classical period, universal religions—faiths that appealed to people from many cultures—became more prominent in Eurasia and North Africa. The decline and collapse of the great Afro-Eurasian empires, from China to Rome, produced political instability and social strife that challenged established ways. In response, universal religions diffused along the trade networks: Christianity from western Asia to Europe, where it soon became the dominant religion; Hinduism throughout India and into Southeast Asia; and Mahayana **(mah-HAH-YAH-nah)** Buddhism into Central and East Asia. These universal religions incorporated existing local beliefs, creating hybrid artistic forms and value systems. The most pronounced synthesis took place in East Asia as Buddhism encountered earlier belief systems such as Confucianism.

Buddhism's arrival proved a momentous transition, fostering the Buddhist Age in both Chinese and Asian history in the fourth through ninth centuries C.E. Buddhism in some form became dominant in much of East, Central, Southeast, and portions of South Asia (see Chapter 5). Basic Buddhist beliefs about overcoming suffering through good deeds and thoughts derived from the sixth-century B.C.E. teachings of the Indian sage known as the Buddha ("the Enlightened One"), but the religion later split into several rival schools. One of these, Mahayana Buddhism, was carried by merchants and missionaries along the Silk Road into Central Asia. From there it spread into western China during later Han times and was firmly established by the fourth century, linking China with distant India. Later the religion spread from China to Korea,

Vietnam, and Japan. Buddhism preached compassion and gentleness, offering hope and meaning to people experiencing hardship, warfare, and instability. It also brought to the Chinese a spiritual outlook largely missing in Confucianism, which appealed to reason and practical ethics but said little about gods or life after death, and in Daoist mysticism, which could not explain the individual's fate in the cosmic order. Mahayana Buddhism promised salvation in an afterlife. But Buddhism also adapted to Chinese traditions. For example, the Buddhist notion of reincarnation clashed with Chinese beliefs in ancestor worship, so most Chinese never accepted this idea.

Traveling peacefully from India through Central Asia, Chinese Buddhism acquired a cosmopolitan outlook and Indian artistic, literary, and cultural influences, as shown by the huge Buddhist sculptures along the Silk Road and in northwestern China. Buddhist missionaries entered China, and several hundred Chinese pilgrims went to India overland or along the sea route through Southeast Asia. The monk Faxian **(fah-shee-en)** spent fifteen years in India and also visited Buddhist centers in Southeast Asia in the fifth century C.E. On their return to China the pilgrims spread knowledge of the societies they encountered.

By the middle of the first millennium C.E., an eclectic Chinese religious tradition embraced three very different viewpoints—Buddhism, Confucianism, and Daoism—known as "the three ways." The schools mixed with each other. Hence, Buddhism influenced popular Daoism, and many Chinese could no longer clearly differentiate between them. An old but still popular Chinese story has Confucius, Laozi, and Buddha walking and talking together, debating the merits of their respective positions; as they cross a bridge, they are obscured in mist. When spotted again, only one somewhat larger figure can be seen in the distance. Yet some distinctions were maintained. Only Buddhism developed a fully organized church, with monks and nuns. Confucianism, a philosophy of social relations rather than a true religion, had no priests. Many Chinese, not identifying themselves exclusively with any of them, saw the belief systems as different roads to the same destination, personal happiness.

Gradually a gap between the educated elite's relatively secular world-view and the common people's popular religion widened. Intellectuals favored Confucian humanism and Daoist naturalism, with moral perfection of humankind as the ultimate goal. Since Confucianism centered on humanity rather than gods, many intellectuals viewed popular religion, with its gods, spirits, ghosts, and magic, as superstition. One Han scholar wrote that "the number of persons who have died since the world began must run into thousands of millions. If everyone of them has become a spirit, there must be at least one to every yard as we walk along the road."[18] Meanwhile, although more Chinese may have been indifferent to religion than was common elsewhere, many peasants, artisans, and merchants believed in thousands of gods and goddesses of Buddhist, Daoist, or animist origin, using shamans to communicate with the spirit realm. They also accepted notions of Heaven and Hell introduced by Mahayana Buddhism, and of **geomancy** **(JEE-u-MAN-see)**, known in Chinese as *feng shui* **(fung shway)** ("wind and water"), a popular Daoist-influenced system for determining the auspicious settings of buildings and graves. Geomancy is still widely employed today in East Asia, and some architects even use it to assess the suitability of modern houses and skyscrapers in North American and European cities.

Science and Technology in the Classical Period

China developed one of the world's oldest scientific and technological traditions, establishing along with the Indians, Mesopotamians, Egyptians, and Greeks, the foundation for modern science. Historians credit the Zhou and Han with many important breakthroughs, including porcelain ("china"), the water-powered mill, the shoulder harness for horses, the foot stirrup (possibly adapted from Central Asian models), the magnetic compass, the seismograph, the wheelbarrow, the stern-post rudder for boats, the spinning wheel, linen, and perhaps the most significant innovation, rag paper. Before paper Chinese scribes wrote with a pointed stylus on strips of wood, bamboo, or woven cloth, but these were difficult to use and store. Eventually an ingenious first-century C.E. artisan beat cloth into fiber and formed thin sheets. To mass-produce Buddhist texts and images and Confucian classics for students preparing for the examinations, Han craftsmen made ink rubbings on paper from stone carvings, often of entire Buddhist books. Elementary block printing was in limited use in China by the sixth century C.E., and by the ninth century woodblock printing had become a major activity in East Asia. Most of these inventions did not reach western Eurasia over the trade routes until a few centuries—in some cases a millennium—later.

The Han innovated in mathematics and science. Besides making the most accurate calculation of *pi* at the time, the Chinese were many centuries ahead of the world in fractions, the concept of negative numbers, and in certain aspects of algebra and geometry. Around 190 C.E. they invented the *abacus*, a primitive computer and unparalleled tool for calculations, constructed by fastening balls on wires attached to a board carved with divisions; this device is still used widely in Asia today. Han astronomers compiled catalogues of stars, speculated on sunspots, and explained the causes of lunar eclipses.

Chinese science, especially medicine, owed much to the cosmological thinking exemplified in yin-yang dualism and also to Daoism, which inspired an interest in nature. An enduring medical discovery, *acupuncture*, developed from the belief that good health was the result of proper yin-yang balance in the body. Thin needles are inserted at predetermined points to alleviate pain or correct some condition. Experts learned the body parts and how to read a pulse. Acupuncture is still practiced today and has spread around the world. The Chinese also stressed good hygiene and preventive medicine, including

geomancy Known in Chinese as *feng shui* ("wind and water"), a system for determining the auspicious settings of human dwellings and graves.

[18]Quoted in Wang, *Images of Women*, 254.

a well-balanced diet and regular exercise. In their quest for the elixir of immortality, Daoist alchemists discovered many edible foods, herbs, and potions that improved health, and they developed the greatest list of pharmaceuticals in the premodern world. Doctors diagnosed gout and cirrhosis of the liver. Many ancient Chinese folk remedies remain popular today in China.

The Chinese continued to develop innovative technologies. Although never a great seafaring people like the Austronesians and Greeks, the Chinese became some of the world leaders in shipbuilding, some taking up maritime trade. Chinese ships carried trade goods back and forth to Korea, Japan, and Southeast Asia. By at least the fifth century C.E. the Chinese had constructed large oceangoing vessels with stern-post rudders for maneuvering, which permitted longer and farther journeys. Chinese ships and navigational skills were probably adequate to even cross the vast Pacific, although there is no compelling evidence that any did so.

The Sui Reunification of China

To a fourth-century observer it might have seemed that the Roman Empire, although visibly weakening, could endure, while the Chinese empire was overrun by "barbarian" invaders, broken apart, and turning to foreign, otherworldly religions. Yet China was eventually reunified under a powerful, centralized government, whereas Rome, facing the same kinds of challenges, fragmented and collapsed. Several factors contributed to China's reassembly. Reestablishment of a centralized state was made easier by China's large population, which by 400 C.E. was some 50 million, probably double Europe's population. More culturally unified than Europe's varied peoples, the Chinese could perhaps more easily absorb the nomadic invaders. Confucian ethical humanism, the merit-based civil service exams, and writing encouraged both cultural and political unity. In contrast, India contained many very different spoken languages and writing systems, while in Europe, speakers of Romance languages based on phonetic alphabets splintered into many competing countries, never to be reunited.

The ruthless Sui **(sway)** dynasty (581–618 C.E.) played the same role in history as the Qin, reuniting China after several centuries of turmoil and division. Tyrants but also patrons of arts and letters, the Sui created the world's largest library. Like the Qin, they were builders, mobilizing 6 million forced workers to construct the Grand Canal linking the Yangzi and Yellow Rivers. At 1,200 miles long, the longest human-made channel ever constructed, the canal ensured the prosperity of later dynasties, as each year huge quantities of grain were shipped north. Tree-shaded parks and inns lined the route. However, like earlier dynasties, the Sui overreached and collapsed. Exhausting campaigns of conquest temporarily extended imperial frontiers into Korea and Central Asia, but the Sui drove the Chinese too hard, causing overwork, food shortages, and soon rebellions. The victor in the ensuing struggles established the Tang **(tahng)** dynasty (618–907 C.E.), which launched China into its great golden age, extending over many centuries, and linked it more closely to Korea and Japan, whose societies we turn to now.

MAKE SURE YOU UNDERSTAND THESE KEY POINTS BEFORE MOVING ON

- **Spurred by invasions of nomadic peoples from the north, the population shifted south, but the invaders were assimilated by existing Chinese government structures.**
- **Buddhism took root in China during this tumultuous period, spreading along the trade routes from India and melding with existing Confucian thought.**
- **The Chinese attitude toward religion was characterized by an easy interchange of beliefs, in which individuals drew from a variety of religious or philosophical perspectives depending on their need.**
- **Daoism promoted the idea of a yin-yang balance in the natural world, influencing developments in science and medicine.**

Korea, Japan, and East Asian Networks

How did the Koreans and Japanese assimilate Chinese influences into their own distinctive societies?

Large, densely populated China dominated East Asia for much of history. Consequently, eastern Asia did not develop the political diversity, with many rival states, that prevailed in India, western Asia, or Europe after Classical times. Korea and Japan adopted intensive farming, becoming receptive to Chinese cultural influence. Although more developed than Japan for many centuries, Korea was often in China's shadow. Separated by water, Japan remained more independent. Yet both Korea and Japan creatively forged distinctive societies.

Korea and China

As a close neighbor, Korea experienced a regular and extensive interaction with China that brought political pressures but also many advantages. Chinese cultural and technological influences permeated the peninsula. Koreans adopted iron technology from China, including advanced weapons, that later fostered agriculture-based states. However, these were soon overwhelmed by Chinese influence. In 108 B.C.E. Wu Di's Han armies, reportedly sixty thousand troops strong, conquered northern Korea against fierce resistance. China ruled for the next four centuries, providing models to the Koreans in government structure, architecture, and city planning. Many Chinese immigrated to the peninsula.

The end of Chinese colonization in 313 C.E. allowed Korean society to flower. Three native kingdoms emerged that dominated Korea between the fourth and seventh centuries, occasionally warring against each other. However, Chinese cultural influences, including the writing system and Confucianism, also spread more widely. Mahayana Buddhism, introduced in 372 C.E., strongly influenced Korean painting, sculpture, and architecture. But the Koreans never became carbon copies of the Chinese. For example, unlike in China, where family status rose or fell with dynastic change and civil service examinations, an inherited aristocracy thrived for most of Korean history. And although most Koreans adopted Buddhism, the long flourishing animism never disappeared.

Eventually one kingdom, Koguryo (Goguryeo) **(ko-GUR-yo)**, based in northern Korea and southern Manchuria, became the most influential state (see Map 6.3). In the fourth century, with China divided, Koguryo expanded far to the north and annexed much of Manchuria and southeastern Siberia, thus becoming one of Eurasia's largest states between 350 and 668 C.E. Historians debate whether Koguryo's people had a close cultural connection to the several smaller states controlling southern Korea. Its army repulsed seven major invasions by the Sui and Tang between 598 and 655 C.E., when a resurgent China was eastern Eurasia's most powerful state. In 612 C.E. Koguryo routed an invading Sui army of some 300,000 troops. In fact, the huge cost of the campaigns in Korea contributed to the Sui dynasty's collapse. Finally, in 668 C.E., Chinese armies, allied with the southern Korean state of Silla **(SILL-ah or SHILL-ah)**, overran Koguryo. Soon Silla drove out the Chinese, reunifying much of Korea in 676.

MAP 6.3 KOREA AND JAPAN IN THE FIFTH CENTURY C.E. During the Classical period Korea was often divided into several states. Koguryo (Goguryeo) in the north was the largest state, ruling part of Siberia. By the sixth century the Yamato state governed much of the main Japanese island, Honshu.

Yayoi and Yamato Japan

Like Korea across the straits, Japan experienced dramatic change. The pottery-making Jomon culture (see Chapter 4) persisted until around 300 B.C.E., when a new culture, Yayoi **(ya-YOI)** (300 B.C.E.–552 C.E.), emerged that was based on productive wet rice farming and had close links with Korea. Some archaeologists think Yayoi culture and rice growing may have begun on the southern island of Kyushu even earlier, perhaps by 1000 B.C.E. Korea remained a source of learning and population for Japan, which received a continuous flow of several million Korean and some Chinese immigrants until 900 C.E., including skilled craftsmen, scribes, and artists. After Korean migrants brought horses, the armored warrior on horseback later became part of Japanese life. In this era the distinction between Korea and Japan may have been murky, but by 600 C.E. the Japanese people as we know them today, and the Japanese language, had coalesced from the genetic and cultural mixing over many centuries of Korean immigrants with the Jomon.

Yayoi Japan traded sporadically with China. A Chinese visitor documented Yayoi society, reporting the preoccupation with taboos, class distinctions, and especially ritual cleanliness. Like modern Japanese, the Yayoi enjoyed dancing, singing, drinking rice wine, and eating raw vegetables; experienced little crime; and revered nature. The Yayoi used the potter's wheel, were expert weavers, and mastered both bronze and iron technology, later fashioning iron into highly effective swords and armor. The Yayoi formed no centralized governments but were organized into many clans, each ruled by a hereditary priest-chieftain. During the second century C.E., with Japan engulfed in conflict, Pimiko **(pih-MEE-ko)** became a powerful queen-priestess who brought peace by imposing strict laws. Chinese observers were fascinated by Pimiko: "Remaining unmarried, she occupied herself with magic and sorcery.... She kept one thousand female attendants, but few people saw her.... She resided in a palace surrounded by towers and stockade, with the protection of armed guards."[19] However, most clan elites were men who governed farmers, artisans, and a few slaves and mobilized people to build hundreds of large earthen tombs, often surrounded by moats, all over south-central Honshu

[19]From Ryusaku Tsunoda et al., eds., *Sources of Japanese Tradition*, vol. 1 (New York: Columbia University Press, 1958), 7.

Gianni Dagli Orti/Private Collection Paris/The Art Archive

PRINCE SHOTOKU This painting from the eighth century C.E. shows Prince Shotoku, one of the major Yamato leaders, and his sons in the Japanese style clothing of the times. Prince Shotoku launched a period of intensive borrowing from China.

Island. The tombs housed the remains of prominent leaders, buried with jewels, swords, and clay figurines.

Japan entered written history in the sixth century C.E. with the Yamato **(YA-ma-toe)** (552–710 C.E.), the first state ruling a majority of the Japanese people. The Yamato kingdom was centered in south-central Honshu, where the cities of Kyoto and Osaka now stand. Not a centralized state like Han China or Koguryo, Yamato erected a national government ruling over territorial clans headed by hereditary chiefs. Eventually it extended its influence into southern Japan while expanding its northern frontier deep into Ainu territory. Like the Yayoi, the Yamato welcomed Korean and Japanese immigrants, and some of them joined the political and cultural elite.

Yamato was headed by emperors and occasionally empresses—all ancestors of the same imperial family ruling Japan today, fifteen centuries later. Political continuity under the same royal family gave the Japanese identity and cultural unity. Japanese mythology portrayed the imperial family as descended from the Sun Goddess. This beautiful spirit, Amaterasu **(AH-mah-teh-RAH-soo)**, and her male consort experienced violent mood swings and periodic conflict, perhaps an expression of the frequent storms, volcanic eruptions, and earthquakes that rock the islands. Despite her tantrums, a female creator deity might reflect the high status of women in early Japan. Chinese visitors reported that the Yayoi made no distinction between men and women, and before the eighth century C.E. around half of the imperial sovereigns were women. However, patriarchy became the common pattern by 1000 C.E.

Shinto ("way of the gods") The ancient animistic Japanese cult that emphasized closeness to nature and enjoyed a rich mythology that included many deities.

Japanese Isolation and Cultural Unity

The Japanese forged a particularly distinctive society through a mixing of the local and the foreign. Over a hundred miles from the Eurasian mainland, Japan had only sporadic communication with Korea. Limited space and resources despite the steadily growing population on the mountainous islands fostered a tightly woven society with intense social pressures, sparking creativity. Since personal privacy became rare in this crowded land, people erected psychological walls that allowed them to "tune out" the surrounding noise and activity.

Isolation also made the Japanese expert at borrowing selectively from the outside during periods of intensive contact. Throughout their history, the Japanese borrowed from Korea, China, and, much later, the West, but they seldom left a borrowed idea in its original form. For example, they adopted the Chinese model of an exalted emperor but not the Mandate of Heaven that justified overthrowing incompetent or tyrannical dynasties. The Japanese also created much of their own culture and technology, including the Classical world's best tempered steel. They created artistic forms and styles of universal appeal, such as carefully planned gardens and *bonsai* **(bon-sigh)** (miniature) trees, as well as ingenious solutions to chronic problems such as urban crowding and limited resources. The Japanese house, containing thick straw floor mats, sliding paper panels rather than interior walls, a hot tub for communal bathing, and charcoal-burning braziers, conserved building materials and minimized fuel needs for heating and cooking.

Japanese Encounters with China

Chinese ideas greatly influenced Japan several times in history, beginning on a large scale in the sixth century C.E. Introduced around 538, Mahayana Buddhism fostered cultural change, bringing, for example, new art forms. Chinese teachers, artisans, and Buddhist monks migrated to Japan, and Japanese journeyed to Korea and China, coming back as Buddhist converts. Just as the Chinese maintained three distinct traditions of thought, in Japan Buddhism coexisted with an ancient animistic cult, centuries later known as **Shinto (SHIN-toe)** ("way of the gods"), which emphasized closeness to nature and enjoyed a rich mythology and many deities.

A growing realization among Japanese leaders that China and Korea were much stronger politically, economically, and culturally spurred deliberate borrowing from China to reshape Japanese society. The Yamato expanded relations with Sui

China and reorganized government structures, integrating Chinese writing and Confucian notions of social organization and morality. The adoption of Chinese ideas accelerated under Prince Shotoku **(show-TOW-koo)** (573–621 C.E.), an ardent Buddhist who sponsored temple building and promoted Confucian values. His ideas foreshadowed the later Japanese emphasis on the group: "Harmony is to be cherished, and opposition for opposition's sake must be avoided as a matter of principle,"[20] he wrote into the first Japanese constitution, issued in 604. Reflecting the Confucian emphasis on the need for ethical government and acceptance of hierarchy, the constitution emphasized cooperation and moral guidance, and Shotoku became one of the most revered figures in Japanese history. Some historians compare him to the Indian king Ashoka, who also embraced Buddhism, and the Roman emperor Constantine, who promoted Christianity. Over the next two and a half centuries many official embassies were exchanged between China and Japan, further promoting the exchange of ideas.

MAKE SURE YOU UNDERSTAND THESE KEY POINTS BEFORE MOVING ON

- **Korea's proximity to China led to the adoption of Chinese writing and other technologies in Korea.**
- **Both Buddhism and Confucianism from China permeated Korean culture and were blended with the native belief system of animism.**
- **The flow of ideas and people from Korea and China to Japan introduced Buddhism, writing, and other influences into Japan, but the Japanese culture, arts, and religion remained distinctive.**
- **The Yamato, Japan's first centralized state, began actively importing cultural and political ideas from China in the sixth century.**

aplia

[20]From David John Lu, ed., *Sources of Japanese History*, vol. 1 (New York: McGraw-Hill, 1974), 21–22.

CHAPTER SUMMARY

The Classical East Asian societies were distinctive in many ways. China was large, densely populated, and an innovator in government, culture, religion, science, and technology. During the warfare and political instability of the late Zhou period, Confucius promoted ethical values and suggested how people could live in harmony with each other through a well-defined and hierarchical social structure. In contrast, the Daoists advocated a life shaped by the natural world, while the Legalists argued that a powerful government must harshly regulate society to preserve order. These Classical ideas persisted in Chinese thought into modern times. The Legalist leaders of the Qin dynasty used brutal policies to transform China into a centralized imperial state. Following the short-lived Qin, the great Han dynasty established a large Asian empire and traded with western Asia and Europe across the Silk Road, becoming a major force in eastern Eurasia. The social structure became more patriarchal, and women were expected to be dutiful to their men.

After the Han collapsed, Central Asians frequently invaded and divided China politically. In this turbulent period, Mahayana Buddhism became popular in China, where it mixed with Confucianism, Daoism, and animism. Eventually the Sui dynasty reunified China, an achievement that contrasted with the Roman Empire in the West, which disintegrated into various fragments. China also became a model for neighboring societies. First the Koreans and then the Japanese adopted many Chinese ideas, including some technologies, writing, Confucianism, and Buddhism. But they also creatively blended them with their own unique traditions, creating a distinctive mix of the imported with the local.

KEY TERMS

Confucianism (p. 122)
The Analects (p. 122)
filial piety (p. 123)
Daoism (p. 124)
Legalism (p. 124)
Sinicization (p. 125)
Silk Road (p. 128)
mandarins (p. 128)
scholar-gentry (p. 128)
geomancy (p. 136)
Shinto (p. 136)

7 Western Asia, the Eastern Mediterranean, and Regional Systems, 600–200 B.C.E.

© Ko.Yo/Shutterstock.com

PERSEPOLIS During the height of their empire, Persian kings built a lavish capital at Persepolis, in today's Iran. This photo shows the audience hall, the part of the grand palace where the kings greeted their ministers and foreign diplomats.

Wonders are many on earth, and the greatest of these is man, who rides the ocean. He is master of the ageless earth. The use of language, the wind-swift motion of brain he learned; found out the laws of living together in cities. There is nothing beyond his power.

—Chorus in *Antigone*, by the fifth-century B.C.E. Greek playwright Sophocles (SAHF-UH-KLEEZ)[1]

IN THIS CHAPTER

Thales (THAY-leez) and Anaximander **(uh-NAK-suh-MAN-der)**, pioneering Greek philosophers and scientists, grew up in prosperous Miletus **(my-LEET-uhs)**, a commercial city on the southwestern coast of Anatolia (modern Turkey) and long a regional crossroads mingling Greek and foreign cultures. Like other young men, they haunted the bustling docks and seaside bars, listening to tales of sailors returning from distant shores and of travelers from foreign lands. Some sailors brought learning from older societies such as Egypt and Mesopotamia, while Milesian merchants sent ships all over the Mediterranean carrying treasured wool developed by Milesian sheep breeders and fine furniture produced by its cabinetmakers. Around the Black Sea, Milesian settlements supplied fish and wheat, enriching the city's traders.

Miletus flourished as a great intellectual center and meeting place for the Greek and Persian worlds. This intermingling fostered new thinking about geography and cartography. Thales worked out a geometrical system to calculate a ship's position at sea, and his student, Anaximander, made the first map of the Mediterranean world and the first Greek astronomical chart. Later Hecataeus **(HEK-a-TAU-us)** of Miletus published a map of the world known to the Greeks, from India to Spain.

The Greeks developed a unique society on the rocky shores of the Aegean Sea. In cities such as Miletus and Athens, they introduced many ideas and institutions that endured through the centuries. The view of humanity's greatness offered by Sophocles in the opening quotation reflects an obsession with individuality and freedom that made the Greeks role models for modern democracies. But Greek achievements are only part of the story. Connected to a wider world, Greeks benefited from regional trade, colonizing other territories and borrowing ideas from neighboring societies. Another creative society and even greater regional power, the Persians, dominated the easternmost Mediterranean and western Asia while introducing many innovations. Ultimately, the rival Greek and Persian societies were temporarily brought together in an empire mixing their two cultures.

[1]Quoted in Norman Davies, *Europe: A History* (New York: Harper, 1996), 117.

The Persians and Their Empire

How did the Persians acquire and maintain their empire?

Although its period of greatest political influence lasted only two centuries, the Persian Empire played an important role in world history. Persians established a larger, more multicultural empire than any people before them, encompassing Anatolian Greeks, Phoenicians, Hebrews, Egyptians, Mesopotamians, and some Indians. Domination of the east-west trade routes made the empire a major meeting ground. The Persians' wars with Greece and their empire building in western Asia also paved the way for an even greater imperial structure under the Greek Alexander the Great and his successors.

Achaemenid The ruling family of the classical Persian Empire.

Building the Persian Empire

The Persian homeland was located on a plateau just north of the Persian Gulf (see Map 7.1). Overland routes connected Mesopotamia and Anatolia to India and Central Asia through Persia's mountains and deserts, where two pastoral Indo-European societies, the Medes **(MEEDZ)** and Persians, competed for power in the early seventh century. Soon the Persians displaced the Medes.

At its peak the Persian Empire, usually known as **Achaemenid** **(a-KEY-muh-nid)** Persia after the ruling family, extended from the Indus Valley in the east to Libya in the

800 B.C.E. | 750 B.C.E. | 700 B.C.E. | 650 B.C.E. | 600 B.C.E. | 550 B.C.E.

GREECE

- **ca. 750–550 B.C.E.** Greek colonization in Mediterranean, Black Sea
- **ca. 594 B.C.E.** Solon's reforms in Athens
- **561–527 B.C.E.** Peisistratus tyrant in Athens

PERSIA

- **600 B.C.E.** Persians become vassals of Medes
- **550–530 B.C.E.** Kingship of Cyrus the Great
- **547–546 B.C.E.** Conquest of Lydia
- **530–522 B.C.E.** Kingship of Cambyses II
- **525–523 B.C.E.** Conquest of Egypt

HELLENISTIC WORLD

west and from the Black, Caspian, and Aral **(AR-uhl)** Seas in the north to the Nile Valley in the south (see Map 7.1). King Cyrus II (Cyrus the Great) began the expansion, and his successors, Cambyses **(kam-BY-seez)** II, Darius **(duh-RY-uhs)** I, and Xerxes **(ZUHRK-seez)** I, continued the conquests. Their autocratic but culturally tolerant government established a model for later Middle Eastern empires and challenged the Greeks in the west.

After first overthrowing the Median king, by 539 Cyrus the Great (r. 550–530 B.C.E.) had conquered Mesopotamia, Syria, Palestine, Lydia (a kingdom in western Anatolia), and all the Greek cities in Anatolia. As much diplomat as soldier, Cyrus followed moderate policies in the conquered territories, making only modest demands for tribute. After conquering Babylonia, he issued a proclamation on a cylinder that some scholars consider the world's first charter of human rights and tolerance: "Protect this land from rancor, from foes, from falsehood, and from drought." Cyrus claimed that the main Babylonian god, Marduk **(MAHR-dook)**, ordered him to help the Babylonians by bringing them "justice and righteousness."[2] He also allowed the Jews taken to Babylon by the Assyrians to return to Palestine and rebuild their temple. When Cyrus was killed while campaigning in Central Asia, his son Cambyses II (r. 530–522 B.C.E.) subjugated Egypt, wisely presenting himself as a new Egyptian ruler who would bring stability, good fortune, health, and gladness.

Cambyses was succeeded by Darius I (r. 521–486 B.C.E.), a usurper who had seized power and who boasted that "over and above my thinking power and understanding, I am a good warrior, horseman, bowman, spear-man."[3] Darius crushed a revolt in Egypt and spread Persian power east and west, even annexing

[2]Quoted in Lindsey Allen, *The Persian Empire* (Chicago: University of Chicago Press, 1959), 27.
[3]Quoted in A. T. Olmstead, *History of the Persian Empire* (Chicago: University of Chicago Press, 1959), 125.

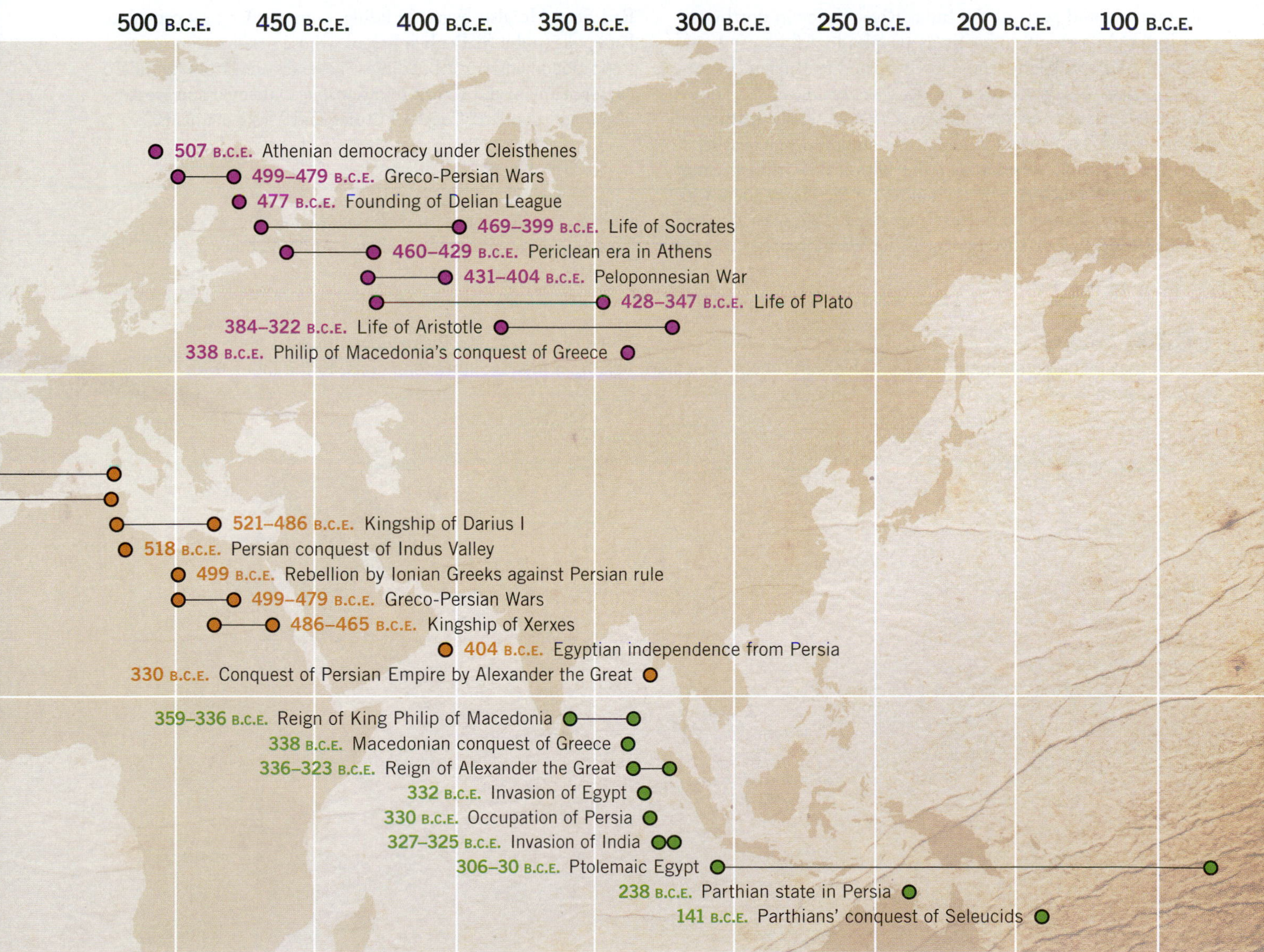

Zev Radovan/BibleLandPictur/www.BibleLandPictures.com/Alamy

BAS RELIEF OF DARIUS AND XERXES HOLDING COURT This relief was carved in one of the palaces at the Persian capital of Persepolis.

Afghanistan and parts of the Indus River Valley in northwestern India. As a result, today many peoples in Afghanistan and Central Asia speak languages closely related to Persian. To promote justice and ensure his posterity as a great lawgiver, Darius fashioned a law code for Babylonia that basically reaffirmed Hammurabi's laws made almost fifteen hundred years earlier.

The Persians were among the Classical world's greatest engineers and builders. For example, to forge closer links with Egypt, Darius completed the first Suez Canal, 125 miles long and 150 feet wide, that briefly connected the Mediterranean and the Red Seas. He also began building a spectacular new capital at Persepolis **(puhr-SEP-uh-luhs)**, on whose massive stone terrace stood monumental royal buildings. Persepolis drew from Egyptian, Mesopotamian, and Greek traditions, its craftsmen and workers including Egyptians, Greeks, Hittites, and Mesopotamians.

Imperial Policies and Networks

Unlike the Assyrians and Babylonians, the Persians used laws, generous economic policies, and tolerance toward the

MAP 7.1 THE PERSIAN EMPIRE, CA. 500 B.C.E. At its height around 500 B.C.E., the Persians controlled a huge empire that included northern Greece, Egypt, and most of western Asia from the Mediterranean coast to the Indus River in India. © 2015 Cengage Learning

conquered to rule successfully. Leading citizens came from many backgrounds. Medes, Armenians, Greeks, Egyptians, and Kurds, a people living in the mountains just north of Persia and Mesopotamia, served as generals. Greeks and Romans imitated some of these Persian techniques when they created even larger empires several centuries later.

Although in theory having absolute power, kings needed to consult with important nobles and judges, who were often in faraway provinces. Each provincial governor, or **satrap (SAY-trap)** ("protector of the kingdom"), ruled according to established laws and paid annual taxes to the king. Communication was aided by the "royal road" stretching 1,700 miles from east to west, and a king's messenger on a horse could cover this road in nineteen days. The Greek historian Herodotus marveled at the extensive, well-protected roads, writing that "neither snow, nor rain, nor heat, nor darkness of night prevents these couriers from completing their designated stages with utmost speed."[4]

The Persian Empire was strengthened by trade, which was promoted both by the highways and by the use of standard weights and measures and minted coins. Instead of stealing their wealth, Persian rulers allowed conquered peoples to maintain their usual economic activities. Phoenicians, for example, continued their Mediterranean trade. To open new trade networks, Darius sent an expedition to India that returned by sailing around Arabia to Suez, laying the foundation for conquering the Indus River Valley and opening more maritime trade.

Perhaps most crucial to their imperial success, the Persians generally treated conquered people and their social and religious institutions with respect. In Egypt, for instance, Cambyses became a pharaoh. The Persians prided themselves on their ability to unify vastly different peoples under the "king of kings," a title that respected other rulers with limited rights in their own territories. Hence, many Greeks fought for Persia in the Greco-Persian Wars. The Persians also utilized various official languages, including Aramaic **(ar-uh-MAY-ik)**, spoken by many peoples of western Asia, and later Greek.

Persian Religion and Society

The Persians made another distinct contribution to later world history by promoting **Zoroastrianism (zo-ro-ASS-tree-uh-niz-uhm)**. Some key ideas in Judaism, Christianity, and Islam are foreshadowed by, and perhaps even derived from, Zoroastrianism, which later became Persia's state religion. Its founder, Zoroaster (whose name means "With Golden Camels"), was one of the first non-Hebrew religious leaders to challenge the prevailing polytheism. Scholars debate whether he lived between 630 and 550 B.C.E. or centuries earlier, perhaps around 1000 or 1200 B.C.E. He may have been a priest in the early Persian religion, which was closely related to the religion of the Aryans who migrated to India.

The early Persians apparently believed in three great gods and many lesser ones, but Zoroaster had a monotheistic vision, preaching that only one of these, ***Ahura Mazda* (ah-HOOR-uh MAZZ-duh)** (the "Wise Lord"), was the supreme deity in the universe, responsible for creation and the source of all goodness. A rival Satan-like entity, Angra Mainyu ("Hostile Spirit"), embodied evil and was the source of all misery, cowardice, lies, and sin. Ahura Mazda allowed humans to freely choose between himself and evil, Heaven and Hell. By serving Ahura Mazda, men and women promoted ultimate goodness and truth. At the end of time, Zoroaster believed, Ahura Mazda would win a final victory over evil and even Hell would come to an end. Zoroaster also banned the use of intoxicants and animal sacrifice. However, some Persians worshiped other gods, and several religions coexisted in Persia.

The Jews may have adopted some ideas about good and evil, God and the devil, Heaven and Hell, and a last judgment from Zoroastrians while held captive in Babylon (586–539 B.C.E.). Christianity later incorporated such ideas, and the Zoroastrian watchwords of "good thoughts, good words, good deeds" became key ideas of several religions. Darius I publicly attributed his victories to Ahura Mazda and honored him for creating earth, sky, and humankind. While Christianity and, later, Islam displaced Zoroastrianism in western Asia, the faith lives on today among small groups in Iran as well as in the wealthy Parsee **(PAR-see)** minority in India, descendants of Persian Zoroastrians.

The Persians were not as politically diversified a society as the Greeks (see Witness to the Past: A Greek Account of Persian Customs). Their system was headed by nobles, many of them warriors who had been granted large estates by the king, followed by priests, merchants, and bankers. In Persian-ruled Babylonian cities these citizens made important judicial decisions in formal assemblies. Zoroastrian priests schooled noble sons to prepare for government careers. The middle class included bakers, brewers, butchers, carpenters, coppersmiths, and potters. At the bottom of the social structure, many peasant farmers were impoverished, becoming poor renters or sharecroppers bound to the land. Slaves, mainly debtors, criminals, and prisoners of war, filled various functions. Some were apprenticed in trades, while others operated small businesses.

Persian society was patriarchal and polygamous. Men believed that the greatest proof of masculinity was to father many sons, and many rich men had several wives. Persian women were usually kept secluded in harems and probably veiled themselves, an ancient practice in western Asia. But some queens and other noble women strongly influenced their husbands, and some controlled large estates. A few women became independently wealthy. For instance, one entrepreneur and

satrap ("protector of the kingdom") A Persian official who ruled according to established laws and procedures and paid a fixed amount of taxes to the emperor each year.

Zoroastrianism A monotheistic religion founded by the Persian Zoroaster, and later the state religion of Persia. Its notion of one god opposed by the devil may have influenced Judaism and later Christianity.

Ahura Mazda (the "Wise Lord") The one god of Zoroastrianism.

[4]Quoted in William H. Stiebing, *Ancient Near Eastern History and Culture* (New York: Longman, 2003), 303.

landowner of commoner origins, Irdabama, controlled a large labor force of several hundred and operated her own grain and wine business.

Warfare and Persian Decline

Persia's rulers eventually encountered major resistance by Scythians and Greeks. Darius campaigned unsuccessfully against the Scythians **(SITH-ee-uhnz)**, the warlike Indo-European pastoral nomads whose territory stretched from Ukraine to Mongolia. Skilled horsemen and master gold and bronze workers, Scythians had both fought and traded with Greek cities. The many Greeks who lived in Persian territories were also rivals for regional power. Inspired by Scythian resistance, some Greek cities on the Ionian **(eye-OH-nee-uhn)** coast of Anatolia rebelled against Persian control (see Map 7.1). In response Darius attacked cities on the Greek peninsula that were supporting the Ionian rebels. During this first Greco-Persian War, the tiny disunited Greek states turned back the world's most powerful empire. While the Persians failed to occupy peninsular Greece, they reclaimed the Ionian cities, brutally punishing the most rebellious. Darius then supported democratic forces in Ionian cities, a tactic that failed to inspire peninsular Greek cooperation with Persian aims.

Xerxes (r. 486–465 B.C.E.), the son of Darius, tried again to conquer the Greeks in 480 B.C.E., attacking with a huge army and naval force. In this fierce two-year struggle, perhaps Xerxes' most effective ally was the Ionian Greek queen

WITNESS TO THE PAST

A Greek Account of Persian Customs

The Persians used several written languages, but few of their nonreligious documents have survived. Much of what we know of Persian life comes from Greek sources, most of them biased against their greatest regional rival and threat. Although his observations must be treated with caution, the Greek historian Herodotus, writing in the later fifth century B.C.E., had a less nationalistic and more universalistic approach, holding some sympathy for Persians. He was born in and traveled widely in the empire, although not to the Persian heartland, and gathered considerable information, including these observations on some Persian customs.

The customs which I know the Persians to observe are the following: they have no images of the gods, no temples nor altars, and consider the use of them a sign of folly. This comes, I think, from their not believing the gods to have the same nature with men, as the Greeks imagine. Their wont, however, is to ascend the summits of the loftiest mountains, and there to offer sacrifice to Zeus [Ahura Mazda], which is the name they give to the whole circuit of the firmament. They likewise offer to the sun and moon, to the earth, to fire, to water, and to the winds. These are the only gods whose worship has come down to them from ancient times....

To these gods the Persians offer [animal] sacrifice in the following manner: they raise no altar, light no fire, pour no libations; there is no sound of the flute, no putting on of chaplets, no consecrated barley-cake; but the man who wishes to sacrifice brings his victim to a spot of ground which is pure from pollution, and there calls upon the name of the god to whom he intends to offer. It is usual to have the turban encircled with a wreath, most commonly of myrtle. The sacrificer is not allowed to pray for blessings on himself alone, but he prays for the welfare of the king, and of the whole Persian people, among whom he is of necessity included....

Of all the days in the year, the one which they celebrate most is their birthday. It is customary to have the board furnished on that day with an ampler supply than common. The richer Persians cause an ox, a horse, a camel, and an ass to be baked whole and so served up to them: the poorer classes use instead the smaller kinds of cattle. They eat little solid food but abundance of dessert, which is set on table a few dishes at a time; this it is which makes them say that "the Greeks, when they eat, leave off hungry, having nothing worth mention served up to them after the meats; whereas, if they had more put before them, they would not stop eating." They are very fond of wine, and drink it in large quantities....

There is no nation which so readily adopts foreign customs as the Persians. Thus, they have taken the dress of the Medes, considering it superior to their own; and in war they wear the Egyptian breastplate. As soon as they hear of any luxury, they instantly make it their own: and hence, among other novelties, they have learnt unnatural lust from the Greeks. Each of them has several wives, and a still larger number of concubines. Next to prowess in arms, it is regarded as the greatest proof of manly excellence to be the father of many sons. Every year the king sends rich gifts to the man who can show the largest number: for they hold that number is strength. Their sons are carefully instructed from their fifth to their twentieth year, in three things alone—to ride, to draw the bow, and to speak the truth. Until their fifth year they are not allowed to come into the sight of their father, but pass their lives with the women. This is done that, if the child die young, the father may not be afflicted by its loss.

THINKING ABOUT THE READING

1. What aspects of religious beliefs and worship does Herodotus stress?
2. How was Persian culture cosmopolitan?
3. What customs made Persian society unique?

Source: William Stearns Davis, *Readings in Ancient History: Illustrative Extracts from the Sources*, vol. 2: *Greece and the East* (Boston: Allyn and Bacon, 1912), 58—61. This text is part of the Internet Ancient History Sourcebook (http://www.fordham.edu/Halsall/ancient/herodotus-persians.asp).

Artemisia **(AHRT-uh-MIZH-ee-uh)**, who was praised for her bravery and the wise counsel she gave the Persian king. But the Persian thrust failed. Although Xerxes still held some of the Greek world and regained control of Egypt, defeat in this second Greco-Persian War proved a turning point in Persian history.

The Persian Empire was not finally conquered until 330 B.C.E., when Alexander the Great's superior army defeated Persian forces. However, the seeds of decline had been planted earlier when Xerxes began imposing heavier taxes. By 424 B.C.E. the Persian Empire suffered from civil unrest caused by fights within the Achaemenid family, disaffected satrapies, currency inflation, difficulty collecting taxes, and high interest rates and debt that ruined many merchants and landlords. Xerxes and his successors also unwisely reversed the inclusive policies of Cyrus and Darius. Some regions rebelled. Egypt ended Persian control in 404 B.C.E., restoring pharaonic rule. Thus support for the increasingly remote kings weakened long before Alexander the Great ended Achaemenid Persia and its once-great empire.

MAKE SURE YOU UNDERSTAND THESE KEY POINTS BEFORE MOVING ON

- **The Persian Empire, centered on a trade crossroads, was larger than any empire that preceded it.**
- **The Persians often won the support of peoples they had conquered through their respect for native cultures and their institution of the rule of law.**
- **The monotheistic Persian religion, Zoroastrianism, may have contributed some key ideas to Judaism, Christianity, and Islam.**
- **The Persian Empire suffered several setbacks, including an unsuccessful campaign against the Scythians and repeated failure to completely conquer Greece.**
- **Though the Persian Empire was conquered by Alexander the Great in 330 B.C.E., it had begun to decline over a century earlier.**

aplia

The Rise and Flowering of the Greeks

What were some features of Greek government, philosophy, and science?

When people today think of the Classical Greeks, they envision the "golden age" of Athenian democracy, with thinkers pondering life's meaning and the scientific mysteries, but these were only part of a complex, often conflicted society. Historians debate how much of their culture the Greeks created and how much they adopted from others. The Mediterranean was a zone of interaction for peoples living around its rim, and by 700 B.C.E. the Greeks were prospering through active participation in maritime trade. The Greeks also struggled to forge democracy. Like people today, they debated how to rule populations, choose leaders, and educate youngsters. But the Greek society modern people admire was also far from egalitarian and had many unattractive features.

The Greek City-States

Varied influences shaped the Greek world. Mountainous terrain, coastal plains, and scattered islands fostered many city-states rather than one centralized state, as well as the maritime trade that brought growth and prosperity between 800 and 500 B.C.E. A growing population, too little good farmland, and commercial interests led many Greeks to emigrate, establishing new settlements along the Ionian coast, around the Black Sea, in Italy, and on the Mediterranean coasts of France and Spain (see Map 7.2). Greeks even visited and lived in Egypt.

Prosperity led to a new conception of the city and the citizen's role. The **polis** **(POE-lis)**, a city-state, became the major institution of Greek life and gave citizens a sense of community, loyalty, personal identity, and meaning. Free male citizens meeting in an open assembly made all decisions, from building a new temple to making war. The worst punishment a Greek could suffer was expulsion from the polis, and some Greeks committed suicide rather than face ostracism. City-states competed fiercely with each other, including in sports events. In the Olympic Games, begun in the eighth century B.C.E. as a religious festival to honor the god Zeus, each polis sent athletes who competed naked in track and field events or personal contests of strength such as wrestling. The idea was to win, even if it meant cheating.

Not all city residents were equal. Many cities developed **oligarchy** **(AHL-uh-gar-kee)**, rule by a small group of wealthy leaders. As much as 80 percent of the population, including women, slaves, children, and resident foreigners, were not citizens and had no right to vote or hold office. Even among citizens, members of old, aristocratic families enjoyed greater respect than others. By the seventh century, however, aristocratic power had weakened. Although aristocrats generally scorned trade in favor of wealth from landowning, growing trade created wealth for other citizens, allowing them to compete with the upper class. Furthermore, a new battle formation relied on infantry more than the aristocracy-dominated cavalry. The city of Sparta perfected the phalanx **(FAY-langks)**, consisting of a square of soldiers moving in unison, each man protected

polis A Greek city-state that embraced nearby rural areas, whose agricultural surplus then helped support the urban population.

oligarchy Rule by a small group of wealthy leaders.

MAP 7.2 CLASSICAL GREECE, CA. 450 B.C.E. Greek settlements, divided into rival city-states, occupied not only the Greek peninsula but also Crete and western Anatolia. Two alliances headed by Athens and Sparta fought each other in the Peloponnesian War (431–404 B.C.E.).

with heavy armor and carrying a sword or spear. Greek armies became citizen-armies, not paid professional forces. As nonaristocrats risked their lives for their polis, they wanted a greater role in governing it.

The new military system, population expansion, and increased wealth from trade with the Ionian Greeks helped foster democracy. Some Greeks combined the contradictory ideas that people are politically free but also owe loyalty to their community. Some also discovered how people could live without being controlled by gods or kings, framing notions of political freedom and equality for adult male citizens. These were radical ideas for that era, or even for ours.

Reform, Tyranny, and Democracy in Athens

The most dramatic political changes occurred in Athens, a polis on the eastern Greek peninsula of Attica that became progressively more democratic. This change was partly the result of a crisis. The soil was wearing out, and farmers were going deeply into debt. As poor wheat harvests continued, farmers sold themselves and their families into slavery. The poor demanded reform. Around 594 B.C.E. Athenians elected Solon **(SOH-luhn)**, a general, poet, and merchant, to lead the city and rewrite the old constitution. To avoid civil war, he canceled debts, forbade enslavement for debt default, made wealth rather than birth the criterion for membership on the city's governing council, and established a Council of 400 to review issues for action by the Assembly of Citizens, a court of appeals where people, rich or poor, could bring cases to court. However, he also reduced the freedom of women by, for example, allowing fathers to sell into slavery daughters who had lost their virginity before marriage.

The Athenian path to more democracy moved from reform to tyranny to democracy. Solon's reforms failed to please either side in this social and economic struggle. The poor wanted land from the rich, while aristocrats resented their loss of power. Tensions returned, allowing Peisistratus **(pie-SIS-truht-uhs)** (r. 561–527 B.C.E.) to seize power as a **tyrant**, not necessarily a brutal ruler but someone ruling outside the law. Peisistratus gave the poor land confiscated from aristocratic estates and launched a building program, including an aqueduct to bring water directly to the city center.

In 507 B.C.E. another aristocrat, Cleisthenes **(KLICE-thuh-neez)**, established genuine democracy in Athens. Instead of emphasizing noble birth or wealth for citizenship, Cleisthenes created geographical units that chose people by lot for a new Council of 500 that submitted legislation to the Assembly, consisting of 40,000 citizens who selected city officials by lot. In the mid-fifth century aristocratic power was further reduced when lower-income citizens were allowed to become officials. Euripides **(you-RIP-uh-deez)** described the system in his play, *The Suppliant Woman*: "The city is free, and ruled by no one man. The people reign, in annual succession. They do not yield power to the rich; the poor man has an equal share in it."[5] Athenians believed that ordinary citizens could serve in any government positions except as military officers, choosing representatives by lot rather than by more divisive elections. However, only a small group of adult males enjoyed these rights. Moreover, many Greeks thought that democracy of any type was a bad thing.

The Spartan System

In the Peloponnese **(PELL-eh-puh-NEESE)** peninsula in southern Greece, the landlocked city-state of Sparta followed a course much different from that of Athens (see Map 7.2). Spartans saw military power as essential for prestige and influence. Short of land, they conquered their neighbors rather than establish overseas colonies and made the conquered peoples agricultural slaves with no political or human rights who could be killed almost at will. Since slaves greatly outnumbered Spartans, a rigid military state emerged, led by two kings and a Council of Elders elected for life by an Assembly of all citizens over thirty who approved or rejected measures prepared by the Council of Elders and the kings. Thus the Spartans discouraged independent thought or behavior. Boys who seemed physically unfit were taken to a remote rural area and left to die. The other boys received rigid military training and were taught that self-discipline and courage were the highest virtues. One legend tells of a young boy who found a small fox and concealed it under his shirt while engaged in military drill. While standing at attention, the boy suddenly fell over dead. The fox had eaten into his vital organs, but self-discipline had kept him from crying out in pain. From ages twenty to thirty, Spartan males served in the army; only after this time were they allowed to live at home with their wives.

Scala/Art Resource, NY

NARRATIVE DRAWING ON POTTERY The Francois vase, made around 570 B.C.E., is considered a masterpiece of narrative drawing on pottery, with fine detail and vivid coloring. It shows scenes of battle.

Although enjoying no political rights, Spartan women acquired a higher status than other Greek women. Their husbands' frequent absences allowed some to acquire wealth and land. Athenian men criticized Spartan women for their independence, portraying them as greedy, licentious, and needing male control. The playwright Euripides scolded the "Spartan maidens, allowed out of doors with the young men, running and wrestling in their company, with naked thighs."[6]

Religion, Rationalism, and Science

The Greeks may have been practical people, but they also respected the supernatural realm. The many gods and legends introduced by the Homeric epics profoundly shaped Greek thinking and values. Greek religion also owed something to Egyptian and Phoenician beliefs. Chief gods and goddesses represented various natural and human activities.

tyrant Someone who ruled a Greek polis outside the law, not necessarily a brutal ruler.

[5] From Loren J. Samons III, ed., *Athenian Democracy and Imperialism* (Boston: Houghton Mifflin, 1998), 216–217.

[6] Quoted in Robert Flaceliere, *Daily Life in Greece at the Time of Pericles* (London: Phoenix, 2002), 56.

Zeus, a sky-god, governed the natural and social order. Other deities included his wife, Hera **(HEER-uh)**, representing marriage and the family; Poseidon **(puh-SIDE-uhn)**, the brother of Zeus, the lord of the sea; Athena, Zeus's favorite daughter, the goddess of wisdom; Apollo, patron of music, philosophy, and other finer things in life; Dionysus **(DIE-uh-NYE-suhs)**, the god of wine; and Aphrodite **(af-ruh-DITE-ee)**, goddess of sex and fertility. Although these deities had human virtues and vices, Greeks viewed them as immortal and more powerful than humans. Defying the gods invited disaster, whereas proper sacrifices to the gods, usually incorporated into festivals and official ceremonies, guaranteed harmony between humans and the heavens.

Interest in life's deeper meaning also fostered a rational approach to the search for truth. The Greeks produced some of history's greatest thinkers, joining the Mesopotamians, Egyptians, Indians, and Chinese in laying the foundation for modern science. Some Greek thinkers questioned supernatural explanations of natural events. The Ionian philosopher Xenophanes **(zi-NAHF-uh-neez)** was skeptical of the gods:

> *Mortals deem that the gods are begotten as they [humans] are, and have clothes like theirs and voice and form.... The Ethiopians make their gods black. The Thracians* **(THRAY-shuhns)** *say theirs have blue eyes and red hair.*[7]

Creative thought sprouted throughout the Greek world. Thales of Miletus (ca. 636–546) was the first known person to perceive the universe as orderly and to seek a natural explanation of phenomena rather than attributing them to gods. Anaximander of Miletus (611–547) believed the first creatures lived in water and came close to the idea, developed several millennia later, that human beings evolved from lower forms of life. Democritus **(di-MAHK-ruht-uhs)** argued that all matter was composed of tiny seeds (atoms) that moved, creating different objects. Heracleitus **(HER-uh-KLITE-uhs)** of Ephasus **(EF-uh-suhs)** in Ionia perceived the universe in a constant state of flux, with only change permanent. The Ionian Pythagoras **(puh-THAG-uh-ruhs)** helped establish modern mathematics by emphasizing the number 10 and developing the multiplication tables and major mathematical theorems.

These early thinkers laid the foundations of natural science and philosophy by emphasizing the explanatory power of human reason and evaluating evidence by human rather than divine standards. However, some Greek thinkers suggested the more troubling idea of relative rather than absolute human standards. The **Sophists** **(SAHF-uhsts)** emphasized skepticism, denying there is ultimate truth. People have struggled with this twin legacy of Greek thinkers ever since.

Sophists Thinkers in Classical Greece who emphasized skepticism and the belief that there is no ultimate truth.

Socratic Method The method, introduced by Socrates, of asking people leading questions to help them examine the truth of their ideas.

Axial Age Philosophy and Thinkers

Three major fifth- and fourth-century Athenian thinkers helped shape world philosophy. The first two, Socrates and Plato, studied the nature of truth; the third, Aristotle **(AR-uh-staht-uhl)**, examined the truth found in nature. These men participated in a philosophical and religious revolution across Eurasia between 600 and 200 B.C.E. that historians often term the Axial Age. The ideas of Buddha in India, Confucius in China, the Hebrew prophets, Zoroaster, and various Greeks shaped Classical societies and remained influential for many centuries.

The earliest seminal philosopher, the Athenian Socrates (469–399 B.C.E.), believed that "the unexamined life" was not worth living. Shabbily dressed, eccentric, passionate, and indifferent to money and pleasure, he asked people leading questions that helped them examine the truth of their ideas, an approach called the **Socratic Method**. Unlike the Sophists, Socrates believed in absolute truths that make people virtuous. But suspicious of democracy, he favored government by the chosen few who acquired superior knowledge. Although considered the founder of Western moral philosophy, some of his elitist views might be unpopular even today. For undermining the polis by asking so many, often embarrassing, questions and "corrupting the youth," Socrates was condemned to death for treason in 399 B.C.E. The prosecutor said of him: "Socrates is an evil doer and a curious person, searching into things under the earth and above the heavens, and making the worse appear the better, and teaching all this to others."[8] Refusing a lighter sentence or exile, Socrates chose death, making him, in modern eyes at least, a martyr for truth and free expression, although most of his contemporaries may not have viewed him this way.

Socrates' leading pupil, Plato (428–347 B.C.E.), became disillusioned with city politics after his mentor's execution. After sojourning in Egypt, Plato founded a school in Athens called the Academy (the source of our word *academic*), where he elaborated Socrates' belief in ultimate truth, beauty, and goodness. He believed that most people, ruled by emotions, cannot see reality. Only a special class who are trained to use reason to control emotions and will, which he called the Guardians, understand ultimate truth and goodness and therefore should govern. Plato later retreated from this elitist conception, suggesting that strong laws could control democratic excesses. Some believe that Plato's thinking sanctioned dictatorships in which a few men claimed special wisdom and virtue.

The Athenian philosopher Aristotle (384–322 B.C.E.) contributed enduring ideas that seem similar to ours today. The son of a Greek physician working for the king of non-Greek Macedonia, Aristotle studied philosophy with Plato and eventually founded his own school. Like Socrates, he was also charged with impiety, but he chose to go into exile. Although distrusting democracy, he encouraged people to pursue their personal desires. Rather than exploring ultimate truths, Aristotle pragmatically emphasized how human nature and physical nature worked. His writings spanned the social sciences, humanities, and natural sciences. One of the first psychologists, he described human

[7]Quoted in Rex Warner, *The Greek Philosophers* (New York: American Library, 1958), 24.
[8]The quote is from Martyn Oliver, *History of Philosophy: Great Thinkers from 600 B.C. to the Present Day* (New York: MetroBooks, 1997), 16–17.

emotions like affection, anger, bravery, fear, hate, joy, and pity. He concluded the world was spherical, classified and analyzed nature, dissected animals, and pioneered zoology, providing a key foundation for both Western and Islamic science. He also studied logic and ethics and studied political systems. In philosophy, Aristotle speculated on **metaphysics**, the broad field that studies the most general concepts and categories underlying people and the world around them (such as "time" and "causation").

Literature

Culturally creative, Athens attracted many writers and artists because prosperity generated spending money for entertainment. Perhaps the Athenians' most enduring contribution, drama, arose from annual religious festivals during which plays based on historical or mythological themes were usually performed in outdoor amphitheaters, accompanied by music. Most plays were tragedies, and the dramatists had different styles. Aeschylus **(ESS-kuh-luhs)** (525–456 B.C.E.) emphasized traditional values, the gods, and justice issues while portraying the disasters brought on by too much pride. Sophocles **(SAUF-uh-klees)** (ca. 497–406 B.C.E.), a humanist, stressed emotional issues. Aristophanes **(AR-uh-STAHF-uh-neez)** (448–380 B.C.E.) wrote comedies ridiculing Athenians and their pretensions. In *The Knights*, a general tries to convince an ignorant sausage seller to unseat the Athenian leader: "To be a leader of the people isn't for learned men, or honest men, but for the ignorant and vile."[9] Some of his criticism reflected Athenian losses during a terrible war. Some playwrights offered vivid images of women who refused to be silenced or abused. In *Agamemnon* **(ag-uh-MEM-non)**, a great tragic drama by Aeschylus, the wife of Agamemnon, the hero of the Trojan War, kills him for sacrificing their daughter to the gods to get a favorable wind to sail to Troy.

Greek lyric poets, especially in Ionia, reflected an individualistic, intellectual approach. Hence, Archilochus **(ahr-KIL-uh-kuhs)** mocked the Spartan battlefield order to "return with your shield—or on it" by writing: "Some lucky Thracian has my shield, For, being somewhat flurried, I dropped it by a wayside bush, As from the field I hurried. To blazes with the shield. I'll get another just as good, When next I take the field."[10] A girl's school director and perhaps the most intensely personal poet, Sappho **(SAFF-oh)**, from the Ionian island of Lesbos, wrote passionate love lyrics to her students: "A host of horsemen, some say, is the loveliest sight upon the earth; some say a display of soldiery; some a fleet of ships, but I say it's whomever one loves."[11] Considered Homer's equal, Sappho wrote poems that were read in the Mediterranean world long after her death.

The Trustees of the British Museum/Art Resource, NY

SOCRATES This statue, made several centuries after his death, celebrates the Athenian philosopher Socrates, who had a strong influence on the thinking of Greek philosophers who came after him, including his student, Plato.

Greek Society

Pronounced differences separated social classes and genders, with freedom reserved primarily for males. Greek society consisted, from top to bottom, of free men (only some of them citizens), many resident foreigners, free women, and slaves. Most free men, if not wealthy landowners or small farmers, worked as laborers, artisans, or shopkeepers. Resident foreigners, including Phoenicians, Lydians, and Syrians, were primarily merchants, bankers, and artisans. Many became wealthy but were required to serve in the military. Free women could not vote, hold office, or serve on juries. Socrates supposedly asked a colleague: "Is there anyone of your acquaintance with whom you have less conversation than your wife?" The reply: "Hardly anyone, I think."[12] Women from elite families generally stayed inside the home, in contrast to many less affluent women.

metaphysics The broad field that studies the most general concepts and categories underlying people and the world around them (such as "time" and "causation").

[9] Quoted in Mortimer Chambers et al., *The Western Experience*, vol. 1, 5th ed. (New York: McGraw-Hill, 1987), 96.

[10] Quoted in C. Warren Hollister, *Roots of the Western Tradition: A Short History of the Ancient World*, 5th ed. (New York: McGraw-Hill, 1991), 109.

[11] From Barbara Hughes Fowler, *Archaic Greek Poetry: An Anthology* (Madison: University of Wisconsin Press, 1992), 131.

[12] Quoted in Robert Flaceliere, "Women, Marriage, and the Family," in *Everyman in Europe: Essays in Social History*, ed. Allan Mitchell and Istvan Deak, vol. 1 (Englewood Cliffs, NJ: Prentice-Hall, 1970), 53.

Slaves, mostly captives taken in battle or debtors, constituted about one-third of the population. They were often household servants, paid artisans, or teachers who instructed young people how to play music and write. Slaves also constructed many great buildings or worked on agricultural plantations or in mines owned by aristocrats. Many slaves faced harsh lives and could be tortured and executed for mere suspicion of a crime.

Like the nuclear family system of the modern West but unlike the extended family pattern of many African and Asian societies, most Greek families consisted of a husband, a wife, and children. Women's principal tasks were to feed and clothe their families and to bear and raise children. While lacking men's sexual freedom, women could own property and divorce their husbands, and they played essential roles in religious festivals. For example, the oracle at the temple of Delphi **(DELL-fye)**, which many leaders consulted to determine the will of Apollo, spoke through a woman's voice.

But women also experienced strong prejudice in a patriarchal society. Aristotle articulated the misogynist, or anti-woman, views of many men in describing women as deformed males. A popular saying expressed male views: "Respectable women should stay at home; the street is for worthless hussies." Some women expressed their discontent, as reflected in a tragic play by Euripides: "[Men] say we lead a safe life at home. What imbeciles! I'd rather stand to arms three times than bear one child."[13] In contrast to political marginalization, Greek literature often portrayed women as powerful and capable of great anger, humor, faithfulness, and intelligence. For example, Penelope, the wife of Ulysses in Homer's *Odyssey*, ruled the state wisely until his return while outmaneuvering many men seeking to marry her. In Aristophanes' bawdy comedy *Lysistrata* **(lis-uh-STRAH-tuh)**, a group of women organize to end war by refusing to have sex with their husbands until the men stop fighting. Lysistrata tells her husband: "We women got together and decided we were going to save Greece. Listen to us and keep quiet, as we've had to do up to now, and we'll clear up the mess you've made."[14]

Some social customs might be considered controversial today. While their wives stayed home, men attended parties, sometimes enlivened by courtesans celebrated for their wit and charm. Some courtesans enjoyed high status and probably a good education. Aspasia **(ass-PAY-zhee-uh)**, a vivacious, literate, and controversial Milesian, probably operated an Athens meetinghouse where educated men, including possibly Socrates, came for sex and conversation with intellectual women. Advocating gender equality, Aspasia became the mistress of the Athenian leader Pericles **(PER-eh-kleez)**, whose enemies, among them dramatists, accused her of writing his speeches, violating the tradition that politics was for men only. Indeed, Greek opinion on her was so divided that it is hard to separate fact from fiction about her life and actions. Unlike some courtesans, most prostitutes were badly exploited slaves.

WOMEN FETCHING WATER The painting on this vase portrays everyday life in a Greek city. Women have congregated at a public fountain to fill jugs with water to be carried back home, where it will be used for drinking, cooking, and cleaning. The women's hair coverings and long robes reflect the fashion of the day.

Homosexuality has existed in all societies from earliest times, but Greek men were particularly open about their same-sex relationships. Artists fashioned many naturalistic statues of naked men and women, and diverse homosexual practices and relationships were tolerated. Bringing up Greek boys and girls separately reduced heterosexual contact. Hence, homosexual behavior between older and younger upper-class men was accepted as part of a training or mentoring relationship for career preparation, with many famous Greeks having such relationships. In Sparta some top military units comprised homosexual couples. But the concepts of same-sex or even opposite-sex relationships twenty-five hundred years ago were not necessarily the same as those today. Men of superior status took for granted that, with or without consent, they could have intimate relations with anyone of inferior status, including servants, slaves, and foreigners. In contrast, nonelite Greeks often condemned homosexual relations between two adults.

[13]From *Medea*, quoted in Frank J. Frost, *Greek Society*, 2nd ed. (Lexington, MA: D.C. Heath, 1980), 94.

[14]From Aristophanes, *Lysistrata and Other Plays*, translated by Alan H. Sommerstein (New York: Penguin, 1973), 200–208.

MAKE SURE YOU UNDERSTAND THESE KEY POINTS BEFORE MOVING ON

- **The mountainous, maritime geography of Greece fostered the development of multiple city-states rather than one centralized state.**
- **The polis system of governance allowed extensive political rights for some but no political rights for many.**
- **Though Greeks had a well-developed religion, they were also notable for their commitment to using reason to understand the world.**
- **Greek drama tended to focus on tragedy, as in the works of Euripides, Aeschylus, and Sophocles; writers like Aristophanes wrote comedies.**
- **Greek women were generally expected to stay at home and out of politics, but they were often featured as powerful characters in plays.**

Greeks, Persians, and the Regional System

In what ways did Persians and Greeks encounter and influence each other?

During the early fifth century B.C.E. peninsular Greek cities successfully fought a series of wars with the greatest power of western Asia, the Persian Empire. But rival Greek states also fought ruinous wars with each other. Both Greeks and Persians borrowed many ideas from neighboring peoples, including the Egyptians and western Asians, causing historians to debate the Classical Greek and Persian legacies for Europe and the Middle East.

The Greco-Persian Wars

The Greco-Persian conflict began in 499 B.C.E., when Athens supported some Greek cities in Anatolia that were rebelling against their Persian overlords. After defeating the rebels in 494, Darius I dispatched a fleet to punish the peninsular Greeks in 492, but storms destroyed his ships. He then sent a larger Persian force, which was defeated at the Battle of Marathon in northern Greece in 490 B.C.E. The Greeks slaughtered the Persians, many of whom drowned in the sea.

The Persians attempted again to conquer Greece in 480 B.C.E., when Xerxes sent a huge army and navy to engage an alliance led by Athens and Sparta. A Spartan force of three hundred fought to the death holding a strategic pass, but they were betrayed by some Greeks who showed the Persians a path around them. The Persians swept down into Athens, burning the city. Expecting final victory, they attacked the trapped Athenian fleet in the Bay of Salamis **(SAL-uh-muhs)**. Surprisingly, however, they were defeated. The large Persian force proved difficult to supply and control effectively, while the Athenians had also developed the world's most advanced fighting ship, the well-armored *trireme* **(TRY-reem)**, which had three banks of oarsmen and deadly bronze rams. The following year (479) the Greeks defeated the remaining Persian forces at the battle of Plataea **(pluh-TEE-uh)**. Some historians argue that the Greek victory over the Persians led to a growing divide between "Europe" and "Asia," with the Greeks increasingly viewing themselves as different from, and superior to, the people to the east.

Empire and Conflict in the Greek World

The declining Persian threat reignited old rivalries between Greek cities, fostering nearly constant warfare between them. To defeat the Persians, the Greek cities had organized the **Delian (DEE-lee-uhn) League**, a defensive alliance led by the richest state and largest naval power, Athens. Other cities contributed funds or ships. But the Delian League changed from a defensive alliance to an Athenian empire. Athens controlled the league treasury, spending some of the money on Athenian civic improvements. Then in 467 Athens took military action to stop the island of Naxos **(NAK-suhs)** from leaving the league. Some Athenians protested that a democracy, which allows varied opinions, could not manage an empire.

Athens reached its golden age under Pericles (ca. 495–429 B.C.E.), a visionary leader and spellbinding orator who promoted democratic legal reforms. Athenians, then numbering some 250,000 to 300,000, were justifiably proud of their city, especially of the magnificent public buildings such as the Parthenon **(PAHR-thuh-nahn)**, a temple dedicated to the city's patron goddess, Athena, on a hilltop called the Acropolis **(uh-KRAHP-uh-luhs)**. But while Athenians embraced self-fulfillment and individualism, some criticized unrestrained freedom, fearing that too much pride or self-expression spelled trouble. Playwrights, poets, and historians argued that arrogance led to punishment by the gods and personal disaster. Despite the warnings, the Athenians' civic pride eventually brought disaster, as increasing resentment of Athenian power by rival cities generated the long **Peloponnesian War** (431–404 B.C.E.) between Athens and Sparta-led alliances. In a famous "funeral oration" to memorialize dead Athenian soldiers, the nationalistic Pericles (r. 460–429 B.C.E.)

Delian League A defensive league organized by Greek cities in the fifth century B.C.E. to defeat the Persians.

Peloponnesian War A long war between Athens and Sparta and their respective allies in 431–404 B.C.E. that resulted in the defeat of Athens.

© irakite/Shutterstock.com

THE ACROPOLIS The Acropolis dominated the surrounding city of Athens. The marble Parthenon at the center, dedicated to Athena, was built during the time of Pericles.

reportedly contrasted Athenian democratic institutions and equality before the law with Spartan discipline and lack of freedom:

> *...We are called a democracy, for the administration is in the hands of the many and not of the few....I have dwelt upon the greatness of Athens because I want to show you we are contending for a higher prize than those who enjoy none of these privileges. For in magnifying the city I have magnified the men whose virtues made her glorious.*[15]

Pericles introduced the novel ideas that war was not just to defend hearth and home but to spread better ideas and systems, and also that free citizens had responsibility to their community. But the assumption that their high ideals made Athenians superior to their neighbors fueled dislike by other Greek cities.

The war proved disastrous for Athens and boosted Sparta. The Athenians' plan to use their navy to combat their enemy's superior land army floundered when a deadly plague hit Athens, killing a third of the population, including Pericles. The Athenians also unwisely attempted to capture Syracuse, a Greek city on Sicily. Later the Spartans, with Persian advice, destroyed the Athenian fleet. The victorious Spartans disbanded the Athenian navy, destroyed the city walls, and killed or exiled thousands of Athenians. Although the war made Sparta the most powerful Greek state, decades of instability followed, and eventually the frequent conflicts between the Greek cities proved too destructive. Less than a century after the Peloponnesian War ended, Greece was conquered by neighboring Macedonia and made the base for a much greater empire.

Historiography: Universal and Critical

The Greeks developed concepts of history that are still used today, but they did so in the context of their connections to other societies. Of course, peoples before them had some sense of history. The legends passed down through oral traditions, such as the stories in the Hebrew Bible and the Homeric epics, were narratives of history, although we cannot prove their accuracy. The Chinese also wrote historical accounts. But the Greeks Herodotus and Thucydides **(thyou-SID-uh-deez)** were the first to pursue critical, analytical, and universal history.

Sometimes called the Father of History, Herodotus (ca. 484–425 B.C.E.) wrote history on a scale never attempted before, providing the main source about the Greco-Persian Wars. Integrating information on geography and culture, Herodotus wrote vividly about neighboring societies. He was born in a Persian-ruled Ionian city, Halicarnasus, and traveled around the Persian Empire and sojourned in Egypt, concluding that some Greek gods could be equated with Egyptian divinities. He also visited Tyre, where he learned that Phoenicians had invented the alphabet. A sophisticated man with an inquiring mind, Herodotus lived for a time in Periclean Athens,

[15]Reported in Thucydides, quoted in L. S. Stavrianos, ed., *The Epic of Man to 1500* (Englewood Cliffs, NJ: Prentice-Hall, 1970), 120–122.

where he met many famous men, and he portrayed the Athenians favorably, attributing the Greeks' victory over the Persians' absolute monarchy to the Greeks' free society. Because his interests and travels went well beyond the Greek world, Herodotus might be considered the first world historian. Although too often reporting unverified hearsay and failing to subject his material to critical scrutiny, he was something of a cultural relativist, avoiding Greek prejudices against other cultures and offering sympathetic views of Persians and criticisms of Greeks.

Our knowledge of Greek politics and wars during the fifth century B.C.E. comes largely from a single book, *The Peloponnesian War*, written by Thucydides (ca. 460–400 B.C.E.), a general exiled from Athens for losing an important battle. Despite his exile, Thucydides objectively evaluated the strengths and weaknesses of his home city, setting an example of careful observation. Unlike earlier writers, he added critical judgments to his narrative, such as by criticizing the Athenians for ignoring Pericles' warnings to attempt no new conquests. He also evaluated democracy's benefits and drawbacks and asked fundamental questions about the nature of power. Thucydides looked for patterns and moral lessons in the past. Whenever historians interpret the past, they are acknowledging a debt to Thucydides, a historian who was not just a teller of tales but also a teacher of wisdom.

Interregional Trade and Cultural Mixing

The Mediterranean Basin remained a vast zone of exchange in which Greeks played the commercial role once dominated by Phoenicians, trading wine and olive oil widely, establishing colonies, and spreading their culture. Like Greeks, Persians welcomed foreign traders. Port cities like Persian-ruled Miletus in Ionia prospered as regional trade hubs, and Persian gold coins were used by many societies. Persian leaders patronized Greek traders living in their domains, and in 510 B.C.E. one of them, Scylax of Caryanda **(SKY-lax of KAR-ee-AN-da)**, headed a Persian trade mission to India. Tribute flowed to the Persian capital, including Arabian and Bactrian camels, Indian gold, Scythian horses, Egyptian bulls, Anatolian leather goods, and Ionian silver.

Long-distance trade was crucial in many ways. Merchants traveling elsewhere to trade eventually evolved into what historians call a **trade diaspora**, living permanently in foreign cities or countries. Most of the shipowners, traders, and moneylenders of Athens came from western Asia or Greek diaspora colonies such as Massalia (today's Marseilles) and the Crimea. Expatriate Greek merchant communities arose in Egypt, western Asia, and around the Black Sea. Trade also spurred a strong Athenian navy, helping Greeks defeat the Persians. Athens, the leading Greek commercial and financial hub, controlled rich silver mines worked by over twenty thousand slaves and imported wheat from Egypt, Sicily, and southern Russia. It gained a reputation as the most profitable and safest city to do business in, where even those of humble origins could achieve wealth.

The Mediterranean Basin brought together southern European, western Asian, and North African cultures. Though highly creative, Persians and Greeks also learned much from other peoples. For example, Persians blended Ionian Greek, Mesopotamian, and Scythian art styles and motifs with their own traditions, while Greeks integrated Phoenician, Lydian, Egyptian, and Mesopotamian influences. Phoenician traders brought art forms and styles that inspired Greeks to modify their columns, pottery, statues, and ceramic styles. Greeks also adopted West Asian musical instruments and melodies, the Phoenician alphabet, and several Phoenician, Egyptian, and Anatolian gods. In addition, many Greek colonists absorbed local influences. For example, Greeks in Massalia, on the southern coast of France, had to understand local Celtic customs and language.

Greeks visited, worked in, settled in, and learned about other societies. For example, many Ionian merchants lived in Egypt. The Athenian lawgiver Solon visited Egypt as a merchant, studied with priests, and wrote poems about living along the Nile, and the influential writings of the Athenian physician Hippocrates **(hip-AHK-ruh-teez)** included some Egyptian medical ideas. Some Greeks even fought as mercenaries for Egyptian kings and worshiped Egyptian gods, while others served in Mesopotamian and Persian armies. The scientist Democritus visited Babylonia and Persia, and both Plato and Aristotle knew something about Zoroastrianism. Cosmopolitan Ionia, where Greek and Asian cultures mixed, produced pathbreaking thinking in philosophy and science, often under Persian patronage. Thales, a Lydian subject, studied geometry in Egypt and was the first Greek to inscribe a right-angled triangle and to determine the sun's course from solstice to solstice, something the Babylonians had long known how to do. The Ionian-born mathematician Pythagoras (ca. 580–ca. 500 B.C.E.) may have visited Egypt and Babylon.

The Persian and Greek Legacies

Both Persians and Greeks left rich legacies for later societies. The Persians built the world's first large empire and flexible, tolerant multinational state, fusing traditions from many cultures while spreading learning, such as Babylonian astronomy, to peoples such as the Greeks. Persians today still revere Cyrus the Great. The Persians' Zoroastrian ideas also influenced Judaism, Christianity, and Islam, and many Persian words entered other languages; for example, the Persian word for "garden" became the English word *paradise*. Persian culture and language strongly influenced Afghanistan and Central Asia, and science and mathematics continued to develop in Ionia and Mesopotamia.

Many historians have admired the Greeks as the direct cultural, intellectual, and political ancestors of modern Europeans and North Americans, perceiving Greek society as culturally richer than any other before modern times. They view the Athenian era of Pericles, Plato, and Aeschylus as a "golden age" that launched Western literature, history, philosophy, science, and the democratic ideal. However, the view of Greece as the fountainhead of Western culture has problems. Many Greek customs and social inequalities, especially their sometimes cruel treatment of women and slaves, appall people today. To critics, Greek thinkers were not very

trade diaspora Merchants from the same city or country who live permanently in foreign cities or countries.

liberal or secular, their democracy was elitist and flawed, and what Greek ideas western Europe inherited came in modified form through the Romans and later through the Arabs. Moreover, modern science is based not only on Greek but also on Chinese, Indian, and Middle Eastern discoveries. As a result, some historians believe the Romans founded the Western tradition, while others see the Greeks as an extension of western Asian and North African societies.

Today the Greeks seem both very strange and quite familiar, and the debate suggests how fascinating the Greeks have been to various societies over the centuries, beginning with the Romans. Middle Eastern societies also treasured Greek thinkers and science, and Greek philosophy influenced some Islamic scholars. The debate also indicates that the Greeks, however imperfect their society, fostered ideas and institutions that were unusual for their time and that have endured for over two millennia.

MAKE SURE YOU UNDERSTAND THESE KEY POINTS BEFORE MOVING ON

- **The Persians attacked the Greeks several times, but the Greeks, against great odds, fended them off.**
- **Following the Greek victory over the Persians, Athens's growing arrogance eventually led to the Peloponnesian War between Athens and Sparta, which ended with Spartan victory.**
- **Herodotus, who wrote of the Greco-Persian Wars, and Thucydides, who wrote of the Peloponnesian War, were the first historians to write critical and analytical history.**
- **The eastern Mediterranean and western Asia were zones of intense trade and cultural mixing.**

The Hellenistic Age and Its Afro-Eurasian Legacies

What impact did Alexander the Great and his conquests have on world history?

Between 334 and 323 B.C.E., Alexander of Macedonia **(MASS-uh-DUHN-ia)**, a student of Classical Greek ideas, created a huge empire that spread Greek culture over a wide area. Alexander's achievements established new networks of communication, and his legacy lived on for centuries in **Hellenism**, a widespread culture that combined western Asian (mainly Persian) and Greek (Hellenic) characteristics. During the Hellenistic Age, Greeks ruled over large parts of western Asia and North Africa, a domination that ended only with the rise of the Roman Empire and new Persia-based empires that continued to influence Middle Eastern history.

Alexander the Great, World Empire, and Hellenism

Greek disunity spawned by the Peloponnesian War opened the door for Macedonia, a state on the northern fringe of Greece, to conquer a vast empire. The war had so weakened all the Greek cities that no one city could unite the peninsula. Led by King Philip II (382–336 B.C.E.), who developed a paid professional army and devised a more effective infantry phalanx, the Macedonian army conquered the Greek cities in 338 B.C.E. But the hard-living, hard-drinking Philip had many enemies among Greeks, Persians, and Macedonian nobles. Two years later, on the eve of an expedition to Asia, Philip was assassinated.

Hellenism A widespread culture flourishing between 359 and 100 B.C.E. that combined western Asian (mainly Persian) and Greek (Hellenic) characteristics.

Philip's twenty-year-old son and Aristotle's former student, Alexander (r. 336–323 B.C.E.), became king following his father's death. A fearless and resolute megalomaniac, his ambitions for conquest were evident as a child. Alexander reportedly lamented that, with such a multitude of other countries, it was a shame that he had not yet conquered even one of them. Later, he wrote to the Persian king that he sought vengeance on Persia for its invasions of Greece a century and half earlier. During his thirteen-year reign, this brilliant military strategist and leader of men used Macedonian, Greek, and mercenary troops to conquer the world from Greece to western India and from the Nile valley to the Caucasus Mountains and Black and Caspian Seas.

Alexander employed ruthless tactics against enemies, sometimes destroying entire cities and slaughtering their inhabitants. In three major battles between 334 and 331, he dismantled the powerful Persian Empire and then burned Persepolis, reportedly after a night of drunken excess, and became Persian ruler. His destruction of many Zoroastrian temples weakened that religion. Alexander's forces then moved through Afghanistan, fighting difficult battles with the tough peoples of that mountainous region, who destroyed their homes and farms rather than surrender. Eventually many of Alexander's horses died and his grain ran out. Finally reaching the Indus Valley, the Macedonian wanted to move into India's heartland, but his exhausted, homesick troops refused, and they made a difficult desert journey back to Mesopotamia.

Alexander saw himself as a world ruler, governing all peoples. His empire incorporated most of the major ancient Afro-Eurasian societies: Egypt, Crete, Mycenae, Phoenicia, Mesopotamia, and the Indus Valley. Alexander initially organized his empire like the Persians. Although he was probably bisexual or homosexual and maintained an intimate relationship with a male adviser, Alexander married a Bactrian

ALEXANDER DEFEATING PERSIANS AT BATTLE OF ISSUS In this Roman copy of an earlier Greek painting, Alexander the Great is shown on his horse in the battle that brought defeat to Persian king Darius III in 333 B.C.E.

(northern Afghanistan) princess, encouraged his soldiers to take Asian wives, and wore the purple and white cloak and head ribbon previously worn by Persian royalty.

After Alexander died in Babylon at age thirty-three, probably from a fever acquired after a night of heavy drinking, the conquered territories retained a mixed Greek-Persian cultural flavor for centuries under the influence of Hellenism. Over the centuries Western observers lionized Alexander, while Persians viewed him as a reckless destroyer and symbol of Western imperialism. The Hellenistic Age lasted several centuries, but the Greek legacy was passed on in a form that fifth-century Greeks might not have recognized, one that emphasized individual freedom and reason less and the emotions more. Farther east, some of Alexander's soldiers settled in Afghanistan and western India, where Greek ideas had an enduring influence on the local art. For centuries afterward people as far away as Ethiopia, Nubia, and western India studied the Greek language and borrowed Greek artistic styles.

Alexander's empire soon fragmented. When asked to whom he left his empire, Alexander allegedly said: "to the strongest." By the end of the fourth century B.C.E., his former generals, all Macedonians, had divided Alexander's empire. A dynasty begun by Ptolemy **(TAHL-uh-mee)** controlled Egypt and the eastern Mediterranean coast; the family of Seleucus **(suh-LOO-kuhs)** controlled Persia, Mesopotamia, and Syria; and followers of Antigonus **(an-TIG-uh-nuhs)** controlled the Macedonian kingdom and northern Greece (see Map 7.3).

Seleucid dominance in Persia and Mesopotamia was ended by the Parthians **(PAHR-thee-uhnz)**, Indo-European pastoral nomads who conquered large parts of Persia, Afghanistan, and Mesopotamia in the second century B.C.E. They expanded their empire into the Caucasus and crushed an invading Roman army in 53 B.C.E. Adopting many Hellenistic traditions, they made Greek the official state language. Gradually Persian influences grew stronger, and the Parthians became Zoroastrians. But frequent wars with the Romans, who replaced the other Hellenistic kingdoms, sapped their strength. A new Persian power, the Sassanians **(suh-SAY-nee-uhnz)**, defeated the last Parthian ruler in 224 C.E. The Sassanians ruled much of western Asia for the next four centuries, coming into frequent conflict with the Romans.

Hellenistic Cities and Economic Networks

Alexander founded many cities named after him, most famously the still-surviving city of Alexandria on Egypt's Mediterranean coast (see Map 7.3). Hellenistic cities were not independent city-states but part of kingdoms, their citizens enjoying little political participation. Wealthy aristocrats, professional soldiers, and bureaucrats ran the cities' governments. Although centers of Greek language and culture, which dominated elite circles, the multiethnic cities also existed in predominantly non-Greek environments and were influenced by local traditions. For example, the Ptolemaic dynasty in

MAP 7.3 **THE HELLENISTIC KINGDOMS** The empire conquered by Alexander the Great was divided into rival Hellenistic kingdoms on his death in 323 B.C.E. By 140 B.C.E. the Parthians had conquered some of the eastern territories.

Egypt ruled with pharaonic pomp. While Hellenistic monarchs relied on Greeks, Persians, and others to govern, they were vastly outnumbered by their Asian and African subjects speaking their own languages.

No longer vibrant democratic communities, Hellenistic urban culture glorified hedonism. The upper classes enjoyed high living, with poets celebrating activities like horse racing, lovemaking, and drinking. A satirical Egyptian poem mocked a drunken and gluttonous harpist who showed up at weddings and festivals: "He disputes with the party-goers, shouting: 'I can't sing when I'm hungry, I can't hold my harp without my fill of wine!' And he drinks wine like two people and eats the meat of three."[16] Hellenistic cities were also cosmopolitan and ethnically diverse. Alexandria, for example, had large Egyptian, Greek, and Jewish populations and was a melting pot where many religions met, new ones sprouted up, and Zoroastrian holy books and the Hebrew Bible were translated into Greek. The Syrian Greek poet Meleager expressed the Hellenistic attitude: "Stranger, we live in the same motherland, the world."[17]

Alexander's conquests also linked the Mediterranean and western Asia in a vast trading network. Alexander had used Persian wealth to build and repair roads and harbors, and Greek colonists introduced or expanded money-based economies. Long-distance trade expanded rapidly as Chinese silk and Indian sugar were traded for Egyptian onions, Macedonian wood products, and Athenian olive oil. As caravans of vegetables and wine moved eastward, they crossed caravans of spices and other goods moving westward out of India, Arabia, and Northeast Africa. This trans-Eurasian trading network remained strong long after the Hellenistic states had disappeared.

Science, Religion, and Philosophy

Hellenistic thinkers maintained the Greek interest in scientific, religious, and philosophical questions. Scientists and mathematicians rigorously collected and evaluated data and then offered hypotheses to explain mathematical problems, natural phenomena, and the workings of the universe. Alexandria, with the ancient world's largest library (700,000 papyrus scrolls), was the chief research center, and Alexandrian thinkers and inventors anticipated modern scientific, mathematical, and technological developments. Here Euclid wrote his text on plane geometry, a book used for two thousand years, and Herophilus **(hair-OFF-uh-lus)** improved the understanding

[16]Quoted in Michael Chauveau, *Egypt in the Age of Cleopatra: History and Society Under the Ptolemies* (Ithaca: Cornell University Press, 2000), 188.

[17]Quoted in Francis Chanoux, *Hellenistic Civilization* (Malden, MA: Blackwell, 2003), 319.

PROFILE

Archimedes, a Hellenistic Mathematician and Engineer

Archimedes was an outstanding mathematician, the greatest engineer of the Hellenistic world, and perhaps the most wide-ranging mind of his time. Some historians consider Archimedes and Aristotle the two greatest thinkers of Greek society. Archimedes was born around 287 B.C.E. to an influential family—his father was apparently an astronomer—in Syracuse, a Greek city on the island of Sicily. He studied in the intellectual capital of the Hellenistic world, Alexandria in Egypt, where inquisitive souls of financial means or, like Archimedes, political connections traveled widely and learned from varied cultures. In this milieu Archimedes became acquainted with famous scientists. Eventually he returned to Syracuse, where he spent the rest of his days. We know little of his personal life and do not know whether he ever married.

In mathematics Archimedes introduced many new ideas, some of which added to Euclid's geometry. He offered a new system of numerals to handle large numbers; calculated the value of *pi*, the ratio of the circumference to the diameter of a circle, more accurately than anyone before him; and discovered the laws for finding the centers of gravity of plane figures. His insights were often visionary. A book he wrote, lost for centuries but recently rediscovered, hints that eighteen hundred years before anyone else he was exploring calculus, the basis for much twenty-first-century technology. Archimedes also studied astronomy and built an ingenious bronze computer-like instrument for measuring the movements of the sun, moon, and planets. This early clock may have inspired later timekeeping inventions.

Archimedes is equally well known for his engineering innovations but wrote much less about his applied than his theoretical studies. Nonetheless, his contributions were immense. He discovered "Archimedes' law," still tested in high school classrooms, which states that a body wholly or partly immersed in a fluid loses weight equal to the weight of the fluid displaced. This insight apparently came to him while in the public baths, as he watched water flow over the side as he entered the pool. According to his later biographer, Plutarch, he leaped from the pool and ran home naked, crying aloud: "Eureka!" ("I have found it!"). (The public nudity would not have astonished Greeks, who were used to seeing people in public without their clothes.) With such discoveries, Archimedes founded the science of hydrostatics, which involves balance and weights.

Archimedes also made other practical contributions. For instance, he supervised construction of the world's first three-masted ship, a huge combination of warship, yacht, and cargo ship that had horse stalls, fish tanks, cargo holds for wheat, and luxurious cabins. He also worked out the law of the lever and the theory of mechanical advantage, using his knowledge to launch his ship with the use of compound pulleys. And he solved a major problem of the time in irrigation and mining by discovering how to move great volumes of water up a steep incline using a large pipe with a tightly fitted screw.

With Roman power on the rise, Archimedes was put in charge of Syracuse defenses. For a while Roman attackers were repulsed by his ingenious weapons, including missiles dropped from cranes that swung out over the fortified walls and darts and balls delivered by catapults. Some legends, which many historians doubt, credit him with experimenting with mirrors to direct the sun's rays at enemy ships to set them on fire.

In 212 the Romans captured Syracuse and killed the aged Archimedes—according to one legend, as the famously absent-minded scientist was working on geometrical diagrams. This Roman triumph helped end the Hellenistic Age and begin the Roman Age in the central Mediterranean. The engineering and mathematical discoveries of Archimedes now became part of Roman and later world traditions.

STR New/Reuters

THE ARCHIMEDES PALIMPSEST In 1889 scholars discovered a crumbling, long-lost parchment containing a copy of a major work by Archimedes, the treatise called "On Floating Bodies." This work, on buoyancy, shows that he was centuries ahead of the rest of the world in his thinking on mathematics and physics, even suggesting ideas that did not reappear until the past several centuries.

THINKING ABOUT THE PROFILE

1. How did Archimedes' career reflect the Hellenistic Age?
2. Why was Archimedes considered one of the major classical engineers and mathematicians?

of the brain and the nervous system. Aristarchus **(AR-uh-STAHR-kuhs)** proposed that the sun rather than the earth was the center of the universe, an idea most Europeans rejected for the next thousand years, while the geographer Eratosthenes **(ER-uh-TAHS-thuh-neez)** calculated the circumference of the earth within about 200 miles. The inventor Hero devised a steam turbine, although it was treated only as an amazing toy. Other major thinkers, such as the engineer and mathematician Archimedes, spent time in Alexandria (see Profile: Archimedes, a Hellenistic Mathematician and Engineer).

Greek philosophy and religion went in new directions during the Hellenistic Age. Some thinkers put less emphasis on reason to solve problems and more on resigning oneself to life in ways that often seemed fatalistic, taking life as it comes. The school of thought known as **Cynicism**, made famous by Ionia-born Diogenes **(die-AHJ-uh-neez)** (ca. 412–ca. 323 B.C.E.), emphasized living a simple life, shunning material things and all pretense. A famous legend of the meeting of Diogenes and a young Alexander conveys the flavor of Cynic philosophy. Diogenes asked Alexander about his greatest desire, and the Macedonian replied, "to subjugate Greece." Next he would subjugate Southwest Asia and then the world. And after that, Alexander said, "I will relax and enjoy myself," prompting Diogenes to reply: "Why not save yourself all the trouble by relaxing and enjoying yourself now?"[18]

Cynicism A Hellenistic philosophy, made famous by the philosopher Diogenes, that emphasized living a simple life, shunning material things and all pretense.

Stoicism A Hellenistic philosophy that emphasized the importance of cooperating with and accepting nature, as well as the unity and equality of all people.

Mithraism A Hellenistic cult that worshiped Mithra, a Persian deity associated with the sun; had some influence on Christianity.

Another Hellenistic philosophy, **Stoicism** **(STOH-uh-siz-uhm)**, emphasized cooperating with and accepting nature, as well as the unity and equality of all people. Founded by Zeno **(ZEE-noh)** (ca. 334–ca. 265 B.C.E.) in Athens, Stoicism was cosmopolitan and optimistic and accepted cultural diversity, teaching that nature's law governing human affairs was common to all people and transcended the limited human laws created by kings. The Stoic emphasis on basic human equality survived over the centuries to influence modern lawmakers.

Hellenistic religion offered people individual happiness and eternal life. The religion of Isis, originally an Egyptian fertility goddess, promised personal salvation. **Mithraism** **(MITH-ruh-iz-uhm)**, a very popular cult that worshiped Mithra, a Persian sun-deity, promised salvation to people who were properly initiated into the faith. Some historians believe that these Hellenistic religions, which shared features with Christianity, help explain the appeal of the teachings and life of Jesus several centuries later. Christianity borrowed from Mithraism the concept of purgatory as well as the winter solstice and birthday of Mithra (December 25). Hellenistic ideas also influenced the Romans (see Chapter 8) and remained important in western Asia and the eastern Mediterranean for many centuries.

MAKE SURE YOU UNDERSTAND THESE KEY POINTS BEFORE MOVING ON

- **After the Peloponnesian War, no Greek city was strong enough to unite the rest of the Greek peninsula.**
- **King Philip II of Macedonia conquered several Greek cities, and, after he died, his ambitious son Alexander the Great established an empire that ranged from Egypt to India.**
- **Alexander's legacy included a vast trading network that linked the Mediterranean, western Asia, and India, as well as the spread of Hellenism, a mix of Greek and Persian culture.**
- **Hellenism was marked by rigorous scientific inquiry, philosophies such as Cynicism and Stoicism that urged people to take life as it came, and mystical religions that had some influence on Christianity.**

aplia

[18]"Diogenes," in *Biographical Encyclopedia of Philosophy* (Garden City, NY: Doubleday, 1965), 76.

CHAPTER SUMMARY

The Greeks and Persians dominated the Mediterranean and western Asia during the early Classical period, influencing many other peoples in the region. The Persians built a huge multiethnic empire. Their emphasis on governing through mutual tolerance, a skillful bureaucracy, and good roads influenced the Macedonian Alexander the Great and his successors, as well as the Roman and Muslim rulers of western Asia after them. Persian religious ideas, including Zoroastrianism, also spread to neighboring peoples such as the Hebrews. The Greeks reached their golden age during the fifth century. The Athenians practiced democracy, however imperfectly, in a society where there were many slaves and where women had few legal rights. Democracy developed as citizens demanded a voice in the decisions that ordered them to war. The Classical Greeks were also pioneers in philosophy and science. Influenced by the increasing emphasis on reason, Greek thinkers like Socrates,

Plato, and especially Aristotle established a foundation for critical thinking and natural science. Their legacy influenced people in both the Middle East and Europe.

The Greeks and Persians were also fierce rivals for regional power, fighting a series of destructive wars but also exchanging trade goods and ideas. The eastern Mediterranean zone fostered cultural mixing, maritime commerce, and the sharing of knowledge and products, and Alexander the Great's conquests made Greek language and culture part of the eastern Mediterranean world for several centuries after his death. The Hellenistic world mixed Greek arts and philosophy with many Persian or western Asian ideas of government. The later Roman, Christian, and then Muslim rulers in these areas retained some of this Greco-Persian heritage.

KEY TERMS

Achaemenid (p. 140)
satrap (p. 143)
Zoroastrianism (p. 143)
Ahura Mazda (p. 143)
polis (p. 145)
oligarchy (p. 145)
tyrant (p. 147)
Sophists (p. 148)
Socratic Method (p. 148)
metaphysics (p. 149)
Delian League (p. 151)
Peloponnesian War (p. 151)
trade diaspora (p. 153)
Hellenism (p. 154)
Cynicism (p. 158)
Stoicism (p. 158)
Mithraism (p. 158)

8 Empires, Networks, and the Remaking of Europe, North Africa, and Western Asia, 500 B.C.E.–600 C.E.

Manuel Cohen/The Art Archive at Art Resource, NY

SANTA SOPHIA The magnificent Santa Sophia Church in Constantinople, rebuilt during the reign of the emperor Justinian in the sixth century C.E., had interior walls covered in gold mosaics that glowed from reflected sunlight. This mosaic from the Zoe panel shows Jesus holding a Bible.

Remember, Roman, that it is for you to rule the nations. This shall be your task: to impose the ways of peace, to spare the vanquished and to tame the proud by war.

—Roman poet Virgil[1]

Around 320 B.C.E. Pytheas **(PITH-ee-us)**, a scientist from the Greek colony of Massalia **(ma-SAL-ya)**, today's city of Marseilles **(mahr-SAY)** on the Mediterranean coast of France, wrote a book about his remarkable travels in Europe. According to his account, the brave and curious Pytheas reached the western coast of France, from where he sailed on a boat owned by local Celtic **(KELL-tik)** people to southwest England. Continuing north through the Irish Sea, he then ventured down Britain's east coast before exploring the North Sea coast as far as Denmark. Some of his contemporaries called him a liar. Today many scholars credit Pytheas for providing Mediterranean societies with their first eyewitness account of the remote northern coast whose mysterious peoples they considered dangerous barbarians.

In Pytheas's time Greeks, Etruscans **(ee-TRUHS-kuhns)**, Carthaginians **(kar-thuh-JIN-ee-uhns)**, and the upstart Romans were part of an interdependent world incorporating southern Europe, North Africa, and western Asia. They competed for economic resources and political power in the western Mediterranean, exchanging ideas and commodities. Three hundred years after Pytheas's travels, the Romans, in Pytheas's time an ambitious but still minor power, had created an empire that more closely linked these European societies.

The Romans' large empire and rich society, celebrated in the opening quote, marginalized or incorporated northern peoples while also transforming North African and western Asian politics, greatly impacting European and world history. When the Roman Empire finally ended after half a millennium, it left several legacies for later European, western Asian, and North African societies. The Romans bequeathed to later Europeans legal and governmental concepts, some derived from the Greeks. Christianity also emerged, forming the cultural underpinning of a post-Roman European society while also spreading in Asia and Africa.

Although the Roman Empire eventually declined, an eastern Mediterranean version, Byzantium **(buh-ZANT-ee-uhm)**, survived, serving as a transcontinental trade center and a buffer between western Europe and West Asian states, including a revived Persian Empire. Byzantine-Persian struggles then set the stage for the rise of another society, the Arabs.

[1]Quoted in Tim Cornell and John Matthews, *The Roman World* (Alexandria, VA: Stonehendge, 1991), 51.

IN THIS CHAPTER

Etruscans, Carthage, Egypt, and the Roman Republic

What were the main political and social features of the Roman Republic?

By 300 B.C.E. the Mediterranean world was politically and culturally diverse, divided between Etruscans, Carthage, Greek city-states, various Hellenistic kingdoms including Egypt, and the rising Romans, who eventually dominated the entire region. The Romans learned much from the older Etruscan society and were influenced by Greek ideas in building their Republic. Eventually Rome conquered peoples in southern Europe and then beyond, establishing the framework of a huge empire.

European Geography, the Etruscans, and Early Rome

Geography and a mild climate shaped western Mediterranean society. Italy's geological spine, the Apennine mountain range, runs down the narrow peninsula's eastern side, while to the west and north spread rich agricultural plains fostering intensive agriculture. Romans exported wine and olive oil

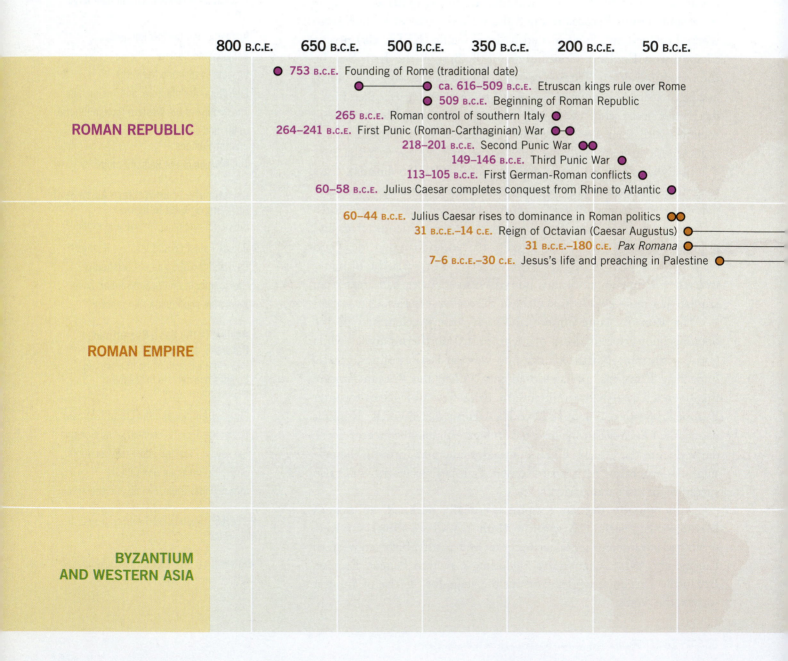

800 B.C.E. | 650 B.C.E. | 500 B.C.E. | 350 B.C.E. | 200 B.C.E. | 50 B.C.E.

ROMAN REPUBLIC

- **753 B.C.E.** Founding of Rome (traditional date)
- **ca. 616–509 B.C.E.** Etruscan kings rule over Rome
- **509 B.C.E.** Beginning of Roman Republic
- **265 B.C.E.** Roman control of southern Italy
- **264–241 B.C.E.** First Punic (Roman-Carthaginian) War
- **218–201 B.C.E.** Second Punic War
- **149–146 B.C.E.** Third Punic War
- **113–105 B.C.E.** First German-Roman conflicts
- **60–58 B.C.E.** Julius Caesar completes conquest from Rhine to Atlantic

ROMAN EMPIRE

- **60–44 B.C.E.** Julius Caesar rises to dominance in Roman politics
- **31 B.C.E.–14 C.E.** Reign of Octavian (Caesar Augustus)
- **31 B.C.E.–180 C.E.** *Pax Romana*
- **7–6 B.C.E.–30 C.E.** Jesus's life and preaching in Palestine

BYZANTIUM AND WESTERN ASIA

while importing grain from the nearby islands of Sicily and Sardinia **(sahr-DIN-ee-uh)** and from northern Africa. Unlike in Greece, agricultural success and easy contact encouraged large states. Indo-European Celtic and Germanic peoples living in the forested hills and plains of western and northern Europe frequently invaded this area using passes through the Alps, a formidable mountain complex.

Romans who expanded beyond Italy drew upon the natural resources of the larger Mediterranean world and beyond (see Map 8.1). Spain offered abundant silver, copper, and tin, while Egypt provided wheat. Beginning about 200 B.C.E., overland trade routes connected the Mediterranean with China along the Silk Road, which brought East Asian products that were bartered in return for gold, silver, precious stones, and some textiles.

The Romans were greatly influenced by the Etruscans, who founded a dozen or so city-states in central and northern Italy by the eighth century B.C.E. Chariot warriors, sailors, and maritime traders, they eventually dominated more of Italy and the island of Corsica but also had contact and sometimes conflict with nearby Greek settlements. They adopted the Greek alphabet and myths, and Greek craftsmen worked in some Etruscan cities.

The Etruscan language is only partially understood, and none of its major literature survives. The Etruscans' well-decorated tombs show they were skilled artists and artisans.

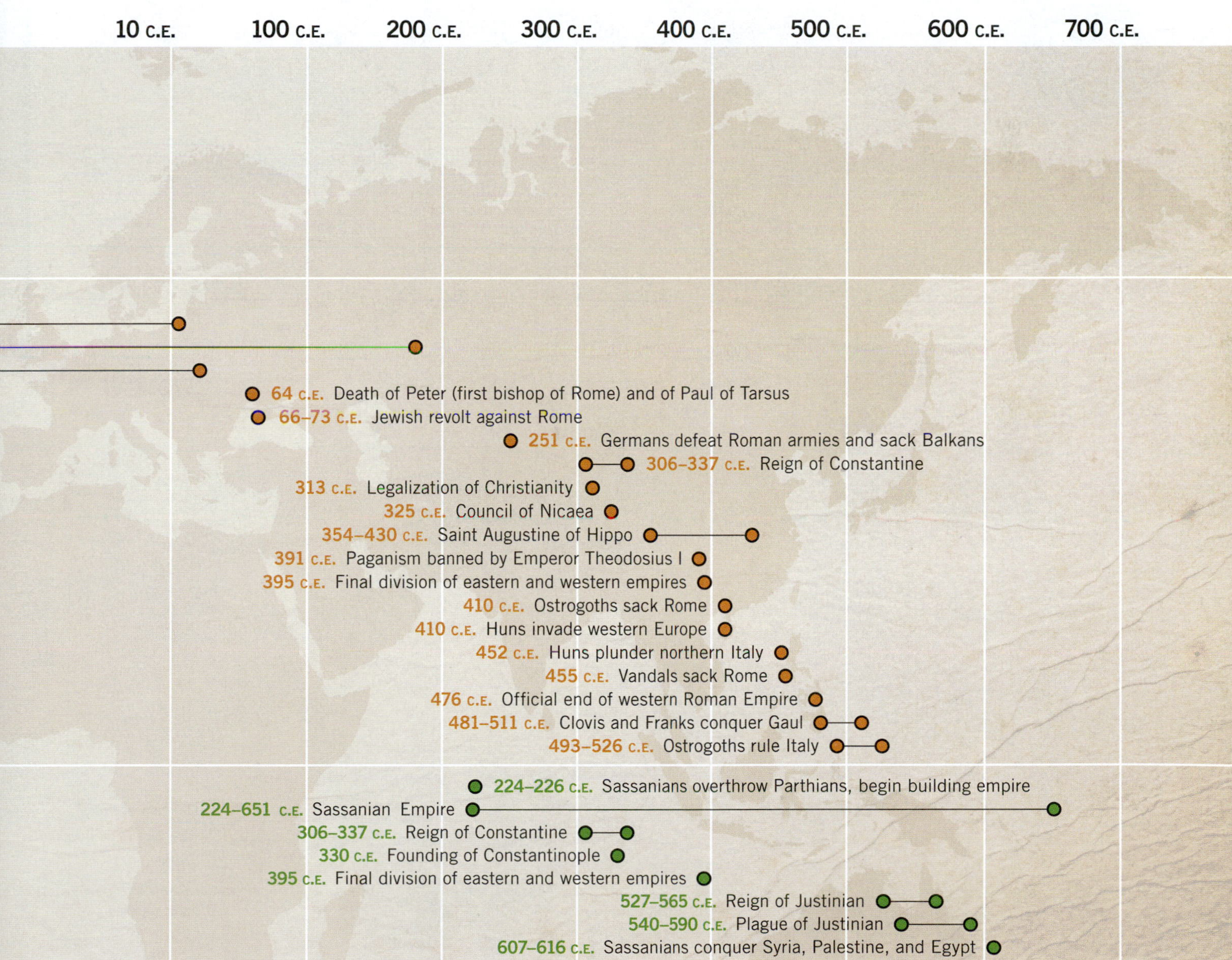

A good road system linked together their well-planned cities, each of which apparently had its own king. Etruscans worked iron ore into excellent iron axes, sickles, and tools. Their rigid social system included slavery, although Etruscan women apparently had a high social status, conversing with men in public, driving their own chariots, owning real estate, and sometimes running businesses like pottery workshops.

In the eighth century B.C.E., Indo-European pastoralists known as the Latins established Rome on seven hills along the Tiber River as a small city-state in central Italy just south of Etruscan territory. Initially Roman-Etruscan relations were peaceful, but the Romans were soon dominated by the Etruscans. The Romans adopted the twenty-six-character Etruscan alphabet borrowed from the Greeks,

MAP 8.1 ITALY AND THE WESTERN MEDITERRANEAN, 600–200 B.C.E. During the early Classical period the Etruscan cities in the north and the Greek city-states in the south held political power in Italy. Carthage held a similar status in Northeast Africa. Eventually the Latins, from their base in Rome, became the dominant political force in the entire region.

as well as the Greek-inspired Etruscan phalanx infantry formation. Skilled Etruscan engineers taught the Romans to make the weight-bearing semicircular arch, which the Romans used to construct city walls, aqueducts to carry water, and doorways. At the end of the sixth century B.C.E., the last Etruscan king was driven out for his brutality, and Rome became independent. Later the Romans conquered and assimilated the Etruscans.

The Roman Republic and Expansion

Using Greek political ideas, in 509 B.C.E. the Romans established a republic, a state in which supreme power is held by the people or their elected representatives. Over the next three centuries, the Romans developed representative government, introducing enduring political ideas. Many modern English words taken from Latin—such as *senate*, *citizenship*, *suffrage* (the right to vote), *dictator* (a man given full power), *plebiscite* **(PLEB-i-site)** (a special vote by citizens on a political issue), and even *republic*—suggest the influence of the Romans on modern political life, including in the United States of America.

Initially, the aristocratic upper class, or **patricians** **(puh-TRISH-uhnz)**, held all power, controlling the Senate, a body that had previously advised the kings, the army, and the legislative body made up of soldiers, the **Centuriate Assembly**. The Senate, composed of three hundred former government officials, ratified resolutions of the Centuriate Assembly before they became law. As the Republic developed, the Centuriate Assembly elected two men each year as **consuls** with executive power.

Commoners, or **plebeians** **(pli-BEE-uhnz)**, heavily outnumbered patricians. As Rome expanded, plebeian soldiers wanted to share in the wealth flowing into Rome. Years of army service had taken them away from their farms and left them in debt, and they demanded a greater political voice and economic equality. A plebeian leader expressed bitterness toward those who opposed reform: "[You] realize vividly the depth of the contempt in which you are held by the aristocracy. They would rob you of the very light you see by; they grudge you the air you breathe, the words you speak."[2] Plebeians believed that political power would allow them to pass laws distributing the state's wealth more fairly.

Gradually social and political rights expanded. In 494 B.C.E. the plebeians selected two of their number, called **tribunes**, to represent their interests in the Centuriate Assembly, much as the consuls represented patrician interests. By 471 a separate new Plebeian Assembly elected tribunes and conducted votes among plebeians, called plebiscites. Plebeians later gained the right to share with the patricians lands won in war, and they won full equality by 267 B.C.E., when their assembly became the state's principal lawmaking body.

To resolve some of its problems, in the fourth century the Roman Republic turned to imperialism, the control or domination by one state over another. A major defeat by the Gauls **(gawlz)**, a Celtic people who plundered Rome in 390 B.C.E., shocked Roman leaders and prompted them to expand Roman territory and move their frontiers further from the city of Rome. As they successfully fought with other Italian city-states, the Romans often granted either full or limited Roman citizenship to the defeated cities' inhabitants. Roman citizenship became a great honor bringing special legal treatment, an honor fathers proudly passed on to their sons. By wisely treating former enemies fairly, Romans spread their power without encouraging revolts and ensured that more men joined their army.

Carthage, Egypt, and Regional Trade

After first conquering the Etruscan cities, which had been weakened by conflicts with the Gauls, the Romans took over the Greek cities in southern Italy and Sicily in 265 B.C.E. Then they encountered their greatest enemy, the Carthaginians. Both Carthage and Egypt played key roles in Mediterranean trade. Carthage **(KAHR-thij)**, a city-state, was originally a Phoenician colony on the North African coast near modern Tunis. In Egypt, the other great power on the Mediterranean's southern shores, the Hellenistic Greek Ptolemaic **(taw-luh-MAY-ik)** dynasty had prospered for over a century.

With a fine harbor and strategic position, Carthage grew into the wealthiest Phoenician outpost, described by a Greek as having "gardens and orchards of all kinds, no end of country houses built luxuriously, land cultivated partly as vineyards and partly as olive groves, fruit trees, herds of cattle and flocks of sheep."[3] However, the autocratic city government experienced political instability as rival leaders vied for power, and differences between the prosperous Phoenician settlers and the native Berbers created tensions. Carthaginians also fought frequent wars with their Greek commercial rivals.

Carthaginian maritime skills fostered trade networks. Around 425 B.C.E. the admiral Hanno led a naval expedition through the Strait of Gibraltar and down the West African coast, seeking markets. He founded trading posts along Morocco's coast and sailed at least as far as the Senegal River. Other Carthaginian expeditions apparently reached the British Isles and perhaps several Atlantic islands off the Northwest African coast. By the third century B.C.E. the Carthaginians had created an empire along the

patricians The aristocratic upper class who controlled the Roman Senate.

Centuriate Assembly A Roman legislative body made up of soldiers.

consuls Two patrician men, elected by the Centuriate Assembly each year, who had executive power in the Roman Republic.

plebeians The commoner class in Rome.

tribunes Roman men elected to represent plebeian interests in the Centuriate Assembly.

[2]Livy, quoted in Frederick Gentles and Melvin Steinfield, eds., *Hangups from Way Back: Historical Myths and Canons*, vol. 1, 2nd ed. (San Francisco: Canfield, 1974), 173.

[3]Diodorus, quoted in Barry Cunliffe, *The Extraordinary Voyage of Pytheas the Greek* (New York: Penguin, 2002), 52.

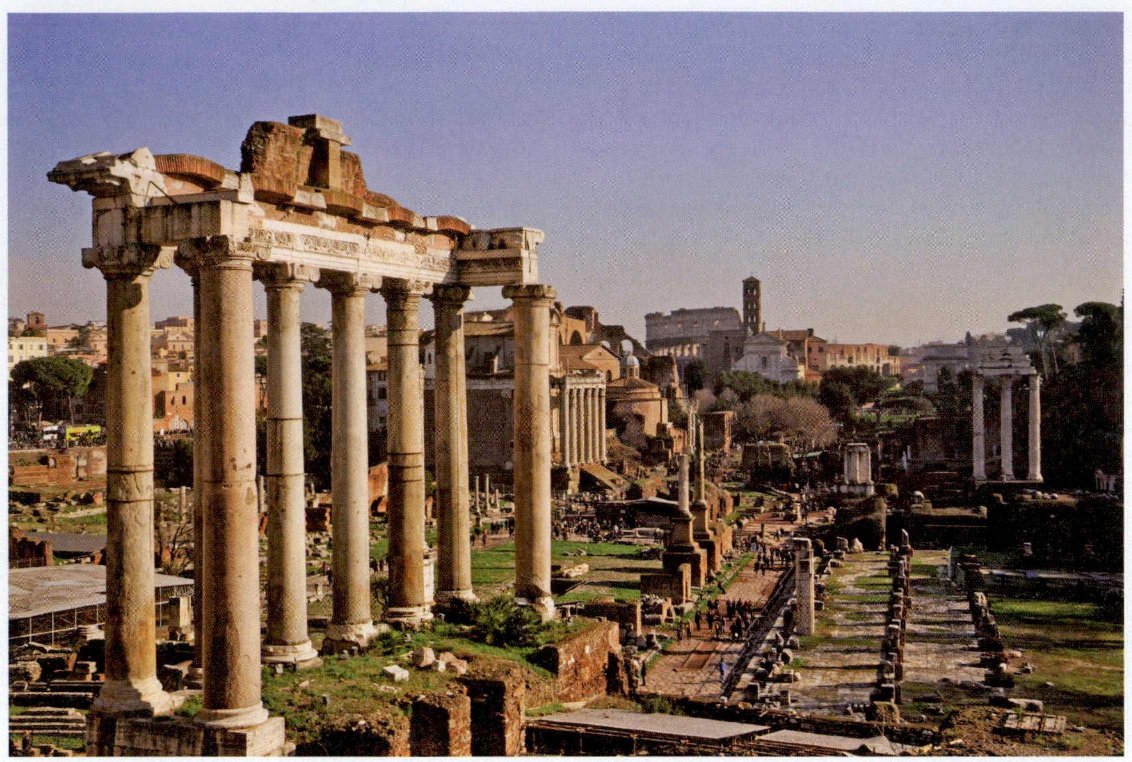

THE ROMAN FORUM The Forum, located amidst various religious and governmental buildings, was the center of Roman political life.

southern and western shores of the Mediterranean Sea, controlling a large part of Spain, much of the North African coast, and the islands of Corsica and Sardinia. In 264 B.C.E. they moved troops to Sicily to aid several Greek cities allied with them against Rome.

By the second century B.C.E., Ptolemaic power in Egypt had become more tenuous as rulers demanded increased agricultural and craft production from workers. Egypt remained a major supplier of wheat and exported papyrus, the preferred medium for scientific, philosophical, and literary texts; textiles; pottery; and metal objects. Greek and Phoenician ships carried some of these goods to foreign ports. Despite the economic growth, many Egyptians tired of foreign occupation, hardship, and high taxes, and several rebellions threatened the government. To maintain their own independence, Egyptian rulers sought alliances with rising Rome. In 180 B.C.E. Cleopatra I became sole ruler, the first in a long chain of assertive queens. Then in 47 B.C.E. an ambitious eighteen-year-old became ruler as Queen Cleopatra VII, just as poor harvests and official corruption fostered more unrest. Her skills enabled the unstable country to maintain domestic peace and deflect Rome for nearly two decades.

The Punic Wars and Afro-Eurasian Empire

The result of Roman expansion southward was three Punic **(PYOO-nik)** Wars between the two major powers and bitter rivals, Rome and Carthage. The first Punic War (264–241 B.C.E.) resulted in Roman naval expeditions against Carthage, finally ending with Roman occupation of Sicily, Corsica, and Sardinia. In the second conflict (218–201), the brilliant Carthaginian general Hannibal (247–182 B.C.E.) led his troops through Spain and France to invade Italy across the Alps, defeating every Roman army sent against them. Modern people may have images in their mind of war elephants, carefully trained to charge and terrify the enemy on the battlefield, used by Hannibal's army lumbering through the rugged mountains. But the elephants and Hannibal's troops, not used to the mountains' snow and ice, perished by the thousands.

The early military success of Hannibal's force alarmed the Romans. With his supply lines overstretched, however, Hannibal could not conquer Italian cities. In contrast, having already absorbed much of Italy, Rome had considerable manpower. Hence Roman generals willingly endured staggeringly high casualties; although fifty thousand soldiers died in the Battle of Canae, Romans would not concede defeat. Eventually the Romans drove Hannibal's forces out and defeated Carthage, which had to surrender all its overseas possessions, including Spain. In the final Punic War (149–146), Romans laid siege to Carthage city and destroyed it. Northwest Africa became a Roman province, a source of copper, grain, and West African gold.

Roman victory encouraged additional imperial expansion, aimed either at punishing Carthage's allies or at restoring stability. In 146 B.C.E. Romans made Greece and Macedonia into a province. Few could resist the Roman infantrymen, armed with swords and rectangular shields, or the armor-clad Roman archers, who rode in carts carrying large crossbows, among the era's most feared weapons. But Romans also employed diplomacy alongside warfare, winning some territories without force. By the mid-first century B.C.E. the Romans had built an empire commanding the entire Mediterranean and its vast resources, binding together Europe, western Asia, and North Africa. The empire included most of Anatolia, Syria, and Palestine, as well as much territory in northern and western Europe. The Ptolemies still controlled Egypt, but they carefully avoided offending the Romans. The Romans also absorbed much of the Hellenistic east, with its web of international commerce. Alexandria in Egypt distributed goods from as far away as India and East Africa.

The Decline of the Republic

But imperial success also fostered major changes in Roman society. The Roman historian Tacitus **(TASS-uh-tuhs)** believed that imperial growth increased the love of power: "It was easy to maintain equality when Rome was weak. World-wide conquest and the destruction of all rival[s] opened the way to the secure enjoyment of wealth and an overriding appetite for it."[4] Indeed, imperial expansion provoked crises that reshaped politics and undermined the Republic, turning representative institutions into window-dressing. As warfare gave military leaders excessive power, the Senate's influence weakened, and growing Roman wealth increased the rich-poor gap. As upper-class families bought farmland from peasants impoverished by long army service, many farmers moved to Rome, where the government supported hundreds of thousands of displaced people to maintain their loyalty. With fewer willing soldiers, the tribune Tiberius Graccus **(tie-BIR-ee-uhs GRAK-uhs)** proposed giving public land to farmers who served in the Roman legions when needed. But when the poor gathered in Rome to support this measure, some wealthy Romans spurred a mob to club Tiberius and many to death, demonstrating rich Romans' determination to maintain power and their ability to mobilize many poor people to support one leader or another.

Changing military power also undermined democracy, as the Senate could not control military leaders. In 107 B.C.E., victorious general Gaius Marius **(GAY-uhs MER-ee-uhs)** was elected consul for five straight years, violating a law limiting the officeholder to one year. Marius and his military veterans pressured the senators to vote for a law giving the veterans public land. Skillful military leaders thereafter used their armies to enhance their political power and outmaneuver civilian leaders, a pattern that resulted in civil and foreign wars. Between 78 and 31 B.C.E., ambitious military leaders expanded Roman territory in Europe and Asia, including Syria and Palestine, while finally destroying republican institutions within Rome itself.

One of these leaders, the ambitious young Julius Caesar, completed the conquest of Europe from the Rhine River west to the Atlantic, sent the first Roman forces into Britain, and then won a civil war against former allies. Caesar also weakened the Senate by enlarging it to nine hundred men, too large for an effective governing body. Finally, in 44 B.C.E. he had himself declared "perpetual dictator," an act that led to his assassination, made famous centuries later in English author William Shakespeare's play, *Julius Caesar*.

Caesar's death led to civil war, the end of any pretense of democracy, and the conquest of Egypt. Caesar's adopted son, Octavian **(ok-TAY-vee-uhn)**, fought Mark Antony, a general who had fallen in love with the Egyptian ruler Cleopatra. A Greek historian described Cleopatra, a remarkable personality who had borne a son by Julius Caesar, as someone whose "presence was irresistible; the attraction of her person, the charm of her conversation, was something bewitching. She could pass from one language to another."[5] The turmoil and the Republic ended when Octavian defeated Antony and Cleopatra at the naval Battle of Actium **(AK-tee-uhm)**, in Greece, in 31 B.C.E. Antony and Cleopatra committed suicide and their armies surrendered to Octavian, giving Rome control of Egypt. The Romans then placed Egypt under a tight grip, imposing heavy taxes and encouraging more wheat production to feed Rome.

MAKE SURE YOU UNDERSTAND THESE KEY POINTS BEFORE MOVING ON

- **The Etruscans formed the first urban society in Italy; they influenced and were eventually conquered by the Romans.**
- **Rome formed a republic, in which citizens rule the state; initially upper-class patricians dominated, but over time the plebeians attained increasing amounts of power.**
- **After a major defeat by the Gauls, the Romans decided that the key to safety was to expand their territory so their frontiers would be safely distant from Rome.**
- **With the shift from Roman Republic to empire, military leaders gained power, farmers grew impoverished, and the people had less voice in government.**

[4] Gentles and Steinfield, *Hangups from Way Back*, 167.

[5] From Plutarch, Life of Antony, in *Readings in Ancient History*, ed. William S. Davis, vol. 2 (Boston: Allyn and Bacon, 1913), 163–164.

The Rise and Decline of Imperial Rome

How did the Romans maintain their large empire?

Athenians had pondered whether empire and democracy were compatible. Likewise, in Rome the clash of personal ambitions and greed created by the wealth gained through conquest led to replacing the Republic with a more autocratic and arrogant imperial system. Imperial rule saw the full development of Roman culture, including those elements such as law that became a significant legacy to European society. The Roman Empire lasted in the West for about five hundred years, ending with a long period of internal and external disorder that undermined the empire. Eventually various population movements put pressure on the empire's frontiers, leading to imperial decline, division, and then collapse.

Augustus and the *Pax Romana*

Emperors (*caesarsi*) who controlled the military and much of the government bureaucracy ruled Rome and its empire. Octavian (63 B.C.E.–14 C.E.), who called himself Augustus, a Latin term meaning "majestic, inspiring awe," was worshiped in some places during his dictatorship and deified after death. His long reign (r. 31 B.C.E.–14 C.E.) established and consolidated a system in which the Senate appointed governors to the peaceful provinces while Augustus governed provinces where troops were stationed. Augustus enacted or vetoed legislation and called the Senate into session. The writer Juvenal **(JOO-vuhn-uhl)** deplored the lost popular voice and its replacement by entertainments to divert public attention: "The people that once bestowed commands now meddles no more and longs eagerly for just two things: bread and circuses."[6]

The period in Roman history from Augustus through the reign of Emperor Marcus Aurelius **(aw-REE-lee-uhs)** in 180 C.E. is known as the ***Pax Romana*** ("Roman Peace"). For the first and last time, the entire Mediterranean world was controlled by one power and the Mediterranean Sea was a "Roman lake," remaining at peace for two centuries (see Map 8.2). Rome experienced few challenges from the Germanic peoples, who mostly remained east of the Rhine and north of the Danube Rivers, while in western Asia the Romans faced only a weak Parthian kingdom in Persia and Mesopotamia. Whether in London or Paris, Vienna or Barcelona—all cities founded by the Romans—people lived under the same laws.

Peace and prosperity encouraged trade and population growth. Great fleets of ships moved goods around the Mediterranean Sea, and trade also flourished along the Silk Road between China and Rome through Central and western Asia. Roman merchants were active many places even before the legions arrived. Rome governed a huge population, estimated at 54 million in the first century C.E., including 6 million in Italy. Rome itself may have been the world's largest city, with a half million to 1 million inhabitants. In this diverse empire the Roman ideal, like that of the Hellenistic Greeks, was cosmopolitan. Hence, Emperor Marcus Aurelius (r. 161–180 C.E.) wrote: "Rome is my city and country, but as a man, I am a citizen of the world."[7] Some non-Romans joined the ruling class, and half of the Roman Senate were non-Italians. Men of wealth and military skill, whatever their ethnic background, could rise to the highest levels in the army and government. Many people migrated to Rome, bringing with them cultural forms such as musical instruments and dances. Thus the empire slowly changed into a multinational state that fostered diversity within unity. Eighteen centuries later the founders of the United States, who admired the Roman Republic model, chose a Latin slogan for their new nation: *e pluribus unum* **(EE PLUR-uh-buhs OO-nuhm)**, "one from many."

Pax Romana The period of peace and prosperity in Roman history from the reign of Augustus through that of Emperor Marcus Aurelius in 180 C.E.

Although Roman thinking owed much to Greek political and ethical philosophy, it was also distinctive, with a practical way of looking at the world. Romans extended the meaning of some Greek ideas, such as citizenship, and developed a concept of civic virtue similar to what people today call public duty. Codified laws underpinned the Roman system, encouraging public responsibility, and several Roman legal principles survived to become part of modern national and international law. The Romans believed that all people, regardless of wealth or position, were equal before the law, and they promoted individual rather than family responsibility for one member's misdeeds. The burden of proof in a trial rested with the person making the charge, not the defendant.

Roman law was influenced by the Greek Stoic belief in eternal truths transcending particular cultures. Leading Roman Stoics, including the philosopher Seneca (4 B.C.E.–65 C.E.), the great Roman lawyer and essayist Cicero (106–43 B.C.E.), and the second-century emperor Marcus Aurelius **(uh-REAL-yus)**, famous for his humanity and justice, believed that all people were alike in their use of reason to determine right from wrong. Stoics promoted tolerance, moderation, and acceptance of life's travails. Because of such beliefs, the Romans generally allowed conquered peoples to govern themselves and to keep their own customs and leaders so long as they paid their taxes and did not revolt.

Religion and Society

Roman religion and society changed over the centuries. Romans worshiped a pantheon of gods and goddesses for practical reasons, such as to ensure good fortune, and specific gods or goddesses were associated with certain tasks, such as agriculture or thievery. Religion was an integral part of civic life, with no "separation of church and state." As state officials, priests performed public sacrifices to please the gods and ceremonies

[6]Quoted in Jerome Carcopino, *Daily Life in Ancient Rome*, 2nd ed. (New Haven, CT: Yale University Press, 1968), 202.
[7]Quoted in Norman Davis, *Europe: A History* (New York: Harper, 1998), 193.

MAP 8.2 THE ROMAN EMPIRE, ca. 120 C.E. The Romans gradually expanded until, by 120 C.E., they controlled a huge empire stretching from Britain and Spain in the west through southern and central Europe and North Africa to Egypt, Anatolia, and the lands along the eastern Mediterranean coast.

Scala/Art Resource, NY

ARA PACIS The Altar of Peace, built in 9 B.C.E., resided in a large enclosure whose walls contain relief sculptures. This scene depicts Mother Earth and her children, with the cow and sheep at her feet representing the prosperity resulting from peace.

promoting the state's welfare. Reflecting these practical goals, Caesar Augustus commissioned the building in Rome of the *Ara Pacis*, or Altar of Peace, a sacrificial marble altar to celebrate the end of the wars of conquest in Gaul and Spain and, hopefully, launch a long era of peace. Not wishing to offend any divinity, Romans also adopted other people's gods and goddesses, equating the Greek deities with their own gods. Thus the leader of Greek gods, Zeus, became the Roman Jupiter, Zeus's wife Hera became the Roman Juno **(JOO-noh)**, and the Greek god of wine, Dionysus, became the Roman Bacchus **(BAK-uhs)**.

Although there was some mobility, Roman society remained stratified into sharply defined upper and lower classes, deeply divided by wealth. The superrich (0.5 percent of the population) held about 80 percent of the wealth, while the poor (65 percent) lived on the edge. Below the upper classes, middle-class merchants and artisans ranked above the urban workers and seriously impoverished peasants. We know something of middle- and lower-class concerns and values from graffiti and tombstone memorials that they left (see Witness to the Past: The Voices of Common Romans).

Slaves, one-third of Italy's population, were mostly war captives, but some people were enslaved as payment for debt or criminal activity. Some slaves earned wages or ran businesses on their owner's behalf, saving until they could purchase their freedom. Others lived very hard lives, working in mines, on vast plantations growing cash crops such as olives and grapes, or as oarsmen of Roman ships. A Roman historian described slaves working in a Spanish silver mine: "The slaves secure for their masters riches which are almost beyond belief. They, however, are physically destroyed, their bodies worn down. Many die because of the excessive mistreatment they suffer. They are given no break from their toil."[8] Most gladiators who fought in the arenas to entertain the public were slaves who had trained at gladiator schools, and few lived to old age. Romans brutally crushed sporadic slave rebellions. Although they often freed slaves after years of good service, ex-slaves remained stigmatized socially.

In this patriarchal society, only men had a political voice, enjoying extensive power over women, children, and slaves. A family's oldest male had the power of life and death over other family members and was even free to kill his children without fear of legal problems. Wives were advised to accept their husband's extramarital sexual exploits: "Let the matron be subject to her husband." Yet, some women stepped outside expected bounds. Seneca criticized those daring women who copied "male indulgences, they keep just as late hours, and drink as much liquor; they challenge men in carousing."[9]

[8]Diodorua Siculus, in Jo Ann Shelton, *As the Romans Did: A Sourcebook in Roman Social History* (New York: Oxford University Press, 1988), 175.

[9]The quotes are from Henry C. Boren, *Roman Society: A Social, Economic, and Cultural History*, 2nd ed. (Lexington, MA: D.C. Heath, 1992), 279, 219.

WITNESS TO THE PAST

The Voices of Common Romans

As with most premodern societies, we know much more from the surviving records and literature about the prominent and wealthy than about the much more numerous common people. But we can learn about the middle and lower classes from their graffiti preserved in ancient city ruins like Pompeii and tombstone epitaphs. Romans used graffiti and epitaphs to voice frank opinions on many matters and to summarize their lives. Like modern graffiti, some of the remarks address sexual activities and bodily functions or insult rivals with profanity. The following are some examples of less profane but often humorous graffiti and epitaphs from various Roman cities.

Graffiti

I'm amazed, O wall, that you've not collapsed under the weight of so much written filth.

A bronze urn has disappeared from my tavern. Whoever returns it will get 65 sesterces reward. Whoever informs on the thief will get 20 sesterces, if we recover it.

Perarius, you're a thief.

No loiterers—scram!

Livia, to Alexander: "If you're well, I don't much care; if you're dead, I'm delighted."

Samius Cornelius, go hang yourself!

Stronnius is an ignoramus.

Crescens is a public whore.

Whoever doesn't invite me to dinner is a barbarian.

Whoever is in love, may he prosper. Whoever loves not, may he die. Whoever forbids love, may he die twice over!

Marcus loves Spendusa.

If you haven't seen the Venus that Apelles painted, take a look at my girl—she's just as beautiful.

Thraex makes the girls sigh.

All the goldsmiths support Gaius Cuspious Pansa for public works commissioner.

The mule-drivers support Gaius Julius Polybius for mayor. Genialis supports Bruttius Balbus for mayor. He'll balance the budget.

I ask you to support Marcus Cerrinus Vatia for public works commissioner. All the late-night drunks back him.

Epitaphs

If you wish to add your sorrow to ours, come here and shed your tears. A sad parent has laid to rest his only daughter, whom he treasured with sweet love as long as the Fates permitted. Now her dear face and form are mere shadow and her bones mere ash.

For my dearest wife, with whom I lived two years, six months, three days, and ten hours. On the day she died, I gave thanks before gods and men.

I was once famous, preeminent among thousands of strong Bavarian men. I swam across the Danube in full armor. I once shot an arrow in the air and split it with a second in midair. No Roman or barbarian ever beat me with a spear, no Parthian with the bow. This tombstone preserves the story of my deeds. But I am still unique, the first to do such things as these.

THINKING ABOUT THE READING

1. What do these graffiti tell us about political life?
2. What do the graffiti and epitaphs reveal about what common people valued?
3. In what ways do the sentiments seem familiar to modern readers?

Adult women also enjoyed some legal rights, including possession of their own property, even if married. Some acquired considerable wealth, using it for such community ends as financing public monuments. Moreover, a wife could escape her husband's legal control by spending three days and nights away from his house, and she could sue her husband if he abandoned her. For example, a woman whose husband had moved to Alexandria and married another woman asked the court to make her husband return the dowry she brought to the marriage. Roman women also had more freedom to leave their homes and travel through the city than did their Greek sisters. Finally, abortion and contraception were common until they were outlawed around 200 C.E.

In the Republic's later years, Romans became free to choose their own spouse. By 17 B.C.E., adultery and avoidance of marriage by both genders had become serious social problems, and some busy prostitutes earned good money. To attempt to halt a population decline among native Italians, a law was passed requiring men to marry or pay higher taxes. At the same time, Romans generally tolerated homosexual activity and did not view it as immoral. Acknowledged homosexuals participated openly in Roman life.

Economy and Trade Networks

The Romans flourished from expanding trade and industry, and Rome became a communications center for a large area of Afro-Eurasia. Industries such as mining and pottery making depended mostly on slave labor, while the wealthy invested in public displays and land rather than business or industry. Romans also built over 150,000 miles of roads, the phrase "all roads lead to Rome" reflecting this accomplishment.

Much of Roman trade depended on maritime trade routes that linked Rome to Asia and Africa. The Egyptian port of Berenike **(BER-eh-nick-y)**, on the Red Sea, was a transfer point for fabrics, spices, gems, and other exotic goods from India and

Southeast Asia, frankincense and myrrh from Arabia, and ivory, drugs, tortoise shells, and slaves from Somalia and Ethiopia. Over a hundred ships a year set off from Berenike and nearby ports for India, while large merchant ships plied the Mediterranean between Egypt and Rome. Archaeologists have uncovered Roman coins in India, China, and Vietnam.

Romans also traded widely over land. Roman-ruled North Africa obtained gold from West African societies across the Sahara Desert, while Chinese products reached Rome over the Silk Road. Romans shipped much gold and silver east in return for spices, jewelry, cut gems, glassware, and silk. But eventually the expanding Roman appetite for Chinese goods harmed Rome's economy. The historian Pliny **(PLIN-ee)** the Elder bemoaned the wealth shipped east and blamed it on Roman women's fondness for silks, pearls, and perfumes: "India and China and [Arabia] together drain our empire. That is the price that our luxuries and our womankind cost us."[10] However, both men and women coveted imported Asian goods.

Literature, Architecture, and Technology

The remarkable achievements of Roman literary culture during the late Republic and early empire mostly reflected the views of the aristocratic elite. Virgil (70–19 B.C.E.), Rome's greatest epic poet, promoted Roman greatness through his *Aeneid* **(i-NEE-id)**, which described the journey of the legendary Trojan hero Aeneas **(i-NEE-uhs)**, who, according to the poem, left Troy and eventually founded the city of Rome. The love poems of Ovid (43 B.C.E.–17 C.E.) were irreverent and erotic, his treatise on the art of love advising men to indulge their sexual cravings. In disgust, the moralistic emperor Augustus eventually sent Ovid into bitter exile along the Black Sea.

Historians also made substantial literary contributions. Tacitus (56–117 C.E.) wrote a history of the early emperors, lamenting the end of the Republic and its more open political atmosphere and sense of equality. He also sympathetically described the Germanic tribes north of the Rhine and Danube, contrasting their sexual purity and other virtues with Roman vices. For example, the corrupt emperor Domitian "fancied that the voice of the Roman people [was] obliterated; he banished teachers of philosophy and exiled every noble pursuit, so that nothing honorable might anywhere be encountered."[11]

The Romans' quest to provide public services fostered notable architecture and engineering. The great dome of the Pantheon **(PAN-thee-ahn)**, or temple to all the gods in Rome, has no interior-supporting pillars and forms a perfect sphere. Rome's Colosseum was the world's largest outdoor arena until the twentieth century. Another architectural wonder was aqueducts, which carried water hundreds of miles from mountains into cities. One of the Romans' most sophisticated engineering projects, public baths, became social centers containing gardens, libraries, and exercise and game rooms. A Roman writer observed that baths, sex, and wine ruin bodies but make life worth living. Wealthy Romans enjoyed many creature comforts, and some of their homes were heated from furnaces under the floor that spread heat to the house through ductwork, similar to the heating systems in Korea. Other inventions included glass windowpanes, scales with weights, chemical fertilizer, theater curtains, door keys, heavy plows, and primitive dental drills. Julius Caesar introduced a calendar creating a year of 365 days and a few minutes. His calendar had to be reformed, but not until the sixteenth century.

The Decline of the Western Roman Empire

Political and economic problems eventually undermined the empire. Roman leaders never found a good way to pass power on to a successor, and reliance on the army to decide who ruled resulted in twelve soldier-emperors between 235 and 260 C.E., none dying peacefully in old age. To control their empire, the Romans spent more wealth supporting a growing bureaucracy and military, pushing the state toward bankruptcy. Paying taxes proved a particular problem in the empire's western half, where serious inflation substantially decreased real wealth. While older, larger cities provided a stronger tax base for eastern provinces, the frontier lands west of Italy consumed more than they produced. To pay for goods and food required finding more precious metals (such as gold and silver) or more slaves to sell or trade to the east for manufactured products.

The empire gradually decayed from within. Leaders were consumed by rivalries, while corruption, ineptitude, and civil wars eroded the government and made the state vulnerable to invaders. In the early third century, increasing costs and the difficulties of controlling a growing empire forced Roman rulers to end further conquests and merely defend existing frontiers, thus cutting themselves off from the income that conquest provided and further impoverishing the government. In addition, some gold and silver mines in the western lands and the fertile soil in Italy became exhausted, making goods more expensive. Romans experienced a steadily widening rich-poor gap, a serious trade deficit with China, declining literacy levels, and growing corruption, apathy, and loss of public spirit. Meanwhile, a cooler climate may have diminished crop yields. Finally, contacts with distant lands made Rome increasingly vulnerable to diseases and epidemics that killed many thousands. Reaching Europe from North Africa, a plague from 251 to 266 C.E. caused dramatic population decline and weakened military forces. At the epidemic's height, five thousand people reportedly died each day in the city of Rome.

Celtic and Germanic Societies and the Romans

The decline of Rome also corresponded with the rise of two northern European societies, Celts and Germans. The Celts, whose culture developed by the twelfth century B.C.E. in the Danube River Basin north of the Alps, occupied large sections of central and western Europe, from Germany and France to

[10]Quoted in Susan Whitfield, *Life Along the Silk Road* (Berkeley: University of California Press, 1999), 21.

[11]Tacitus, Agricola, quoted in Moses Hadas, ed., *A History of Rome from Its Origins to 529 A.D. as Told by the Roman Historians* (Garden City, NY: Doubleday Anchor, 1956), 126–127.

Alinari/Art Resource, NY

ROMAN ARMY CAMP This carving shows a camp being built by Roman legionnaires during a military campaign. Soldiers' helmets, shields, and pikes are propped up at the right side. Some men build walls and dig ditches.

the British Isles and Spain. The Celtic peoples resisted the expanding Romans. Powerful chiefs ruled small Celtic states, and priests, known as *druids*, organized the worship of their many gods. Many Celts lived in large fortified towns or produced a substantial agricultural surplus, and some had coins and writing. Aided by bronze and then iron technologies, they were fierce warriors and fine horsemen. By 400 B.C.E. Celtic tribes were raiding into Italy, sacking Rome and weakening the Etruscan states. In Gaul their armies' many trumpeters and horn blowers, as well as war cries, terrified their opponents.

However, the well-drilled, disciplined Roman legions overwhelmed the Celtic fighters, which were divided by tribal rivalries, and eventually Romans colonized or Germans dislodged most of the Celts. In 225 B.C.E. the Romans overran the Celts in northern Italy, and first Carthaginians and then Romans crushed Celtic power in Spain. Julius Caesar conquered the Celts of Gaul. In 60–61 C.E., however, the Romans faced a temporary setback when Celts led by a warrior-queen, Boudica **(boo-DIK-uh)** (d. 61 C.E.), destroyed several Roman settlements in England. Boudica had good reason to despise the Romans, who had pillaged her territory, flogged Boudica, and raped her daughters. A Roman historian lamented the defeat brought by a woman, which caused the Romans great shame. In retaliation, the Romans sent in a larger force, killing 80,000 of Boudica's subjects. The queen committed suicide rather than surrender.

Celtic societies and culture remained strong mostly in Ireland and the rugged hills of Wales and Scotland, where long lines of communication kept the Romans from extending their rule. The Roman emperor Hadrian **(HAY-dree-uhn)** built a remarkable 73-mile-long rock wall across northern England to keep Celtic tribes out of Roman territory. Christianity, which reached Ireland in the fifth century, eventually modified Celtic culture. Today the Irish, Scottish, and Welsh people still honor their Celtic heritage, but few speak their ancestral Celtic languages. In most of mainland Europe and England, Celtic culture gradually became Latinized and Germanized, although pockets of Celtic identity survive in Brittany **(BRIT-uhn-ee)** (western France) and northwest Spain.

Germanic peoples living in Scandinavia and the northern plains of Germany also pressured Rome's northern borders and eventually began migrating into the empire. No known German cities or states existed, but Germanic peoples inflicted several defeats on Roman legions in Gaul in 113 B.C.E. Although the Romans ultimately crushed the Germans, fear of Germanic invasions helped prompt Roman expansion northward. Some Germans were brought into the Roman fold, some serving in the Roman army. The Roman historian Tacitus praised Germans for their hospitality, noting that they considered it a crime to turn any visitor away from their door. However, most Romans viewed Germans as dangerous "barbarians."

For the next several centuries Romans and Germans watched each other warily on the empire's fringes. When German tribes formed confederations, their combined strength made them a greater threat. Pushed by their own enemies such as westward-moving Huns from Central Asia, some Germans moved on to Roman lands, intensifying German-Roman conflict. In 251 C.E. Germans defeated a Roman army and plundered the Balkans. The Romans could not field enough high-quality soldiers to defeat the invaders because their shrinking population meant that men needed to farm could not be spared for the army. In 381 the Romans began drafting men, but many draftees mutilated themselves to avoid service.

German expansion greatly impacted Roman society. High taxes to support the armies alienated all classes but fell primarily on poor peasants, many of whom lost their land and became workers on large landed estates. Sometimes, giving up their freedom, whole villages placed themselves under a wealthy landlord's protection, with men and women working their patron's land. Meanwhile, the upper classes increasingly escaped cities for their country estates. Thus Roman cities slowly but steadily shrank in size and wealth as fewer children were born and the upper classes moved away.

The Division of the Roman Empire

The mounting problems led to the empire's division. Emperor Diocletian **(DIE-uh-KLEE-shuhn)** (r. 285–305) recognized the western province's weakness and divided the empire in half, making the Adriatic Sea an east-west dividing line. He ruled the east from Nicomedia **(NIK-uh-MEED-ee-uh)** in Anatolia and appointed another man, Maximian, as western emperor. A later emperor, Constantine (r. 306–337), temporarily reunited the empire under one ruler, establishing a new capital on the Straits of Bosporus **(BAHS-puhr-uhs)**, first named New Rome and then Constantinople **(cahn-stan-tih-NO-pul)**—today's Istanbul **(IS-tahn-BUL)**. In 395 Constantinople became the capital of the eastern, or Byzantine, Empire, which survived the western Roman Empire by nearly a thousand years.

Gilles Mermet/Art Resource, NY

LIFE ON A LATE ROMAN EMPIRE ESTATE The painting, of a fortified manor house and its surroundings, shows typical farming activity for each season.

The worst Roman military defeats, in the fourth and fifth centuries C.E., forced emperors to abandon claims to many territories, including Britain. In 410 the Germanic Ostrogoths **(AH-struh-GAHTHS)** (eastern Goths) plundered the city of Rome while a branch of the Huns, fierce horse-riding pastoralists, conquered Hungary and later pushed various Germans west into Gaul, Italy, and Spain. Led by the able warrior Attila **(uh-TIL-uh)** (406–453), Huns ravaged the Balkans and Greece before plundering northern Italy in 452. Hun power soon collapsed, but Rome was again sacked by another German group, the Vandals, in 455 C.E. In 476, Germans deposed the last Roman emperor, marking the official end of the western empire.

Romance languages
Languages that derive from Latin, such as French, Italian, and Spanish.

Various Germanic kingdoms, including the Vandals in Northwest Africa, the Visigoths **(VIZ-uh-gahths)** in Spain, and the Ostrogoths in Italy, now ruled the western Mediterranean world. Another German group, the Franks, under their leader Clovis **(KLO-vuhs)**, conquered what is now France and western Germany. Meanwhile, Germanic Angles and Saxons migrated into England. These Germanic peoples adopted a considerable amount of Roman culture, and some used local versions of Latin, forming the basis for **Romance languages** such as French, Italian, and Spanish.

MAKE SURE YOU UNDERSTAND THESE KEY POINTS BEFORE MOVING ON

- **The Romans set long-lasting legal standards and offered allegiance to a wide variety of gods, many of them borrowed from other peoples.**
- **Roman society was highly stratified; slaves performed much of the manual labor, and women, although accorded some significant legal rights, were generally subjugated.**
- **Rome served as a nexus for trade and communication and excelled in architecture and engineering.**
- **The Celts, who were fierce warriors, posed a threat to the Romans, but they were eventually conquered and Latinized except for some in rugged areas of the British Isles.**
- **The Roman Empire had trouble fielding enough soldiers or gathering enough money to fend off the German threat.**

aplia

Christianity: From Western Asian Sect to Transregional Religion

How did Christianity develop and expand?

The Christian church played a vigorous role in Roman cities even in the western empire's final decades. Christianity arose in Palestine (in western Asia) in the first century C.E. as a Jewish sect (see Map 8.3), and Christian religious and social institutions then accompanied Greco-Roman culture into the new Germanic kingdoms. Together they defined the culture that dominated Europe in the centuries following the Classical period. The transformation of Christianity from small Jewish sect to the faith of emperors and the empire provides one of the Roman era's most dramatic legacies. To understand the history of Western societies requires analyzing Christianity's rise and values.

Roman Palestine and Jesus of Nazareth

Christianity was founded on the teachings of Jesus of Nazareth, a Jewish teacher in first-century C.E. Roman-ruled Palestine. Palestine and the surrounding region contained diverse traditions. Most people, including Jews, spoke Aramaic **(ar-uh-MAY-ik)**, the later Persian Empire's official language, and most literate people wrote in Greek, a legacy of Hellenism. Various Egyptian, Mesopotamian, Phoenician, Persian, and Greek traditions undoubtedly influenced the Jewish and then Christian faiths. Palestine was one of the most restless Roman provinces and had a history of rebellion against Rome. Moreover, Jewish society had diverse beliefs and practices. Over the centuries Hebrew prophets, such as Isaiah in the eighth century B.C.E. and Jeremiah, Ezekiel, and the "Second" Isaiah during the early Axial Age, explored the relations of the Hebrews to their God and other peoples. At the same time, various mystical sects rejected both Hellenistic cosmopolitanism and the formal Jewish leadership. Jesus inherited these prophetic traditions and spoke of himself as the fulfillment of Jewish law.

Much uncertainty surrounds the life of Jesus. Roman records confirm religious conflicts and instability in Palestine but make no mention of Jesus. According to Christian tradition, Jesus was a Jewish carpenter, teacher, and healer who probably lived from around 7 or 6 B.C.E. to 30 C.E. As with Buddha and Confucius, our knowledge of Jesus and his career comes from his followers' writings, primarily through the four gospel (literally "good news") accounts, the centerpieces of the Christian New Testament. The earliest narrative, the Gospel of Mark, was written around 70 C.E., some forty years after Jesus died. The four gospels in the official canon, compiled in the mid-second century C.E., were written not as historical

MAP 8.3 SPREAD OF CHRISTIANITY Christianity arose in Palestine in the first century C.E. and gradually gained footholds in parts of western Asia, North Africa, and southern Europe by 300 C.E. Over the next five centuries Christianity became the dominant religion in much of western and central Europe and expanded its influence in western Asia and North Africa.

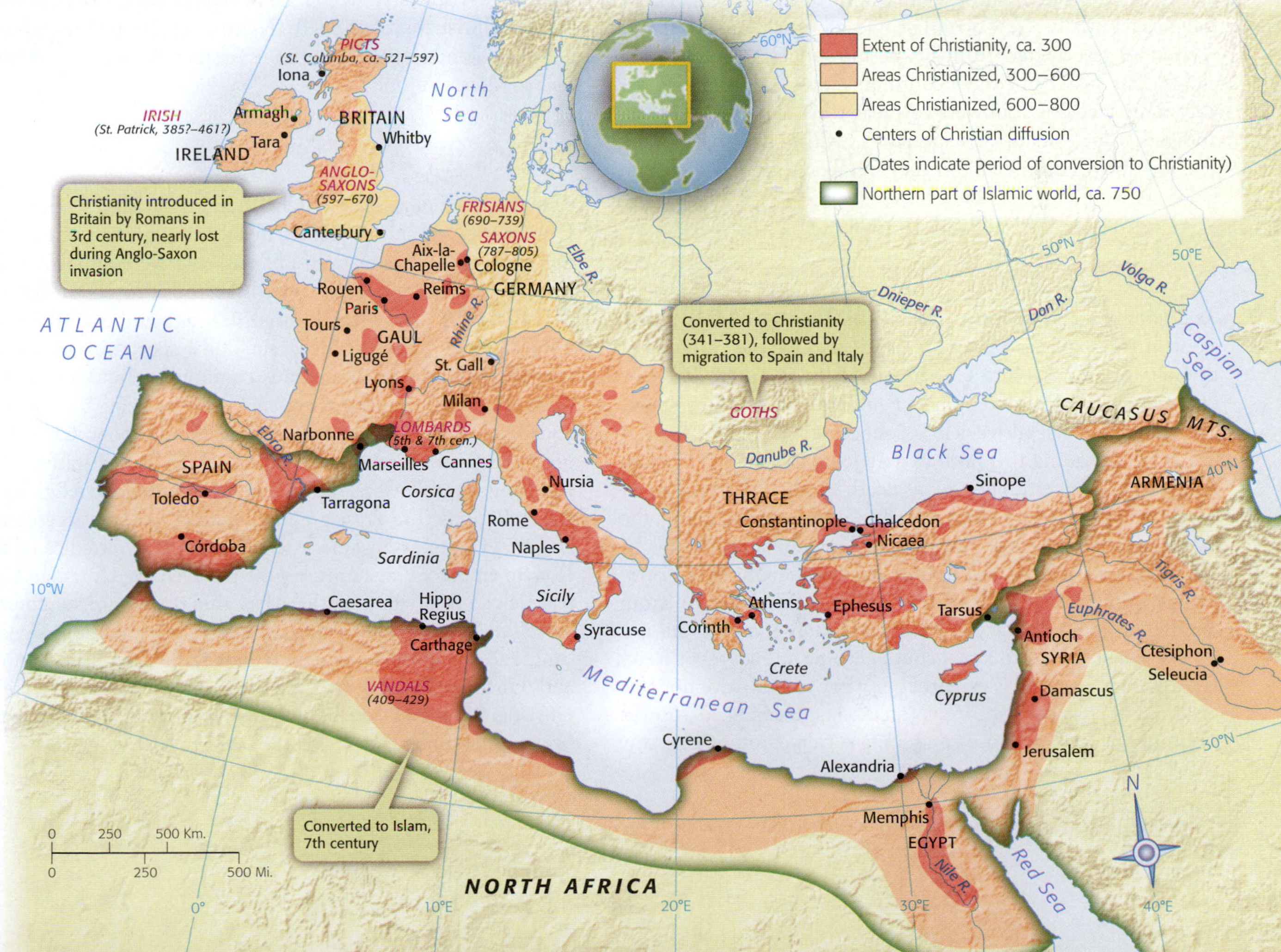

accounts but as faith statements, a "witness" to God's power in the lives of early Jesus followers. As a result, modern theologians and historians vigorously debate the gospel accounts' historical accuracy. Several dozen other gospels or gospel fragments were excluded from the Christian Bible, some differing considerably from the official gospels. Whether the gospel accounts were based largely on eyewitness testimonies, oral traditions, or earlier writings since lost remains unclear.

The gospels describe Jesus as, among other things, a moral reformer who confronted the Jewish leaders, especially the *Pharisees* **(FAR-uh-seez)**, a group emphasizing ritual purity, obeying strict ceremonial laws, and awaiting the coming of a messiah who would free them from the Romans. Jesus favored a simple life, loving others, forgiving enemies, accepting the poor and other despised groups, and opposing excessive legalism and ceremony. According to the Gospel of Matthew, Jesus summed up his teachings in two commandments: "Love God with all your heart, soul, and mind; and love your neighbor as yourself."[12] Matthew reported that Jesus angered influential Jews and Romans by advising the wealthy to give their money to the poor since rich people were unwelcome in God's kingdom. Although his followers considered Jesus much more than a teacher, modern theologians debate whether Jesus ever claimed to be divine, a "son of God," or viewed himself as a healer and wisdom teacher.

Jesus's enemies, especially the Roman governor and a few Jewish religious leaders, accused him of treason against Rome and tried, convicted, and executed him by crucifixion. Jesus's followers, initially a few dozen people, all Jews, claimed he was revived or resurrected from death and "appeared to" his disciples. This belief in Jesus's continuing divine presence probably motivated his followers to preach his message to others and gather for worship as a special sect within the first-century C.E. Jewish community. Soon they numbered several thousand believers.

Paul and the Shaping of Christianity

The activities and writings of Paul of Tarsus **(TAHR-suhs)**, a port city in southeast Anatolia, greatly affected the evolution of the religion of Jesus into Christianity. A first-century Romanized Jew from a Pharisee family, Paul said he was miraculously converted to belief in Jesus as a young man. He spent the rest of his life spreading this faith to non-Jews, traveling to western Asian and Greek cities before his death in a Rome prison about 64 C.E. Paul's teaching emphasized Jesus as a divine being, the "son of God" who earned forgiveness for humankind's sins by his death on the cross. Accepting Jesus as the Christ (*Christus* meant "anointed one"), Paul taught, could save a person from damnation to an eternity in Hell, and a non-Jew who did not follow Jewish laws and ritual could become a follower of Jesus. By arguing that there was neither Jew nor Greek, slave nor free person, but instead a spiritual equality, he challenged Roman assumptions such as those condoning slavery, prompting many Roman citizens to regard Christians as a threat. Paul's patriarchal views also strongly influenced Christian thinking. He valued celibacy above marriage and urged wives to be subject to their husbands and remain silent in church.

Paul disagreed strongly with those who believed that Christians had to follow Jewish laws. His decision to exempt converts from undergoing the circumcision required by Jewish law was crucial for Christianity's success; in those days before antibiotics and anesthesia, such operations would have discouraged many. Peter, Jesus's chief disciple, finally agreed, on Paul's urging, that God made no distinction between Jews and others, and he later became the first bishop of Rome (and hence the first pope). Peter was probably killed in Rome during the persecution of Christians in 64. Eventually, most Christians believed they were saved by faith in Jesus, not by following any Jewish tradition.

Paul's victory in convincing Peter to include non-Jews was crucial in establishing Christianity as a world religion (see Map 8.3). A Jewish revolt from 66 to 73 C.E. resulted in the Roman destruction of the Jewish temple in Jerusalem and the dispersion of many Jews to other lands. During the revolt the *Zealots*, a group of Jewish rebels, held out in a hilltop fort known as Masada **(muh-SAHD-uh)** overlooking the Dead Sea. Although the Romans eventually took the fort, Masada stood through history as a symbol of Jewish resistance to oppression. Jews became discredited in Roman eyes, making it fortunate that early Christians had broken with Judaism. While Jews scattered across Eurasia and North Africa, non-Jewish Christians continued to grow as the religion spread along trade networks throughout western Asia, North Africa, and southern Europe.

Christianity in the Mediterranean Zone

The Roman context shaped Christian growth and institutions. Christianity had similarities to "mystery religions," some rooted in Persian and Hellenistic traditions, that were popular in the Roman world at the same time. Like the followers of Mithra **(MITH-ruh)** or Isis **(ICE-uhs)**, Christians believed in life after death and had practices, such as a special initiation rite (baptism), that fostered religious community. But Christianity offered a greater emotional appeal by emphasizing the spiritual equality of all people and a concern for the poor. Christians used the terms *heathen* and *pagan*, which had negative connotations, for followers of polytheistic or animistic religions or the irreligious. The faith gradually gained greater acceptance, and in 313 C.E. it became a legal religion by an edict of the Roman emperor Constantine, who believed the Christian God had helped him win a battle. After this the organized church, loosely headed by the bishop of Rome, became more significant, and by 400 C.E. non-Christian faiths had been banned and Christianity had become the official Roman religion. Christianity united state and church in a troubled marriage for over a millennium.

[12]Matthew 22: 37–39, in *The Holy Bible*, King James Version (Chicago: Thomas Nelson, 1982), 957.

But Christians also contended with theological divisions. For example, the sect of **Arianism** **(AR-ee-uh-niz-uhm)** taught that Jesus was not divine but rather an exceptional human being. In 325 C.E., to combat what most Christians saw as heresies and to establish core beliefs, Constantine called a church council at Nicaea **(nye-SEE-uh)**, in Anatolia, where he ordered the bishops to resolve their doctrinal differences and determine which beliefs to follow. The **Nicene (NYE-seen) Creed** they produced became the official doctrine of the early church and is still recited in many denominations.

Early Christians borrowed much Greco-Roman culture but refused to acknowledge the emperor's official divine status, prompting sporadic persecution. Nevertheless, as Christianity spread, most believers were left alone to worship freely. Many acquired a Roman education and even celebrated Roman festivals along with the new Christian ones. For example, they celebrated Jesus's birthday on the date of the old Roman and Mithraist winter solstice festival. Early Christians also generally adopted the Greco-Roman tolerance toward homosexuality. Yet tensions between Christians and non-Christians simmered, such as those leading to the murder of the philosopher Hypatia **(hye-PAY-shuh)** by Christian mobs in Alexandria around 416 C.E. (see *Profile:* Hypatia of Alexandria, a Pagan Philosopher). Some early church leaders also blamed the Jews for the death of Jesus. In general, however, Christians adapted successfully to Roman life.

By the early fifth century, Christians were the political and social leaders in most Roman cities, but some became troubled by their success. Followers of Jesus were supposed to focus on spiritual instead of worldly success, on Heaven instead of earth. This questioning fostered monasticism, a life of penance, prayer, and meditation, either alone or in a community of other seekers. For instance, Benedict of Nursia (ca. 480–ca. 543) became so disillusioned by hedonistic Roman life that he moved into a cave and later founded western Europe's first monastic order, the Benedictines **(ben-uh-DIK-teenz)**. Benedict formulated monastic rules explaining how to live a spiritually fulfilling life. For many monks and nuns, the practice of **asceticism**, or austere religious practices such as intense prayer, helped to strengthen spiritual life and seek a deeper understanding of God. Some church leaders also reemphasized the superiority of virginity over marriage, a value earlier stressed in the writings of Paul.

Augustine and Roman Christianity

Christianity expanded, producing church institutions and thinkers who shaped the theology. In the empire's declining decades, the North African bishop Augustine of Hippo (354–430 C.E.) redefined Christianity's relation to the Roman world, and his concepts of Christian morality and history dominated western European culture for a thousand years. Augustine tried several faiths before becoming a convinced Christian, priest, and, in 395, bishop of Hippo, a city near Carthage. Like many Roman cities, Hippo had followers of many faiths, including various pagan and Persian traditions, all seen as heretical by the established church. After the Ostrogoths sacked Rome in 410, Augustine, troubled by the pagan accusation that Christians' refusal to fight (many early Christians were pacifists) and abandonment of the Roman gods caused Roman society to wither, wrote *City of God*, completed in 427. Defending Christianity against its critics, he argued that the "city of God" comprised all who followed God's laws (i.e., Christians), while the "city of man" consisted of non-Christians, who ignored God's teachings and would be damned in a final judgment at the end of time. Contending that all of history was in God's hands, he promoted a view of history as a straight line of progress from past to future, in which, at the end of history, Jesus would return to judge all humanity, living and dead.

Viewing Christian morals as superior to that of the tolerant Roman culture, Augustine urged Christian men and women to remain celibate; marriage was only for those with low self-control. He criticized sex outside of marriage, sanctioned sex within marriage only for procreation, and proclaimed men superior to women. Augustine's writings and theology strongly influenced the Roman Catholic tradition, as Christians increasingly separated themselves from hedonistic Roman practices. For example, in 498 Christian leaders introduced an annual feast day in honor of Saint. Valentine to replace a holiday honoring Juno, the Roman goddess of love and marriage, and a popular, somewhat raunchy, Roman fertility festival.

Christianity filled the vacuum as Roman government collapsed and many people left cities in the fifth century. The city of Rome's population fell from 800,000 in 300 to 60,000 in 530, with the Christian clergy often providing the only semblance of order for those remaining. Church officials also achieved a huge boost when the Germanic Franks converted to Latin Christianity under their ruler Clovis. Then, in the late sixth century, Europe was hit by many disasters, enumerated in 599 by an alarmed Pope Gregory: "as the end of the world approaches, many things menace us which never existed before: inversions of the climate, horrors from the heavens and storms contrary to the season, wars, famine, plagues, earthquakes."[13] But the widespread mood of doom proved premature. A new age was dawning in western Europe, largely German and Christian in tone, with a Greco-Roman overlay of language and culture.

Arianism A Christian sect that taught that Jesus was not divine but rather an exceptional human being.

Nicene Creed A set of beliefs, prepared by the council at Nicaea in 325 C.E., that became the official doctrine of the early Christian church.

asceticism Austere religious practices, such as intense prayer, that were used to strengthen spiritual life and seek a deeper understanding of God; began to be used in the Christian church in the fifth and sixth centuries C.E.

[13]Quoted in Michael McCormick, *Origins of the European Economy: Communication and Commerce, A.D. 300–900* (New York: Cambridge University Press, 2001), 27.

PROFILE

Hypatia of Alexandria, a Pagan Philosopher

Hypatia, a female philosopher and mathematician, lived in the Hellenistic Egyptian city of Alexandria, part of the Roman Empire. As Christianity became more influential, she followed a non-Christian polytheistic religion, making her in Christian eyes a "pagan." Perhaps nothing better shows the complex relationship between Christians and pagans, and the tension within the Christian community itself, than her murder at the hands of a Christian mob in 415 C.E. To critics of religious intolerance such as the eighteenth-century English historian Edward Gibbon, Hypatia was a beautiful woman torn to pieces by a fanatic mob because she believed in the Greek spirit of reason instead of, in his view, Christianity's irrational beliefs. But it was not that simple.

Born around 355 C.E., the daughter of a well-educated mathematician and astronomer, the young Hypatia studied the works of the mathematician Euclid and other great Hellenistic thinkers and became known for making geometry intelligible to students. She also studied philosophy, but not the purely rational sort Gibbon imagined. She became a neo-Platonist, viewing philosophy as almost a religion, a way to discover the hidden divine spirit within each person. She also stressed the feminine aspects of culture, arguing that women benefited from honoring goddesses. Hypatia wrote commentaries on mathematical and astronomical subjects, lived quietly as a teacher, did not publicly participate in pagan worship, and, like many Christian women of her day, practiced celibacy, although she was married to another philosopher. Women philosophers were uncommon in those days, but Hypatia's wisdom and learning became celebrated. Admirers claimed she had "the spirit of Plato and the body of Aphrodite [the Greek goddess of love]." She taught both pagan and Christian students, one of whom became a Christian bishop in Anatolia but remained Hypatia's lifelong friend.

Conditions in Alexandria changed after 391 C.E., when the Roman emperor Theodosius forbade pagan worship. During the next twenty years, many Christians determined to eradicate all non-Christian religions, spurring violent attacks on Jews and pagans. Now a majority of Alexandria's population, Christians were divided into feuding factions. Tensions grew worse in the city after Cyril, a fanatic intolerant of non-Christians, won election as bishop in 412. Since Hypatia was a close friend and supporter of Orestes, the city's Christian governor, his bitter rival Cyril spread the rumor that the widely respected Hypatia was a witch and practiced black magic. He also encouraged attacks on Jews.

In 415 a semimilitary gang of young Christians allied with Cyril dragged Hypatia from her carriage, stripped off her clothes, murdered her, and burned her body. Cyril had not ordered this, but he had created a social climate that made such a crime possible. Alexandria became a more thoroughly Christian city, expelling the Jews, who had been a substantial community in Alexandria for over six hundred years. Cyril was never punished for his part in Hypatia's death.

Later critics wrongly viewed Hypatia mostly as a martyr for her non-Christian beliefs. She was also, at least partly, a victim of a jealous bishop. However, Gibbon and others correctly saw her as one of the last representatives of a tolerant paganism rooted in the Hellenistic and Roman culture's cosmopolitan ethos, now replaced by an intolerant form of Christianity. Her death also represented the displacement of philosophers from the public forum by religious men who claimed that the ideas they preached were superior because they came from God rather than from book learning.

STATUE OF HYPATIA This statue honors the great pagan philosopher and mathematician of fifth-century Alexandria who was murdered by Christian rivals.

THINKING ABOUT THE PROFILE

1. What does Hypatia's career tell us about Alexandrian society?
2. What does her experience reveal about conflicts between Christians and non-Christians in the late Roman Empire?

Note: Quotation from Maria Dzidzka, *Hypatia of Alexandria* (Cambridge: Harvard University Press, 1995), 5.

MAKE SURE YOU UNDERSTAND THESE KEY POINTS BEFORE MOVING ON

- **Christianity was born in Palestine, an area with a tradition of rebellion against Rome, and grew out of the Jewish prophetic tradition.**
- **Paul was instrumental in spreading and shaping Christianity after Jesus's death, as well as in arguing that one did not have to be Jewish to become a Christian.**
- **Aided by the popularity of mystery religions similar to it and by the decline in quality of life, Christianity took hold and became the official Roman religion.**
- **In defending Christianity against its critics, Augustine distinguished between Christians, who would be saved, and non-Christians, who would be damned, and he also argued for strict standards of sexual morality that favored celibacy.**

Revival in the East: Byzantines, Persians, and Arabs

How did the Byzantine and Sassanian Empires reinvigorate the eastern Mediterranean world?

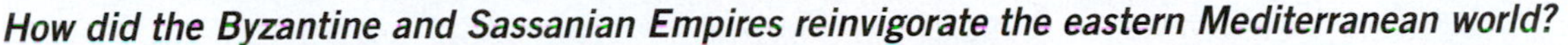

A century after Roman emperor Constantine dedicated his new capital city, later known as Constantinople, in 330 C.E., the western part of the empire fell to various German groups while the eastern empire fostered a new and distinctive society, Byzantium. Byzantium viewed itself as continuing the Roman Empire but developed a different political structure and a culture and church more Greek than Latin. By taking the brunt of attacks by resurgent western Asian peoples such as the Sassanian Persians, Byzantium gave the struggling new states in western Europe time to develop into a separate Latin Christian culture. The Persian-Byzantine conflict also helped shape the rising Arab society.

Early Byzantium and the Era of Justinian

Byzantium emerged as the most powerful state in the eastern Mediterranean region, maintaining this status for many centuries. Constantinople straddled the narrow waterway linking the Aegean and Black Seas and separating Europe from western Asia, symbolically linking diverse peoples and traditions. The large eastern Roman Empire initially encompassed the Balkans, Greece, Anatolia, Syria, Palestine, and Egypt. Few emperors in Rome enjoyed the power Byzantium's government had over its people, economy, and religious institutions.

Byzantium's most important early ruler, the Emperor Justinian **(juh-STIN-ee-uhn)** (r. 527–565 C.E.), spurred on by his powerful and ambitious wife, Theodora **(THEE-uh-DOR-uh)**, was determined to defeat the German states in the west and reunite the old Roman Empire. His armies reconquered a large part of the western territories, defeating the Ostrogothic kingdom in Italy in 563. But long years of fighting left Rome devastated, with only a few thousand impoverished, disease-ridden inhabitants. Moreover, Justinian's victories required ever higher taxes, and he was barely able to defend his own domains from Huns, Persians, and various peoples migrating into Europe. During the first half of the seventh century, Justinian's successors fought the Sassanian Persians, losing control of the western lands (see Map 8.4).

Justinian also established a political pattern of despotism in which Byzantine subjects treated the emperors as near-gods with absolute power over most areas of national life. They presided over a centralized and complex bureaucracy (hence our term *byzantine* for complicated and puzzling systems). Spies monitored the population. Justinian had many critics, among them the great Byzantine historian Procopius, who described the emperor as "at once villainous and amenable; as people say colloquially, a moron. He was never truthful with anyone. His nature was an unnatural mix of folly and wickedness."[14] But Justinian also collected all existing Roman laws into one legal code, preserving Roman legal principles for later generations.

In 540 the Byzantines encountered one of the most terrible epidemics in world history, often known as Justinian's plague. The sickness, probably bubonic plague, spread along the trade routes from Egypt into western Asia before reaching Europe. At its height some ten thousand people a day perished. Ships were loaded with corpses, rowed out to sea, and abandoned. Agriculture largely halted, leaving many communities abandoned. A Christian bishop in Palestine wrote that "all the inhabitants, like beautiful grapes, were trampled and squeezed dry without mercy."[15] The plague returned several times until 590. When Justinian died at age eighty-three, his empire was much poorer, weaker, and less populated than it had been when he took power.

Byzantine Society, Economy, and Religion

Despite its many political misfortunes, the Byzantine Empire survived for centuries because of its social and economic strengths, including more urbanization than western Europe. Constantinople grew to perhaps a million people, described by a visitor as "a splendid city, how stately, how fair. It would be wearisome to tell of the abundance of all good things."[16]

[14]From A. Atwater, trans., *Procopius: The Secret History* (Ann Arbor: University of Michigan Press, 1963), 8.
[15]Quoted in Daniel Del Castillo, "A Long-Ignored Plague Gets Its Due," *Chronicle of Higher Education*, February 15, 2002, A22.
[16]Quoted in Philip Sharrard, *Byzantium* (New York: Time-Life, 1966), 36.

MAP 8.4 THE BYZANTINE AND SASSANIAN EMPIRES By 600 C.E. the Byzantine Empire controlled much of southern Europe and the eastern end of the Mediterranean Basin, and the Sassanian Empire dominated most of the rest of western Asia, part of Turkestan, and Egypt. Various Germanic kingdoms held political sway in far western Europe, northern Europe, and northeast Africa.

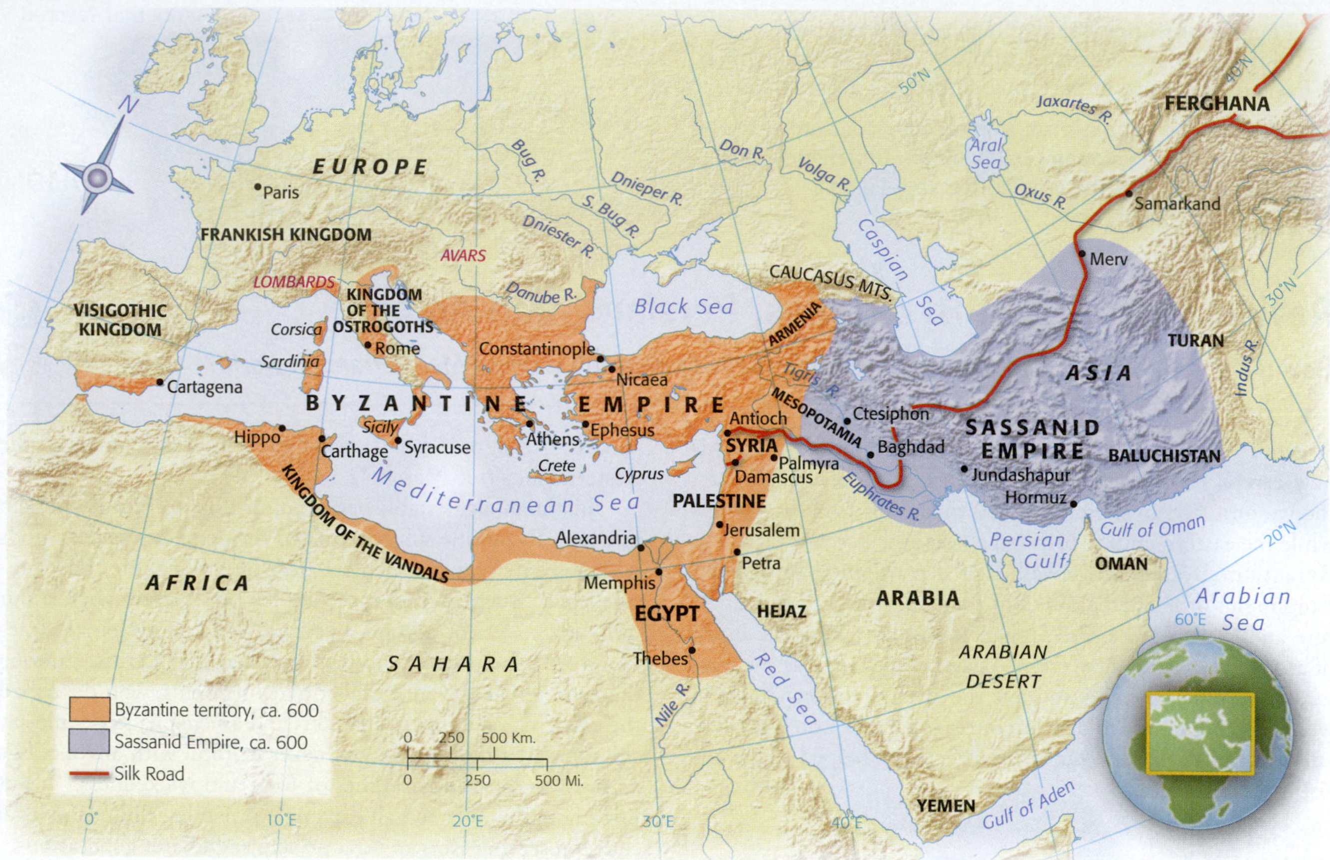

The urban wealthy lived in splendor, enjoying luxury goods like silk clothes, carpets, and elegant tapestries provided by local industry. A huge gap separated them from the poor peasants, who faced unique restrictions; peasants living many years in one place were required to remain there, and they eventually became bound to the soil and controlled by powerful landlords. Despite patriarchy, urban upper-class women enjoyed influence, and some queens exercised considerable power. Women could control their own property and have their dowry returned if their husbands divorced them. However, men enjoyed greater legal safeguards, and wife-beating was common. Maternal and infant mortality rates were high, pregnancy remaining hazardous and childbirth dangerous.

Byzantium had a flourishing economy. As prominent members of the urban aristocracy, merchants and bankers benefited from Constantinople's position astride the principal trade routes between Europe and Asia. The government taxed all goods passing through the capital, including spices, cotton, and copper from India and Southeast Asia; jewels, silk, gold, and silver from China and Central Asia; gold, ivory, and slaves from Africa; cotton and grain from Egypt; grains, wool, and tin from northwestern Europe; olive oil and silver from Spain and Italy; and timber, fur, copper, hides, and slaves from Russia and Scandinavia. Byzantine coins have been found as far away as China. But most trade with China and India had to go through Persian-controlled lands, and Persian-Byzantine relations alternated between uneasy peace and armed conflict.

Monophysites A heretical sect that argued that Jesus had a single divine nature rather than both a divine and a human form.

Byzantine society and culture, fundamentally Hellenistic Greek, inevitably diverged from the western Roman tradition in many ways, especially in religion and culture. Byzantines preserved and later passed on to the Latin west (often through Muslims) the works of Plato, Aristotle, Homer, Sophocles, and other Greeks. The eastern Christian church separated from its Latin counterpart, evolving into the Greek Orthodox Church, with many customs and viewpoints foreign to the Roman Church. Religion permeated Byzantine life. The church, especially monasteries, gained control of considerable land and hence wealth. From the ruler, who controlled both temporal and religious affairs, to the ordinary citizen, Byzantines avidly discussed religious questions, and emperors proposed church reforms and called church councils to address what mainstream Christians considered heresies. These included the **Monophysites** **(muh-NAHF-uh-sites)**, who argued that Jesus had a single divine

Werner Forman / Art Resource, NY

INTERIOR OF SANTA SOPHIA CATHEDRAL The great cathedral of Santa Sophia in Constantinople, rebuilt for Byzantine emperor Justinian, was famous for its spectacular interior.

nature rather than both a divine and human form; and the **Nestorians**, who believed that Jesus's divine and human natures existed independent of each other. Christianity also shaped gender relations. A goddess representing urban prosperity was replaced by the much beloved Christian image of the Holy Virgin Mary, giving women moral stature. But the church also viewed women as weak and inferior, both physically and morally, and easily tempted by sin.

Over time theological disputes between the Greek and Latin Churches grew. In general, Greek Christians emphasized ritual and refused to accept the bishop of Rome (later known as the pope) as superior in authority to other bishops. In the eleventh century such conflicts over authority and doctrine contributed to a final split between the two churches. Meanwhile, Monophysites formed the Armenian, Coptic, and Syrian Orthodox Churches. Nestorians migrated to Persia, becoming the basis of the modern Chaldean and Assyrian Churches, and from Persia they spread their faith along the Silk Road into India and China.

Strongly influenced by western Asian traditions, Byzantine art and architecture reflected the cultural diversity of this huge empire. The fusion of Persian and Greco-Roman influences can be seen in the great dome in Constantinople's Church of Santa Sophia (Holy Wisdom), built under Justinian. Symbolizing inner Christian spirituality in contrast to human pride, the church has a modest external appearance but a richly decorated interior that includes mosaics, marble columns, tinted glass, and gold leaf.

Sassanian Persians and Their Networks

Both the Romans and Byzantines had to deal with Persian revival under the Sassanian dynasty, which generated frequent conflict. Considering themselves the successors to the Achaemenids a half millennium earlier, the Sassanian court, based in modern Iraq, fostered a brilliant culture mixing Hellenistic and Persian influences. The Sassanians overthrew the Parthians in 224 and spent the rest of the third century building their own empire. In the east they fought with the Kushans **(KOO-shans)**, whose Afghanistan-based empire controlled parts of western India and Central Asia. Eventually the Sassanians occupied much of Afghanistan and some of the Central Asian Silk Road cities, but they lost some territories to the Huns in the fourth century C.E. To the west the Sassanians expanded into the Caucasus and Mesopotamia, creating chronic conflict with Rome in and around Syria. They also occupied parts of Arabia, including Yemen **(YEM-uhn)** in the south. In the sixth and early seventh centuries the Sassanians conquered the eastern Byzantine Empire, including Syria, Palestine, and Egypt (see Map 8.4). But years of war with Byzantium weakened both societies. In 651 the last Sassanian king was murdered and Arab Muslim armies gained control of all Sassanian territories.

Controlling much of the Persian Gulf, Sassanian Persia became a contact zone for international trade. Sassanian trade links stretched east as far as India, Central Asia, and China and south into Africa, and Silk Road cities used Byzantine and Sassanian coins as currency. Persians produced some of the world's finest pottery, silver plates, pearls, brocades, carpets, and glassware, exchanging these for gems, incense, perfume, and ivory.

Sassanian Religion and Culture

In contrast to the religiously tolerant Achaemenids, the Sassanians mandated a state religion, Zoroastrianism, supporting the priesthood and sometimes persecuting other religions. However, state religions tend to decay. The Zoroastrian establishment became corrupt and rigid, and by the fifth century the faith's influence and followers diminished. Yet Zoroastrianism spawned various mixed religions. One of them, Mithraism, became popular in the Roman Empire and spread as far west as England. Another new religion, **Manichaeism (man-uh-KEE-iz-uhm)**, founded by the

Nestorians A heretical Christian sect that believed that the divine and human natures of Jesus were independent of each other.

Manichaeism A blend of Zoroastrianism, Buddhism, and Christianity, founded by Mani, that emphasized a continuing struggle between the equal forces of light and dark.

Persian Mani **(MAH-nee)** (216–277 C.E.), blended Zoroastrianism, Buddhism, and Christianity, emphasizing continuing struggle between the equally powerful forces of light and dark. Although Mani was executed for heresy, his faith suppressed by both the Sassanians and Christians, Islam and some Christian sects later incorporated his religious dualism.

With Zoroastrianism less influential, the state became more tolerant of diversity, turning the capital city, Jundashapur, into a cosmopolitan intellectual center. Christian minorities such as the Armenians of the Caucasus region generally enjoyed religious freedom, and the Sassanians welcomed Nestorian Christians fleeing Byzantine repression. Foreign scholars migrated to the newly tolerant state, as did Jews and others fearing persecution in Christian Europe. The Sassanians collected scientific and literary books from many neighboring peoples, translated Greek writings, and established a renowned hospital and medical school. Sassanian Persia's multiculturalism provided a framework that enabled later Islamic governments to rule diverse peoples and faiths. But Zoroastrianism, too closely connected to Sassanian domination, became only a minor faith after Islam swept through the region.

Interregional Trade, Cities, and the Arabs

Arab culture was fostered by the ebb and flow of long-distance trade in western Asia, often influenced by Hellenistic Greek, Roman, Byzantine, and Sassanian activities. Diverse Semitic societies lived in the Arabian peninsula, whose mountains, dry plains, and harsh deserts stretch from the Jordan River and Sinai southeast to the Indian Ocean. Most Arabian peoples were traders, farmers, and pastoral nomads divided into tribes. Roman sources described the mobile pastoralists: "All alike are warriors of equal rank, ranging widely with the help of swift horses and slender camels."[17] Eventually all of these groups coalesced into the Arab society.

Arab society arose in part from the Nabataeans **(NAB-uh-TEE-uhnz)**, who traded all over the Middle East and into Europe by land and sea and whose writing system became the inspiration for Arabic script. The Nabataeans established a kingdom and in the fourth century B.C.E. built a major trading city, Petra **(PE-truh)**, in a narrow gorge in today's Jordan, astride the overland caravan routes. With a population of thirty thousand at its peak, Petra eventually flourished as a crossroads for goods moving between India, Arabia, Greece, and Egypt. Its residents developed an ingenious system of dams, pipes, channels, and underground cisterns for collecting and storing rainwater while also growing wheat, grapes, and possibly olives in this arid region. Petra's spectacular ruins, with their elaborate facades carved into rock, still astonish visitors.

In 106 B.C.E. the Romans occupied Petra, beginning a long decline as trade shifted north to Palmyra **(pal-MY-ruh)**, on the Euphrates River in today's Syria. After conquering this prosperous trading city in 114 B.C.E., the Romans had cultivated Palmyra to protect their eastern frontier. Palmyra thrived until 273 C.E., when the Romans crushed a revolt led by the shrewd and ambitious Queen Septimia Zenobia **(zuh-NO-bee-uh)**. Taking advantage of Roman wars with the Goths, Zenobia sent her army into Egypt, gained control of the Roman grain supply, and then occupied much of Roman Asia. She invited Greek thinkers to Palmyra and encouraged religious tolerance. After fierce battles the Romans reoccupied Palmyra and took Zenobia to Rome, where she died.

Arab culture was also shaped by successive farming-based kingdoms in Yemen in southern Arabia that had existed since the days of the fabled Queen of Sheba around 1000 B.C.E. Living in high, cool mountains and well-watered valleys, the Yemenites produced impressive civil engineering and architecture, abundant harvests aided by elaborate dams and terraces, and splendid cities. City-states emerged, among them Saba, possibly the Hebrew Bible's Sheba. Yemenites traded by sea with India and East Africa, as well as across Arabia with the eastern Mediterranean and Mesopotamia. The region's frankincense was prized as far away as Rome.

In the sixth century C.E. Arabian conditions changed as political disarray, an Ethiopian invasion, and commercial depression undermined Yemenite society and power. To the north, renewed Sassanian-Byzantine conflict led both to actively seek allies in central Arabia, making Arabia a political pawn caught between Orthodox Byzantium, Zoroastrian Persia, and Coptic Ethiopia. Yet increasing overland trade fostered settlement by many Christian and Jewish merchants in desert towns like Mecca **(MEK-uh)**. Some Arabs adopted these religions, and in the seventh century these trends fostered the emergence of a new Arab faith, Islam, out of Classical roots. Eventually Islamic armies overran most of the Byzantine Asian territories and the Sassanian Empire.

MAKE SURE YOU UNDERSTAND THESE KEY POINTS BEFORE MOVING ON

- **Justinian ruled the Byzantine Empire absolutely and tried to retake the western Roman Empire, with mixed results.**
- **More urban and wealthy than western Europe, the Byzantine Empire served as a trading hub for goods from across Europe and Asia.**
- **Byzantine culture became more Greek and less Roman, and the Byzantine Church denied the authority of the pope and came to emphasize ritual and doctrine to a greater degree than did the Roman Church.**
- **The Sassanians revived the strength of Persia and adopted Zoroastrianism as a state religion.**
- **Arab culture began to rise out of tribes of pastoral nomads, the trading cities of Petra and Palmyra, and the farming-based kingdoms of Yemen.**

[17] Quoted in Patricia Crone, "The Rise of Islam in the World," in *The Cambridge Illustrated History of the Islamic World*, ed. Francis Robinson (New York: Cambridge University Press, 1966), 4–5.

CHAPTER SUMMARY

The activities and cultures of the Romans, Germans, Greeks, and Persians largely shaped the middle and late Classical period in the Mediterranean world and western Asia. Romans adopted and spread some Classical Greek values while also making major contributions in government, law, and architecture. For several centuries they had a Republic in which some of the people had a voice in government and elected Rome's leaders. To acquire more resources and preempt challengers, the Romans gradually expanded their territory until it encompassed much of Europe, North Africa, and western Asia, in the process defeating and conquering rivals, including the Etruscans, Carthage, Egypt, and the Celts. Eventually a more autocratic system led by powerful emperors replaced the Republic. Controlling far-flung territories proved expensive, however, and the Roman forces became overextended. Soon the Romans were also defending their territories against the incursions of the Germanic peoples.

New forces also developed in the eastern end of the Mediterranean Basin. Christianity arose out of Jewish society in Palestine and spread throughout the Mediterranean world, western Asia, and North Africa. The power of the Christian church rose as Roman political power declined. In the east Byzantium emerged out of the eastern Roman Empire, developing into a distinct society that incorporated Hellenistic Greek political and cultural traditions. It also fostered the Greek Orthodox Church. Meanwhile, the Sassanians reinvigorated Persian society and built a large empire, eventually putting pressure on Byzantium. These conflicts increased travel over the trade routes and generated new currents in Arab society.

KEY TERMS

patricians (p. 165)
Centuriate Assembly (p. 165)
consuls (p. 165)
plebeians (p. 165)
tribunes (p. 165)
Pax Romana (p. 168)
Romance languages (p. 174)
Arianism (p. 177)
Nicene Creed (p. 177)
asceticism (p. 177)
Monophysites (p. 180)
Nestorians (p. 181)
Manichaeism (p. 181)

9 Classical Societies and Regional Networks in Africa, the Americas, and Oceania, 600 B.C.E.–600 C.E.

Werner Forman / Art Resource, NY

AKSUM STELE Early in the Common Era the kings of the African state of Aksum, in what is today Ethiopia, decorated their capital city with tall, flat-sided pillars known as steles, some nearly 70 feet high, possibly as monuments to the royal family.

When the day dawns the trader betakes himself to his trade; the spinner takes her spindle; the warrior takes his shield; the farmer awakes, he and his hoe handle; the hunter awakes with his quiver and bow.

—Ancient Yoruba proverb about daybreak in a West African town[1]

In the classical world, few settlements were as specialized as those serving the caravans crossing the trackless sands of Africa's vast Sahara Desert, a barren landscape where scorching sun and arid soil made planting crops or trees nearly impossible. Rest stops at isolated oasis towns with gardens, date palms, and flocks of sheep allowed weary travelers to find fresh water and restock before resuming their journeys. The round trip of many weeks between North African coastal zone cities and those on the desert's southern fringe held many dangers besides thirst and discomfort, including fierce raiders on horseback. Camels, the major beast of burden in the caravan trade, were often uncooperative animals, waging battles of wills with their handlers, but they could travel many days without water. Thanks to these caravans and the brave men who led them, sub-Saharan African products reached a wider world while goods and ideas from North Africa and Eurasia found their way to peoples living south of the Sahara.

The diverse societies in sub-Saharan Africa, the Americas, and Oceania (the Pacific Basin) were partly shaped by their environment, whether deserts like the Sahara, rugged highlands, flood-prone river valleys, rain forests, savannahs, seacoasts, or small islands. Contacts with other peoples, whether friendly, hostile, or both, also influenced societies. Various Africans established connections with the wider world through long-distance trade, especially by the trans-Saharan camel caravans or boats around the Indian Ocean, ensuring that few societies remained completely isolated. The various societies that developed in sub-Saharan Africa, the Americas, Australia, and, thanks to intrepid mariners, the Pacific islands worshiped their own deities, created their own artistic styles, valued some products more than others, and evolved their own social and political structures, including some states. At the same time, they had much in common.

[1]From *The Horizon History of Africa* (New York: American Heritage, 1971), 207.

IN THIS CHAPTER

Classical States and Connections in Northeast Africa

What were some of the similarities and differences between Kush and Aksum?

In Classical times tropical Africa and Eurasia were connected largely through intermediaries, including North Africans linked to the trans-Saharan caravan trade and Indian Ocean maritime traders. Kush **(koosh)** in Nubia and Aksum **(AHK-soom)** in Ethiopia became trading hubs and powerful states, both enjoying close ties with Egypt and western Asia.

Iron, Cities, and Society in Kush

The kingdom of Kush in Nubia, along the Nile south of Egypt, existed from about 800 B.C.E. to 350 C.E., flourishing as the major African producer of iron and an important crossroads for trade between sub-Saharan Africa and the Mediterranean (see Map 9.1). Its capital city, Meroë **(MER-uh-wee)**, became an industrial powerhouse of the Classical world. Kush had many sources of iron ore, as evidenced by the heaps of iron slag littering the ruins of Meroë today. Kushites imported pottery, fine ceramics, wine, olive oil, and honey from Egypt and western Asia, and they exported iron and cotton cloth.

Both Greeks and Romans admired the Nubians. Some Nubians apparently visited Greece, others served in Persian armies that attacked Greece, and Africans, possibly Nubians, went to Rome to trade or work as musicians, actors, gladiators, athletes, and day laborers. A grand city of perhaps twenty-five thousand, Meroë contained massive temples, large brick-lined pools possibly used for public baths, and rows of many spectacular pyramids, similar to those in Egypt but smaller, where kings and queens were buried in splendor. The highly skilled builders used masonry, stonework, fired brick, and mud brick. As in the Indus cities, washing and sanitation facilities, with many latrines, serviced Meroë's population.

Although influenced by Egypt, Kushite society and culture were distinctive. Topping the social hierarchy, absolute monarchs, including some queens, both governed and served as guardians of the state religion and temples. Besides worshiping some Egyptian gods, Kushites considered their monarchs, like Egyptian pharaohs, divine, and inscriptions testify to the rulers' piety. Roman sources report kings guided by laws and traditions:

> *It is their custom that none of the subjects shall be executed, even if the person condemned to death appears to deserve punishment. Instead the king sends one of his servants bearing a symbol of death to the criminal. He upon seeing [it], immediately goes to his own house and kills himself.*[2]

[2]Quoted in Stanley Burstein, ed., *Ancient African Civilizations: Kush and Axum* (Princeton, NJ: Markus Wiener, 1998), 41.

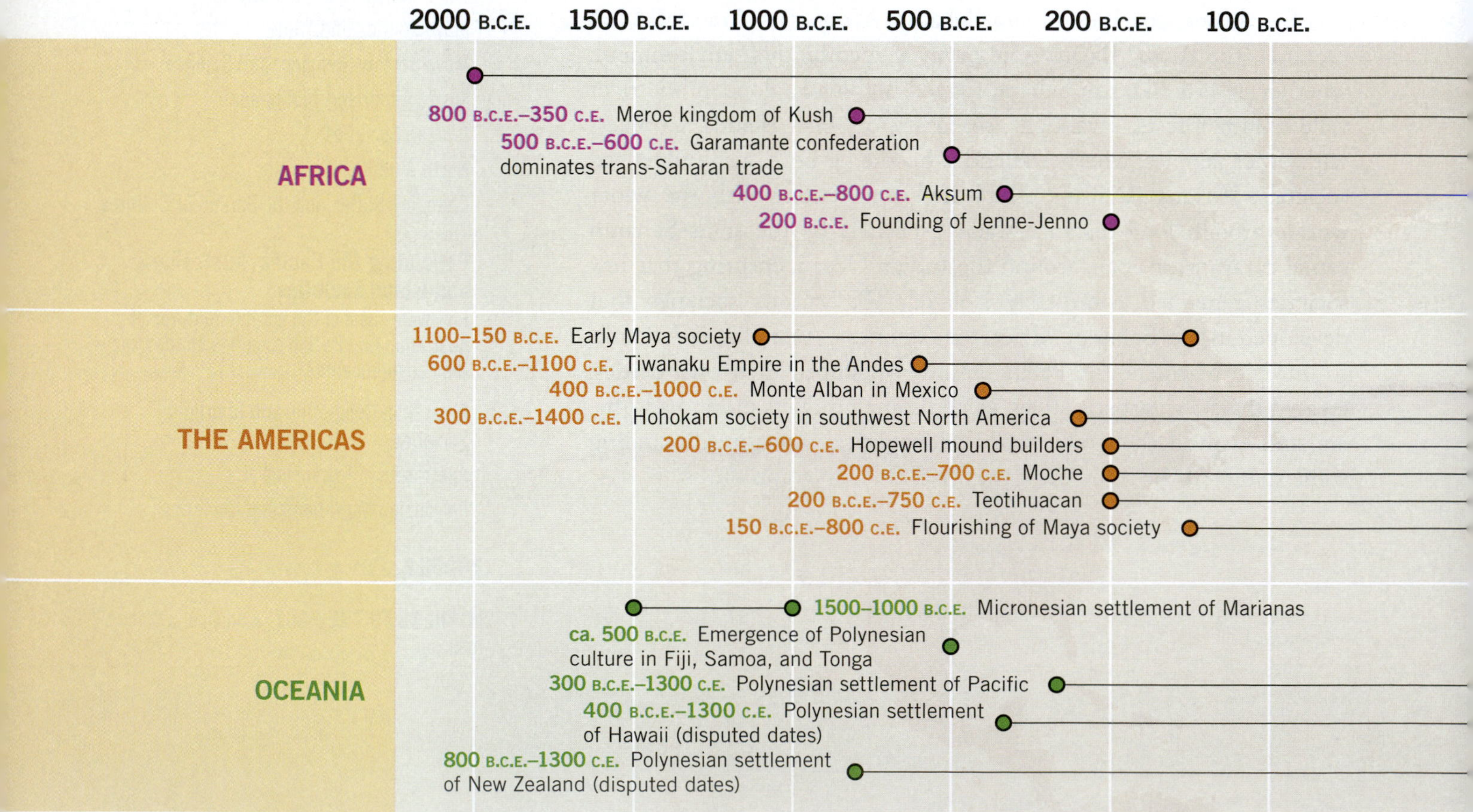

2000 B.C.E. | 1500 B.C.E. | 1000 B.C.E. | 500 B.C.E. | 200 B.C.E. | 100 B.C.E.

AFRICA

800 B.C.E.–350 C.E. Meroe kingdom of Kush
500 B.C.E.–600 C.E. Garamante confederation dominates trans-Saharan trade
400 B.C.E.–800 C.E. Aksum
200 B.C.E. Founding of Jenne-Jenno

THE AMERICAS

1100–150 B.C.E. Early Maya society
600 B.C.E.–1100 C.E. Tiwanaku Empire in the Andes
400 B.C.E.–1000 C.E. Monte Alban in Mexico
300 B.C.E.–1400 C.E. Hohokam society in southwest North America
200 B.C.E.–600 C.E. Hopewell mound builders
200 B.C.E.–700 C.E. Moche
200 B.C.E.–750 C.E. Teotihuacan
150 B.C.E.–800 C.E. Flourishing of Maya society

OCEANIA

1500–1000 B.C.E. Micronesian settlement of Marianas
ca. 500 B.C.E. Emergence of Polynesian culture in Fiji, Samoa, and Tonga
300 B.C.E.–1300 C.E. Polynesian settlement of Pacific
400 B.C.E.–1300 C.E. Polynesian settlement of Hawaii (disputed dates)
800 B.C.E.–1300 C.E. Polynesian settlement of New Zealand (disputed dates)

Queen mothers apparently played influential political roles. Below the ruler were the bureaucratic and military elite. Military officers led an army feared for both its weapons and the soldiers' appearance, as described by the Greek historian Herodotus:

> *[They] were clothed in panthers' and lions' skins, and carried long bows made from branches of palm trees, and on them they laced short arrows made of cane tipped with stone. Besides this they had javelins, and at the tip was an antelope horn, made sharp like a lance; they also had knotted clubs. When they were going into battle they smeared one half of their body with chalk, and the other half with red ocher.*[3]

Free peasants and slaves constituted the lower classes. Women had various economic roles, working in gold mining, farming, and craft production. They also served as priestesses, perhaps specializing in the honoring of female deities.

Kushites enjoyed a rich culture. Some Greek-speaking teachers apparently lived at Meroë, and at least one Kushite king studied Greek philosophy. Meroë artists produced highly polished, finely carved granite statues of their monarchs. Music played on trumpets, drums, harps, and flutes accompanied ceremonial and religious life, some instruments perhaps imported from Egypt and Greece. People of all classes and both genders wore jewelry. They also drank heavily, as evidenced by thousands of goblet fragments littering a ruined tavern. Finally, the presence of writing on numerous tombstones as well as graffiti suggests widespread literacy among all classes. The Kushite alphabet, **Meroitic** **(mer-uh-WIT-ik)**, a cursive script that can only be partly read today, gradually replaced Egyptian hieroglyphics in monumental inscriptions, as Egyptian influence apparently faded over time while indigenous culture flourished.

The Legacy of Kush

After a millennium of power and prosperity, by 200 C.E. Kush declined. Just as widespread climate change may have hastened Han Chinese and Roman decline, Kush suffered because environmental deterioration caused by centuries of deforestation and overgrazing helped produce a drier climate. Chronic warfare with Aksum, an Ethiopian state, also contributed to Meroë's problems. In 350 C.E. an Aksumite invasion destroyed what remained of the Kush kingdom.

However, Kushite culture remained alive in neighboring African societies. Similar political traditions in some West African societies suggest that some Kushites, including the

Meroitic A cursive script developed in the Classical period by the Kushites in Nubia that can only be partly read today.

[3]Quoted in Derek A. Welsby, *The Kingdom of Kush: The Napatan and Meroitic Empires* (Princeton, NJ: Markus Wiener, 1996), 40.

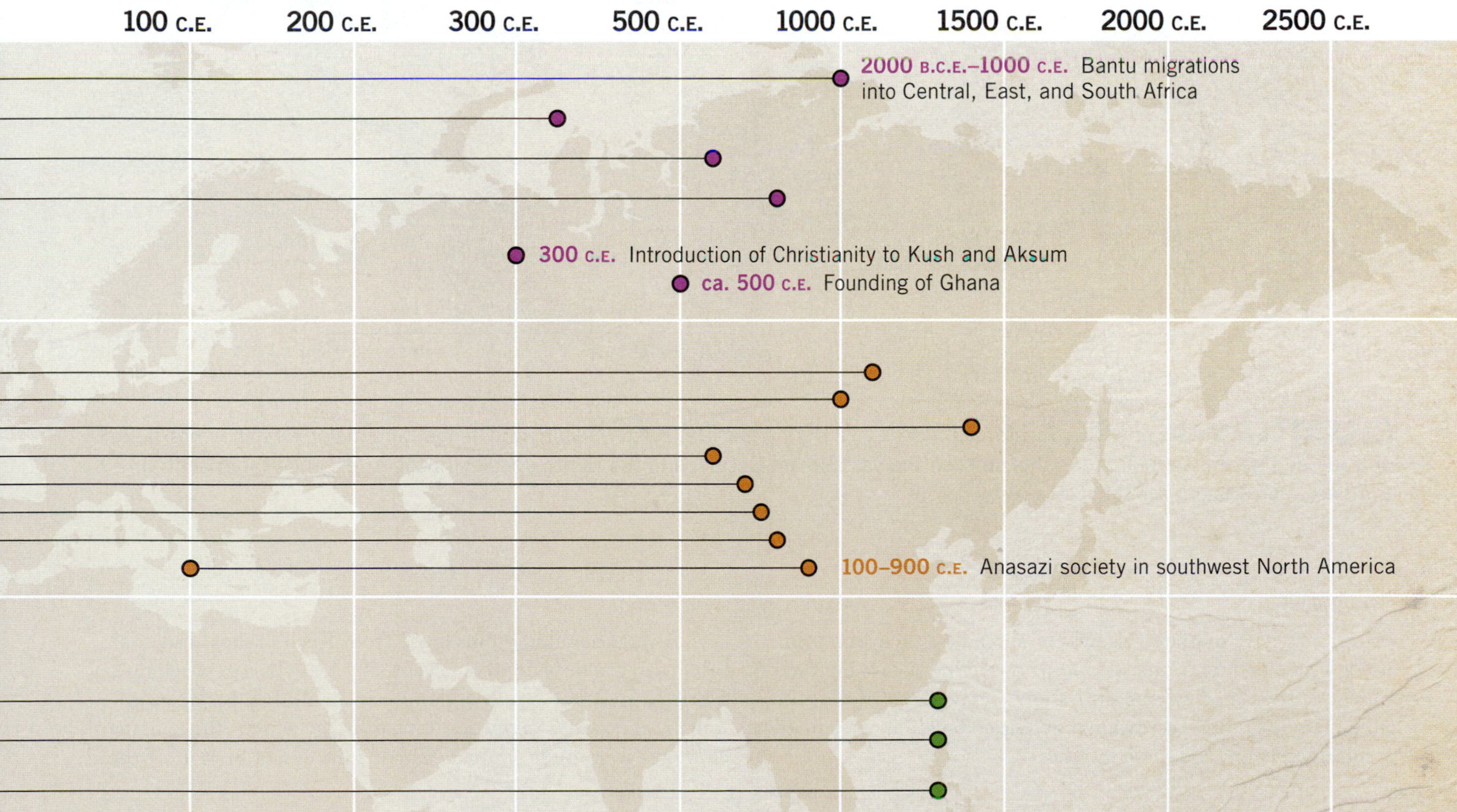

MAP 9.1 CLASSICAL AFRICA, 1500 B.C.E.–600 C.E. During this era, Kush, Aksum, and Jenne were major African centers of trade and government. Trade routes crossed the vast Sahara Desert, and the Bantu-speaking peoples expanded into central, southern, and eastern Africa.

rulers, may have migrated elsewhere, spreading their iron technology and culture. Some peoples now living a few hundred miles southwest of Meroë still show many signs of Kushite influence, including recreational activities (such as wrestling), fashion, body art, and material life.

Several new kingdoms arose from Kush's ashes, and contacts with the outside world eventually brought a new religion, Christianity, that became dominant in Nubia between the fourth and sixth centuries C.E., during which time many churches were built. Nubian Christianity was a branch of the

Coptic (KAHP-tik) Church, which followed Monophysite thought (see Chapter 8) and had become influential in Egypt. Many Copts still live in Egypt, but Nubia's Christian kingdoms, isolated from other Christians by the Islamic conquest of Egypt in the seventh century C.E., gradually faded. Around 1400 C.E. Muslims conquered the last Christian Nubian state, and most people converted to Islam. Today only the ruins of Christian churches and monasteries remain, along with Meroite pyramids, the material legacy of Kush.

Werner Forman Archive/Glow Images

QUEEN AMANITERE Queen Amanitere ruled Meroë along with her husband, King Natakamani, around 2,000 years ago. In this relief on the Lion Temple at Naqa, Kush, she holds vanquished foes by the hair while brandishing swords, thus demonstrating the power of the royal couple and the Kushite state.

The Aksum Empire and Society

Another literate urban African state, **Aksum**, emerged near the Red Sea in the rocky but fertile Ethiopian highlands beginning around 400 B.C.E. Despite an unpredictable climate and deep gorges that inhibited communication, Aksumities traded with Egypt and benefited from proximity to the Red Sea, the major maritime route linking the Mediterranean Sea and the Indian Ocean. At the Red Sea's narrowest point, only 20 miles of water separates Arabia's southern tip from Northeast Africa, and many Semitic people from Arabia crossed into Ethiopia and settled. This accessibility to Arabia greatly benefited northern Ethiopians, allowing links to the Hebrews. Ethiopian legends claim that the Queen of Sheba **(Saba)**, who, according to biblical accounts, met the Hebrew king Solomon, was in fact an early Ethiopian monarch, Queen Makeda **(ma-KAY-da)**, who went to Israel in search of knowledge. In the tale Makeda supposedly told her people:

> *Let my voice be heard by all of you, my people. I am going in quest of Wisdom and Learning. My spirit impels me to go and find them out where they are to be had, for I am smitten with the love of Wisdom and I feel myself drawn as tho by a leash toward Learning. Learning is better than treasures of gold, better than all that has been created upon earth.*[4]

Semitic immigrants from Yemen, the probable location of ancient Sheba, may have brought the story with them to Ethiopia and adapted it for local needs. The son of Solomon and Makeda, Menelik **(MEN-uh-lik)**, supposedly founded a new kingdom, Aksum. Ethiopian legends portray the young Menelik smuggling out from Jerusalem the Ark of the Covenant, which holds the holy tablets Hebrews believe God gave to Moses. Ethiopian Christians claim the Ark remains enshrined in an Aksum cathedral, with viewing restricted to only a few people.

Aksumites, ancestors of the Amharic **(am-HAR-ik)** people who today dominate central Ethiopia, worked both bronze and iron. Between 400 B.C.E. and 100 C.E. they built their first temples and palaces of masonry, as well as a city, dams, and reservoirs. Irrigation and terracing supported productive farming. The Aksumites also developed an alphabet and enjoyed close economic and cultural exchange with both southwestern Asia and eastern Africa. In about 50 C.E. they built an empire that dominated some of Northeast Africa and that flourished chiefly from trade. Soon Aksum eclipsed Meroë, gaining control of trade between the Red Sea and the central Nile. The Persian prophet Mani included Aksum among the world's four great kingdoms, along with Persia, Rome, and China.

The Aksumites traded all over the Middle East, eastern Mediterranean, and East Africa, and their trade networks also reached Sri Lanka and India; many Indian coins have been found at Aksum (see Witness to the Past: A Shopper's Guide to Aksum). Aksumites exported ivory, gold, obsidian, emeralds, perfumes, and animals while importing

Coptic Church A branch of Christianity, based on Monophysite ideas, that had become influential in Egypt and became dominant in Nubia between the fourth and sixth centuries C.E.

Aksum A literate, urban state that appeared in northern Ethiopia before the Common Era and grew into an empire and a crossroads for trade.

---

[4]From *Horizon History*, 78.

[5]Quoted in Graham Connah, *African Civilization. Precolonial Cities and States in Tropical Africa: An Archaeological Perspective* (Cambridge: Cambridge University Press, 1987), 78.

metals, glass, fabrics, wine, and spices. They used the Greek language in foreign commerce and became the first sub-Saharan Africans to mint their own coins.

Aksum had various links to other societies. Byzantium sent envoys to the court, seeking alliances against common enemies in Arabia, and extensive ties with Yemen's Semitic peoples fostered genetic and cultural intermixing between these two peoples. The Amharic language, **Geez (gee-EZ)**, blends African and Semitic influences. Hebrew culture also influenced Ethiopian literature and religion. The modern Amharic royal family, descendants of Aksumite kings, claimed ancestry from King Solomon and Queen Makeda. The Jewish communities known as *Falasha* **(fuh-LAHSH-uh)** have lived in northern Ethiopia for many centuries.

Kings claiming a paternalistic attitude toward their people dominated Aksum's social structure. A fourth-century C.E. monarch left an inscription boasting that he "will rule the people with righteousness and justice, and will not oppress them."[5] Judging from their spectacular palaces, kings also enjoyed great wealth and power. A sixth-century Byzantine ambassador reported on the royal family's pomp and ceremony, noting that the king wore

> *a golden collar. He stood on a four-wheeled chariot drawn by four elephants; the body of the chariot was high and covered with gold plates. The king stood on top carrying a small gilded shield and holding in his hands two small gilded spears.*[6]

Below the royal family, an aristocracy supplied the top government officials, a substantial middle class included many merchants, and peasants and slaves occupied the lowest tier, subject to conscription for massive building projects.

The capital city of Aksum, a wealthy and cosmopolitan trading center widely known for its monumental architecture, boasted magnificent pillars, thin stylized representations of multistoried buildings (some over 100 feet high), many stone platforms, and huge palaces. Making and transporting the monoliths and stone slabs required remarkable engineering skills.

Geez The classical Amharic language of Ethiopia, a mixture of African and Semitic influences.

The Aksum Legacy

With Christian missionaries traveling the trade routes from western Asia, Christianity became influential just as Aksum reached its height of economic and military power in the fourth century C.E. The king adopted the faith, making Christianity the kingdom's official religion. According to a Roman source, he "began to search out Roman merchants [at Aksum] who were Christian and to give them great influence and to urge them to establish [churches], supplying sites for buildings, and in every way promoting the growth of Christianity."[7] The king had political reasons for conversion, since he wanted closer relations with Rome, Byzantium, and Egypt. But the Amharic population only slowly adopted the new faith. Ethiopian Christianity resembled Egypt and Nubia's Coptic churches but also incorporated long-entrenched spirit worship and various Hebrew practices, including the Jewish sabbath and kosher food.

Aksum eventually collapsed. By 400 C.E., reduced rainfall and the resulting pressure on the land had produced an ecological crisis, and political problems added to imperial decline. In addition, the conquest of southern Arabia by Aksum's enemy, Sassanian Persia, in 575 diverted the Indian Ocean commerce from the port of Adulis. Then the rapid Islamic conquests of western Asia and North Africa beginning in the mid-seventh century cut Aksum off from the Christian world. Aksum's trade withered, spawning economic stagnation, cultural decline, and political instability, and by 800 C.E. the Aksumites had abandoned the capital city. But unlike Kush, Ethiopian society persisted in recognizable form. Over the centuries Christianity became a deeply ingrained local religion in the Ethiopian highlands, with the unique Ethiopian church, closely connected to the monarchy, owning many landed estates. Ethiopians remained relatively isolated in their mountain fastness for the next ten centuries.

MAKE SURE YOU UNDERSTAND THESE KEY POINTS BEFORE MOVING ON

- **The kingdom of Kush in Nubia, with its capital city of Meroë, was a major African iron producer and crossroads of trade between sub-Saharan Africa and the Mediterranean.**
- **Kush was influenced by Egypt but was also remarkable for its rich culture and its fearsome warriors and absolute monarchs.**
- **Aksum, in the Ethiopian highlands, had contact with Egypt and Arabia, may have forged links with the Hebrews, and after a time eclipsed Meroë as the region's primary trade center.**
- **Aksum's king converted to Christianity as a means of establishing closer relationships with Rome, Byzantium, and Egypt.**
- **Like Kush, Aksum may have declined in part because of climate change, but it was also hurt by the Islamic conquest of its neighbors; unlike Kush, however, the society endured into modern times.**

[6]Quoted in Robert W. July, *A History of the African People*, 5th ed. (Prospect Heights, IL: Waveland, 1998), 45.
[7]Rufinus, quoted in Burstein, *Ancient African Civilizations*, 95.

WITNESS TO THE PAST

A Shopper's Guide to Aksum

The following account of Aksum's trade comes from the Periplus of the Erythrean Sea, *written by an unknown Greek in the second half of the first century* C.E. *The* Periplus, *a guide prepared for merchants and sailors, outlines commercial prospects in Arabia, the Indian Ocean, and the Persian Gulf. It also describes many of the region's bustling ports. Hence, the* Periplus *provides excellent material for understanding Classical exchange networks. In this excerpt, we learn about the port city of Adulis* **(A-doo-lis)** *on the Red Sea. Now called Massawa* **(muh-SAH-wuh)**, *Adulis was the chief Aksumite trade distribution center where goods from the Ethiopian interior and from faraway places such as India, Egypt, and the Mediterranean were brought for sale or transshipment.*

Adulis [is] a port . . . lying at the inner end of a bay. . . . Before the harbor lies the . . . Mountain Island, . . . with the shores of the mainland close to it on both sides. Ships bound for this port now anchor here because of attacks from the land [by bandits]. . . . Opposite Mountain Island, on the mainland, . . . lies Adulis, a fair-sized village, from which there is a three day's journey to Coloe, an inland town and the first market for ivory. From that place to the [capital] city of the . . . Aksumites there is a five day's journey more; to that place all the ivory is brought from the country beyond the Nile. . . .

There are imported into these places [Adulis], undressed cloth made in Egypt for the Berbers; robes from . . . [modern Suez]; cloaks of poor quality dyed in colors; double-fringed linen mantles; many articles of flint glass, and others of . . . [agate] made in . . . [Thebes, Egypt]; and brass, which is used for ornament and in cut pieces instead of coin; sheets of soft copper, used for cooking utensils and cut up for bracelets and anklets for the women; iron, which is made into spears used against the elephants and other wild beasts, and in their wars. Besides these, small axes are imported, and adzes and swords; copper drinking cups, round and large; a little coin for those coming to the market; wine of Laodicea [on the Syrian coast] and Italy . . . ; olive oil . . . ; for the King, gold and silver plate made after the fashion of the country, and for clothing, military cloaks, and thin coats of skin. . . . Likewise from the district of Ariaca [on the northwest coast of India] across this sea, there are imported Indian cloth [fine-quality cotton]. . . . There are exported from these places ivory, and tortoise-shell and rhinoceros-horn. The most [cargo] from Egypt is brought to this market [Adulis] from the month of January to September.

THINKING ABOUT THE READING

1. What were some of the societies that were linked to the trade at Adulis?
2. What does this reading tell us about the networks of exchange that connected Aksum to a wider world?

Source: W. H. Schoff, trans. and ed., *The Periplus of the Erythraen Sea: Travel and Trade in the Indian Ocean by a Merchant of the First Century* (London, Bombay & Calcutta, 1912).

The Blossoming of West and Bantu Africa

How did the spread of the Bantus reshape sub-Saharan Africa?

Complex urban societies also arose in West Africa, especially in the Sudanic region on the Sahara's southern fringe, among peoples like the Mande **(MAHN-day)**, who were linked to North Africa and beyond by trade networks. Meanwhile, Bantu-speaking Africans spread their languages, cultures, and technologies widely, occupying the southern half of Africa. Some connected to trade networks linked to east coast port cities.

Sudanic Farming, Cities, and the Trans-Saharan Networks

In the vast but dry grassland region known as the Sudan **(soo-DAN)**, lying in West and Central Africa between the Sahara and tropical forests, societies adapted their economic life to the prevailing ecology. Most Sudanese became farmers in small, largely self-sufficient villages, growing vegetables and cereal crops, especially millet and sorghum, that needed little water. West Africans also grew cotton and developed richly colored cotton clothing. The food grown in a large fertile delta along the Niger **(NYE-juhr)** River helped to feed the trading cities.

Some Sudanese along the Niger River congregated in large towns and cities that reached 30,000 or 40,000 in population. The major hub, Jenne-Jenno, in today's nation of Mali, developed as early as 200 B.C.E. Residents built circular straw houses coated with mud and worked copper, gold, and iron obtained from mines several hundred miles away. Gold dust and small copper ingots **(ING-guhts)** apparently served as Sudanic currency. By 400 C.E. Jenne-Jenno had become a crucial transshipment point for goods brought by camel or donkey caravans and Niger River boats. It flourished as a commercial center for many centuries, closely tied, like other Sudanic cities, to the trans-Sahara caravans. Eventually a wall a mile in circumference surrounded the city to protect the residents. Built upon a productive agriculture, Jenne-Jenno exported grain, fish, and animal products in exchange for metals. It and other commercial centers in the Niger Valley were probably independent city-states for most of the first millennium C.E.

Large cities and states were less common in sub-Saharan Africa than in Eurasia and North Africa. The African agricultural system, mostly based on shifting cultivation, suited the soils but could not generally support large settled populations. In the first century C.E. Africa contained perhaps between 15 and 25 million people, much less than half that of China. About half lived in Egypt, Kush, and along the Mediterranean coast. With small population densities, societies did not require a powerful state to maintain order and could be held together by social and economic ties.

Beginning well before the Common Era, various caravan routes crossing the Sahara's barren sands greatly aided Sudanic growth by fostering interregional trade. Eventually a large trade system spanned the Sahara, linking Sudanic towns with southern Mediterranean coastal societies such as Carthage. Salt moved south while gold moved north, and gold used in Carthage coins may have come from western Africa. Sudanic cities also shipped north cotton cloth, leather goods, pepper, and slaves, which the merchants in North Africa then sold to Europe.

Although largely self-sufficient, Sudanic societies needed salt mined in the central Sahara and along the West African coast. The *Garamante* tribal confederation, which inhabited a large desert region north of the Sudan, mostly controlled the salt trade. These Berber **(BUHR-buhr)** people, who created the Sahara's most elaborate urban society, dominated the caravan trade routes as intermediaries from around 500 B.C.E. to 600 C.E., managing a vast commercial network and apparently selling African slaves to the Carthaginians, Romans, and Greeks. The Garamantes used camels as pack animals and horses to pull light chariots. To the Greeks and Romans, they were warlike barbarians, but these Saharans made the parched desert livable by combining pastoral stock raising with irrigated farming. They constructed several thousand miles of underground canals to cultivate their farms, lived in walled cities and villages, built stone citadels as military outposts, and were apparently governed by royal families. Their state collapsed around the same time as the Roman Empire, the remnants later overrun by Muslims.

Werner Forman/Universal Images Group/Getty Images

A JENNE WARRIOR This statuette, about 2 feet tall and made of a baked clay known as terracotta, likely portrays a warrior in Jenne, probably of high status, although some experts believe it portrays a founding ancestor.

West African States and Peoples

As in Kush and Aksum, commerce stimulated state building in the Sudan and West Africa. Kingdoms apparently grew out of markets, taxing the trade in gold and other commodities. The Soninke **(soh-NIN-kay)** of the middle Niger Valley formed the first known major Sudanic state, **Ghana (GAH-nuh)**. Although existing by at least 700 C.E., Ghana probably emerged several centuries earlier, and its probable capital city was built of stone sometime between 500 and 600 C.E. Ghana reached its height as a trade-based empire in the ninth century and flourished until the thirteenth.

Ghana The first known major Sudanic state, formed by the Soninke people of the middle Niger Valley.

Mande Diverse Sudanic peoples who spoke closely related languages, shared many customs, and dominated the western Niger River Basin and adjacent areas of West Africa.

Diverse **Mande (MON-day)** peoples perhaps typified Classical Sudanic societies. The Mande spoke closely related languages, shared many customs, and dominated the western Niger River Basin and adjacent areas. Mande-speakers included such ethnic groups as the Soninke (who established Ghana), Mandinka **(man-DING-goh)**, Malinke **(muh-LING-kee)**, and Bambara **(bam-BAHR-uh)**. By 900 or 800 B.C.E. Mande farmers lived in large walled villages, and they may have built Jenne-Jenno. Later, Mande-speakers dominated much of the western Sudan.

The Mande groups shared many social, political, and religious traditions. Their societies included aristocratic, warrior, and commoner classes and ritual and religious specialists. Eventually they developed theocracies with chiefs and village heads combining religious and secular duties. A respected class of oral historians and musicians known widely as **griots** **(GREE-oh)** memorized and recited the community's history, emphasizing leaders' deeds. Many Mande of all classes enjoyed considerable prosperity, making and trading widely their elaborate and beautiful cotton clothing. Mande and other Sudanic peoples also developed some common ideas about religion, including animism. Although they believed in a distant creator god, spirits of nature and ancestors loomed large in daily life. The Mande drew no neat line between the living and the dead while wanting to keep the favor of good spirits and avoid the hostility of bad ones.

Over time various peoples possessing new tools and agricultural techniques, including some from the Sudan, migrated into the Guinea **(GIN-ee)** coast, a land of forest and swamp with few edible plants or game animals that stretched some 2,000 miles from modern Senegal **(sen-i-GAWL)** to southeastern Nigeria **(nie-JEER-ee-uh)**. Mixing Sudanic and other traditions produced unique new societies. To survive their challenging environment, people lived mostly in small, self-sufficient villages with rich social networks, practicing subsistence agriculture, with yams and bananas as staple crops, and often working the land communally. The Guinea peoples traded with the Sudan by traveling over land or by boat up the rivers such as the Niger and Volta **(VAHL-tuh)**, becoming linked to wider economic and cultural exchange networks. Many coastal societies practiced some common customs, including Sudanese traditions such as theocratic political systems and pronounced social-class divisions.

The Bantu-Speaking Peoples and Their Migrations

Over several thousand years, many iron-using speakers of Bantu languages migrated from their original homeland in eastern Nigeria into Central and East Africa (see Chapter 3). Some scholars argue that the diffusion of Bantu culture and technology proceeded even without large numbers of migrants. During the Classical period, Bantu peoples accelerated their expansion to the south and east, some moving into the drought- and disease-prone southern Congo grasslands region known as Katanga **(kuh-TAHNG-guh)**. South of the Congo Basin rain forest, most land is relatively arid because of irregular rainfall. Fortunately, Bantus successfully adapted sorghum and millet from the Sudan and Ethiopia to this dry southern climate. From Katanga many Bantus moved to the west, south, and east. By 200 B.C.E. they had reached the Zambezi **(zam-BEE-zee)** River Basin, and by the third century C.E. they had entered what is now South Africa. Trade and migration networks spanning vast distances eventually connected Africa's southern third to the Sudan and the East African coast.

As Bantu migrants encountered local peoples, they incorporated new influences. Being ironworkers, Bantus possessed more effective military and agricultural technologies than many non-Bantu peoples, who were sometimes pushed into marginal economic areas suitable only for hunting and gathering. For example, the Mbuti Pygmies of the Congo region moved into thick rain forests, while many of the Khoisan **(KOY-sahn)** peoples in southern Africa, such as the !Kung, became desert dwellers. But many Bantus intermingled with, and probably culturally assimilated, those they met. Sudanese cultural forms carried by Bantus, such as drums and percussive music, woodcarving, and ancestor-focused religions, became widespread. The process worked both ways. For example, Xhosa **(KOH-sah)** and Zulu peoples, settling along the far southeastern coast, mixed their languages and cultures with local Khoisan cattle herders, incorporating cattle herding into their economic life.

The migrating Bantus gradually absorbed various East African societies, including pastoralists and farmers. Relationships were sometimes hostile with various ironworking pastoralists from the eastern Sudan who were also settling in East Africa, known as **Nilotes** **(nie-LAHT-eez)** because they speak Nilotic **(nie-LAHT-ik)** languages very different from Bantu tongues. Some Bantus began herding cattle and goats; others mastered new crops, including Southeast Asian foods like bananas, coconuts, sugar cane, and Asian yams brought to East Africa, along with domesticated chickens and possibly pigs, outrigger canoes, and musical instruments, by Indonesian mariners and migrants early in the Common Era and possibly centuries earlier. Some Indonesian mariners apparently established coastal trading posts and married local people. Between 100 and 700 C.E. Indonesians settled the large, previously uninhabited island of Madagascar, implanting there a mixed Indonesian-Bantu culture and language that still survive.

Maritime Trade and the East African Coast

Maritime trade fostered a cosmopolitan society on the East African coast. Winds and currents in the Indian Ocean reverse direction every six months, allowing boats from southwestern and southern Asia to sail to East Africa and back each year. Trading ports dotted the coast from Somalia to present-day Tanzania, and the main port, Rhapta **(RAHP-ta)** in Tanzania, had a large Arab merchant community.

Coastal trade grew slowly. A first-century C.E. Greek reported ships leaving Egypt's Red Sea ports and then visiting Adulis and Somalian ports before sailing to East African ports such as Rhapta. They then headed to India rather than venturing farther down what they considered the mysterious southern coast and ocean. East Africa exported ivory, rhinoceros horn, and tortoise shell to Egypt, India, and western Asia, importing iron goods, pottery, and glass beads. Egyptian, Roman, and West Asian coins found in the region indicate trade with Mediterranean peoples, and Persian pottery was common along the coast and inland. Eventually, coastal culture mixed Bantu and southwestern Asian ideas. But it took many centuries before any ships established contact with the Western Hemisphere, to which we now turn.

griots A respected class of oral historians and musicians in West Africa who memorized and recited the history of the group, emphasizing the deeds of leaders.

Nilotes Ironworking pastoralists from the eastern Sudan who settled in East Africa and there had frequent interactions with the Bantus.

MAKE SURE YOU UNDERSTAND THESE KEY POINTS BEFORE MOVING ON

- **The Sudan region included trading hubs such as Jenne-Jenno, but the population was not dense enough to require a powerful state; Ghana was the first state to arise, probably around 500 C.E.**
- **The Garamante peoples controlled the extensive Sahara Desert caravan routes to bring salt from the African Mediterranean coast to Sudan, which exported gold in return.**
- **The Bantu peoples, equipped with iron tools, continued to migrate south and east, mixing with and sometimes pushing out other peoples, as they made their way to South Africa by the third century C.E.**
- **Indonesian mariners settled on the East African coast and, to a greater extent, in Madagascar, where a mixed Indonesian-Bantu culture survives to this day.**

Classical Societies and Networks in the Americas

How did the Mesoamerican, Andean, and North American societies compare with each other?

As in Eurasia and Africa, the first cities and states in the Americas developed during ancient times, including Mesoamerica and the Andes (see Chapter 4). Population increase helped foster more urban societies during the Classical period. By around 1 C.E. around 15 million people lived in the Americas, over two-thirds of them in Mesoamerica and western South America, where several cities became centers of prosperous states. Most of these societies thrived from highly productive agriculture, developing diverse cultures, governments, and ways of life.

The Emergence of the Early Maya

In the lowland rain forests of Central America and southeast Mexico's Yucatán **(YOO-kuh-TAN)** Peninsula, the **Maya** **(MIE-uh)** became the most long-lasting and widespread Mesoamerican society, forging a literate but often brutal culture that excelled in some sciences and mathematics (see Map 9.2). Building on earlier regional traditions, probably including the Olmec culture to the northwest, they practiced shifting cultivation agriculture and ceramic making from at least 1100 B.C.E. They also introduced intensive farming of maize (corn) and other foods into tropical forests. According to Maya legends, the gods had fashioned people out of corn. Farmers built artificial platforms and terraces for growing enough crops to also support a ruling elite, and they constructed large underground reservoirs to store groundwater where rainfall was scarce. As more productive agriculture fostered larger populations, the Maya spread southward into the mountains and coastal zones of today's Chiapas **(chee-AHP-uhs)** (Mexico), Guatemala **(GWAHT-uh-MAHL-uh)**, Honduras, El Salvador, and Belize **(buh-LEEZ)**.

Maya The most long-lasting and widespread of the classical Mesoamerican societies, who occupied the Yucatán Peninsula and northern Central America for almost 2,000 years.

With increasing power, Maya elites organized ambitious building projects, constructing their first pyramids and elaborate stone buildings by 600 B.C.E. Unlike Egyptian pyramids, which were burial tombs for top leaders, Maya pyramids were built for religious worship and ceremonies, with temples on top to house the gods. According to Maya folklore:

> *There had been five generations of people since the origin of light, of life and of humankind. And they built houses for the gods, putting these in the center of the highest part of the citadel. After that their domains grew larger and more crowded.*[8]

As divine kingship notions became widespread, the Maya made stone statues and carvings of their rulers while painting sophisticated murals illustrating Maya myths.

At their cultural height, 150 B.C.E.–800 C.E., the Maya built many cities boasting masonry buildings, large temples, spacious plazas and pyramid complexes, and elaborate carvings. Suburbs containing residences, markets, and workshops stretched out from the city centers. In the major early city, El Mirador, the earliest Maya writing was inscribed on pot fragments and sculpture. Influenced by Olmec models, the Maya developed the Americas' most comprehensive writing system, a hieroglyphic script used for calendars, religious regulations, many sacred books, and recordings of dynastic histories, genealogies, and military successes. A later Spanish observer admired "those who carried with them the black and red ink, the manuscripts and painted book, the wisdom, the annals, the books of song."[9]

Tikal **(ti-KAHL)**, in eastern Guatemala, a major Maya city between 200 and 900 C.E. housing fifty thousand or more people at its height, contained three hundred large ceremonial buildings dominated by temple pyramids 200 feet high that were decorated with stucco plaster carvings. The first ruler used the jaguar to symbolize kingship, military bravery, and religious authority. His descendants, King Great Jaguar Paw and General

[8]From the *Popul Vuh*, quoted in Brian M. Fagan, *Kingdoms of Gold, Kingdoms of Jade: The Americas Before Columbus* (London and New York: Thames and Hudson, 1991), 94.

[9]Father Bernardino de Sahagun, quoted in Richard E. W. Adams, *Prehistoric Mesoamerica* (Boston: Little, Brown, 1977), 110.

MAP 9.2 MAJOR CLASSICAL SOCIETIES IN THE AMERICAS Various societies in the Americas lived largely from agriculture in this era and were connected to trade networks. Some, like the Mayans and Teotihuacan in Mesoamerica and Moche, and Tiwanaku in South America, developed cities and states while various North Americans, such as the Anasazi, Hohokam, and Hopewell, lived in towns.

Smoking Frog, led Tikal to a great victory over the rival city Uaxactun in 378 C.E., ensuring Tikal's regional supremacy for the next two hundred years. Tikal's success and survival also owed much to engineering projects, including the Maya world's largest dam, 260 feet long and 33 feet high, built of stone, rubble, and dirt, to collect, store, and filter rainwater for use in periodic droughts.

ROBERT MICHAEL/AFP/Getty Images

MAYA CODEX Only three Maya books (or codices) are known to have survived the Spanish conquest. This beautiful illustrated folding-screen book, the Dresden Codex, compiled around 1200 C.E., records astronomical calculations, tables of eclipses, and ritual detail. It is written on a long strip of bark paper coated with stucco.

Maya Politics and Trade

With Maya identity being more cultural than political, much cultural uniformity persisted among the competing cities, probably because of the region's dense population and the cities' close proximity with one another. Perhaps 10 million people lived in the Maya lowlands by 600 C.E., and a few cities, such as Tikal, now dominated others in the region. But no united Maya state or empire ever existed. With warfare between competing city-states over resources frequent and brutal, prisoners of war were usually enslaved or sacrificed. As in various Eastern Hemisphere and American societies, human sacrifice was common. Captured leaders from other cities faced especially agonizing deaths.

Maya ruling families were interconnected, with sons or daughters often being married into ruling families of rival cities to cement alliances or discourage attack. Cities were ruled by kings and sometimes queens who combined political, military, and religious leadership, consolidating their position by linking themselves to gods and ancestors and erecting stone monuments glorifying their deeds and ancestry. Because the scribes writing these inscriptions gained respect and influence, they might also be killed when their city-state and king lost a war.

Maya cities were linked by interregional trade networks hacked through the often dense rain forests. While rulers taxed and may have distributed goods, many cities had marketplaces for traders. They also traded widely with non-Maya societies, some hundreds of miles away in central Mexico or deep into Central America. Dugout canoes carried Maya and Central American goods to eastern Caribbean islands beginning at least fifteen hundred years ago, and Maya trading rafts probably sailed up and down the Central American coast and to some islands. Merchants from the great non-Maya city of Teotihuacan **(teh-o-tee-WAH-kahn)**, near today's Mexico City, lived in Maya cities, and Maya merchants and craftsmen settled in Teotihuacan. Unlike Eastern Hemisphere societies, the Maya did not work bronze or iron, but they did use copper and imported gold from Panama. They especially prized jade, a very hard stone obtained through long-distance trade. Skilled Maya artists carved in jade, as well as in stone and wood, and traded their jade products over great distances.

Maya Society, Religion, and Science

In the hierarchical Maya social structure, the upper class included nobles, who staffed the bureaucracy, architects, priests, and scribes. Below them were many artisans, including sculptors, potters, painters, and stoneworkers. Laborers and farmers supplying manual work and food occupied a lower rung. Slaves, mostly criminals, war prisoners, orphans, or children sold by debtors, did manual work for wealthy households. The strict legal code forced convicted robbers to restore stolen goods, pay for them, or work for the victim as a slave until they repaid the debt.

In the Maya's extended, multigenerational patrilineal family structure, each person had two names, one from the father's family and one from the mother's. Parents arranged marriages for their children at an early age. Maya society accorded men more rights, prestige, and privileges, and boys and young men often lived apart from their families in special communal houses, learning the arts of war. Mothers kept their daughters close, giving them a strict upbringing and punishing girls, but not boys, for compromising their chastity. Yet, some royal women wielded considerable power behind the kings, and a few served as rulers, sometimes very powerful warrior queens. Recent studies contend that women had influence as healers, oracles, and midwives.

City people enjoyed leisure activities. Regular festive local markets featured dancing to drums and flutes as well as ball games. All settlements featured ball courts with a stone ring, often 20 or 30 feet high, in the middle. Players used a

Georg Gerster/Science Source

TEOTIHUACAN This overview shows the two largest pyramids at Teotihuacan, the Pyramid of the Moon (bottom center) and the Pyramid of the Sun. There were six hundred smaller pyramids in the city.

6-inch-diameter rubber ball, which they could only hit with their buttocks, fists, and elbows. The rapid action was exhausting, making the main goal, directing the ball through the ring, difficult; teams were probably also rewarded for keeping the ball in play as long as possible. In an important match involving war captives, losers were sometimes sacrificed. Some Mexican villages still play the game, now over two thousand years old, but without dire consequences for losing.

Each Maya city was fed by thousands of peasants growing maize and *cacao* **(kuh-COW)**, from which chocolate is made, and raising turkeys domesticated in central Mexico. Cacao cultivation might go back to the Olmec. Although each farm family had their own plot, they cleared and cultivated communally with neighbors. Since the Maya and other Americans had no draft animals for farming, the intensive agriculture practiced in the Eastern Hemisphere was impossible. Instead peasants worked small plots, for perhaps fifty days a year. They were also subject to labor on public works or to military duty.

Maya religion, science, and mathematics were linked together. The Maya worshiped a creator god and many other deities. The only surviving book of Maya religion, the *Popul Vuh* ("Book of Council"), recognized a sacred earth, with humankind "given memory to count the days, [to be] bearers of respect for its divinity; to keep the rituals which connect humanity, nature and the heavens."[10] Obsessed with placating gods through ritual practices, including human sacrifice, the Maya believed the gods needed victims, as did kings, to maintain their reputations for power. They also emphasized body purification, patronizing sweat baths, buildings fashioned to contain heat and steam generated by hot rocks. Sometimes these baths were used for religious ceremonies.

Concerned with correct times and seasons for religious celebrations, the Maya made calendars and studied astronomy. Cosmic phenomena determined the best days for war, marriage, trade, rituals, and other activities. Conceiving time as cyclical, priests observed the movement of planets and stars. The Maya had the world's most accurate secular calendar, based on a solar

[10]Quoted in Michael Wood, *Legacy: The Search for Ancient Cultures* (New York: Sterling, 1994), 166.

year at 365 days, before the sixteenth century. However, they based their religious calendar on 260 days. The two calendars coincided every fifty-two years, prompting great festivals and religious observances.

The interest in time contributed to a mathematics system simpler and easier to use than Roman numerals. Like India's mathematicians, the Maya introduced the concept of zero. Unfortunately, the Spanish invaders in the 1500s C.E. destroyed most Maya books (known as codices). Zealous Christians, many Spanish considered the writing pagan, one arguing that the "books contained nothing [but] superstition and lies of the devil, [so] we burned them all which caused [the Maya] much affliction."[11] This terrible loss has made it much more difficult for historians to understand Maya history and culture.

Studying the sun, stars, and planets proved wise because cyclical variations in solar energy caused debilitating droughts roughly every two hundred years. Perhaps climate changes undermined the legitimacy of leaders linked to gods and provoked wars over scarce resources. Eventually increasing droughts probably contributed to Maya cities' collapse.

Monte Alban and Teotihuacan

Some other Mesoamerican peoples also developed cities and states. By 400 B.C.E. small states had emerged among the Zapotec **(ZAHP-uh-TEK)** people in southern Mexico, especially around Monte Alban **(MON-teh ahl-BAHN)**, a hilltop city and large ceremonial center ruled by hereditary kings and priests, with several huge pyramid platforms. Many large carved stones, possibly portraits of slain war captives, suggest military activity. Thanks to population growth and migration, the capital city may have housed 25,000 to 30,000 people at its peak between 300 and 750 C.E. The Zapotec developed a complex alphabet and calendar similar to, and possibly derived from, those of the Olmec. Around 750 C.E. Monte Alban city began a long decline and was abandoned by 1000 C.E..

Other major urban societies emerged in the large Valley of Mexico (the site of present-day Mexico City), long a center for mining *obsidian* **(uhb-SID-ee-uhn)**, a glassy, volcanic rock prized for its razor-sharp edges. By 200 B.C.E. **Teotihuacan** ("the City of the Gods") became the Americas' largest city and the capital of an empire in central Mexico that extended its influence over much of Mesoamerica, and by 600 C.E. it was one of the world's half dozen largest cities, with between 120,000 and 200,000 inhabitants. Laid out on a north-south axis bisected by wide avenues, the city boasted plazas, markets, apartment buildings, palaces, and hundreds of temples. As in India's Harappan cities, a complex drainage system removed unwanted water. In the city's ceremonial center, a huge Pyramid of the Sun rose over 200 feet high, built from 3 million tons of volcanic rock dug up and then transported without iron tools or beasts of burden to pull wheeled vehicles. American pyramids, smaller in size and built differently than the great Egyptian and Nubian pyramids, nonetheless demonstrate that people can create the same symbols, however widely separated by geography and time. Teotihuacan also contained ball courts.

Teotihuacan ("the City of the Gods") The largest city in the Americas and the capital of an empire in central Mexico during Classical times.

Moche A prosperous, powerful state that formed along the northern Peruvian coast from 200 B.C.E. to 700 C.E.

Teotihuacan was a political, religious, and economic center. The kings, apparently viewed as divine, left administration to bureaucrats and aristocrats. The people had writing and an ingenious numbering system, which no doubt assisted trade and administration. Priests and artisans, perhaps a quarter of the city's population, resided in houses built around small courtyards, where some fashioned obsidian tools or manufactured ceremonial pottery. Teotihuacan functioned as the hub for trade networks spanning Mesoamerica and extending far to the north and south. Some neighborhoods housed merchants and sojourners or settlers, many of them traders and artisans, from Maya cities and other regions, and Teotihuacan merchants also traveled widely. Maya-carved jade statues were common. There may also have been close links between Teotihuacan and Maya royal families.

Eventually Teotihuacan society collapsed. Rulers became increasingly militaristic and human sacrifice more common, earning Teotihuacan enemies and harming trade. The causes of the collapse may have been environment disaster (such as a prolonged drought) or internal revolts or invasions by a rival state. In 750 C.E. invaders burned the city down, and the population scattered. But even in ruins the city's splendor lived on. A millennium later the Aztecs who had settled the area told the Spanish conquerors of their reverence for the sacred spirit of the pyramids: "And this they call Teotihuacan, because it is where they bury the lords."[12]

Andean Societies

Other societies emerged and often flourished in South America. Chavín, the Andes state, had collapsed by 200 B.C.E., but some of its architectural and religious patterns spread through the Andes and into adjacent lands. **Moche (MO-che)**, a prosperous and powerful state or, as some research suggests, grouping of affiliated communities, formed around 200 B.C.E. in the desert along the northern Peruvian coast. In this dry region farming required maintaining irrigation canals that channeled runoff from the Andes to grow corn, beans, peppers, squash, and cotton, which Moche skillfully wove into textiles. They also exploited the abundant, protein-rich maritime resources just offshore, including fish and mollusks.

The Moche were part of a distinctive culture that built monumental architecture, with platforms and courtyards, and fashioned beautiful jewelry, mirrors, and pottery. Coastal peoples traded some of their agricultural and maritime bounty to

[11] Frey Diego de Landa, quoted in T. Patrick Culbert, *Maya Civilization* (Washington, DC: Smithsonian, 1993), 22.

[12] Fra Bernardino de Sahagun, quoted in Juan Schobinger, *The First Americans* (Grand Rapids, MI: William B. Eerdmans, 1994), 97.

PROFILE

A Moche Lord

Outside of Mesoamerica, no American society left written records to help us understand individual lives. Nearly all we know of the Moche comes from recent archaeological investigations. As in Egypt, an arid climate preserved many objects, including jewelry, weapons, clothing, ceramics, and skeletons. Pottery paintings portray Moche life, and excavations at royal tombs reveal how Moche leaders lived and died, even if we do not know their names, personalities, family ties, or precise governmental functions. We can now trace the experiences of one leader, probably a warrior-priest, known to archaeologists as one of the lords of Sipan, a Moche city, who was buried in his mid-thirties around 390 C.E.

Archaeologists know what Moche men and women looked like. Men were stocky, averaging about 5 feet 3 inches in height, but this lord was 3 inches taller. He cut his hair in bangs over his forehead, wore it long in back, pierced his ears and nose, painted his face, and tattooed his arms and legs. Moche women, such as those in the lord's family, stood about 4 feet 7 inches tall and wore their hair long, often braided with colorful woolen strands. At ceremonies women's dress consisted of a multicolored woven smock heavily laden with long strands of beads. Women lived much longer than men, but men had far richer costumes.

Buried in all the finery he probably wore in his official and ceremonial life, the Sipan lord dressed ostentatiously, demonstrating his wealth and power. He wore a long tunic completely covered with gilded copper platelets, with copper sandals on his feet. On his wrists he sported large beaded bracelets of turquoise, gold, and shell. A beaded chest-plate and a spectacular necklace of gold and silver beads covered his chest and shoulders, probably gleaming like the sun. Around his waist a belt supported crescent-shaped bells. A crescent-shaped gold nose ornament completely covered his mouth and lower face, and his large ear ornaments were inlaid with gold and turquoise. On his head, the Sipan lord wore a large, crescent-shaped headdress ornament made of gold. In one hand he held a gold and silver scepter, signifying high rank. Moche art frequently depicted high-status men dressed like the Sipan lord.

The lord led a privileged life, but it also held many dangers. Most Moche were poor; only a few people, like the lord, lived in extreme opulence. Every valley may have had one or more royal courts connected to one another through marriage alliances and trade, like the Maya kings. Moche art frequently depicts warriors parading in front of royalty, perhaps preparing for war against rival courts. Like Maya royalty, perhaps the lord of Sipan went into battle to personally fight rival lords.

Battle was a grueling and fateful experience. Warriors used clubs to beat the enemy's heads or hurled stones and arrows with a sling. Like Roman gladiators, Moche warriors participated in hand-to-hand combat, with the ultimate goal of capturing the enemy for torture and sacrifice. Complex rules may have governed warriors' conduct on and off the field. Battles ended when one warrior caught hold of another's hair and dragged him down. The loser, stripped of his clothes and weapon, was paraded before the royalty of the winners. Painted bottles show the victorious lord presiding over a horrific sacrificial ceremony, drinking a goblet of blood drawn from the slit throats of captive enemy warriors. The lord of Sipan never suffered that fate. He was buried along with several young women, perhaps wives, concubines, or attendants; two burly men armed with shields and war clubs, possibly to protect him in the afterlife; and a dog, probably the lord's pet hound.

A MOCHE LORD This Moche lord, memorialized for posterity in ceramic, wears the headgear and ear ornaments common to the Moche nobility. The potter skillfully captured the lord's facial features, giving the portrait a lifelike quality.

THINKING ABOUT THE READING

1. How do burials and paintings on pots help us understand Moche life?
2. What do the lord's clothing and symbols of royalty tell us about Moche society?
3. What role did warfare play in the life of a Moche lord?

Andes societies for potatoes and other highland crops. Eventually trade networks linked societies over western South America. Some took up seagoing trade. Between 500 B.C.E. and the 1600s C.E., the Manteno people from coastal Ecuador used balsa wood rafts equipped with sails and loaded with textiles, ceramics, precious metals, and prized shells to forge a coastal trade network stretching from Mexico to Chile. Because of these trends, coastal and interior peoples depended on each other, encouraging state formation in both places.

The well-planned Moche capital city, centered around two massive brick pyramids dedicated to the sun and moon, contained perhaps ten thousand people. Separate and perhaps hostile city-based Moche kingdoms were spread over hundreds of miles, all with similar customs, buildings, and pyramids. Burial chambers and clay pottery painted with highly realistic scenes of social activity provide knowledge of Moche society, such as the sometimes elegant, sometimes brutal life of the elite (see Profile: A Moche Lord). While male warrior-priests were powerful, priestess-queens seem to have occasionally ruled some cities. Enormous amounts of gold and silver artifacts were buried with dignitaries.

Revealing everyday life, painted pots show midwives attending birthing mothers, women carrying babies on their backs in shawls, and men with tatooed faces. Nearly everyone wears headgear, from the elite's feathered headdresses to the common folks' decorated cotton turbans. Like most Andes peoples, Moche consumed maize beer. The paintings also portray erotic lovemaking between men and women and between gods and humans, as well as war leaders drinking their unfortunate captives' blood. While many customs shock us and may not have made them popular neighbors, the Moche should be remembered for more than bloodshed. Excellent gold workers, they also made products from a copper and gold alloy as well as silver. They created one of the world's finest ceramic traditions and apparently also developed a mathematical system based on 10.

Eventually the Moche faced challenges they could not overcome, including natural disasters, among them prolonged drought, massive earthquakes, and severe *El Ñinos* **(el NEEN-yoz)**, the periodic warm water currents in the Pacific that bring higher temperatures and torrential rain. Moche leaders may have responded to the resulting food shortages with increasing warfare to obtain resources and human sacrifice to appease the gods. The ecological and political crises these disasters generated brought Moche collapse by 650 or 700 C.E.

While Moche dominated the northern Peruvian coast, various states rose and fell in the Andes and along the southern Peruvian coast. In the Lake Titicaca **(tit-i-KAHK-uh)** region (in modern Bolivia and southern Peru) of the Andes highlands between 600 and 100 B.C.E., the ancestors of the Aymara **(AYE-muh-RAH)** people built a state and constructed impressive stone sculpture. Even in ruins, their plazas, palaces, and brightly colored temples decorated with gold-covered reliefs impressed the Spanish fifteen hundred years later; one wrote: "There is a hill made by the hands of men, on great foundations of stone. What causes most astonishment are some great doorways of stone, some made out of a single stone."[13] The capital city, Tiwanaku **(tee-wah-NA-coo)**, over 10,000 feet above sea level, emerged by 100 C.E. and reached its height in 600 C.E. with a population of perhaps forty thousand, controlling much of the southern Andes. A statue of the sun-god atop a platform greeted visitors, and the city center featured a huge, sacred platform 650 feet long and 50 feet high. The rulers staged elaborate festivals with much drug and alcohol consumption to recruit labor for public works projects. Little is known of gender relations, but in the neighboring and rival state of Wari, just to the north, women of elite status operated a mountaintop brewery, making hundreds of gallons of corn beer every week.

Tiwanaku influenced a large region of western South America. Its art and religion, probably involving human sacrifice, spread into neighboring societies. Tiwanuku's hinterland, rich in llama herds and copper mining, flourished from raised field agriculture—seeds planted on long artificial ridges separated by ditches—which improved drainage, replaced nutrients in the poor soil, and protected crops such as potatoes from frost, making agriculture some 400 percent more productive than the region's farming today. Like other Andean peoples, the Aymara also skillfully used fibers. Weaving together reeds, they made boats to sail on the lake. But by 1100 C.E. the capital and surrounding fields were abandoned, perhaps because climate change generated a drought so severe that rivers dried up.

Another peoples, the Nazca **(NAHZ-kuh)**, a decentralized agrarian society in southern Peru's harsh desert that flourished from 200 B.C.E. to 600 C.E., manufactured beautiful multicolored pottery and textiles while constructing ceremonial centers. But the Nazca are most famous for creating geometric lines along their windswept plateau by clearing away surface stones to reveal the underlying rock and then laying the stones along the edges of the lines. Constructed on a huge scale, the lines depict either geometric shapes or animals such as monkeys and birds. These enigmatic markings have puzzled modern observers; scholars think they were created to mark the seasons, communicate with gods believed to dwell in the nearby mountains, or mark water sources. Or they may have just been artistic expressions of shapes and animals.

North American Societies

Sophisticated societies also emerged in North America. Several cultural traditions and permanent towns emerged among the desert farmers of the American Southwest, including the Hohokam **(huh-HOH-kuhm)**, Anasazi **(ah-nah-SAH-zee)**, and Mogollon **(MOH-guh-YOHN)**.

By around 300 B.C.E. the Hohokam of southern Arizona and northwest Mexico were trading extensively with other southwestern peoples and the southern California coast.

[13]Cieza de Leon, quoted in Fagan, *Kingdoms of Gold*, 192.

Hohokam farmers used advanced irrigation, dams, terraces, and other strategies to grow maize, beans, squash, and cotton. The Hohokam also built large towns; the total population in the vicinity of present-day Phoenix may have reached forty thousand. The presence of ball courts and rubber balls, as well as Mesoamerican-style platform mounds, indicates Mesoamerican influence. But no evidence for human sacrifice or warfare has been found. Eventually overpopulation, deforestation, and drier climates increased stress and conflict, and Hohokam settlements were abandoned by the fifteenth century. Their modern descendants include the Pima and Papago Indians of Arizona.

The Anasazi and closely related Mogollon culture were the direct ancestors of the Pueblo Indians in today's Arizona and New Mexico. The widespread Anasazi culture, which arose around the first century C.E., reached its high point between 750 and 900 C.E. with towns in Arizona, Utah, and Colorado. The Mogollon culture, emerging around 200 B.C.E., stretched from central Arizona and New Mexico into northern Mexico. These societies flourished from corn growing and skillful gathering until the fifteenth century C.E.

Other cultures were mound builders, following a tradition that had begun in North America around 2500 B.C.E. (see Chapter 4). Between around 500 B.C.E. and 400 C.E., a new mound-building culture became even more widespread, encompassing the Mississippi, Ohio, Tennessee, and lower Missouri River Basins and their tributaries as well as the South Atlantic coast, a total area larger than India. The most prominent mound builders, known today as Hopewell, lived in the Ohio River region. Hopewell artistic styles, maize cultivation, religious beliefs, ceremonial traditions, and burial customs spread throughout the eastern woodlands. Without any large state, the Hopewell created extraordinary earthworks and other engineering projects. Elaborate geometric designs such as hexagons and circles marked their mounds, some of which served as burial chambers for the elite. The spectacular Great Serpent Mound, built on an Ohio hilltop around two thousand years ago, was shaped like a snake, ran 800 feet long from head to tail, and was 4 feet tall and 20 feet wide. The Ortuna, a Hopewell culture in northern Florida, built 20-foot-wide canals that allowed dugout canoes to reach both Atlantic and Gulf coasts, thus connecting them to a trading network stretching north to Ohio.

Two major economic changes supported the mound-building cultures. Agriculture became more intensive, especially after maize cultivation spread, and long-distance trade networks expanded over much of North America. Along the river trade routes moved obsidian from the Rocky Mountains, copper from the Great Lakes and later southern Appalachia, ceramic figurines and vessels from the lower Great Lakes, ore from Kansas, silver from Ontario, shells from the Gulf of Mexico and Florida, freshwater pearls from the Mississippi, and marine products from the Gulf coast such as sharks' teeth and turtle shells. Sharks' teeth have been found in Illinois, over a thousand miles from the Caribbean.

The Hopewell culture began declining around 300 C.E. and collapsed by 600 C.E. Overpopulation and the resulting competition for land may have stressed the environment and economic system while disrupting trade networks. The climate cooled and maize crop diminished. In addition, around 300 C.E. someone invented or imported the bow and arrow, altering the power balance and stimulating warfare.

Changing States and the Spread of Cultures

While Olmec and Chavín traditions remained influential in Mesoamerica and the Andes region, much change occurred over the Classical centuries, although often on a different timeline from the Eastern Hemisphere. Around 200 or 300 C.E., small states such as Monte Alban, Teotihuacan, Tikal, and Tiwanaku grew into larger states, often regional empires. Long-distance trade increased, merchants became more influential, and ideas (such as Mesoamerican writing and ball games) spread more widely. Many American peoples revered the land as the source of both physical and spiritual life, with a close relationship to the supreme spirits or gods. Hence, the Maya and some North American societies considered maize sacred, a gift from the gods.

Except for the exceptionally enduring Maya and Tiwanaku, South American and Mesoamerican states rose and fell after a few centuries, perhaps because environmental and climate changes affected agriculture and fishing while fostering chronic warfare. Although establishing frameworks for later empires such as the Aztec and Inca, the Classical states did not survive in their original form, as the Chinese and Ethiopian states did.

The widespread presence of pyramids in Mesoamerica and South America has prompted some speculation about possible contacts across the Atlantic to North Africa and the Mediterranean long before the arrival of Norse Vikings around 1000 C.E. and, five centuries later, Spanish ships. But no firm archaeological evidence exists for any Eastern Hemisphere connections, and most specialists doubt any such contacts. Pyramids are based on practical principles of monument construction that are probably available to builders anywhere. Some American peoples built mounds nearly as early as the first Egyptian pyramids.

Pottery design, artwork, and plants along the American west coast, from California to Chile, hint at trans-Pacific contacts, provoking occasional speculation about possible Chinese, Japanese, or Polynesian voyages to the Americas. Some studies claim to find Japanese **(Jomon)** pottery and genes in Ecuador, Olmec hieroglyphics resembling Shang Chinese characters, Polynesian musical instruments and loan words in western South America, or Polynesian words and boat designs along the California coast. Skilled mariners, Polynesians were capable of trips over several thousand miles of uncharted ocean, and a few could have occasionally visited the American coast. This might explain South American sweet potatoes in Polynesia by 1000 C.E. However, no conclusive proof exists for any trans-Pacific contacts, and if any voyages did occur, they left no obvious long-lasting influence.

MAKE SURE YOU UNDERSTAND THESE KEY POINTS BEFORE MOVING ON

- **The Maya society on the Yucatán Peninsula developed a comprehensive writing and numbering system, studied astronomy and devised accurate calendars, and built impressive buildings and large pyramids that served as religious centers.**
- **Teotihuacan, near present-day Mexico City, grew into one of the largest and best-designed cities in the world and had an extremely advanced infrastructure, including a complex drainage system.**
- **In the Andes, Chavín was succeeded by Moche, whose pottery depicts a violent culture of war and sacrifice but also of advanced metalwork and architecture.**
- **In the desert Southwest of North America, the Hohokam people developed extensive irrigation systems, and their cultural artifacts show some Mesoamerican influence.**
- **Supported by corn and expanded trade networks, mound-building cultures spread across eastern North America.**

Populating the Pacific: Australian and Island Societies

How were some of the notable features of Australian and Pacific societies shaped by their environments?

Although the original settlers of Australia and the Pacific islands migrated from or through Southeast Asia, the societies they developed remained largely isolated from the historical currents of Eurasia for many centuries. Australian Aborigines mastered a hostile environment and flourished from hunting and gathering. In extraordinary voyages, Austronesians migrated over thousands of miles of open ocean to inhabit most of the Pacific islands, adapting to new environments, creating diverse cultures, and developing long-distance trade networks.

Australian Geography and Aboriginal Societies

Australia was settled at least fifty thousand years ago, and by 1000 B.C.E. Aboriginal tribes spoke some two hundred distinct languages. Australia's environments included tropical, heavily forested north and northeast coasts, temperate southeast and southwest river basins and coasts, and deserts dominating much of the interior. Aboriginal life, based largely on hunting and gathering, exploited many food sources such as coastal marine life and wild plants and insects in the harsh desert interior. Women gathered plants and small animals, prepared family meals, looked after children, made clothing, and built huts, while men fished, hunted large animals, and manufactured implements. Aborigines developed an intimate understanding of weather patterns and their relationships to plants, animals, and land, knowledge used by meteorologists today.

Most Aborigines ate as well as peoples in Afro-Eurasia, with malnutrition and starvation largely unknown. However, agriculture never developed because of mostly infertile land and erratic rains, and no native plants or animals were capable of domestication. Even today large-scale irrigation sustains farming, and, as in Mesopotamia, it increases the groundwater's salt content, endangering fresh water supplies. Instead, Aboriginal societies developed land management and usage that conserved their resources over thousands of years, evolving a close relationship to the earth that remained central to their customs and beliefs. Studying the night sky to survive the challenging landscape, they used stories to explain the tides, eclipses, the rising and setting sun and moon, and the changing positions of stars and planets throughout the year. The sky served as a calendar for when seasons changed and certain foods were available.

Many Aboriginal practices made use of environmental realities. For example, fire could clear land, encouraging the regrowth of edible plants and natural ecosystem rejuvenation. Whether deliberate or natural, fires have always occurred regularly in Australia, but they complicate modern urbanized life. Beginning around 6000 B.C.E., one Aboriginal society, the Gunditjmara in southern Australia, built an ingenious artificial lake for operating eel farms and traded the abundant eels around southern Australia. The Gunditjmara may also have lived in a permanent town with stone houses.

Aboriginal societies shared many similar customs and beliefs. Needing to move by foot with the seasons to maximize food availability, most owned few possessions, expressing pride in their mobility. Aboriginal men carried spear throwers and spears while women carried digging sticks and baskets to hold foodstuffs. They relocated to the same camps every year over regular trails. Aboriginal tribes were organized either through the patrilineal or the matrilineal line, and nuclear families operated with considerable independence and flexible relations between genders. Although few tribes had chiefs, older males exerted influence in religious and social life, while women made critical decisions about the campsite and controlled their own ceremonial life. Periodic disputes between neighboring tribes sometimes led to fighting, which was usually settled by diplomacy involving the tribal elders.

Spending only about three days a week in search of food, Aborigines had time for rituals, ceremonial expression, and religious matters, including a widely shared belief in the mythology

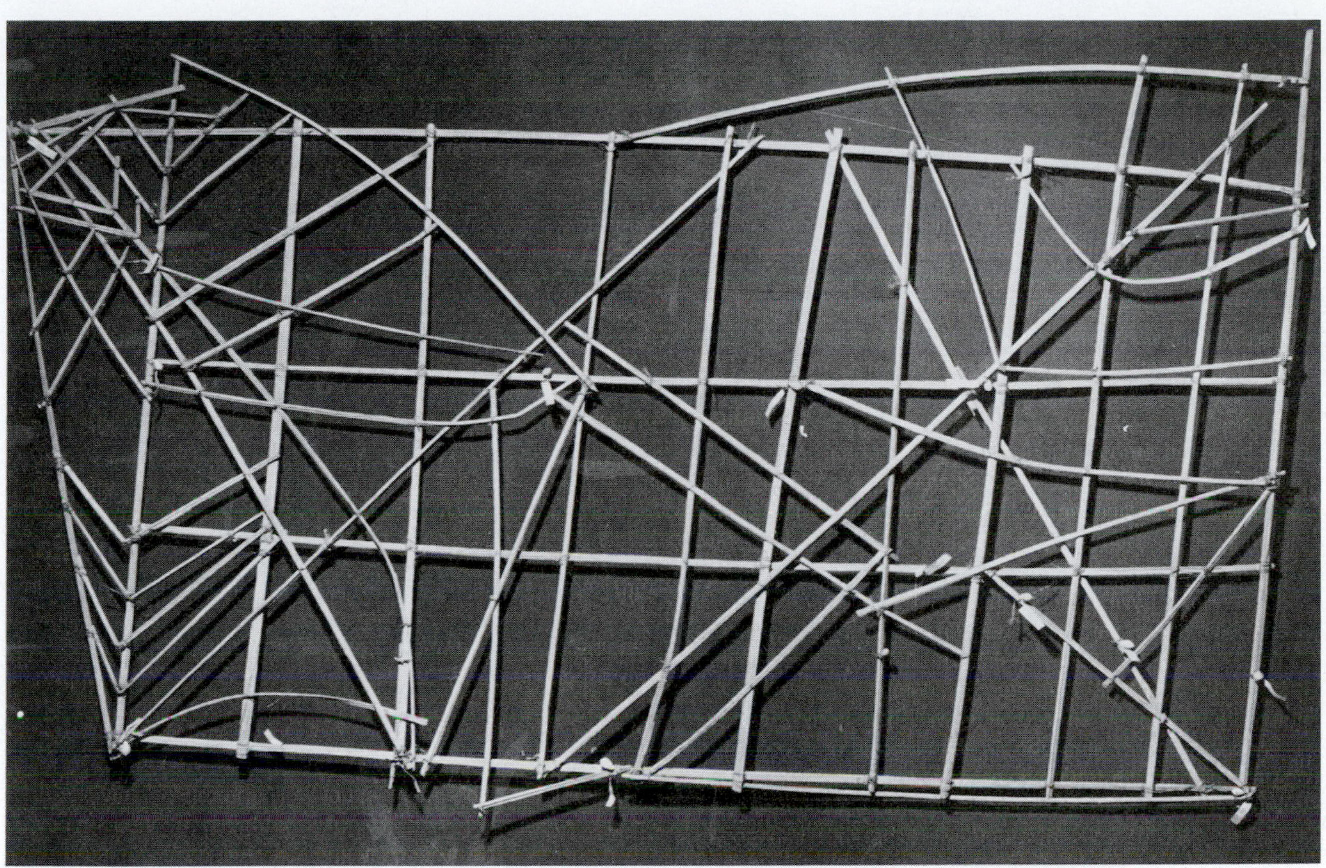

POLYNESIAN PALM-FROND NAVIGATIONAL MAP This nautical map, made in the Marshall Islands from palm fronds, shows distances between islands as measured by time traveled. The map may have originally had bits of shell or coral to mark islands. Polynesians and Micronesians often made such maps for their ocean voyages.

of the **dreamtime**, the distant past when the spiritual ancestors gave order and form to the universe at the world's creation. Dreamtime myths were remarkably consistent around Australia, passed down through countless generations by a rich oral literature. Aborigines recognized an animistic world of many spirits and ghosts. Their art had a religious base, including body decoration, bark paintings, and especially rock carvings and paintings.

A complex trade system spanned the continent. Northern coast pearls and shells reached southern Australia, and quartz, flint, and other tool-making stones, as well as animal skins, wood products, and ornaments, were exchanged over wide areas. By Classical times Indonesian trading ships probably visited the northwest coast to obtain pearls. Later, Chinese ships may have done the same. But these outside contacts had little influence on most Australian societies. Today, after two centuries of change brought by European conquest and settlement, the life that sustained Aborigines for thousands of years has largely passed. Whereas once they sang songs about their lands and history, today, largely settled on rural land reserves or in poor urban neighborhoods, Aborigines lament the loss of their traditions. Their stories still recollect tribal pasts and beliefs, but the storytellers inhabit a very different reality than did their ancestors.

Austronesian Expansion

Today some twelve hundred different Austronesian languages are spoken from Madagascar eastward through Indonesia, Malaysia, the Philippines, and most of the Pacific islands. No premodern peoples, including Indo-Europeans and Bantus, migrated over as wide an area in so short a time as did Austronesians. In ancient times some Austronesian-speaking peoples moved from Southeast Asia into the western Pacific islands just northeast of Australia, encountering Melanesians **(mel-uh-NEE-zhuhnz)** who had earlier migrated from Southeast Asia (see Chapter 4). Over time the two traditions mixed, and Melanesians adopted Austronesian languages. Eventually some Austronesian-speaking peoples from the western Pacific sailed farther east and north to colonize other islands, in the process fostering new groups later known as Polynesians **(PAHL-uh-NEE-zhunz)** and Micronesians **(MIE-kruh-NEE-zhunz)**.

Overpopulation on islands with limited resources, fresh water, or fertile land spurred these intentional migrations. Islanders learned to limit population growth to avoid

dreamtime In Aboriginal Australian mythology, the distant past when the spiritual ancestors gave order and form to the universe at the world's creation.

MAP 9.3 PACIFIC MIGRATIONS IN THE CLASSICAL ERA During this era, Austronesian peoples scattered across the vast Pacific Basin, using ingenious canoes and navigation techniques to settle nearly all the inhabitable islands. From bases in Tonga and Samoa in the west, the Polynesians settled a large expanse of the basin ranging from Hawaii in the north to Easter Island in the east and New Zealand in the south.

deforestation and natural resource depletion, which would generate conflict or migration. Using only the stars, moon, sun, winds, and waves to guide them, a strategy they term "wayfinding," migrants endured the hardships of long open-sea voyages to discover new islands, some mountainous and covered by dense rain forests, others flat atolls only a few feet above sea level. Navigation and boat building were a science; voyagers spent many days selecting the right tree for their canoes because worm-ridden wood might prove disastrous at sea. An ancient Tahitian prayer reveals the voyagers' fears: "O gods! Lead us safely to land. Leave us not in the ocean. Give us a breeze. Let the weather be fine and the sky clear."[14] Excellent naval technology made these migrations possible: each double-hulled outrigger canoe, up to 100 feet long with two hulls and a platform lashed between them for living, cooking, work space, and storage, could carry up to eighty people, along with foods, plants, and animals.

Micronesians, who settled many central and north Pacific islands, made ingenious navigation charts from cowrie shells tied together. The Austronesian-speaking ancestors of Micronesians colonized many small islands in the central Pacific, among them the Marianas **(MAR-ee-AN-uhz)**, including the islands of Guam and Saipan, and the Carolines. The Chamorro **(cha-MOR-roe)** people of the Marianas grew Asian rice, suggesting they had continuing connections with the Philippines.

Polynesian Migrations and Societies

Polynesian culture flowered first in the neighboring Fiji, Tonga, and Samoa **(suh-MO-uh)** island groups around 500 B.C.E. (see Map 9.3). Scholars vigorously debate the timing of later Polynesian migrations. Some contend that around 300 or 200 B.C.E. Tongan mariners may have reached the Marquesas **(mar-KAY-suhs)** Islands and soon thereafter Tahiti **(tuh-HEE-tee)**, 1,500 miles east of Tonga. Other studies place these events much later, around 1000 to 1100 C.E. Polynesians sailed from Samoa 1,500 miles north to the

[14]Quoted in Judy Thompson and Allan Taylor, *Polynesian Canoes and Navigation* (Laie, Hawaii: Institute of Polynesian Studies, 1980), 32.

Kiribati **(kear-uh-BAH-tee)** Islands and then to the Marshall Islands. Scholars similarly disagree as to whether Marquesas mariners settled Hawaii between 400 and 600 C.E. or much later, around 1200 to 1300, after crossing over 2,000 miles of ocean, followed by a migration from Tahiti 2,500 miles east to Easter Island. Finally, sometime between 800 and 1300 C.E., some Tahitians moved west another 2,500 miles to Aotearoa **(ow-TEH-a-ROW-uh)** (which a Dutch explorer later named New Zealand), the largest Polynesian-settled landmass. These settlers, the ancestors of the Maori **(MAO-ree)** people, faced a very different climate and topography from the tropical islands, as well as new plants and animals. Conceivably Polynesian sailors also visited the Peruvian coast, perhaps explaining the presence of sweet potatoes, a South American crop, in eastern Polynesia and New Zealand for at least one thousand years.

Polynesian agriculture emphasized Southeast Asian crops such as yams, taro, bananas, coconuts, and breadfruit and animals such as pigs, chickens, and dogs. But survival required modifications, including elaborate terracing, artificial ponds, irrigation, and exploitation of local food sources such as coconuts and of marine life in lagoons, coral reefs, and the deep sea. Cloth made from bark furnished clothing. But fragile island ecologies became easily unbalanced. Imported animals like pigs, dogs, and (unintentionally) rats consumed birds, and overhunting of local species and deforestation created problems. As an extreme example, Easter Island, which was heavily forested when Polynesians arrived, became completely denuded over the centuries, the people reduced to poverty and chronic conflict over ever scarcer resources.

Early Polynesians lived in clans that were generally dominated by hereditary chiefs who controlled the lands. Conflict between rival clans over status and land led to tensions and sometimes war. Eventually the most elaborate social hierarchies emerged in Tonga, Tahiti, and Hawaii, with paramount chiefs ruling many thousands of followers and controlling much of the economy. While men held most political power, women often enjoyed a high status. Most Micronesian and some Polynesian societies were matrilineal. Polynesian women often ranked higher than their brothers in spiritual and ritual authority and, by marrying into other clans or ruling families, could help political relations. The Polynesian societies also shared many other cultural traits, including elaborate facial and body tattooing (the word *tattoo* is of Polynesian origin), myths, reverence for ancestors, and art forms such as woodcarving. Many of these customs were also common in Melanesia and Micronesia.

The huge triangle of Polynesia, anchored at the ends by Hawaii, New Zealand, and Easter Island, is one of the world's largest territorial expanses. One of the first outsiders to explore the area, British captain James Cook, wrote in 1774: "It is extraordinary that the same [people] should have spread themselves over all the isles in this vast Ocean, almost a fourth part of the circumference of the Globe."[15] But migration over such vast distances did not necessarily mean isolation. Thanks to a large maritime network, obsidian mined on New Britain island, northeast of New Guinea, was distributed from Borneo to Fiji, 4,000 miles apart. Moreover, nearby island groups maintained trade and social links. For example, the families of Tongan and Fijian chiefs frequently intermarried. But the sailing required remarkable observation and could be dangerous, as Captain Cook reported from Tonga in 1777: "In these Navigations the Sun is their guide by day and the Stars by night; when these are obscured they have recourse to the points from whence the Wind and waves come upon the vessel. If [these] shift, they are bewildered."[16] Even today Polynesian traditions honor great navigators of the past such as Moikeha and Pa'ao, who sailed back and forth between the Marquesas and Hawaii over a millennium ago.

MAKE SURE YOU UNDERSTAND THESE KEY POINTS BEFORE MOVING ON

- **Aboriginal Australians developed great understanding of natural phenomena and were very successful hunters and gatherers for thousands of years.**
- **Aborigines across Australia believed in the dreamtime of the mythic past and felt that spirits and ghosts inhabited much of the physical world.**
- **Polynesian culture probably began in Fiji, Tonga, and Samoa, but it spread out over a remarkable expanse of the Pacific Ocean.**
- **An extensive trading network developed among the Pacific islands, and, despite their isolation from each other, the islands' cultures remained quite homogenous.**

[15]Quoted in Peter Bellwood, *The Polynesians: Prehistory of an Island People*, revised ed. (London: Thames and Hudson, 1997), 7.

[17]Quoted in Peter Bellwood, *Man's Conquest of the Pacific: The Prehistory of Southeast Asia and Oceania* (New York: Oxford University Press, 1979), 300.

CHAPTER SUMMARY

During the Classical Era some sub-Saharan Africans became more closely linked by trade with North Africa and Eurasia. Kush became a center for iron production, and Aksum flourished as a trading hub. The cities and small states that emerged in West Africa's Sudanic region participated in the growing trans-Saharan caravan trade network, which linked them with the Mediterranean world. Cities also appeared along the East African coast, tied by trade networks to the Mediterranean, western Asia, and India. Bantu-speaking peoples settled the southern half of Africa, carrying with them iron technology and many Sudanic influences.

Various urban societies dominated Mesoamerica and the Andes, including the Maya, Moche, Tiwanaku, Teotihuacan, and Monte Alban. The Maya forged a particularly enduring society based on competing city-states, developed a writing system, and understood much about astronomy and mathematics. The Moche on the Peruvian coast and Tiwanaku in the highlands formed empires. In Mesoamerica, Teotihuacan became the greatest city in the Americas and a major trading hub. In North America many peoples adopted farming, built permanent towns, and took up mound building. In the Pacific, Australian Aborigines adapted well to their harsh environment, flourishing for millennia from hunting and gathering. And various Austronesian peoples, particularly the Polynesians, made spectacular migrations into the vast Pacific Ocean by using remarkable seagoing technologies and adapting to diverse island environments.

KEY TERMS

Meroitic (p. 187)
Coptic Church (p. 189)
Aksum (p. 189)
Geez (p. 190)
Ghana (p. 192)
Mande (p. 192)
griots (p. 193)
Nilotes (p. 193)
Maya (p. 194)
Teotihuacan (p. 198)
Moche (p. 198)
dreamtime (p. 203)

HISTORICAL CONTROVERSY

The Afrocentric Challenge to Historians of Antiquity

For many years the writings by Western scholars about world history emphasized Europe, a biased perspective known as Eurocentrism. In the conventional story line, history began in Egypt, Mesopotamia, and Palestine before moving to Greece and Rome and then on to northwestern Europe and eventually to North America. The rest of the world, except perhaps for India and China, constituted an exotic aside to the European mainstream. The academic fields of classics (the study of the Greco-Roman world) and Egyptology specialized in the ancient Mediterranean world, mostly excluding the rest of Africa and Asia. Before the 1970s most Western historians either ignored Africa or argued that Africa was unimportant throughout world history.

The Problem

Today a historical perspective incorporating Africa is common, but for much of the twentieth century many scholars agreed with an eminent British historian, who wrote in 1928 that Africa had no history and that most Africans had stayed stagnant and sunk in barbarism for many centuries. In reacting to racial discrimination and lingering contempt for Africa's historical legacy, many historians have made a convincing case for the importance of Africa and its critical role in world history. But questions remain. Was Africa a key part of the larger ancient and Classical world? Was Egypt essentially an African or a Mediterranean society? Finally, did Egypt strongly influence Classical Greece?

Alinari/Art Resource, NY

ATHENA, GREEK GODDESS OF WISDOM Some scholars suspect that some Greek deities, such as Athena, portrayed here in a Greek sculpture, were based on Egyptian deities.

The Debate

In dramatic contrast to Eurocentrism, an alternative approach known as Afrocentrism emphasizes Africa's, rather than Europe's, centrality in history. The more radical Afrocentrists provide a mirror image to the Eurocentric model, dismissing the older history as a lie designed to glorify European culture and perpetuate the power of white people. They assert that Africa was the fountainhead of Mediterranean culture and that a new way of understanding world history must be developed. Afrocentrists like the Senegalese Cheikh Anta Diop and the American Molefe Asante argue that black Africans, including Egyptians, originated and developed many of the arts, philosophies, and technologies of the ancient and Classical Mediterranean societies.

Critics accuse the radical Afrocentrists, like the rigid Eurocentrists, of exaggeration and selectivity in their use of historical evidence, charging that they rely on largely outdated and discredited sources. Some Afrocentrists, for example, offer unsubstantiated theories that Egyptian queen Cleopatra (a Hellenistic Greek) and Athenian philosopher Socrates were black, or that African mariners established the Olmec society of Mexico. British scholar Stephen Howe even asserts that Afrocentric writings replace outmoded Eurocentric scholarship with a misleading version that offers a fictional history.

One prong of the debate is whether ancient Egypt should be seen as essentially Mediterranean or as an African society rooted in African traditions. Most scholars now acknowledge extensive Egyptian connections to Africa, western Asia, and southeastern Europe. African ties were certainly extensive. The ancient Egyptian language was closely related to many African tongues. Historians of Africa believe that many ideas Egyptians shared with African peoples diffused to Egypt from the south, including the notion and rituals of divine kingship that underpinned Egyptian royalty, various myths and gods, and much material culture. But Egypt's connections were diverse. Populated by migrants from all directions, Egypt produced people of many skin colors and physical features. As a trade crossroads, it maintained trade relations with Africans, Asians, and Europeans. People moved around and intermarried. Thus the Nile Valley was a zone of contact between many groups; considerable mingling of people occurred and, with that, creative cultural borrowing and invention, making it difficult to precisely identify foreign influences on Egyptian culture.

Another controversy concerns whether Egypt spread African ideas and influences to the Greek culture emerging across the Mediterranean. In his three-volume study, *Black Athena*, the British-born, U.S.-based scholar Martin Bernal

(Continued)

contended that, until the early nineteenth century, Western historians stressed the Afro-Asiatic origins of Greek culture, acknowledging Egypt and Phoenicia as core influences. Then, he argued, because of increasing racism toward black people and rising European imperialism and nationalism, Western scholars began to stress the Greeks as being a creative source of culture rather than derivative—the pure and original source of European society. African and Middle East influences, such as those from Egypt and Phoenicia, were removed from the scenario.

To support his point, Bernal used the myths and historical writings of the Greeks themselves, including, for example, the claims by Greek historian Herodotus that Egyptians invented mathematics and that the names of Greek gods originated in Egypt. Herodotus spent time in Egypt around 450 B.C.E. and admired the Egyptian heritage. Influenced by his views, Bernal agrees with Diop that a significant proportion of Greek religion, political philosophy, architecture, science, and even language was imported from Phoenicia and Egypt. For example, Bernal suggests that Athena, the Greek goddess of wisdom and patron goddess of Athens, was a transplanted version of Neith, a goddess from the Nile Delta.

Bernal's work provoked a storm of controversy. Critics accuse Bernal of misreading Greek myths and historical accounts. They suggest that the Greeks credited Egypt with these accomplishments because they wanted to legitimize their own position by connecting with the older and much respected Egyptian culture. Furthermore, as most historians are aware, Herodotus often exaggerated or relied on unreliable hearsay, and so is not always a convincing source. Reliance on Herodotus, critics charge, led Bernal to unsubstantiated links, such as one tracing the origins of Greek philosophy to Egyptian literature on wisdom, despite many differences. In one of the stronger critiques, Mary Lefkowitz links Bernal to radical Afrocentrism (an approach he criticizes), deploring his scholarship for disputing that the Greeks invented democracy, philosophy, and science.

In this debate, few classicists disagree that the Greeks admired the Egyptians and traded with them extensively. Some leading Greek thinkers, including Herodotus, Solon, Plato, Thales, and Euclid, visited or studied in Egypt. But, like Lefkowitz, many classicists believe that Bernal greatly overstates Afro-Asian influence, underestimates Greek genius, and misuses linguistic and archaeological evidence. At the same time, however, many other scholars defend Bernal or praise him for stimulating needed debate. Some, including the Africanist Basil Davidson and the classicist Jacques Berlinblau, take a middle view on Bernal's work. And the controversy has also inspired more studies placing Egypt and Africa in a larger regional or world context, such as those by Schofield and Davies and by Gilbert and Reynolds.

Evaluating the Debate

Both sides of the debate have been accused of having a political agenda: to influence how the histories of Europe and Africa are taught in North American and European schools. Hence, the controversy illustrates the danger of what historians call "present-mindedness," the tendency to interpret the past largely in light of present social and political concerns. While we can never entirely escape this tendency, we can try to see the people of the past as they saw themselves. This means not using their experiences as ammunition in current social and political debates. Since the issues of how much Egypt contributed to Greece and how much it reflected or stimulated sub-Saharan African cultures are legitimate subjects for historical investigation, the debates will continue.

THINKING ABOUT THE CONTROVERSY

1. What is the Afrocentric criticism of Eurocentrism?
2. What is the classicists' criticism of Afrocentrism?
3. What are the insights and problems of Bernal's Black Athena?

Exploring the Controversy

Afrocentric history was pioneered by Cheikh Anta Diop in *Civilization or Barbarism: An Authentic Anthropology* (Brooklyn: Lawrence Hill, 1991) and *The African Origin of Civilization: Myth or Reality* (New York: Lawrence Hill, 1974). A more radical approach can be found in Molefe Asante's *Afrocentricity* (Trenton: Africa World Press, 1988) and *The Afrocentric Idea* (Philadelphia: Temple University Press, 1987). The most significant scholarly challenge to the views of mainstream classicists can be found in Martin Bernal, *Black Athena: The Afroasiatic Roots of Classical Civilization*, 3 vols. (New Brunswick, NJ: Rutgers University Press, 1987, 1991, 2001). Bernal responds to his critics in *Black Athena Writes Back* (Durham, NC: Duke University Press, 2001). The major rebuttals to Bernal and Afrocentrism include Stephen Howe, *Afrocentrism: Mystical Pasts and Imagined Homes* (London: Verso, 1998); Mary Lefkowitz, *Not Out of Africa: How Afrocentrism Became an Excuse to Teach Myth as History* (New York: Basic Books, 1996); and Mary Lefkowitz and Guy MacLean, eds., *Black Athena Revisited* (Chapel Hill: University of North Carolina Press, 1996).

For thoughtful discussions of the Afrocentrist controversy, see Basil Davidson, *The Search for Africa: History, Culture, Politics* (New York: Times Books, 1994); and Jacques Berlinblau, *Heresy in the University: The "Black Athena" Controversy and the Responsibility of American Intellectuals* (New Brunswick, NJ: Rutgers University Press, 1999). Useful studies of Egypt and Africa in world history include Louise Schofield and W. Vivian Davies, eds., *Egypt, the Aegean and the Levant: Interconnections in the Second Millennium* (London: Trustees of the British Museum, 1995); and Erik Gilbert and Jonathan T. Reynolds, *Africa in World History: From Prehistory to the Present*, 3rd ed. (Upper Saddle River, NJ: Prentice-Hall, 2011).

SOCIETIES NETWORKS TRANSITIONS

PART III

Encounters and Transformations in the Intermediate Era, ca. 600–1500

CHAPTER OUTLINE

Scholars often refer to the time frame from 600 to 1500 as the medieval period, or "middle ages." The term *medieval* suggests societies with relatively weak governments, rigid social orders, and one dominating religion, a description that best fits Europe in this era and perhaps Japan and parts of India. However, the term has little relevance for China, the Islamic states, and most of Africa, Southeast Asia, and the Americas. *Intermediate Era* is a more neutral term to describe this creative period, which saw worldwide innovations, the emergence of new trade networks, and vigorous new cosmopolitan societies. The Intermediate Era differed from preceding eras by virtue of the increasing contacts between peoples. Today the term *globalization* refers to the increasing interconnectedness of peoples around the world through international trade, investment, ideas, popular culture, and travel. This part examines some early forms of globalization during the Intermediate Era, such as the spread of world religions and the social changes they fostered, long-distance trade, the spread of disease, and the connections sparked by the major transitions of the Mongol expansion, climate change, and, in the Late Intermediate Era, the acceleration of maritime exploration.

Networks
The Spread of Universal Religions

Thanks to the expansion of universal religions over the networks of exchange, by 1500 the religious map of the Eastern Hemisphere looked very different than it had in 600. The power and reach of universal, or world, religions such as Buddhism, Christianity, and Islam increased markedly during the Intermediate Era, as millions of people embraced ideas, beliefs, and ways of life vastly different from those of their ancestors. Islam became the most widespread religion, rapidly expanding through Western Asia and North Africa, eventually claiming Central Asia and parts of Europe, and finally gaining large followings in West Africa, the East African coast, South Asia, China, and Southeast Asia.

Older faiths also spread in this era. Theravada Buddhism became established in Sri Lanka and then expanded into mainland Southeast Asia, where it gradually displaced earlier faiths and reshaped cultures. Mahayana Buddhism became entrenched in Japan, Korea, Vietnam, Mongolia, and Tibet. Buddhist networks fostered the movement of pilgrims, such as the seventh-century Chinese monk Xuan Zang (swan tsang), who sojourned in India for several decades. By 1200 Christianity had also expanded to encompass nearly all of Europe in its fold, filtering north into the Germanic and Celtic lands and east among the Slavs. Eventually the Roman Catholic Church dominated the west while the Orthodox Church claimed Russia and much of eastern Europe. Although Christianity was pushed back by Islam in western Asia and North Africa, sizable Christian communities grew and sometimes flourished in these regions.

Universal religions generally promoted moral and ethical values that helped preserve harmony in societies that were increasingly cosmopolitan. The Christian injunction to "love thy neighbor as thyself," the Buddhist emphasis on good thoughts and actions, and the Muslim ideals of social justice and the equality of believers fostered goodwill and cooperation. Nonetheless, chronic tensions arose between Christian Europe and the Islamic world, derived from political and economic conflicts as well as a clash between the strong missionary impulses of both religions. Christians and Muslims often viewed each other as barbarians. A tenth-century Arab geographer argued after visiting Europe that the manners of Christian Europeans "are harsh, their understanding dull and their tongues heavy. Those of them who are furthest to the north are the most subject to stupidity, grossness and brutishness."[1] Tensions between the two rival faiths generated the European Crusades to regain the Holy Land, which left a legacy of bitterness on both sides.

A commonality shared by all religions was a reverence for learning, as the spread of world religions facilitated access to knowledge through the creation of libraries and various centers of scholarship. The House of Wisdom in Abbasid-ruled Baghdad attracted scholars from all over the Islamic world and beyond. Some Buddhist centers of higher education, such as the university at Nalanda in India and the monasteries in Sumatra, attracted students from all over Asia. In Europe, various Christian orders and thinkers encouraged the preservation of knowledge, laying the foundation for universities, such as Paris and Oxford, and spurring philosophical speculation. Eventually the European universities broadened their studies, mixing theology with secular subjects such as science and logic. But under religious influence, many societies became more patriarchal and less tolerant of lifestyles that strayed from what religious teachings deemed appropriate.

Societies
Gender Roles and Family Patterns

The expansion of universal religions, combined with increasing trade, influenced many aspects of social life, thought, and attitudes. While the status of women varied around the world, most religions had patriarchal structures. Islam incorporated many Arab and Persian customs that constrained women, including those that prescribed female seclusion and modesty. However, Islamic patriarchy was modified where pre-Islamic cultures had less rigid gender roles, as in Spain, Southeast Asia, and West Africa. The pious Arab traveler Ibn Battuta, for example, was astonished that, in his view, the Mali women wore much too revealing clothing and seemed to have a higher status than the men. Most Christian thinkers believed that women belonged in the home. A fifteenth-century Italian warned that "it would hardly win us [men] respect if our wife busied herself among the men in the marketplace. It also seems somewhat demeaning to me to remain shut up in the house among women when I have manly things to do among men."[2]

As Confucianism dug deeper roots in East Asia, patriarchy became a stronger force there. By the 1400s it was more common to seclude upper-class Chinese women, and even bind their feet. Japanese society also became more patriarchal, as the warrior culture replaced the aristocratic system in which elite women had flourished. But some Mahayana Buddhists favored gender equity, at least in principle. The Japanese Zen master Dogen **(DOE-joan)** argued that there was nothing special about masculinity: "The elements that make up the human body are the same for a man as for a woman. You should not waste your time in futile discussion of the superiority of one sex over another."[3] In Southeast Asia, Theravada Buddhism proved a generally moderating force in gender relations, although men had more opportunity than women to acquire the merit needed to reach nirvana because only men could become monks.

Religious values shaped public roles, family patterns, and sexual attitudes. In societies as different as Byzantium, Carolingian France, West Africa, Southeast Asia, and the Inca Empire, individual women could still gain power as queens or as powers behind the throne. But in most societies, religious hierarchies, military organizations, and schools remained mostly male, with priesthoods, warfare, and literacy giving men more access to prestige and resources. Islam allowed men to have four wives, but polygamy for some men meant that women were unavailable to others. While Christian teachings favored monogamy and marriage, many men and women joined clerical orders or for other reasons never married. And in Europe and many societies around the world, men of elite status, such as kings, had multiple wives and concubines. Only a minority of western Europeans, mostly middle class, lived in nuclear families like those common today in the West, and only a few societies allowed women to have more than one husband.

Attitudes toward homosexuality and gender identity varied widely. Followers of Christianity, Judaism, Islam, and Confucianism all shared an aversion to homosexual relations, in part because they did not produce children. But this sexual behavior had long been practiced and even sometimes tolerated in these traditions. Christian tolerance turned to fierce repression only in the thirteenth century, and such repression was not a global pattern. Perhaps because there were many unmarried Muslim men and rigid segregation of the sexes, some Islamic societies ignored homosexual activity. The Japanese, Chinese, and some Southeast Asian and Native American societies also tended to accept homosexuality as part of life. Gender categories could be flexible. Some Asian and American tribal peoples identified more than two genders, including homosexual or heterosexual men who lived as women and served the village as shamans.

Societies
Slavery and Feudalism

Most societies were hierarchical, and, whatever the predominant political and social system, many people lived in slavery or faced severe restrictions on their freedom. Sanctioned by various religions or simply by custom or economic necessity, slavery had long been common throughout the world and remained so in the Intermediate Era, except for East Asia, where it largely died out by 1000. Islam permitted slavery but encouraged owners to treat slaves well. In Arab, Persian, and Turkish societies, the availability of slaves to do the physical work made the seclusion of elite women

[1]Quoted in Peter N. Stearns, *Western Civilization in World History* (New York: Routledge, 2003), 52.

[2]Leon Batista Alberti, quoted in Jeremy Brotton, *The Renaissance Bazaar: From the Silk Road to Michaelangelo* (London: Oxford University Press, 2002), 73–74.

[3]Quoted in Peter N. Stearns, *Gender in World History* (New York: Routledge, 2000), 52.

WORLD RELIGIONS AND TRADE ROUTES, 600–1500 Much of the Eastern Hemisphere was linked by land and maritime trade routes. Along with goods and travelers, Buddhism, Christianity, and Islam spread along these trade routes, attracting believers from many societies.

SILK ROAD TRAVELERS The Silk Road remained a key trade route during this era. This painting, from a fourteenth-century atlas made in Spain, shows one of the horse and camel caravans that traveled between China and Central Asia.

bpk, Berlin/(name of museum)/(name of photographer)/Art Resource, NY

possible. Many African societies, whether Muslim or non-Muslim, had slaves, including the West African kingdoms and East African city-states. Africans had been shipped north to Arab and Persian societies for centuries. Slaves were also common in Southeast Asian societies such as Angkor and Siam. In the Americas, various peoples, among them the Maya and Aztecs, enslaved prisoners of war, debtors, and criminals. After the end of the Roman Empire, slavery declined in Europe and was gradually replaced by serfdom, a less restrictive form of bondage, but the slave market did not end. Some slaves still labored in parts of western Europe, sometimes even on lands of Christian monasteries, and an active Mediterranean slave trade shipped Slavs, Greeks, and Turks from the Black Sea region to southern Europe and North Africa. Some northwestern Europeans were also sold as slaves to Mediterranean societies. Eventually Africans appeared in southern European slave markets.

In most feudal societies, political, military, and religious elites lived off wealth from the primary producers, such as peasants, herders, and artisans. Relations between people of different status, especially between lords and vassals, were prescribed by agreements or law, and governments were weak or decentralized. The feudal model, which included lords and knights, independent manors, serfdom, small states, and chronic warfare, was best represented by some medieval western European societies between 800 and 1300. In medieval Europe the dominant Christian church encouraged people who wanted to reap rewards in Heaven to accept the social order. Some historians also apply feudalism to Japan under the warrior class, and others to parts of India and Southeast Asia, where many small states competed for power. In both western Europe and Japan, feudalism established a basis for future change by building up intense pressures that eventually erupted. Many societies were not feudal, however. Large centralized states such as Song dynasty China, Abbasid Iraq, Mali, or the Inca Empire employed a system whereby emperors or kings exercised great power over the population through bureaucracies.

Networks
Long Distance Trade

Long-distance trade had long linked faraway societies, most commonly by land. Since 200 B.C.E. the Silk Road had allowed trade goods, ideas, religions, technologies, and people to move between China and the Mediterranean basin. Trade routes also connected West Africa and the Mediterranean across the Sahara Desert, and peoples in the Americas traded goods over long distances. The Mongol conquests had fostered extensive trade, but with the Mongol Empire's demise and the security of Silk Road travel reduced, maritime trade became more crucial and naval technology improved considerably. By 1000 an increasingly lucrative maritime trade had grown in the Eastern Hemisphere, despite the dangers from pirates and storms. Much trade crisscrossed the Mediterranean, with Venice, Genoa, Constantinople, Aleppo in Syria, Alexandria, and Algiers serving as major ports. Sailing networks along Europe's Atlantic coast later linked the Baltic and North Seas to Mediterranean ports.

Farther east, the Indian Ocean routes became the heart of the most extensive maritime trade network, a "maritime Silk Road", involving the world's most populous societies and linking China, Japan, Vietnam, and Cambodia in the east through Malaya, Indonesia, India, and Sri Lanka to Persia, Arabia, Russia, the eastern Mediterranean, and the East African coast. Over these routes the spices of Indonesia, the gold and tin of Malaya, the textiles, sugar, and cotton of India, the cinnamon of Sri Lanka, the gold and ivory of East Africa, the coffee of Arabia, the carpets of Persia, and the silks, porcelain, and tea of China moved to distant markets. Europe proved a huge market for Asian spices.

An English book from the early 1400s reported the popularity of black pepper, which helped disguise the bad taste of heavily salted preserved meat during the long European winter: "Pepper is black and has a good smack, And every man doth it buy."[4] The Indian Ocean network's trade dynamism depended on cosmopolitan port cities, especially hubs such as Hormuz (Persia), Kilwa (Tanzania), Cambay (northwest India), Calicut (southwest India), Melaka (Malaya), and Quanzhou **(chwan-cho)** (southern China), which all became vibrant centers of international commerce and culture drawing populations from various societies.

The hemispheric trade system that eventually developed was primarily fueled by China and India, the great centers of world manufacturing in this era (see Historical Controversy: Eastern Predominance in the Intermediate World). Together China and India probably produced over three-quarters of all world industrial products before 1500. China exported iron, steel, silk, refined sugar, and ceramics, while India was the great producer of textiles. Their industrial products might be transported thousands of miles. Hence, the work of a cotton weaver in India might be sold in China or East Africa, and Chinese ceramics might reach Zimbabwe and Mali. The Muslim soldiers who resisted the Christian crusaders in the Middle East used steel swords smelted in India from East African iron. Merchants from all over Afro-Eurasia—Arabs, Armenians, Chinese, Indians, Indonesians, Jews, Venetians, Genoese—traveled great distances in search of profits, fostering numerous networks and often forming permanent trade diasporas. Hence, one Cairo-based Jewish family had branches in India, Persia, and Tunisia. The fame of Melaka, Calicut, Hormuz, and other Asian ports as commercial hubs for valuable goods reached Europe, and by the late fourteenth century some European merchants and monarchs were beginning to dream of a sea route to the East that would enable them to trade directly with China and the Indies. This dream would lead to maritime exploration in the 1400s.

Transitions
The Mongol Empire

Perhaps the greatest transition of the era was fostered by the Mongols, pastoralists and tough steppe herders of horses and camels who brutally conquered the largest land empire in world history, stretching from the western shores of the Black Sea east to China and Korea. Genghis Khan (ca. 1162–1227) was a visionary leader who effectively united the Mongol tribes. His mounted, well-armed warriors, aided by siege weaponry and innovative military strategies of rapid attack, made a formidable fighting force. Within the span of a century, approximately 1250 to 1350, the Mongol armies, supported by a Mongol population of less than 2 million, swept out of their arid Central Asian grasslands to put over 200 million people under their control. Competition for limited resources caused by ecological instability, climate change, or population growth may have prompted the Mongols to undertake their conquests. Whatever the reasons, the Mongol expansion, which united a large chunk of the Eurasian population and indirectly affected millions of other people, was one of the most crucial developments in world history. Mongol armies conquered Central Asia, Tibet, Russia, part of eastern Europe, Afghanistan, Persia, Iraq, Anatolia, and later China and Korea. The Mongols were at the Danube, preparing to sweep through Hungary into western Europe, when Genghis Khan's successor, died, aborting that thrust. Thus western Europe did not suffer the ravages experienced by other peoples and eventually benefited from the Mongols, who thus served as great equalizers.

Some world historians consider Genghis Khan the most crucial figure of the second millennium C.E. because, despite his brutality, the Mongol conquests he led established an early form of globalized communication characterized by technology and product transfer moving chiefly from east to west along the Silk Road. During the Mongol era Chinese inventions such as the spinning wheel, medical discoveries, and domesticated fruits and plants such as the orange and lemon reached Europe and the Middle East. The Mongols also unwittingly set in motion changes that allowed Europeans to acquire and improve Chinese technologies such as printing, gunpowder, and the magnetic compass while developing new inventions of their own. These Chinese inventions had a major impact in Europe. In the seventeenth century the English philosopher Francis Bacon noted that Chinese printing, gunpowder, and the magnet "changed the whole face and state of things" in European literature, warfare, and navigation.[5] As Europeans improved Chinese weapons such as flamethrowers and primitive guns, late medieval warfare became far deadlier, while gunpowder and Chinese military technology, coming by routes opened by the Mongols, also helped reshape Middle Eastern politics and fostered the rise of the Ottoman Empire.

During Mongol times many men of talent moved from west to east, as travel from one end of Eurasia to the other became easier than ever before, fostering greater hemispheric connections. In China the Mongols relied administratively on a large number of foreigners who came to serve in the civil service. These included many Muslims from West and Central Asia and a few Europeans such as the Italian Marco Polo who found their way to the fabled land the Europeans called Cathay. Polo's reports on his travels increased European interest in Asia and inspired later explorers, such as Christopher Columbus, to seek a sea route to East Asia. People moved the other way too. A Chinese Nestorian Christian monk of Turkish ancestry, Rabban Sauma, even visited Rome, France, and England in 1287 as a diplomat for the Mongol ruler of Persia, the first known visitor to western Europe from East Asia and an early example of politics on a hemispheric scale. By reopening Central Asian trade routes closed by political turmoil and by connecting with many different

[4]Quoted in M. N. Pearson, "Introduction," in *Spices in the Indian Ocean World*, ed. M. N. Pearson (Aldershot, United Kingdom: Valorium, 1996), xv.

[5]Quoted in L. S. Stavrianos, *Lifelines from Our Past: A New World History*, rev. ed. (Armonk, NY: M.E. Sharpe, 1997), 58.

CATAPULTS The Mongols used advanced military technology, including catapults, to conquer cities. This battle scene, painted by a Persian artist, shows the Mongols attacking a city around 1300.

Ms Or 20 f.124v Mahmud ibn Sebuktegin attacks the rebel fortress of Zarang in Sijistan in 1003, miniature from the 'Jami' al-Tawarikh' of Rashid al-Din, c.1307 (vellum), Islamic School, (14th century)/Edinburgh University Library, Scotland/With kind permission of the University of Edinburgh/The Bridgeman Art Library

countries, the Mongols fostered communication networks and the transfer of technology between once remote parts of the Eastern Hemisphere. In doing so, they were major catalysts of change, laying a foundation for the gradual transition from the Intermediate to the Early Modern Era.

Transitions
Consequences of Disease in an Increasingly Global World

The worst disease pandemic in world history, known in the West as the Black Death, capitalized on the expanding trade networks and disrupted the complex system of interregional trade and communication that had flourished around Eurasia in the thirteenth and fourteenth centuries, causing unexpected economic and political transitions. In its wake agricultural and industrial production declined and financial crises and labor shortages wrecked economies from China to France. The pandemic also helped undermine Mongol rule in East Asia and the Middle East, in part because of huge population losses. Ironically, it may have resulted from the Mongol conquests, in particular the greater contact they brought between Eurasian societies. Climate change may also have been a factor. Eurasia was unusually wet during the 1300s, perhaps increasing the number of fleas and rats, through which the disease was thought to be spread.

The Black Death, which most scholars think was chiefly caused by bubonic plague, apparently originated in China or Central Asia, where it killed millions. An increasingly complex system of global networks contributed to its spread. By the mid-1300s it had been carried by merchants and soldiers along the Silk Road to southern Russia. Ships leaving the Genoese trading colony at Calfa, on the Crimean peninsula at the north end of the Black Sea, carried it unwittingly to the Middle East and Europe, where it raged through cities and towns. In the affected societies, from China to Egypt to England and even to fishing villages in remote Greenland, perhaps a third of the total population died in the first outbreak, the higher mortality being in congested cities. Surveying the damage, the Italian writer Petrarch wrote that future generations would be "incredulous, unable to imagine the empty houses, abandoned towns, the squalid countryside, the fields littered with dead, the dreadful silent solitude which seemed to hang over the whole world. Physicians were useless, philosophers could only shrug their shoulders and look wise."[6] Millions more died as the pandemic reappeared in intervals in western Eurasia over the next century.

[6]Quoted in Frederick F. Cartwright, *Disease and History: The Influence of Disease in Shaping the Great Events of History* (New York: Thomas Y. Crowell, 1972), 37.

When the Black Death came to an end, a spurt of growth saw population levels soar from East Asia to Europe, which may have encouraged overseas explorations in search of resources. By 1500 the world population had reached between 400 million and 600 million people, about twice the population of 1000. China accounted for a fourth of the total, and India for at least a fifth. Europe, including Russia, grew rapidly to 70–95 million. In contrast, unaffected by the Black Death, sub-Saharan Africa and the Americas each probably had 60 to 80 million people by 1500.

Transitions
Consequences of Climate Change

Climate change has helped shape, and sometimes destroy, societies since the dawn of humankind. It spurred the transition to farming in western Asia 10,000 years ago, undermined the Mesopotamian and Indus societies 4,000 years ago, and hastened the decline of the Chinese Han and Roman Empires around 200 C.E. Eurasian weather became more erratic during the 1200s, and the fluctuations may have helped prompt the Mongol expansion by bringing drought to the grasslands. In South Americas, climate change probably contributed to the collapse of various societies, including Tiwanaku, Moche, Teotihuacan, and the southern Maya. In North America great droughts in the 1200s may have fostered decline in the Mississippi Basin societies and caused the dispersal of the Pueblo peoples of the southwestern deserts, who responded to hard times by migrating in search of wetter lands, as they said in their songs and poems: "Survival, I know this way. It rains. Mountains and canyons and plants grow. We traveled this way."[7]

Around 1300 an unusually warm period gave way to much cooler weather that lasted until 1850, sparking what scientists call the "Little Ice Age," with serious results for societies. Whatever the causes, which are still debated, longer and more frigid winters periodically affected Europe, North America, Central Asia, and China. Bitter cold drove the Norse Vikings out of Greenland, and Icelandic farming floundered. Severe storms and flooding in Europe were followed by drought and crop failures, causing widespread famine. As rivers and canals froze, boat traffic was inhibited. Between 1315 and 1317 perhaps 15 percent of Europe's population starved to death, and malnutrition made northern Europeans and Chinese less resistant to the Black Death. In addition, rainfall declined in India and Africa, drying up many lakes. The North Atlantic climate became even colder from the mid-1600s to mid-1700s, and such discomfort may have inspired some adventurous Europeans to seek greener pastures abroad, in the Americas.

Transitions
Overseas Explorations

The forces of the era, including long-distance trade, the Mongol expansion, and climate change, fostered another great transition, the great voyages of discovery. By the early 1400s the Chinese had the most advanced ships and navigational techniques. Anxious to reassert their regional influence after overthrowing the Mongol rulers, they took the initiative of exploration, dispatching unprecedented voyages of discovery. In a series of expeditions in the early 1400s, huge Chinese ships followed long-established maritime networks as far as East Africa and Arabia, reflecting the crucial role played by Afro-Eurasian maritime commerce. However, this Chinese thrust did not have lasting effects on the world. Although they had the naval capability, the Chinese, unlike the Europeans, lacked the economic incentive and religious zeal to sail around Africa in search of Europe.

The Portuguese and then the Spanish, both peoples with long maritime traditions and coastal locations, used Chinese, Arab, and European naval technology to construct ships and equip crews for successful long-distance voyages. In search of gold, spices, slaves, and other resources, Portuguese ships sailed south to West and Central Africa, where they established outposts and eventually colonies. By the end of the fifteenth century the Portuguese had rounded the Cape of Good Hope to reach the Indian Ocean, the East African trading ports, and finally India. The Portuguese were not the only Europeans dazzled by Asian wealth. A historian in the early 1500s reported on another mariner and his ambitions:

> *Christopher Columbus, a Genoese, proposed to the Catholic King and Queen [of Spain] to discover the islands which touch the Indies. He asked for ships, promising not only to propagate the Christian religion, but also certainly to bring back pearls, spices and gold beyond anything imagined.*[8]

The Spanish expedition led by Columbus landed in the Americas in the 1490s. With these new networks of communication between distant societies, the history of the world was profoundly altered. An even more connected world—a great global network—and the Early Modern Era were at hand.

[7]Quoted in Brian Fagan, *The Long Summer: How Climate Changed Civilization* (New York: Basic Books, 2004), 224.

[8]Peter Martyr, quoted in Jack Turner, *Spice: The History of a Temptation* (New York: Vintage, 2004), xi.

10 The Rise, Power, and Connections of the Islamic World, 600–1500

Apic/Hulton Archive/Getty Images

PILGRIMAGE CARAVAN Every year caravans of Muslim pilgrims converged on Islam's holiest city, Mecca, in Arabia. This painting shows such a caravan led by a band. In this era pilgrims came from as far away as Morocco and Spain in the west and Indonesia and China in the east.

Then came Islam. All institutions underwent change. It distinguished [believers] from other nations and ennobled them. Islam became firmly established and securely rooted. Far-off nations accepted Islam.

—Ibn Khaldun, fourteenth-century Arab historian[1]

In 1382 the fifty-year-old Arab scholar Abd al-Rahman Ibn Khaldun **(AHB-d al-ruh-MAHN ib-uhn kal-DOON)** left his longtime home in Tunis in North Africa and moved east to Egypt. He was already well-traveled and renowned as a thinker; his work, like his life, reflected the expansive Islamic society's cosmopolitan nature, crossing many geographical and cultural borders. He had recently completed his greatest work, a monumental history of the world known to educated Muslims and the first attempt by a historian anywhere to discover and explain changes in societies over time. Rational, analytical, and encyclopedic in coverage, it also offered a philosophy of history rooted in the scientific method.

With roots in Arabia, Ibn Khaldun's family later migrated to Spain and several generations later to Tunis. Ibn Khaldun visited and worked in various cities of North Africa and Spain, serving diverse rulers as a jurist, adviser, or diplomat. He then settled in Cairo, Egypt, a city he praised as the "metropolis of the world, garden of the universe, meeting-place of nations, ant hill of peoples, high place of Islam, seat of power."[2] There he served as a judge and a teacher, wrote voluminously, and traveled with high Egyptian officials to Palestine, Syria, and Arabia. Six centuries after his family left Arabia for the western Mediterranean, he could feel at home in their ancestral homeland. The Islamic world he chronicled enjoyed an extraordinary unity of time and space.

The rise of Islam that produced Ibn Khaldun was a major historical turning point that led to widespread social, cultural, and political changes over the centuries. Islamic expansion launched a thousand-year era, from the seventh to the seventeenth century, that brought many Afro-Eurasian peoples into closer contact with one another and allowed for a mixing of cultures within an Islamic framework. The religion originated in seventh-century Arabia and eventually spread across several continents. Today Islam is, after Christianity, the world's largest religion, embraced by about one-fifth of humanity. A dynamic faith in dialogue with, and often tolerant toward, other traditions, Islam adapted to new cultures while remaining close to its founding ideals. For nearly a thousand years Islamic peoples greatly influenced or dominated much of the Eastern Hemisphere. During this period, Muslim thinkers salvaged or developed major portions of the science and mathematics that shaped later industrial society, while Muslim sailors and merchants opened or extended networks that spread goods, technologies, and ideas throughout Afro-Eurasia.

[1]From *The Muqaddimah: An Introduction to History*, translated by Franz Rosenthal and edited by N. J. Dawood (Princeton: Princeton University Press, 1967), 25–27.

[2]Quoted in Albert Hourani, *A History of the Arab Peoples* (Cambridge: Belknap Press, 1991), 3.

IN THIS CHAPTER

Early Islam: The Origins and Spread of a Continuous Tradition

How did Islam arise and spread?

The Islamic religion was founded in the Arabian peninsula, a parched land inhabited mainly by nomads living on the fringes of more powerful societies. The visions of one man, Muhammad **(moo-HAM-mad)**, inspired this fervently monotheistic faith influenced by Jewish and Christian thought. Islam's explosive energies propelled it from a small Arab sect into the dominant faith of many millions from one end of the Eastern Hemisphere to the other. Within 130 years of Islam's birth, Arab armies and navies had conquered lands from Spain to Persia, and in the following years Islam took root in India, Central Asia, and China. These conquests and the spread of the new religion dramatically reshaped many societies across the Afro-Eurasian zone. Arab language and culture spread with Islam, providing a new identity for the once diverse Middle Eastern societies.

The Middle Eastern Sources of Islam

In Muhammad's day the Middle East—western Asia and North Africa—enjoyed great cultural diversity, a major factor in Islam's rise. The Byzantine Empire filled the vacuum left by the collapse of Roman control in western Asia and North Africa,

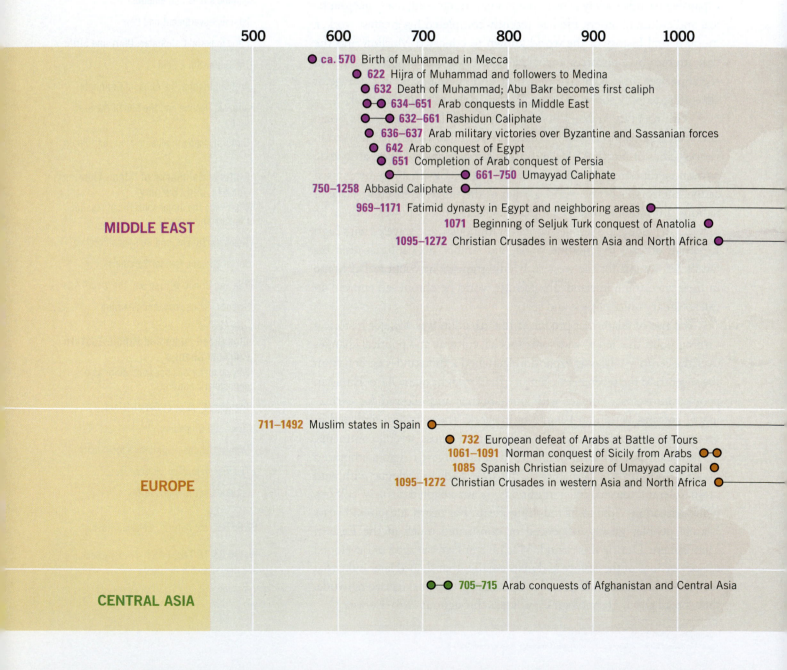

500 600 700 800 900 1000

MIDDLE EAST

- **ca. 570** Birth of Muhammad in Mecca
- **622** Hijra of Muhammad and followers to Medina
- **632** Death of Muhammad; Abu Bakr becomes first caliph
- **634–651** Arab conquests in Middle East
- **632–661** Rashidun Caliphate
- **636–637** Arab military victories over Byzantine and Sassanian forces
- **642** Arab conquest of Egypt
- **651** Completion of Arab conquest of Persia
- **661–750** Umayyad Caliphate
- **750–1258** Abbasid Caliphate
- **969–1171** Fatimid dynasty in Egypt and neighboring areas
- **1071** Beginning of Seljuk Turk conquest of Anatolia
- **1095–1272** Christian Crusades in western Asia and North Africa

EUROPE

- **711–1492** Muslim states in Spain
- **732** European defeat of Arabs at Battle of Tours
- **1061–1091** Norman conquest of Sicily from Arabs
- **1085** Spanish Christian seizure of Umayyad capital
- **1095–1272** Christian Crusades in western Asia and North Africa

CENTRAL ASIA

- **705–715** Arab conquests of Afghanistan and Central Asia

and between 611 and 619 Sassanian Persia conquered Syria, Palestine, and Egypt. The Persians, Byzantines, and Ethiopians all interfered in Arabian politics. Many Middle Eastern people were Christians, including sects such as the Monophysites (among them the Copts of Egypt) and Nestorians, which were considered heretical by Roman Christians. These diverse traditions eventually influenced Islam.

However, Islam was produced by a distinctive Arab society and culture. The Arabs, a Semitic people, occupied a desolate environment where only scattered oases and a few areas of fertile highlands sustained life. Survival in a sparsely populated environment depended on cooperation within families, clans, and tribes. A council of senior males governed each tribe, selecting a supreme elder respected for his generosity and bravery. Some Arabs, like the Nabataeans, became traders who ranged widely in the Middle East; trading cities and farmers flourished in Yemen in the south. But many Arab tribes were tent-dwelling nomadic pastoralists, known as **Bedouins (BED-uh-wuhnz)**, who wandered in search of oases and grazing lands, some raiding trade caravans. Revering poetry, one month a year, Arabs halted raids and battles so that poets could gather and compete. Later Christian crusaders may have taken the Arab romantic poetry tradition to Europe, where it probably influenced the chivalric love songs of medieval European performers known as troubadours.

Diverse religious traditions saturated Arabia, including Judaism, Christianity, and Zoroastrianism. Like Hebrews, Arabs believed they descended from Abraham. While some Arabs

Bedouins Tent-dwelling nomadic Arab pastoralists who wandered in search of oases, grazing lands, or trade caravans to raid.

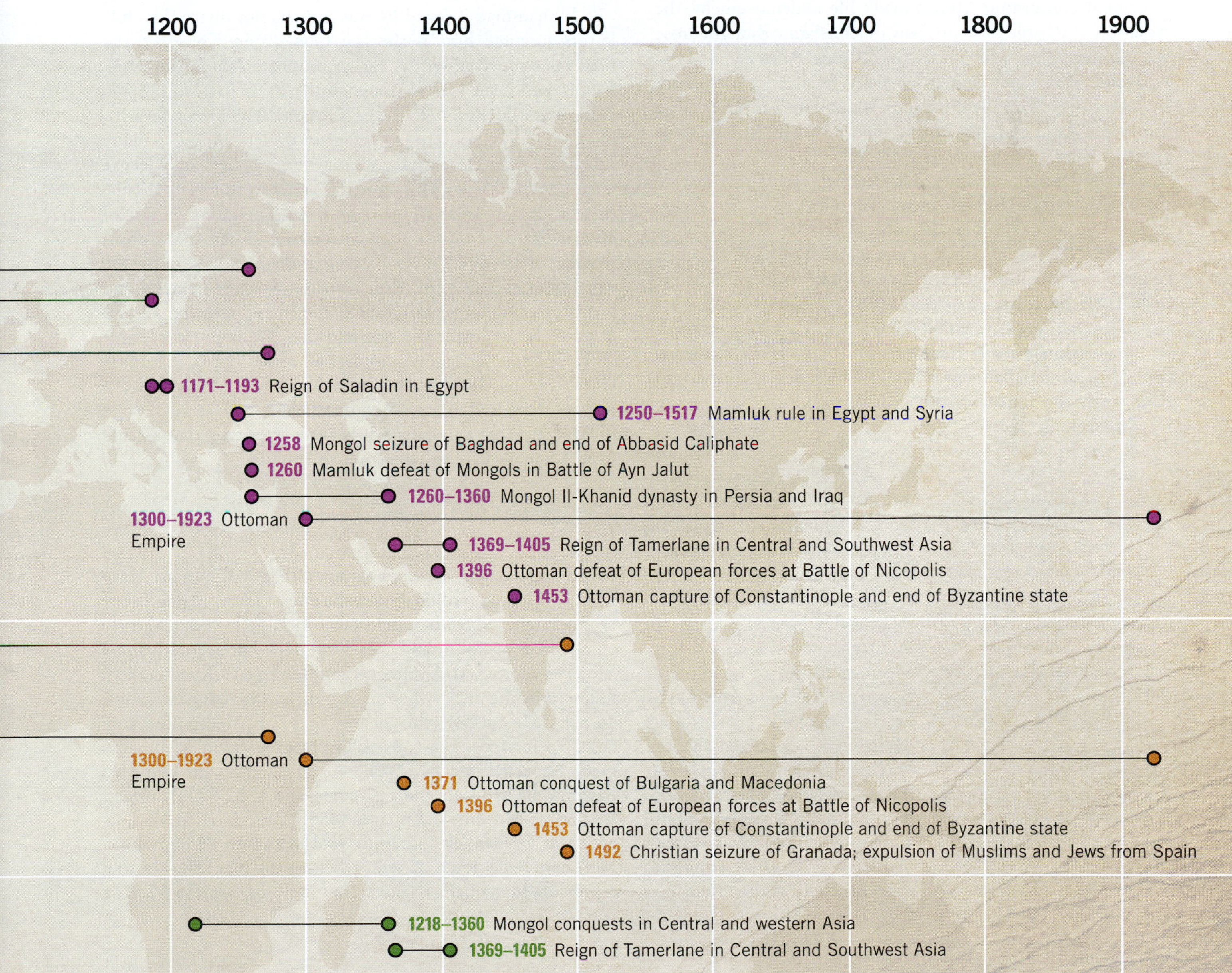

had adopted Judaism or Christianity, most were polytheistic, believing in many gods, goddesses, and spirits. Some tribes believed that the chief god was housed in a huge sacred cube-shaped structure made out of stone, known as the **Ka'ba (KAH-buh)**, in Mecca, a bustling trading city in central Arabia near the Red Sea to which people made annual pilgrimages. Meccan merchants obtained hides, leather goods, spices, and perfumes in Yemen and exchanged them in Syria for textiles, olive oil, and weapons.

The Prophet Muhammad and His Revelations

The founder of Islam was Muhammad Ibn Abdullah (ca. 570–632). Just as scholars debate the historical accuracy of the Hebrew Bible and the Christian gospels, and lack adequate sources for the lives of the Buddha and Confucius, there is disagreement concerning Muhammad's life and movement, the evolution of Islamic precepts, how much Islamic thought arose out of older ideas, and the factors shaping Arab and Islamic expansion. The main sources on early Judaism, Christianity, and Islam were compiled decades, sometimes centuries, after the events described and can be interpreted by historians in different ways.

In traditional accounts, Muhammad was a member of the Hashimite **(HASH-uh-mite)** clan of the prosperous mercantile Quraysh **(KUR-aysh)** tribe of Mecca. Raised by an uncle after his parents died, he became a merchant, shipping goods for a wealthy twice-widowed older woman, Khadija **(kah-DEE-juh)**, who had capitalized on opportunities that city life sometimes gave ambitious women. They soon married. Although Muhammad's trade caravans flourished, he considered Meccan merchants greedy and materialistic, contrary to Arab traditions of generosity.

In seeking answers, Muhammad often meditated in the barren mountains around Mecca. In 610 he had visions in which, he believed, God revealed the secrets of existence. Muhammad reported visitations by an angel bringing God's command to "recite in the name of your lord who created the human."[3] One of his wife's cousins, a monotheist, encouraged him to accept the visions as revelations from God. Fearing demonic possession, Muhammad agonized about the visions, which continued over the next twenty-three years, but he eventually accepted their authenticity largely because of his wife Khadija's support: "She believed in me when no one else did. She considered me to be truthful when the people called me a liar. She helped me with her fortune when the people had left me nothing."[4] Muhammad began preaching the new faith of Islam ("submission to God's will"). The early believers, or Muslims **(MUZ-limz)** ("those who had submitted to God's will"), mostly came from his middle-class friends, relatives, and a few other Meccans, some from lower-class backgrounds. Gradually some rich Quraysh also joined.

Ka'ba A huge sacred cube-shaped stone in the city of Mecca to which people made annual pilgrimages.

Quran ("Recitation") Islam's holiest book; contains the official version of Muhammad's revelations, and to believers is the inspired word of God.

Hadith ("Narrative") The remembered words and deeds of Muhammad, revered by many Muslims as a source of religious guidance and law.

hijra The emigration of Muslims from Mecca to Medina in 622.

In the 650s, several decades after Muhammad's death, followers compiled his revelations into an official version, the **Quran (kuh-RAHN)**, meaning "Recitation." Beloved for its beautiful poetic verses, it became Islam's holy book, to believers the inspired word of God. A second book revered as a source of religious guidance and law, the **Hadith (hah-DEETH)**, meaning "narrative," compiled during the ninth and tenth centuries, collected the remembered words and deeds of Muhammad himself.

Muhammad insisted he was human, not divine. His followers accepted him as the last God-inspired prophet, the final voice superseding the earlier prophets Adam, Abraham, Moses, and Jesus (see Witness to the Past: The Holy Book, God, and the Prophet in the Quran). Muhammad's faith mixed older traditions with new understandings, many principal ideas clearly resembling some beliefs of Mecca's Christians and Jews. Muhammad's views were strictly monotheistic, putting aside all other gods, with believers assured of an afterlife. In contrast to Arab customs, Islam guaranteed women certain rights formerly denied them and promoted the equality of all believers. Muhammad advocated equality and justice, sharing all wealth, living simply, and creating a spirit of unity. Some historians contend that Muhammad's movement was ecumenical, welcoming all monotheists, including Christians and Jews, as "believers," and only after his death became more exclusive, adding new beliefs such as pilgrimage to Mecca; other scholars, while often agreeing that Islam's form gradually evolved, question this thesis.

Emigration and Triumph

Muhammad soon faced challenges that led him to leave Mecca. Mecca's political and business leaders and many Quraysh rejected Muhammad's views and followers as threatening their position, and some enemies harassed Muslims and even plotted Muhammad's murder. In 619 Khadija died, followed by the uncle who raised him, leaving Muhammad in despair. Meanwhile, the nearby city of Medina became engulfed in strife. The contending factions invited Muhammad, respected for his fairness and honesty, to come to Medina and arbitrate their disputes, and in 622 Muhammad led seventy Muslims and their families from Mecca to Medina, an event known as the **hijra (HIJ-ruh)**, or "emigration." Hence, to believers, 622, which begins the Muslim calendar, represents humanity's response to God's message. In Medina

[3]Quoted in Jonathan Bloom and Sheila Blair, *Islam: A Thousand Years of Faith and Power* (New Haven, CT: Yale University Press, 2002), 29.
[4]Quoted in Wiebke Walther, *Women in Islam* (Princeton: Markus Wiener, 1993), 104.

WITNESS TO THE PAST

The Holy Book, God, and the Prophet in the Quran

The Quran is organized according to the individual chapter's length, with early and later revelations mixed together rather than a rigid organization of thoughts. English translations lose most of the nuances of the Arabic language, obscuring the beautiful, powerful, poetic writing style. In Arabic the Quran is both a scripture and an elegant literature that has inspired millions. The following brief excerpts present some basic ideas about the holy book itself, the monotheistic God's unity and power, and the recognition of Muhammad as a human prophet or apostle to God.

In the name of the Merciful and Compassionate God. That is the Book! There is no doubt therein; a guide to the pious, who believe in the unseen, and are steadfast in prayer, and of what we have given them expend in alms; who believe in what is revealed to thee, and what was revealed before thee, and of the hereafter they are sure. These are in guidance from their Lord, and these are the prosperous....

God, there is no god but He, the living, the self-subsistent. Slumber takes Him not, nor sleep. His is what is in the heavens and what is in the earth. Who is it that intercedes with Him save by His permission? He knows what is before them and what behind them, and they comprehend not aught of His knowledge but of what He pleases. His throne extends over the heavens and the earth, and it tires him not to guard them both, for He is high and grand.... On Him is the call of truth, and those who call on others than Him shall not be answered at all, save as one who stretches out his hand to the water that it may reach his mouth, but it reaches it not! The call of the misbelievers is always in error.... In the name of the Merciful and Compassionate God, Say "He is God alone!"

Muhammad is but an apostle; apostles have passed away before his time; what if he die or is killed, will ye retreat upon your heels? He who retreats upon his heels does no harm to God at all; but God will recompense the thankful.... Muhammad is not the father of any of your men, but the Apostle of God, and the Seal of the Prophets; for God all things doth know!

THINKING ABOUT THE READING

1. What is the purpose of the Quran?
2. What are the powers of God?
3. What is the relationship between Muhammad and God?

Source: Excerpts taken from Chapters 2, 3, 13, and 33 of the Quran, as reprinted in L. S. Stavrianos, ed., *The Epic of Man to 1500* (Englewood Cliffs, NJ: Prentice-Hall, 1970), 210–211.

the Muslims formed a new community of believers, or **umma**. Many Medinans accepted Muhammad as the Prophet, and he built his first mosque for worship and prayers.

Having a forceful personality and leadership skills, Muhammad also wisely tolerated differences, for example, by accommodating Jews and respecting the stories of their past prophets. Muhammad said their original teachings had been distorted by Jews and Christians.

In Medina Muhammad also took new wives. Because frequent warfare and raiding killed off many men, Arab men often had several wives so they could protect vulnerable women and procreate more children. Concerned for the welfare of women without husbands, Muhammad urged his men to marry widows and required that all wives be treated equally and fairly.

Muhammad's growing popularity earned him more enemies. Some Medina Jews mocked his beliefs. Muhammad urged his followers to respect sympathetic Christians and Jews, saying, "Dispute not with the People of the Book. We believe in what has been sent down to us, and what has been sent down to you; our God and your God is One."[5] But, needing strong methods to preserve his umma, he expelled two Jewish tribes and killed all the men of another suspected of aiding his opponents. Muhammad's followers won various military skirmishes, usually against much larger armies. The Muslims, mostly city dwellers, quickly learned desert warfare. In general Muhammad proved a flexible, pragmatic leader, usually negotiating and compromising rather than shedding blood, but his brilliant military victories and shrewd diplomacy made him Arabia's most powerful man. Muhammad pardoned most of his foes and assumed power in Mecca, sharing taxes from trade with those who became Muslim.

Amidst social and economic changes in western Arabia, Muhammad's message of monotheism, community, equality, and justice proved a powerful attraction, dissolving social barriers between tribes and encouraging a larger spiritual community. In his last sermon, Muhammad told his audience to deal justly with each other, treat women kindly, and consider all Muslims as brothers. His message emphasized the one and only, all-powerful God, **Allah** **(AH-luh)**: "He knows what is hidden and what is evident. He is the merciful lord of mercy. There is no God but him. He is the king, the holy, the peace, the faith keeper, the preserver, the strong, the all-disposing."[6] Thanks to expanding long-distance trade, some Meccans became richer and others poorer, fostering social instability. But Muhammad, like Jesus of Nazareth, emphasized social justice, winning support among the poor.

umma The community of Muslim believers united around God's message.

Allah To Muslims the one and only, all-powerful God.

[5]Quoted in Karen Armstrong, *Muhammad: A Biography of the Prophet* (San Francisco: Harper San Francisco, 1992), 160.

[6]Quoted in Francis Robinson, *The Cultural Atlas of the Islamic World Since 1500* (Oxford: Stonehenge, 1992), 180.

The faithful before the Kaaba in Mecca, from the 'Siyer-i Nebi' (gouache on paper), Turkish School,(16th century)/Topkapi Palace Museum, Istanbul, Turkey/Bildarchiv Steffens/The Bridgeman Art Library

THE PILGRIMAGE TO MECCA This sixteenth century Turkish painting portrays faithful pilgrims before the Ka'ba, Islam's most sacred site, in Mecca.

When Muhammad died at age sixty-two, the umma faced a challenge because Muhammad had left little guidance on future leadership Disagreements arose. The four men closest to him formed a **caliphate** **(KAL-uhf-uht)**, an imperial state headed by an Islamic ruler, or *caliph* **(KAL-uhf)**, considered the successor of the Prophet in civil affairs. Muhammad's four consecutive successors, known later as the Rashidun ("rightly guided") caliphs, ruled from Medina between 632 and 661, but disagreements about suc-

Caliphate An imperial state headed by an Islamic ruler, the caliph, considered the designated successor of the Prophet in civil affairs.

Ramadan The thirty days of annual fasting when Muslims abstain from eating, drinking, and having sex during daylight hours, to demonstrate sacrifice for their faith and to understand the hunger of the poor.

haj The Muslim pilgrimage to the holy city of Mecca to worship with multitudes of other believers from around the world.

jihad Effort to live as God intended; a spiritual, moral, and intellectual struggle to enhance personal faith and follow the Quran.

Islamic Beliefs and Society

Like Christians, Muslims, considering their faith the last revealed religion, possessed a strong missionary impulse to share their faith with all people. The basic tenets provided a new world-view that changed history and a sense of community in the wider brotherhood of believers. Believers have clear duties. The "five pillars" include, first, the profession of faith: "There is no God but Allah and Muhammad is his messenger." Muhammad is not considered divine but a teacher chosen by God to spread the notion of a monotheistic God: eternal, all powerful, all knowing, and all merciful. Second, formal worship is performed with words and action five times daily. The third pillar, assistance to the poor and disadvantaged, requires Muslims to donate a tenth of their wealth, an act that also benefits the giver. The fourth pillar, the annual fast or **Ramadan** **(RAHM-uh-dahn)**, lasts one month, during which time Muslims abstain from eating, drinking, and having sex during daylight hours, to sacrifice for their faith and to understand hunger. Families and friends gather to eat just before sunrise and then again following sunset. Finally, if possible, at least once in their lives Muslims make a pilgrimage, or **haj** **(HAJ)**, to Mecca, worshiping with other believers from around the world. Among other spiritual activities, pilgrims circle the great Ka'ba shrine, as Arabs had done before Islam.

Islam places other demands on believers. A puritanical moral code prohibits adultery, gambling, usury, or the use of intoxicating liquors. Like Judaism, Islam has strict dietary laws, including a ban on pork. Muslims strive to live as God intended through effort, or **jihad** **(ji-HAHD)**, a spiritual, moral, and intellectual struggle to enhance personal faith and follow the Quran. However, a zealous minority has interpreted jihad as military conflict or violent struggle with nonbelievers or enemies, somewhat like the Christian crusading tradition. As with Judeo-Christian beliefs, Muslims believe in angels, heavenly servants who serve as God's helpers, and a Devil who flouts God's command; they also anticipate a last judgment where each individual is held accountable for his or her own actions. The good attain Heaven, a garden paradise, while the wicked suffer an eternity in Hell.

The search for social unity fostered a moral and divinely guided community that regulated how people lived together, asking people to pursue justice, avoid excesses, and practice mercy. Viewing Christians and Jews as "protected peoples," Islamic laws recognized the freedom of religious minorities to worship and promoted toleration. The Quran stated: "Lo! those who believe [in Islam], and those who are Jews and Christians, whoever believeth in Allah on the last day and doeth right—surely their reward is with their Lord, and no fear shall come upon them, neither shall they grieve."[7] Some Christians and Jews, angry with the Byzantine Empire's corruption and occasional repression, aided Muslim expansion and viewed Arabs as liberators.

Islamic ideas improved the position of women in Arab culture. Before Islam, Arab women, often secluded, had few rights. Under Islam, men could have up to four wives if they could support and treat them equally and had more rights than women under divorce and inheritance rules. However, women enjoyed some legal protection, could own property and engage in business, and were considered partners before God alongside men. Scholars debate how Muhammad viewed women's roles. He enjoyed women's company, helped with household chores, listened with interest when his wives asserted their opinions, and emphasized that men should treat women kindly. He took more wives after Khadija's death; his favorite, A'isha, played a prominent political role, especially after his death. Muhammad encouraged female modesty in dress, suggesting that women draw their cloaks about them when they went out. Whether this meant full veiling of the face remains disputed. Since ancient Mesopotamia, veiling was common in Middle Eastern societies, and eventually it became expected of devout women. While this enforced modesty restricted women, many Muslim men and women believed that the custom protected women's dignity and virtue. This practice separated the sexes, preventing what most Muslims considered inappropriate romantic entanglements.

Arab Conquests and the Making of an Islamic World

The Arabs rapidly expanded from their base in central Arabia. Between 634 and 651 Muslim armies conquered Iraq, Syria, Palestine, Egypt, and Persia, while Arab ships sailed into the Mediterranean, taking Cyprus (649), Carthage (698), Tunis **(TOO-nuhs)** (700), and then Spain (711–720). In 732 Islamic expansion in Europe was finally stopped in southern France, at the Battle of Tours (toor), by a combined Christian force. Had Arab forces won that conflict, the history of Europe might have been different. Within two centuries, Islam became the dominant religion in the Middle East and North Africa, at the expense of Christianity and Zoroastrianism. Later, it spread across the Sahara to West Africa, down the East African coast, and north into Anatolia and then the Balkans. Adoption of the Arabic language, identity, and Islam united diverse peoples in western Asia and North Africa by transforming them into Arabs.

Arabs also expanded eastward, carrying Islam with them. After completing the conquest of Sassanian Persia, they conquered Afghanistan, Sind (sind) in the lower Indus Basin, and Central Asia between 705 and 715 (see Map 10.1). By 751 Arab armies had reached the Chinese Empire's western fringes, winning a fierce engagement at the Talas River, blocking Chinese westward expansion, and turning Central Asian Turks away from China and toward the Islamic world. Muslims now controlled most Silk Road cities, such as Samarkand and Bukhara. Muslim Arabs and Persians already carried out seaborne trade with China, and some merchants settled in coastal cities there. In the eleventh century, Muslims began ruling large parts of India, and later, in the fifteenth and sixteenth centuries, Islam spread through the Southeast Asian islands. The Arabic script was now used for writing various Asian and African languages, including Urdu in India, Malay in Southeast Asia, and Hausa in West Africa. Even in places like Java, where spoken Arabic never displaced local languages, children were often taught to read and recite the Quran in Arabic.

Historians debate the energies involved in the rapid Arab expansion. Factors in Arabia, including long-term drought, poverty, and overpopulation, may have spurred Muslims to seek new lands. Perhaps Arab leaders needed to capture lucrative trade routes and productive lands to support their followers. The Byzantine and Sassanian Empires, exhausted from warfare and infighting, made an easy target for conquest. Furthermore, Arab fighters were often motivated by religious faith. Yet Muslims apparently made no systematic attempt to impose their religion on the conquered. Some historians suggest that Islam was still defining itself and was not yet clearly differentiated from Judaism and Christianity.

Fragile Islamic community dynamics also provided a motive for expansion. Muhammad's death created a crisis because his followers had lost their charismatic spiritual leader. By providing a common cause, conquest discouraged leaving the community. Warfare also capitalized on a long tradition of tribal fighting. Arab armies were cohesive, mobile, and well led. To prevent the rise of rival factions, Muhammad's first successor, his best friend Abu Bakr **(ab-boo BAK-uhr)**, forbade people from leaving the umma and declared Muhammad God's final prophet. Abu Bakr allied with other tribes, among them the often feuding nomadic Bedouins, whose fighting spirit could be turned against non-Arab foes. Arab fighters divided up each conquest's spoils, spreading wealth within the community, maintaining unity, and keeping the allegiance of those favoring a radical egalitarianism that challenged those with wealth and power.

By the eleventh century Islam had grown from an Arab cult into the dominant religion over a wide area of Afro-Eurasia, joining older universal religions such as Buddhism and Christianity. Late-seventh and early-eighth-century Muslims thought of themselves as carriers of a global movement and a new religion encompassing many peoples, including self-governing communities of Greek Orthodox Christians, Nestorians, Copts, Zoroastrians, Manicheans, and Jews. Rather than remaining minority rulers over non-Muslim majorities, Arab Muslims began encouraging conversion and cultural synthesis. But conversion by force was the exception rather than the rule. Many found the religion and the increasingly cosmopolitan community of believers an attractive alternative to their old traditions.

[7]Quoted in Henry Bucher, *Middle East* (Guilford, CT: Dushkin, 1984), 19.

MAP 10.1 EXPANSION OF ISLAM, TO 750 C.E. The Arabs rapidly conquered much of western Asia, North Africa, and Spain, in the process expanding Islam into the conquered territories. By 750 their empire stretched from Morocco and Spain in the west to western India and Central Asia.

MAKE SURE YOU UNDERSTAND THESE KEY POINTS BEFORE MOVING ON

- **Islam was born in Arabia, a harsh land where many people lived in cooperative tribes or clans.**
- **Muhammad's teachings were monotheistic (like Christianity and Judaism) and emphasized equality and mutual respect among peoples from different tribes.**
- **Islam's foundation is the five pillars: profession of faith; formal worship; charity; annual fasting, or Ramadan; and the pilgrimage, or haj, to Mecca.**
- **Islam spread extremely rapidly via Arab conquest of the Middle East, North Africa, Central Asia, and parts of India and Europe.**
- **Explanations for the rapid Arab expansion include the need for resources, the weakness of other empires, and the need for a common cause to hold the Arabs together.**

Early Islamic States and Empires

What were the major achievements of the Islamic states and empires?

Islamic expansion allowed powerful states to rule millions of Muslims and non-Muslims, aided by unique concepts of government and law. For over half a millennium Arabic-speaking Muslims governed a large segment of the Eastern Hemisphere. Great states and empires dominated the Middle East, and Islamic states on the fringe of Christian Europe passed on knowledge. Peoples and ideas spread widely, fostering a dynamic mix of Arab, Persian, Indian, and Greek cultures. But Islam also divided into rival sects, creating enduring tensions that influenced Middle Eastern politics for many centuries.

sultan A Muslim ruler of only one country.

Islamic Government and Law

Since Muslims viewed government and religion as the same, Islamic states tended to punish Muslims who violated religious prohibitions. Combining political and religious power produced a theocracy headed by a caliph or more commonly a **sultan**, a Muslim ruler of only one country. Such far-reaching power was easily misused, but respected religious scholars' moral authority could sometimes check political abuses. The Islamic legal code, or **Shari'a** **(shah-REE-ah)** ("the way to the watering hole"), regulated social and economic as well as religious life, providing a comprehensive guide to issues such as divorce, inheritance, debts, and morality. It also evolved over time. Based chiefly on the Quran and the Hadith, augmented by Islamic legal scholarship, the Shari'a was also rooted in Arab, Persian, and Byzantine cultural traditions and customs. But conflicts over Quranic interpretation and application fostered several competing interpretative traditions that differed slightly in emphasis on such tools as reasoning and scriptural authority. Some interpreted the Shari'a as moderate, tolerant, forgiving, and rationalist; others as austere, rigid, and harsh, to be interpreted literally.

Religious scholars such as judges, preachers, and prayer leaders elaborated the Shari'a and sustained Islamic culture, providing a cohesion and stability that was independent of the rise and fall of rulers. Muslims valued education based on studying with renowned religious and legal scholars, and by the tenth century they had created religious boarding schools, known as **madrasas** **(muh-DRAH-suhz)**, that were headed by religious scholars. Today thousands of these schools flourish all over the Muslim world.

© Waj/Shutterstock.com

THE GREAT UMAYYAD MOSQUE IN DAMASCUS This mosque, built between 709 and 715, is the oldest surviving monumental mosque.

Early Imperial Caliphates: Unity and Strife

Beginning with the Rashidun, imperial caliphates attempted to maintain unity but also faced challenges. After 661 political power shifted outside of Arabia with two successive imperial dynasties, the Umayyad **(oo-MY-ad)** and the Abbasid **(ah-BASS-id)**, both installed by members of Muhammad's Quraysh tribe as power shifted away from Arabia. While Mecca and Medina remained spiritual hubs, reinforced by annual pilgrimages, new cities emerged as major political and economic centers.

Political conflict increased with growth. The early conquests enriched Medina and Mecca merchant clans, but criticism of the new materialism eventually prompted a full revolt against the Rashidun leadership. Dissidents murdered the unpopular third caliph, Uthman **(ooth-MAHN)**, installing Ali **(ah-LEE)** (ca. 600–661), Muhammad's son-in-law, as the fourth caliph. Although well qualified, pious, and generous, Ali proved weak, and moving the capital from Medina to Kufah **(KOO-fa)** in Iraq provoked challenges to his leadership. The opposition to Ali, rallied by Muhammad's widow, A'isha, resulted in civil war and Ali's murder. Ali's death ended the Rashidun era, but the divisions generated a permanent split in the Islamic world. Centuries later, many Muslims viewed the Rashidun period as a golden age of simple government and righteous cause, with some calling for a new caliphate to rule the Muslim world.

Shari'a The Islamic legal code for the regulation of social and economic as well as religious life.

madrasas Religious boarding schools found all over the Muslim world.

The Umayyad dynasty (661–750) seized power and moved the caliphate to Damascus **(duh-MAS-kuhs)** in Syria. Men with no direct connection to, or descent from, the Prophet now led the Islamic empire, and large bureaucratic states with remote leaders who passed on their rule to their sons defined Arab politics. Umayyad caliphs extended the Islamic empire deep into Byzantine territory. However, rulers soon faced unrest because, although encouraging Islam and calling themselves deputies of God, they ignored Islamic morality. The Umayyads' legendary drinking, womanizing, and lax religious devotion generated civil war and division, which eventually led to their downfall. Umayyad opponents emphasized Muhammad's role as God's prophet, clearly setting Islam apart from rival monotheistic religions. Among the challengers, the Prophet's only remaining male heir, his grandson Husayn **(hoo-SANE)**, attracted support from those who believed the caliph must be Muhammad's direct descendant. However, Husayn's rebellion in 680 failed, and he was killed in the Battle of Karbala **(KAHR-buh-LAH)**, a city in Iraq, becoming, along with his murdered father Ali, a martyr against the Umayyads.

The Sunni-Shi'a Split

After Ali's death, Islam began to split into two main branches due to disagreements over the umma's nature and the full meaning of Muhammad's revelations. The main branch, **Sunni** **(SOO-nee)** ("The Trodden Path"), accepted the Prophet's practices and the historical succession of caliphs. In their view, governments guarantee political independence and religious integrity. Today about 85 percent of all Muslims, including most in North Africa, Turkey, the Balkans, South and Southeast Asia, and China, as well as the majority of Arabs, are Sunni. Sunni embraces diverse opinions and practices, adhering to one of four main schools of Islamic law and a broad view of who qualifies for political power.

The other main branch began in a dispute over leadership. The **Shi'a** **(SHEE-uh)** ("Partisans" of Ali) revered Muhammad's family and recognized only leaders descended from Muhammad through his son-in-law, Ali, to them the Prophet's rightful successor. Karbala and nearby Najaf **(NAH-jaf)**, where respectively Husayn and Ali are buried, became holy Shi'ite pilgrimage centers. Shi'ites provided an alternative to Sunni Islam but divided into three rival schools based on which leader after Ali should be followed. The main Shi'ite populations live today in Iran, Iraq, Lebanon, and the Persian Gulf states. Smaller minorities are scattered across Central Asia, western India, and Pakistan.

Sunni ("The Trodden Path") The main branch of Islam, comprising those who accept the practices of the Prophet and the historical succession of caliphs.

Shi'a ("Partisans" of Ali) The branch of Islam emphasizing the religious leaders descended from Muhammad through his son-in-law, Ali, who they believe was the rightful successor to the Prophet.

Although the two branches of Islam share many commonalities, Sunni-Shi'a differences run deep. Like some Christians, ultra-Orthodox Jews, and Hindu sects but unlike Sunnis, many Shi'ites followed strong religious leaders they considered divinely inspired. Like Catholics and Protestants in some Western countries, Sunnis and Shi'ites sometimes fought each other. Sunni majorities sometimes persecuted Shi'ite minorities, producing a Shi'ite martyrdom complex and dissent against Sunni rulers. Over the centuries Shi'ite states often ruled uneasily over Sunni majorities.

Arabian Nights: The Abbasid Caliphate

The Ummayads were replaced by the Abbasid Caliphate (750–1258). which enjoyed great power and fostered a dynamic society, surviving for half a millennium, embodying the unity of the Islamic umma, and establishing a pattern for later Muslim rulers. The Abbasids, who were Sunni Quraysh descended from Muhammad's uncle, Abbas, attracted support from both Sunnis and Shi'ites to defeat the Umayyad army. The lone Umayyad survivor fled to Spain and there established a state that flourished for three centuries. Abbasid forces expanded the empire eastward and maintained pressure against Byzantium in the west. By 800 the Abbasid Empire ruled some 30 million people (see Map 10.2).

Moving the capital to Baghdad, where the Tigris and Euphrates Rivers come closest together in Iraq, placed the Abbasid government alongside major trade routes and fertile irrigated fields. Boasting joint-stock companies and banks, Baghdad became one of the world's greatest hubs, its bazaars filled with goods from as far away as China, Scandinavia, and East Africa. To publically demonstrate their piety and generosity, the Abbasids employed thousands to build palaces, schools, hospitals, and mosques. Some Baghdad citizens, however, openly flouted Islamic prohibitions against hedonistic behavior, and Baghdad generally reflected Islamic society's cosmopolitan flavor. In the 1160s a visiting rabbi from Muslim-ruled Spain, Benjamin of Tudela, wrote of the ethnically diverse city and its large Jewish community:

> *This great Abbasid [caliph] is extremely friendly towards the Jews, many of his officers being of that nation. Baghdad contains about one thousand Jews, who enjoy peace, comfort, and much honor. Many of the Jews are good scholars and very rich. The city contains 28 Jewish synagogues.*[8]

Islam flourished by receiving and absorbing culture from all over the Eastern Hemisphere. For example, Persian influence on the Abbasid system was strong, and many Persians occupied high government positions. The Abbasids acquired knowledge from faraway lands, such as papermaking technology from Chinese captured in the Battle of Talas of 751; by 800 Baghdad had its first paper mill. Papermaking allowed for wider distribution of the Quran, helping to spread Islam.

[8]Quoted in Manuel Komroff, ed., *Contemporaries of Marco Polo* (New York: Horace Liveright, 1928), 286–292.

MAP 10.2 THE ABBASID EMPIRE, CA. 800 C.E. The Abbasids, a dynasty based in what is today Iraq, established the largest Muslim empire in the Early Intermediate Era, ruling lands from Central Asia to Egypt before losing most of their territories. Among other major Islamic states, the Umayyads ruled Spain and Northwest Africa and the Fatimids ruled Egypt and neighboring lands.

The height of Abbasid Baghdad conjures up the images of affluence and romance reported in *The Arabian Nights*, stories that later influenced European writers, artists, and composers. For example, the nineteenth-century Russian composer Nikolai Rimsky-Korsakov's **(RIM-skee KAWR-suh-kawf)** famous *Scheherazade* symphony evokes Abbasid Baghdad's atmosphere. The original *Arabian Nights* stories, augmented over several centuries, incorporated Persian, Egyptian, Indian, and other traditions and encompassed many subjects and moods, among them fantasy, comedy, piety, sex, tragedy, brutality, sentimentality, and obscenity. Some scholars perceive feminist values reflected in the proactive female characters. Some misleading images of old Baghdad, based loosely on the great literary work, come from fanciful children's books and films featuring flying carpets and genies in magic lamps, which in the stories appeared mostly in dreams. Life under the most famous Abbasid caliph, Harun al-Rashid **(hah-ROON al-rah-SHEED)** (786–809), lacked flying carpets and magic lanterns, but it did include a large harem of wives, concubines, and slave girls numbering perhaps two thousand. These royal harems suggested a secluded world of luxury, idleness, and endless plotting for royal favor. Like some other Abbasid rulers, Harun reputedly drank heavily and pursued the temptations of the flesh.

Adopting some customs from the conquered gradually transformed Arabs from desert herders and traders into imperial rulers. The Abbasids often ruled through traditional leaders, such as Egypt's Coptic Church patriarchs. In Iraq they resolved disputes among Nestorian Christians just as the Sassanian governors had done. Like the Sassanians, the caliphs patronized a state religion, now shifted from Zoroastrianism to Islam, and lavishly supported arts and crafts. They also appointed Muslim judges and built mosques.

Urban growth followed conquests. The caliphates' administrative centers drew in surrounding people seeking work. Hence Baghdad rapidly swelled to perhaps a million people by 900, becoming the world's largest city. Like the Sassanians, the caliphs divided cities into wards marked by ethnic and occupational groups, governing them through their own leaders.

Abbasid Decline and the End of the Arab Empire

Like all empires, the Abbasids eventually faced mounting problems, gradually losing their grip on power by the tenth century. As Turkish soldiers guarding the caliphs became more powerful and disaffected Shi'ites fomented bloody revolts, the caliphate became a mere figurehead and parts of the empire broke away. Anti-Abbasid Shi'ites claiming descent from Fatima, Muhammad's daughter, established the Cairo-based Fatimid **(FAT-uh-mid)** Caliphate in Egypt and North Africa, after which Cairo became Baghdad's rival as an intellectual and economic center. The university founded in Cairo by the Fatimids in 970, Al-Azhar, became the most influential in the Islamic world and remains the unrivaled center of Islamic higher learning. Shi'ites also ruled various smaller states in which most of the population remained Sunni or non-Muslim yet generally enjoyed religious freedom. Finally, the wealth of the Abbasid realm attracted the Mongols, Central Asian nomads who in the thirteenth century built a great regional empire stretching from East Asia to eastern Europe (see Chapter 11). In 1258 Mongol armies sacked and destroyed Baghdad and executed the last Abbasid caliph, shattering the symbolic unity of the Muslim world. Now Persians, Berbers, Kurds, Turks, and Mongols challenged Arab dominance.

Despite these setbacks, political weakness and declining cultural dynamism only become evident in the Islamic world in the sixteenth and seventeenth centuries. Yet, although few later Muslim rulers could match the power of the early Abbasids, Islam accelerated its diffusion to new peoples, and between 1258 and 1550 the territorial size of the Islamic world doubled. Scholars, saints, and mystics assumed leadership throughout this world, establishing legal structures, dogmas, social forms, standards of piety, aesthetic sensibilities, styles of scholarship, and schools of philosophy that helped define the vital core of Islamic culture.

© julius fekete/Shutterstock.com

ALHAMBRA, COURT OF LIONS The Alhambra, or Palace of Lions, built in Granada in southern Spain in the fourteenth century, is one of the finest architectural treasures from Muslim Spain. It features a courtyard with a fountain.

Cultural Mixing in Muslim Sicily and Spain

Islamic culture also flourished in Sicily and Spain, where it fostered a cosmopolitan mixed society characterized by prosperity and shared scientific knowledge. Between 825 and 900 Muslim forces conquered Sicily, the largest Mediterranean island, thus tying it closer to the Arab-dominated maritime trade system. Muslim rulers repaired long-decayed Roman irrigation works, vastly increasing agricultural production. Many Arabs, Berbers, Africans, Greeks, Jews, Persians, and Slavs gravitated to the island, mixing with local peoples. The Muslim capital, Palermo, was larger than any other European city except Constantinople. But Muslim political divisions left the island open to gradual Christian reconquest. Between 1061 and 1091 Normans, descendants of Vikings who had settled in France, replaced a Muslim government with their own, and by 1200 Christian German rulers had established a Sicilian state. The persecution of Muslims and Jews gradually brought to an end the dynamic fusion of Islamic and Christian traditions.

A more enduring Muslim society emerged in Spain, which was mostly conquered by Umayyad forces between 711 and 720. Their capital, Cordoba **(KAWR-duh-buh)**, became Europe's largest city by 1000, home to half a million people. For several centuries a famed center of culture and learning, Umayyad Spain drew scholars and thinkers from all over Europe and the

Islamic world. Cordoba's library held 400,000 volumes, when Christian Europe's libraries owned only several hundred. Tolerance generated a productive relationship between diverse peoples and traditions, with Christian, Muslim, and Jewish thinkers working together to share and advance knowledge. An Arab poet called Cordoba the garden of the fruits of ideas. Here intellectuals discussed ancient Greek thought and the latest astronomical discoveries and translated books from and into Arabic. This cosmopolitan intellectual culture passed on to Europe much of the Classical Greco-Roman heritage, Islamic and Indian science and mathematics, and some Chinese technology, such as papermaking. Europe also received Arab vocal and instrumental music, important in Islamic ceremonies, pleasure, and worship. Arab folk songs and musical instruments, such as the guitar and lute, diffused northward, influencing the courtly love songs of European troubadours and, later, Western popular music.

By 1000 civil wars and factionalism fostered decline, and the Umayyad government fragmented into smaller, often warring states. Intolerant Muslim invaders from Morocco conquered some regions, persecuting anyone not sharing their rigid interpretation of Islam. Many Spaniards, remaining loyal to Catholicism, provided a support base for reconquest efforts, and northern Spain gradually came under Christian control. In 1085 Christian knights conquered Cordoba, the center of Islamic power. Constant Christian military pressure gradually pushed Muslim rule into southern Spain, and by 1252 Christian princes controlled much of Spain and Portugal. Finally, in 1492, Christians took the last Muslim stronghold at Granada **(gruh-NAHD-uh)**. The new Christian rulers, militant and intolerant, forced Muslims and Jews to either convert to Christianity or face expulsion. Many converted but thousands fled, usually to Muslim countries in North Africa or to Anatolia.

MAKE SURE YOU UNDERSTAND THESE KEY POINTS BEFORE MOVING ON

- **Due to different views of Muhammad's teachings and the rightful succession of caliphs, Islam began to split into two branches, the Sunni majority branch and the Shi'a dissident branch.**
- **The Umayyad dynasty, which succeeded the Rashidun Caliphate, was led by men with no connection to Muhammad who extended the empire into Byzantine lands.**
- **Under the Abbasid Caliphate, which provided the setting for *The Arabian Nights*, Baghdad became a cosmopolitan hub of trading and culture.**
- **As they expanded, Arabs adopted the imperial ruling structures of the peoples they conquered and were targeted by numerous invaders, including the Mongols.**
- **Muslims ruled Spain and Sicily for several centuries, but Christians gradually reclaimed them and failed to maintain the tolerance of the early Muslim rulers.**

Cultural Hallmarks of Islam: Theology, Society, and Learning

What were the major concerns of Muslim thinkers and writers?

Islamic expansion launched a thousand-year era, from the seventh to the seventeenth century, that brought many Afro-Eurasian peoples into closer contact with one another. Muslims synthesized elements from varied traditions, including Arab, Greek, Persian, and Indian, producing a durable hybrid culture rooted in theology, social patterns, literature, art, science, and learning. Several distinct strands of thought and behavior combined to produce a distinctive social system and a renowned cultural heritage. Islamic scholars contributed major scientific achievements and historical studies to the world.

Theology, Sufism, and Religious Practice

Debates over theological questions led to divergent interpretations of the Quran and diverse views about the great questions of life and death, reflecting the mixing of intellectual traditions. Some Muslim thinkers emphasized reason and free will, while others believed that Allah preordained everything. Some influential thinkers mastered several fields of knowledge. Abu Yusuf al-Kindi **(a-BOO YOU-suhf al-KIN-dee)** (ca. 800–ca. 870), an Iraqi Arab, praised the search for truth and popularized Greek ideas. Although stressing logic and mathematics, he also published work on science, music, medicine, and psychology. The philosopher and medical scholar Abu Ali al-Husain Ibn Sina **(a-BOO AH-lee al-who-SANE IB-unh SEE-nah)** (980–1037), known in the West as Avicenna **(av-uh-SEN-uh)**, was a native of Bukhara **(boo-CAR-ruh)**, a Silk Road city in Central Asia, who mostly worked in Persia. Ibn Sina believed that everyone could exercise free will but that the highest goal was communion with God. Afghanistan-born Abu Hamid al-Ghazali **(AH-boo HAM-id al-guh-ZAL-ee)** (1058–1111), a Baghdad teacher, used Aristotelian logic to justify Islamic beliefs. This rationalistic approach lost support among Sunnis from the fourteenth century onward.

Among both Sunnis and Shi'ites a mystical approach and practice called **Sufism** **(SOO-fiz-uhm)** gained many followers. Sufism emphasized personal spiritual experience rather than nitpicking theology, stressing the superiority of the heart over the mind and the search for communion with God. Much as the Quran sanctioned mysticism—"Wherever ye turn there is the face of God"[9]—a famous Persian Sufi poet, Baba Kuhi, saw God in everything: "In the market, in the cloister—only God I saw; In the valley and on the mountain—only God I saw. Him I have seen beside me oft in tribulation; in favor and in fortune—only God I saw."[10] Many Sufis exchanged information with Christian, Hindu, and Jewish mystics, willingly synthesized Islam with other ideas, and considered their practices useful even for non-Muslims. Sufis were instrumental in spreading Islam to South Asia, Indonesia, and West Africa, all regions where Sufism remains strong today. But Sufism constituted a supplement rather than a challenge to conventional Islam.

Sufis congregated in orders led by masters who taught prescribed techniques. One of the most famous Sufi orders, Turkey's whirling *dervishes* **(DUHR-vish-iz)**, practiced special exercises and methods, including trance dancing, to achieve a state of divine ecstasy. Several Sufi orders gained renown as being peace-loving and tolerant of different views and customs. As followers credited some Sufi masters with magical powers, their tombs became pilgrimage destinations. Sufis also produced most Islamic poetry. Millions revere the Persian Sufi poet Hafez **(hah-FEZ)** (1326–1389), who loved both God and the grape: "Here we are with our wine and the ascetics with their piety. Let us see which one the beloved [God] will take."[11] However, Sufism remained controversial. While tolerating religious flexibility won Sufis converts, many non-Sufis condemned the suspension of Islamic biases against wine, drugs, and music in worship.

Spreading into diverse cultures, Islam developed several patterns of practice. Adaptationists willingly adjusted to changing conditions, providing the base for reform and modernizing movements. Conservatives, mistrusting innovation, strove to preserve established beliefs and customs, such as the rigid gender division. The most dogmatic conservatives argued that Muhammad's divine revelations set a permanent, unchangeable authority for judging existing conditions. Finally, some stressed personal aspects of the faith. These diverse patterns all have large followings among both Sunnis and Shi'ites, fostering political and social conflict in Muslim societies.

Sufism A mystical approach and practice within Islam that emphasized personal spiritual experience.

Social Life and Gender Relations

As Islamic culture expanded and matured, the social structure became more complex and marked by clear ethnic, tribal, class, occupational, religious, and gender divisions, especially in the Middle East. Arabs generally enjoyed a higher social status than Turks, Berbers, Africans, and others. Those claiming descent from Muhammad and his Hashimite clan held an especially honored status in Islamic societies. Many Arabs were also members of tribes. Because the first Muslims were merchants, Islam attracted people in the commercial sector, who could spiritually sanction their quest for wealth by financing pilgrimages to Mecca and helping the poor through almsgiving. However, Christian and Jewish minorities did not always have the same rights as Muslims. Because they paid higher taxes and could not own weapons, they were exempt from military duty, and they enjoyed some legal protections. These communities were generally allowed to follow their own laws, customs, and beliefs and maintain their own religious institutions.

Slavery was common. Slaves served as bureaucrats and soldiers, business and factory workers, household servants and concubines, musicians, and plantation laborers. One Abbasid caliph kept eleven thousand slaves in his palace. Islamic law encouraged treating slaves with consideration, and many were eventually freed. Many slaves were war captives and children purchased from poor families or from European states like Byzantium and Venice. For over a dozen centuries, especially after 1200, an Arab-dominated slave trade brought perhaps 10 to 15 million African slaves to the Middle East across the Sahara or up the East African coast. African slave soldiers were common in Egypt, Persia, Iraq, Oman **(oh-MAHN)** in eastern Arabia, Yemen, and South Asia.

Families anchored the social system, arranging marriages to cement social or business ties between two families. Although Shari'a law allowed men up to four wives at a time, this privilege remained largely restricted to the rich and powerful. Many poor men, unable to afford the large bridal gifts expected, never married at all. While divorce was theoretically easy for men, marriage contracts sometimes specified a large gift to the wife upon divorce. Parents expected children to obey and respect them, even after they became adults. Family gatherings, usually segregated by gender, often involved poetry recitations, musical performances, or Quran readings. Although Islamic law harshly punished homosexuality, homosexual relationships were not uncommon, with same-sex love often reflected in poetry and literature, especially in Muslim Spain. The tolerant attitudes of Arabs, Persians, and Turks toward homosexual romantic relationships often shocked European visitors.

For centuries both Western and Islamic observers have debated women's status in Islamic society. Hence, the

[9]Quoted in Alfred Guillaume, "Islamic Mysticism and the Sufi Sect," in *The Spread of Islam*, ed. Claire Swisher (San Diego: Greenhaven Press, 1999), 153.

[10]"Baba Kuhi of Shiraz," translated by Reynold A. Nicholson. Quoted in Mary Ann Frese Witt et al., *The Humanities: Cultural Roots and Continuities*, vol. 1, 7th ed. (Boston: Houghton Mifflin, 2005), 270.

[11]Quoted in Adam Goodheart, "Pilgrims from the Great Satan," *New York Times*, March 10, 2002, A12.

PERSIAN WOMEN AT A PICNIC This miniature from sixteenth-century Persia around 1600 shows women preparing a picnic. The ability of women to venture away from home varied widely depending on social class and regional traditions.

philosopher Ibn Rushd **(IB-uhn RUSHED)** (1126–1198), known in the West as Averroes **(uh-VER-uh-WEEZ)**, attacked restrictions on women as an economic burden, arguing that "the ability of women is not known, because they are merely used for procreation [and] child-rearing."[12] Although the Quran recognized certain women's rights, prohibited female infanticide, and limited the number of wives men could have, it also accorded women less standing in courts of law and only half the inheritance of men. While some Muslims criticized restrictions on women as institutionalizing their social inferiority, other Muslim men and women contended that they liberate women from insecurity and male harassment. Scholars also disagreed over whether customs such as veiling and seclusion were based on Quranic mandates or patriarchal, pre-Islamic Arab, Middle Eastern, and Byzantine customs. Some Muslim communities in the Middle East, and many outside the region, never adopted these practices.

Women played diverse roles. During Abbasid times some elite women, while excluded from public life, enjoyed considerable power behind the scenes. For instance, Khayzuran, noted for her compassion and generosity, rose from a simple Yemenite slave girl to become the great love and wife of the Caliph Mahdi, dominating his harem and investing in land reclamation and charitable works. On his death, she helped smooth the transition to the rulership of her son, Harun al-Rashid. Some exceptional women circumvented restrictions. Umm Hani (also known as Mariam) in fifteenth-century Cairo studied law and religion with famous teachers, wrote poetry, owned a large textile workshop, and became a renowned teacher and scholar of the Hadith. She also had seven children by two husbands and made thirteen pilgrimages to Mecca. In the lower classes, while formal education for girls remained limited, women monopolized occupations such as spinning and weaving and worked in the fields or some domestic industries beside men. And among some Muslims, particularly sub-Saharan Africans and Southeast Asians, women often enjoyed relative independence, dressing as they liked, socializing outside the home, and earning money. Turks and Mongols were more liberal on gender issues than Arabs and Persians. Hence, gender relations varied considerably.

Pen and Brush: Writing and the Visual Arts

Although Islamic societies became identified with literacy and literature, the Arabic alphabet originated in southern Arabia long before Muhammad's time. Islam enhanced the script by emphasizing literacy, the Quran stating: "Read, and thy Lord is most generous, Who taught with the pen, Taught man what he knew not."[13] Muslims adopted the Arab poetic tradition but modified romantic ideas into praise not for a lover but for the Prophet and Allah.

One of the greatest Abbasid writers was the Persian astronomer and mathematician Omar Khayyam **(OH-MAHR key-YAHM)**. In his famous poem *Rubaiyat* **(ROO-bee-AHT)**, he noted life's fleeting nature: "One thing is certain, that Life

[12]Quoted in Walther, *Women in Islam*, 40.

[13]Quoted in Mervyn Hiskett, "Islamic Literature and Art," in Swisher, ed., *Spread*, 120.

flies; and the rest is Lies; the flower that once has blown forever dies." This led him to regret never knowing the purpose of existence:

> *Ah, make the most of what ye yet may spend, Before we too into the Dust descend; Dust unto Dust, and under Dust to lie, [without] Wine, Song, Singer, and End! Into this Universe, and Why not knowing, Nor Whence, like Water willy-nilly flowing; And out of it, as Wind along the Waste, I know not Whither, wily-nilly blowing.*[14]

The most famous Sufi poet, the thirteenth-century Afghanistan-born Persian Jalal al-Din Rumi **(ja-LAL al-DIN ROO-mee)**, blended liberal spirituality with humor in writings about love, desire, and the human condition. Often dancing while reciting his poems, Rumi was optimistic, joyful, and ecumenical, stating: "I am neither Christian, nor Jew, nor Zoroastrian, nor Muslim."[15] Over seven hundred years after his death, Rumi became the best-selling poet in the United States after his poems were translated into English.

The study of history and social sciences, especially geography, owes much to Muslim writing. With the expansion of Islam and Arab traders around Afro-Eurasia, some Muslims traveled to distant lands, and educated Muslims enjoyed reading these travelers' accounts of other countries. Modern historians are indebted to travelers such as the Moroccan jurist Ibn Battuta **(IB-uhn ba-TOO-tuh)** for knowledge about sub-Saharan Africa and Southeast Asia from the ninth to the fifteenth centuries (see Profile: Ibn Battuta, a Muslim Traveler). Geographers and cartographers such as Al-Idrisi **(al-AH-dree-see)** from Muslim Spain also produced atlases, globes, and maps.

The well-traveled North African Ibn Khaldun (1332–1406) was the first known scholar anywhere to ponder patterns and structure in history. His monumental work connected the rise of states with a growing solidarity between leaders and their followers. His recognition of the role of "group feeling" (what today we call ethnic identity) and religion was pathbreaking. In studying other cultures, he advocated "critical examination":

> *Know the rules of statecraft, the nature of existing things, and the difference between nations, regions and tribes in regard to way of life, qualities of character, customs, sects, schools of thought, and so on. [The historian] must distinguish the similarities and differences between the present and the past.*[16]

calligraphy The artful writing of words.

Ibn Khaldun put the Arab expansion into the broader flow of regional history.

Visual arts flourished. Since Arabic is written in a flowing style, **calligraphy (kuh-LIG-ruh-fee)**, the artful writing of words, became an admired art form offering both a message and decoration. Islamic Persia, India, and Central Asia also fostered painting, especially landscapes, and Muslims produced world-class architecture, including lavishly decorated buildings such as India's Taj Mahal. Some architecture, such as mosques with domes and towers, reflected Byzantine church influence. Then as now, Muslims produced carpets and fabrics valued in many non-Muslim societies.

Science, Technology, and Learning

While many creative thinkers emerged, Muslims also borrowed, assimilated, and diffused Greek and Indian knowledge and were familiar with some Chinese technologies. Hence, certain Classical and Hellenistic Greek traditions of philosophy and science nearly forgotten in Europe survived in the Middle East. Muslim thinkers synthesized learning from other societies with their own insights, fostering advances in science and medicine. For example, Nestorian Christians taught Greek sciences under Abbasid sponsorship. Abbasid caliphs opened the House of Wisdom in Baghdad, a research institute with schools, observatories, and a huge library, staffed by scholars who translated Greek, Syrian, Sanskrit, and Persian books on philosophy, medicine, astronomy, and mathematics into Arabic. Aristotle's writings were particularly influential. Other scientific centers arose, from Spain and Morocco to Samarkand in Central Asia. In the tenth and eleventh centuries the Shi'ite Fatimids built the House of Knowledge in Cairo with a massive library holding 2 million books, many on scientific subjects.

Arab and Persian scholars actively assimilated the imported knowledge. As the influential eleventh-century Persian philosopher Al-Biruni **(al-bih-ROO-nee)** wrote: "The sciences were transmitted into the Arabic language from different parts of the world; by it [the sciences] were embellished and penetrated the hearts of men, while the beauties of [Arabic] flowed in their veins and arteries."[17] The diversity of ideas produced an open-minded search for truth apparent in Ibn Khaldun, Ibn Sina, al-Kindi, and Ibn Rushd. For instance, the philosopher al-Kindi wrote that Muslims should acknowledge truth from whatever source it came because nothing was more important than truth itself. Ibn Rushd (Averroes), who lived in Cordoba, influenced Christian thinkers by his writings on Aristotle and by asserting the role of reason. In the eleventh century, Christian Europe became aware of the Muslim synthesis of Greek, Indian, and Persian knowledge from libraries in Spain. But religious conservatives increasingly criticized philosophy as anti-God; Averroes was banished from Cordoba in 1195 for his views.

Muslims also advanced medicine. Although influenced by Greek ideas, medical specialists did not accept ancient wisdom

[14]Excerpted in John Yohannan, ed., *A Treasury of Asian Literature* (New York: New American Library, 1965), 261–262.
[15]Quoted in Jonathan P. Berkey, *The Formation of Islam: Religion and Society in the Near East, 600–1800* (New York: Cambridge University Press, 2003), 233.
[16]Quoted in Hourani, *A History of Arab Peoples* (Cambridge: Belknap Press, 1991), 201.
[17]Quoted in Bernard Lewis, *The Arabs in History* (New York: Harper and Row, 1960), 131.

Ibn Battuta, a Muslim Traveler

Among Islamic travelers who journeyed to, and often sojourned in, distant lands, the most famous, Abdallah Muhammad Ibn Battuta, a gregarious and pious fourteenth-century Moroccan, spent thirty years touring the length and breadth of the Islamic world, as far east as Southeast Asia and, he claimed, coastal China. He was a pilgrim, judge, scholar, Sufi, ambassador, and connoisseur of fine foods and elegant architecture. Ibn Battuta's writings about his remarkable journeys, the autobiographical *Rihla* (Book of Travels), provide detailed, often unique eyewitness accounts of many societies. A collaborator compiled the *Rihla* in a literary form near the end of the adventurer's life.

Born in Tangier, Morocco, to a Berber family of scholars and trained in Islamic law, at twenty-one Ibn Battuta left home in 1325 to seek adventure and learning. His wanderlust proved difficult to quench. Expected to stay close to home and family, no woman, Muslim or otherwise, could have undertaken such extensive travel in that era. Traveling by camel, horse, wagon, or ship, Ibn Battuta covered between 60,000 and 75,000 miles, visiting dozens of countries. He never had a conventional family life and married several times for short periods, leaving children all over the hemisphere. The politically ambitious jurist often sojourned in a society for months or years, his longest career stint being seven years' service in the Delhi Sultanate of northern India. Wherever he went, Ibn Battuta made observations on many subjects, from cuisine and botany to political practice and Sufi mystics. For example, he reported on the "continuous series of bazaars [along the Nile] from Alexandria to Cairo. Cities and villages succeed one another without interruption." And, coming from a more patriarchal North African society, he marveled at the "respect shown to women by the [Central Asian] Turks, for they hold a more dignified position than the men. Turkish women do not veil themselves."

Although he was a repeated visitor to Mecca and the Islamic heartland, Ibn Battuta's experiences in Islam's frontier regions, such as India and the Maldive Islands, Southeast Asia, the East African coast, the western Sudan, Turkish Central Asia, Anatolia, and Mongol-ruled southern Russia, provide the most useful information, revealing an expanding, vigorous Islamic realm encountering diverse structures, peoples, and practices. For example, we learn about the sexual customs of the Maldive Islands, where he married a sultan's widow, and the Arab religious scholars, Persian merchants, and Chinese painters who gathered at Delhi "like moths around a candle."

Whereas the Christian Marco Polo a century earlier was always a stranger in his Asian travels, in most places Ibn Battuta encountered people who shared his world-view and social values. From Morocco to Central Asia and around the Indian Ocean Rim, people worshiped in mosques and used Shari'a law. Ibn Battuta enjoyed the company of merchants, scholars, Sufis, and princes, conversing with them in Arabic on many topics, including developments in faraway lands. His knowledge of Islamic law and Arabic allowed him to work as a judge and legal scholar from Morocco to India. But, while cosmopolitan and open-minded by the era's standards, he was uncomfortable in mostly non-Islamic societies such as China and in frontier cultures where local custom greatly modified Islamic orthodoxy, such as Mali in West Africa. The traveler finally returned home to Tangier, where he died around 1368.

THE JOURNEY TO MALI No known paintings of Ibn Battuta exist. However, this map of Africa and the Mediterranean world, made by a Jewish cartographer in Spain in 1375, features a drawing of a camel-riding Muslim traveler that some historians think represents the journey of the Moroccan to Mali.

THINKING ABOUT THE PROFILE

1. Why was Ibn Battuta one of the great travelers of the Intermediate Era?
2. What do his travels tell us about the values and reach of Islamic religion and culture?

Notes: Quotations from Ross Dunn, *The Adventures of Ibn Battuta: A Muslim Traveller of the 14th Century* (Berkeley: University of California Press, 1986), 45, 183; Nikki R. Keddie, "Women in the Middle East Since the Rise of Islam," in *Women's History in Global Perspective,* ed. Bonnie G. Smith, vol. 3 (Urbana: University of Illinois Press, 2005), 81.

uncritically, instead developing an empirical tradition. Baghdad hospitals were the world's most advanced. Muslim surgeons used opium for anesthesia, extracted teeth and replaced them with false teeth made from animal bones, removed kidney stones, and did colostomies. Islamic medical books translated into Latin in the twelfth century became Europe's major medical texts for the next five centuries. Two medical scientists, Abu Bakr al-Razi **(a-boo BAH-car al-RAH-zee)** (ca. 865–ca. 932) and Ibn Sina (Avicenna), compared Greek ideas with their own research. Al-Razi, a Persian, directed several hospitals and wrote more than fifty clinical studies as well as general medical works including the *Comprehensive Book,* an eighteen-volume medical encyclopedia used in Europe into the 1400s. Al-Razi also studied what we would today call sociological and psychological aspects of medicine; a century later Ibn Sina stressed psychosomatic medicine, treated depression, and pioneered the study of vision and eye disease, performing complicated eye operations. His medical encyclopedia provided about half of the medical curriculum in medieval European universities. Muslims also pioneered many of the apparatus, techniques, and language of chemistry later adopted in the West.

Arab and Indian mathematics made possible the later Scientific Revolution in Europe. In Baghdad the Persian Zoroastrian al-Khuwarizmi **(al-KWAHR-uhz-mee)** (ca. 780–ca. 850) developed the mathematical procedures he called algebra, building on Greek and Indian foundations. Omar Khayyam, the Persian poet at Baghdad's House of Wisdom, helped formulate trigonometry. From Indian math books Muslims adopted a revolutionary system of numbers, today known as Arabic numerals because Europe acquired them from Muslim Spain. They were not only more convenient but also used a dot (eventually a zero) to indicate an empty column. Advances in mathematics and physics made possible improvements in water clocks, water wheels, and other irrigation apparatuses that spread well beyond the Islamic world.

Muslim astronomers combined Greek, Persian, and Indian knowledge of the stars and planets with their own observations. Applying mathematics to optics, they constructed a primitive telescope. One astronomer reportedly built an elaborate planetarium that reproduced the movement of the stars, and a remarkable observatory built at Samarkand in Central Asia in 1420 produced charts for hundreds of stars. Some astronomers noted the eccentric behavior of the planet Venus, challenging the widespread notion of an earth-centered universe. Indeed, many Muslim astronomers accepted a round earth. Calculating the size of the Earth, Al-Biruni even postulated large unknown landmasses west of Eurasia.

Between the eighth and thirteenth centuries, Islamic societies also made agricultural innovations, expanding production in a "green revolution." Improved diets and health spurred dramatic population growth. When Arab conquests opened the door to India, the Middle East obtained South Asian crops such as cotton, hard wheat, rice, and sugar cane; fruits such as the coconut palm, banana, sour orange, lemon, lime, mango, and watermelon; and vegetables such as spinach, artichokes, and eggplant. These imports from wetter lands encouraged better irrigation, including the use of enormous water wheels to supply water. The spread of agricultural products was one of the Islamic peoples' major contributions to world history. Most of these crops filtered westward to Spain, where they thrived, and cotton became a major crop in West Africa. While many crops reached Christian Europe from Spain and Sicily, they were adopted only slowly, since Europe at that time had a lower population density and limited irrigation technology.

MAKE SURE YOU UNDERSTAND THESE KEY POINTS BEFORE MOVING ON

- **Sufism, a mystical approach to Islam that emphasized flexibility and a personal connection with God, drew both Sunni and Shi'ite followers.**
- **Although the Quran and most Muslim societies restricted women, some Muslim societies did not, and both Muslims and non-Muslims have debated the origins and benefits of such practices as wearing a veil.**
- **Literature, especially poetry, was very important in Islamic culture, as was calligraphy, the artful writing of words.**
- **Islamic science and medicine were very advanced and pioneered such practices as anesthesia and the replacement of false teeth; Islamic mathematicians were instrumental in propelling the Scientific Revolution.**

Globalized Islam and Middle Eastern Political Change

Why do historians speak of Islam as a hemispheric culture?

Dar al-Islam ("Abode of Islam") The Islamic world stretching from Morocco to Indonesia and joined by both a common faith and trade.

Between the eighth and seventeenth centuries, Islam, the product of a once parochial Arab culture, expanded out of its Arabian heartland to become the dominant religion across a broad expanse of Africa and Eurasia, with Muslim minorities emerging in places as far afield as China and the Balkans. This expansion created **Dar al-Islam** (the "Abode of Islam"), the Islamic world stretching from Morocco to Indonesia and the Philippines,

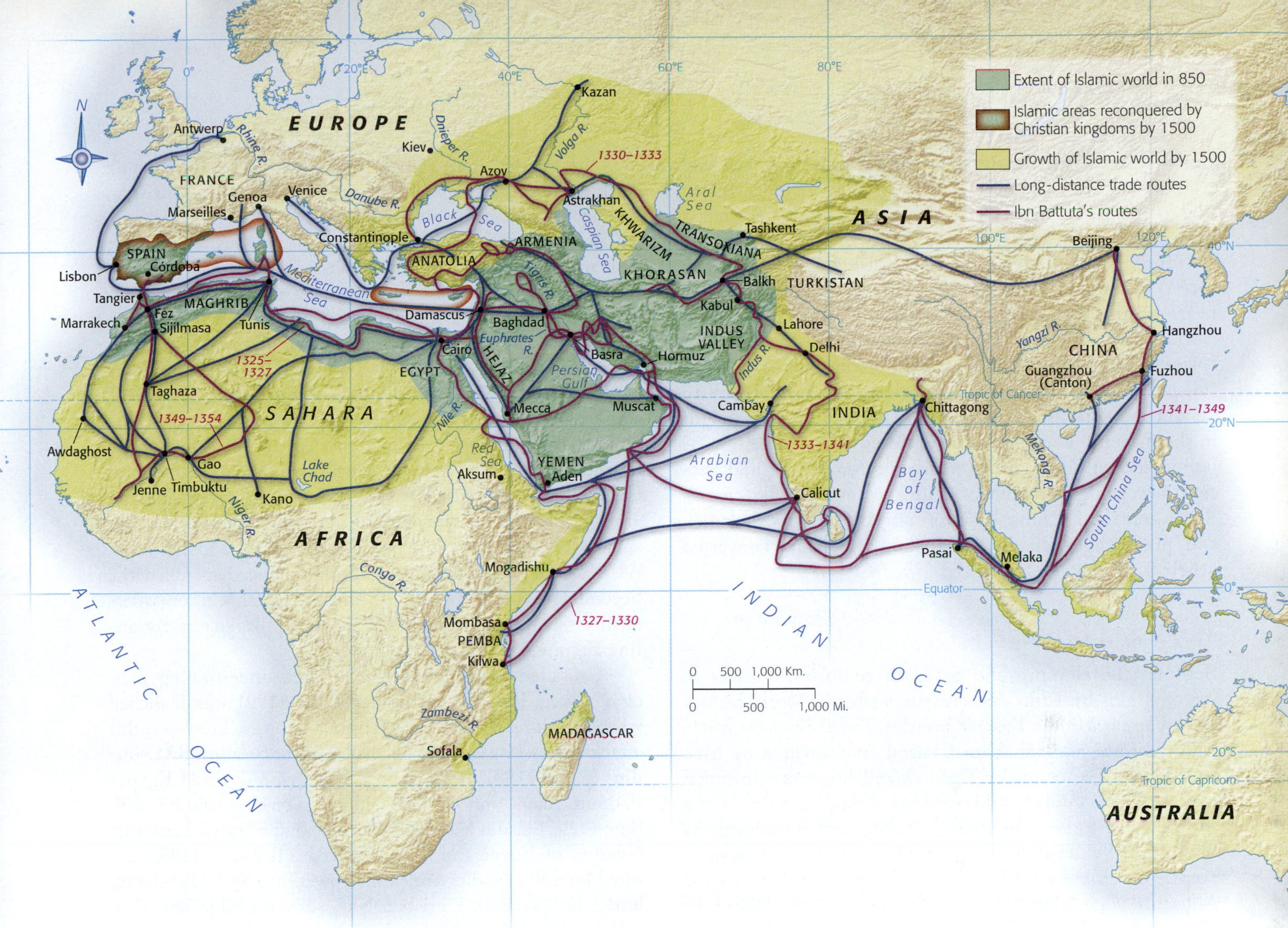

MAP 10.3 DAR AL-ISLAM AND TRADE ROUTES, CA. 1500 C.E. By 1500 the Islamic world stretched into West Africa, East Africa, and Southeast Asia. Trade routes connected the Islamic lands and allowed Muslim traders to extend their networks to China, Russia, and Europe.

joined by both a common faith and trade. Islam-fostered networks reached from the Atlantic eastward to the Pacific, spreading Arab words, names, social attitudes, cultural values, and the Arabic script to diverse peoples. Eventually several powerful military states emerged that ruled over large populations of Muslims and non-Muslims. The Islamic world also faced severe challenges—expanding Turks, Christian crusaders, Mongol conquerors, and horrific pandemics—setting the stage for new political forces in the fifteenth and sixteenth centuries. Yet, the Islamic tradition was resistant, overcoming factionalism and political decay to remain creative well past the 1400s.

The Global Shape of Dar al-Islam

More than half of the world's 1.5 to 2 billion Muslims today live outside the Middle East, the majority in South and Southeast Asia, with Arabs significantly outnumbered by non-Arab believers. After the Abbasid Caliphate's demise, Arab political power diminished, but Islam grew rapidly in both Africa and South Asia (see Chapters 12–13). Dozens of prosperous Muslim trading cities, from Tangier in Northwest Africa to Samarkand in Central Asia to Melaka in Malaya, offered goods from distant countries. Beginning in the thirteenth century, Muslims constructed a hemisphere-spanning system based on economic exchange and a shared understanding of the world and the cosmos, linked by informal networks of Islamic scholars and saints. The Quran and its message of a righteous social order provided a framework for Dar al-Islam.

Islam's spread corresponded with growing Muslim-dominated long-distance trade, especially the maritime trade around the Indian Ocean Basin. Except for the Chinese, Arabs enjoyed the world's most advanced shipbuilding and navigation between 1000 and 1450. The lateen sails that Arabs devised, or perhaps adapted from Southeast Asians, later allowed European ships to undertake long-distance voyages in the 1400s. An increasingly integrated Muslim-dominated maritime trading system gradually linked the eastern Mediterranean, Middle East, East African coast, Persia, and India with East and Southeast Asia (see Map 10.3). One Arab merchant expressed his commercial ambitions: "I want to send Persian saffron to

China, where I hear that it fetches a high price, and then ship Chinese porcelain to Greece, Greek brocade to India, Indian iron to Aleppo [a Syrian city], Aleppo glass to the Yemen and Yemeni material to Persia."[18]

The Straits of Melaka in Southeast Asia and Hormuz **(HAWR-muhz)** at the Persian Gulf entrance stood at the heart of the key mercantile system of the Intermediate world. Over these sea routes Indonesian and East African spices, Malayan gold and tin, Indian textiles, southern African gold, and Chinese silks, porcelain, and tea traveled to distant markets. The maritime network achieved its height in the fifteenth and sixteenth centuries, when Muslim economic and cultural power remained strong. Arab and Persian merchant communities could be found as far east as Korea and south China. By intermarrying with local women and practicing their faith, Muslim merchants converted others to Islam.

Turks and Crusaders

Between the eleventh and fifteenth centuries, a series of interventions by Turks and crusaders affected world history by reshaping Middle Eastern politics. The Turks were originally pastoral nomads from Central Asia divided by tribe and dialect. For centuries these skilled horsemen intruded into Chinese, Indian, and western Asian societies, some adopting Nestorian Christianity, Judaism, or Buddhism. As they gradually drew closer to Middle Eastern cultures, most eventually embraced Islam. Some Turks sent boys to the Abbasids, where they trained to become Abbasid soldiers or administrators.

Late in the tenth century, Muslim Turks called the Seljuks **(SEL-jooks)** achieved regional power. Recruiting other Turkish tribes, they expanded from Central Asia and swept through Afghanistan and Iran into Iraq. Allied with the declining Abbasids, Seljuk forces conquered many Muslim and Christian societies in the Caucasus region, eventually creating a large empire stretching from Palestine to Samarkand. In 1071 the Seljuks seized much of Anatolia, populated largely by Greek-speaking Orthodox Christians, from the weakening Byzantine state. Even when the Seljuks' power soon diminished elsewhere and their empire crumbled, they continued to govern Anatolia.

By the eleventh century some Islamic states faced increasing challenges from European Christians. Between 1095 and 1272 Christians from various European societies launched a long series of Crusades to win back what they viewed as the Christian Holy Land from Muslim occupation (see Chapter 14). The First Crusade capitalized on Muslim weakness: feuding Muslim states could not cooperate; some states, such as Fatimid Egypt, maintained lucrative trade ties with Europe; and some Middle Eastern societies had substantial Christian and Jewish populations and many dissident Muslims. In the end, however, the Crusades failed to achieve their long term goals.

The First Crusade (1095–1099) was triggered by Seljuk Turk encroachment on Byzantine territory and a Christian church division into rival branches in 1054. Roman popes, worried about Seljuk expansion and anxious to reassert primacy over the breakaway Constantinople-based Greek Orthodox Church, promoted the idea of positive violence to defend the faith. Using untrue stories of Muslim atrocities against Christians in Palestine, Pope Urban II called on Christians to reclaim the Holy Land and protect Jerusalem's churches and relics. Some 100,000 European volunteers, some pious, others just hungry for booty, responded. The crusaders fought their way to Jerusalem in 1099, taking the city and killing thousands of Muslims, Jews, and even local Christians. Some crusaders stayed on to guard the sites but also to colonize the surrounding territory, establishing four small Crusader states in what is today Israel and Lebanon. As Muslim forces regrouped, another pope dispatched the Second Crusade (1147–1149), during which the crusaders mostly slaughtered Jews in Europe and pillaged the Byzantine Empire.

Crusaders often fought each other, undermining their own power. The Third Crusade (1189–1192) was launched when Muslims pushed back Christian forces. However, this attack was met by General Salah al-Din, or Saladin **(SAL-uh-din)** (1138–1193), an Iraqi-born Kurd who deposed Egypt's Fatimid rulers and became sultan, replacing Shi'ite with Sunni rule. Saladin led Muslim armies that stopped a crusader invasion of Egypt and then, between 1187 and 1192, captured Jerusalem and extended his power into Syria. A tolerant leader, he spared the Christians who surrendered in Jerusalem and employed the great Cordoba-born Jewish sage and legal authority Moses Maimonides **(my-MAHN-uh-deez)** (1135–1204) as his physician. His military exploits made Saladin a hero in Muslim eyes, and he is still revered today. The final six Crusades failed to wrest control of North Africa, Jerusalem, and Anatolia from Muslim hands.

Historians still debate the Crusades. Many crusaders were inspired by sincere religious zeal to preserve access to Christian holy sites, but many also looted captured cities, including Orthodox Constantinople. Muslim armies often showed little mercy on their enemies. Some believe that the militant Christian challenge to Islam ultimately made both religions less tolerant and more zealous, complicating relations. For centuries afterward some Muslim rulers viewed their Christian subjects as untrustworthy, while Christians persecuted the remaining Muslim populations in southern Europe. Even today, hundreds of years later, Islamic militants capitalize on lingering resentment against Western "crusaders."

Mongol Conquests and the Black Death

The Mongols **(MAHN-guhlz)**, Central Asian pastoral nomads, constituted a much greater short-term threat to Islam than Christian crusaders sweeping into western Asia. Led by

[18]Hariri, quoted in Fernand Braudel, *A History of Civilizations* (New York: Penguin, 1995), 71.

Genghis Khan **(GENG-iz KAHN)** (ca. 1162–1227), the Mongols, prompted perhaps by environmental stress and overpopulation, began expanding out of Mongolia in the late twelfth century. Between 1218 and 1221 they fought their way through lands inhabited mostly by Turkish-speaking Muslims, destroying several great Silk Road cities. The Mongol attack destroyed states, created instability, and unwittingly laid the foundation for a hemisphere-wide pandemic causing much devastation and death.

Mongol atrocities became legendary. For example, to paralyze Muslim societies with fear and to prevent opposition, the Mongols killed 700,000 mostly unarmed residents in the Persian city of Merv. Fear usually worked. An Arab chronicler wrote of Mongol invaders that "in the countries that have not yet been overrun by them, everyone spends the night afraid that they may appear there too."[19] After Genghis Khan's death in 1227, the Mongols turned to conquering China, Russia, and eastern Europe but also put pressure on the Caucasus and Anatolia. In 1243 they defeated the remnants of the Seljuk Turks.

In 1256 a grandson of Genghis Khan, Hulegu **(hoo-LAY-goo)** (1217–1275), led new attacks with more lasting consequences for the Middle East. In Iraq in 1258, Hulegu's army, faced with fierce resistance, pillaged Baghdad, burning schools, libraries, mosques, and palaces, killing perhaps a million people, and executing all the Abbasids, a fateful turning point for Arab society that ended the prosperity and intellectual glory once represented by the now-gutted city. Hulegu's forces pushed on west, occupying Damascus and destroying Aleppo **(uh-LEP-oh)**. The pastoralist Mongols also disrupted agriculture, returning some farms to pasture and dispersing the peasants. In some places farming never recovered.

But the Islamic tradition proved resilient. When Hulegu's armies invaded Egypt in 1260, they were defeated at the battle of Ayn Jalut by the Mamluks **(MAM-looks)**, ex-slave soldiers of Turkish origin who had taken power there. Hulegu's Mongols stayed in Iraq and Persia, calling themselves the Il-Khanid **(il-KHAN-id)** dynasty, assimilating Persian culture, and eventually adopting Islam. Descendants of Mongol invaders in Russia, known as Tartars, also became Muslim. The Il-Khanids practiced religious toleration and encouraged monumental architecture, learning, and literary renaissance; and scholars wrote pathbreaking world histories telling us much about the Mongol empire.

By building a large empire across Eurasia, the Mongols fostered overland trade and travel, but they also provided a path for deadly diseases to spread. Like Europe and China, the Islamic world was deeply affected by the terrible fourteenth-century pandemic known in the West as the Black Death, a catastrophic disease, probably bubonic plague, that killed quickly and spread rapidly. Initially carried into the Black Sea region from eastern Asia by fleas infesting rats that stowed away on Silk Road caravans or trading ships, the pandemic hit the Middle East repeatedly over a century, reducing Egypt and Syria's population by two-thirds. Ibn Khaldun wrote that "cities and towns were laid waste, roads and way signs were obliterated, settlements and mansions became empty. The entire inhabited world changed."[20] Ibn Khaldun felt he might be living at history's end. But by the 1400s the Middle East had stabilized and regained some economic and cultural dynamism.

The Rise of Muslim Military States

In the thirteenth and fourteenth centuries, several powerful Muslim military states arose, including the Mamluks in Egypt, the Timurids in Central Asia, and the Ottoman Turks in Anatolia. Gunpowder, a Chinese invention that moved along the Silk Road during Mongol times, forever changed warfare and also impacted politics. After 1350 firearm possession gave some states and groups advantages over rivals and led to stronger, more bureaucratic states.

The Mamluks ruled Egypt and Syria from 1250 to 1517, making Egypt the richest Middle Eastern state. After expanding into Arabia and capturing Mecca and Medina, they controlled and taxed the flow of Muslim pilgrims. They also enjoyed an active trade with Genoa and Venice, the major Italian trading cities that supplied Asian goods to Europe. Venetian merchants established trading posts around Mamluk lands, exchanging timber, metals, and gold for spices, dyes, and Indian textiles. Eventually, however, Mamluk corruption and increasing taxes prompted seafaring European merchants to seek a maritime route to the East. In 1516–1517 another Turkish group, the Ottomans, defeated the Mamluks and absorbed their lands into the growing Ottoman Empire (see Map 10.4).

In Central Asia, Tamerlane **(TAM-uhr-lane)** (1336–1405), a ruthless Muslim prince of Turkish and Mongol ancestry who was crippled by an arrow wound as a young man but hoped to emulate Genghis Khan, made the Timurid state the dominant power for over a century. From his capital, Samarkand, Tamerlane's army rampaged through the Caucasus, southern Russia, Persia, Iraq, and Syria, killing thousands and destroying cities and farms. He then wreaked havoc in northern India (see Chapter 13). Only Tamerlane's death in 1405 halted his forces from invading China and Ottoman Turkey. Although Tamerlane protected merchants and Sufi mystics, his heritage largely consisted of smoking ruins and pyramids of human heads. However, his successors built mosques and patronized scholars, and later his grandson established a great empire in India in the early 1500s.

The Ottoman **(AHT-uh-muhn)** Turks established the most powerful and enduring military state. The Ottomans originated as a small Anatolian kingdom led by a chief named Osman **(ohs-MAHN)** (Ottoman means "followers of Osman"). Osman was influenced by Sufis dedicated to destroying Byzantium, which was reeling from temporary crusader occupation

[19]Ibn Al Athir, quoted in Mike Edwards, "Genghis Khan," *National Geographic* (December 1996): 9.

[20]Quoted in Francis Robinson, *The Cambridge Illustrated History of the Islamic World* (Cambridge: Cambridge University Press, 1996), 198.

of Constantinople and weakening influence in Anatolia. Capitalizing on this vacuum, by 1300 the Ottomans had raided and then annexed remaining Byzantine strongholds in Anatolia. Using gunpowder weapons, they ultimately conquered much of the Byzantine Empire, creating a dynamic state in western Eurasia and a link between Middle Eastern Islam and European Christianity. Once great Byzantium increasingly became a shell surrounding Constantinople.

Soon the Ottomans moved into the Balkans, where they defeated Serbia, the strongest Christian power in southeastern Europe. The Ottomans favored Muslims in taxes, and many Albanian and Serb-speaking Christians adopted Islam, some for economic reasons, creating a division in the Balkans between Catholic, Orthodox, and Muslim peoples that complicates politics even today. At the Battle of Nicopolis **(nuh-KAHP-uh-luhs)** in 1396, the Ottomans defeated a Hungarian-led force drawn from throughout Europe to oppose Ottoman expansion. In 1453 Sultan Mehmed **(MEH-met)** the Conqueror (1432–1481) finally took Constantinople and converted the city into the Ottoman capital, which was eventually renamed Istanbul.

millet The nationality system through which the Ottomans allowed the leaders of religious and ethnic minorities to administer their own communities.

The Ottoman Empire was now the major regional power and Istanbul a major trade hub, attracting a multiethnic, multireligious population. Patronizing the arts, Mehmed the Conqueror invited famous Italian artists and architects to work in his cosmopolitan capital, by 1500 Europe's largest city. Ottoman sultans used subject peoples' administrative and military skills and promoted talented men regardless of background. Moreover, through the **millet** ("nationality") system, leaders of religious and ethnic minorities were allowed to administer their own communities. Hence, the Greek patriarch had

MAP 10.4 THE OTTOMAN EMPIRE, 1566 Between 1300 and the mid-1500s the Ottoman Turks expanded out of western Anatolia to conquer a large empire in western Asia, Egypt and North Africa, and eastern Europe, making the Ottomans one of the world's largest states.

Réunion des Musées Nationaux/Art Resource, NY

VENETIAN AMBASSADORS VISITING MAMLUK DAMASCUS Venetians and Genoese merchants, fierce rivals, regularly visited the Middle East to acquire silks, spices, and other valuable products. This painting from the 1400s shows Venetians being received by the Mamluk governor of Damascus, who wears a horned hat and sits on a low platform, in today's Syria.

authority over all Orthodox Christians in Ottoman territory, while Christians and Jews generally practiced their religions freely. The millet system allowed Turks to divide and hence rule diverse peoples.

A dynamic and militarily powerful Ottoman state continued to expand, by 1500 solidifying control over Greece and the Balkans (see Map 10.4). In the 1500s, Ottoman rule extended over much of western Asia as far east as Persia and North Africa from Egypt to Algeria. In the 1500s the Ottomans also played an ambitious naval role in the Indian Ocean for several decades, expanding trade and confronting Portuguese expansion while establishing an alliance with the Indonesian Muslim state of Acheh on Sumatra. Ottoman, and Islamic, expansion in western Eurasia finally came to an end when the Ottomans were defeated while attempting to take Hungary in 1699. However, the Ottoman Empire continued until 1923.

Islamic Contributions to World History

By linking peoples of varied cultures, ideas, religions, and languages, Arab expansion fostered intellectual and artistic creativity, while the Islamic faith and culture profoundly influenced South Asian, African, and European societies. For example, the gradual Islamic conquest of India posed an alternative to Hinduism. As Islamic influence and Arab merchants traveled south across the Sahara and along the East African coast, various African societies also adopted Islam and some Islamic customs and technologies. From the ninth through eleventh centuries, Arabs in Sicily and Spain passed on to Europe some of the advanced science, mathematics, and technology of the Middle East, India, and China. In many respects, Muslims linked the Classical Greeks and Indians with late medieval Europeans, whose universities now studied Greco-Roman and Islamic learning. Eventually this exchange of knowledge helped spark a scientific and technological revolution in Europe as well as a questioning of the entrenched Christian church, ultimately leading to more diverse ideas within Western societies. But the exchange was not one way, as Muslims also benefited from European medicine, science, and art.

The mixture of Arab, Persian, Turkish, Byzantine, Christian, Jewish, African, and Indian influences created a hemispheric-wide Islamic world that connected culturally and politically diverse societies sharing a common faith and, often, values. While most Iraqis, Syrians, Egyptians, and North Africans adopted the Arabic language and called themselves Arabs, Persians and Turks maintained their own spoken languages but now wrote using Arabic script. Indeed, for many centuries

Persian remained a language of government and the elite, from the Seljuk Turkish empire to various Muslim states in India and Central Asia.

Non-Muslims played key roles, especially in commerce. From the eighth through eleventh centuries Jews were the key middlemen between Christian Europe and the Muslim world. Hence, Jews from southern France traded in Spain, North Africa, and the eastern Mediterranean, many becoming fluent in Arabic. After the eleventh century Jews lost ground as intermediaries to Italians in the west and Armenian Christians in the east.

Muslim scholars were proud of their expansive horizons. For example, the Egyptian Jalal al-Din al-Suyuti **(juh-LALL al-din al-sue-YOU-tee)** (1445–1505) boasted that he and his books had traveled as far as West Africa and India. Yet, after the last Muslim kingdom in Spain fell in 1492, he believed the Muslim world needed intellectual and social renewal. Although the Ottoman Turks were rising, al-Suyuti could not know that after 1500 Muslim states would also have a resurgence in Persia and India, nor that various Europeans, benefiting from the encounter with Islam, would become serious rivals to Muslim power and challenge the interconnected Islamic world.

Several powerful Islamic states, including the Ottoman Empire, enjoyed political and economic influence in the sixteenth and seventeenth centuries. But, with the occasional exception of Ottoman Turkey, technological innovation, scientific inquiry, and the questioning of accepted religious and cultural ideas fell off in the Middle East. Most madrasas, while training Muslim clerics and providing spiritual guidance, had narrow, theology-based curriculums that deemphasized secular learning. These trends diminished the humanist, tolerant tradition of Islamic scholarship represented by Baghdad's House of Wisdom and the schools in Muslim Spain. Over the next three centuries, Middle Eastern peoples who had boasted innovative and cosmopolitan traditions for a millennium gradually lost military and economic power while Europeans surged.

MAKE SURE YOU UNDERSTAND THESE KEY POINTS BEFORE MOVING ON

- **Trade routes spread Islam throughout the hemisphere, eventually creating Dar al-Islam, an Islamic world stretching from Indonesia to Morocco, in which Arabs constituted a minority of Muslims.**
- **The Mongols, led by Genghis Khan and Hulegu, ruthlessly attacked Muslims in Central Asia and sacked Baghdad, but the Islamic tradition continued throughout Mongol rule.**
- **The arrival of gunpowder from China allowed Muslim military states, such as the Mamluks and the Timurids, to gain power.**
- **The Ottoman Turks established an extremely successful empire in the territory of the former Byzantine Empire by allowing subject minorities to administer their own affairs.**
- **By conducting and preserving a great deal of scientific and philosophical learning, the Muslims contributed much to European culture.**

CHAPTER SUMMARY

The rise of Islam in Arabia during the seventh century changed world history, forging a community of believers around a set of monotheistic ideas. Muhammad's message proved so popular that, within a few decades, Muslim Arabs had conquered a large empire and spread Islam to many Arab and non-Arab peoples. Islam offered distinctive religious, political, and social ideas, such as pilgrimage, annual fasting, a legal code, and an emphasis on social justice, but it also was influenced by Christian, Jewish, Persian, and other traditions. Islamic societies flourished under powerful theocratic governments, such as the Umayyad and Abbasid Caliphates, while Islamic writers and scientists assimilated and developed knowledge from many societies. Muslim thinkers preserved Classical Greek learning while pioneering new ideas in astronomy, mathematics, the physical sciences, and agriculture. Arab links also contributed knowledge to medieval Europe, spurring the scientific and technological rise of the West.

The Islamic world became a cosmopolitan network of peoples linked by trade and religious scholars. While the Abbasid collapse brought some political fragmentation, Islam still expanded, overcoming several challenges in the millennium after Muhammad. By 1500 the Ottoman Turks controlled a vast empire. Stretching from western Africa and southwestern Europe eastward to Southeast Asia and western China, Islam became a hemispheric culture, even extending its influences into non-Islamic regions. After 1500, however, the Islamic Middle East began to fade as a political power and a center for intellectual inquiry.

KEY TERMS

Bedouins (p. 219)
Ka'ba (p. 220)
Quran (p. 220)
Hadith (p. 220)
hijra (p. 220)
umma (p. 221)
Allah (p. 221)
caliphate (p. 222)
Ramadan (p. 222)
haj (p. 222)
jihad (p. 222)
sultan (p. 224)
Shari'a (p. 225)
madrasas (p. 225)
Sunni (p. 226)
Shi'a (p. 226)
Sufism (p. 230)
calligraphy (p. 232)
Dar al-Islam (p. 234)
millet (p. 238)

11 East Asian Traditions, Transformations, and Eurasian Encounters, 600–1500

Rafael Macia/Photo Researchers/Science Source

GIANT JAPANESE BUDDHA AT KAMAKURA During this era, most Japanese adopted Buddhism, some expressing their faith in art. This gigantic statue, erected in the city of Kamakura in 1252, shows the Buddha in meditation.

China is a sea that salts all rivers that flow into it.

—Italian traveler Marco Polo (1275 C.E.)[1]

Early in the twelfth century the Chinese artist Zhang Zeduan, noted for his realistic drawings, painted a massive scroll of people at work and leisure throughout Kaifeng **(KIE-FENG)**, then China's capital city and home to perhaps 1 million people. Set during the annual spring festival, the huge scroll portrays a bustling city, from its riverside suburbs to the towering city gates to the downtown business district, during one of China's most creative and prosperous eras. The scroll features people (mostly men) going about their daily activities, including foreign merchants, streetside hawkers, fortune tellers, scholars, and monks. Some people work in warehouses, iron smelters, arsenals, and shipyards. Zhang's vivid record of Kaifeng's commercial life shows building material suppliers, textile firms, drug and chemical shops, hotels, food stalls, teahouses, and restaurants. Cargo and pleasure barges cruise the river, while camels heavily laden with goods enter the city. The scroll remains a fascinating window onto the Song era, when China truly was the center of the world.

Much of the prosperous city life Zhang portrayed was familiar to Chinese of earlier and later generations, for Chinese society demonstrated considerable continuity over time. The Han's eventual succession by the Sui and then by the Tang **(tahng)** and Song **(soong)** dynasties ensured that Chinese society continued largely along traditional lines, in contrast to the dramatic changes taking place in Japan, the Middle East, India, Southeast Asia, and Europe during the Intermediate Era. Once the Tang adopted a modified version of the Han system, the ensuing millennium proved a golden age, broken only occasionally by invasion or disorder. Some scholars call the Intermediate Era in world history the "Chinese Centuries," with China perhaps the world's richest, most populous society, enjoying a well-organized government and economy, a flourishing artistic and literary culture, and technological and scientific creativity. Commercial and cultural networks connected China to the rest of Eurasia, influencing Korea and Japan, which adopted aspects of Chinese culture while also forging distinctive societies. China did indeed, as Marco Polo recognized, influence or awe all those with whom it came into contact.

[1]Quoted in John Merson, *The Genius That Was China: East and West in the Making of the Modern World* (Woodstock, NY: Overlook Press, 1990), 14.

IN THIS CHAPTER

Tang China: The Hub of the East

What role did Tang China play in the Eurasian world?

The harsh Sui dynasty ruled China for only a short time (581–618 C.E.) before rebellions ended the regime. The victor in the ensuing struggles between rival rebel forces established the Tang dynasty (618–907), whose three centuries of rule set a high point in many facets of Chinese life, providing a cultural and political model for neighboring societies. The only comparable power in Eurasia at that time was the Muslim Abbasid empire; India and Europe were divided into many small states often threatened by invaders. Tang models shaped China until the early twentieth century.

The Tang Empire and Eurasian Exchange

In the seventh and eighth centuries Tang China was earth's largest, most populous society, with some 50 or 60 million people and immense influence in the eastern third of Eurasia (see Map 11.1). Like the earlier Han, the Tang launched ambitious campaigns that brought Central Asia (as far west as the Caspian Sea), Tibet, Mongolia, Manchuria, and parts of Siberia under Chinese rule. Vietnam had long been a colony. The Koreans became a vassal state, and the Japanese established close ties. Chinese garrisons protected the Silk Road, fostering trade and migration.

As the most outward-looking Chinese dynasty, Tang China became a world market of ideas, people, and things arriving over the exchange networks. The Silk Road across Central Asia remained a transcontinental highway for traders, adventurers, diplomats, missionaries, and pilgrims traveling east or west, carrying goods and ideas. Nestorian Christian, Manichean, Buddhist, and Muslim missionaries arrived, while merchants from around Asia, many coming by sea, formed communities in Chinese cities. A lively sea trade or maritime Silk Road linked China with Southeast Asia, India, and the Middle East. Arab, Persian, Indian, Cambodian, and Malay immigrants constituted perhaps two-thirds of the 200,000 residents of the southern port of Guangzhou **(gwahng-jo)**, also known as Canton, which boasted both Sunni and Shi'ite mosques. Indian astronomers and mathematicians joined the Tang government as scientific officials, and several thousand people of foreign birth, mainly Central Asians, served as government officials or army officers. One early Tang emperor boasted that "in antiquity everyone

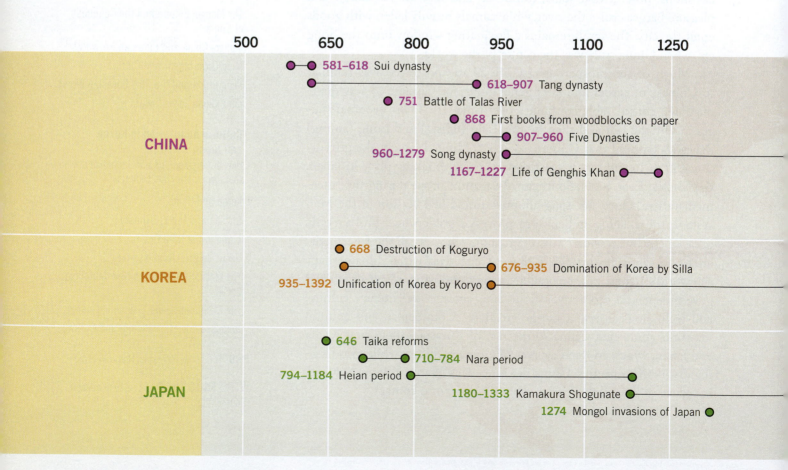

500 650 800 950 1100 1250

CHINA

- **581–618** Sui dynasty
- **618–907** Tang dynasty
- **751** Battle of Talas River
- **868** First books from woodblocks on paper
- **907–960** Five Dynasties
- **960–1279** Song dynasty
- **1167–1227** Life of Genghis Khan

KOREA

- **668** Destruction of Koguryo
- **676–935** Domination of Korea by Silla
- **935–1392** Unification of Korea by Koryo

JAPAN

- **646** Taika reforms
- **710–784** Nara period
- **794–1184** Heian period
- **1180–1333** Kamakura Shogunate
- **1274** Mongol invasions of Japan

honored Chinese and looked down upon barbarians…[but now he] loved them all."[2] Meanwhile, several hundred Chinese scholars visited or sojourned in India, most of them seeking Buddhist literature.

China and the World

Tang wealth and power stimulated commerce throughout Eurasia. By land or sea, many Chinese inventions reached western Eurasia. In 753 C.E. a Chinese craftsman reported that, in Baghdad: "As for the weavers who make light silks, the goldsmiths who work gold and silver there, and the painters; the arts which they practice were started by Chinese technicians."[3] Europeans and Middle Easterners prized Chinese products such as silk and porcelain, and Chinese culture also spread to Korea and Japan. This multicultural exchange benefited China. Societies such as Burma, Java, and Nepal regularly sent embassies to the Tang court bearing gifts, and renewed contacts with India and the Middle East fostered China's creativity. New products, most notably tea from Southeast Asia, appeared, first as medicine and then beverage, fostering teahouses in every marketplace. The chair, imported from the Middle East, replaced seating pads, making the Chinese East Asia's only chair users. However, some Chinese scholars criticized cosmopolitan attitudes and foreign culture.

The Eurasian exchange fostered dynamic, culturally rich cities. Tang China boasted many cities larger than any in Europe or India. The capital, Chang'an **(CHAHNG-ahn)**, present-day Xi'an **(SHEE-AHN)**, had 2 million inhabitants. The world's largest city, Chang'an reflected urban planning, its streets carefully laid out in a grid pattern, the city divided into quadrants, and broad thoroughfares crowded with visitors and sojourners from many lands, including Arabs, Persians, Syrians, Jews, Turks, Koreans, Japanese, Vietnamese, Indians, and Tibetans. Many foreign artists, artisans, merchants, and entertainers, such as Indian jugglers and Afghan actors, worked in the capital, which contained four Zoroastrian temples, two Nestorian Christian churches, and several mosques. The only contemporary cities rivaling Chang'an in size and amenities were Baghdad, the powerful Abbasid Caliphate's capital, and Byzantine-ruled Constantinople.

[2]Quoted in Charles Holcombe, "Immigrants and Strangers: From Cosmopolitanism to Confucian Universalism in Tang China," *T'ang Studies* 20–21 (2002–2003): 72—73.

[3]Quoted in John A. Harrison, *The Chinese Empire* (New York: Harcourt Brace Jovanovich, 1972), 239.

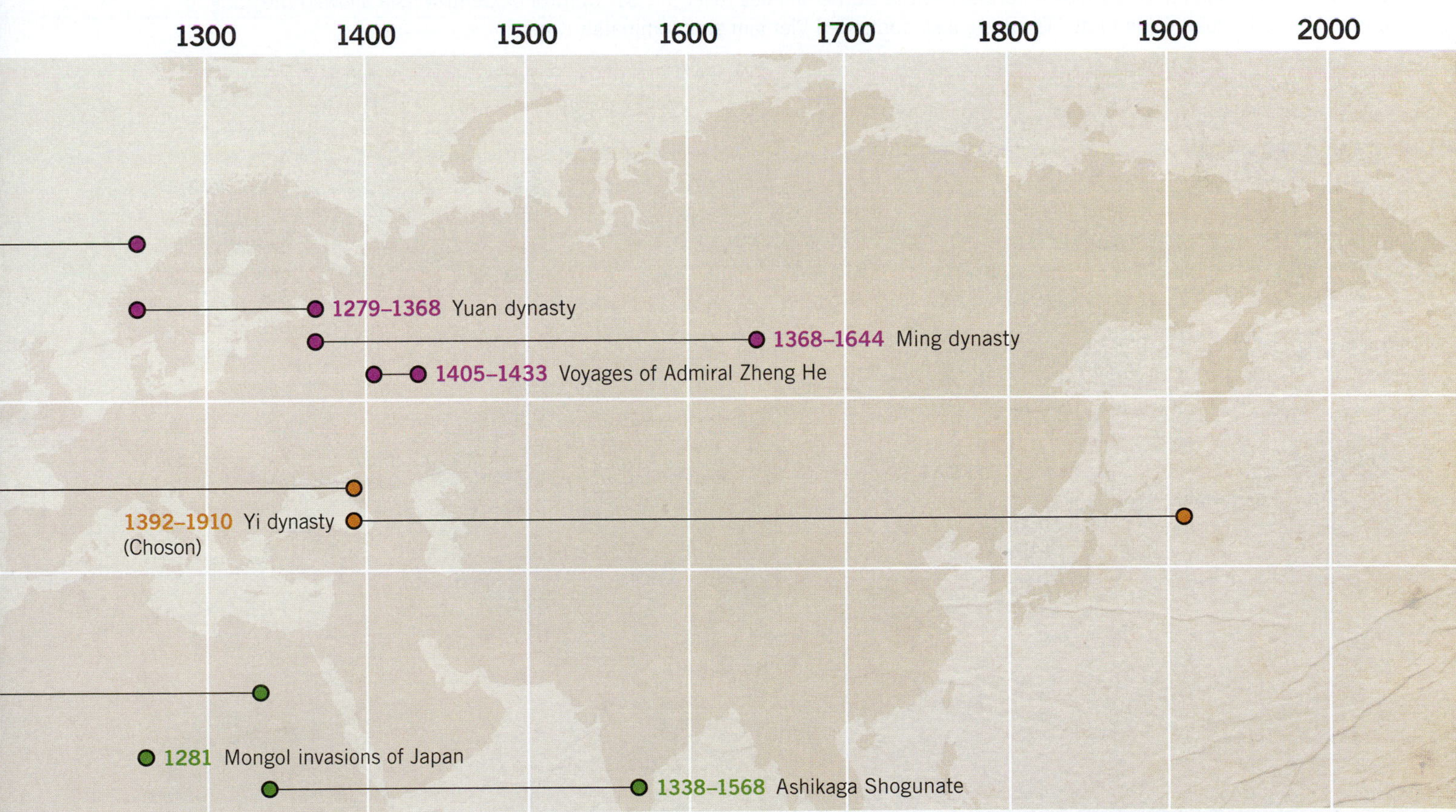

Imperial Government and Economic Growth

China's centralized and highly efficient imperial government maintained one of the world's most productive economies. Despite bloody rebellions, invasions, assassinations, palace coups, and dynastic upheavals, stability marked China's political system for many centuries. Later dynasties followed the Tang model. According to Confucian theory, the state emulated the family, with the emperor serving as the people's symbolic father, governing by moral example, not physical force. Chinese considered the emperor the Son of Heaven—not divine but the intermediary between the terrestrial and supernatural realms—and the country's first scholar. During daily audiences, foreign diplomats sometimes presented gifts symbolizing their submission to his authority. In return he ceremoniously bestowed on them a title, state robes, and gifts, followed later by a banquet.

While women sometimes had power behind the throne, only one, the Empress Wu Zhao **(woo chow)** (625–705), ever officially led the government. An imperial concubine at age thirteen, she used her political skills and ruthless ambition to eventually displace the sickly emperor and maintained power for five decades. While Empress Wu generally ruled ably, Chinese scholars considered her an evil usurper and warned future generations against women rulers.

In theory emperors held absolute power, but their actual power was circumscribed. The Censorate, an agency unique to China, monitored government workings, rooted out corruption, proposed state policy changes, and criticized government failings. Only the strongest emperors could punish the Censorate for criticism. Furthermore, the Mandate of Heaven doctrine, which gave people a right to overthrow an evil, corrupt, or ineffective government, meant that emperors had to consider their policies and behavior.

Because administering a large, diverse empire required a competent bureaucracy, the Tang revived the Han dynasty's competitive civil service exams. Believing that government officials, known as mandarins, should be the country's wisest and ablest men, they used merit-based exams to recruit talented individuals, regardless of birth, for government service. A national university and hundreds of local-level academies helped train potential officials. During the Tang and succeeding Song dynasties, perhaps 15 percent of the mandarins did not come from upper-class backgrounds, indicating some social mobility. And yet, the Tang was also, like the Han, an age of aristocratic power, with men from great families boasting rich pedigrees dominating public life and the civil service.

The system consisted of examinations at local, provincial, and national levels. Usually less than 5 percent of candidates

MAP 11.1 THE TANG EMPIRE, CA. 750 C.E. The Tang dynasty forged a large empire across Central Asia into Turkestan before their expansion was halted by Muslim armies at the Battle of Talas River in 751. Control of Central Asia allowed the Tang to protect the Silk Road trade route. The Tang also controlled Vietnam and dominated Korea.

Mansell/Time Life Pictures/Getty Images

TANG EMPRESS WU ZHAO A portrait of seventh century Tang Empress Wu Zhao, the only woman to officially lead China's government in the imperial period.

passed and moved on to the next level. Passing the highest level earned the equivalent of a PhD degree, a prerequisite to hold office. Largely testing knowledge of literary composition and the Confucian classics, the competitive merit exam system contributed greatly to China's long political stability, giving the ruling elite a shared Confucian ideology emphasizing ethics and loyalty. The Tang bureaucracy numbered around fifteen thousand officials, a small number for a huge country and an indication that they ruled with the people's cooperation or acquiescence. From now on China's leaders ruled through the bureaucracy of scholars.

Tang officials pursued economic growth, especially agricultural production. A Tang official explained the system: "Grain and cloth are produced by the [peasants], natural resources are transformed by the artisan class, wealth and goods are circulated by the merchant[s], and money is managed by the ruler."[4] The 80 percent of Chinese tilling the soil were generally able—often just barely—to produce a food surplus for the 20 percent in towns and cities. But the Chinese achieved better yields, becoming some of the world's most efficient farmers. To circumvent powerful landowning families, Tang officials experimented with land reform. The "equal field system" assigned each peasant family a plot of around 19 acres, in the hope that this allotment provided enough for the family's needs. The reforms brought the peasantry some prosperity, but the system disintegrated when the Tang declined after some 120 years. Still, throughout history some emperors and officials sought a more equitable land system.

Religion, Science, and Technology

Buddhism flourished in Central, Southeast, and East Asia during the Early Intermediate Era. Under the Tang, Buddhism became a dominant faith, while Confucianism and Daoism remained influential. Buddhist monks, pilgrims, and artists traveled between India and China, drawing the two societies into closer contact. However, competing Buddhist sects presented the Tang with problems. Furthermore, because Buddhist monasteries controlled vast tax-exempt lands and wealth, they became alternative power centers that sparked a mid-ninth-century government crackdown on Buddhist institutions. Emperor Wuzong **(woo-chong)** (840–846), desperate for more revenues, seized forty-six hundred monasteries, defrocking all monks under fifty. Although Wuzong's successors restored the monasteries, his actions reduced the Buddhist orders' political and economic power enough to ensure they never again exercised secular power.

Some new religions moved east along the Silk Road. Nestorian Christianity, considered heretical in Byzantium, gained a small following, and Islam became strong in northwest China and parts of southwest and southern China. Jewish merchants, mostly from Persia, settled in several northern China cities, founding small but enduring Jewish communities. Unlike Wuzong, the Tang court generally took a tolerant, ecumenical view of religion, one emperor proclaiming: "The Way [truth] has more than one name. There is more than one sage. Doctrines vary in distant lands, their benefits reach all mankind."[5]

Scholars and craftsmen made scientific and technological achievements. Astronomers established the solar year at 365 days and studied sunspots, and some also argued that the earth was round and revolved around the sun. They were the first anywhere to analyze, record, and predict solar eclipses. Tang engineers also built the first load-bearing segmental arch bridge. After perfecting gunpowder, an elaboration of the firecracker, by mixing sulphur, saltpeter, and charcoal, Chinese military forces used primitive cannon and flaming rockets to protect their borders or resist rebels. Finally, the Chinese made great advances in printing. For centuries they had carved texts into stone and made ink rubbings for mass distribution of religious and

[4]Po Chu-I, quoted in William H. McNeill, *The Pursuit of Power: Technology, Armed Force, and Society Since A.D. 1000* (Chicago: University of Chicago Press, 1982), 28.

[5]Quoted in C. P. Fitzgerald, *China: A Short Cultural History* (New York: Praeger, 1961), 336.

Confucian texts. As demand soared, some creative men began carving texts into wooden blocks and then reproducing text on paper with ink; the first known paper book was issued by 868. Woodblock printing provided texts for the civil service exams and spread Buddhist writings. Possessing an insatiable desire to classify past wisdom for use by future generations, Chinese compiled encyclopedias to record their accumulated knowledge. Woodblock printing also gave rise to a written popular culture.

The Arts and Literature

Some of China's greatest painters and sculptors lived in Tang times. Scholars and government officials avidly pursued painting and calligraphy, the beautiful rendering of Chinese characters to record a meaningful poem, quote, or passage in a refined, balanced form. Both calligraphers and painters used brush and ink on silk or paper. Chinese paintings were generally restrained, understated, and philosophical. Influenced by Daoism, many painters specialized in landscapes. An eleventh-century writer explained why: "Why does a virtuous man take delight in landscapes? That in a rustic retreat he may nourish his nature; amid the carefree play of streams and rocks, he may take delight. Haze, mist, and the haunting spirits of the mountains are what human nature seeks, and yet can rarely find."[6] But Confucian ideas were also expressed, with people usually a small part of the picture. Like Confucian philosophy, Chinese arts stressed order, morality, and tradition. Yet, some free-spirited artists experimented wildly; one eccentric flipped ink-soaked hair at silk, and another splashed while dancing. Artists also reflected their times. Wind-tossed bamboo and choppy water, for example, might indicate turbulent politics. Chinese also experienced art when sipping tea from nearly transparent porcelain cups, the world's most sanitary utensils at that time. China became famous for splendid lacquer ware, furniture made with mother of pearl, gold and silver inlay, and luxurious brocades.

Many of China's greatest poets lived in this era. Annual literary festivals, held in Chang'an, selected prizewinners. Many poems depicted life's hardships—poverty, war, romantic love's ups and downs, the passing of time, the imminence of death. But lyrical poems explored life's wonders and the parting of friends. Chinese poems usually blended emotion with restraint, reflecting their Daoist and Buddhist influences. For example, Wang Wei **(wahng way)** expressed a Daoist appreciation of nature: "Walking at leisure we watch laurel flowers fall. In the silence of this night the spring mountain is empty. The moon rises, the birds are startled, As they sing occasionally near the spring fountains." The poem describes a changing landscape of falling laurel leaves, a quiet spring mountain, a rising moon, and birds singing, all creating Daoist feelings of peace, detachment, and purity.

The two giants of Tang poetry were Li Po **(lee po)** and Du Fu **(too foo)**, close friends but very different in their personalities and styles. The eccentric free spirit Li (701–762) was romantic, disrespectful of authority, and humorous but often melancholy. Influenced by Daoism, Li said that a good person must be carefree, maintaining a child's heart and mind. He apparently drowned on a boat trip while reaching out in a drunken ecstasy for the moon's reflection in the water. In "The Joys of Wine" he wrote: "Since Heaven and Earth love wine, I can love wine without shaming Heaven. With three cups I penetrate the Great Dao. Take a whole jugful and I and the world are one. Such things as I have dreamed in wine, Shall never be told to the sober."[7] Li also occasionally wrote

SONG LANDSCAPE This painting, completed around 1000 C.E., shows a Buddhist temple dwarfed by towering mountain peaks.

[6]Quoted in Derk Bodde, *China's Cultural Tradition: What and Whither?* (New York: Holt, Rinehart and Winston, 1957), 31.

[7]The Wang and Li poems are from Robert Payne, ed., *The White Pony: An Anthology of Chinese Poetry* (New York: Mentor, 1960), 154, 174.

about public issues. He outlined the hardships of conscripted soldiers during the Tang military campaigns in Central Asia, wondering who would cultivate their fields.

A Confucian humanist, Du Fu (712–770), Li Po's opposite, was the preeminent poet of social consciousness, deeply concerned with the human condition. Du's poems held up a mirror to his times. His antiwar poems remain powerful even a millennium later: "When will men be satisfied with building a wall against the barbarians? When will the soldiers return to their native land?" He sympathized with soldiers and their families rather than with imperial aims:

> *The war-chariots rattle, The war-horses whinny. Each man of you has a bow and quiver in his belt. Father, mother, son, wife, stare at you going. At the border where the blood of men spills like the sea. And still the heart of Emperor Wu is beating for war. Do you know that, east of China's mountains, in two hundred districts, And in thousands of villages, nothing grows but weeds? And though strong women have bent to the ploughing, East and west the furrows are all broken down.*

Du also showed tenderness, celebrating everyday life's pleasures: "Clear waters wind, Around our village. With long summer days, Full of loveliness. My wife draws out, A chessboard on paper, While our little boys, Bend needles into fish hooks. What more could I wish for?"[8]

Changes in the Late Tang Dynasty

Significant changes took place in China between the eighth and tenth centuries. The overwhelming majority of Chinese now lived in central and south China, the fertile Yangzi Basin becoming the most productive economic region. New crop strains from Southeast Asia made possible two crops of rice a year. Combined with better transportation, this fostered more trade and increasing urban population. Crafts and merchant guilds and the world's first paper money appeared, and Chinese traders visited Southeast Asia to obtain luxury goods.

Like the Han, the Tang ultimately found its empire too expensive to maintain and difficult to defend. After a bitter defeat by Arab forces at the Battle of Talas River (near Samarkand) in 751, Tang military power declined in Central Asia. Muslim forces and Islam filled the vacuum in Turkestan and in the Xinjiang **(shin-jee-yahng)** region just west of China proper. Climate change, especially a long dry spell between 840 and 940 that caused food shortages, may have contributed to Tang decline. Finally the Tang lost control of China itself. The country broke apart; in 907 Chinese rebels, spurred by famine and drought, sacked Chang'an. The Tang demise allowed Vietnam to finally free itself from Chinese rule.

For five decades, China was divided into several competing states known as the Five Dynasties. But Chinese society was now too massive and deeply rooted to tolerate centuries of anarchy; from the Tang onward the interludes of disorder between great dynasties proved brief. Perhaps China might have remained more innovative if smaller competing states had replaced imperial unity, as in western Europe. But the Chinese deplored disunity. A proverb stated: "Just as there cannot be two suns in the sky, there cannot be two rulers in China." The centralized imperial system remained in place for nearly a millennium after the Tang.

MAKE SURE YOU UNDERSTAND THESE KEY POINTS BEFORE MOVING ON

- **The Tang Empire was marked by ambitious expansion, visitors and residents, and the spread of Chinese goods across Eurasia.**
- **Stability was maintained by keeping the emperor's authority somewhat in check and by rewarding high achievers through the civil service exam system.**
- **Buddhism reached its peak influence during the Tang but was greatly weakened when Emperor Wuzong seized Buddhist monasteries.**
- **During the Tang, the first books were printed using woodblocks.**
- **Poetry and other arts were very popular; while usually stressing Daoist harmony, they sometimes expressed criticism of the government.**

Song China and Commercial Growth

Why might historians consider the Song dynasty the high point of China's golden age?

The next great dynasty, the Song **(Sung)** (960–1279), presided over a sophisticated period of achievement. Although lacking the Tang's empire building and world leadership, the Song was in many respects more refined in the arts of living, technological development, and material richness. Some historians describe the Song as premodern China's most exciting period, characterized by innovation, economic dynamism, urban sophistication, and cultural flowering. Late Song China, stretching a thousand miles

[8]Du's poems are from Cyril Birch, ed., *Anthology of Chinese Literature from Early Times to the Fourteenth Century* (New York: Grove Press, 1965), 240—241; and *Tu Fu: Selected Poems* (Peking: Foreign Languages Press, 1962), 100.

east to west and north to south, contained perhaps 120 million people, between a quarter and a third of the world's total.

Cities, Economies, and Technologies

Song China boasted the world's largest cities, at least five having populations over a million, and nearly fifty others each containing over 100,000 people. Meanwhile, once-great western Eurasian cities had fallen in population: Rome to 35,000 and Baghdad to 125,000. Chinese urban residents enjoyed a high quality of life. A modern scholar described the vibrant activity in one of these cities:

> *The day started with the booming of temple bells. Peddlers began to make their way up and down the streets, calling out the foods they had for sale. Carts laden with meats and vegetables moved in toward the markets. Businesses of all kinds opened. Many…, such as the tailors, hairdressers, dealers in paper and brushes, and caterers, served the city's taste for luxury. As night fell, lanterns lit up taverns and restaurants, the largest of which had staffs of hundreds. In the theater district dozens of houses offered varied bills, including the latest songs, puppet shows, acrobats, wrestlers, storytellers, and comedians.*[9]

In the later Song era, when nomadic invaders had pushed the government south of the Yangzi River, the capital was Hangzhou **(hahng-jo)**, a city of several million on the southern end of the Grand Canal (see Witness to the Past: Life in a Major Chinese City). A later and well-traveled Italian visitor, Marco Polo, called it unquestionably the world's greatest city. Nanjing in the fifteenth century, and Beijing from the sixteenth into the nineteenth centuries, followed Hangzhou as the world's largest cities.

The Song marked the high point for Chinese commerce and foreign trade. The merchant class grew substantially, with tax revenues three times higher than for the Tang. The Grand Canal linking the Yellow and Yangzi River Basins allowed mass movement of goods between north and south. To support this commerce, China developed the world's first fully monetized economy, putting paper money and silver coins into wide use. Song China also enjoyed the world's most advanced farming. Farmers doubled the rice crop and vastly increased the growing and marketing of sugar, once a minor crop. Meanwhile, foreign trade flourished from maritime networks connecting China to the rest of Afro-Eurasia. Chinese merchants regularly visited Southeast Asia and traded around the Indian Ocean, and Chinese industrial and food products found markets in Persia, East Africa, and Egypt. Thousands of foreigners, including Arab, Indian, Persian, and even East African merchants, lived in the cosmopolitan southern seaports of Guangzhou (Canton) and Quanzhou (Zayton). Both cities contained numerous mosques and Hindu temples.

Song China had the world's most advanced industry, reflected in its export of manufactured goods (silks, porcelain, books) and import of raw materials (spices, minerals, horses). Chinese porcelain traded all over Asia, the Middle East, and parts of Africa, its ethereal beauty and great strength fostering a reputation for magical or spiritual power. The name *china* became synonymous with the world's finest porcelain products. China's iron industry, the world's largest before the eighteenth century, also produced fine steel for tools, weapons, stoves, ploughshares, cooking equipment, nails, building materials, and bridges. Mass production and metal-casting techniques supplied standardized iron products to the world's largest internal market. The Song mined coal for fuel, produced salt on an industrial scale, and had the world's best maritime technology. Trade also spurred a significant shipbuilding industry. Some

SCROLL OF KAIFENG This segment from the scroll "Spring Festival on the River," discussed in the chapter opening, shows people thronging the Rainbow Bridge while boatmen lower their masts to pass under the cantilevered structure. Along the streets and bridge stalls merchants sell their goods.

[9] John Meskill, "History of China," in *An Introduction to Chinese Civilization*, ed. John Meskill (Lexington, MA: D.C. Heath, 1973), 127—128.

WITNESS TO THE PAST

Life in a Major Chinese City

The following excerpts are from a description by Marco Polo of Hangzhou, the capital city of China during the southern dynasty and still an important cultural, political, and economic center during Mongol rule in the late 1200s, when Polo witnessed the city life he discusses.

There were in this city twelve guilds of the different crafts.... All these craftsmen had full occupation, for many other cities of the kingdom are supplied from this city with what they require.... The number and wealth of the merchants, and the amount of goods that passed through their hands, were so enormous that no man could form a just estimate thereof.... Neither...[the crafts masters] nor their wives ever touch a piece of work with their own hands, but live as nicely and delicately as if they were kings and queens. The wives indeed are most dainty and angelical creatures!

Inside the city there is a [large] Lake...and all round it are erected beautiful palaces and mansions, of the richest and most exquisite structure that you can imagine, belonging to the nobles of the city.... Both men and women are fair and comely, and for the most part clothe themselves in silk, so vast is the supply of that material.... All the streets of the city are paved with stone or brick...so that you ride and travel in every direction without inconvenience.... The city...has some 3000 [hot] baths, the water of which is supplied by springs..., and the people take great delight in them, frequenting them several times a month, for they are very cleanly in their persons....

Everything appertaining to this city is on so vast a scale, and the Great Khan's yearly revenues therefrom are so immense...it seems past belief.... The city...has on one side a lake of fresh and exquisitely clear water..., and on the other a very large river. The waters of the latter fill a number of canals of all sizes which run through the different quarters of the city, carry away all impurities, and then enter the Lake..., thus producing a most excellent atmosphere. By means of these channels, as well as by the streets, you can go all about the city. All the ten marketplaces are encompassed by lofty houses, and below these are shops where all sorts of crafts are carried on, and all sorts of wares are on sale, including spices and jewels and pearls. Some of these shops are entirely devoted to the sale of wine made from rice and spices, which is...sold very cheap.

Certain of the streets are occupied by...women [courtesans and prostitutes).... Strangers who have once tasted their attractions seem to get bewitched, and are so taken with their blandishments and their fascinating ways that they never can get these out of their heads. Hence...when they return home they say they have been to...the City of Heaven, and their only desire is to get back thither as soon as possible. Other streets are occupied by the Physicians, and by the Astrologers, who are also teachers of reading and writing; and an infinity of other professions have their places round about those squares....

There is such a degree of good will and neighborly attachment among both men and women that you would take the people who live in the same street to be all one family.... They also treat the foreigners who visit them for the sake of trade with great cordiality, and entertain them in the most winning manner, affording them every help and advice on their business....

THINKING ABOUT THE READING

1. What impression of the city do you get from Polo's account?
2. What does the reading tell us about the city's economy?
3. How does Polo evaluate the roles of men and women?

Source: From *The Book of Ser Marco Polo the Venetian Concerning the Kingdoms and Marvels of the East*, trans. and ed. by Henry Yule, 3rd ed. revised by Henri Cordier (London: John Murray, 1903), Vol II. Pp. 185–193, 200–205, 215–216. This text is part of the Internet Medieval History Sourcebook (http://www.fordham.edu/halsall/source/polo-kinsay.asp).

huge compartmentalized ships, with four decks and four to six masts, were capable of carrying five hundred sailors and extensive cargo. Thousands of cargo ships plied the rivers and canals.

In technology and science, the Chinese produced a majority of the world's major inventions between the first and fifteenth centuries C.E. For example, they built the world's longest bridge (2.5 kilometers) and expanded the use of water-powered clocks and mills. Many inventions later spread throughout Eurasia, including the magnetic compass (for naval navigation), sternpost rudder, and spinning wheel. Song craftsmen also made movable type from fired clay and then tin or copper, greatly facilitating book printing. In weaponry, Song technicians developed fire lances, bamboo tubes filled with gunpowder that were the precursors of the metal-barrel gun. Fitted with missile launchers, flamethrowers, cannon, and bombs, Song ships protected the coast. Half a millennium before western Europe's Industrial Revolution, Song engineers also invented the world's first industrial machine, a mechanized spinning process for reeling silk and later hemp thread. There were also advances in astronomy. Astronomers still use data the Song collected from observing the skies, such as on the supernova that created the Crab Nebula, and a Song calendar precisely measured the solar year (365.2425 days). In medicine, Chinese doctors inoculated against smallpox, a disease that ravaged much of Afro-Eurasia. Some Chinese medical ideas reached the Middle East and Europe by the thirteenth century.

Society and Religion

An urbane elite culture thrived. Printed books fostered the spread of education, exposing a wider audience to the social and political elite's values, and the government established schools in every district. Although only a small percentage of students ever became mandarins, a degree or some educated background brought status. The cultivated gentleman, whether or not in government service, was expected to master music (especially lute playing), chess, calligraphy, poetry, and painting.

However, women experienced more restrictions than in earlier centuries. Tang paintings and statues showed aristocratic women in swept-up hair riding horses or standing dignified in loose-fitting gowns. Now women's status declined. Fearing that new economic opportunities for women might undermine patriarchy, conservatives limited women's roles. Men more often took concubines (official mistresses) in addition to their wives, and families increasingly frowned upon widows remarrying. Yet, some women from elite families became literate, reading and writing mostly for their own pleasure. Meanwhile, peasant wives worked in the fields alongside men and were therefore crucial to the family economic livelihood. They also operated restaurants and sold fish and vegetables in markets. Still, children belonged to the father's family, and the husband's mother ruled the wife. Divorce, possible but uncommon, disgraced the woman. Poor women also faced a difficult old age, as a male writer sympathetically described:

> *For women who live a long life, old age is especially hard to bear, because most women must rely on others for their existence. Some wives with stupid husbands are able to manage the family's finances. But the most remarkable are the women who manage a household after their husbands have died leaving them with young children.*[10]

Another source of suffering for women, footbinding, was introduced during the Song among the elite and some common folk. Mothers tightly bound the feet of five- or six-year-old daughters to prevent normal growth, crippling a girl's feet and giving her a dainty walk that men viewed as erotic. Because they needed women's labor for family survival, many peasants rejected the practice as physically debilitating. However, footbinding became widespread in later dynasties.

The Song period also saw the rise of **neo-Confucianism**, a form of Confucianism incorporating many Buddhist and Daoist metaphysical ideas that was associated particularly with Zhu Xi **(JOO shee)** (1130–1200), a child prodigy and one of China's most influential thinkers. Believing that original Confucian ideas had become rigid and misunderstood, Zhu resigned from government service in disgust at corruption and advocated rediscovering Confucianism's original essence. Daoism also influenced Zhu's rational and humane approach, which recognized a dualism between the material world and the energy the Chinese believed pervaded the universe, or **qi** (ch'i). *Tai qi* (tai ch'i), exercises to build mind and body, harnessed qi for personal centering. Like Confucius, Zhu identified reason or principle as the unchanging law and morality for measuring all human affairs: "For every person the most important thing is the cultivation of himself as an ethical being."[11] However, Zhu's indifference to natural science diminished scientific inquiry. Although he praised accomplished women and urged them to pursue book learning at home, his writings also strengthened gender distinctions. Over time neo-Confucianism became the elites' dominant mindset and a force for stability but not innovation. At the same time, many peasants and town dwellers, disinterested in or unaware of theological debates, revered local cults and gods, some only loosely linked to Buddhism, Daoism, or Confucianism.

neo-Confucianism A form of Confucianism arising in China during the Song period (960–1279) that incorporated many Buddhist and Daoist metaphysical ideas.

qi In Chinese thought, the energizing force pervading the universe.

The Song in World History

The Song could have proved a turning point in Chinese and world history, but they did not foster a major transition. The profound economic, technological, and urban developments remind some historians of eighteenth-century Europe at the dawn of rapid industrialization, but the commercial and agricultural dynamism never revolutionized Chinese society. Instead, China contained and absorbed these developments. The Chinese possessed the technology to sail the seas and colonize other lands, but being largely self-sufficient, they lacked the incentive. Moreover, since the highly bureaucratic empire easily adjusted to economic change, it prevented merchants from disrupting China's social order. With productive agriculture to feed a huge population, convenient transportation by water through canals, and many natural resources, Chinese felt no need for additional mechanized technologies. The Mongol conquest of the Song, a cooler climate by the thirteenth century, and the Black Death pandemic in the fourteenth also undermined economic dynamism. Population pressure became a growing burden as farmland filled up.

Confucian disdain of merchants eventually led to stagnation and allowed the imperial government to contain economic growth. Although the large number of mandarins from wealthy merchant families in this period supported commercial growth, many essential commodities remained government monopolies, such as iron, grain, cloth, and salt, while taxes on the wealthy financed public granaries to check famine. These monopolies over essential products enriched the state and protected the population from price and supply problems, but they also restricted merchants to handling nonessential products.

The Song, more interested in economic growth than empire, generally avoided military expansion. Prosperity, trade, and urban living made peace more attractive than conquest. Meanwhile, Central Asian pastoralists gained an edge on complacent China by importing Chinese military technologies and experts, including ironworkers and engineers. Another problem was that, although maintaining the world's largest army, the Song, unlike the Han and Tang, reduced military leaders' power so they could not threaten civilian authority, a chronic Tang problem. Hence, adopting a passive attitude toward pastoral nomads across the border, the Song attempted to appease them with generous payments. Ultimately the policy failed. In the twelfth century one group, the Jin (Chin), conquered northern China, forcing the Song court south across the Yangzi, where it continued to rule central and southern China from Hangzhou until it was invaded by the Mongols.

[10] Yuan Tsai, from Patricia Buckley Ebrey, ed., *Chinese Civilization and Society: A Sourcebook* (New York: The Free Press, 1981), 96.

[11] From Dun J. Li, ed., *The Essence of Chinese Civilization* (Princeton, NJ: Van Nostrand, 1967), 88.

MAKE SURE YOU UNDERSTAND THESE KEY POINTS BEFORE MOVING ON

- The Song dynasty was notable for its bustling urban life, its maritime trade, and its advanced economy.
- Song China made great advances in the manufacture of porcelain, ships, and bridges and in the prevention of disease.
- During the Song, the pursuit of education and cultivation became widespread among the elite; however, the status of women declined, and footbinding began to be practiced by the elite and some commoners.
- The Song's achievements did not lead to a major historical transition because China at this time felt self-sufficient, was not interested in conquest, and kept merchants out of important industries; it also tried to deal with neighboring pastoral nomads peacefully, a strategy that ultimately failed.

Mongol Conquest, Chinese Resurgence, and Eurasian Connections

How did China change during the Yuan and Ming dynasties?

From the thirteenth through the nineteenth centuries the Chinese way of life maintained great continuity. Three ruling houses held power between the Song downfall and the imperial system's demise in the twentieth century, an almost unprecedented record of political stability, perhaps matched only by the ancient Egyptian kingdoms. Disorder occurred chiefly during years of dynastic decline and replacement. Two of the three dynasties were conquest dynasties imposed by non-Chinese nomadic peoples riding in on horseback. The two dynasties that held power between the thirteenth and seventeenth centuries were the Yuan **(yu-wenn)**, established by invading Mongols, and the Ming, which marked a return to Chinese rule.

The Mongol Empire and the Conquest of China

For several millennia Chinese feared what they considered "barbarian" Central Asians who killed, looted, and took captives. The strongest rulers controlled these peoples by conquest or divide-and-rule diplomacy. Enduring Central Asian influence on China's political life resulted from the close proximity of the arid grasslands north and west of China, suitable only for mobile herding, to China's lush farmlands, with contrasting environments producing very different societies. Central Asia's pastoral economy and few resources necessitated seasonal migration and chronic poverty for the tough, self-reliant herders. When China was weak, the Great Wall proved no major barrier to peoples envious of China's affluence. In the thirteenth century China's worst nightmare occurred when a confederation of warlike peoples, the Mongols, conquered all of China.

Before invading China the Mongols conquered much of Eurasia, including eastern Europe and western Asia. Traditionally divided into feuding tribes, the Mongols became united under the ruthless but brilliant Temuchin (ca. 1167–1227), who defeated or co-opted his rivals and then changed his name to Genghis Khan **(GENG-iz KAHN)** ("Universal Emperor"). Of humble origins, he had simple motives: "A man's greatest pleasure is to defeat his enemies,...drive them before him,...take from them that which they possessed,...see those whom they cherished in tears,...to ride their horses,...hold their wives and daughters in his arms."[12] Skilled horse soldiers, more agile than their foes, Mongols proved formidable opponents. Their well-organized fighting units possessed powerful bows lethal at 600 feet, disc-shaped stirrups giving the rider maneuverability, and the world's most advanced siege weaponry, including catapults. China's strength made it one of the last Mongol conquests. Genghis Khan conquered parts of northern China in 1215, and the rest of China fell fifty years after Genghis's death under his grandson, Khubilai Khan **(koo-bluh KAHN)** (r. 1260–1294), who created a new dynasty, the Yuan (1279–1368). China then became part of a great world empire stretching from eastern Europe and the Black Sea to Korea (see Map 11.2).

The Mongols imposed a distinctive government and fostered new cultural forms. Khubilai Khan proved a rather enlightened ruler, less cruel and more pragmatic than most Mongol leaders elsewhere in Eurasia. He patronized Buddhism, built granaries for food storage, operated an efficient postal system, and improved the transportation network. But Chinese historians condemned Khubilai Khan for Mongol sins generally, such as maintaining Mongol cultural identity and actively resisting assimilation into Chinese society. Later Chinese viewed the Yuan as China's darkest hour, an intolerable rule by aliens who refused to be absorbed. Khubilai Khan moved the capital to Beijing ("Northern Capital"), a provincial city close to the Great Wall and alongside major highways leading north and west. Except for brief periods since, Beijing has remained China's capital, eclipsing more ancient cities like Chang'an and Hangzhou. Reflecting his nomadic heritage, Khubilai preferred sleeping in tents, including one erected in the imperial palace gardens.

The Mongols mistrusted intellectuals but were tolerant in religion, inviting missionaries from all over Eurasia to come to the court for religious debates, including Christians of various sects (including Catholics). Khubilai Khan's mother

[12]Quoted in H. D. Martin, *The Rise of Chingis Khan and His Conquest of North China* (Baltimore: Johns Hopkins University Press, 1950), 5.

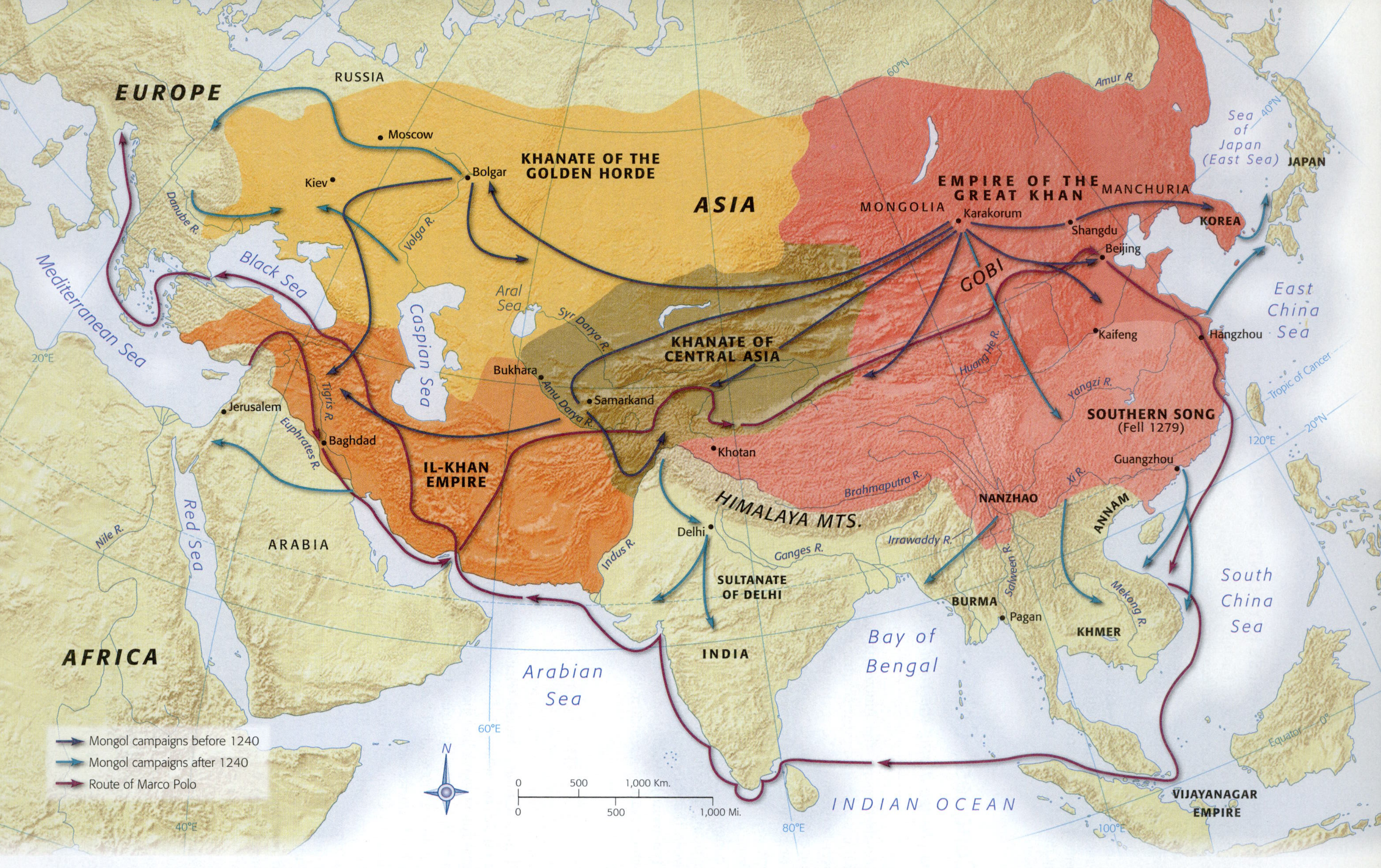

MAP 11.2 **CHINA IN THE MONGOL EMPIRE** After the Mongols conquered much of Central Asia, western Asia, and eastern Europe, they added China and Korea to their huge empire, the largest contiguous land empire in world history. During the Mongol era many Asians and some Europeans, including the Italian Marco Polo, visited or worked in China.

KHUBILAI KHAN AND HIS ENTOURAGE HUNTING This painting by a Chinese artist of the time shows Khubilai Khan, dressed in ermine, and Mongol colleagues, including a woman, hunting on horseback, a popular activity among Mongols.

was a Nestorian Christian of Turkish ancestry, but, like many Mongols, he adopted Tibetan Buddhism. Governing a religiously diverse society, Khubilai Khan wanted to avoid conflict. However, Mongols had even more rigid gender expectations and marriage practices than the Chinese, expecting widows to remain chaste and dutifully serve their parents-in-law. Chinese men now demanded that women remain at home and emphasize feminine behavior, including the growing fashion of tightly bound feet.

Mongol China and Eurasian Networks

The Mongols reopened China's doors to the world and protected the Silk Road, reviving the exchange of goods, ideas, and technologies between East and West. Chinese inventions like gunpowder, printing, the blast furnace for cast iron, silk-making machinery, paper money, and playing cards moved westward. Many foreigners came to Mongol China by land and sea. Although Khubilai Khan sought Chinese support by modeling his government along Chinese lines and performing Confucian rites, most scholars and bureaucrats refused cooperation. Mongols were forced to rely administratively on foreigners coming to serve in what was effectively an international civil service, including many Muslims from Central Asia, western Asia, and North Africa and a few Europeans who found their way to "fabled Cathay," as they called China.

One of the European visitors, the Italian merchant Marco Polo (ca. 1254–1324), initially traveled to China with his father and uncle seeking trade goods but spent seventeen years there, mostly in government service. Eventually Polo returned to Italy and told of the wonders he had encountered or heard about to unbelieving Europeans who knew little about the world east of Palestine. Most dismissed Polo's book as full of lies, but historians confirm the general accuracy of his account. A keen observer, he recorded Chinese resentment toward the Mongols, who once slaughtered a city's entire population for the killing of one drunk Mongol soldier. Polo wrote of China's great cities, such as Beijing and Hangzhou. Standing along the shores of beautiful West Lake in Hangzhou, he wrote that "the city is beyond dispute the finest and noblest in the world in point of grandeur and beauty as well as in its abundant delights. The natives of this city are of peaceful character, thoroughly honest and truthful and accustomed to dainty living."[13] The city boasted parks, a fire department, garbage collection, a pollution-control agency, and paved streets—all things nonexistent in Polo's much smaller Venice, a major European city.

[13] R. E. Latham, trans., *The Travels of Marco Polo* (Baltimore: Penguin Books, 1958), 184—187.

Indeed, China was far more developed in many fields than the rest of Eurasia, probably enjoying the world's highest standard of living. Polo noted, for example, that the Chinese had for a thousand years burned black stones (coal) for heat and took regular baths, astonishing information to medieval Europeans, who seldom if ever bathed.

Mongol control had enormous consequences for Central Asia, the Middle East, and Europe, and the Mongols dominated regions such as Russia and Turkestan for a long time. But Mongol rule in China, lasting only a century, did not leave a deep imprint. Most Chinese hated the Mongols, whose leadership deteriorated after Khubilai Khan's death. Furthermore, Mongols lost their fighting toughness, desiring luxury more than sacrifice. As Mongols in Central Asia and Persia adopted the cultures and religions of the conquered, Mongol unity fragmented and power struggles grew rampant. Adding to these troubles, a terrible plague (probably bubonic) outbreak raged and the Yellow River flooded severely, bringing famine. Historians still debate whether the pandemic, which killed many millions of Chinese, traveled west along the Silk Road to cause the terrible Black Death that greatly reduced the population of the Middle East and Europe in the fourteenth century; see Chapters 10 and 14. Some recent studies suggest that the Black Death plague originated in Turkestan. Soon rebellions broke out all over China. Eventually a Chinese commoner established a new dynasty, and Mongol military forces returned to Central Asia. Today Mongols venerate Genghis Khan as their greatest leader, building memorials and even a theme park to honor the conqueror.

Detail from a vase depicting silk weaving (ceramic), Chinese School, Ming Dynasty (1368-1644)/Golestan Palace, Tehran, Iran/Giraudon/The Bridgeman Art Library

MING SILK WEAVING This detail from a Ming ceramic vase depicts women weaving silk, a craft dominated by women.

Ming Government and Culture

The new Ming dynasty (1368–1644) fostered orderly government, social stability, and cultural richness. The founder, Zhu Yuanzhang **(JOO yu-wen-JAHNG)** (1328–1398), a former Buddhist monk and son of an itinerant farm worker, rose, like the founder of the Han, from abject poverty through sheer ability and ruthless behavior in a time of opportunity. Ming China's people lived for nearly three centuries in comparative peace and prosperity, enjoying living standards among the world's highest and mortality rates among the lowest. During this time China more than doubled in population, from around 80 million to between 160 and 180 million.

Ming government resembled the Han and Tang but was somewhat more despotic and isolated. Perhaps because of the bitter Mongol rule, Ming emperors exercised more power than earlier emperors and placed the bureaucracy under closer scrutiny, eliminating the office of prime minister, who had monitored the country's pulse. A more timid Censorate reduced checks on royal abuses. Like previous dynasties, some Ming emperors had male lovers as well as many wives and concubines, reflecting the tolerance of same-sex relationships among many Chinese court officials and commoners.

Order infused the arts. Although culture in the Mongol period had proved relatively sterile, musical drama (Chinese opera) had become a popular entertainment, appealing to common folk rather than the elite. In the Ming, however, theater reached its highest level. Chinese operas included extended arias and spoken dialogue, each performance aimed at harmonizing song, speech, costume, makeup, movement, and musical accompaniment. Chinese music, mostly composed for operas or for ritual and ceremonial purposes, included string, wind, and percussion instruments, especially flutes, lutes, and zithers.

The Chinese also began writing novels in Yuan times, an elaboration of age-old storytelling. The first novelists were intellectuals who refused to work for the Mongols and made a living by writing books for a popular audience, including some of the world's first detective stories. Fiction, considered worthless by most Ming scholars, had a large audience. Most novels had a Confucian moral emphasizing correct behavior, but some offered social criticisms or satires. Perhaps the greatest Ming novel, *The Water Margin* (also known as *All Men Are Brothers*), presented heroes who were also bandits, Robin Hoods driven into crime by corrupt officials. Meanwhile, to encourage intellectual pursuits, rulers expanded the Hanlin ("Forest of Culture") Academy established in the Tang, assigning some of the brightest scholars there to read and write whatever they liked. Ming scholars compiled an 11,000-volume encyclopedia (with 20,000 chapters) and a 52-volume study of Chinese pharmacology.

Ming China and the Afro-Eurasian World

The early Ming rulers pursued territorial expansion, including a failed attempt to recolonize Vietnam. But China was now oriented more to the sea. Rather than send armies far into Central Asia, the emperor dispatched a series of grand maritime expeditions to southern Asia and beyond to reaffirm China's preeminence in eastern Eurasia. Admiral Zheng He **(jung huh) (Cheng Ho)** (ca. 1371–1435), a huge man and trusted court eunuch of Muslim faith, commanded seven voyages between 1405 and 1433, a feat of seamanship that was unprecedented in world history. The largest fleet comprised sixty-two vessels carrying twenty-eight thousand men, and the largest "treasure ships," as they were known, weighed 1,500 tons, were 450 feet long, boasted nine masts nearly 500 feet high, and carried a crew of five hundred. These ships must have astounded observers, and, although undertaking only a few military actions, perhaps intimidated them as well. A few decades later Christopher Columbus sailed from Spain in three tiny vessels carrying a total of only about a hundred men.

Zheng He's extraordinary voyages carried the Chinese flag through Southeast Asia to India, the Persian Gulf, the Red Sea, and the East African coast (see Map 11.3). Had they continued, the fleet could have sailed around Africa to Europe or the Americas, but they had no incentive to do so. Some thirty-six countries in southern and western Asia officially acknowledged Chinese preeminence. The ruler of Malindi, an East African city, sent ambassadors bearing tribute, including a giraffe.

Historians still debate the reasons for Zheng's great voyages. Some point to the desire to have foreign countries reaffirm the emperor as the Son of Heaven. Zheng may also have sought a deposed boy emperor who had disappeared, possibly fleeing into exile. Others suspect the ambitious emperor wanted to demonstrate China's military capabilities. As these voyages coincided with increased activity by Chinese merchants

MAP 11.3 THE VOYAGES OF ZHENG HE After replacing the Mongols, the Ming reestablished a strong Chinese state, attempted to recolonize Vietnam, and rebuilt the Great Wall. Ming emperors also dispatched a series of grand maritime expeditions in the early 1400s that reached the Middle East and East Africa.

in Southeast Asia, some historians see commercial motives as primary. Many thousands of Chinese visited or settled in the Philippines, Indonesia, Siam, and Vietnam, creating a closer commercial link to China, while Yuan and Ming porcelain was sold as far west as South-Central Africa.

Zheng He's voyages may also have revitalized a tribute system which during Han and Tang times shaped China's relations with its neighbors. China considered friendly East, Southeast, and Central Asian states as vassals, granting them trade but rarely intervening to support their allies. In return tributary states sent periodic envoys bearing gifts to the emperor, confirming his superiority and playing along to gain China's goodwill and trade goods. In Ming times tribute came regularly from states in Korea, Vietnam, Cambodia, Borneo, Indonesia, South Asia, and Central Asia.

Inevitably the Chinese saw themselves as the Middle Kingdom, surrounded by barbarian societies. Never recognizing any other society as equal, they felt superior not just materially but also culturally, with barbarians unable to resist their appeal, a view reinforced when other East Asians borrowed from China and others sent tribute missions. To be civilized, they believed, was to embrace Chinese culture, and a virtuous ruler irresistibly attracted barbarians. Thus tribute-bearers performed a rite, the **kotow**, that involved prostrating themselves before the emperor, a practice from which we get the modern English word *kowtow* ("to pander to authority"). This practice, above all others, left little doubt as to who was superior and who was inferior, reflecting a Confucian sense of hierarchy.

Ming China Turns Inward

In the early Ming, China remained perhaps the world's wealthiest, most developed country. Hindu India faced Muslim conquests, Middle Eastern societies struggled to overcome setbacks, and western Europeans were just beginning to foster political and economic dynamism. Commercially vibrant and outward-thrusting, Ming China had the capability to open maritime communication between the continents and become the dominant world power. Instead China turned inward. The grand voyages and the commercial thrust to distant lands came to a sudden halt when the Ming emperor ordered them ended, banned construction of deep-sea vessels, and soon outlawed Chinese emigration altogether. But some Chinese continued to illegally travel or settle abroad for trade; frustrated Ming officials admitted that "powerful families traded overseas with large ships. Scoundrels secretly profited from it."[14] Foreign merchant ships still came to China, with the tribute system providing cover for extensive trade and smuggling.

kotow The tribute-bearers' act of prostrating themselves before the Chinese emperor.

The stunning reversal of official Chinese engagement with the world that, in the perspective of later history, seemed so counterproductive sparks scholarly debate. Perhaps Zheng He's voyages, which brought back few valuable resources, were too costly even for the wealthy Ming government. Unlike Christians and Muslims, the Chinese lacked missionary zeal, having little interest in spreading religion and culture except to near neighbors like Vietnam. Furthermore, despite flourishing guilds and frequent wealth, merchants held a low status in the Confucian social system. Ming leaders believed profit was evil, and mercantile interests inevitably conflicted with political ones. A later Ming scholar wrote that "one in a hundred [Chinese] is rich, while nine out of ten are impoverished. The poor cannot stand up to the rich. The lord of silver rules heaven and the god of copper cash reigns over the earth."[15] Hence many mandarins despised merchants and opposed foreign trade. But some merchants, seeking respect and status, emulated the Confucian scholars by, for example, collecting art, engaging in philanthropy, and educating their sons.

Military factors also influenced the turn inward. With Mongols regrouping in Central Asia and memories of oppressive Mongol rule still fresh, the Ming shifted resources to defend the northern borders and the pirate-infested Pacific coast, rebuilding and extending the Great Wall. The Great Wall near Beijing mostly reflects work done by the Ming. In addition, military operations along the northern border and an ill-fated invasion of Vietnam generated a fiscal crisis that weakened the government.

Finally, the catastrophe of Mongol rule made the Chinese more ethnocentric and antiforeign. Always land-based, self-centered, and self-sufficient, the Chinese now believed they needed little from outside. China remained powerful, productive, and mostly prosperous, enjoying generally high living standards, well into the eighteenth century, when profits from overseas colonies and the Industrial Revolution tipped the balance in favor of northwest Europe. By the later Ming, China had entered a period of relative isolation that was ended only by the forceful intrusion of a newly developed Europe in the early 1800s.

MAKE SURE YOU UNDERSTAND THESE KEY POINTS BEFORE MOVING ON

- **The ancient Chinese fear of Central Asian nomads was realized when the Mongols, under Genghis and Khubilai Khan, conquered China and established the Yuan dynasty.**
- **Khubilai Khan made improvements in China's transportation system and moved the capital to Beijing.**
- **Because of lack of cooperation from Chinese scholars and bureaucrats, the Mongols established an international civil service, in which Marco Polo served.**
- **After the end of Mongol rule, the Chinese enjoyed three centuries of prosperity under the Ming dynasty, and their sense of well-being was displayed in Zheng He's grand sailing expeditions, which enhanced China's position among its neighbors.**
- **For reasons still debated, the Ming emperor suddenly ordered all overseas activity halted and China turned inward, beginning an isolation that ended only in the 1800s.**

[14]Quoted in Philip A. Kuhn, *Chinese Among Others: Emigration in Modern Times* (Lanham, MD: Rowman and Littlefield, 2008), 9.

[15]Zhang Tao, quoted in Timothy Brook, *The Confusions of Pleasure: Commerce and Culture in the Ming* (Berkeley: University of California Press, 1998), vii.

Cultural Adaptation in Korea and Japan

How did the Koreans and Japanese develop their own distinctive societies?

As East Asia's cultural heartland, China influenced its three large neighbors of Vietnam (see Chapter 13), Korea, and Japan. All derived considerable culture from China, including writing systems, philosophies, and political institutions. At the same time, they adapted these influences to their indigenous customs, maintaining their cultural identity. Eventually the Japanese developed a very different way of life and outlook than they had a few centuries earlier.

Korea and China

Several strong states emerged on the Korean peninsula. In the mid-seventh century the southern state, Silla **(SILL-ah)**, defeated its main rival, Koguryo (Goguryeo), and eventually united most Koreans. Political unity fostered homogenization of Korean culture. Like earlier states, Silla became China's vassal, borrowing Chinese culture and institutions. Buddhism triumphed as many Korean Buddhist monks traveled to China, and the Tang system became the government model, with Confucianism as a political ideology. But Koreans borrowed selectively. They placed more emphasis than the Chinese did on inherited status instead of merit, and the rich-poor gap was wider. Moreover, Silla's rulers included three queens, suggesting less gender bias than in China. For example, Queen Sondok (r. 632–647) fostered science and promoted a tolerant mixing of Buddhism and shamanism. Silla women generally shared in their menfolk's social status and enjoyed many legal rights.

During the period of Silla domination (676–935), Koreans adapted Chinese writing to their own very different spoken language and created a distinctive literature in history, religion, and poetry. To mass-produce these works, Silla craftsmen developed woodblock printing as early as China, and the world's oldest extant woodblock printing, a Korean Buddhist writing, dates from 751. In astronomy, a great observatory is one of East Asia's oldest. Korea also formed connections with the wider world. Buddhist pilgrims came from India, and many Arabs traded or settled down there. One Arab wrote that "seldom has a stranger who has come there from Iraq or another country left it afterwards. So healthy is the air there, so pure the water, so fertile the soil and so plentiful of all good things."[16]

Gradually Silla declined as the result of elite rivalries, corruption, and peasant uprisings. The new dominant state, Koryo **(KAW-ree-oh)**, lasted for over four centuries (935–1392). Chinese influence continued in politics and philosophy, with Koreans erecting an examination system and importing neo-Confucianism. During this time the Koreans developed a publishing industry, inventing the world's first metal movable-type printing by 1234. But they retained a distinctive political and social system. Court, military, and aristocratic landowning families influenced kings, who were never as strong as Chinese emperors. Another difference was that Korean farming relied on large estates. Women's status also changed. In contrast to Silla women, Koryo court women mainly exercised influence behind the scenes. For example, Lady Yu successfully urged her reluctant husband, Wang Kon, the Koryo dynasty founder, to seize power from a despotic ruler, arguing, "It is an ancient tradition to raise a banner of revolt against a tyrant. How can you, a great military leader, hesitate?"[17] While most Koryo women played a lesser role in public affairs, they farmed and took full responsibility for family affairs.

Korean Buddhism, assimilating many animist elements, gradually became a powerful economic and political force. But the involvement of monks in political life fostered religious corruption and a worldly orientation, alienating some believers.

© Rakkandee/Shutterstock.com

KING SEJONG This modern statue portrays the Yi dynasty King Sejong, revered by Koreans for his political, economic, and scientific achievements, such as observing stars and supervising book printing. Sejong patronized learning, supported agricultural innovations that increased crop yields, introduced humane laws, and fostered economic growth.

[16]Quoted in Bruce Cumings, *Korea's Place in the Sun: A Modern History* (New York: W.W. Norton, 1997), 37.

[17]Quoted in Yung Chung Kim, ed. and trans., *Women of Korea: A History from Ancient Times to 1945* (Seoul: Ehwa Women's University Press, 1977), 32.

Hence, although for fifteen hundred years Koreans have been nominally Buddhist, the religion gradually lost influence.

Choson and the Yi Dynasty

When the Mongols conquered the peninsula, the Koreans resisted. The Mongols responded by devastating the land, carrying off hundreds of thousands of captives, and imposing heavy taxes. Yet, during the Mongol era closer links to trade networks brought to Korea more Chinese and western Asian learning and technology. In 1392 a new Korean dynasty, the Yi **(yee)**, whose state was known as Choson **(cho-suhn)**, meaning "Fresh Dawn," replaced Mongol rule and lasted 518 years, until 1910 (see Map 11.4).

dyarchy A form of dual government that began in Japan during the Nara period (710–784), whereby one powerful family ruled the country while the emperor held mostly symbolic power.

Choson maintained a tribute relationship with China while expanding Chinese social and political models. Government careers required mastering Confucian scholarship, with Confucianism legitimizing government by a virtuous ruler. Education expanded to prepare students for civil service exams. Confucian influence also remade Korean social institutions such as the family. Believing Korean women had too much freedom and hence behaved immorally, the Yi encouraged women's seclusion at home, arranged marriages, face veiling when out in public, female chastity, and strict obedience to husbands and fathers. However, commoner women, needed for work in the fields, usually had more freedom of movement. Today Confucianism is arguably stronger than Buddhism, especially in rural Korea.

Choson remained among the more creative Late Intermediate societies, encouraging literature, technology, and science. For example, Koreans created the world's first rain gauges and installed them throughout the country to keep accurate rainfall records. King Sejong **(say-jong)** (r. 1418–1450), respected by Koreans for improving the economy, helping poor peasants, and prohibiting cruel punishments, strongly supported scientific progress. Sejong wrote agricultural books and formed a think tank, the Hall of Worthies, where scholars invented a phonetic system for pronouncing Chinese characters and writing the Korean language. But Koreans still used Chinese for serious scholarship.

MAP 11.4 KOREA AND JAPAN, CA. 1300 Japanese society developed in an archipelago, the major early cities rising in central Honshu. In 1274 and 1281 the Japanese repulsed Mongol invasions by sea. Throwing off the Mongols, Korea was unified under the Yi dynasty in 1392.

Japan in the Nara Era

Although adopting many Chinese and Korean influences, Japan produced a robust, highly distinctive society. In the mid-sixth century the Japanese embarked on three centuries of deliberate cultural borrowing from China with the *Taika* **(TIE-kah)** ("Great Change") reform of 646 C.E., which rulers hoped would transform Japan into a centralized empire like Tang China. The new governmental system resembled, on the surface, China's centralized bureaucracy. The Japanese now used the Chinese writing system to record their history and conduct daily activities. Adopting Buddhism also brought a rich art and architecture tradition to Japan. Meanwhile, Koreans continued to migrate to Japan.

Conscious borrowing from China peaked in the Nara **(NAH-rah)** era (710–784), named for Japan's first capital city, which was modeled on the Tang capital, Chang'an, and home to some twenty thousand people. Japan's total population probably numbered 5 or 6 million. The Nara regime nationalized land in the emperor's name and, using Tang models, reallocated it on an equal basis to peasants, who then paid a land and labor tax. Abandoned as unworkable after a few decades, the system illustrated that in agrarian societies like Japan land control supported political power.

Despite changes designed to strengthen imperial authority, the emperor never became an activist Chinese-style ruler. Powerful aristocrats controlled the bureaucracy while retaining large tax-exempt landholdings. Japan became a **dyarchy**, a dual government whereby one powerful family filled the highest government posts and dominated the emperors, whose power was mostly symbolic. Emperors lived in luxurious seclusion, guaranteeing an unbroken succession through having sons. This system remained in place into the nineteenth century.

Nara leaders promoted aspects of Chinese culture, blending them with Japanese traditions. Imperial court rituals and ceremonies, largely based on Tang models and still maintained today, included stately dances and orchestral music using Japanese versions of Chinese musical instruments such as the flute, lute, and zither. Chinese writing also gained great prestige, with Chinese ideographs adapted to Japan's very different nontonal spoken language, a difficult conversion process. Chinese literary forms, including poetry and calligraphy, also became popular.

The Japanese adopted and reshaped the Chinese philosophical and religious doctrines they found appealing. They modified Confucianism's ethical and political doctrines to suit their own society and adopted Mahayana Buddhism, whose view that all things are impermanent greatly influenced their art and literature. Many artists and poets focused on passing time and changing seasons. Hence, one writer ruminated in 1212, "The river's waters are always changing. The foam on the pond appears, disappears. So is it in this world with men and their houses."[18] But the Japanese also retained their animist nature worship, known today as Shinto, which probably incorporated some Chinese (especially Daoist) influences as it became an imperial cult. Shinto and Buddhism addressed different needs and easily coexisted. Shinto deities were not gods but beautiful natural phenomena such as Mount Fuji **(FOO-jee)**, waterfalls, thunder, or stately trees. Shinto also stressed ritual purity, encouraging bathing and personal cleanliness. It offered no coherent theology, moral doctrine, or concept of death or an afterlife.

Economic unrest disrupted late Nara society. Resenting forced labor and military conscription, which often caused economic ruin, many peasants abandoned their fields and became wandering *ronin* **(ROH-neen)** ("wave people"), some of whom were hired by large landowners as workers. To stop people from becoming ronin, the government abolished compulsory service and gave responsibility for policing and defense to local officials. Eventually the ronin these officials hired as troops became the provincial warrior class, armed with bows and arrows and curved swords, who reshaped Japanese life.

Heian Cultural Renaissance

During the Heian **(HAY-en)** period (794–1184), when the capital moved from Nara to Heian, or Kyoto, 28 miles north, imitating and borrowing from China gradually ended and was replaced by relative isolation. Heian leaders discontinued foreign contacts in the ninth century and set about consciously absorbing and adapting imported Chinese cultural patterns under the slogan "Chinese learning, Japanese spirit." At the same time, Buddhism gradually harmonized with Shinto beliefs while generating new sects, art, and temple building. A unique court society also arose that fostered a distinctly Japanese writing system, literary styles, arts, and world-view. The development of **kana** **(KAH-nah)**, a phonetic script consisting of forty-seven syllabic signs derived from Chinese characters, allowed Japanese to write their language phonetically, especially when kana letters were combined with Chinese characters. This system is still used today.

Heian elite culture, enormously remote from us today in time, attitudes, and behavior, reached its high point around 1000 C.E., flourishing among a small group of privileged families in Kyoto, a city of around 100,000. Many elite residents thrived from bureaucratic jobs and land ownership. This aristocracy, extraordinarily withdrawn from the outside world, created a culture governed by standards of form and beauty, making no distinction between art and life. Passionately concerned with social rank, they created some of Japan's greatest literature and art while admiring the ability to write artistically, compose a graceful poem, and create an elegant costume. They energetically created beauty, such as by putting together harmonious syllables and lines of ink on the page or perfumes on the body. The Heian period was unique for the careful attention spent in choosing an undergarment or the time taken in writing a love note, with perhaps a tastefully faded chrysanthemum to emphasize the melancholy nature of the contents. The superficial Heian aristocrats, not interested in pure intellect or social morality, were obsessed by mood, especially the sense of beauty's transience.

Women from affluent families enjoyed their highest status during Heian times, with romantic affairs and sexual promiscuity tolerated for both men and women. Aristocratic women spent their days playing games, writing diaries, listening to romantic stories, or practicing art. Some, such as the novelist Lady Murasaki **(MUR-uh-SAH-kee)**, gained a formal education and wrote because, without demanding jobs, they had abundant free time and could focus on their feelings (see Profile: Lady Murasaki, Heian Novelist). A poet might deftly turn a scene of nature into one of emotion: "The flowers withered, their color faded away, while meaninglessly, I spent my days in the world, and the long rains were falling."[19]

The Heian aristocracy saw love as an art; people wrote poems before meeting their lover and then the following morning, such as these two morning-after poems from the diary of a prominent woman writer, Izumi Shikibu:

> *Woman: "painful though it were, to see you leave before dawn [to avoid discovery], better by far than when the dawn's grey light, so cruelly tears you from my side."*
> *Prince: "to leave you while the leaves are moist with dew, is bitterer by far, than if I were to say farewell at night, without a single chance to show my love."*[20]

Heian women wore their hair long to the ground, applied white skin powder and lipstick, plucked their eyebrows, and blackened their teeth with dye. In one novel, a lady refuses to

kana A Japanese phonetic script developed in the Heian period (794–1184) that consisted of some forty-seven syllabic signs derived from Chinese characters.

[18] Komo no Chomei, from "Hojoki: My Ten-By-Ten Hut," in William McNaughton, *Light from the East: An Anthology of Asian Literature* (New York: Laurel, 1978), 249.

[19] Quoted in Donald Keene, "Literature," in *An Introduction to Japanese Civilization*, ed. Arthur E. Tiedemann (Lexington, MA: D.C. Heath, 1974), 395.

[20] Quoted in Ivan Morris, *The World of the Shining Prince: Court Life in Ancient Japan* (New York: Kodansha, 1994), 229.

PROFILE

Lady Murasaki, Heian Novelist

Women produced much of the best Heian literature. A lady-in-waiting, Lady Murasaki (Murasaki Shibiku), wrote the greatest book, *The Tale of Genji*, the world's first psychological novel, beginning around 1008. Murasaki worked as the maid to Empress Akiko, the emperor's consort and daughter of a political leader. We know only a little of Murasaki's life, much of it from a diary she kept. She was born around 978 into a leading aristocratic family steeped in literature, her grandfather being a famed poet and her father a provincial governor who, apparently lamenting she was not a boy, allowed her to study. Murasaki's writing showed familiarity with Chinese history, literature, and poetry. Indeed, she criticized young people who expected good jobs without undergoing appropriate training.

Culture Club/Hulton Archive/Getty Images

LADY MURASAKI This eighteenth-century painting of Lady Murasaki writing The Tale of Genjii while observing the moon reflected the styles of the artist's times but also suggests the continuing significance of the beloved Heian-era writer.

Perhaps because she avidly pursued learning, Murasaki was married late, at age twenty, but her much older husband died only a few years later from illness. She had at least two children, including a daughter who later became a well-known writer. Murasaki probably died sometime between 1025 and 1031, perhaps after several years as a Buddhist nun. Her self-description in her diary suggests an introverted woman:

> *Pretty yet shy, unsociable, fond of old tales, conceited, so wrapped up in poetry that other people hardly exist, spitefully looking down on the whole world—such is the unpleasant opinion that people have of me. Yet when they come to know me they say that I am strangely gentle, quite unlike what they had been led to believe.*

The Tale of Genji is much more sophisticated in language and thoughtful in sensibility than earlier Japanese literature. In *Genji* Murasaki made contemporary language rather than formal Chinese writing style an artistic medium. Even today words and phrases from *Genji* are common in Japanese language. She also had other goals, claiming that the novel should always have "a definite and serious purpose." In focusing on her characters' emotional and psychological interplay, her writing betrays a strongly feminine perspective. A treasure trove on social history, *Genji* reveals much about the times.

The engaging story chronicles the life and amorous adventures of handsome Prince Genji, an emperor's son and model for the qualities of taste and refinement admired by the Kyoto aristocracy. Genji is an accomplished poet, painter, dancer, musician, and athlete. But his supreme gift is the art most prized: "pillowing" (lovemaking). Genji and his friends, devoting little time to their government jobs, spend their days largely searching for pleasure, attending countless ceremonial functions, reciting poetry endlessly, and moving from one romantic affair to another. The novel's mood is subdued melancholy and nostalgia for the passing of lovely things. Both men and women freely express their emotions. Hence, Genji shows a keen sensitivity to nature: "I hope that I shall have a little time left for things which I really enjoy—flowers, autumn leaves, the sky, all those day-to-day changes and wonders that a single year brings forth; that is what I look forward to." The novel ends with Genji making plans to give up his posts and retire to a mountain village, perhaps to continue with his poetry, music, and painting while focusing more on religious knowledge.

THINKING ABOUT THE PROFILE

1. What sort of background did Murasaki come from?
2. Why is *Genji* such an important work of literature?

Notes: Quotations from Ivan Morris, *The World of the Shining Prince* (New York: Kodansha, 1994), 251; Ryusaku Tsunoda et al., eds., *Sources of Japanese Tradition*, vol. 2 (New York: Columbia University Press, 1958), 178–179; and Mikiso Hane, *Japan: A Historical Survey* (New York: Charles Scribner's, 1972), 56.

do these things, disgusting her attendants: "Those eyebrows of hers, like hairy caterpillars, aren't they; and her teeth—like peeled caterpillars."[21] Equally concerned with their personal dress and appearance, men also used cosmetics.

However, only a tiny fraction of Japan's population could afford this hedonism so removed from real life. The common people outside Kyoto had vastly different experiences, usually working at bare subsistence levels as farmers and craftsmen. Generally illiterate and saddled by unremitting work, most knew nothing of Heian court life or Chinese literature. Heian aristocrats called the provinces "uncivilized, barbarous, wretched" places.[22] But late Heian literature also reflected a growing pessimism that the Kyoto elite's world might soon vanish. Social and economic changes were clearing the path for a more decentralized system, as powerful regional families gained wealth and built up their own warrior bands, based on kinship and vassal ties to their lord, to keep the peace. By the twelfth century, Japan was moving into a new historical phase and a much different social system.

The Warrior Class and a New Japanese Society

The provincial warrior class, who would shape Japan's future, assimilated the residue of Chinese culture from the Heian elite. As Heian governors, too fond of Kyoto life, delegated their local powers to subordinates, this warrior class gradually became the dominant force in Japanese politics and society, producing a very different culture. Rural society changed, with powerful, land-hungry, tax-exempt families and Buddhist communities often seizing land by force and increasing the tax load on peasants. Some peasants fled to remote areas or joined roving bands of unattached ronin; others signed over themselves and their lands to lords of manors, becoming bound to the soil and supplying food in exchange for protection. Thus Heian era estates were replaced by lords ruling over the villages on their land. By around 1200 perhaps only 10 percent of the cultivated land remained taxable, and a new rural aristocracy held local power. Soldiers and ronin became military retainers to aristocratic landowning families headed by mounted warriors. As the end of conscription weakened imperial forces, political and military power dispersed to rural areas. Overpopulation also contributed to periodic fighting, with too many people competing for control of too little good land.

The warrior class fostered a social and political system more like Zhou China or medieval Europe than the centralized Tang state. Historians disagree as to when between the twelfth and fourteenth centuries the transition to a new Age of Warriors was completed, but the system continued in some form to the nineteenth century. Rights to land and lord-vassal relations lubricated military, political, and economic power. Despite many similarities between post-Heian Japan and medieval Europe, Japanese rulers were often stronger than most European kings.

The warrior class, or **samurai** **(SAH-moo-rie)** ("one who serves"), gradually assumed military supremacy over the emperor and the court. Rural lords and their military retainers forged a relationship based on an idealized feudal ethic later known as **Bushido** **(boo-SHEE-doh)** ("way of the warrior"), that was not completely developed until the seventeenth century. The samurai had two great ideals: loyalty to leaders, and absolute indifference to all physical hardship. They enjoyed special legal and ceremonial rights and expected in return to give their lords unquestioning service. Although only a few women from samurai families engaged in combat, most received some martial arts training to help run and defend the family estates.

Although heading the social system, samurai constituted a small percentage of the population. If a samurai failed to do his duty or achieve his purpose, suicide was a purposeful and honorable act that served as conclusive evidence that here was a man who could be respected by friend and enemy alike for his physical courage, determination, and sincerity. Homosexuality was also common among the samurai, as among several other warrior castes in history, such as the Spartans in classical Greece, perhaps because of male bonding and an ethic extolling male values. Japanese society generally tolerated same-sex relationships. Such unique cultural patterns as Zen Buddhism and the tea ceremony also rose to prominence among the samurai class.

The Shogunates and Economic Change

With Japan controlled by competing bands of feudal lords, civil war broke out between two powerful families and their respective allies. One lord, Minamoto-no-Yoritomo **(MIN-a-MO-to-no-YOR-ee-TO-mo)**, emerged victorious and set up a military government in Kamakura **(kah-mah-KOO-rah)**, near Tokyo **(TOE-kee-oh)**, that lasted from 1180 to 1333. The emperor commissioned him **shogun** **(SHOW-guhn)** ("barbarian-subduing generalissimo"), or military dictator controlling the country in the name of the emperor, who remained in seclusion in Kyoto. Responsible for internal and external defense, the shogun could nominate his own successor. No shogun seriously attempted to abolish the imperial house, which, though politically impotent, symbolized the people and land. Kamakura shoguns, nominally subordinate to the emperors, had real power, but before 1600 the system was not very centralized.

samurai ("one who serves") A member of the Japanese warrior class, which gained power between the twelfth and fourteenth centuries and continued until the nineteenth.

Bushido ("Way of the Warrior") An idealized ethic for the Japanese samurai.

shogun ("barbarian-subduing generalissimo") A Japanese military dictator controlling the country in the name of the emperor.

[21]Quoted in ibid., 204.

[22]Quoted in Mikiso Hane, *Japan: A Historical Survey* (New York: Charles Scribner's, 1972), 56.

Mongols failed twice, in 1274 and 1281, to invade Japan. Khubilai Khan sent messengers imperiously demanding that Japanese leaders acknowledge a subservient tributary relationship to his regime: "You, stupid little barbarians. Do you dare to defy us by not submitting?"[23] Knowing less about Mongols than most Asians, they refused, outraging Khubilai. The 1281 attempt involved up to 150,000 men transported by over 4,000 conscripted Chinese ships, some armed with ceramic bombs, the world's first known seagoing exploding projectiles. On both occasions, Mongol armies landed, met fierce resistance, and were destroyed when great storms scattered and shipwrecked their fleets. These divine winds, or *kamikaze* **(KAHM-i-KAHZ-ee)**, convinced the Japanese of special protection by the gods, and any inferiority complex toward China ended. Japan was not successfully invaded and defeated until 1945.

In 1333 the Kamakura Shogunate collapsed through intrigues and civil wars and was replaced by a government headed by the Kyoto-based Ashikaga **(ah-shee-KAH-gah)** family (1338–1568). But Ashikaga shoguns never had much real power beyond the capital. Political power became increasingly decentralized as local lords struggled to obtain more land, leading to the rise of several hundred landowning territorial magnates called **daimyo** **(DIE-MYO)** ("great name"). Each daimyo monopolized local power, had his supporting samurai, and derived income from the peasants working on his land.

Between 1200 and 1500 Japan experienced rapid change in both economic and political spheres. Agriculture became more productive, and an increasingly active merchant class lived in the fast-growing towns. The Japanese developed a new interest in foreign trade, with Japanese sailors and merchants traveling to China and Southeast Asia. Chinese merchants also settled in several southern ports. These new energies strained the rigid political and social system. In the 1500s civil war and the arrival of European merchants and Christian missionaries aggravated these problems, resulting in a dramatic modification of the political system.

daimyo ("great name") Large landowning territorial magnates who monopolized local power in Japan beginning with the Ashikaga period (1338–1568).

Zen A form of Japanese Buddhism called the meditation sect because it emphasizes individual practice and discipline, self-control, self-understanding, and intuition.

Noh Japanese plays that use stylized gestures and spectacular masks; began in the fourteenth century.

Japanese Society, Religion, and Culture

Shaped by the warrior class, Japanese society and culture became even more rigid than before. Inequality started in the family, which was headed by a patriarchal male: children owed obedience to their parents, and the young honored the old. Expected to be dutiful, obedient, and loyal to their menfolk, women moved into their husband's household after marriages arranged for family interests, not romantic love. Marriage became more durable and divorce more difficult, giving married women more security, and aristocratic women dominated the imperial court staff and ran the emperor's household. As in China, group interests outweighed individual rights and freedoms.

Many Buddhist sects emerged during this time, but three became most significant. The largest, the *Pure Land*, emphasized prayer and faith for salvation, stressed the equality of all believers, and rejected reincarnation, maintaining that believers went straight to nirvana; it became very popular among the lower classes. The *Nicheren* **(NEE-chee-ren)** sect has sometimes been compared to Christianity and Islam because of its militant proselytizing and concern for the afterlife. Whereas most Japanese Buddhists were peaceful and tolerant, Nicherens were angry, seeing rival views as heresy. The third major Buddhist sect, **Zen**, originating in China under Daoist influence, emphasized meditation, individual practice and discipline, self-control, self-understanding, and intuition. Knowledge came from seeking deep into the mind, rather than from outside assistance. One Zen pioneer wrote, "Great is mind. Heaven's height is immeasurable but Mind goes beyond heaven; the earth's depth is unfathomable, but Mind reaches below the earth. Mind travels outside the macrocosm."[24] Zen practitioners expected enlightenment to come in a flash of understanding. Zen culture, devised to bring people in touch with their nonverbal, nonrational side, stressed simplicity and restraint, contending that "great mastery is as if unskillful."[25]

Zen values permeated the arts, including rock gardens, landscape gardening, and flower arrangements. Gardens, ponds, and buildings, such as the beautiful thirteenth-century Golden Pavilion of Kyoto, emphasized harmony with their natural surroundings. The highly formalized tea ceremony, emphasizing patience, restraint, serenity, and the beauty of simple action involving the commonplace preparing and drinking of tea, could last two hours, suggesting withdrawal from the real world. Japanese ceramics and pottery later gained world respect for their subtlety and understated beauty. Potters made cups, bowls, and vases using rough textures and irregular lines to suggest weathering and the effects of time, a Japanese preoccupation. An old art, painting stressed not creativity or self-expression but skill and technique through self-discipline. The **Noh** drama, which included stylized gestures and spectacular masks, also appeared in this era.

[23]Quoted in Lo Jung-Pang, *China as a Sea Power, 1127–1368*, ed. Bruce Elleman (Hong Kong: Kong University Press, 2012), 89.
[24]From Ryusaku Tsunoda et al., eds., *Sources of Japanese Tradition*, vol. 2 (New York: Columbia University Press, 1958), 236.
[25]Quoted in Noel F. Busch, *The Horizon Concise History of Japan* (New York: American Heritage, 1972), 58.

MAKE SURE YOU UNDERSTAND THESE KEY POINTS BEFORE MOVING ON

- **The Korean state of Silla was subordinate to China and borrowed a great deal from China's culture, adapting it to Korean traditions.**
- **Ruling Korea after the Mongols, the Yi sought good relations with China and instituted the Chinese educational and civil service exam system.**
- **In the Nara period, Japan borrowed heavily from Chinese culture, but its government was a dyarchy in which one powerful family dominated the emperor, and imports such as Buddhism were melded with native cultural features such as Shinto.**
- **In the Heian period, borrowing from China ended, foreign contacts were stopped, and a small elite group, concerned almost exclusively with the pursuit of aesthetic beauty, created some of Japan's best art and literature.**
- **In Japan, the warrior class, or samurai, gradually attained supremacy over the emperor and the court, and an organization like that of medieval Europe, based on lords and vassals, became dominant.**

CHAPTER SUMMARY

The Intermediate Era was in many respects a golden age for much of East Asia. The Tang and Song dynasties represented perhaps the high point of Chinese history and culture. While the Tang enjoyed great external power, the Song featured dramatic commercial growth. The Chinese continued to develop distinctive forms of literature, visual arts, philosophy, and government, as well as new technologies and scientific understandings. The Mongol conquest and brief period of rule weakened China's dynamism but extended overland trade routes that linked China even more closely to the outside world and promoted the spread of Chinese science and technology to western Eurasia. During the Ming, China briefly reasserted its transregional power and maintained an advanced technology. But, in part because of the experience of Mongol rule, Ming China also increasingly turned inward, becoming less involved in world affairs.

The Koreans and Japanese synthesized Chinese learning, writing, Confucianism, and Buddhism with their own native traditions to produce highly distinctive societies. Significant change occurred in Japan as it moved from the aristocratic court culture of Heian to a warrior-dominated culture based on large landowning families and their military retainers, or samurai. By the end of the 1400s the East Asian societies remained strong but faced new challenges when Europeans began to expand their power in the world.

KEY TERMS

neo-Confucianism (p. 252)
qi (p. 252)
kotow (p. 258)
dyarchy (p. 260)
kana (p. 261)
samurai (p. 263)
Bushido (p. 263)
shogun (p. 263)
daimyo (p. 264)
Zen (p. 264)
Noh (p. 264)

12 Expanding Horizons in Africa and the Americas, 600–1500

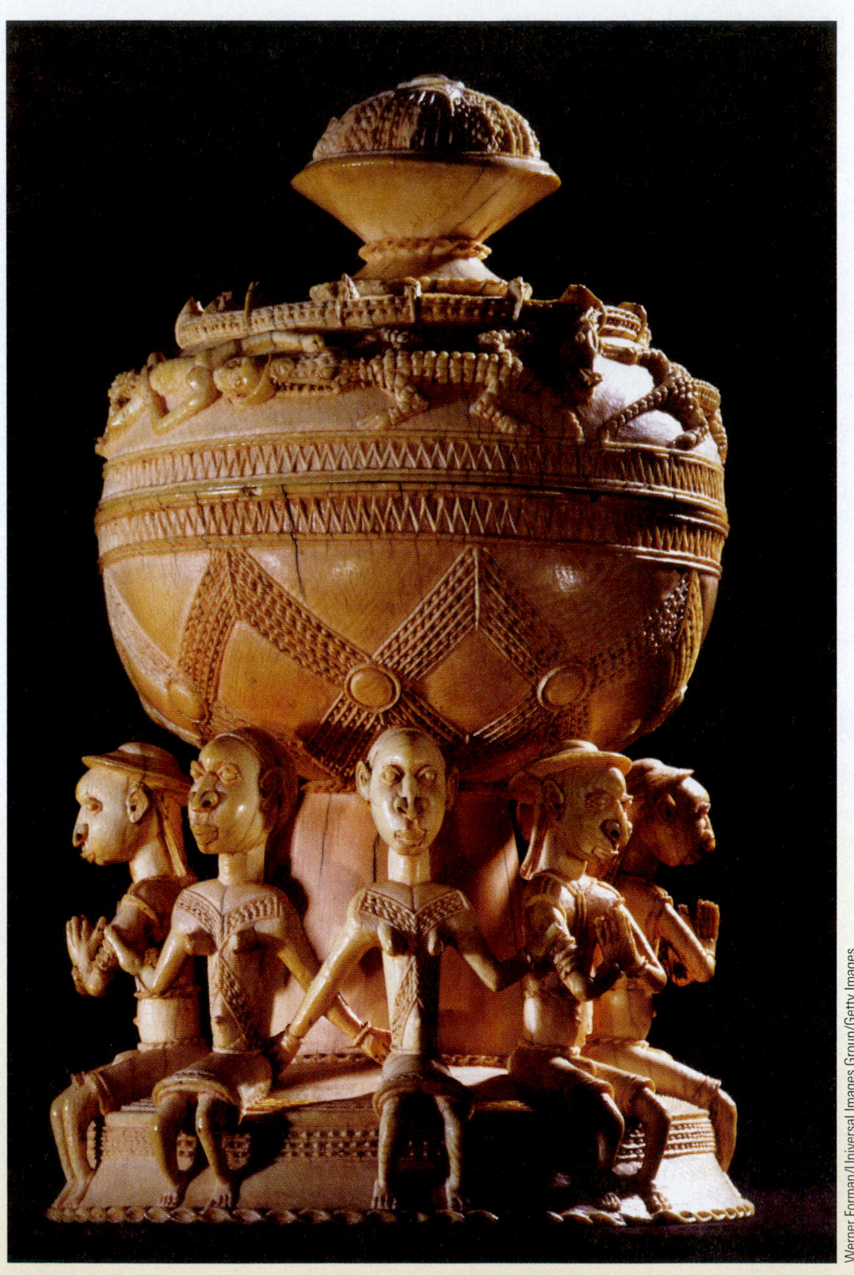

Werner Forman/Universal Images Group/Getty Images

SAPE IVORY SALTHOLDER Africans had traded and carved ivory since ancient times. This magnificent ivory carving, probably made in the fifteenth century by an artist of the Sape people, who lived in what is today Sierra Leone in West Africa, was used to store salt. The carving reflected artistic influence brought to the region by the earliest Portuguese explorers and traders.

A long time ago, when the Arabs arrived in Lamu [a port in today's Kenya, East Africa], they found local people there. The Arabs were received with friendliness and they wanted to stay on. The local people offered to trade land for cloths. Before the trading was finished, the Arabs had the land, and the [local people] had the cloth.

—A Lamu oral tradition[1]

IN THIS CHAPTER

Around 912 the Baghdad-born Arab geographer Abdul Hassan Ibn Ali al-Mas'udi sailed to East Africa with mariners from Oman, in eastern Arabia, on their regular trading expedition to what Arabs described as *Zanj* ("the land of black people"). The journey along the East African coast could be perilous, with reefs and strong winds generating high waves. Al-Mas'udi visited ports as far south as Sofala **(so-FALL-a)**, in Mozambique **(moe-zam-BEEK)**. After travels to Persia, India, and China, al-Mas'udi settled in Cairo, where he wrote scholarly books. The most influential, *Meadows of Gold and Mines of Gems*, described changing East African societies while also recording the links between these coastal towns, Arabs, and other Eurasian societies. Al-Mas'udi praised the coast's energetic traders and skilled workers, reported that the Sofala region exported abundant gold, and described how Arabs carried ivory from Zanj to Oman, from where they shipped it to India and China. He wrote that "in China the Kings and military and civil officers use ivory [to decorate furniture]. In India ivory is much sought after. It is used for the handles of daggers. But the chief use of ivory is making chessmen and backgammon pieces."[2]

During the Intermediate Era many East Asians, Southeast Asians, South Asians, West Asians, North Africans, and Europeans benefited from exchanging technologies, products, religions, and ideas. As al-Mas'udi confirmed, some sub-Saharan Africans connected to this vast network as trade expanded. African peoples like the gold producers near Sofala became integral parts of hemispheric commerce. But many sub-Saharan Africans had only indirect links, and the American societies across the Atlantic Ocean no known links, to these busy Afro-Eurasian networks. Despite lacking contact with each other, Africans and Americans shared some social and political patterns and challenging desert, forest, or highland environments. States and empires rose and fell. However, unlike in more densely populated areas of Eurasia, where people lived in large, centralized states, many Africans and Americans lived in self-governing villages. Western Hemisphere geography also inhibited the growth of long-distance networks such as those linking East Africa to China. Only after 1492 did maritime exploration permanently connect African, American, and Eurasian peoples.

[1]Quoted in Patricia W. Romero, *Lamu: History, Society, and Family in an East African Port City* (Princeton: Markus Wiener, 1997), 14.
[2]Quoted in Esmond Bradley Martin and Chryssee Perry Martin, *Cargoes of the East: The Ports, Trade and Culture of the Arabian Seas and Western Indian Ocean* (London: Elm Tree Books, 1978), 9.

Diverse African States and Peoples

How did contact with Islamic peoples help shape the societies of West and East Africa?

Several important kingdoms arose in the Sudanic region and along the Guinea coast. As in Eurasia, empires sprouted, flourished, and decayed. Scholars studied and disputed in centers of learning, and what Chinese artists accomplished with ink and Europeans with paint, African artists achieved with bronze and wood. The rise of great Sudanic kingdoms coincided with Islamic expansion and a global commerce linking West Africa with North Africa, the Mediterranean Basin, and western Asia. Along the East African coast, Islam spread in a flourishing mercantile region linked to Eurasia. The Bantus also continued to expand as they settled the vast expanses of central, eastern, and southern Africa, some building great kingdoms. Like Sudanic kingdoms and most Eurasian societies, some Bantu peoples built cities, kept records, engaged in extensive trade, and boasted diverse social classes. Indeed, many Africans were well integrated into the hemispheric system, with people, objects, and ideas circulating within Africa as well as to and from the world outside.

Trade, State Building, and Islamic Expansion in the Sudan

For hundreds of years camel caravans transporting gold, salt, ivory, slaves, and ceramics between West and North Africa had crossed the trackless Sahara sands, where dry conditions, towering sand dunes, and searing sun conspired against crops, grasses, and trees. The trade benefited people in the Sudan, the largely grasslands region just south of the Sahara, where generally flat geography and the long but sluggish Niger River made it a meeting place of people and ideas.

Beginning in the 800s, Islam filtered down Saharan trade routes much as it spread in Southeast Asian islands (see Chapter 13), carried peacefully by merchants, teachers, and mystics. Muslim merchants settling in Sudanic towns helped form stable governments to protect the trade, as many political and economic leaders, and eventually most Sudanic peoples, embraced Islam, introducing changes in customs, names, dress, diet, architecture, and festivals. Islamic schools spread literacy in Arabic, and the religious atmosphere promoted tolerance, by Muslims toward animists and vice versa. Still, Islamic practice was often superficial, and it took several centuries for the religion to permeate into villages.

A few kingdoms already existed before Islam reached the Sudan. Considered divine in these animist societies, kings remained aloof from the common people, ruling through bureaucracies. But elders or chiefs often played a role, electing kings and needing to approve major decisions, such as going to war. Women in royal families enjoyed some power and, in

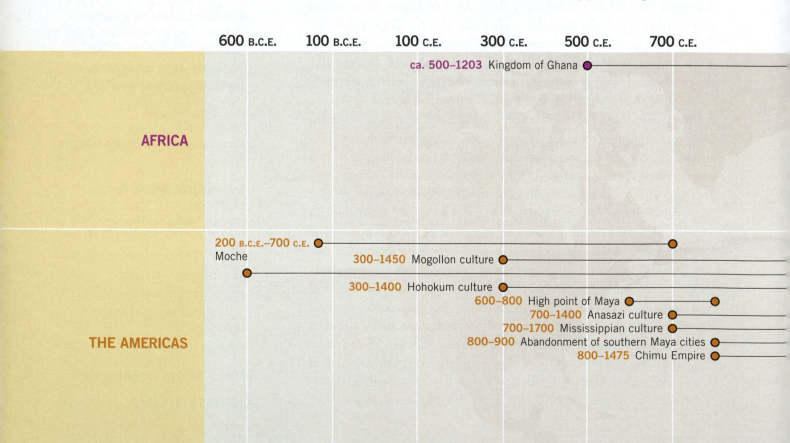

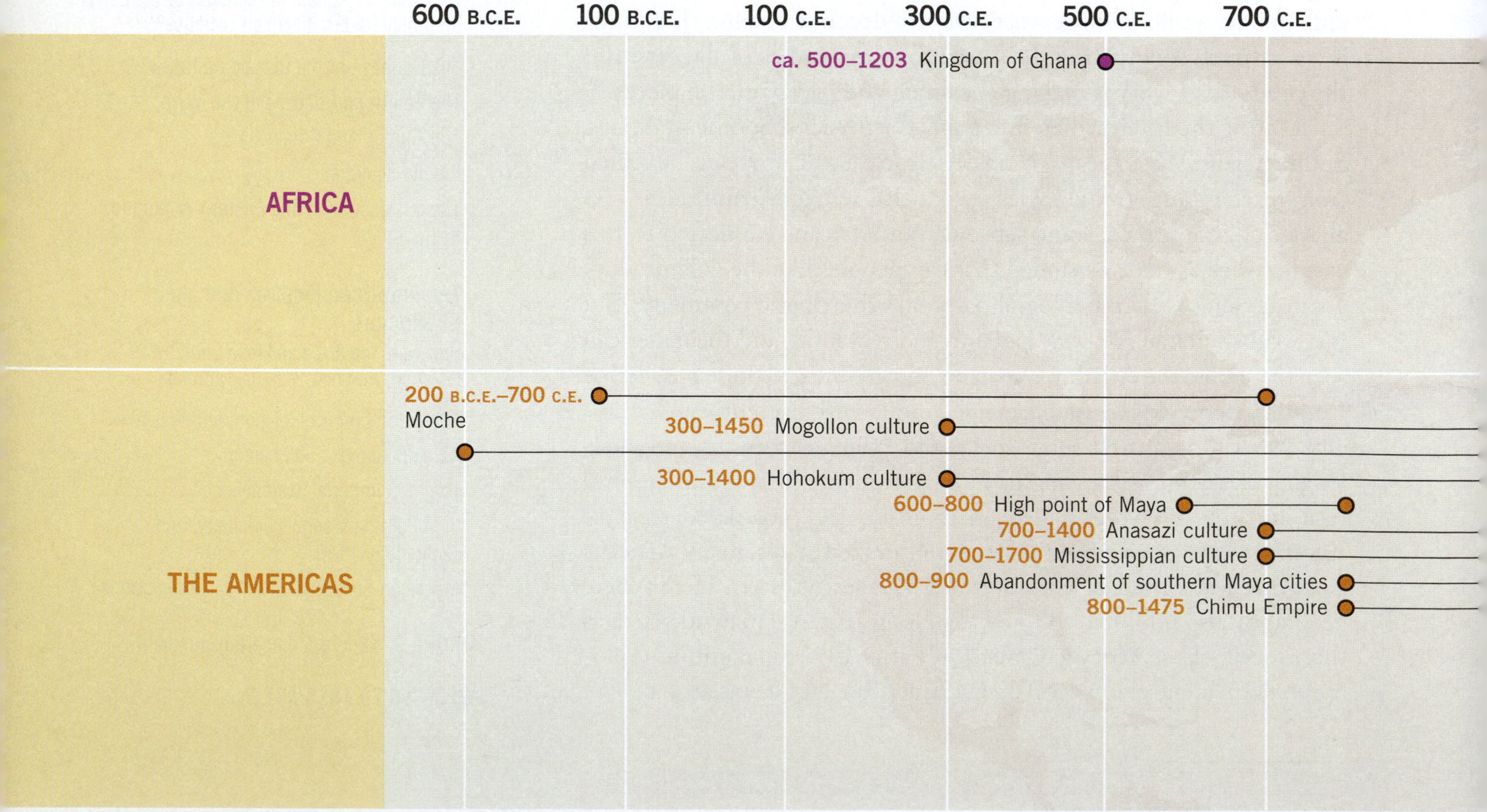

600 B.C.E. | 100 B.C.E. | 100 C.E. | 300 C.E. | 500 C.E. | 700 C.E.

AFRICA

ca. 500–1203 Kingdom of Ghana

THE AMERICAS

200 B.C.E.–700 C.E. Moche

300–1450 Mogollon culture

300–1400 Hohokum culture

600–800 High point of Maya

700–1400 Anasazi culture

700–1700 Mississippian culture

800–900 Abandonment of southern Maya cities

800–1475 Chimu Empire

a few societies, could rule as queens. Some kingdoms became empires. But states were inherently unstable, having no fixed territorial boundaries but only fluctuating spheres of influence, and often included diverse ethnic groups.

The earliest known Sudanic kingdom was Ghana, centered on the northwestern Niger River (see Map 12.1). Mande speakers of the Soninke **(soh-NIN-kay)** ethnic group probably established Ghana around 500 C.E. (see Chapter 9), but it reached its golden age in the ninth and tenth centuries, prospering from controlling the trans-Saharan gold trade. Of Ghana and its profitable commerce, the Spanish Muslim traveler Abu Hamid al-Andalusi wrote: "In the sands of that country is gold, treasure immeasurable. Merchants trade salt for it, taking the salt on camels from the salt mines. They travel on the desert as if it were a sea, having guides to pilot them by the stars or rocks."[3] Many of the twenty thousand inhabitants of Ghana's capital, Koumbi, were immigrants, including Arab and Berber merchants and some scribes who helped communicate with North Africa. Ghana's rulers converted to Islam, increasing the royal court's wealth and splendor. An Arab visitor wrote that the king's attendants had gold-plaited hair and carried gold-mounted swords, and that even guard dogs wore collars of gold and silver. Eventually mosques and Quranic schools dotted the capital. But a civil war erupted, and Berbers from North Africa attacked and destroyed the kingdom in 1203.

Mali and Songhai: Islam and Regional Power

The greatest Sudanic empire, Mali **(MAHL-ee)**, was formed in 1234 by another Mande-speaking group, the Malinke **(muh-LING-kay)**, led by the Keita **(KAY-ee-tah)** clan, whose leader, Sundiata **(soon-JAH-tuh)**, became the **mansa** **(MAHN-suh)**, or king (see Profile: Sundiata, Imperial Founder). Farmers and traders, the Malinke conquered much of the western Sudan, including most of the former Ghana territories. Stretching some 1,500 miles east to west, Mali incorporated dozens of ethnic groups. The Malinke mansa, both a secular and religious leader, displayed wealth and ceremonial regalia and expected his subjects to approach him on their knees, instilling respect and obedience in his people. Sundiata apparently converted to Islam, perhaps to secure better relations with North Africa, but never seriously practiced the religion and also used Malinke animism and magic.

Increasing Islamic influence expanded communication and travel. Some Mali emperors made glittering pilgrimages to Mecca. Sundiata's descendant, Mansa Musa **(MAN-sa MOO-sa)** (r. 1312–1337), went to Mecca in 1324 on a white Arab horse, taking along fifty slaves bearing golden staffs, one thousand followers, and one hundred camels, each loaded with 300 pounds of gold. An Arab official recorded

mansa ("king") Mande term used by the Malinke people to refer to the ruler of the Mali Empire.

[3]Quoted in *Africa's Glorious Legacy* (Arlington, VA: Time-Life Books, 1994), 90.

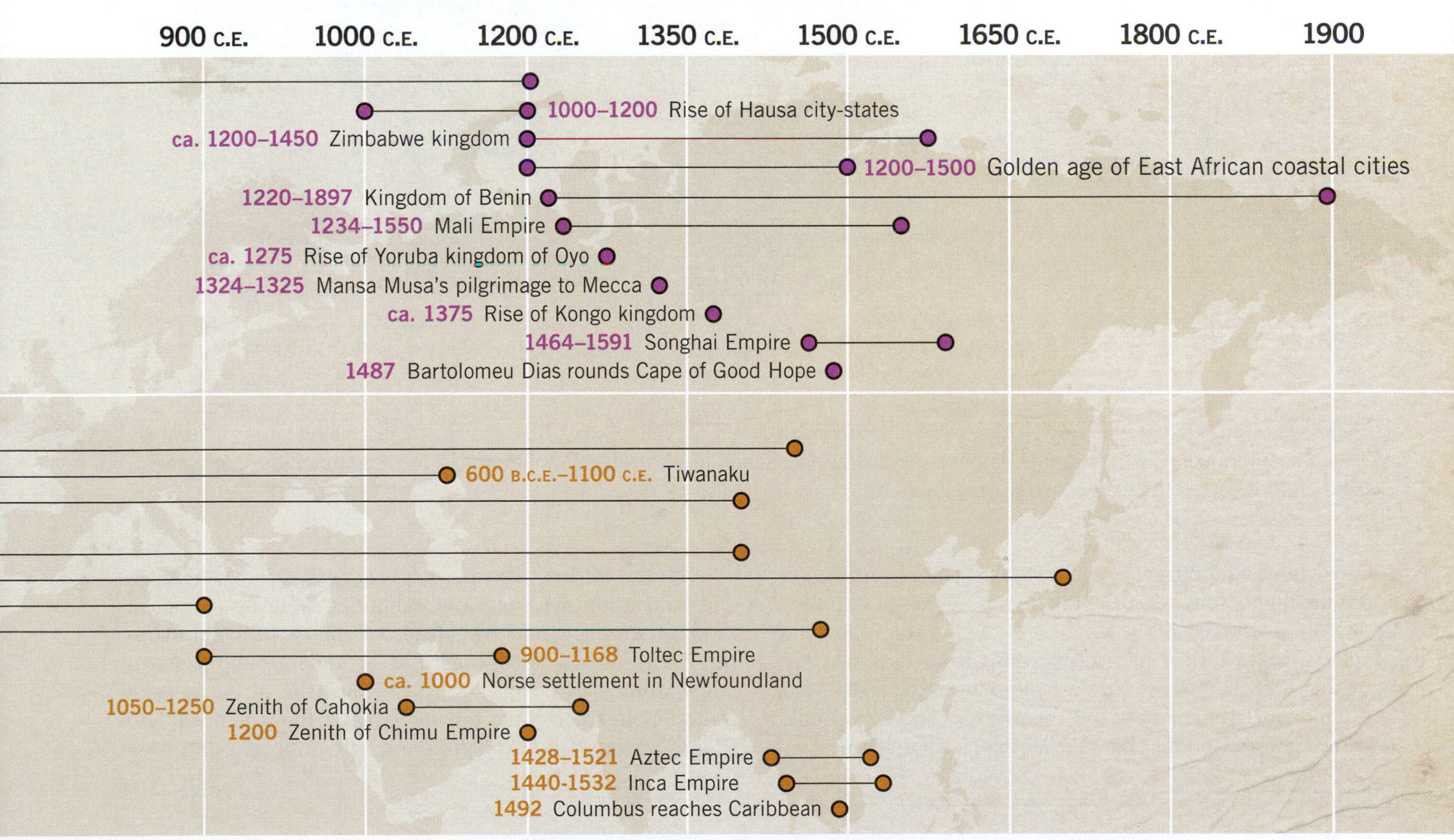

MAP 12.1 MAJOR SUB-SAHARAN AFRICAN KINGDOMS AND STATES, 1200–1600 C.E. Many large kingdoms and states emerged in Intermediate Africa. Large empires dominated the Sudan in West Africa, while prosperous trading cities sharing a Swahili culture dotted the east coast.

Mansa Musa's visit to Egypt en route to Arabia: he "spread upon Cairo the flood of his generosity; there was no person or holder of any office who did not receive a sum of gold from him. The people of Cairo earned incalculable sums from him, whether by selling or gifts."[4] Mansa Musa built grand mosques in Mali and imported Islamic jurists. But the majority of Mali's people remained animist and the elite were lax in practicing Islam.

Most Malians lived in small villages, fishing, herding, and cultivating rice, sorghum, or millet. Mali also supplied most of Europe's, and two-thirds of the world's, gold supply. Men mined gold in open pits or underground passages while women extracted gold dust from the dirt dug from mines. Gold traders met salt merchants from the north and silently matched piles of gold and salt until agreeing on a

[4]Quoted in E. Jefferson Murphy, *History of African Civilization* (New York: Dell, 1972), 120.

PROFILE

Sundiata, Imperial Founder

According to tradition, Sundiata Keita, the "Lion Prince" of the Malinke people, founded the great Mali Empire. Separating myth from fact about his life is difficult, but, since Arab historians such as Ibn Khaldun, who surveyed Mali's history, mention him, most historians believe Sundiata did exist. Nonetheless, any account must use oral epics, which glorify his heroism and reflect a Malinke view of a glorious past.

When Sundiata was born in the early thirteenth century, Ghana was collapsing and various other groups were contending to fill the power vacuum. One of twelve sons of a Malinke king, Nare Fa Maghan, and Sogolon Conde, a hunchback, Sundiata as a child was sickly and had stiff legs that made walking difficult. Hence he was spared when a rival state, Kaniaga, under their brutal king, Sumaguru, conquered Sundiata's town, Niane, and executed all his brothers as potential threats. According to the oral epic:

> *He had a slow and difficult childhood. At the age of three he still crawled along on all-fours. He had nothing of the great beauty of his father. He had a head so big that he seemed unable to support it. He was taciturn and used to spend the whole day just sitting in the middle of the house. Malicious tongues began to blab. All Niane talked of nothing but the stiff-legged son.*

However, soothsayers predicted greatness for him. Eventually he overcame his physical problems so that "at the age of eighteen he had the stateliness of the lion and the strength of the buffalo."

As a young man Sundiata went into exile and then returned to rally his people against the tyrannical Sumaguru: "The sun will arise, the sun of Sundiata." Determined and diplomatic, he skillfully used traditional clan and kinship groups as well as a reputation for possessing magic to build and solidify his power. Persuading other Malinke chiefs to surrender their titles to him, he became his peoples' sole king, enhancing his position in preparation for war.

SUNDIATA This modern depiction of Sundiata Keita memorializes the legendary founder of the Mali Empire. Even today, nearly a millennium after his death, Sundiata remains a hero to Africans for his political and military skills.

From Ada Konare Ba, Sunjiata: Le Fondateur L'Empire du Mali (Dakar: Nouvelles Editions Africaines, 1983)

Sundiata put together a military force, and around 1235 he triumphed over Sumaguru in the battle of Kirina, after which he conquered much of the old Ghana territories.

As king, Sundiata acquired the power to reshape Malinke government and society. According to the epics, "He left his mark on Mali for all time and his [rules] still guide men in their conduct [today]." As ruler for over two decades, Sundiata transformed his small state into the core of an imperial system based in his hometown of Niane, alongside the Niger River and near valuable gold fields. His rule brought peace, happiness, prosperity, and justice: "He protected the weak against the strong. The upright man was rewarded and the wicked one punished." The epic account is undoubtedly an idealized version of truth, but it also recorded that Sundiata punished his enemies. Malinke custom allowed high-status men to have many wives, and Sundiata, like his father, followed this practice, leaving many descendants.

Sundiata died about 1260, but his legend lived on. As the epics retold even today put it:

> *Sundiata was unique. In his time no one equaled him and after him no one had the ambition to surpass him. Men of today, how small you are beside your ancestors. Sundiata rests but his spirit lives on and today the Keitas still come and bow before the stone under which lies the father of Mali.*

THINKING ABOUT THE PROFILE

1. What does Sundiata's career tell us about the personal qualities admired by the Malinke people and helpful in forging a Sudanic empire?
2. How do the epic stories told over the centuries remember Sundiata and his deeds?

Note: Quotations from D. T. Niane, *Sundiata: An Epic of Old Mali* (London: Longman, 1965), 15, 40, 47, 81, 83–85.

THE SANKORE MOSQUE This fourteenth century mosque in Timbuktu was built in a traditional Sahel style of mud bricks and wooden beams. Periodic repairs can be made from ladders propped against the beams.

fair exchange. Imports also came to Mali from as far away as China and India. The Mali trading city of Timbuktu **(tim-buk-TOO)** emerged as the major southern terminus of the trans-Saharan caravan trade. Islam's international links and trans-Saharan commerce enticed visitors and sojourners to Mali, including poets, architects, teachers, and traders from places such as Spain and Egypt, and at least one Italian merchant reached Timbuktu. The fourteenth-century Moroccan traveler Ibn Battuta, who spent months in Mali, praised Malians for their many "admirable qualities," commenting that "they are seldom unjust, and have a greater abhorrence of injustice than any other people." He also found that "neither traveler nor inhabitant in it has anything to fear from robbers or men of violence."[5] But the pious Muslim frowned on what he considered women's immodest dress and independent behavior.

Mali rapidly declined in the 1400s because of internal factionalism and raids by other peoples. Soon the fringes broke away, and by 1464 Songhai **(song-GAH-ee)**, a kingdom formed by several ethnic groups, replaced Mali as the dominant Sudanic empire. By 1550 what remained of the Mali empire had disintegrated. Some Songhai rulers were nominal Muslims, others devout. The most revered leader, Aksia **(ACK-see-a)** the Great (1483–1528), possibly of slave origin, was humane, pious, tolerant, and devoted to learning. The substantial imperial capital, Gao (ghow) on the Niger River, contained perhaps 100,000 people. As North African and European demand for gold and slaves increased, Songhai flourished from trans-Saharan trade, receiving glass, copperware, cloth, perfumes, and horses. Many slaves, obtained from nearby peoples and sold in the Gao slave market, were taken on the arduous journey to the Mediterranean societies.

Timbuktu became a major intellectual center with a famous Islamic university that taught astronomy, astrology, medicine, history, geography, Arabic, and Quranic studies. The city's many scholars and students patronized bookstores and libraries containing thousands of books, many in African languages using Arabic script. In recent years over thirty thousand lost books on many subjects, hundreds of years old and revered by local people, have been found hidden underneath Timbuktu's mud houses and in nearby desert caves. When Islamic militants seized and held Timbuktu for some months in 2012–2013, they destroyed some books, but local residents hid most of the others again or smuggled them out for safekeeping.

Timbuktu prospered as part of the Songhai kingdom. One visiting North African noted many shops and abundant food, describing the people as "of a gentle and cheerful disposition, and spend a great part of the night in singing and dancing through all the streets of the city."[6] Songhai flourished until 1591, when Moroccans destroyed its military power.

The Central Sudan and Guinea Coast

After 1000 another dynamic Sudanic society developed farther east, in northern Nigeria, eastern Niger, and southern Chad, where the Hausa **(HOUSE-uh)** people formed fiercely competitive city-states, ruled by kings, that dominated some trans-Saharan trade. As its prosperity attracted non-Hausa immigrants, including Arabs and Berbers, Hausa society became increasingly Islamic. Hausa cities such as Kano **(KAHN-oh)** were centers for manufacturing cotton cloth and leatherwork, some sold as far away as Europe. The Hausa were also farmers, famed craftspeople, and, later, skilled traders, pursuing wealth all over West Africa. Today the Hausa language, which mixed Arab, Berber, and West African influences, remains the central Sudan's major trading language and sub-Saharan Africa's most widely spoken language.

[5]The quotes are from E. W. Bovill, *The Golden Trade of the Moors*, 2nd ed. (London: Oxford University Press, 1970), 95.
[6]Leo Africanus, quoted in Kevin Shillington, *History of Africa*, rev. ed. (New York: St. Martin's Press, 1995), 105.

BENIN KING This brass plaque from the royal palace depicts the Benin king on horseback, supported by two retainers.

Werner Forman/Universal Images Group/Getty Images

Like many Sudanic peoples, the Hausa possessed a strong class system that was headed by royal families and aristocrats, followed by Islamic intellectuals, such as teachers, and wealthy merchants. Hausa women enjoyed a high status compared with many African women. A fifteenth-century queen, Amina, who ruled a major Hausa state, Zaria **(zah-REE-uh)**, was praised as "like the moon at its full, like the morning star. She is a lion as precious as gold among all women."[7]

Along the Guinea coast, a region of rain forest and grasslands just south of the Sudan, Sudanic influence and trade fostered state building among societies like the Yoruba **(YORE-uh-buh)**,who settled in southwestern Nigeria around 1000 B.C.E. By 1275 these societies had developed a state in western Nigeria, Oyo **(OY-oh)** that encompassed most Yoruba. Oyo remained the area's most powerful state, flourishing until the late eighteenth century. Eventually various leaders established other Yoruba states, some linked to Oyo and each based on a large city ruled by a king or prince. While powerful and considered sacred, kings were influenced by elders and aristocrats. By modern times Yoruba identity was based more on common language and culture, including complex animistic traditions still influential today, than politics.

Many Yoruba towns served as both commercial and political centers ruled by elaborate bureaucracies, producing cloth, iron, brasswork, and terracotta figures. Enjoying respect, merchants were closely connected to north-south trade. Not expected to work in the fields, many Yoruba women developed wealth and influence as traders. Yoruba artists achieved fame. For example, Yoruba at Ife **(EE-fay)** cast beautiful bronze portraits of their rulers. Since Yoruba culture prized submissiveness to superiors and discouraged conflict, crime was rare.

East of Yoruba territory, another great kingdom, Benin **(buh-NEEN)**, was the state of the Bini **(bean-ee)** people, who shared some Yoruba traditions. Benin emerged around 1220 and established an empire in the mid-1400s under King Ewuare **(ee-WAHR-ee)** the Great. While Ewuare was a warrior, later kings became spiritual leaders, leading secluded lives with their many wives but subject to influence by powerful local chiefs. Benin artists cast beautiful bronzes and carved ivory glorifying the king and state. Located near the Atlantic coast, Benin was one of the first African kingdoms to be visited by Europeans in the 1400s, who wrote of the prosperous society they admired.

Protected by high walls, Benin city included an elaborate royal palace, neat houses with verandas (porches), and neighborhoods linked by broad avenues. Bini merchants, trading with the Hausa, Yoruba, and Songhai, dealt in woodcarvings, foodstuffs, ironwork, farm tools, weapons, and later cloth. As producers of most of the cloth, Bini women benefited from this trade. The upper classes dressed and dined well, consuming beef, mutton, chicken, and yams, while the poor ate yams, dried fish, beans, and bananas. However, an innovative welfare system protected the poor from becoming beggars by supporting those unable to work. Benin began to decline in 1550 but only collapsed in 1897.

The Bantu Diaspora

The expansion of Bantu peoples, introduced in Chapter 9, continued during the period discussed in this chapter. Historians debate whether this involved large-scale human migration or instead small numbers of Bantu speakers, carrying advanced farming and an iron-using material culture, who moved to a new area and mixed with local people who eventually adopted Bantu language, perhaps initially as a lingua franca. As mentioned in Chapter 9, in eastern Africa migrating Bantu encountered Nilotic-speakers, who had migrated from North-Central Africa. Bantus and Nilotes **(NAI-lots)** competed over good grazing land and salt, but they also traded, coexisted, and sometimes mixed together. For example, in Kenya the Bantu Gikuyu **(kee-KOO-yoo)** intermarried, traded, and sometimes fought with the Nilotic Masai **(mah-SIE)**, who were mainly cattle herders.

Over time Bantu languages spread over forest, savannah, and highlands in the southern half of Africa, with the speakers developing diverse cultures, languages, political systems, and economic patterns but also maintaining many common traditions. Most Bantu-speakers remained farmers, practicing shifting cultivation where necessary but using more complex methods where possible. Bananas became East Africa's staple crop. Some Bantus lived in towns and centralized kingdoms on the Sudanic model, especially in the Great Lakes region. But most kings had religious and ceremonial rather than real political power, and villages usually remained autonomous.

East African Commerce and Swahili Culture

Expanding Islam and global commerce integrated East African coastal peoples, including many Bantus, into Dar al-Islam and the wider world. The 1,200 miles of coast stretching from

[7]Quoted in Constance B. Hilliard, ed., *Intellectual Traditions of Pre-Colonial Africa* (New York: McGraw-Hill, 1998), 311–312.

Somalia down to Mozambique proved a cultural melting pot, fostered by trade linking East Africa with societies around the rim of the Indian Ocean and bringing in diverse cultures, languages, and religions. Prevailing monsoon wind patterns made sailing up and down the coast relatively easy, fostering regular contact with seafaring folk from Arabia, Persia, India, and Southeast Asia. Indonesians visited East Africa for several centuries, some perhaps intermarrying with East Africans, and brought with them bananas, coconuts, and yams, which spread throughout tropical Africa. Some Indonesians also settled on Madagascar. Eventually seafaring Arabs from the Persian Gulf, Oman, and Yemen dominated coastal trade, seeking ivory, tortoise shell, leopard skin, and later gold and copper.

As trade increased, many city-states developed, among them Mogadishu **(mo-ga-DEE-shoo)**, Lamu **(LAH-moo)**, Malindi **(ma-LIN-dee)**, Mombasa **(mahm-BAHS-uh)**, Zanzibar **(ZAN-zuh-bahr)**, Kilwa **(KILL-wa)**, and Sofala. These states governed only a small hinterland and were chiefly interested in trade rather than military expansion. Settlers came from Arabia, Persia, and India. A royal court, often claiming Persian or Arab ancestry, and powerful trading families dominated each city-state. Trade networks into the interior expanded with the discovery of gold in the Zimbabwe **(zim-BOB-way)** highlands. With access to these gold fields, Sofala at the mouth of the Zambezi **(zam-BEE-zee)** River became a wealthy city.

The coast reached its golden age from the twelfth through the fifteenth centuries as Islam became entrenched. Ships from Arabia, Persia, and India regularly visited. One passenger, the Moroccan jurist Ibn Battuta, traveled as far south as prosperous Kilwa, on an island off Tanzania, describing it as "one of the most beautiful and well-constructed towns in the world, elegantly built [with] good buildings of stone and mortar, entirely surrounded by a wall and towers."[8] With perhaps twenty thousand people, Kilwa was a collection hub for goods coming in from north and south. Its upper classes built three-story stone houses with indoor plumbing and acquired large quantities of gold and silver jewelry as well as Chinese silk and porcelain. Ibn Battuta described Kilwa's Muslims as devout, chaste, and virtuous and its rulers, a family claiming Yemenite descent, as humble and pious. Still, he disliked some local customs, such as their rich diet. He approved of chicken, meat, fish, vegetables, and mangoes but not rice cooked with butter and yogurt chutney, probably of South Asian origins. His reports show East Africans closely linked to the Islamic world by trade and religion but also maintaining various local customs.

East African city-states became integral to the Intermediate world's greatest maritime trading network, whose ports and trade routes linked economies around the Indian Ocean rim stretching from Indonesia to the Persian Gulf and East Africa. Foreign traders brought pottery, Chinese porcelain, glass beads, and Indian cotton to East Africa, trading them for iron, ivory, tortoise shell, leopard skins, gold, and slaves. The beautiful homes in coastal cities, some with tropical gardens, fountains, and pools, attested to the upper- and middle-class wealth.

Swahili Name for a distinctive people, culture, and language, a mix of Bantu, Arab, and Islamic influences, that developed during the Intermediate Era on the East African coast.

Intermarriage and blending of Bantu, Arab, and Islamic influences in coastal cities produced a distinctive new African culture and language, **Swahili** (Arab for "people of the coast"). While Arabic script was used to produce poetry, historical legend, religious speculation, and commercial accounts, Swahili became the coastal region's major trading language, its influence reaching as far inland as the eastern Congo River Basin. Today Swahili is second only to Hausa as a first or second language in sub-Saharan Africa.

Swahili favored Arab architectural styles, ideas of inheritance, and dress, including long gowns for men and modest attire for women. Whereas interior Bantu peoples practiced either patrilineal or matrilineal descent, the Swahili were, like Arabs, firmly patrilineal. However, Islam only slowly penetrated the hinterland, spreading in part because it was flexible, tolerating Bantu beliefs in spirits and ancestor worship. Today Muslims are numerous in all East African countries, but five hundred years ago Islam was found mostly in coastal towns.

Zimbabwe and the Kongo

East African trading cities were only part of the wider Bantu diaspora, which also included various kingdoms in Central and southern Africa. On South-Central Africa's fertile plateau a great kingdom, Zimbabwe ("houses built of stone"), flourished from trade with the coast. Today little remains of the kingdom's monumental buildings except for dozens of impressive stone ruins dotting the landscape for hundreds of miles, constructed by Shona **(SHO-nah)** people between the thirteenth and fifteenth centuries. The granite buildings had various functions. Some were walls enclosing towns, and others were apparently courts. In the capital city, probably containing 10,000 to 20,000 people, the largest enclosure, Great Zimbabwe, an oval space surrounded by a wall 1,800 feet long, 32 feet high, and 17 feet thick, may have housed the royal family or perhaps served as a sanctuary where they worshiped their patron deity.

Although the Shona farmed and herded, it was mining that fostered Zimbabwe's prosperity. The Shona had migrated from the southern Congo River Basin, an area of many copper mines. After discovering gold, copper, and iron ore on the plateau, they extracted it from open-pit and occasionally underground mines and traded these minerals down the Zambezi River to the coast. By 1500 some ten thousand Arab and Swahili traders lived along the river, buying and exporting the gold to the Middle East and India through Sofala and Kilwa. Shona exports corresponded to the rapid growth in the world demand for gold, and in return Zimbabwe received Indian textiles and Chinese ceramics. Shona artists also produced copper, bronze, and gold ornaments.

Perhaps due to overpopulation, soil exhaustion, and cattle overgrazing, in the 1400s the empire split into two rival states, and the capital city was largely abandoned by 1450. As Zimbabwe declined, trade routes and then the government may have shifted north to the upper Zambezi River Valley, but the Shona continued to export gold to the coast.

[8]Quoted in John Middleton, *The World of the Swahili* (New Haven, CT: Yale University Press, 1992), 40.

THE GREAT ZIMBABWE COMPLEX Great stone enclosures, most probably used as royal residences or religious sanctuaries, were built around the Zimbabwe kingdom. This one, surrounded by high walls, was at the center of the kingdom's capital city.

In the 1300s the Bakongo **(bah-KOHNG-goh)** people established another great kingdom, Kongo, near the Atlantic coast of northern Angola and western Congo, whose population eventually reached 2.5 million. In the capital city of Mbanga **(um-BAHN-ga)**, royal musicians bearing drums and ivory trumpets announced visitors and ceremonies to the king's compound, which was nearly a mile around. High-status people wore finely woven cloth fabrics, beautifully dyed, that European visitors compared to velvet, silk, and brocade. Theoretically absolute and divine, the king was elected by elders and governors and had to seek advice from a council formed by heads of leading clans.

Kongo village chiefs settled disputes but referred serious quarrels or crimes to district judges. Villagers lived in houses with walls of palm matting and thatch roofs. Every day women ground millet into a white flour and stirred it in boiling water to make a stiff porridge that was eaten with peas or beans and spicy sauces made of palm oil. Meat such as chicken, fish, or game, as well as bananas, yams, and pumpkins, provided some variety. Trade flourished, with people using a seashell-based currency to buy salt, colored cloth from India, palm cloth, palm belts, and animal skins.

MAKE SURE YOU UNDERSTAND THESE KEY POINTS BEFORE MOVING ON

- The area south of the Sahara, known as the Sudan, benefited most from the Sahara caravan trade and gradually embraced Islam.
- South of the Sudan, on the Guinea coast, the Yoruba developed a balance of power between kings and aristocrats and were generally peace-loving traders and artists, and the prosperous kingdom of Benin developed an innovative welfare system.
- The Bantus continued to expand across eastern and southern Africa and established numerous coastal city-states that were greatly influenced by trade with Arabs.
- The East African coast became largely Muslim, though retaining a great deal of its native African culture along with influences from such cultures as Arabia and South Asia.
- Zimbabwe rose to prosperity from mining and built large granite buildings whose precise use is still debated by historians.

African Societies, Thought, and Economies

What were some distinctive patterns of government, society, thought, and economy in Intermediate Africa?

Societies across Africa shared many common patterns of social organization, religion, culture, and economy. Nonetheless, they also varied considerably, depending on their connections to the Islamic world and whether they had centralized or village-based governments. While intensive agriculture did not develop to the same extent as in Eurasia, trade with the wider world attracted European explorers to the region.

Political and Social Patterns

Although many Africans were governed by powerful kingdoms such as Mali, Benin, and Zimbabwe, many other people lived in decentralized, stateless societies featuring self-governing villages that focused on family relationships. Here councils of elders normally assisted chiefs and applied customary law to regulate conduct. Some of these stateless societies were small and some large, but each was unique. For example, the Tiv **(tihv)** of eastern Nigeria developed an egalitarian society with kinship-based legal and economic rights. Using a form of local democracy, village elders and family heads allocated land, administered justice, and organized community activities, with custom influencing leaders' and citizens' behavior. Women controlled their own fields and did much of the farmwork but were aided by men in harvesting and planting. Another society, the Gikuyu **(kee-KOO-you)**, were Bantu farmers in the temperate, green highlands around Mount Kenya in East Africa who mostly lived in individual family homesteads. They had no local chiefs; instead, a senior male in each extended family represented the family to the broader society. Younger Gikuyu men formed a council that handled military affairs, while village councils elected representatives to district councils of elders. This democratic Gikuyu system relied heavily on group discussion and public opinion.

Whether living in kingdoms or stateless societies, individuals were connected to others through social networks and cooperation. An economic unit, the family frequently included all living relatives, with their spouses and children. Some societies practiced matrilineal kinship, tracing descent and inheritance through the female line. In kingdoms, the queen sister or queen mother usually enjoyed high respect. For example, the Bini people still revere Idia, an early-sixteenth-century queen mother who raised an army and used her magical powers to help her son overcome his enemies. Queen mothers often controlled access to rulers, managed treasuries, presided over court systems, and helped enthrone or depose rulers. Some queens ruled in their own right. However, women's status varied widely. Men dominated most families and often had multiple wives. With children the chief goal of marriage, a woman could rise in status by bearing many children. Women also looked to children rather than husbands for support in old age.

A web of associations defined socially acceptable behavior. Families were part of clans or lineages that traced descent to a common ancestor. Work or music groups, secret societies, religious cults, and age grades promoted cooperation between people of the same generation. Most groups prized collective effort and responsibility instead of individual initiative. *The ethnic group*, often mistakenly called the "tribe" by modern observers, included people, not necessarily related by kinship ties, who spoke the same language, practiced similar customs, and lived in the same general territory. Some ethnic groups, like the Yoruba and Hausa, numbered in the millions and were divided into multiple states. Distinct cultures, languages, and religions marked off groups such as the Yoruba, Hausa, Shona, and Gikuyu.

oral traditions Verbal testimonies concerning the past; the major form of oral literature in cultures without writing.

Like many societies around the world, some sub-Saharan peoples condoned slavery and traded slaves, which were often war captives or debtors. Ibn Battuta wrote that, in Sudanic cities, the wealthy "vie with one another in regard to the number of their slaves and serving-women. They never sell the educated female slaves, or but rarely and at a high price."[9] Slaves filled diverse social and economic roles: the Wolof **(WOH-lohf)** tribe of Senegal did housework, Kongo slaves worked as soldiers or plantation workers, and the Akan **(ah-KAHN)** on the Guinea coast worked in gold mines. Some Hausa slaves enjoyed a high social status as palace advisers. Some families considered slaves members of their household, and many slaves could marry and have their children freed. While slave life was often hard, African slaves often had more rights and enjoyed better treatment than slaves in most European, Islamic, Asian, and American societies.

Religious and Artistic Traditions

Diverse African religions included Muslim and Christian believers but also millions practicing monotheism, polytheism with many gods and spirits, animism (spirit worship), or a mix of the three. Africans often recognized a supernatural world of sorcery, magic, spirits, ancestors, and multiple gods mediated by shamans, male or female specialists skilled in curing disease and with knowledge about the spiritual realm. Understanding that many illnesses had spiritual and psychological as well as physical dimensions, shamans often succeeded as healers. Some male elders, considered sages, collected wisdom and challenged individuals to become better and more knowledgeable. Scholars compare these sages, in their constant probing for truth, to Classical Greek, Indian, and Chinese philosophers. Reverence toward cosmic forces blended into worship and spirituality. Many Africans believed in a life force that was part of all living and material entities. They also revered deceased family members and ancestors, who were considered present in spirit. Since most societies envisioned an unapproachable high god holding himself aloof from daily affairs, people prayed to ancestors and spirits.

The Dogon people, who live on an arid plateau in today's nation of Mali, may represent what African society and religion were like before states formed and outside religions arrived. Ruled by priest-chiefs, the Dogon work the fields collectively, center their lives on community religious festivals and arts, and order their society through myths that perceive the cosmos as dualistic, mixing male and female, order and change.

Africans developed oral and written literatures. Most societies relied on **oral traditions**, verbal testimonies concerning the past that were passed through generations by professional rememberers, known as *griots* in West Africa, who served as local historians, recordkeepers, and sometimes councilors to kings and tutors to princes. Griots recounted past events and royal genealogies while updating their stories with contemporary happenings, becoming walking libraries that who transmitted knowledge to their successors. As a modern griot explained: "We are vessels of speech, the repositories which harbor secrets many centuries old. We are the memory of mankind."[10] Based on oral traditions, a chronicle recognizing the reigns and genealogy of sixty-seven kings in a central Sudanic kingdom, Kanem-Borno, spans the

[9]Quoted in Bovill, *Golden Trade*, 96.

[10]Djeli Mamoudou Kouyate, quoted in D. T. Niane, *Sundiata: An Epic of Old Mali* (London: Longman, 1965), 1.

ninth through nineteenth centuries. Many top West African writers and popular musicians today come from griot families.

Possessing written languages such as Arabic, Hausa, Amharic, and Swahili, some African peoples produced poetry and philosophical speculation. However, writing spread slowly because most Africans, relying on well-defined customs to maintain order, did not need written laws. With communal ownership, they also had no need to track land use and inheritance. Merchants in Sudanic and East African cities recorded large purchases or sales in Arabic or Swahili, but elsewhere writing was difficult, since paper deteriorates quickly in the tropical climate.

Africans produced a rich artistic heritage, including sculpture, dance, and music. Paleolithic Africans were among the first people anywhere to paint on rocks and cave walls. When farming developed, painting declined and sculpture in wood, clay, ivory, bronze, or gold became the major visual art form. African wooden masks for religious festivals, as well as carvings of animal, human, and spiritual figures, have influenced modern artists around the world. Music and dance, closely integrated into work, leisure, and religion, usually involved everyone's participation. Musical groups often accompanied people working in the fields, and at day's end farmers and musicians returned to the village for an impromptu party. While African musicians emphasized percussion, using many types of drums, they also played wind and string instruments. African musical traditions filtered into the Middle East, influencing Islamic music, and beginning in the 1500s, African slaves carried their musical traditions to the Americas, blending them with European and Native American styles to foster many twentieth-century popular music forms, such as blues, jazz, rock, calypso, salsa, and samba.

Agriculture and Trade

Sub-Saharan Africans successfully exploited their tropical environment's resources to foster farming and trade. Unlike in Eurasian societies, which had horses and oxen to pull plows and large wheeled carts, in Africa various tropical diseases or insect pests prevented breeding or maintaining these animals except in the northeast highlands and the dry Sudan and Sahara. With economic production and transportation relying mainly on human muscles, most Africans were small farmers who produced food primarily for their own use. With often poor soils, irregular rainfall, and no manure from draft animals for fertilizer, Africans could not match the highly productive agriculture found in China, India, and Europe. Instead many practiced shifting cultivation, a practical adaptation to local conditions that worked well if population densities remained small. By 1500 probably some 40 million people lived in sub-Saharan Africa, compared to over 100 million in China. However, Africans used more sophisticated techniques such as irrigation or terracing where possible.

Trading networks interlaced tropical Africa. Great markets emerged at Sudanic cities such as Gao and Timbuktu, where traders bought and sold ivory, ebony, and honey from the Guinea coast and books, wheat, horses, dates, cloth, and salt from the north. Most market traders were women, and most traveling merchants men. Renowned as long-distance traders, Hausa merchants traveled to the Guinea coast to buy kola nuts, a rain forest tree crop that can be made into one of the few stimulants allowed Muslims. Tropical Africans exported various items, including gold, ivory, and kola nuts, to North Africa, Asia, and Europe. Both gold and cowry **(KOW-ree)** shells, collected on the Indian Ocean coast, served as local currency.

In local trade people bought and sold things needed for everyday life, such as salt, ironware, and copper, while women made cloth from cotton and bark. Because sources of abundant salt were rare, it commanded a high price, and traders sometimes obtained it from hundreds of miles away. Iron ore was more common. Although Africans valued copper for making bangles and bracelets, few good sources existed. The most extensive copper mining took place in the copper-belt region south of the Congo Basin and in South Africa.

Africans, Arab Slave Traders, and the Portuguese

Africans connected to Eurasia primarily by trade across the Sahara Desert or along the East African coast. For example, Arab, Berber, and African traders shipped African slaves north to be sold in North Africa, Iberia, Arabia, Persia, India, and Christian Europe. Between 650 and 1500 trans-Saharan caravans transported perhaps 2 to 4 million slaves from West Africa to Mediterranean societies, while 1 to 2 million were shipped from East Africa and 1.6 million (mostly Nubians and Ethiopians) from Red Sea ports. Though these numbers were significant, the trade was smaller in scale than the trans-Atlantic slave trade carried out by Western nations between 1500 and 1900. African slaves in the Middle East became domestic servants, laborers, soldiers, and even administrators. Perhaps 250,000 descendants of African slaves, traders, and sailors live in India and Pakistan today.

The trans-Saharan slave trade inspired western Europeans to eventually seek slaves directly in West Africa. In search of Asian spices, African gold, and slaves, well-armed Portuguese began sailing south along the West African coastline in the early 1400s, sporadically planting 7-foot-high stone pillars topped with a cross, inscribed in Latin and Portuguese, to symbolize their achievements and claims to discovered lands (see Chapter 14). This exploration began a new era in African history. The Portuguese colonized the Cape Verde **(VUHRD)** Islands in the Atlantic and nearby coastal Guinea-Bissau **(GIN-ee bis-OW)** while also establishing trading forts. Some West Africans acquired artistic and religious ideas from Portuguese merchants and Christian missionaries.

In 1487 a Portuguese expedition led by Bartolomeu Dias rounded the Cape of Good Hope at Africa's southern tip and sailed into the Indian Ocean, thus opening a whole new chapter in Western exploration and intensifying Portuguese interest both in Africa and the world to the east. Even after Christopher Columbus, sailing for Spain, announced his "discovery" of what he thought was India in 1492, the Portuguese concentrated on the sea route around Africa. In 1497 Portuguese ships commanded by Vasco da Gama sailed up the East African coast to the trading city of Malindi and, engaging an Indian or Arab pilot, sailed on to southern India. Da Gama had discovered the fastest oceanic path from Europe to the Indian Ocean maritime trading network.

In the 1480s the Portuguese began a long relationship with the Kongo kingdom by sending Catholic missionaries and skilled craftsmen to that area. In 1491, after two Kongolese court officials claimed the Virgin Mary appeared to them in dreams, King Nzinga a Nkuwu **(en-ZING-a ah en-KOO-WOO)** and some aristocrats adopted Christianity and sent their children to Portugal for study. The king actually wanted Portuguese teachers, craftsmen, and weapons to use against a rival kingdom. By the early 1500s, however, after realizing the economic possibilities in the Americas, the Portuguese became far more interested in obtaining slaves than in helping Kongo's economy or treating the Kongolese as equals. In 1514 they began exporting Kongolese slaves to nearby islands and, eventually, to the Americas, beginning a new era for Africa and a direct relationship with Europe and the Americas, the region to which we now turn.

MAKE SURE YOU UNDERSTAND THESE KEY POINTS BEFORE MOVING ON

- **Many Africans lived in "stateless societies" in which family relationships, rather than rulers or governments, organized people's lives.**
- **In addition to Muslims and Christians, many Africans were polytheistic, believers in multiple gods and spirits.**
- **In Africa the oral tradition was much stronger than the written one, and writing spread slowly because African custom did not depend on recordkeeping and important knowledge was passed down orally by griots.**
- **African agriculture faced a number of challenges, including poor soil, irregular rainfall, and the difficulty of obtaining and using draft animals.**
- **Several million African slaves were shipped to the Middle East, and the Portuguese laid the groundwork for the much larger European slave trade to the Americas.**

American Societies in Transition

What factors explain the collapse of the Early Intermediate Era American societies?

Like Africans, most Americans creatively exploited their environments, whether in urban societies or smaller agricultural or nomadic communities. Whereas many Africans had direct or indirect contact with Eastern Hemisphere networks, Americans remained a world apart from that interconnecting zone. Furthermore, these American societies were often separated from each other by great distances and more geographical barriers—high mountains, harsh deserts, and thick forests—than their Eurasian counterparts. Yet cultures, technologies, and trade goods spread over a wide area. Powerful states with dense populations in Mesoamerica and the Andes, such as the Maya, declined or collapsed, while less centralized governments formed elsewhere, including North America.

The Collapse of the Classical States

Unlike Afro-Eurasian states such as Rome, Gupta India, and Han China, most major Classical Era American states survived into the Early Intermediate Era. Great cities such as Teotihuacan, Tikal in the Maya lands, and Tiwanaku and Wari in the southern Andes had flourished for centuries, supported by productive and innovative farming, trade, and metalworking, often combined with subduing their neighbors. Creative plant breeders, Americans combined nutritious maize with beans, squash, and fish or game for a well-balanced, healthy diet while discovering many plant drugs, including quinine and coca that are still used today to cure disease or alleviate pain.

However, newer centers of religious, economic, or political power now replaced older ones. In eighth-century Mesoamerica, Monte Alban declined while Teotihuacan collapsed, removing a unifying commercial and political hub. Although the Maya flourished for centuries, by 900 they had abandoned many cities. In South America, Moche collapsed around 700 and and Wari Tiwanaku around 1000. The reasons for these rapid political and economic transitions remain debated, but climate change probably played a role. In Mesoamerica and South America's Pacific coast, a warming climate baked the land as failing rains brought drought. Grassy hillsides turned brown, streams dried up, and crops withered.

The Zenith and Decline of the Maya

The Maya of Yucatán and northern Central America declined rapidly and then suddenly collapsed, allowing new powers to rise. Maya society peaked between 600 and 800, with growing populations (3–5 million people), creative irrigation systems, and massive monument building. Population densities reached a staggering 600 people per square mile, similar to China today, testifying to Maya success in mastering a marginal environment for farming. Tikal may have contained 50,000 people.

Warfare between states, mostly for royal glory and economic predominance, not conquest, was frequent, but victories were short-lived. The Maya enjoyed close commercial contact with central Mexico; for example, in Teotihuacan a whole neighborhood was reserved for Maya merchants. Maya also sometimes ventured by boat to Caribbean islands, trading jade, salt, feathers, and chocolate. They were excellent sculptors, builders, astronomers, and mathematicians and, with a well-developed writing system that could express any thought or concept, produced thousands of folding-screen books called codices, made of bark paper, although only a handful survived after the Spanish conquest. The early Maya evidently practiced forest conservation, considering certain groves of trees sacred, but they cut down forests for building large temples.

Between 800 and 900 the Maya deserted most cities in the southern lowlands, and the whole region lost perhaps two-thirds of its population. Multiple factors fostered the collapse. Climate change apparently caused a century-long drought, emptying the complex system of canals and reservoirs that collected rainwater for farming and drinking. Overpopulation prompted attempts to increase agricultural productivity on marginally fertile land, which led to soil degradation and deforestation that may have caused crop failures. Trade networks shifted from inland river-based cities to the coastal states. The Maya experienced reduced rainfall, famine, malnutrition, starvation, epidemics, and increased warfare, while increasingly unstable governments prompted revolts. Some people moved to fortified villages in remote areas. The political and religious hierarchy of kings, aristocrats, and priests collapsed, and merchants, scribes, and craftsmen ceased their work.

These dramatic developments missed northern Maya cities on the Yucatán Peninsula such as Uxmal **(oosh-MAHL)**, which flourished until around 1000, but more frequent warfare engulfed this region, and human sacrifice increased. The city of Chichen Itza **(chuh-chen uht-SAH)**, founded around 800, dominated northern Yucatán between 1000 and 1250 until it was succeeded by Mayapan **(MY-uh-PAHN)**, itself destroyed by a rebellion in 1441. By the 1500s the Yucatán Maya were fragmented into small states in chronic conflict with each other. The remnants of the Maya people, mostly reduced to subsistence farming, still lived over a wide area of Mesoamerica, but their once-brilliant history was fading from memory.

PYRAMID AT TULA Each figure on this pyramid at the Toltec capital is made of fitted stone sections and represents a warrior carrying a throwing stick in one hand and a bag of incense in the other.

The Toltecs and Chimu

As the older Mesoamerican and Andean states declined or collapsed, powerful states not unlike West African kingdoms emerged. The Toltecs **(TOLL-teks)**, moving into Mexico's central valley from the desert north, created an empire lasting from 900 to 1168 and systematically recorded their history in writing. Their empire involved a loose military alliance of newcomers mixing with local people with roots in Teotihuacan. Toltecs adopted the cult of **Quetzalcoatl** **(kate-zahl-CO-ah-tal)**, the feathered serpent, which goes back deep in Mesoamerican history. In Toltec tradition, Quetzalcoatl was a human leader banished to sea by war-gods, a story probably based on Topiltzin **(to-PILLT-sen)** (b. ca. 947), a cult high priest who succeeded his father as Toltec king but whose opposition to human sacrifice and promotion of peace angered more warlike leaders. Forced into exile, the man gradually blended into the god in myth. But the legend also said that the banished man-god, bearded and of fair complexion, would return to seek revenge. This prophecy haunted later Mesoamericans.

The Toltecs achieved wide influence, even over some northern Maya cities. Their capital city, Tula, filled with ceremonial architecture and with 30,000 to 60,000 people, was a center for obsidian mining, with Tula craftsmen producing obsidian and copper tools. The Toltecs may have established some contact with Andean societies, and some Toltec trade goods reached as far north as New Mexico and Arizona. But in the twelfth century the Toltec state, weakened by long-term drought, famine, and war, collapsed, disrupting the trade routes.

Along South America's Pacific coast, the Chimu **(chee-MOO)** Empire, whose ruling class may have descended from Moche nobles, rose to prominence around 800. By 1200 it was a sizable empire stretching some 600 miles north to south, with a capital, Chan Chan **(CHAHN CHAHN)**, that boasted many adobe-walled compounds and 25,000 to 50,000 people. Chimu lords, living in magnificent walled palaces up to three stories high, had elaborate funerals that involved the sacrifice of several hundred men and women to serve as attendants in the afterlife. Conscripted workers labored on vast construction and irrigation projects, including 25-foot-wide roads. To irrigate fields of maize, beans, cotton, gourds, squash, peanuts, and fruits, they constructed hundreds of miles of terraces and large storage reservoirs that controlled the water flow down the mountainsides. These activities helped Chimu avoid all but the most severe droughts and achieve two or three crops a year. Eventually, however, Chimu faced challenges it could not overcome. El Niño climate changes disrupted irrigation, and by the fourteenth century Chimu declined, perhaps because of overpopulation and increased soil salinization. Around 1475 the Inca conquered and incorporated the Chimu into a vast Andean empire.

Pueblo Societies

While only a few American societies formed kingdoms or built large cities, many peoples

Quetzalcoatl The feathered serpent, a symbol that goes back deep in Mesoamerican history.

MAP 12.2 MAJOR NORTH AMERICAN SOCIETIES, 600–1500 C.E. Farming societies were common in North America. The Pueblo peoples such as the Anasazi in the southwestern desert and the mound builders in the eastern half of the continent lived in towns. The city of Cahokia was the center of the widespread Mississippian culture and a vast trade network.

creatively farmed in challenging environments and supported towns and long-distance trade. Some of the most successful societies developed in the southwestern desert of North America, whose modern descendants are known as the Pueblo Indians because of their permanent towns, called *pueblos* in Spanish. Learning to farm this dry region, Pueblo peoples survived and sometimes flourished by selecting just the right soils for maize, growing cotton, weaving cotton cloth, and often building towns around human-made dams, terraces, irrigation canals, and reservoirs. Even though they had to travel everywhere by foot, Pueblo peoples traded with central Mexico and the Pacific coast, mining and exchanging turquoise with Teotihuacan and the Toltecs for craft goods. Some Mesoamerican religious beliefs and customs, such as the feathered serpent tradition and ball courts and games, also filtered north.

By 700 the Hohokum and Mogollon dominated parts of southern Arizona, New Mexico, and northern Mexico (see Map 12.2). Around 1325 in Casa Grande, a town of over two thousand people in northern Mexico, the Hohokum constructed a building three stories high of thick adobe atop a platform mound. By 1000 the neighboring Mogollon people had developed masonry technology for house building. But climate change caused drought in the 1300s, and both the Hohokum and Mogollon settlements were eventually abandoned.

The Anasazi **(ah-nah-SAH-zee)**, meaning "ancient ones" in the Navaho **(NAH-vuh-ho)** language, flourished between 700 and 1400, reaching their height between 900 and 1250. Anasazi towns, featuring masonry houses constructed of huge sandstone blocks, wood beams, and clay carried from distant forests, dot large sections of Arizona, Colorado, New Mexico, and Utah, including major centers at Mesa Verde and Chaco **(CHAHK-oh)** Canyon. Mesa Verde, ingeniously built into steep cliff walls, probably housed 2,500 people, with another 30,000 living in the surrounding area. In Chaco Canyon, eight adobe towns sat in or on the rim of the canyon, with multistoried houses, some six stories high, built around central plazas. Wide roads connected the Chaco pueblos with Anasazi towns a hundred miles away. Probably numbering 100,000 people, the Anasazi, like many Pueblo Indians, lived in egalitarian communities that practiced matrilineal kinship and matrilocal residence, with men moving into their wife's household. Women owned the houses, crops, and fields, but men dominated the council of elders who administered each town.

Environmental challenges eventually precipitated collapse, and by 1200 Anasazi agriculture declined from severe drought. Deforestation, soil erosion, disease epidemics, and invasions by outsiders may also have been factors. Hard times fostered increased warfare between pueblos, with some pueblos, their social order undermined, possibly resorting to human sacrifice or cannibalism. By 1300 many Anasazi had moved to the Rio Grande River Valley, mixing with other newcomers to produce the Pueblo peoples of central and northern New Mexico, and by 1400 Anasazi culture had collapsed, with Chaco and Mesa Verde long since abandoned. Those Anasazi who survived were probably the ancestors of southwestern tribes like the Hopi **(HOH-pee)** and Zuni.

The Mississippian and Eastern Woodlands Societies

In eastern North America's vast and fertile Mississippi and Ohio River Basins, mound-building cultures flourished that were based on trade and shifting cultivation of maize (see Chapter 9). The Mississippian culture, widespread between 700 and 1700, featured several cities, monumental architecture, social hierarchies, and religious art. The main Mississippian center, Cahokia **(kuh-HOH-kee-uh)**, strategically located near the juncture of the Mississippi and Missouri Rivers near today's Saint Louis, probably contained some 30,000 to 60,000 at its peak between 1050 and 1250, making it the North American counterpart to Teotihuacan and Tula. People came from hundreds of miles around to live, work, and participate in mass ceremonies.

Showing Mesoamerican influences, Mississippian communities like Cahokia had central plazas with platform mounds topped by temples and elite houses, probably surrounded by markets. The largest of many Cahokia pyramids, 1,000 feet long, 700 feet wide, and 100 feet tall, was larger than Egyptian pyramids and had a circumference greater than Teotihuacan's Pyramid of the Sun. Circles of standing timbers tracked the seasons by marking the sun's position. As in Mesoamerica, Cahokia's priest-rulers probably presided over lavish rituals atop the pyramids, with the chief religious cult worshiping the sun and revering mythical creatures. At a ruler's death priests sacrificed some commoners to accompany him to the hereafter.

In the matrilineal Cahokia society, divided into distinct classes, a lord showed his status by riding in a flotilla of large canoes decorated with gold objects. Warfare over territory may have been common. Cahokia artisans made baskets, pottery, shell beads, leather clothes, copper ornaments, wooden utensils, and stone tools, and they carved artistic images into their buildings. The major hub of a vast trade network stretching from the Great Lakes to the Rockies to the Gulf Coast along the Mississippi, Missouri, and Ohio Rivers, Cahokia imported Great Lakes copper to make jewelry and drinking cups, as well as marine shells, shark teeth, and barracuda jaws from the Gulf Coast. Cultural influences from Cahokia also spread through the eastern woodlands, including new strains of maize better adapted to cooler climates.

Cahokia was largely abandoned around 1300, probably from some combination of drought, floods, deforestation, a destructive fire around 1170, and a political-ideological crisis. The greater Mississippian culture collapsed by 1550, and the Mississippi River Basin population dwindled, probably because of overpopulation, soil depletion, epidemics, and a cooling climate that damaged agriculture. Growing tensions between elites and commoners may also have undermined the political system. By the early 1700s malaria and smallpox brought by Europeans had devastated the surviving Mississippian peoples, and French colonizers wiped out the last mound builders, the sun-worshiping Natchez people in the lower Mississippi Valley, in a battle in 1731.

In North America's eastern woodlands, few states developed, with most farming communities resembling African stateless societies such as the Tiv. Village chiefs, often elected by elders, had little authority, and every family participated in decision making. Eastern woodland farming produced abundance. An English observer visiting Massachusetts in 1614 noted that the land was "so planted with gardens and corn fields, and so well inhabited with a goodly, strong people [that] I would rather live here than anywhere."[11] While men cleared the fields, they were often gone hunting or fighting. Warfare using bows and arrows, though common, generally led to few casualties. Women, working in groups, produced most of the food and thus had high social and political status in these often matrilineal societies. Women elders often could approve or prohibit warfare, and frequently a senior clan mother known for her wisdom nominated a new chief for election or rejection by the tribe. This relative freedom fostered a stronger emphasis on romantic courtship.

[11]John Smith, quoted in Charles Mann, "The Pristine Myth," *The Atlantic Online*, March 7, 2002 (http://www.theatlantic.com/unbound/interviews/int2002-03-07.htm).

MAKE SURE YOU UNDERSTAND THESE KEY POINTS BEFORE MOVING ON

- **American Classical states survived longer than their counterparts in Eurasia, though they ultimately declined, perhaps because of climate change.**
- **The Maya supported an extremely dense population, but by 900 C.E. the southern Maya had collapsed, while the northern Maya continued on fitfully before collapsing by 1500.**
- **The Toltecs, a loose military empire based in central Mexico, adopted the cult of Quetzalcoatl, the feathered serpent.**
- **The Pueblo peoples of the American Southwest, largely egalitarian and matrilineal, thrived on maize and grew and wove cotton.**
- **In the Mississippi and Ohio River Basins, mound-building cultures thrived on the fertile land and built some of the world's largest structures.**

The American Empires and Their Challenges

How were the Aztec and Inca Empires different, and how were they similar?

With Maya collapse and Toltec and Chimu decline, the Aztecs **(AZ-tek)** and Inca **(IN-kuh)** built the largest empires and most sophisticated states in the pre-Columbian Americas (see Map 12.3). Thanks to strong armies and well-organized governments, both empires dominated large regions but rapidly collapsed when confronted in the 1500s with Spanish military forces and the epidemic diseases they brought from the Eastern Hemisphere.

The Aztec Empire, Religion, and Warfare

Aztec society was founded by the warlike Mexica, Nahuatal **(NAH-what-uhl)**-speaking immigrants from the north. An early leader told them that "we shall conquer all peoples of the universe. I shall make you lords and kings of all that is in the world."[12] Taking pride in their warrior reputation and writing about their history, Mexica identified themselves as the Toltecs' successors, adopting many Toltec gods, rituals, and cultural forms. By 1325 they had established a strong state controlling much of the lake-filled Valley of Mexico, where Teotihuacan once flourished. There they built their capital, Tenochtitlan **(teh-noch-TIT-lan)**, expanding into neighboring regions in 1428. Their greatest ruler, Moctezuma **(mock-teh-ZOO-ma)** I (1440–1468), declared that war was the greatest Aztec preoccupation, with its purpose to gain new territories while acquiring prisoners for sacrifice to the gods. By 1519 the Aztec Empire controlled much of central and southern Mexico, even collecting tribute from people as far south as Guatemala and El Salvador. Tribute from the conquered became an important revenue source.

Religion supported warfare. Aztecs believed the sun was a warrior-god daily battling his way across the skies to prevent the universe's destruction by the forces of darkness. To help the sun-god remain fit for this struggle, Aztecs fed the deity with blood from non-Aztec warriors captured in their frequent fighting, regularly sacrificing them in gruesome rituals. In Aztec myths, their god Huitzilopochtli **(wheat-zeel-oh-POSHT-lee)** ("The Hummingbird Wizard") commanded them to feed him with human hearts torn from the recently sacrificed. Aztecs practiced human sacrifice on a greater scale than any other major society, sacrificing several thousand captured warriors a year. Other central Mexican people practiced blood sacrifice as well.

By 1500 the Aztecs faced growing economic, political, and military problems. The need for a regular supply of captives created a permanent state of war and terror, fostering political instability and fierce resistance. The conquered peoples paid tribute but frequently rebelled, providing an excuse to fight and obtain more captives. Brutal Aztec policies created many enemies, and some later proved willing to cooperate with the Spanish to invade Tenochtitlan. Even before this, Aztec leaders, haunted by bad portents, apparently felt a deepening insecurity. These worries increased in 1518, when word reached Tenochtitlan of winged towers (Spanish ships) bearing bearded white men on Mexico's east coast. Because Spanish arrival coincided with Quetzalcoatl's prophesied return, historians debate whether Emperor Moctezuma II identified Spaniards with the god and thus lost the will to resist. However, Aztec tools and weapons, still based on sharp minerals such as obsidian, were no match for Spanish guns and steel swords. Although the Spanish encountered a vigorous Aztec society, Spanish conquest and occupation in 1521 ended the Aztec era.

Aztec Economy and Society

Aztecs developed a prosperous economy and dynamic social system. Tenochtitlan (the site of today's Mexico City), on a swampy island in a large lake, was one of the world's great cities, where large palaces, temples, forty pyramids, and diverse markets served some 150,000 to 300,000 residents. Spaniards marveled at the markets selling each kind of merchandise in its respective street (see Witness to the Past: An Aztec Market). Thousands of canoes carrying passengers or produce traversed the six major canals daily. The city awed the first Spaniards in 1519:

> *And when we saw all those towns and villages built in the water, and other great towns on dry land, and that straight and narrow causeway leading to Mexico [Tenochtitlan], we were astounded. These great towns and buildings rising from the water, all made of stone,*

[12]Quoted in Richard F. Townsend, *The Aztecs*, rev. ed. (New York: Thames and Hudson, 2000), 59.

MAP 12.3 SOUTH AMERICA AND MESOAMERICA, 900–1500 C.E. The Maya and Aztecs in Mesoamerica and the Inca in the Andes forged the most densely populated societies, the most productive farming, and the best-organized governments. The Inca built one of the world's largest empires. Other urban societies also flourished in Mexico and South America.

seemed like an enchanted vision. Indeed, some of our soldiers asked whether it was not all a dream[13].

Highly productive farming and trade underpinned the Aztec economy. The Aztecs grew their food on artificial islands, called **chinampas**, that were built on the central valley lakes, a technology dating back hundreds of years. Miles of shallow canals irrigated the islands, which produced 5-6 crops a year. Tenochtitlan served as the core of a trade system stretching into North America and Central America, and whole villages produced copper items or textiles. Merchants enjoyed a privileged position but carefully maintained the state's goodwill, some probably serving as spies in outlying areas.

Emperors, true despots who were considered semigods and selected by high officials, priests, and warriors, headed the hierarchical social structure. Then came the warrior-noble caste, with men divided into war lodges such as the eagle knights and jaguar knights. If

chinampas Artificial islands built along lakeshores of the central valley of Mexico for growing food.

[13]Quoted in Brian M. Fagan, *Kingdoms of Gold, Kingdoms of Jade: The Americas Before Columbus* (London: Thames and Hudson, 1991), 7.

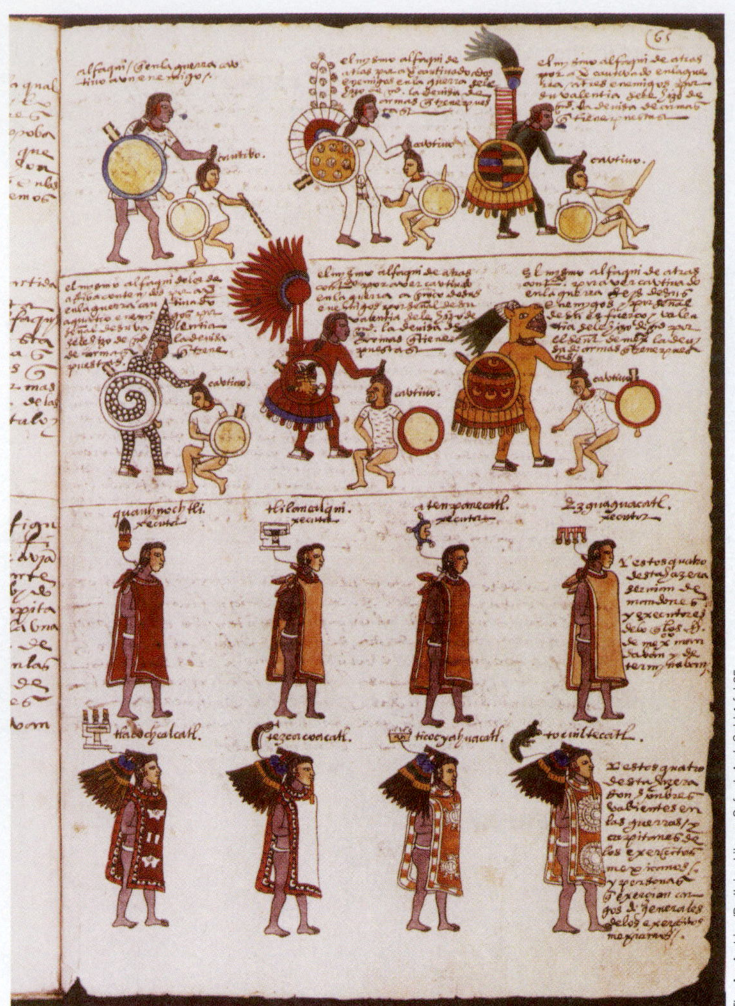

The Art Archive/Bodleian Library Oxford, Arch Seld 1 fol 65r

AZTEC WARRIORS These drawings, made by a sixteenth-century Aztec artist, show Aztec warriors, wearing costumes that reflect their status. Some have defeated their opponents and forced them to kneel in submission. Many such captives would later be sacrificed.

captured by the enemy, they were expected to die with honor. According to an Aztec poem: "There is nothing like death in war. Far off I see it; my heart yearns for it!"[14] The priesthood, mostly celibate, played a key role, preparing calendars and most books. An Aztec remembered the priests as "sages wise in words. They watch over, they read, they lay out the books. They lead us, they tell us the way."[15]

Commoners, held in contempt by the elite, included artisans who created beautiful representations of the human figure. Indeed, Aztec sculptures, painted codex books, and murals were traded all over Mesoamerica. Many commoners worked as tenant farmers on noble-owned land. While upper classes enjoyed sumptuous meals of meat, tortillas, and tamales, followed by a chocolate drink, commoners lived on ground maize meal, beans, and vegetables, cooked with chili, and rarely ate meat. Numerous slaves, often debtors or criminals, occupied the lowliest position.

Men and women led very different lives. While their menfolk served the state, elite women had two main roles: childbearer and weaver. Noble fathers advised their daughters "to learn very well the task of being a woman, which is to spin and weave. It is not proper for you to learn about herbs or to sell wood, peppers, [or] salt on the streets"[16] (like commoner women). While elite girls remained at home until their arranged marriage, when they moved into their husband's family, commoner women were freer to pursue careers such as street vendors and midwives. Many young boys learned religion, history, rhetoric, and the arts of war in schools, but girls, preparing for marriage, were taught domestic skills and religion.

The Inca Imperial System

The Inca conquered an empire in the Andes much larger than the Aztec Empire. Inca society, led by warrior chiefs, came together in central Peru around 1200. In the early 1400s a new leader, Viracocha **(VEE-ruh-KOH-chuh)** Inca, claiming to be a living god, launched campaigns of conquest with an army led by professional officers. By 1440 Viracocha's son, the pragmatic and visionary Pachacuti **(PA-cha-koo-tee)** ("World Remaker") (r. 1438–1471), the major empire builder, eventually conquered the Lake Titicaca Basin and Chimu Empire. By 1525, after uniting both highlands and the coastal zone for the first time, the Inca dominated from southern Colombia to central Chile. Their capital city, Cuzco **(KOO-skoh)**, contained between 60,000 and 100,000 people, and the empire, stretching for nearly 3,000 miles, much of it above 8,000 feet in altitude, became the most politically integrated in the Americas. The Inca treated conquered peoples more generously than did the Aztecs, incorporating them into their armies, rewarding their service, and tolerating their religions and cultures.

Inca imperialism was spurred by religion and concepts of kings as divine offspring of the sun and responsible for defending the cosmic order. Kings enjoyed great wealth and pomp. According to a Spanish observer, the king in a royal procession, wearing a collar of huge emeralds, was borne on a massive gold sedan throne lined with tropical bird feathers and studded with gold and silver plates. Kings' bodies, mummified on their death, became the center of a cult. With deceased kings still considered owners of their property and land, their successors had an incentive to seek new conquests for acquiring their own property and land.

The Inca conquered or frightened into submission nearly all the farming societies, but their culture and power did not permeate far into rain forests and deserts. Deliberately resettling peoples to prevent rebellion or develop new districts, the Inca, unlike the Aztecs, faced relatively few rebellions. Many non-Inca appreciated the peace imposed after several centuries of warfare. To win support, Inca also encouraged sons of

[14]Quoted in Fagan, *Kingdoms of Gold*, 224.
[15]Quoted in Robert M. Carnack et al., *The Legacy of Mesoamerica: History and Culture of a Native American Civilization* (Upper Saddle River, NJ: Prentice-Hall, 1996), 415.
[16]Quoted in Marysa Navarro, "Women in Pre-Columbian and Colonial Latin America," in *Restoring Women to History* (Bloomington, IN: Organization of American Historians, 1988), 6.

WITNESS TO THE PAST

An Aztec Market

The wealth of foods and other trade goods available in markets in and around Tenochtitlan impressed Spanish conquistadors on their first visit in 1519, two years before their conquest. This account by Bernal Diaz del Castillo **(DEE-as del kah-STEE-yoh)**, *a Catholic priest who observed the Spanish conquest, describes the great market of Tlatelolco, near Tenochtitlan, which was thronged with as many as 25,000 people every day. Special market days might have attracted twice that number.*

We were astounded at the number of people and the quantity of merchandise that [the market] contained, and at the good order and control that was maintained, for we had never seen such a thing before.... Each kind of merchandise was kept by itself and had its fixed place marked out. Let us begin with dealers of gold, silver, and precious stones, feathers, mantles, and embroidered goods. Then there were other wares consisting of Indian slaves, both men and women.... Next there were other traders who sold great pieces of cloth and cotton, and articles of twisted thread.... There were those who shod cloths of hennequen [a tough fiber] and ropes and the sandals with which they are shod....

Let us go and speak of those who sold beans and sage and other vegetables and herbs,... and to those who sold fowls, cocks,... rabbits, hares, deer, mallards, young dogs and other things of that sort in their part of the market, and let us also notice the fruiterers, and the women who sold cooked food, dough and tripe;... then every sort of pottery made in a thousand different forms from great water jars to little jugs;... then those who sold... lumber, boards, cradles, beams, blocks and benches.... Paper... and reeds scented with liquid [amber], and... tobacco, and yellow ointments....

I am forgetting those who sell salt, and those who make the stone knives,... and the fisherwomen and others who sell some small cakes... [and] a bread having a flavor something like cheese. There are for sale axes of brass and copper and tin, and gourds and gaily painted jars made of wood. I could wish that I had finished telling of all the things which are sold there, but they are so numerous and of such different quality and the great market place with its surrounding arcades was so crowded with people, that one would not have been able to see and inquire about it all in two days.

THINKING ABOUT THE READING

1. What does the reading tell us about Aztec society and its material culture?
2. In what ways does the Aztec market remind you of a modern supermarket or department store?

Source: Bernard Diaz del Castillo, "The Discovery and Conquest of Mexico," translated by A. P. Maudslay (New York: Farrar, Straus and Cudahy, 1956).

non-Inca leaders to attend school with Inca nobles in Cuzco, where they studied history, geometry, military tactics, and oratory. Goodwill and cooperation among the conquered were fostered by festivals featuring vast quantities of maize beer. While the Inca also practiced human sacrifice, they did so on a smaller scale than the Aztecs, mostly on ceremonial occasions. Several children from noble families of conquered peoples might be killed on a mountaintop as honored gifts to the mountain gods and their bodies were then mummified by the cold.

In the hierarchical and rigid Inca system, the royal family kept their bloodline undiluted by siblings marrying each other. Each ruler had many concubines and a chief queen, his sister, with her own magnificent palace and often considerable power behind the scenes. The queen headed a moon cult, led ceremonies for major goddesses, and gave birth to male heirs. Rebellions eventually became more frequent, and rivalry for the throne sometimes led to civil war. Such a conflict had just ended in 1532, weakening Inca resistance and allowing the newly arrived Spanish to triumph militarily and replace the Inca political system with Spanish rule.

Inca Political Economy, Society, and Technology

The most productive agriculture and creative technology in the Americas supported Inca society. Unlike with the Aztecs, the state, not merchants, operated the imperial economy by collecting and distributing goods, and imperial storehouses collected food for distribution as needed. The state required army service and work on state-owned farms or public works projects. Officials regularly visited villages to monitor work productivity or sanitation.

Inca society was patriarchal, with most commoners members of large extended families. Both men and women made pottery and worked in the fields, the men plowing and the women sowing the seeds. Each day peasant women spent time weaving and collecting firewood or llama dung for cooking. The ancient Andean creator-god and chief Inca deity, Viracocha, had both male and female characteristics, and the Inca worshiped several female deities, including the Earth Mother.

Whereas Aztecs mainly pursued sacrificial victims, Inca wanted control of labor and land. They built administrative centers throughout their territories, some as retreats for the elite, such as Machu Picchu **(MAH-choo PEE-choo)**, a spectacular collection of buildings built high atop a narrow mountain ridge above a remote river valley. With communications a priority in ruling conquered lands, 14,000 miles of roads, many graded and paved with gutters for drainage, radiated out from Cuzco to link this vast empire. Inca engineers even tunneled through rocks and built suspension bridges across gorges and pontoon bridges of reeds across rivers. The road system awed the Spanish, one writing, "I believe there is no account of a road as great as this, running through deep valleys, high mountains, banks of snow,

MACHU PICCHU This dramatic mountaintop settlement in the high Andes was probably built as a spiritual retreat for Inca royalty, who enjoyed its well-constructed drains, baths, fountains, and administrative buildings.

torrents of water, living rock, and wild rivers."[17] Along these roads relay runners, averaging some 150 miles per day, conveyed administrative messages, and llama pack trains carried supplies.

Unlike Mesoamericans, the Inca had no formal writing system, but they used an efficient form of recordkeeping that involved differently colored knotted strings, called **quipus**, to record commercial dealings, property ownership, and census data. An oral literature with narrative power, including tales, prayers, and plaintive love songs, was passed down through the generations.

The Inca excelled in technology and science. Vast agricultural engineering projects, such as terraces and irrigation canals, generated widespread prosperity, surpassing most Eastern Hemisphere counterparts. Inca agriculture, far more productive than Peruvians can manage today, emphasized potatoes, maize, peanuts, and cotton. Practicing soil conservation, the Inca rarely experienced famine. They also developed sophisticated medicine and surgical techniques, including simple anesthesia procedures. Copper, bronze, and silver were fashioned into beautiful metal objects. Master cloth makers, the Inca wove luxurious woolen fabrics from alpaca fleece and made bridges from cords and roofs from fibers. Engineers built fortresses and temples with great blocks of stone so perfectly joined that even a knife could not be inserted between them.

American Societies and Their Connections

Although thousands of miles of forests and mountains limited direct contact, American societies exchanged ideas and goods with each other over extended networks. Thanks to trade and conquest, many western South American peoples worshiped the same gods, shared mythologies, practiced human sacrifice, and made similar textiles, artworks, and metal products. Mesoamerican religious ideas, such as the Quetzalcoatl cult, influenced the Anasazi and even reached the Mississippi Valley, and Mesoamericans traded with the Pueblo peoples for turquoise and with Central Americans for jade. Traders known as the Manteno, from coastal Ecuador, also sailed large balsa rafts carrying cargo up and down the Pacific coast from Chile to Mexico, fostering some north-south communication.

quipus Differently colored knotted strings used by the Inca to record commercial dealings, property ownerships, and census data.

Geographical barriers did not prevent Andean and Mesoamerican societies from developing some common social and political features. Hence, both regions had similar gender relations. Unlike in North America, where matrilineal patterns were common, these were patriarchal societies, with men dominating central governments, village life, and extended family households while women prepared food, wove cloth, and ran households. Unlike kings and noble men, who might have several wives, most commoners practiced monogamy. Warfare, common but ritualized, involved much protocol, including declarations of war. Armies in close formation fought hand to hand, hoping to capture rather than kill opponents. Since most battles occurred far from cities, civilians and settlements were largely left alone.

Historians debate the size of the Western Hemisphere population in the late 1400s, but recent studies estimate 60 to 75 million, far fewer people than in the Eastern Hemisphere. Mesoamerica had the most population, perhaps 20 to 30 million, while 12 to 15 million lived in the Andes region. Perhaps 7 million occupied North America, two-thirds in the eastern woodlands and southwest. Compared to inhabitants of the Eastern Hemisphere, Americans faced fewer deadly diseases, and some peoples were quite healthy. Yet, farmers and urbanites, especially Maya, experienced more health risks than hunters and gatherers. General health seems to have deteriorated for some centuries prior to the Columbian voyages. Famine caused by sporadic climate change posed a bigger problem.

Eventually, American societies faced challenges coming from the Eastern Hemisphere. The only known European visits to the Americas before 1492 occurred in eastern Canada. Around 1000 C.E. a small group of Greenland-based Norse (Norwegian) Vikings, led by Leif Ericson, visited the area and established a base camp in Newfoundland (see Chapter 14). Alienating the local people, they abandoned their settlement after a few years, but occasional Norse trading visits may have continued for decades, even centuries. Recent DNA studies among Icelanders found that several long established families carry some Native American genes, suggesting that Norse visitors may have taken at least one woman back with them. The isolated Norse did not publicize their discoveries to Europe, although Portuguese fishermen visiting Iceland may have heard some stories.

Five centuries later a more enduring trans-Atlantic connection was forged. In search of Asia, a Spanish expedition

[17]Pedro Cieza de Leon, quoted in Terence N. D'Altroy, *The Incas* (Malden, MA: Blackwell, 2002), 3.

led by an Italian mariner, Christopher Columbus, ventured out in three small ships, eventually reaching the Bahamas. In later voyages Columbus visited more of the Caribbean and the South American coast. Even before 1492 some Americans had premonitions of a coming disaster. A few years earlier the Tarascan **(tuh-RAH-skuhn)** people of western Mexico, rivals of the Aztecs, forecast a time when

> *there will be no more temples or fireplaces, everything shall become a desert because other men are coming to the earth. They will spare no end of the earth, and everywhere all the way to the edge of the sea and beyond.*[18]

Despite creating technologies and ways of life that met their needs, thousands of years of isolation left Americans vulnerable to devastating diseases and the more effective steel weapons brought from more densely populated Afro-Eurasia. The new oceanic link altered American history forever, as epidemics wiped out millions of people, great empires fell, and Europeans colonized the hemisphere.

MAKE SURE YOU UNDERSTAND THESE KEY POINTS BEFORE MOVING ON

- **The Aztecs lived in a state of constant war and conquest, sacrificing thousands of enemy warriors a year, but their enemies helped the Spanish to conquer them.**
- **The Aztecs were productive farmers and active traders, with a hierarchical social structure in which priests played a central role.**
- **The Inca conquered a wide area in the Andes and had a hierarchical social structure, but they were far more inclusive and tolerant than the Aztecs.**
- **Trade in the Inca Empire was tightly controlled by the state, and an extensive irrigation system and soil conservation program yielded a consistent and abundant food supply.**
- **Despite extremely limited contact between Andean societies and Mesoamerican ones, they were similar in terms of gender relations and warfare protocols.**

[18] "The Chronicles of Michoacan", quoted in Melvin Lunenfeld, ed., *Discovery, Invasion, Encounter: Sources and Interpretations* (Lexington, MA: D.C. Heath, 1991), 262.

CHAPTER SUMMARY

African and American societies were separated by a vast ocean but shared certain patterns. They both formed some great centralized kingdoms and empires as well as many village-based stateless societies, and their contacts with Eurasian states and networks ranged from modest to none. Most Africans were settled ironworking farmers. The Sudanic kingdoms of Ghana, Mali, and Songhai had a complex political, cultural, and intellectual life, as well as trade connections to the Mediterranean. The increase in long-distance trade and the widespread acceptance of Islam helped integrate West Africa into hemispheric networks. Similar trends reshaped the East African coast, where city-states emerged and became linked to the Middle East and the great Indian Ocean maritime trade networks. Some coastal Bantus blended Islam and Arab culture with their own traditions, creating a Swahili culture. Other Bantus formed great kingdoms such as Zimbabwe, which flourished from gold exports. Throughout Africa, however, many people lived in small stateless societies. African religion included both polytheistic and monotheistic traditions, and many people believed in diverse spirits.

Across the Atlantic in the Americas, Classical states, including the long-enduring Maya, eventually collapsed from climate change and chronic warfare and were replaced by vigorous new peoples, such as the Toltecs and Chimu. The Aztecs and Inca built the largest empires that ever existed in the Americas. The Americans also showed a pattern of continuity with the past, with both the Aztecs and Inca making use of long-established religious traditions and highly efficient agricultural techniques. The Aztecs practiced human sacrifice and commerce on a much greater scale than the Inca, while the Inca were outstanding engineers and road builders. Both empires had productive agriculture and well-organized states, but neither was prepared for the diseases and iron weapons that were brought by the Spanish.

KEY TERMS

mansa (p. 269)
Swahili (p. 274)
oral traditions (p. 276)
Quetzalcoatl (p. 279)
chinampas (p. 283)
quipus (p. 286)

13 South Asia, Central Asia, Southeast Asia, and Afro-Eurasian Connections, 600–1500

The Return to China, illustration from 'Myths and Legends of China', by Edward T.C. Werner, pub. by George G. Harrap & Co., 1922 (colour litho), English School, (20th century)/Private Collection/The Bridgeman Art Library

XUAN ZANG ARRIVING IN CHINA A seventh-century C.E. Buddhist Chinese pilgrim, Xuan Zang, spent many years traveling in India, collecting Buddhist wisdom and observing Indian life. This modern Chinese painting shows him and his caravan returning to China with pack loads of Buddhist manuscripts.

Indian government is founded on benign principles. The taxes on the people are light. Each one keeps his own worldly goods in peace. The merchants come and go in carrying out their transactions. Those whose duty it is sow and reap, plough and [weed], and plant; and after their labor they rest awhile.

—Xuan Zang, seventh-century Chinese visitor to India[1]

In 630 C.E. a determined Chinese Buddhist monk, Xuan Zang **(swan tsang)** (ca. 602–664), traveled the Silk Road to India on an extended pilgrimage to collect holy books, spending fifteen years visiting every corner of the subcontinent. Very observant and politically astute, he also chafed at many Indian Buddhists' perception that China was too remote to truly claim Buddhism. In a debate at the great Nalanda **(nuh-LAN-duh)** Monastery, Xuan Zang told the monks that

> *Buddha established his doctrine so that it might be diffused to all lands. Who would wish to enjoy it alone? Besides, in my country humanity and justice are highly esteemed.*[2]

Xuan Zang admired much in India, including the tolerance for diverse viewpoints. Although various Hindu traditions were dominant, Buddhism enjoyed protection and royal patronage. Xuan Zang described an Indian society with a rigid social structure but also creative and open to foreign influences, including regular contact with China, Europe, the Middle East, and Indonesia. He praised India's high standard of living, efficient governments, and generally peaceful conditions. But he criticized caste restrictions, such as confining untouchables to their own shabby neighborhoods. After traveling some 40,000 total miles, Xuan Zang returned to China in 643 with hundreds of Buddhist books to be translated into Chinese, and fostered closer relations between India and China.

India's cultural diversity and openness to foreign influence resulted in part from repeated invasions by Central Asians that Hindu society eventually absorbed. Groups with differing customs generally lived peacefully, and Indian ideals spread to neighboring peoples. But Hindu political domination and cultural assimilation of newcomers faced a particularly severe challenge when Muslims gained control over large parts of the subcontinent. Islam's arrival constituted a turning point in India's development, comparable to the Aryan migrations into India several millennia earlier.

Southeast Asians also adopted new political systems and religions some strongly influenced by Indian culture. By the fifteenth century new faiths from outside, Theravada Buddhism and Islam, reshaped the political and cultural map.

[1]From L. S. Stavrianos, *The Epic of Man to 1500* (Englewood Cliffs, NJ: Prentice-Hall, 1970), 160, 162–163.

[2]Quoted in Tansen Sen, *Buddhism, Diplomacy, and Trade: The Realignment of Sino-Indian Relations, 600–1400* (Honolulu: University of Hawaii Press, 2003), 11.

IN THIS CHAPTER

Hinduism, Buddhism, and South Asian Society

How did Hinduism and Buddhism change in this era?

No Hindu leaders recreated an empire like the Maurya or Gupta Empire. Instead India encompassed many states, cultures, and languages. Despite a broad Hindu tradition and the common heritage it created, India became a collage of microcultures, with many images on the same canvas shaping one another while retaining their own distinctive character. This mixing demonstrated one of Indian history's themes: diversity in unity. Although it divided into competing schools of thought and practice, Hinduism experienced a Renaissance, growing in popularity and increasingly shaping Indian life, while Buddhism faded but found new influence in neighboring societies. Hindu culture flourished in India for half a millennium before facing the concerted challenge from Islamic peoples.

Unity and Disunity in Hindu India

The political disunity that followed the Gupta Empire's demise in the fifth century proved a long-term pattern. The exception was the reign of King Harsha Vardhana (600–647), who came to power at sixteen and briefly united parts of north India, amassing a formidable army of 100,000 cavalry and 60,000 elephants. Harsha skillfully held together his small empire while cultivating close relations with Tang China. He enjoyed philosophy and renown as a poet and, while enjoying royal pomp, listened patiently to his humbler subjects' complaints. A strong Buddhist like Ashoka, he tolerated all faiths but also prevented his beloved sister, a Hindu, from committing sati at her husband's cremation. Harsha ruled for forty-one years, but his empire collapsed on his death.

Rajputs ("King's Sons") A Hindu Indian warrior caste formed by earlier Central Asian invaders.

Despite Harsha's brilliant reign, dozens of states proliferated in the subcontinent. Many Hindu states were absolute monarchies whose rulers owned many economic resources, such as forests, mines, and weaving operations, and controlled outlying regions through appointed governors. Holding precarious power, they buttressed their rule by claiming a divine mission and employed brahmans (Hindu priests; see Chapter 2) as court advisers for legitimacy.

North and south India developed somewhat different political patterns. Some north Indian states were controlled by **Rajputs** ("King's Sons"), members of a Hindu warrior caste formed by earlier Central Asian invaders who were raised in traditions of chivalry, honor, and courage not unlike Japanese samurai or medieval European knights. Their code emphasized mercy toward enemies and precise rules of conduct in warfare. However, Rajput-led kingdoms often fought each other for regional power. In contrast, many south Indian states, oriented to the sea, specialized in piracy and foreign trade. Merchants here had more political influence and continued their lucrative maritime trade with Southeast Asia, China, and the Middle East. Indeed, many visited or settled in Southeast Asia, bringing with them lasting south Indian ideas on art, politics, and religion.

However fragmented were India's politics and regions, the countless villages reflected cultural continuity, remaining

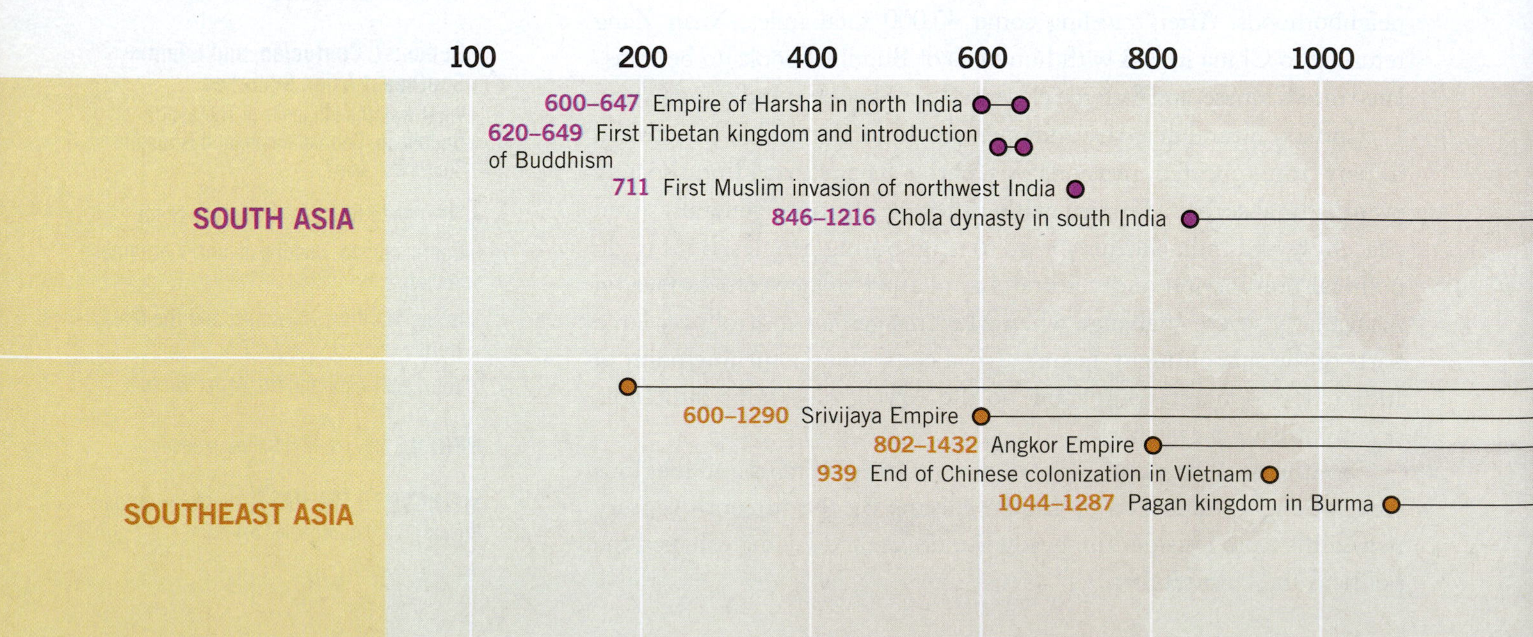

the basic unit of Indian life. Even today, about 80 percent of Indians live in villages. Farmers had to feed a population that reached around 100 million by 1500. Since the ruler owned all the land and was therefore entitled to tax or share the produce, the land tax remained the main source of state revenue and the main burden on villagers. By regularly meeting their tax obligations, peasants had the hereditary right to use the land they farmed. Village governments included a council elected annually from among village elders and caste leaders that dispensed local justice and collected taxes.

Villages remained largely self-sufficient and organized through the caste system, which promoted stability. Different castes lived in their own neighborhoods, but all contributed to the community's livelihood. Each village was essentially a symbiotic community, with a potter, carpenter, blacksmith, clerk, herdsman, teacher, astrologer, priest, and many farmers serving each other on a barter basis. Some modern writers romanticize traditional village life as peaceful coexistence, and certainly it offered psychological and economic security. Each villager had a recognized status, rights, and duties, a supportive caste community, and many personal relationships. When rulers maintained peace, repressed banditry, and kept the tax burden reasonable, most people were probably contented.

Many Indians also lived in towns and cities. Merchants helped administer the towns but, as in China, were heavily taxed and not allowed to become too independent of government. During the eighth century, to escape the Islamic conquest of Persia, some Zoroastrians fled to western India and formed the distinctive *Parsee* (Persian) community, which became known for its businessmen and manufacturers. Indeed, India was one of the world's leading manufacturing centers, with urban workshops producing cloth, textiles, pottery, leather goods, and jewelry for local use or export to markets as distant as China, Africa, and eastern Europe. India and China provided most of the world's industrial goods until the eighteenth century, the average per capita incomes for Indians remaining high by world standards.

The Hindu Social System and Scientific Traditions

Hindu society demonstrated great continuity over the centuries and, as in China, subordinated the individual to the group. Indians owed their most basic obligations to their extended family, a relationship described in an old saying as "joint in food, worship, and property." The family included several generations living together in the same household, enforcing caste regulations and collectively owning their economic assets, such as farmland. Sharing family wealth constituted an effective social security. Most families, especially in north India, were patriarchal, headed by a senior male, although older women enjoyed considerable influence. Children lived in close contact with cousins, aunts, uncles, and grandparents, making child rearing a group obligation.

Marriage customs reflected regional differences. North Indian parents arranged marriages, marrying girls off young usually to a boy in a neighboring village. Because the bride's family paid for the wedding and gave lavish presents, families preferred sons. South Indian girls often married boys they already knew, frequently a cousin. In Kerala **(CARE-a-la)** in southwestern India, one group practiced **polyandry**, marriage of a woman to several husbands. Most Indians considered divorce humiliating.

polyandry Marriage of a woman to several husbands.

Men enjoyed many privileges. Obsessed with social

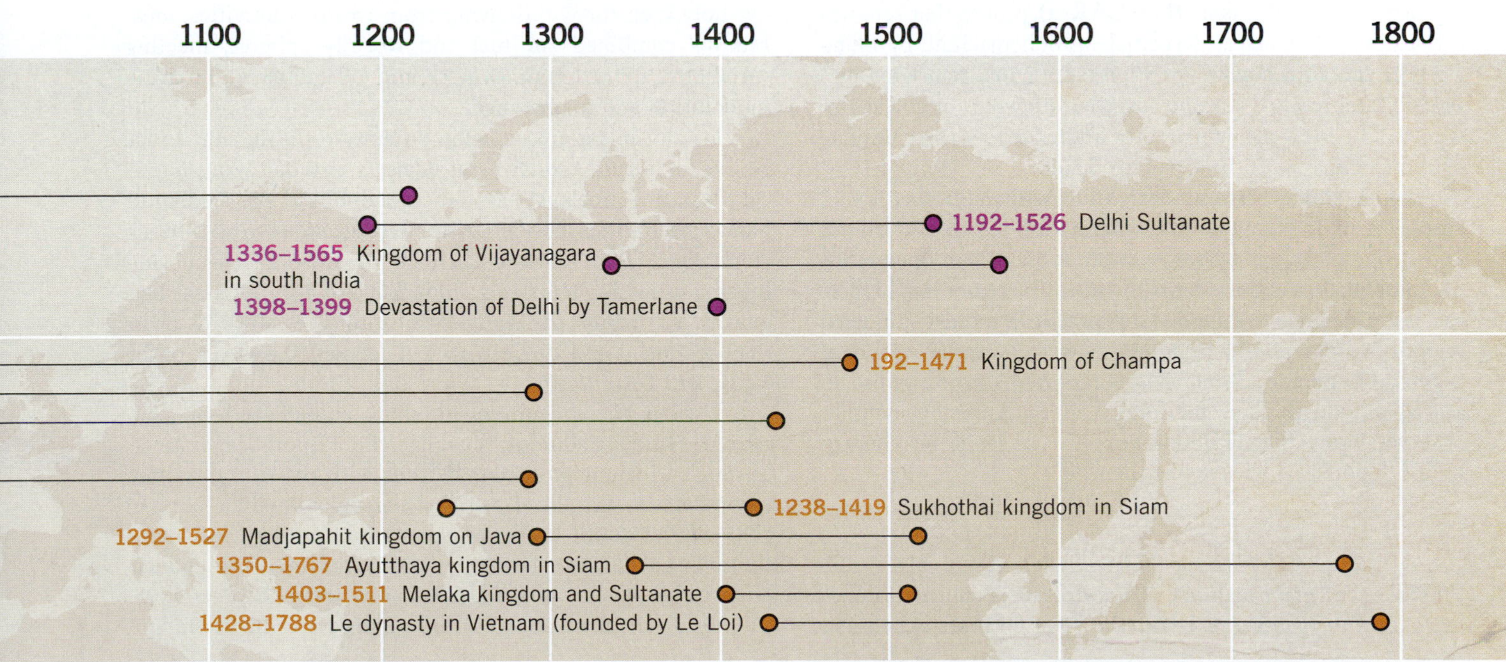

stability and controlling female sexuality, fathers of all castes taught females to avoid all men except their closest relatives after puberty. Expected to stay at home, high-caste women only occasionally visited friends or family. Low-caste and untouchable women, who needed to earn incomes for family survival, enjoyed more mobility. Most women led lives marked by obedience, sacrifice, and service, submitting to parents, husband, and children. Brides, usually much younger than husbands, moved into their husband's household and obeyed their new mother-in-law. Yet husbands often treated brides indulgently. Indians also revered motherhood. Bearing children (especially sons) improved the wife's status considerably, bringing more respect. Growing older and becoming a mother-in-law gained women even more influence.

Women also enjoyed some legal rights; although it was undoubtedly common, society condemned ill-treatment of women. However, widowhood proved catastrophic if a woman had no son. Because Hindu custom frowned on remarriage, a young and childless widow faced a difficult situation. To avoid surviving their deceased husband, some women, especially in north India, chose or were forced to die on their husband's funeral pyre. An ancient Indian expression captures the challenge for women: "As a girl she is under the tutelage of her parents; as an adult her husband; as a widow her sons." Some women, such as actresses, singers, and prostitutes, flouted social custom and mainstream values, ensuring their low status.

Indians held diverse views about sex. Many books commended celibacy, advising married men to exercise their sexual prerogatives sparingly for better health and virtue. Yet, many Indian texts such as the *Kama Sutra*, a manual of lovemaking and related matters, reflect more worldly views. Hindu gods and goddesses, portrayed in art and writings as highly sexual beings, were very unlike the virginal Madonna and celibate Jesus of Christian tradition, the spiritually and morally pure Buddha, and the image of women reflected in puritanical Islamic restrictions.

Indians made many contributions in mathematics and science. In the twelfth century one of the greatest mathematicians and astronomers, Bhaskara **(bas-CAR-a)**, proved that zero was infinity and designed a perpetual motion machine by filling a wheel rim with quicksilver. Bhaskara's book, translated into Arabic, later reached Europe, inspiring drawings of quicksilver wheels. His ideas also apparently influenced the first weight-driven clocks, built in Europe after 1300.

Some Indian astronomers and mathematicians found employment in Tang China, where they fostered a fruitful knowledge exchange. However, while Indians developed rational mathematics and the basis for scientific reasoning, higher-caste indifference to applied or practical inquiry hindered scientific progress. As brahman power increased, technical expertise lost status. Some visitors reported a growing disdain among Hindu thinkers for foreign ideas. An astute Muslim observer wrote that "Hindus believe ...there is no country, king, religion, [or] science like theirs."[3]

Hindu Diversity and Renaissance

Providing the great majority of South Asians' spiritual framework until the coming of Islam, the diverse Hindu beliefs and practices accommodated all classes, personalities, and intellects, giving scholars and mystics abstract and speculative thought and the more worldly a wealth of ritual, art, and gods for every occasion. Although Hindu values permeated society, Hindus relied on no fixed and exclusive theology. As the earliest Hindu holy book, the *Rig Veda*, put it: "Reality is one; sages speak of it in different ways."[4] Concepts of spiritual power ranged from an indescribable but all-pervading, omnipotent God, to personal gods with human attributes, to demons and spirits. Some historians doubt that Hinduism existed as a cohesive religion at this time, postulating instead hundreds of competing loosely linked devotional sects, cults, and theological strains with a few common ideas such as karma. Hinduism remained undogmatic, a philosophy and way of life with no central institution or church to monitor faith or codify beliefs. Hindus even disagreed on which sacred writings were most important. It was Muslims who introduced the collective term Hindu, from the Persian term for "Indians," to describe the varied Indian sects and cults, and it was nineteenth-century Europeans who began referring to the diverse collection of beliefs as "Hinduism."

Hindu tolerance suggested that all approaches to God were valid, although mystics and intellectuals considered their approaches superior. For example, mother-goddess worship, common among the lower castes, especially in south India, was less popular among higher castes. Worship of the many gods and goddesses varied. Many cults, believing that the wives and consorts (companions) of the main male gods responded more to their needs, worshiped goddesses like Shiva's wife, Shakti **(SHAHK-tee)**, who was revered as kind and beautiful but also cruel and fearsome. Most Hindus perceived the world as a collection of temporary living quarters for individual souls going through a succession of lives. The most devout sought liberation from human consciousness, which would free them from the endless cycle of birth and rebirth, but only a small minority seriously sought escape from the earthly world's pain and pleasures. While respecting wandering holy men for withdrawing from worldly activities, most Hindus combined spiritual and worldly spheres, meeting social obligations to family, caste, and village while practicing moderation and temperance.

Hinduism fostered a common culture throughout India. Brahmans served monarchs as advisers, standardizing political ideas and rituals. While they monopolized the reading of Sanskrit scriptures, Hindu classics were available to all through storytellers. The Vedas, collections of ancient prayers and hymns, were also translated from Sanskrit into regional languages. Yet, before the eighteenth century few Indians other than brahmans and intellectuals had detailed knowledge of the Vedas and *Upanishads*.

During these centuries thinkers embellished or revitalized Hindu traditions, sparking the Hindu Renaissance. Through itinerant preaching, debates with rivals, and written commentaries on the *Upanishads*, Shankara **(shan-kar-uh)** (788–820), a south Indian brahman child prodigy, revitalized the mystical *Vedanta* tradition, which emphasized the underlying unity of all reality and illusion of the phenomenological world. To Shankara, all Hindu gods were manifestations

[3] Al-Biruni, quoted in Romila Thapar, *Early India: From the Origins to AD 1300* (Berkeley: University of California Press, 2002), 437.
[4] Quoted in Paul Thomas Welty, *The Asians: Their Evolving Heritage*, 6th ed. (New York: Harper and Row, 1984), 68.

Caroline Vancoillie/Shutterstock

THE KHAJURAHO TEMPLE COMPLEX Built between 950–1150, these Hindu temples contain many erotic sculptures that may reflect Tantric influences.

of the impersonal, timeless, changeless, and unitary Absolute Reality, *Brahman*, the individual soul only a tiny part of the universes' unity. While accepting Hindu scriptures as divine revelation, he tried to prove them through logical reasoning and debates with other thinkers all around India, including Buddhists, Jains, Tantrics, and atheists; some debates lasted fifteen days. Yet Shankara also argued that all knowledge was relative because ignorance warps humankind's grasp of reality; the truth of existence is only understood through ascetic meditation. Shankara's views remain very popular among modern Indian intellectuals.

Other philosophers offered different visions. Opposing Shankara and Vedanta, Ramanuja **(RAH-muh-NOO-ja)**, a Tamil brahman, emphasized **bhakti**, devotional worship of a personal god, arguing that the gods should be accessible without priestly help. A few centuries later some Christian reformers in Europe developed a similar notion of personal relationships with God without priestly aid. Bhakti tradition emphasized pilgrimage to holy places such as the city of Benares **(buh-NAHR-uhs)** (Varanasi), alongside the Ganges; Hindus who died in Benares had their sins washed away. Many early bhakti thinkers, most of them nonbrahmans, also opposed or downplayed the caste system. The bhakti tradition appealed particularly to women, illiterates, and the lower castes. An early female poet, Antal, urged women devotees to revere Lord Krishna (an incarnation of Vishnu). Later the bhakti movement became part of mainstream Hinduism.

The Hindu Renaissance spurred the building of flamboyant temples whose sculptural art illustrated the faith's intricate mythology. Hence, in a temple constructed in Khajuraho **(kah-ju-RA-ho)** dedicated to Vishnu, sculptures carved into the temple walls suggested delights enjoyed by the gods, including lovemaking. The erotic, sexually explicit paintings or carvings in many Hindu temples reflected an open portrayal of sexuality.

Transitions in Indian and Tibetan Buddhism

While Hinduism experienced resurgence, Buddhism's influence gradually declined except in northeast India, where governments patronized the religion's institutions, such as the Nalanda Monastery's college, which attracted religious students from around Asia. Pilgrims from distant lands, such as Xuan Zang, exemplified Buddhism's spread to Central Asia, Tibet, China, Korea, Japan, and Southeast Asia and its adaptation to different cultures. Northeast India's intellectual environment also promoted an interfaith dialogue that created new schools of Buddhist and Hindu thought. One new Buddhist school, the **Vajrayana** ("Thunderbolt"), featuring female saviors and magical powers, spreaded during the eighth century into Nepal and Tibet.

In Bengal the contact between Mahayana Buddhists

bhakti Devotional worship of a personal Hindu god.

Vajrayana ("Thunderbolt") A form of Buddhism that featured female saviors and the human attainment of magical powers.

and Hindu followers of Shiva who revered his consort, the goddess Shakti, led to **Tantrism (TAN-triz-uhm)**, which worshiped the female essence of the universe. Both Tantric and Vajrayana schools exalted female power as earth mother and divine strength, and Tantric sects developed within both Hinduism and Buddhism. Some mystical sects presented male-female sexual union as a symbolic unity between earthly and cosmic worlds, while other sects promised release from life's pain in a single lifetime to those cultivating hedonism, pleasure, and ecstasy. Tantric Hindus often opposed the caste system. But most Hindus and Buddhists denounced Tantrism as an excuse for debauchery and sexual desire, and gradually Tantrism became a minor strand in the two religions.

While Buddhism declined in India, the remote high Tibetan plateau became its refuge. The first known pre-Buddhist Tibetan state emerged when Songsten-gampo **(SONG-sten-GOM-po)** (r. 620–649 C.E.) unified several tribes. Interested in connecting to Asian neighbors, he established close relations with Tang China, marrying a Chinese princess. Although not a Buddhist, he allowed missionaries into his kingdom. Tibetans also made India's Sanskrit script their written language. By the eighth century Buddhism had become Tibet's dominant faith, its monasteries enjoying many legal protections and government financial support. But many Tibetans still followed the ancient folk religion, *bon*. The two faiths competed for popular support and political influence, with violent conflicts destroying the unified state.

In the thirteenth century many Buddhist monks fled to Tibet to escape Islamic persecution in India, reinvigorating both Tibetan Buddhism and state building. Political relations with the predominantly Buddhist Mongols, who had conquered China and established some control in Tibet, also boosted Tibetan Buddhism. A unified Tibetan government, reestablished in 1247 under one Buddhist sect and then by aristocratic families, persisted into the seventeenth century.

Tibet's distinctive Buddhism is often termed **Lamaism (LAH-muh-iz-uhm)** because of the centrality of monks, or *lamas* **(LAH-muhz)**, and huge monasteries; perhaps a quarter to a third of male Tibetans became career monks. Buddhism eventually permeated every aspect of Tibetan life. Believers practiced magic, made pilgrimages to shrines, and provided generous support to monasteries and teachers. Tibetans also blended Buddhism with strong beliefs in the supernatural, including evil spirits. For example, people spun hand-held or roadside prayer wheels and carved prayers into stones, seeking the Buddha's help.

MAKE SURE YOU UNDERSTAND THESE KEY POINTS BEFORE MOVING ON

- **In the Intermediate Era, India was fragmented into many small states; the north was influenced by earlier Central Asian invaders and the south by maritime trade with Southeast Asia.**
- **In the Hindu social system, the individual was subordinate to the group and people tended to live in extended families that supported their members.**
- **Hinduism adapted itself to the needs of a wide variety of people, from the worldly to the scholarly, and helped to establish a common culture throughout India.**
- **Buddhism became the dominant religion in Tibet, where it became Lamaism, and many Indian Buddhist monks took refuge there to escape Islamic persecution.**

The Coming of Islam to India and Central Asia

How did Islam alter the ancient Indian pattern of diversity in unity?

The spread of Islamic religion and government in India proved a major transition, as important as the Aryan migration several millennia earlier. With Muslims and Hindus almost exact opposites in beliefs, Islam created a great divide in South Asian society. As Al-Biruni, an eleventh-century Muslim scholar, put it: "Hindus entirely differ from us in every respect. In all manners and usages they differ from us to such a degree as to frighten their children with us."[5] For centuries Hindu society had absorbed invaders and their faiths, but Islam, a self-confident, missionary religion, could not be assimilated. Tensions between the two faiths sometimes caused conflict. However, Islam enriched Indian culture, establishing new connections with western Asia as Muslims spread Indian ideas, especially in mathematics and science, to the Middle East and Europe. Many Indians embraced the new faith, and Muslims also gained political dominance over large parts of India.

Tantrism An approach within both Buddhism and Hinduism that worshiped the female essence of the universe.

Lamaism The Tibetan form of Buddhism, characterized by the centrality of monks (*lamas*) and huge monasteries.

Early Islamic Encounters

Islamic forces reached Central Asia and India within a few decades of the religion's founding. Centuries before Islam's rise, Arab sailors had linked India by trade to western Asia and East Africa. The Silk Road trade had also made western Asians well

[5]Quoted in Lucille Schulberg, *Historic India* (New York: Time-Life Books, 1968), 11–12.

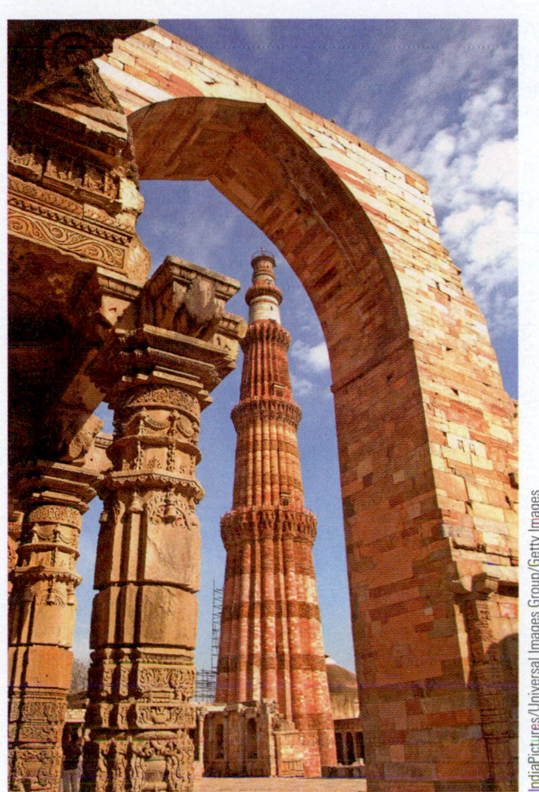
IndiaPictures/Universal Images Group/Getty Images

THE KUTB MINAR TOWER IN DELHI The 240-foot-high Kutb Minar temple in Delhi was built between the twelfth and fourteenth centuries to celebrate Muslim victory in north India.

aware of India's riches. Islamic rulers hoped to dominate these valuable regions.

After expanding into Afghanistan, by 673 Arab armies had moved into Silk Road cities such as Bukhara and Samarkand, dominated by Sogdian **(SOG-dee-uhn)** merchants, mostly Buddhists and Zoroastrians. Rival Central Asian city-states could not cooperate against the dynamic Arabs. Although many Sogdians resisted, by the early eighth century Arabs had conquered most of the cities. With the Arab defeat of Chinese forces at the Battle of Talas River in 751, serious resistance to Muslim dominance in Central Asia ended, and eventually most Central Asians adopted Islam. However, six centuries later, after Mongol rule in China ended, Central Asian economies suffered as the Silk Road trade declined, in part because China developed more interest in maritime trade.

Islamic expansion through western and Central Asia challenged Indians. The first invasion of northwest India took place in 711. After Indian pirates plundered an Arab ship near the mouth of the Indus River, Arab armies responded by briefly conquering the western Indus Basin. But not all encounters were violent. Arab traders from Yemen also brought Islam by settling in southwestern Indian ports.

By the eleventh century Turkish peoples had formed Islamic sultanates in Afghanistan, with Ghazni **(GAHZ-nee)** the most powerful. Sultan Mahmud **(MACH-mood)** of Ghazni (r. 997–1030) led campaigns into India, as much for plunder as for conquest. Seeing the many Hindu idols as an abomination to Islamic monotheism, the invaders destroyed Hindu temples while looting cities and killing Hindus. The vast wealth they took back to Ghazni helped that city become a great center of Islamic learning and arts, attracting famed scholars such as the Persian Al-Biruni.

Rajputs led opposition to Muslim invaders, maintaining a spirited Hindu resistance for many decades. Indian wars were traditionally fought largely between rulers and their respective warrior castes rather than by conscripted civilians. The caste system allowed only warriors such as Rajputs to have arms training, and they could not effectively mobilize other Indians to fight. Eventually the more mobile, horse-riding Muslims defeated Rajput armies, who also used outdated military tactics and had divided political loyalties.

The pillaging, destruction, and killing or enslaving of Hindus by early Muslim invaders fostered long-term Hindu antipathy. Even Al-Biruni concluded that Mahmud "utterly ruined [India's] prosperity. To Mahmud the Hindus were infidels, to be dispatched to hell as soon as they refused to be plundered."[6] Muslim newcomers zealously persecuted Buddhists as well, destroying monasteries and schools, including the Nalanda complex. With thousands of monks either killed or fleeing to sanctuary in the Himalayas or Tibet, Buddhism nearly disappeared from the land of its birth. In 2011 an international group of thinkers and educators announced plans to rebuild Nalanda as an ecumenical university.

The Rise and Fall of the Delhi Sultanate

In 1191 a Turkish prince, driven by religious fervor and lust for riches, conquered most of northern India and founded the Delhi Sultanate (1192–1526), which reached its height in the 1200s and 1300s. Islamic authority and religion spread throughout north India, bringing political unity for the first time in centuries (see Map 13.1). But the unstable Delhi system experienced frequent bloodshed and treachery as leaders competed for power.

Some Delhi sultans patronized the arts, supported science, treasured Greek philosophy, and built architecturally splendid structures. Many others, tyrannical and cruel, routinely killed rivals and their families. Some ruined the country with reckless spending. All employed Persian-style royal pomp, but they also styled themselves after Hindu monarchs, demanding prostration and toe-kissing from subordinates. This blending of ruling styles suggests that Muslim and Hindu cultures mixed among the elite. Some sultans expanded Delhi's power into central India and, briefly, south India, creating an empire larger than the Gupta realm.

Two of the most able Delhi sultans were Iltutmish **(il-TOOT-mish)** (1211–1236), who built the most powerful north Indian state, and his remarkable daughter, Raziya (r. 1236–1240). Iltutmish kept out Genghis Khan's Mongol armies by skillful diplomacy, gradually followed more tolerant policies toward Hindus, and welcomed Muslim refugees,

[6]Quoted in Debiprasad Chattopadhyana, *History of Science and Technology in Ancient India*, vol. 3 (Calcutta: Firma KLM Private Ltd., 1996), 60.

MAP 13.1 INDIA AND THE DELHI SULTANATE, CA. 1300 C.E. At its height, the Delhi Sultanate controlled much of northern India. South India was divided into many major states, with the Cholas and Pandyas the largest. Indian ports were connected by a vigorous maritime trade to the Middle East, East Africa, and Southeast Asia.

among them scholars and artists, fleeing the Mongols. Their large numbers helped keep Hinduism from gradually absorbing Islam. Iltutmish's chosen successor, Raziya, became the only female Muslim ruler in Indian history, praised for fostering trade, building roads, planting trees, supporting poets and artists, and opening schools. A male Muslim observer described her as "a great monarch, wise, just and generous. She was endowed with all the qualities befitting a king, but she was not born of the right sex, and so in the estimation of men all these virtues were worthless."[7] Resented as a female leader in a patriarchal society, she offended Muslim conservatives by abandoning the veil, dressing in male garb, and having a close, perhaps romantic, relationship with a male personal attendant. She died defending her position from male rivals.

By the mid-fourteenth century the Delhi Sultanate went into a rapid decline, devastated by rebellion, civil war, and severe drought and famine caused in part by climate change. Meanwhile, a new Muslim threat appeared in the northwest, the Mongol and Turkish forces of Tamerlane (1336–1405). The ruthless warrior had already conquered Central Asia and

[7]Minhaju-s Siraj, quoted in John Keay, *A History of India* (New York: Atlantic Monthly Press, 2000), 245.

Persia, creating the Timurid Empire based at Samarkand (see Chapter 10). In 1398 Tamerlane's forces invaded India, looting Delhi, killing perhaps 100,000 people, mostly Hindus, and dragging away thousands more as slaves. Tamerlane defended his actions: "although I was desirous of sparing them it was the will of God that this calamity should befall the city."[8] Tamerlane and his army returned to Central Asia, leaving Delhi's few surviving inhabitants to perish by plague or starvation. His invasion destroyed Delhi and with it political unity in north India. The Delhi Sultanate survived for several centuries in a shrunken form, but by the fifteenth century India was fragmented into dozens of Muslim and Hindu states.

Hindu Politics and Culture

Various Hindu monarchies governed parts of south and east India. Like post-Heian Japan and medieval Europe, these states featured economic self-sufficiency and political decentralization, with warriors receiving land from the monarch in exchange for military service. Commerce flourished, especially in south India. Merchants on the southwest coast, including Jews and Arabs, maintained close ties to western Asia and North Africa. An inscription from a merchant guild in 1055 boasted that they were "famed throughout the world, adorned with many good qualities. Born to be wanderers over many countries, the earth as their sack."[9] Wealthy ports such as Cochin **(KOH-chin)** and Calicut **(KAL-ih-cut)** in Kerala and Cambay **(kam-BAY)** in Gujarat **(GOO-jur-ot)** played major roles in Indian Ocean trade.

The Tamil **(TAA-mill)** people of southeast India, controlled by a Hindu dynasty, the Cholas **(CHO-luhs)** (846–1216), profited from both piracy and foreign trade. The powerful Chola navy controlled the eastern Indian Ocean, conquering both Kerala and Sri Lanka (Ceylon). Chola merchant castes organized a dynamic maritime trade that brought great wealth to their society and revenue to kings. Sometimes Chola seafaring led to plunder and conquest as far away as Southeast Asia, especially Sumatra and Java. Chola rulers established close diplomatic and trade ties to Burma, Cambodia, and China.

Tamils developed an outstanding artistic tradition, including many fabulous Hindu temples featuring magnificent bronzes. Some unknown tenth-century genius created perhaps the greatest artwork, a bronze figure of Shiva portrayed as "Lord of the Dance," ready to commence the cosmic dance of life and restore vitality to the world. For centuries artists and historians have praised this work, one writing that

> *rarely has an artist achieved such perfect balance and harmony in any medium as in this metal statue, whose symbolism embraces all of Hindu civilization in its mythic power.... The workmanship of the artists was flawless in its beauty, magically transmuting metal to fleshlike texture, imparting the breath of life to their subjects.*[10]

SHAUN CURRY/AFP/Getty Images

SHIVA AS LORD OF THE DANCE This famous bronze statue of Shiva as Lord of the Dance was made by Chola artists in southeast India. Displaying himself as a god of many qualities, Shiva grasps the flame of destruction in one hand and the drum of creation in another. The small figure under his foot represents the illusions that Shiva undermines.

The Cholas declined, and the power vacuum was eventually filled in 1336 by another Hindu kingdom, Vijayanagara **(vij-uh-yuh-NUHG-uhr-uh)** ("City of Victory"). This militarily powerful state, eventually dominating much of south and central India, built a magnificent temple-filled capital city but was destroyed by rivals in 1565. The persistence of Hindu rule in southern India preserved Hindu customs and institutions disappearing in some northern areas.

Muslim Rule and the Reshaping of Indian Life

The growing number of Muslims and Islamic political power changed Indian history. Muslims and Hindus experienced chronic conflict from tensions created by their very different values. Hinduism, with its many deities, elaborate rituals, powerful priests, fondness for images, and preference for eating pork but not beef, constituted the opposite of all Islam held sacred. Hindus despised some Muslim rulers' intolerance and desperately resisted Muslim control. Muslim governments, not wanting to permanently alienate their Hindu subjects, a huge majority of the population, made some compromises. Although Muslim rulers often confiscated Hindu nobles'

[8]Quoted in Ibid., 274.

[9]Quoted in Hermann Kulke and Dietmar Rothermund, *History of India*, 3rd ed. (New York: Routledge, 1998), 245.

[10]Stanley Wolpert, *A New History of India*, 5th ed. (New York: Oxford University Press, 1997), 113.

WITNESS TO THE PAST

The Songs of Guru Ravidas, an Untouchable Poet-Saint

Ravidas was widely considered a saint despite his humble origins. Born near Benares to an untouchable family of cobblers and shoemakers, his devotional poems and songs reflected his social reality. Some observers emphasize his protest against the unfair caste system; others contend they celebrate equality only in spiritual terms. Arguing that all can read the Vedas and worship without brahmanic mediation, Ravidas suggested that caste and gender divisions should end if people would strive together for a higher spiritual unity. His work earned respect from some brahmans and outraged others. He also influenced other bhakti poets and the founders of Sikhism, and he is revered by many Hindus and Sikhs today. The reading is excerpted from several poems.

Who could long for anything but you [God]?
My master, you are merciful to the poor;

You have shielded my head with regal parasol.
Someone whose touch offends the world
You have enveloped with yourself....
Oh well born of Benares, I too am born well known:
My labor is with leather. But my heart can boast the Lord....

A family that has a true follower of the Lord
Is neither high caste nor low caste, lordly or poor.
The world will know it by its fragrance.
Priests or merchants, laborers or warriors,
Halfbreeds, outcastes, and those who tend cremation fires—
Their hearts are all the same.
He who becomes pure through love of the Lord
Exalts himself and his family as well.
Thanks be to his village, thanks to his home,
Thank to that pure family each and every one....
No one equals someone so pure and devoted—
Not priests, not heroes, not parasolled kings.
As the lotus leaf floats above the water, Ravidas says,
So he flowers above the world of his birth.

THINKING ABOUT THE READING

1. How do these poems reflect Ravidas's social status?
2. How does he perceive God?
3. How do the poems foster debate over his purposes?

Source: John Stratton Hawley and Mark Juergensmeyer, *Songs of the Saints of India* (New York: Oxford University Press, 1988), 24–25.

wealth, life in villages went on largely undisturbed. Eventually many Muslim scholars and leaders respected Hindus and the small Zoroastrian community as peoples of the book, counterparts to Christians and Jews in western Asia. But non-Muslims still faced second-class status and special tax payments.

Over the centuries many Hindus converted to Islam, especially in the Indus River Valley in the northwest and Bengal in the northeast. A much smaller proportion of southerners embraced Islam. Converts included rich Hindus who wanted to safeguard their positions and secure government offices in Muslim-ruled states, as well as many poor Hindus who wanted to escape low or untouchable status and avoid heavier taxes on non-Muslims. Over 90 percent of today's South Asian Muslims, one-fourth of the region's population, descend from converts rather than Muslim immigrants. Sometimes Muslims, occasionally including rulers, adopted Hinduism. Sufi mystics seeking personal union with god prompted many Hindus' conversion. Bengali folk tradition celebrates a Sufi who moved to a village and built a mosque: "For the whole day [he] sat under a fig tree. His fame soon spread far and wide. Everybody talked of the occult [healing and psychic] powers he possessed."[11] People respected the Sufis' intense spiritual discipline and deep religious understanding. Perhaps the close resemblance to bhakti Hinduism, which also emphasized emotional commitment, helped the Sufi effort. Today many South Asian Muslims and some Hindus still venerate Sufi mystics of earlier centuries as saints.

Religious and cultural mixing occurred. Some Hindu and Muslim mystics came together to emphasize love of god, and some poets, honored later as saints, blended Sufi and bhakti ideals, among them Kabir **(kah-BEER)** (1440–1518), from a low-status caste of weavers in Benares. Although blind and illiterate, Kabir wrote poetry that is still revered today by both Hindus and Muslims. His writing rejects religious prejudice and the caste system while extolling love for a monotheistic god: "I am neither in temple nor in mosque; I am neither in Kaaba [Muslim shrine] nor in Kailash [abode of Shiva]. Neither am I in rites and ceremonies, nor in Yoga and renunciation....Hari [Lord Vishnu] is in the East; Allah is in the West. Look within your heart,...All the men and women of the world are His Living Forms. Kabir is the child of Allah and of Ram [God]."[12] Some revered bhakti poet-saints came from untouchable backgrounds, most notably Guru Ravidas in the fifteenth century (see Witness to the Past: The Songs of Guru Ravidas, an Untouchable Poet-Saint).

The cultural mixing fostered a new language used by many Muslims in north and northwest India. Urdu **(ER-doo)** combined Persian, Turkish, Arabic, and Indian words superimposed

[11]Quoted in Richard Eaton, "Islamic History as Global History," in *Islamic and European Expansion: The Forging of a Global Order*, ed. Michael Adas (Philadelphia: Temple University Press, 1993), 21.

[12]William Theodore De Bary, ed., *Sources of Indian Tradition*, vol. 1 (New York: Columbia University Press, 1958), 355–357.

on a Hindi grammar and written with Arabic script. In addition, Hindu social life incorporated Muslim influences, including Persian words and food, male Muslim clothing styles, and, among some north Indians, the custom of **purdah**, seclusion of women. Some intermarriage also occurred, and, at the village level, Muslims fit themselves into the caste system to some extent. Thus Muslim Indian society, like Hindu society, was not egalitarian but led by an upper class descended from immigrants.

However, despite some mixing, from the thirteenth century onward, Indian life became two distinct currents flowing side by side. Challenged by missionary Islam, Hinduism became more conservative, emphasizing tradition and priestly leadership. Refusing assimilation into Hindu culture, Muslims mostly remained disdainful of Hindus and the caste system. But, unlike Buddhism, which was centered in vulnerable monasteries, Hinduism's decentralized structure proved stable. Thus Hindus and Muslims mingled to some extent along the lines of contact but never formed a single stream. This persistent division greatly affected twentieth-century India, when the British colony of India (ruling most of the subcontinent) was eventually divided into separate nations, Hindu-dominated India and Muslim-dominated Pakistan. The island of Sri Lanka remained a bastion of Theravada Buddhism.

MAKE SURE YOU UNDERSTAND THESE KEY POINTS BEFORE MOVING ON

- **Hindu warriors fended off Muslim invaders for a time, but they were outmatched and eventually defeated by their aggressive opponents.**
- **The Islamic Delhi Sultanate brought unity to north India for the first time in centuries, but its rulers ranged from the enlightened to the tyrannical.**
- **Various Hindu monarchies, including the Cholas, maintained power in southern and eastern India, while Hindu traditions died out in the north.**
- **Muslim and Hindu beliefs were radically opposed, but over time Muslim rulers came to tolerate Hindu subjects, many of whom eventually converted to Islam.**

Cultural Adaptation and Kingdoms in Southeast Asia

What political and religious forms shaped Southeast Asian societies in the Early Intermediate Era?

Owing partly to stimuli from India and China, several great Southeast Asian kingdoms with fluctuating borders developed near the end of the first millennium C.E., establishing their main centers in Cambodia, Burma, the Indonesian islands of Java and Sumatra, and Vietnam (see Map 13.2). Southeast Asian societies mixed outside influences with their own traditions.

Indianized Kingdoms and Societies

From early in the Common Era until the 1400s, many Southeast Asian societies selectively adapted Indian models to shape their political patterns, a collaborative process some historians term Indianization, that produced a convergence of cultures. Some rulers declared themselves god-kings, not just China-style intermediaries between the human and cosmic realms but rather reincarnated Buddhas or Shivas worthy of cult worship. By maintaining order in this world, they ensured cosmic harmony. Kings enjoyed enormous prestige but also faced continuous threats from neighboring states and from rivals, who often succeeded in acquiring the throne.

The economic foundations of Indianized kingdoms differed, with some based largely on agriculture and others, especially alongside the Straits of Melaka, dependent on maritime trade. These contrasting patterns represented skillful adaptations to differing environments. In agriculture-based economies, rice-growing technology became productive enough to sustain large centralized states, but in swampy places lacking good farmland, people maximized their access to the open sea frontier.

Migrations and mixing of peoples and cultures were significant themes in Southeast Asia, as in India, Europe, and Africa. Hence, the Burmans **(BUHR-muhnz)** in the ninth century and the Tai **(tie)** from the seventh to thirteenth centuries moved from Tibet and China into mainland Southeast Asia. The Burmans established the dynamic state of Pagan **(puh-GONE)** in central Burma (1044–1287).

Religion played a central political role. While peasants chiefly remained animists, elites adopted Hinduism and Mahayana Buddhism (and in Burma Theravada Buddhism). In the twelfth century, the city of Pagan was one of the world's architectural wonders, filled with magnificent temples and shrines glorifying Buddhism and Hinduism. Religion in Indianized states often infused government and the arts, with Hindu priests becoming advisers on court rituals. With Hindu Indian epics such as the *Ramayana* and *Mahabharata* deeply imbedded in the cultures, Hindu kings, gods, and demons animated the arts. Many Southeast Asian written languages, such as Khmer, Burman, and Thai, used Indian scripts, fostering

purdah The Indian Muslim custom of secluding women.

MAP 13.2 MAJOR SOUTHEAST ASIAN KINGDOMS, CA. 1200 C.E. By 1200 the Khmer Empire (Angkor), which once covered much of mainland Southeast Asia, had declined. Sukhothai, Pagan, Srivijaya, Champa, and Vietnam were other major states.

poetry, religious speculations, and historical chronicles, all important components of elite culture.

Southeast Asian societies shared many common features. Extensive land and maritime trade networks linked the region from earliest times, with many people specializing in local or foreign commerce. Most larger states had multiethnic populations, including foreign merchants, that encouraged a cosmopolitan attitude. Still, most Southeast Asians were farmers and fishermen, lived in villages, and cooperated for mutual survival. Differing social and cultural traditions separated the royal courts and capital cities from the villages.

Southeast Asian family patterns ranged from flexible arrangements to a few patriarchies and matriarchies. Unlike in patriarchal India and China, some women enjoyed relatively high status. A few, like the Burmese queen Pwa Saw **(pwah saw)**, exercised political influence behind the scenes (see Profile: Pwa Saw, a Burmese Queen). Yet, in some pageantry-filled courts, women in royal harems and their many female attendants were expected to be grateful. One Javanese male poet noted: "the women's quarters seemed to radiate a shimmering light / It was as if the amazing beauty emanated from heaven."[13]

The Angkor Empire and Society

In Cambodia the Khmer people created the greatest Indianized kingdom, Angkor **(ANG-kor)**, which means "Holy City" in Sanskrit. A visionary king, Jayavarman **(JAI-a-VAR-man)** I (r. 802–834), identifying himself with the Hindu god Shiva, established the state in 802. His successors extended the kingdom, which persisted until 1432. Magnificent temples still standing today testify to Angkor's prosperity and organization. By the twelfth century the bustling capital, Angkor Thom **(ANG-kor tom)**, contained perhaps a million people, much larger than medieval European and most Chinese and Arab cities. Although Angkor traded with China and other countries, with many Chinese merchants living in the kingdom, agriculture remained the economic foundation.

At its height Angkor's empire, acquired and maintained by warfare, diplomacy, and pragmatism, controlled much of Cambodia, Laos, Thailand, and southern Vietnam, with regional governors enjoying considerable autonomy. The many kings who patronized art and built roads and temples bragged about their achievements, as in a monument praising a late-ninth-century king: "In all the sciences and in all the sports, in dancing, singing, and all the rest, he was as clever as if he had been the inventor of all of them"[14] Zhou Daguan **(joe ta-kwan)**, China's ambassador in 1296, left vivid descriptions of Angkor, including the justice system: "Disputes of the people, however insignificant, always go to the king. Each day the king holds two audiences for affairs of state. Those of the functionaries or the people who wish to see the king, sit on the ground to wait for him."[15] The well-financed state held much power over people but supported substantial public services, including hospitals, schools, and libraries. Exhibiting some of the premodern world's most advanced civil engineering, conscripted workers constructed extensive canal and reservoir networks for efficient water distribution and storage. Although historians debate how much farming depended on irrigation from these canals, the Khmer had one of the world's most productive agricultures and produced three to four crops of rice a year.

The Angkor government, which resembled a theocracy, presided over a cult for god-king worship, with priestly families

[13]Quoted in Helen Creese, *Women of the Kakawin World: Marriage and Sexuality in the Indic Courts of Java and Bali* (Armonk, NY: M.E. Sharpe, 2004), 44.

[14]Quoted in W. Robert Moore, "Angkor, Jewel of the Jungle," *National Geographic* 117, no. 4 (April 1960): 540.

[15]Quoted in Christopher Pym, *The Ancient Civilization of Angkor* (New York: New American Library, 1968), 118.

PROFILE

Pwa Saw, a Burmese Queen

Women in royal families were politically influential in many Southeast Asian states, mostly behind the scenes, but few enjoyed the influence of thirteenth-century Queen Pwa Saw of Pagan. Much of what we know about her life comes from a chronicle of the country's history compiled by Burmese scholars in the nineteenth century. Modern historians debate whether it represents more myth than fact. Whatever the accuracy, in their traditions the Burman people remember Queen Pwa Saw as witty, wise, beautiful, and instrumental in shaping politics for forty years during one of their most difficult periods.

The girl who would become queen was born to a prosperous peasant family in a remote village around 1237. According to legends, a deadly king cobra approached as she slept but failed to attack, considered a favorable omen, and a jasmine bush she tended astonished her neighbors by blooming in three colors. This unusual event drew the attention of the young King Uzana (r. 1249–1256), a playboy fond of hunting and drinking who was visiting the district with a large entourage of attendants. The unexpected visit of a king and his party riding on elephants spurred the villagers into frenzied preparations for a proper reception to demonstrate their respect. Infatuated with the bright, pretty, graceful, and talkative sixteen-year-old girl, Uzana took her back to Pagan as one of his many wives and appointed her a deputy queen. A short time later, Uzana died in an accident while hunting wild elephants.

With her husband's death, Pwa Saw was thrown into the royal court's schemes and rivalries as various factions maneuvered for power. Placed in a precarious position as a young bride resented by rival queens, she quickly forged an alliance with the able and wily Chief Minister Yazathingyan **(YAH-za-THING-yan)**, who feared the accession of the king's oldest son, the unpopular Prince Thitathu **(thee-TAH-thoo)**, with whom he had long quarreled. Together they convinced officials to support another son, Narathihapade **(NAR-a-THITH-a-PAH-dee)** (r. 1256–1287), as king and make Pwa Saw chief queen. But the young king proved arrogant, quick-tempered, and ruthless, alienating many at court and earning the nickname "King Dog's Dung." While the economy declined, the king boasted that he was "the commander of 36 million soldiers, the swallower of 300 dishes of curry daily," and had 3,000 concubines. His zeal to build an expensive Buddhist pagoda fostered the proverb that "the pagoda is finished and the great country ruined." Pwa Saw remained loyal but lost respect for the king.

After her ally Yazathingyan died leading royal forces to suppress a rebellion in the south, Pwa Saw skillfully survived the king's paranoid suspicions and the constant intrigues of court nobles, attendants, and other queens. Because the king trusted the widely revered queen, she could often overrule his destructive tendencies and talk him into making wiser state decisions. She also convinced the erratic king to appoint capable officials. But she had to maintain her wits. Increasingly paranoid, Narathihapade executed any perceived enemies and burned another queen to death. In the 1270s, anxious to prove himself a great leader, he rejected Pwa Saw's advice to meet Mongol demands for tribute and avoid conflict, instead escalating tensions and bringing on war, disaster, and temporary Mongol occupation of Pagan.

Luca Tettoni/Robert Harding Picture Library Ltd/Alamy

COURT LIFE OF PWA SAW No known paintings of Pwa Saw exist. This fresco, from the Ananda Buddhist temple at Pagan, shows rich court ladies, much like Pwa Saw herself, relaxing in an upstairs room of a magnificent Buddhist temple while, downstairs, stallholders hawk their wares to visitors.

Even as the Pagan state declined, Pwa Saw asserted a benevolent influence. For instance, in 1271 she donated some of her lands and properties to a Buddhist temple, expressing hope that in future existences she would "have long life, be free from illness, have a good appearance, melodic of voice, be loved and respected by all men and gods, [and] be fully equipped with faith, wisdom, nobility." In 1287 one of his sons murdered the mad king. In 1289 Queen Saw and surviving ministers selected a new king, Kyawswar **(kee-YAH-swar)** (1287–1298). With that last effort to help her country, she retired in style to her home village.

THINKING ABOUT THE PROFILE

1. What skills did Pwa Saw use to influence the court?
2. What does this profile tell us about the relations between queens and kings at Pagan?

Notes: Quotations from D. G. E. Hall, *A History of South-East Asia*, 4th ed. (New York: St. Martin's Press, 1981), 169; and Michael Aung-Thwin, *Pagan: The Origins of Modern Burma* (Honolulu: University of Hawaii Press, 1985), 41.

Tim Hall/Robert Harding World Imagery/Getty Images

ANGKOR WAT TEMPLE COMPLEX This photograph shows the inner buildings of the Angkor Wat temple complex in northern Cambodia. The towers represented the Hindu view of the cosmos. Mount Meru, the home of the gods, rises 726 feet in the middle.

holding privileged positions. Numerous temples and Hindu priests controlled massive wealth. Theater, art, dance, and the many magnificent stone temples, some as huge as small mountains, reflected Hindu values. Designed to represent Hindu cosmic thinking on the gods' abode, temples also symbolized a monarch's earthly power, with construction involving amazing engineering and massive conscripted labor. Some seventy thousand workers built the premodern world's largest religious complex, Angkor Wat **(ANG-kor waht)**, in the twelfth century. Reliefs carved into stone at Angkor Wat and other temples illustrate daily life, showing fishing boats, midwives attending a childbirth, merchant stalls, festival jugglers and dancers, peasants bringing goods to market, crowds at a cockfight, and men playing chess.

Khmer commoners tolerated highly inequitable wealth and power distribution and substantial labor demands. Although no India-style caste system existed in the rigid social structure, each class had its appointed role: below the king were priests, and below them trade guilds. Most people were of the farmer-builder-soldier class or slaves and people in temporary servitude. Rich families often owned more than a hundred slaves, and merchants ten or twenty. Slaves dredged irrigation canals, rowed war boats, worked quarries, and helped build the great temples. In this matrilineal society women played a more important role in social life and politics than in most other societies, operating most retail stalls. According to Zhou Daguan: "In this country it is the women who are concerned with commerce."[16] Some royal women participated in intellectual or service activities. Jayarajadevi **(JAI-ya-RAJ-adeh-vee)**, King Jayavarman VII's first wife, took in hundreds of abandoned girls and trained and settled them. After her death the king married Indradevi **(IN-dra-deh-vee)**, a renowned scholar who lectured at a Buddhist monastery. Women also participated in the arts, especially as poets. They dominated the palace staff, some even serving as gladiators and warriors. Chinese visitors were shocked by the liberated behavior of Khmer women, who went out in public as they liked.

[16]Quoted in David Chandler, *A History of Cambodia*, 2nd ed. updated (Boulder, CO: Westview Press, 1996), 74.

Indianized Urban Societies in Java and Sumatra

Several Indianized states developed in the Indonesian archipelago on the large islands of Java and Sumatra. Encounters in Java between Indian influence and local traditions produced a distinctive religious and political blend known as Hindu-Javanese, which perceived the earthly order mirroring and embodying the cosmic order. Hence, people must avoid disharmony and change to preserve the cosmic order, which required the god-king to prevent social deterioration and maintain order in a turbulent human world. The greatest Javanese kingdom, Madjapahit **(MAH-ja-PA-hit)** (1292–1527), reaching its peak in the fourteenth century under the fabled Prime Minister Gajah Mada, loosely controlled much of present-day Indonesia. As in Angkor, Javanese kingdoms like Madjapahit built capitals and palaces to imitate the cosmic order. Temple complexes such as Borobodur **(BOR-uh-buh-door)** in central Java, as well as shadow puppet plays, or **wayang kulit (WHY-ang KOO-leet)**, based on Hindu epics like the *Ramayana* but having much local content as well, reflected Hindu-Buddhist ideas.

Social inequality permeated Hindu-Javanese society, with complex etiquette regulating relations between people of different status. Aristocrats, who administered the realm, expected deference from commoners, most of whom lived in village cultures differing substantially from royal capitals. A tradition of mutual aid fostered communal effort in village work. Peasants identified more with their village than with distant kings in their palaces.

Unlike in agricultural kingdoms on Java and in Cambodia, international trade largely shaped Sumatran coastal states. The Straits of Melaka separating Sumatra from the Malay Peninsula provided a major passageway for a complex maritime trading system linking the eastern Mediterranean, Middle East, East African coast, Persia, and India with East and Southeast Asia. Between 600 and 1290 many small trading states in the Straits region came under the loose control of Srivijaya **(SREE-vih-JAI-ya)**, based in southeastern Sumatra, which helped shape the region's international commerce and maintained trade relations with powerful China. Srivijaya's naval force both fought and engaged in piracy. Becoming a major center of Buddhist study, Srivijaya attracted thousands of Buddhist monks and students from many countries.

International Influences and the Decline of the Indianized States

Most Indianized states declined and collapsed from internal and external challenges between the thirteenth and fifteenth centuries. Several problems challenged Angkor: military expansion overstretched resources; increased temple building spurred higher tax levies and forced labor, antagonizing many commoners; growing breakdown of the irrigation system required more labor for maintenance; and increasingly unpredictable rains due to climate change overstretched the hydraulic system.

States also faced challenges from outsiders. Over several centuries groups from mountainous southwestern China speaking Tai languages migrated into Southeast Asia, some of them setting up states in the Mekong Basin and northern Thailand. The Tai, ancestors of the closely related Siamese **(SYE-uh-meez)**, today known as the Thai, and the Lao **(laow)** peoples, conquered or absorbed local peoples while also adopting some of their cultural traditions. Eventually they came into conflict with Angkor, repeatedly sacking the capital and seizing much of the empire's territory. The Khmer Empire soon disintegrated, with the capital city abandoned. As jungles overtook the monuments to their glorious past, Khmers became pawns perched uneasily between the expanding Vietnamese and Siamese states.

Meanwhile, Mongols threatened Angkor's neighbors. After conquering China, in 1288 they attacked Pagan, which refused to recognize Mongol overlordship. The Mongols soon withdrew, leaving instability in Burma as rival groups competed for power. Elsewhere in Southeast Asia the Mongols found mostly frustration. Although a land-and-sea invasion of Vietnam and Champa inflicted terrible damage, a temporary Vietnamese-Cham military alliance ultimately triumphed. A Vietnamese general, Tran Hung Dao, inspired resistance fighters by having his soldiers tattoo "Kill the Mongols" on their right arms. A Mongol naval expedition to Java also proved a costly failure. Southeast Asians were among the few peoples to successfully resist Mongol conquest and power.

Religion proved another force for change. By the early second millennium, Theravada Buddhism and Islam began filtering peacefully into the region. Theravada Buddhism had long influenced Burma, but a revitalized form from Sri Lanka provided a challenge to Indianized regimes. The Buddhist message of egalitarianism, pacifism, and individual worth proved attractive to peasants weary of war, public labor projects, and tyrannical kings. Theravada Buddhism, a tolerant religion, coexisted with animism, with peasants honoring the Buddha while worshiping local spirits. By the fourteenth century most Burman, Khmer, Siamese, and Lao peasants had adopted Theravada Buddhism, while elites mixed the faith with older Hindu–Mahayana Buddhist traditions.

From the thirteenth through sixteenth centuries, Sunni Islam filtered in from the Middle East and India, spreading widely. Like Buddhism, Islam offered an egalitarian message and a complex theology that appealed to peasants and merchants in the Malay Peninsula, Sumatra, Java, and some other Indonesian islands. Some adopted Sunni Islam in a largely orthodox form, while others mixed it with animism or Hinduism-Buddhism. Sufism also blended well with the existing mysticism. Only a few scattered peoples maintained Indianized societies. Among the Balinese **(BAH-luh-NEEZ)** on the Indonesian island of Bali, Hinduism and other classical patterns remained vigorous, emphasizing arts like dancing, music, shadow plays, and woodcarving. Thus visitors to Bali today glimpse patterns once widespread in the region.

wayang kulit Javanese shadow puppet play based on Hindu epics like the *Ramayana* and local Javanese content.

MAKE SURE YOU UNDERSTAND THESE KEY POINTS BEFORE MOVING ON

- **Most Southeast Asian states were multiethnic and influenced by immigrants and the migration of Mahayana Buddhism and Hinduism from India.**
- **The Indianized kingdom of Angkor controlled a large swath of Southeast Asia and completed advanced civil engineering projects, such as an extensive canal system and the huge temple complex of Angkor Wat.**
- **Hindu priests played a very important role in Angkor, and the social structure was extremely rigid, though an Indian-style caste system did not take hold and women were more important in society and politics than in most places in the world.**
- **Southeast Asians fended off the Mongols, but new peoples such as the Tai invaded and destroyed Angkor, and the gradual introduction of Theravada Buddhism and Sunni Islam challenged the hierarchical order and displaced Indian influence in many states.**

Buddhist, Confucian, and Islamic Southeast Asian Societies

What was the influence of Theravada Buddhism, Confucianism, and Islam on Southeast Asia?

By the fifteenth century Southeast Asia had experienced a major transition. Less despotic states gradually replaced Indianized kingdoms, and networks of trade and religion expanded, linking the region even more closely to Afro-Eurasia. Major Southeast Asian societies diverged from earlier Indian and Chinese-influenced patterns as Theravada Buddhism, Confucianism, and Islam permeated into the countryside. By the 1400s three broad but distinctive social and cultural patterns had developed: Theravada Buddhist, Confucian-Buddhist Vietnamese, and Malayo-Muslim or Indonesian.

Theravada Buddhist Society in Siam

Siamese established several states in northern and central Thailand. Sukhothai **(SOO-ko-TAI)** (1238–1419), founded by former Angkor vassals, controlled much of Thailand's central plains. While some modern historians are skeptical of the stories, according to Siamese tradition, Rama Kamkheng **(RA-ma KHAM-keng)** ("Rama the Brave"), a shrewd diplomat, established Sukhothai's glory and a tributary relationship with China. Sukhothai adopted Khmer script and incorporated Khmer influences in literature, art, and government. Siamese chronicles portray Rama as a wise and popular ruler. A temple inscription tells us that

> *the Lord of the country levies no tolls on his subjects. If he sees someone else's wealth he does not interfere. If he captures some enemy soldiers he neither kills them nor beats them. In the [palace] doorway a bell is suspended; if an inhabitant of the kingdom has any complaint or any matter irritates his stomach and torments his mind, and he desires to expose it to the king ring the bell.*[17]

This probably exaggerated his merits, but Thais credit Rama with making Theravada Buddhism the state religion and adopting humane laws. By 1350, another Siamese state with its capital at Ayutthaya **(ah-YUT-uh-yuh)** had eclipsed Sukhothai, developing a regional empire and influence extending into Cambodia and small Lao states along the Mekong River. Ayutthaya's rivalry with Burmans and Vietnamese for regional dominance occasionally led to war.

Theravada Buddhist kings, popularly viewed as semidivine reincarnated Buddhas, lived in splendor, advised by brahman priests in ceremonial and magical practices. Their many wives and sons, all possible rivals for the throne, and unclear political succession rules, caused chronic instability. Despite bureaucratic government, royal power lessened as distance to the capital increased.

Siamese society resembled that of other Theravada Buddhists: Khmer, Burmans, and Lao. Siamese social order, divided into a small aristocracy, many commoners, and some slaves (many of them prisoners of war), expected deference to higher authority and respect for status differences. Unlike China or India's extended families, small nuclear families were the norm. While Theravada peoples encouraged cooperation within family and village, they also valued individualism. Although not enjoying absolute equality and expected to show their respect for men, free women enjoyed many rights, inheriting equally with men, able to initiate marriage or divorce, and operating most of village or town market stalls. The relative freedom of Siamese women shocked visitors from China, India, Europe, and the Middle East. A Muslim Persian diplomat in Ayutthaya wrote that "it is common for women to engage in buying and selling in the markets and even to undertake physical labor, and they do not cover themselves with modesty. Thus you can see the women paddling to the surrounding villages where they successfully earn their daily bread with no assistance from the men."[18]

Siamese society reflected Theravada Buddhist values, such as gentleness, meditation, and reincarnation, as well as belief

[17]From ibid., 41.

[18]Ibn Muhammad Ibrahim, from Michael Smithies, *Descriptions of Old Siam* (Kuala Lumpur: Oxford University Press, 1995), 91.

in *karma*, the idea that one's actions in this life or past lives determine one's destiny. To escape the endless round of life, death, and rebirth, believers attained merit by performing generous deeds, with the ultimate goal of reaching *nirvana*, release from suffering. Many men became Buddhist monks, playing key roles in local affairs and operating village schools; consequently, Theravada societies had some of the premodern world's highest literacy rates (especially for males). Women could not gain merit as monks, although some became nuns. Most Siamese, tolerant of the less devout, believed that individuals were responsible for their own spiritual state. Peasants supported their local Buddhist temple while placating animist spirits in the fields.

Confucianism, Buddhism, and Vietnamese Society

Vietnam, another important state, was a Chinese colony for over a thousand years, but in 939 it finally pushed the Chinese out and established independence. Vietnam continued to borrow Chinese ideas and even became a vassal state, sending tribute missions. Confucians and Buddhists competed for influence. By the fourteenth century Vietnam offered a striking contrast to Theravada Buddhist societies.

Despite Vietnam's formal subservience, Chinese forces occasionally attempted a reconquest, inspiring Vietnamese to become masters at resisting foreign invasions. In 1407 the new Ming dynasty invaded and conquered Vietnam. In response to harsh Chinese repression, Le Loi **(lay lo-ee)** (1385–1433), a mandarin from a landowning family, organized resistance and struggled tenaciously for two decades. After finally expelling the Chinese in 1428, Le Loi founded a new Vietnamese dynasty, the Le (1428–1788). His social and economic reforms and victory over Chinese domination made him a hero of Vietnam's long struggle for independence. Le Loi told his people: "Over the centuries, we have been sometimes strong, sometimes weak; but never yet have we been lacking in heroes. In that let our history be the proof."[19] Over the centuries, common identity and national feeling greatly aided Vietnamese survival on powerful China's fringe. With peace, literature, poetry, and theater flourished.

Vietnam's imperial system was modeled on China's, with the emperor considered a "son of heaven," an intermediary between the terrestrial and supernatural realms ruling through the Mandate of Heaven. As in China, emperors governed through a bureaucracy staffed by scholar-administrators (*mandarins*) chosen by civil service examinations to recruit men of talent. The official ideology, Confucianism, stressed ethical conduct, social harmony, and hierarchy. Vietnam sought to influence or control highland peoples as well as neighboring Cham, Khmer, and Lao states.

Peasant society differed considerably from the imperial court and political elite, with religious life mixing Mahayana Buddhism, Confucianism, and Daoism, all adopted from China, with spirit and ancestor worship. Peasants had to be respected; an old proverb advised that "the scholar precedes the peasant, but when the rice runs out, it's the peasant who precedes the scholar." Another expression, "the authority of the emperor ends at the village gate," reflected the autonomy of largely self-governing villages. Villages reserved communal land for landless peasants. Despite the patriarchal social system, women dominated town and village markets, buying and selling food and crafts, and saw their influence increase with age. By the 1400s the Vietnamese also became more involved with maritime trade.

By the tenth century, some Vietnamese, supported by imperial forces, left the overcrowded Red River Valley and Tonkin Gulf and migrated southward. In the 1440s they overran northern Cham states in central Vietnam, and by the sixteenth century, Vietnamese migrants had pushed toward the Khmer-dominated Mekong River Basin in southern Vietnam, displacing southern Cham states. With these migrations, the Vietnamese became more involved with Southeast Asia, and the central and southern dialects and cultures gradually differed from the northern Vietnamese.

Islam, Maritime Networks, and the Malay World

Southeast Asians long excelled as seafaring traders, traveling as far as East Africa. Port cities became essential intermediaries in the trade between China, India, and the Middle East. This trade fostered contact with Muslim merchants from Arabia, Persia, and India, who spread Islam along Indian Ocean trading routes. Commercial people adopted a religion sanctioning wealth accumulation and preaching cooperation among believers. Some Hindu-Buddhist rulers of coastal Malay Peninsula and Indonesian states, eager to attract Muslim traders and impressed by Islam's cosmopolitan universality, embraced the faith, converting themselves into sultans. Increasing trade spurred city growth and new maritime trading states, giving merchants more influence in local politics. As the transformed international maritime economy created unprecedented commercial prosperity and cosmopolitan culture in Southeast Asia, agricultural advances, including new crops and rice varieties, fueled population increase, migration, and more bureaucratic states.

Islamic expansion coincided with, and was spurred by, the rise of the great port of Melaka **(muh-LACK-uh)** on Malaya's southwest coast facing the Straits of Melaka. In 1403 the city's Hindu ruler, Parameswara, adopted Islam and became a sultan. Melakans blended Islamic faith and culture with older Hindu-Buddhist and animist beliefs in an eclectic cultural pattern. With regional Islam closely identified with Melaka's Malay people, some historians describe Muslim Southeast Asian societies as Malayo-Muslim. Malay identity, including the practice of Islam and the use of the Malay language, spread to many societies in Malaya, Sumatra, and Borneo.

[19] Quoted in Ralph Smith, *Viet-Nam and the West* (Ithaca, NY: Cornell University Press, 1971), 9.

©Stefano Ember/Shutterstock.com

ROYAL PALACE IN JAVA The kings and then sultans of the region lived on the grounds of this palace in Jogjakarta for generations, along with many retainers and functionaries.

Melaka replaced Srivijaya as the region's economic power, becoming the crossroads of Asian maritime commerce. Its rulers sent tributary missions to China and made their port a waystation for Zheng He's Chinese voyages to the western Indian Ocean (see Chapter 11). In exchange for Melaka's service, the Ming supported the young state in regional disputes. Soon merchants from around Asia arrived, transforming the port into the archipelago's major trading hub and the Indian Ocean network's southeastern terminus. One of the world's major emporiums, Melaka rivaled other great trading ports such as Calicut, Cambay, Guangzhou (Canton), Hormuz, Alexandria, Genoa, and Venice. In 1468 Melaka's sultan Mansur wrote to the king of the Ryukyu Islands, "We have learned that to master the blue oceans people must engage in commerce. All the lands within the seas are united in one body. Life has never been so affluent in preceding generations as it is today."[20] Gradually, Melaka built a highly decentralized empire that dominated much of coastal Malaya and eastern Sumatra.

Melaka flourished until 1511 as a vital link in world trade. An early-sixteenth-century Portuguese visitor wrote that it had "no equal in the world," extolling Melaka's importance to peoples and trade as far away as western Europe: "Melaka is a city . . . made for merchandise, fitter than any other in the world. Commerce between different nations for a thousand leagues on every hand must come to Melaka."[21] Melaka enjoyed a special connection to Cambay, an Indian port nearly 3,000 miles away. Every year trading ships from around the Middle East and South Asia gathered at Cambay and Calicut to make the long voyage to Melaka, carrying with them grain, woolens, arms, copperware, textiles, and opium. Goods from as far north as Korea reached Melaka.

By the late 1400s Melaka's 100,000 to 200,000 people included 15,000 foreign merchants speaking some eighty-four

[20]Quoted in Anthony Reid, *Southeast Asia in the Age of Commerce, 1450–1680*, vol. 2 (New Haven: Yale University Press, 1993), 10.

[21]Tome' Pires, quoted in Paul Wheatley, *The Golden Khersonese* (Kuala Lumpur: University of Malaya Press, 1961), 313.

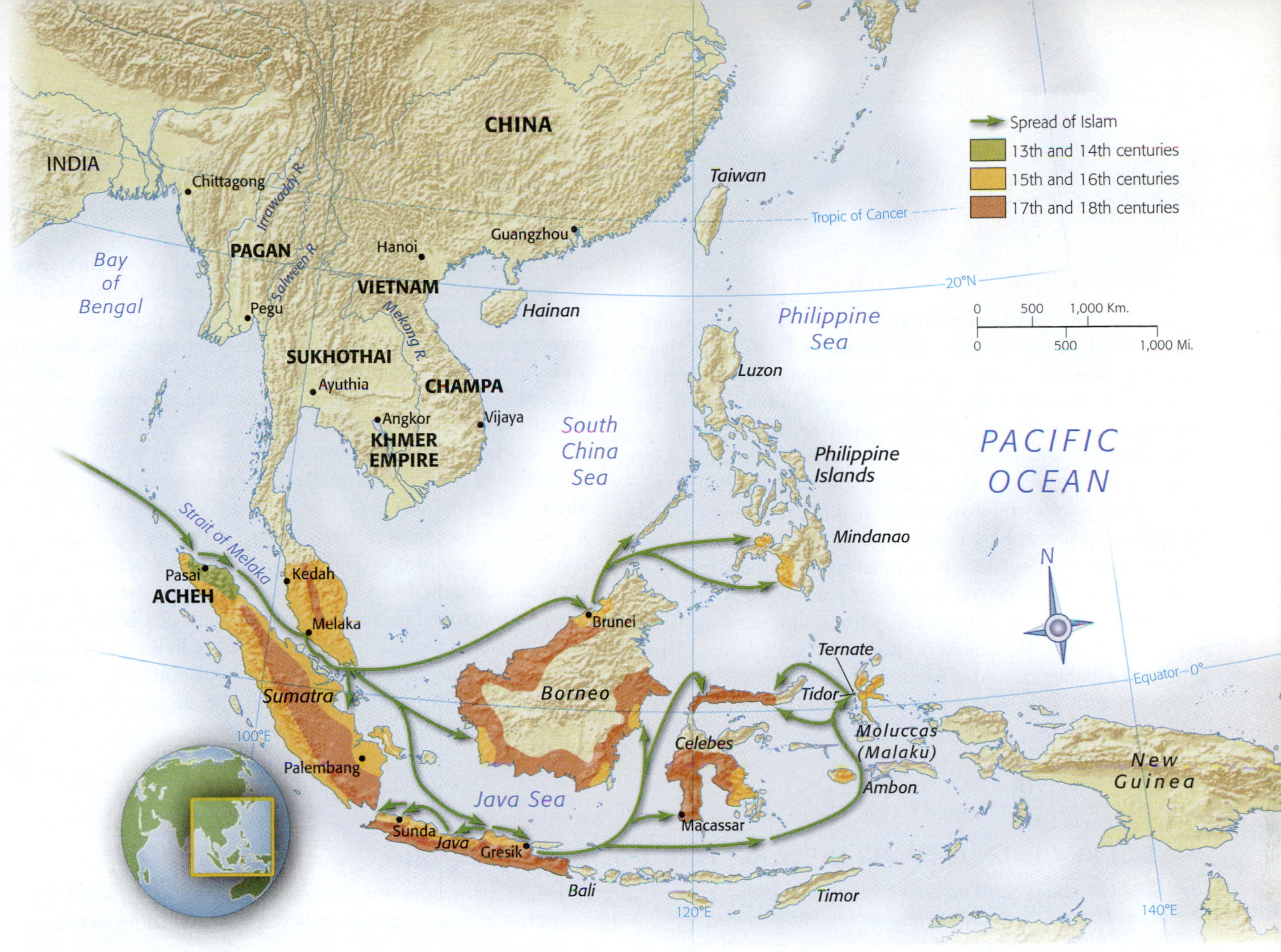

MAP 13.3 THE SPREAD OF ISLAM IN ISLAND SOUTHEAST ASIA Carried by merchants and missionaries, Islam spread from Arabia and India to island Southeast Asia, eventually becoming the major faith on many islands and in the Malay Peninsula.

languages, whose diversity reflected Melaka's global importance: from the west Arabs, Egyptians, Persians, Armenians, Jews, Ethiopians, Swahilis, Burmese, and Indians; from the east and north Vietnamese, Javanese, Filipinos, Japanese, and Chinese. Visitors claimed that more ships crowded Melaka's harbor than any other port, attracted by a stable government and free trade policy. City shops offered Indian textiles, Middle Eastern books, Maluku cloves and nutmeg, Javan batiks and carpets, Chinese silk and porcelain, and Philippine sugar. Gold brought from various places was so plentiful that children played with it.

From Melaka Islam spread around the Malay Peninsula and western Indonesian archipelago (see Map 13.3), spurring political change and economic growth. Some Islamic states, such as Acheh **(AH-chay)** in northern Sumatra, became regional powers. The sultanates of Ternate **(tuhr-NAH-tay)** and Tidor **(TEE-door)** in the Maluku **(muh-LUKE-uh) (Moluccan)** Islands of northeastern Indonesia prospered from producing spices (especially cloves and nutmeg) prized in Europe and the Middle East. Gradually many people, following their ruler's example, adopted Islam, joining Southeast Asia to the wider Islamic world. But many village-based societies, some still practicing animism, remained in more remote areas such as central Borneo and the Philippine Islands, with no political authority higher than local chiefs.

Various patterns of Islamic belief and practice, more diverse than elsewhere, emerged. In many cases Islam did not completely displace older customs. For example, on Java Indianized kings and courts combined Islamic beliefs with older Hindu-Buddhist ceremonies and mystical traditions. Women often retained some political influence, and Muslim courts were filled with hundreds, sometimes thousands of women, as concubines, attendants, staffers, guards, and textile workers. Many peasants maintained mystical animist beliefs and practices under an Islamic veneer, tolerating diverse religious views, while others (especially merchants) adopted more orthodox beliefs, following prescribed Islamic practices and looking toward the Middle East for models. In the hierarchical Javanese social system, sultans remained aloof from common people, while aristocrats remained obsessed with practicing refined behavior rooted in mystical Hinduism.

Javanese of all classes placed a great value on avoiding interpersonal conflict.

Southeast Asia and the Wider World

Southeast Asia had long been and remained a cosmopolitan region where peoples, ideas, and products from many lands met. The intrepid Italian traveler Marco Polo passed through in 1292 on his way home from his long China sojourn. His writings praising the wealth and sophistication of Champa, Java, and Sumatra aroused European interest in seeking direct trade connections with these seemingly fabulous lands. Polo wrote that "Java is of unsurpassing wealth, producing all kinds of spices, frequented by a vast amount of shipping. Indeed, the treasure of this island is so great as to be past telling."[22] Chinese merchants played significant roles in many ports by the 1400s, often marrying local women and settling down. Their trade networks linked Southeast Asia to China, Japan, and the Ryukyu Islands. Agrarian-based societies such as Vietnam and Siam became more involved in international trade by the 1400s.

Indeed, the Southeast Asia Marco Polo and other travelers such as the Moroccan Ibn Battuta encountered was one of the world's more prosperous and urbanized regions. Major cities like Ayutthaya, Melaka, and Hanoi (Vietnam) were as large as major European urban centers like Naples and Paris. By the 1400s, China and India's dense populations still dwarfed Southeast Asia's 15 to 20 million people. Yet, blessed with fertile land and extensive trade, Southeast Asians often enjoyed better health, more varied diets, and adequate material resources than most peoples.

Southeast Asia's connections to the wider world, as well as its famed wealth, eventually attracted less welcome arrivals. By the beginning of the sixteenth century a few Portuguese explorers and adventurers, with deadly weapons, state-of-the-art ships, Christian missionary zeal, and desire for wealth, reached first India and then Southeast Asia seeking "Christians and spices." Siam, Vietnam, Melaka, and Java probably enjoyed higher standards of living than Portugal, but the Portuguese previewed what became a powerful, destabilizing European presence that gradually altered the region after 1500.

MAKE SURE YOU UNDERSTAND THESE KEY POINTS BEFORE MOVING ON

- **Siamese states such as Sukhothai and Ayutthaya were Theravada Buddhist monarchies that valued individualism and peacefulness, offered women a fair amount of freedom, and were permeated by Buddhist values.**
- **Despite gaining freedom from Chinese rule, Vietnam retained a great deal of Chinese cultural influence.**
- **Inhabitants of the Malay and Indonesian archipelagoes embraced Islam, which arrived via increasing maritime trade, and grafted it onto Hinduism and Buddhism to create many different patterns of Islamic belief, while native animist traditions survived to some extent in the villages.**
- **Melaka displaced Srivajaya as the center of Southeast Asian trading power and became an international crossroads.**

[22]Quoted in Kenneth R. Hall, *Maritime Trade and State Development in Early Southeast Asia* (Honolulu: University of Hawaii Press, 1985), 210.

CHAPTER SUMMARY

Although many earlier patterns of life and thought persisted in India and Southeast Asia during the Intermediate Era, these regions also experienced tremendous changes. A constant stream of West Asian and Central Asian peoples into India brought more diversity to social patterns and beliefs. Although India remained politically fragmented, Hinduism enjoyed a kind of renaissance. Most people owed allegiance to their family, caste, and village. Hinduism spawned diverse ideas and cults and gradually brought some cultural unity, while Buddhism gradually lost influence in much of India. Hindu society faced its greatest challenge from Muslim conquerors, who became politically dominant in north India. Muslims would not be assimilated, although there was some mixing of Hindu and Muslim traditions. Islam added a major new strand to India's heritage, influencing the political, religious, and cultural realms but increasing diversity at the expense of unity.

Hindu and Buddhist ideas along with various other Indian traditions diffused to Southeast Asia, where they helped foster the rise of great kingdoms. The Angkor Empire dominated much of mainland Southeast Asia by mixing Indian and local patterns. New religions and new peoples, especially the Tais, eventually reshaped Southeast Asia. Theravada Buddhism became a major influence in several societies, including Siam, while Islam became strong in peninsula and island societies such as Melaka and Java. International trade fostered economic dynamism, and Melaka served as a major international port in which many cultural traditions flourished.

KEY TERMS

Rajputs (p. 290)
polyandry (p. 291)
bhakti (p. 293)
Vajrayana (p. 293)
Tantrism (p. 294)
Lamaism (p. 294)
purdah (p. 299)
wayang kulit (p. 303)

14 Christian Societies in Medieval Europe, Byzantium, and Russia, 600–1500

© Philip Lange/Shutterstock.com

WELLLS CATHEDRAL The importance of Christianity in European life was symbolized by magnificent cathedrals. This cathedral, built in the English town of Wells in the thirteenth century C.E., was designed to reflect the glory of God.

The most Christian man beloved by God, the glorious king of the Franks, while he was building this [Christian] monastery, wished that [its] consecration and the battles which he [waged] should not be consigned completely to oblivion.

—Monastery dedication attributed to Charlemagne, ninth-century Frankish Emperor[1]

IN THIS CHAPTER

In 800 C.E. the city of Rome, filled with magnificent buildings and monuments, was the majestic center of western Christendom. Along one of many roads connecting the fabled metropolis to a wider Europe, the most powerful ruler in Europe, Charlemagne **(SHAHR-leh-mane)**, the king of the Germanic people called the Franks, arrived from his capital of Aachen **(AH-kuhn)**, some 700 miles away in northwest Germany, to celebrate Christmas mass with Pope Leo III, Christendom's head. Wearing a Roman toga and Greek cloak, the towering Charlemagne, 6 feet 4 inches tall, entered spectacular Saint Peter's cathedral. When the Christmas service ended, the pope placed upon Charlemagne's head a golden crown encrusted with sparkling jewels while the crowd chanted, "Crowned by god, great and peace-loving Emperor of the Romans, life and victory."[2] For the first time the pope had crowned an emperor of a new, church-blessed Roman Empire. In the following centuries, complex relations between the Roman Church and diverse European states helped shape European life, as popes tried to influence secular affairs and shape monarchies, while kings worked to control the church and, like Charlemagne, used religion—even building monasteries—for their own purposes.

Fifteenth-century Italian historians first coined the term **medieval** to describe the centuries between the Classical Romans and their own time as a superstitious and ignorant "Dark Age." But the reality of what later scholars often called the "Middle Ages" in Europe was more complex. Linked by faith and culture, western Europeans combined Christianity with practices inherited from both Romans and Germanic groups like the Franks. Although mixing religion and politics went back to ancient times, in both western Europe and Byzantium, the presence of strong Christian church influences in all aspects of society, including politics, was an innovation. Medieval people perceived themselves as part of Christendom rather than Europe. As Christian culture spread into northeastern Europe and Russia, Europeans also borrowed much from other cultures, especially Islam. Finally, Europe's many tensions—including conflicts among Christian leaders, kings, and nobles for power; debates over reconciling faith and reason; and the differing priorities of the rural-based aristocracy and urban merchants—fostered a competitive spirit, helping spur overseas exploration in the fifteenth century.

medieval A term first used in the 1400s by Italian historians to describe the centuries between the Classical Romans and their own time.

[1]From a fourteenth-century legend, quoted in Amy G. Remensnyder, "Topographies of Memory: Center and Periphery in High Medieval France," in *Medieval Concepts of the Past: Ritual, Memory, Historiography*, ed. Gerd Althoff et al. (New York: Cambridge University Press, 2002), 214.
[2]Quoted in *What Life Was Like in the Age of Chivalry: Medieval Europe, AD 800–1500* (Alexandria, VA: Time-Life Books, 1997), 17.

Forming Christian Societies in Western Europe

How did Europeans create new societies between 500 and 1000?

The western Roman Empire's disintegration in the fifth century led to political and social instability, clearing the ground for the rise of new societies between 500 and 1000. The mixing of Roman and Germanic traditions as well as relations with non-European peoples spurred creativity. Diverse western European societies developed many common features, including a dominant Christian church and similar social, political, and economic systems. Economic change and technological development also fostered a new Europe.

Environment and Expanding Christianity

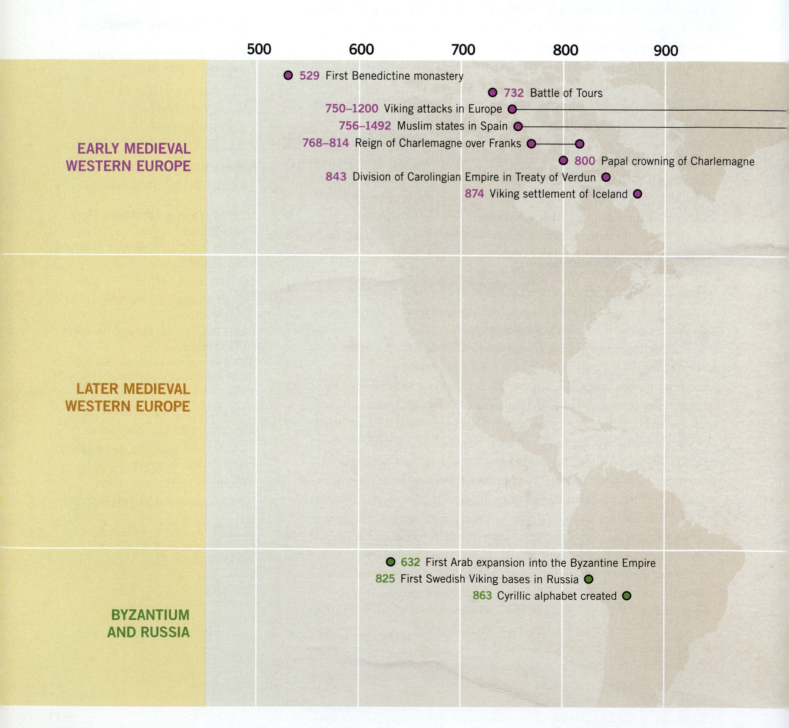

Climate change and disease shaped post-Roman Europe. Between 500 and 900 a cooling climate brought shorter growing seasons before warmer trends returned, while the terrible plague that devastated Europe during Justinian's time occasionally reappeared. Given these challenges, not surprisingly people turned to religion for support. Between 200 and 800 western Europe also suffered repeated incursions by migrating peoples. Various Germanic groups destroyed forever the western Roman Empire and culture, preventing any imperial restoration like China's, where Classical society reemerged during the Tang dynasty. Today few people study Latin, once the Mediterranean world's dominant language.

Yet, Europe's favorable geography enabled similar religious, social, economic, and political patterns to spread. Much of western and central Europe benefited from fertile, well-watered plains rich in minerals and a long coastline offering many fine harbors along the Mediterranean and Baltic Seas and the Atlantic Ocean. Long navigable rivers such as the Danube **(DAN-yoob)** and Rhine, as well as accessible mountain passes through the Alps, made communication much easier than in Asia, Africa, and South America. Hence, land and sea networks linked diverse societies, fostering the movement of ideas, products, peoples, technologies, and diseases.

As Roman power melted away, the church became the major authority, with local bishops and monasteries often the only government in rural areas. Over time the Roman bishops

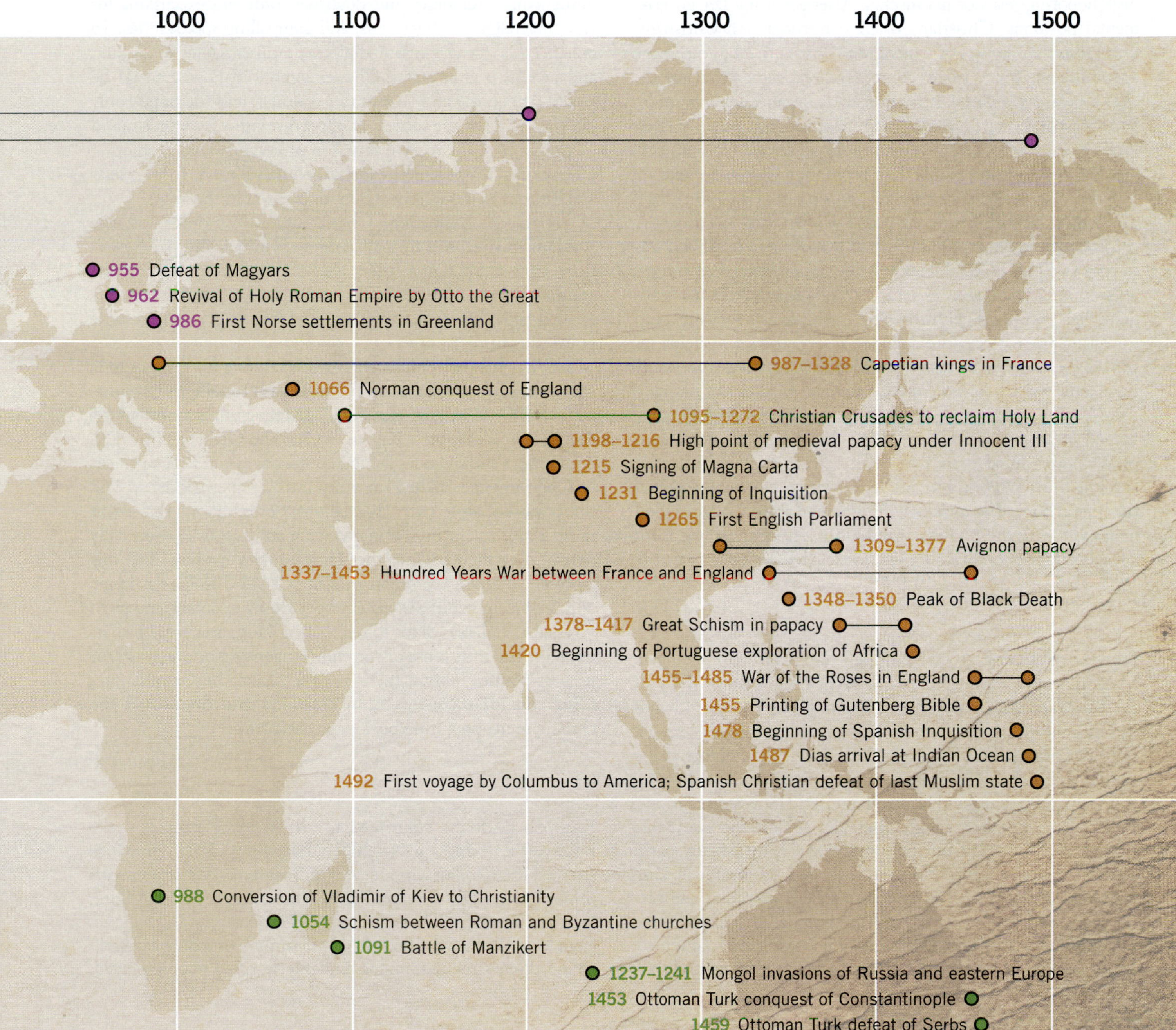

gained authority, eventually claiming the title of pope (Holy Father) and heading the vast church apparatus, and increasingly the papacy symbolized an independent church not controlled by any one government and asserting influence over kings. Popes continued efforts to spread the faith to those Germanic peoples still following their ancient gods. Around 600 Pope Gregory I sanctioned turning pagan worship sites into churches rather than destroying them. The Anglo-Saxon kingdom of Kent in England converted and dispatched missionaries to German lands, most famously Boniface **(BON-uh-face)** (ca. 675–754), a member of the Benedictine order, who won many converts.

Christians blended German values and practices into their faith. Hence, they changed the pagan use of special amulets or charms to ward off evil to wearing Christian medals around the neck honoring Jesus or his mother. After acquiring key governmental positions, Christians often persecuted non-Christians, destroying their houses of worship or denying them government appointments. Since many church bishops came from upper-class German families, Christian leaders began valuing warriors and fighting, never a prominent feature of early Christianity. Even local church leaders often seemed more concerned with protecting their territory and family than promoting Christian values.

The church also sponsored religious orders. From Christianity's earliest centuries, some men and women tried to escape the corruptions and temptations of cities by moving to isolated places to pray and prepare for Heaven. Many monks joined monasteries, communities for men who had taken holy orders. Monasteries grew their own food, with monks clearing forests for crops, and some larger monasteries provided social services such as shelter for travelers, emergency food, and clothing for the poor. At the same time, some women joined convents for lives of service or prayer.

While monks and nuns tried to escape society, they helped create a new culture. With the slogan "to work is to pray," monks filled their lives with activity to avoid idleness, and one form of work, copying manuscripts, eventually created the bound book. The monks' willingness to serve God and their neighbors with their hands and their hearts gave manual labor a respect it never enjoyed in the Classical Mediterranean world.

The Frankish and Holy Roman Empires

Between 500 and 1000 Europe's political map changed. Muslim armies conquered North Africa, the eastern shore of the Mediterranean, and most of Spain during the seventh and eighth centuries (see Chapter 10), and Muslim bands raided Italy and France. Frankish ruler Charles Martel's victory at the Battle of Tours in 732 finally stopped these raids. Following this victory, the Franks created a large state in western Europe. In 753 Pope Stephen sought their aid against the Germanic Lombard kingdom in northern Italy, which threatened papal control of central Italy. He then anointed the Frankish king Pepin **(PEP-in)** the Short as Italy's special protector, indicating the sacred nature of kingship in Christian thought and the pope's belief in his right to designate political rulers. In return, Pepin defeated the Lombards and donated land in central Italy to the pope, the foundation for small Papal States surrounding Rome that remained under papal control for over one thousand years. Western Europe's chief religious leaders became divided between their spiritual and earthly concerns.

The papal-Frankish special relationship grew during a new dynasty known as the Carolingians **(kah-roe-LIN-gee-uhnz)** after their greatest ruler, Charlemagne (r. 768–814), was crowned by the pope in Rome. Charlemagne spread Frankish power from France and northern Italy deep into the lands of another Germanic people, the Saxons, in north and central Germany, temporarily uniting the heart of western Europe (see Map 14.1). Taking great interest in his peoples' religious lives, Charlemagne promoted both education and Christianity, using the church to strengthen his empire by appointing bishops and priests, influencing ceremonies and doctrines, ordering executions for violating religious obligations, and controlling monasteries. To enhance his power, he sent diplomatic missions to Byzantium and various Islamic states. Charlemagne told Pope Leo III he would defend the church from its enemies, and the pope's only job was "to assist the success of our arms with your hands raised in prayer to God."[3] In return for protecting and promoting Christianity, Carolingians expected church leaders, from priests and bishops to monastery abbots, to be loyal to the king.

Although crowning Charlemagne "Emperor of the Romans" revived the Roman Empire symbolically, papal relations with Carolingian rulers also ensured later church-state conflict. Popes argued that lay control over church matters needed papal approval, while later German rulers wanted some political control in Italy.

Charlemagne's empire was divided among his three grandsons in the Treaty of Verdun **(vuhr-DUN)** in 843, and eventually other Germanic peoples challenged the Franks for influence. The Saxon ruler Otto I, known as Otto the Great (r. 936–973), built a new empire, establishing control over rebellious princes in Germany and leading an army into northern Italy; in 962 the pope declared Otto "Roman Emperor." From this point until 1806, rulers in Germany retained this title, eventually proclaiming their lands as the "Holy Roman Empire." But this empire had little in common with the Classical Roman Empire. Much of its territory was never under Roman control, and most Germans, Italians, Slavs, Czechs, and Hungarians within its domains had little sense of common citizenship or much awareness of politics beyond the local level. Like the Carolingians, Otto and his successors both defended and dominated the church, even appointing bishops in their lands.

Vikings and Other Invaders

Europe's heartland continued to attract other peoples seeking wealth. Vikings, or Northmen, facing population pressures that led them to launch raids out of Scandinavia, a region with limited productive farmland, posed the biggest threat. Viking warriors burned and looted towns and monasteries in England, France, Holland, and Ireland. While rumors probably exaggerated Viking atrocities, understandably terrified people prayed:

[3]"Charlemagne's letter to Pope Leo III, 796," from C. Warren Hollister et al., *Medieval Europe: A Short Sourcebook*, 2nd ed. (New York: McGraw-Hill, 1992), 78.

MAP 14.1 EUROPE DURING THE CAROLINGIAN EMPIRE At the height of their power under Charlemagne, the Carolingian rulers of the Franks controlled much of northwestern Europe, including what is today France, the Low Countries, western and southern Germany, and northern Italy.

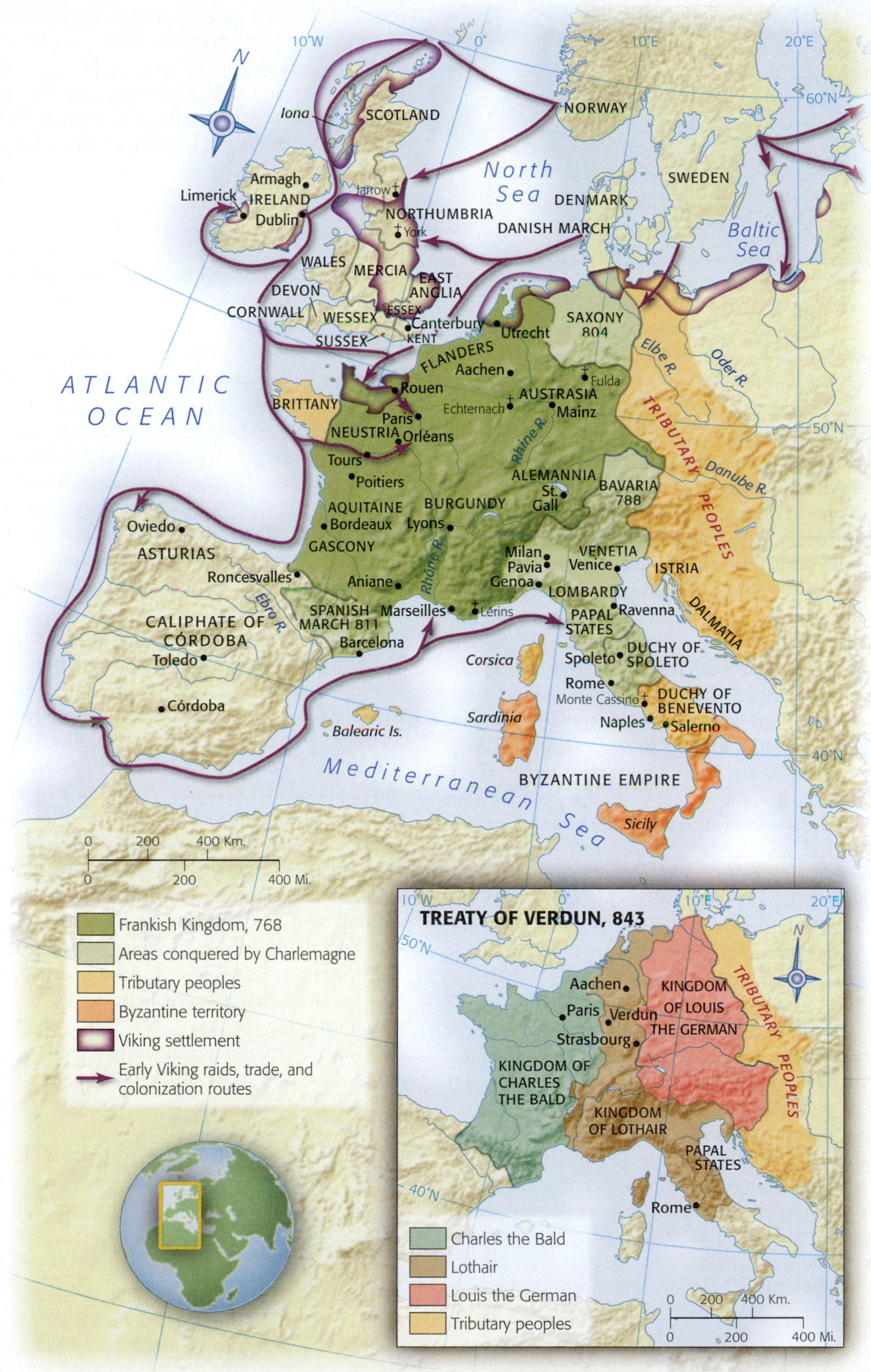

Maurice ROUGEMONT/Gamma-Rapho/Getty Images

VIKING LONGSHIP This longship from the ninth century, excavated from a burial mound in Norway in 1904, boasted intricate decorations and carvings. Probably used for ceremonial purposes, it became the burial chamber of a royal Viking woman.

"From the violence of the men from the north, O Lord, deliver us."[4] Skilled craftsmen, Vikings built ingenious shallow-draft boats capable of both oceanic and riverine voyages.

Between 750 and 1200 various Vikings raided, traded, and settled around Europe, seeking plunder and often captives. An account of a ninth-century attack on a Scottish town reported: "They [Vikings] were four months besieging it [Strathclyde]; and at last reducing the people who were inside by hunger and thirst…, they broke in upon them afterwards…all the riches…were taken; a great host [of people was taken] out of it in captivity."[5] Eventually Scandinavians adopted Christianity and established the kingdoms of Denmark, Norway, and Sweden. Some Swedish Vikings moved east into Russia, establishing several states and sailing downriver to the Black Sea to trade with Byzantium and the Middle East. Danish and Norse Vikings also established permanent settlements in coastal England, Ireland, and the islands north of Scotland, founding towns that later became cities like Dublin and York; recent DNA studies show widespread Viking ancestry in the British Isles. Other Vikings settled down in western France, in Normandy (named after Normans or Northmen). Normans descended from these Vikings conquered England in 1066.

Eventually Vikings gave up raiding for trade and farming. Those settling outside Scandinavia adopted the local Celtic, Latin, Germanic, or Slavic cultures. But their heritage remains in many place names and words in local languages. Vikings left other legacies as well. Among the world's greatest maritime explorers, Norse Vikings began settling Iceland in 874 and founded several settlements on Greenland around 986. Around 1000 a few Greenland Vikings established an outpost along the coast of eastern Canada, apparently making occasional trading visits for the next several centuries. These Viking explorers also fostered a democratic ideal, as shown by the Icelanders' elected assembly that was created in 930 to make and administer laws.

Two other warlike peoples, Bulgars **(BUL-gahrz)** and Magyars **(MAG-yahrz)**, migrated from Russia into central Europe. The Slavic Bulgars, contained by Byzantine armies, eventually converted to Eastern Orthodox Christianity and settled in the eastern Balkan region known as Bulgaria. Magyars, excellent horsemen speaking a Ural-Altaic language related to Turkish, moved into the Hungarian plain, threatening Germany and Italy. However, German forces under Otto the Great crushed a large Magyar army in 955; Magyars then settled permanently in Hungary, adopting Roman Christianity.

Early Medieval Trade, Muslim Spain, and Technology

While most Europeans were peasants, growing food or raising livestock, merchants traded wool hides, salt, fish, wine, and grain over long distances, often by sea or riverboat. Eastern Mediterranean trade continued briskly, tightly controlled by Byzantine rulers, and east-west trade grew dynamic. Venice, an Italian city, was an active trading center throughout the Middle Ages, competing with Genoa to dominate trade with the Middle East and Byzantium. Other Italian cities remained connected to the Byzantine economy. Merchants occasionally visited even remote towns, and aristocrats purchased luxury goods such as silk produced in the East. By 800, multiple networks of exchange reconnected western Europeans to each other and to eastern Europe and the increasingly Islamic Middle East.

Europeans benefited from growing connections with the Muslim world, as Islamic expansion stimulated a movement of people, goods, and information, such as Asian science and Classical Greek thought, that influenced many Afro-Eurasian societies. For example, intellectual life benefited from the exchange of products and ideas between Christian Europe and cosmopolitan Islamic Spain and Sicily. Scholars and merchants from all over the Mediterranean and the Frankish kingdom gravitated to Spanish cities such as Cordoba and Toledo, where Christian, Jewish, and Muslim traditions interacted. Hence, the philosophical, scientific, and technological writings of many Classical Greek and Indian as well as Persian and Arab thinkers spread among educated Europeans. In the 1140s, an Italian translator of Arabic texts wrote that "it befits us to imitate the Arabs especially, for they are our teachers and the pioneers."[6]

Various technological improvements, some originating in Asia, now came into common use in western Europe, laying the basis for European expansion after 1000. Some major technological innovations improved agriculture, spurring higher grain yields that fostered European population growth. The rugged *moldboard plow*, with a blade that dug the earth and an attached moldboard that turned over the furrow, enabled farmers to turn and drain the heavy, wet soil of northern Europe, where difficult farming conditions kept populations sparse. Horseshoes, adopted from Central

[4]Quoted in F. Donald Logan, *The Vikings in History*, 2nd ed. (New York: Routledge, 1991), 15.

[5]Quoted in Angelo Forte et al., *Viking Empires* (New York: Cambridge University Press, 2005), 88.

[6]Hugo of Santalla, quoted in Jerry Brotton, *The Renaissance Bazaar: From the Silk Road to Michelangelo* (Oxford: Oxford University Press, 2002), 195.

Asians in the ninth century, allowed farmers to expand their use of horses to plow fields, especially when combined with horse collars. Invented in China, horse collars distributed the weight across the animal's shoulders so the horse could pull more weight and work longer hours. The most crucial improvement, the three-field system, replaced the Roman two-field system. Europeans divided their fields into three parts and let only one-third lie fallow each year, increasing their yield by planting winter and summer wheat in the other two fields. Increased grain consumption produced a better-balanced diet.

Other innovations fostered industry. First invented in Roman times, watermills built along rivers and streams generated power, freeing up human and animal labor for other tasks. By 1056 over 5,600 watermills in England provided power for such activities as sawing logs and grinding wheat into flour, allowing mechanization of some industries, and by the 1100s Europeans used windmills, invented in Persia, to generate power for such industries as grinding grain. The wheelbarrow also reached Europe from China.

TILLING THE FIELDS Most medieval Europeans were peasants growing food. This French painting from the 1400s shows peasants working land on a manor.

MAKE SURE YOU UNDERSTAND THESE KEY POINTS BEFORE MOVING ON

- **With the Roman Empire's decline, the Christian church became a power in its own right with influence over kings; monasteries created a new culture that respected manual labor.**
- **Under Germanic influence, Christians more aggressively spread their faith, assimilating pagan practices and transforming them into Christian ones.**
- **During this time the Papal States were created, Charlemagne's Carolingian empire temporarily united much of Europe, and Otto the Great began the tradition of calling Germany the "Holy Roman Empire."**
- **The Vikings of Scandinavia, who raided European lands for over four centuries, were also good traders and eventually settled in Iceland, Greenland, and various European territories.**
- **As merchants engaged in growing networks of exchange, trade with the expanding Muslim world and contact with Muslim Spain introduced Europeans to Classical Greek, Indian, Arab, and Persian ideas.**

Medieval Societies, Thought, and Politics

What institutions and ideas shaped medieval European life?

Three institutions dominated medieval Europe between 800 and 1300: the papacy in religion and church state relations, feudalism in politics and social structure, and manorialism in the economic realm. Both feudalism and manorialism developed from late Roman Empire roots, varying greatly across western Europe. The pluralism of religious, social, political, and economic institutions forged in early medieval Europe, combined with an unusually warm climate, spurred many changes between 1000 and 1300. In this period, called the "High Middle Ages," growing church and papal power fostered conflict with rulers and intellectuals. Tensions between religious and lay rulers, between Roman and Byzantine Christian leaders, and between Christians and Muslims, along with growing divergence between cities, with their merchant classes, and traditional feudal aristocrats ruling in the countryside, helped reshape European society.

The Emergence of Feudalism

Although some historians consider the concept misleading and overgeneralized, most characterize the complex and decentralized social, political, and economic system in these centuries as **feudalism**, a

feudalism A political arrangement characterized by a weak central monarchy ruling over smaller states or influential families that were largely autonomous but owed service obligations to the monarch.

political arrangement in which a weak central monarchy ruled over smaller, largely autonomous states and aristocratic families that owed military and labor service obligations as vassals to the monarch. In turn, these nobles ruled as lords over warriors and farmers on their estates, who owed them service as **vassals**. Church leaders supported this arrangement, arguing that "it is the will of the Creator that the higher shall always rule over the lower. Each individual and each class should stay in its place [and] perform its tasks."[7] This feudalistic political and social formation was strongest in France, England, and parts of Italy. Although many monarchs had little power beyond their capital and hinterland, some small states were part of a larger unit, such as the Holy Roman Empire, with their princes owing allegiance to the king but exercising power in their domains.

Despite the Christian church's role in creating a common culture and strong rulers such as Charlemagne and Otto the Great, certain forces fostered the decentralization that characterized feudalism. The old Roman roads fell into disrepair, disrupting transportation and trade, and Europe remained sparsely populated with few cities. By 1000 France, the most densely populated region, had only 8 or 9 million people, England a million and a half, and Europe as a whole around 40 million, less than half of Song China's 100 million. With both money and talent scarce and land the source of wealth, Charlemagne rewarded his best soldiers and officials by giving them control over land. Vassals who held such land grants, called **benefices**, took an oath of personal loyalty to the king, promising him military service in exchange for a free hand governing their territory, collecting taxes from the inhabitants, and administering justice.

Feudalism also refers to legal relations between lords and vassals, including the **fief**, the thing granted in a feudal contract, usually land but sometimes something such as the right to collect tolls on a bridge. With a large enough fief of land, the vassal could subdivide it and have his own vassals. Feudalism allowed a king to rule a large country without personally administering it. Ruling through subordinates was most common in England, especially after William, Duke of Normandy, invaded in 1066, forming a feudal monarchy.

Feudal society included **knights**, armored military retainers swearing allegiance to their lord, who fought mostly on horseback while bearing the heavy expense of warhorses and elaborate armor. Knights had a rigid code of behavior, including a sense of duty and honor known as **chivalry**. A thirteenth-century French writer explained the chivalric ideal: "A knight must be hardy, courteous, generous, loyal and of fair speech; ferocious to his foe, frank and debonair to his friend. [He] has proved himself in arms and thereby won the praise of men."[8] Despite romantic images of knights wielding lances in jousts or defending maidens from fire-breathing dragons, the reality was usually more mundane. Knights wore 60 pounds of chain-mail armor and often collapsed from heat exhaustion, and the steel suits of armor seen in museums were not generally used until the 1400s. Regular fights between rival states and lords kept knights busy, and successful knights might acquire wealth and marry into an aristocratic family. The stirrup, brought by Central Asians, enabled knights to stand when delivering blows, making the blows more powerful than if delivered while seated.

vassals In medieval Europe, a subordinate person owing service to a lord.

benefices In medieval Europe, grants of land from lord to vassal.

fief In medieval Europe, the thing granted in a feudal contract, usually land.

knights In medieval Europe, armored military retainers on horseback who swore allegiance to their lord.

chivalry The rigid code of behavior, including a sense of duty and honor, of medieval European knights.

manorialism The medieval European system of autonomous, nearly self-sufficient agricultural estates.

serfs In medieval Europe, peasants legally bound to their lord and tied to the land through generations.

Manors, Cities, and Trade

The rural economy was based on **manorialism**, a system of autonomous, nearly self-sufficient agricultural estates. As Roman cities had become expensive, wealthy Romans had retreated to their large country estates and hired low-wage agricultural workers. Eventually these Roman estates and villages became manors, each supplying its own needs, from mills for grinding grain to blacksmiths for shoeing horses. Often organized around a castle, manors were owned by nobles with rights to the produce grown by hereditary **serfs**, peasants legally bound to their lord and tied to the land through the generations. Tilling the lord's fields as well as their own, serfs had use of the manor's resources, such as farming tools or crafts, and protection in the manor house or castle if the settlement was attacked. Although they could not change their status or leave without permission, they could not be dispossessed unless they failed to satisfy their obligations. Warned to work hard to receive their eventual reward in Heaven, they paid for security with a lifetime of drudgery. Occasional peasant revolts indicated some dissatisfaction.

Although serfdom became far more pervasive, slavery did not disappear altogether in Europe. Mostly farmers or domestic servants, slaves constituted perhaps 10 percent of the English population until the eleventh century, were common in Italy and Spain, and also worked papal estates and the farms of French monasteries. Leading Christian thinkers like Saint Thomas Aquinas argued that slavery was morally justified and an economic necessity. An active Byzantium-based Mediterranean slave trade acquired slaves, mostly Slavs, Greeks, and Turks, from the Black Sea region, shipping them to southern Europe and North Africa. Carolingians and Venetians also sold European slaves to Arabs, while Vikings sold English and French slaves to Byzantium and Islamic Spain. By the 1400s Arabs and Portuguese were selling enslaved West Africans in

[7]Quoted in John M. Hobson, *The Eastern Origins of Western Civilization* (New York: Cambridge University Press, 2004), 113.
[8]Quoted in Jo Ann H. Moran Cruz and Richard Gerberding, *Medieval Worlds: An Introduction to European History, 300–1492* (Boston: Houghton Mifflin, 2004), 388.

southern Europe, and by the end of the fifteenth century black Africans constituted some 40 percent of the slaves in the Spanish city of Valencia; the remainder were mostly Muslims, Russians, Greek Orthodox Christians, Canary Islanders, and Jews.

Populations, towns, and cities grew. Compared to Byzantium, China, and the Islamic world, early medieval western Europe was economically underdeveloped and had small cities: by 1000 Rome had only 35,000 people, Paris 20,000, and London 10,000. By contrast, Constantinople had 300,000, Kaifeng in China had 400,000, Cordoba in Muslim Spain nearly 500,000, and the world's largest city, Baghdad, a million people. However, between 1000 and 1300 new methods of growing crops spurred a doubling of Europe's population to about 75 million, and western European cities became centers of trade and industry. Milan and Paris grew to almost 100,000, and London had 30,000 people and a problem with air pollution due to burning coal.

As today, some considered cities degenerate places. An eleventh-century English monk detested London:

A MEDIEVAL TOWN This painting shows a variety of town enterprises, including a tailor's shop, a barbershop, and an apothecary.

> *I do not like that city. All sorts of men crowd together there from every country. Each race brings its own vices. No one lives in it without falling into some sort of crime. Actors, jesters, smooth-skinned lads, flatterers, effeminates, pederasts, singing and dancing girls, quacks, belly-dancers, sorceresses, extortioners, magicians, mimes, beggars, buffoons: all this tribe fill all the houses. Therefore, if you do not want to dwell with evildoers, do not live in London.*[9]

Nevertheless, urban life and its economic opportunities attracted people. A German expression, "city air makes one free," confirmed that a serf who left the manor and spent "a year and a day" in a city without being caught was considered legally free. Thus cities increasingly operated outside the feudal social and political structure. City craftsmen and merchants organized themselves into fraternal organizations called **guilds** to protect members' economic interests and to win exemptions from feudal obligations. Eventually city charters, secured from the local lord or king who needed the wealth that city commerce and payments brought, allowed cities to have their own courts and other self-government privileges.

Although merchants benefited from cities and commercial expansion, they had to overcome social prejudices. In feudal society, people belonged to one of three categories, in order of importance: "those who prayed" (churchmen, priests, and monks), "those who fought" (aristocratic warriors, knights), and "those who worked" (peasants). Merchants and bankers had no place in this hierarchy unless they married an impoverished aristocrat's daughter and hence acquired land. But most merchants also shared society's values and Christian faith. Hence, the English merchant Godric of Pinchale (ca. 1069–1170) left home as a teenager to peddle goods in nearby villages and then traded goods by sea between England, Scotland, Denmark, and Holland. Eventually he owned a small fleet of vessels, becoming quite wealthy and making pilgrimages to Jerusalem. He never married and later in life gave away all his wealth to the poor, became a hermit, wrote religious poetry, and gained fame for his piety.

People resented merchants for selling goods for more than they paid for them and consorting with foreigners. With greed considered a serious sin, loaning money at interest was regarded as **usury**, a sin because the lender made a profit without doing any labor. But moneylending was necessary to commerce, and even popes borrowed money at interest. While Italians became renowned bankers, moneylending was often left to Jews, allowing Christians to benefit from borrowing money without committing usury. Gradually using and lending money became more acceptable.

Long-distance trade reached its peak between 1100 and 1350 as western Europeans shipped woolen textiles, flax, hemp, wines, olive oil, fruit, and timber to the East in return for luxury goods from Byzantium and Asia such as spices, silk, perfumes, and

guilds In medieval Europe, collective fraternal organizations of craftsmen and merchants designed to protect the economic interests of their members.

usury The practice of loaning money at interest; considered a sin in medieval Europe, although necessary to commerce.

[9] Richard of Devizes, quoted in Jacques Le Goff, ed., *The Medieval World* (London: Postgate Books, 1997), 139.

precious gems. As trade and commerce around Europe grew, prejudice against merchants declined. Cities such as Constantinople, Venice, Genoa, Bruges **(broozh)** and Amsterdam in the Low Countries, and Strassburg in the Rhineland became major commercial hubs. Italian merchants acquired goods from the Middle East and Byzantium, shipping them to Belgium and Holland for woolen textiles. One French ruler, the Count of Champagne **(shahm-PAHN-yuh)**, established the "Champagne fairs", when goods were displayed at town fairs lasting seven weeks. The wealth created fostered a commercial revolution, making merchants and bankers more influential.

Eventually commerce became more central to Europe's economy than agriculture, although the broad repercussions—the rise of capitalism; incorporation of merchants as a vital social class; stronger monarchies; and weakening of both feudalism and the Christian church—became clear only centuries later. While both popes and political leaders in Europe remained powerful, the merchant class gradually gained political and economic influence to challenge feudal nobles and eventually monarchies.

Social Life and Groups

Medieval society was patriarchal, though family life and gender relations varied with social status and local customs. Generally, men supported their families while women ran households and raised children. Parents preferred sons, who passed on the family line, property, and name, to daughters and arranged most marriages. Society allowed men to have sex outside marriage but valued women for their virginity and faithfulness. The church considered marriage a necessary evil, with sex only for procreation, not pleasure. A leading theologian, Saint Thomas Aquinas, contended that "woman was created to help man, but only in the act of procreation, because in all other tasks he can find far better support elsewhere." One priest even warned married people to avoid sex on the Sabbath because "monsters, cripples, and all sickly children [are] conceived on Saturday nights."[10] However, rulers often flouted custom. Charlemagne enforced rigid Christian morality on his people while also marrying four times, having five mistresses, and siring eighteen children.

Today's Western middle-class model of a husband, wife, and their unmarried children living in one independent household, separate from the larger family, was the exception. Many women married late, and many men and women remained unmarried. Children often left their birth families at an early age to become apprentices in a trade, servants, or novices in religious orders. Laws favoring men spurred many women to join convents, all-female Christian communities that offered physical and social protection and leadership possibilities.

courtly love A standard of polite relationships between knights and ladies that arose in the 1100s in medieval Europe. Courtly love was celebrated in song by wandering troubadours.

Medieval society had contradictory views of women. Biblical gender stereotypes fostered the belief that women had to be subordinate to men, were depraved, led men into sin, and were intellectually inferior. Yet, Mary, the Virgin Mother of Jesus, became one of the most popular objects of devotion, with many cathedrals named after Notre Dame **(NO-truh DAHM)** ("Our Lady"). Furthermore, women could inherit property and worked in many occupations, including farming, ale making, small-scale trade, glassmaking, and the textile industry.

Probably originating in Muslim Spain, where women poets flourished, by the 1100s **courtly love**, a new concept of passionate but pure relationships between knights and ladies and celebrated in song by wandering troubadours, brought romance to male-female relations and, combined with the Virgin Mary cult, elevated aristocratic women's status. But whether courtly or not, romantic love existed mostly outside of marriage. In medieval tales, knights often sought the favors of fair maidens (usually the wife of another, perhaps their lord) who were unattainable. With adultery considered a high crime, the knight's love was usually unrequited.

Early Christian tolerance of homosexuality survived through the Early Middle Ages. Although various church leaders and rulers condemned what they called "sodomites," after the immoral biblical city of Sodom, public attitudes were often more accepting, with considerable homosexual fiction and poetry published in the eleventh and twelfth centuries, and several prominent bishops and English kings thought to be homosexuals. By the thirteenth century, public attitudes shifted. Growing states promoted uniformity in social relations and religious views, fostering suspicion of those outside the mainstream. The church launched a violent campaign against heresy and unconventional behavior, often targeting suspected homosexuals. Whereas in 1250 homosexual behavior was legal in most of Europe, by 1300 it was a capital offense in many societies.

Tightly ordered medieval society was rife with tensions, with violent crime common and daily life precarious for rich and poor alike. Most groups disliked the Romany (or Gypsies), a wandering group originally from India who arrived in Europe from the Middle East between 1,000 and 1,500 years ago. Many tensions also arose from major distinctions between Christians and "outsiders"—nonbelievers, Muslims, Jews, heretics. Christians described Muslims as "pagans," who reciprocated by calling Christians "infidels" (unbelievers). The drive to destroy all beliefs outside of the Christian mainstream eventually led to a long series of Crusades against Islam and persecution of Jews.

Many European towns had Jewish communities. Although Jews worked in many occupations, they were best known as merchants and bankers because Christians were forbidden to loan money at interest. Resentment of their commercial success and moneylending made them scapegoats for hard-to-explain misfortunes, such as epidemics. While Christians mostly tolerated Jews before 1150, anti-Semitism **(AN-tee-SEM-uh-tiz-uhm)** increased dramatically as more Christians took up banking or more militantly asserted their faith. In 1182 France ordered Jews to leave, an expulsion imitated in other countries during the next three

[10]The quotes are from Frederic Delouche et al., *Illustrated History of Europe: A Unique Portrait of Europe's Common History* (New York: Barnes and Noble, 2001), 170; and Georges Duby, "Marriage in Early Medieval Society," in *Love and Marriage: The Middle Ages*, translated by Jane Dunnett (Chicago: University of Chicago Press, 1994), 11.

centuries. Governments also restricted Jewish businesses and residences to certain districts. Our modern term ghetto originally described medieval city neighborhoods where Jews were compelled to live. Many expelled Jews migrated to Poland and Byzantium, which developed large Jewish populations.

Struggling to differentiate correct belief from heresy, Christians directed disdain at alleged heretics. While some devout Christians criticized church corruption, ill-educated priests, and arrogant bishops, church leaders viewed reformers as heretics. Hence, they organized military attacks on the Albigensians **(AL-buh-JEN-shunz)**, a group in southern France who criticized the church's material wealth, urged clerical poverty, and wanted the Bible translated from Latin into the vernacular languages such as French and German so that ordinary people could read it for themselves. The church destroyed the Albigensians by killing their followers and confiscating their property.

The Church as a Social and Political Force

The church enjoyed social and political power but also experienced turmoil during the High Middle Ages. Massive cathedrals with lofty spires inspired deep emotions. Medieval Christians registered births and marriages and paid taxes in the village church, and they measured the stages of their lives by sacraments such as baptism and matrimony, which priests had to administer. Able to deny someone the sacraments, considered necessary for salvation, medieval priests had enormous power. They could also **excommunicate**, or expel a person from the church and its sacraments, a psychologically devastating act.

Not all priests and bishops lived up to their responsibilities or growing expectations for celibacy. Many priests had little education and could barely recite the Latin liturgy, and some were corrupt and took bribes. Many priests and monks were also married. Reformist church leaders, believing priests should not be distracted by families and not wanting priests to pass on their parishes to their children, attempted to crack down. Nonetheless, even after the final ban many priests were married, kept mistresses, or were either homosexual or assumed to be so. Many people had ambivalent attitudes toward the clergy, fearing priests because of their power and ridiculing them because of their shortcomings.

In the eleventh century, reformers attempted to change the church and end abuses by priests, monks, and high officials. New religious orders tried to restore monastic life to its original purity, insisting that all monks remain celibate. Several German rulers also appointed reform-minded popes who tried to end **simony (SIGH-muh-nee)**, a common practice whereby wealthy families paid to have their sons appointed bishops, who collected significant revenues in their territories. Attempting to keep European rulers from interfering in papal elections, the church established the College of Cardinals in 1059 to elect the pope. Churchmen made Roman law the basis of church law because it referred all matters to the person at the top, in this case the pope.

Growing papal political power became clear when a major church-state conflict erupted over the appointment of bishops. For centuries rulers had appointed leading nobles to key church offices. But in 1075 Pope Gregory VII (ca. 1020–1085) excommunicated the German emperor for appointing the archbishop of Milan **(mi-LAHN)**. Gregory had a low opinion of kings, who "derive their origin from men ignorant of God who raised themselves above their fellows by pride, plunder, treachery, murder, at the instigation of the Devil."[11] In 1122 both men compromised, agreeing that both emperor and pope would invest new bishops. This dispute strengthened papal authority and weakened German emperors. As German rulers intervened in Italian politics to regain control over the church, they lost influence over their own princes at home, leading eventually to decentralized government and political warfare in German-speaking lands. Another pope, Innocent III (r. 1198–1216), dramatically extended papal authority over secular rulers, using his control over the sacraments to force King John of England to accept the pope's candidate for archbishop of Canterbury and requiring the French king to take back a wife he had divorced. He also required Jews to wear distinctive clothing and aggressively punished "heretical depravity."

The papal drive to investigate and eliminate heresy led to the **Holy Inquisition**, a church court created in 1231. Churchmen tried thousands of people with views outside the mainstream, with popes sanctioning torture and starvation to induce confessions. Those found guilty faced punishments, including penances, banishment, prison, mutilation, and death. Over two centuries several thousand people were executed. The most notorious inquisition began, under state rather than church control, in Spain in 1478 and perpetrated brutal persecution of Jews and Muslims, burning at least two thousand people at the stake. The inquisitions continued into the 1600s and included bans on books viewed as dangerous to the faith.

Christians adopted ancient Jewish ideas about nature and history, including the concept of progress. Early Christian thinkers believed that human society improved with time, an idea then foreign to most of the world. Originating with the seven-day creation story in Genesis, this linear rather than cyclical concept viewed history as moving progressively from one point to another. To many Christian thinkers, God planned the world, including the natural environment, for human benefit, an idea that necessitated exploiting nature. With no item having any purpose but to serve humans, God wanted people to improve land by clearing forests and wetlands, which some monasteries did with enthusiasm. This crass attitude toward nature justiied the great technological and economic development to later emerge in the West and also caused environmental problems.

excommunicate To expel a person from the Roman Catholic Church and its sacraments.

simony In medieval Europe, a practice whereby wealthy families paid to have their sons appointed bishops.

Holy Inquisition A church court created in 1231 in medieval Europe to investigate and eliminate heresy; inquisitions continued into the 1600s.

[11]Quoted in Cruz and Gerberding, *Medieval Worlds*, 277.

Some Christian and Jewish thinkers dissented from these views and affirmed nature as God's creation that required care and stewardship. Saint Francis of Assisi (1182–1226), who renounced wealth to found a new religious order, the Franciscans **(fran-SIS-kuhnz)**, dedicated to lives of poverty, humility, and serving the urban poor, saw all creatures as part of God's plan. The twelfth-century Jewish philosopher Moses Maimonides wrote that "it should not be believed that all beings exist for the sake of the existence of man."[12] Furthermore, kings and lords often protected the forests where they enjoyed hunting.

New European States

Threatened by increasing papal power, and with growing economies reducing the need for feudal vassals, rulers sought more control over their lands (see Map 14.2). English kings were most successful at centralizing power. After conquering England, William of Normandy (1027–1087) divided the land among his chief vassals, but by the 1100s William's successors had reduced the local nobility's authority and were appointing justices and tax collectors. King Henry II (r. 1154–1189), who invaded Ireland in 1171 and established control of the island's eastern region, expanded the royal courts' power over feudal and church courts.

However, some English rulers unintentionally laid the foundations for later representative government. John (Prince John of the Robin Hood legend) weakened royal power in 1215 by signing the **Magna Carta** **(MAG-nuh KAHR-tuh)** or "Great Charter," an agreement that limited the feudal and taxation rights of the king and his officials while protecting the rights of the church, lords, and merchants. The Magna Carta was later used to support the notion that rulers had to have their subjects' consent, a foundation of modern English constitutional monarchy. Another step toward representation was taken because of Henry III's (r. 1216–1272) incessant demands for taxes to fight foreign wars. In 1265, rebellious barons called together a parliament (literally, a "speaking place") including middle-class townspeople and knights to air their grievances and demand that the king consider their views. This parliament became the model for later meetings called by kings to secure approval of their policies.

Like the English kings, the Capetians **(kuh-PEE-shuhnz)**, who succeeded the Carolingians as kings in France (987–1328), also tried to increase their power and expand their territory. King Philip II (r. 1180–1223) gained control over Normandy and replaced noblemen with paid officials more loyal to the crown. Louis IX, or Saint Louis (r. 1226–1270), a pious man, curbed the nobility's power while persecuting heretics and Jews. Philip the Fair (r. 1285–1314) may have had the most impact on France and Europe. To raise money for his wars, he arrested all the Jews, seizing their property before expelling them in 1306, and had the leaders of a militant religious order, the Knights Templar **(TEM-plahr)**, burned at the stake as heretics so he could default on a loan. When Pope Boniface VIII (r. 1294–1303) challenged Philip's growing power, Philip accused him of sexual perversion and murder and sent a force to Italy to arrest him. Townspeople rescued the pope by driving French troops away. For the next seventy years (1305–1377), the College of Cardinals, bowing to French pressure, elected popes, mostly French, who chose to live in Avignon **(ah-vee-NYON)**, a papal territory in southern France. Philip's ruthless action showed that papal control over European rulers was ending. France emerged as the strongest western European kingdom.

Magna Carta ("Great Charter") An agreement signed by King John of England in 1215 that limited the feudal rights of the English king and his officials while protecting the rights of the church, lords, and merchants.

The German Hohenstaufen **(HO-uhn-SHTOU-fuhn)** dynasty (1152 and 1254), in trying to control Italy while the feudal German nobility remained powerful, had less success centralizing their lands. Frederick I (r. 1154–1190) reasserted his authority as Holy Roman Emperor over the wealthy northern Italy cities, but the pope organized an Italian coalition and defeated Frederick's forces. Frederick I's successors gradually lost power to German princes. Italy, divided into small papal-ruled and nonpapal states. Only seven hundred years later did Germany finally achieve the territorial unity enjoyed by France and England.

The Crusades and Intellectual Life

The religious and political tensions helped foster the Crusades, a series of military expeditions or holy wars between 1095 and 1272 to reclaim the "Holy Land," Palestine, from Muslim control (see Chapter 10). European Christians had long made pilgrimages to Jerusalem and considered the city part of their world. Crusading began after the Byzantine emperor sought help to dislodge the Muslim Seljuk Turks, who now dominated much of western Asia. Medieval Christians had a militant zeal to spread their faith and destroy Islam, through the use of force if necessary, and early Christian thinkers like Augustine of Hippo sanctioned war to defend the faith. Except for Islam, no other world religion maintained a strong missionary impulse to convert the world to what its believers considered the only true faith. Religious beliefs and idealism, often mixed with lust for wealth and land, motivated crusaders. Political rivalries between European leaders also played a role.

In 1095 Pope Urban II urged Christian rulers to protect the Christian holy sites, prompting the first of nine crusades by land and sea. Fabricating or exaggerating stories of Muslim atrocities against Christians, he proclaimed that the Turks "have completely destroyed some of God's churches. They ruin the altars with filth and defilement. They are pleased to

[12]Quoted in Clive Ponting, *A Green History of the World: The Environment and the Collapse of Great Civilizations* (New York: Penguin, 1991), 144.

kill others. And what shall I say about the shocking rape of the women."[13] Various kings, nobles, and bishops joined the cause. Crusaders temporarily occupied parts of the Holy Land, including Jerusalem, even establishing crusader-led states, but eventually they were forced out. Other crusaders ransacked Constantinople and Egypt.

Looting and pillaging cities, crusaders often slaughtered thousands of Muslims, Jews, and Byzantine Christians, burning mosques and synagogues with people inside. In Germany in 1096 crusaders slaughtered twelve thousand Jews. Non-Christians viewed crusaders as terrorists. In response, Muslim defenders killed local Christians; Jerusalem's streets, it was said, ran ankle-deep in blood. In the thirteenth century, crusading energies dissipated, but the remaining bitter Christian-Muslim animosity still complicates political and cross-cultural relations today.

Some medieval tensions derived from robust intellectual debates, often in universities, involving theologians and philosophers. By the twelfth century, guilds of scholars formed centers of higher learning, most famously at Paris, Oxford in England, and Salerno and Bologna **(boe-LOAN-yuh)** in Italy. Whereas earlier universities in India and the Islamic world mostly specialized in religious studies, European universities taught both religion and secular knowledge, such as Aristotle's philosophy, raising eyebrows among church leaders (see Profile: Heloise, a French Scholar and Nun). Students learned the

[13]Quoted in Thomas F. Madden, *A Concise History of the Crusades* (Lanham, MD: Rowman and Littlefield, 1999), 8–9.

MAP 14.2 MEDIEVAL EUROPE, 900–1300 During the High Middle Ages, the Holy Roman Empire, comprising dozens of smaller states, covered much of what is today Germany, Austria, eastern France, and northern Italy. France, England, Hungary, and Poland were also major states.

PROFILE

Heloise, a French Scholar and Nun

A scandalous love affair between two brilliant people, Abelard and Heloise, reveals much about medieval life and values, including church politics and attitudes toward sexuality. Ever since the romance and its sad repercussions have inspired countless works of poetry and prose. Often portrayed as a forbidden affair between a smitten schoolgirl and her unprincipled teacher, a famed but controversial theologian, the relationship between the two figures was far more complex.

Coming from a wealthy, influential family, Heloise (1101–1164), the niece of a high church official in Paris, had more educational opportunities than most women of her time and studed at a well-financed convent where she showed a keen intelligence. In 1117 her uncle Fulbert, a high-ranking cleric, arranged for the seventeen-year-old to study with Peter Abelard (1079–1142), a famous teacher but a nonclergyman, at the Notre Dame Cathedral school. Born into an aristocratic family in Brittany, Abelard studied with renowned teachers and taught at several schools. Notorious for both his arrogance and intellect, he made enemies in the church by championing reason, logic, and progressive thinking on religious doctrine.

RMN-Grand Palais/Art Resource, NY

HELOISE AND ABELARD This painting, from a fourteenth-century French manuscript, shows Heloise (in nun's habit) and Abelard in conversation, years after their torrid love affair had shocked church authorities.

Despite a twenty-year age difference, Abelard and Heloise fell passionately in love. Abelard wrote of how they went from reading books to kissing and composing love songs and letters to each other. But their affair also reflected friendship and intellectual respect, her letters revealing good knowledge of Roman and Christian writers. The two lovers tried to keep their affair quiet and were secretly married after she became pregnant. Their son, raised by Abelard's sister, eventually became a church official. Their romance came at a time when the church was not just encouraging but mandating that clergy as well as secular teachers, such as Abelard, and students in church schools remain celibate. Abelard realized his marriage would end his current position and future church career. But Heloise's family, upon learning of the affair, sought revenge, and Fulbert hired two men to beat and then castrate Abelard. Now disgraced, Abelard joined a Benedictine monastery, and, at his encouragement, Heloise entered a convent, eventually becoming the community's director.

Although separated, Heloise and Abelard continued to write to each other. Expressing her affection, Heloise wrote him that "I seek to please thee rather than [God]. Thy command brought me, not the love of God, to the [nunnery]." Strongly influenced by Aristotle's thought, Abelard restored his scholarly reputation by writing books and essays about mixing philosophy and religion, views his critics considered heresy. Later, as an abbot (head) of a large monastery, while maintaining a personal distance he helped Heloise and her nuns establish a new convent. Her ability to gain support and funding helped her convent flourish. She remained ambivalent about her career, however, writing Abelard that "I am judged religious at a time when there is little in religion that is not hypocrisy." Heloise became known for her learning, and one top male cleric praised her knowledge of the liberal arts: "You have surpassed all women and have gone further than almost every man." However, Heloise resented Abelard's desire to remain aloof from her, writing: "Of all the wretched women I am the most wretched, for the higher the ascent, the heavier the fall."

Although dying twenty years apart, the pair was buried alongside each other at the convent, a fitting conclusion to a relationship and an era. Heloise was one of the last educated churchwomen to maintain close contact with male scholars and church officials. Obsessed with celibacy, the church increasingly separated men and women engaged in religious life.

THINKING ABOUT THE PROFILE

1. What does the love affair and its consequences tell us about life at this time?
2. How did the different ways in which Abelard and Heloise rebuilt their lives reflect the values of medieval people?

Notes: Quotations from Barbara A. Hanawalt, *The Middle Ages: An Illustrated History* (New York: Oxford University Press, 1998), 88; Jane Slaughter and Melissa K. Bokovoy, *Sharing the Stage: Biography and Gender in Western Civilization*, vol. 1 (Boston: Houghton Mifflin, 2003), 255, 261–262; and James Burge, *Heloise and Abelard: A New Biography* (San Francisco: HarperSanFrancisco, 2003), 271.

"seven liberal arts"—astronomy, geometry, arithmetic, music, grammar, rhetoric, and logic—before specializing in medicine, law, or philosophy. As today, students did not spend all of their time studying. When one student wrote home for money because "the city is expensive and makes many demands," his father replied: "I have recently learned that you live dissolutely, preferring play to work, and strumming your guitar while others are at their studies."[14]

Heated debates over faith and reason, often against church opposition, contributed much to later Western thought. Thomas Aquinas **(uh-KWINE-uhs)** (1225–1274), an Italian Dominican monk and professor at the University of Paris, argued that reason could determine much, even God's existence, but that eventually a believer had to accept on faith many mysteries. He also believed that God mandated human domination over nature and that women were passive and incapable of moral perfection. Some thinkers influenced by Aristotle argued that real knowledge came only from direct observation, a position that supported scientific inquiry.

Medieval literature was diverse. The *Song of Roland*, from twelfth-century France, described the great deeds of a loyal knight who died fighting in Charlemagne's army. But the epic's warlike tone contrasted with many French lyric poems and stories exalting personal happiness and romantic love in a society that generally arranged marriages. Another story, the Celtic legend of British King Arthur and his court, was addressed by writers all over Europe. In some versions Arthur's wife, Guinevere **(GWIN-uh-veer)**, and his best friend, Lancelot, follow their hearts, becoming doomed lovers. There was also lighter writing, such as this parody of the Christian Apostles' Creed written by a student more delighted by spirits than by the Spirit: "I believe in the tavern of my host, More than in the Holy Ghost. The tavern will my sweetheart be, and the Holy Church is not for me."[15]

MAKE SURE YOU UNDERSTAND THESE KEY POINTS BEFORE MOVING ON

- **Feudalism was a medieval political arrangement in which a king gave nobles the right to rule over sections of his territory in exchange for their allegiance.**
- **Medieval society was patriarchal, considering women inferior to men; children usually left home early; and parents arranged most marriages.**
- **Many of the tensions in medieval society were caused by the intolerance for "outsiders": non-Christians and heretics, Muslims, and Jews, all of whom were disdained and treated harshly, killed (as in the Crusades), or expelled.**
- **Christians adopted the Jewish belief in progress over time and the belief that everything in the world was for the use of humans, a view that laid the ground for later industrialization in the West.**

Eastern Europe: Byzantines, Slavs, and Mongols

How did Byzantine society differ from that of western Europe?

Byzantium, and the eastern European societies it influenced, remained very distinct from western Europe. Despite Christianity and long-standing trade connections, deep political, economic, and religious differences separated them and still do. Byzantium demonstrated remarkable longevity, serving as a buffer zone protecting central and western Europe against Muslim, Slavic, and Mongol invaders, but, from the eleventh century on, it experienced steady political decline until it was finally defeated by the Ottoman Turks in 1453. Most Slavic societies in eastern Europe adopted Eastern Orthodox Christianity, and the Russians eventually created a powerful state.

Byzantium and Its Rivals

Byzantium faced nearly continuous pressure from neighboring peoples. In the sixth and seventh centuries Sassanian Persians and Byzantines fought wars, weakening both empires and making Arab conquest of their lands easier. Arabs attacked Constantinople in 673 and 717, but the Byzantines survived. For the next three and a half centuries they also faced challenges from various Slavic peoples who migrated into and settled eastern Europe, dominating this vast region of mountains, forests, and grasslands stretching north from Greece to the eastern Baltic and eastward through Russia. The major Slavic threats came from Bulgars and Serbs. The Byzantine ruler known as "Basil the Bulgar-Slayer" defeated a Bulgar army in 1014, blinding fifteen thousand Bulgarian prisoners of war before releasing them to return home. The Bulgar defeat opened the door to Serbs, who set up several small states in the Balkans, sparking conflict with Byzantium. After a series of wars, Ottoman Turks conquered the Serbs in 1459.

Byzantine political fortunes declined. In 1071, Norman knights drove Byzantine forces from southern Italy, and in 1091, at the Battle of Manzikert **(MANZ-ih-kuhrt)**, Seljuk Turks seized eastern Anatolia. The shrunken Byzantine territories now faced regular attacks from both east and west.

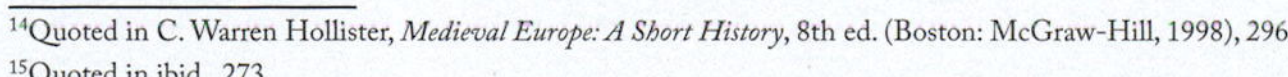

[14]Quoted in C. Warren Hollister, *Medieval Europe: A Short History*, 8th ed. (Boston: McGraw-Hill, 1998), 296.
[15]Quoted in ibid., 273.

Turks soon completed the conquest of Anatolia, leaving Constantinople a beleaguered fortress. Desperate Byzantines requested help from western knights to defend them against the Turks; instead crusader armies occupied Palestine and Syria between 1096 and 1200. The Byzantines also did not expect crusaders in 1204, bribed by the Venetians, Byzantine trading rivals, to use a disputed imperial succession as an excuse to conquer Constantinople itself, which they governed until forced out in 1261. Capitalizing on these disasters, expanding Ottoman Turks finally conquered Constantinople and the surrounding territory in 1453, ending the Byzantine state and transforming the capital city, which the Turks eventually renamed Istanbul.

Despite its many misfortunes, Byzantium's economic and religious strengths enabled it to survive for a long time. Located astride the principal trade routes between Europe and Asia, Constantinople's merchant class remained vital. Traders shipped eastern European slaves, including many Slavs (source of the English term *slave*) from the Black Sea region, for sale in the Mediterranean. Taxes from these goods and people as well as silk production enriched the treasury, and Byzantine coins were used around Eurasia.

With Byzantine church and state intertwined, Christianity and its rituals influenced all aspects of society, fostering lengthy religious ceremonies and an intense prayer life. Unlike in western Europe, governments dominated the church, with rulers regularly interfering in church affairs. Byzantines also engaged in hair-splitting theological disputes, bitterly disagreeing on the use of icons, painted images of holy figures, and over whether the Holy Spirit proceeded from God or from both God and Jesus. Byzantine Christians refused to recognize the bishop of Rome's supremacy over other bishops. These conflicts over theology and authority spurred the final split between the Roman Catholic and Greek Orthodox Churches, which came when the pope and the patriarch of Constantinople angrily excommunicated each other in 1054.

Although the Byzantine church supported male power, a few women achieved political or intellectual influence. Empress Irene, an orphan who married an emperor, ruled Byzantium for two decades (780–802). Although her detractors considered her cruel and ruthless, Irene fostered prosperity, made peace with Muslim states, and temporarily resolved the dispute over icons. Byzantium's best-known historian, the princess Anna Comnena (1083–1148), studied literature, astronomy, medicine, and Greek philosophy.

Byzantium, Russians, and Mongols

Byzantine culture and religion spread north and east and survived the empire's defeats. Differing eastern and western versions of Christianity offered eastern European peoples a choice of which to adopt. In the ninth century, two Byzantine brothers, known later as Saints Cyril and Methodius **(mi-THO-dee-uhs)**, converted many Slavs to eastern Christianity. Devising an alphabet, known as Cyrillic **(suh-RILL-ik)**, for the Slavs, Cyril translated the Bible and other church writings from Greek. Bulgars, Serbs, Russians, and many Ukrainians eventually adopted Byzantine culture, including Orthodox Christianity. Russians and other societies they influenced, including Georgians in the Caucasus, embraced ideas such as an autocratic emperor and close church-state relations, in contrast to western Europe, where church-state conflicts remained common. Other Slavs, among them Croats **(KRO-ATS)**, Czechs **(checks)**, Lithuanians **(lith-oo-ANE-ee-uhnz)**, Poles, Slovaks **(SLO-vaks)**, Slovenes **(SLO-veenz)**, and many Ukrainians, adopted Roman Catholicism. Eastern and western European cultures remain distinct even today, partly because of the differences between the Greek and Roman churches of one thousand years ago.

Russian identity descended from the Rus **(roos)**, whose capital was at Kiev **(KEE-yev)**, in today's Ukraine **(you-CRANE)**. Swedish Vikings who founded trading cities in the Slavic regions became the Rus ruling class, both trading with and raiding the Byzantines. Viking trade networks crisscrossed the Russian and Ukrainian plains, and Slavs eventually assimilated the Vikings. From the tenth to the twelfth centuries, the Russians expanded, forming settlements as far north as Novgorod **(NOHV-goh-rod)** and shipping timber south to the Black Sea. The Rus ruler Vladimir **(VLAD-ih-mir)** I (ca. 956–1015) in Kiev had several wives and eight hundred concubines but, hoping for political advantage, sought marriage to a Byzantine princess. After she refused to marry a pagan polygamist, he agreed to accept Orthodox Christianity in 988 and make her his only wife. Ordering his soldiers to be baptized, Vladimir guaranteed that much of eastern Europe would become Eastern Orthodox.

By the time western Europeans heard rumors about the brutal Mongols, the Russians had already encountered them. Mongol armies conquered Central Asia and parts of China and the Middle East (see Chapters 10 and 11) and repeatedly sacked Russian cities beginning in 1237. A papal envoy who visited Kiev after an attack reported, "We found lying in the fields countless heads and bones. [The city] has been reduced to nothing: barely 200 houses [still] stand there."[16] Until the fifteenth century most Russians remained subject to the Golden Horde, a Mongol state on the lower Volga River. Muscovy **(MUSS-koe-vee)**, a Russian state centered on Moscow, benefited, since the Golden Horde treated its ruler as the senior Russian leader.

Western Europe was fortunate to escape Mongol conquest. In 1241, Mongol armies moved far into Europe, crushing Polish and Hungarian forces sent against them. Standing at the Danube, they contemplated invading German lands. But Mongol generals returned to Mongolia when their leader, Ogodei, died, sparing Germans and Europeans farther west. Had the Mongol conquests continued westward, European history might have been very different. But Europe was much less tempting than far richer China and Islamic western Asia.

Eventually Muscovy became the dominant Russian state as Mongol political power declined and the head of the Russian Orthodox Church, appointed by the Constantinople patriarch, moved from Kiev to Moscow. Under Ivan III (1440–1505), Muscovy escaped Mongol control and established domination over other Russian states. Ivan began to call himself czar

[16]Quoted in Nicholas V. Riasanovsky, *A History of Russia*, 5th ed. (New York: Oxford University Press, 1993), 72.

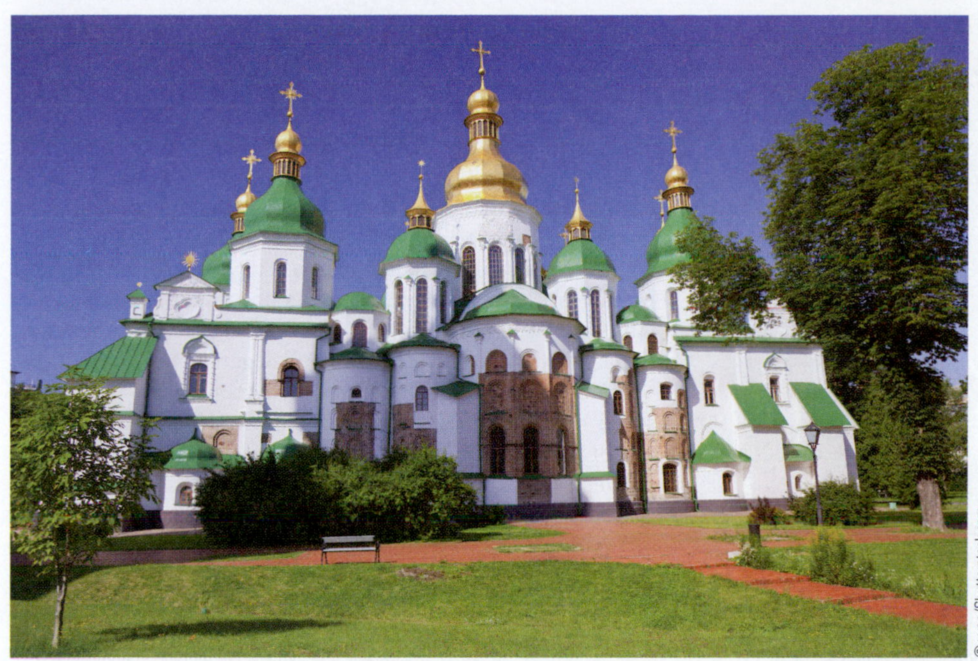

© vvoe/Shutterstock.com

ST. SOPHIA CATHEDRAL IN KIEV. Built in the early eleventh century, possibly by Vladimir I, to rival Hagia Sophia in Constantinople,the cathedral symbolized Kiev and Rus as the "new Constantinople."

(meaning "caesar"), indicating his superiority over lesser rulers, and married the last Byzantine emperor's niece. The Russian Orthodox Church broke with the patriarch of Constantinople, and Russian clergy referred to Moscow as the Third Rome, successor to Constantinople. A monastery abbot proclaimed: "The Church of old Rome fell for its heresy; the gates of the Second Rome, Constantinople, were hewn down by the axes of the infidel Turks; but the Church of Moscow, the Church of the New Rome, shines brighter than the sun in the whole universe."[17] Russians also expanded into the territories of the Catholic Lithuanians, adding religious antagonisms to political tensions between Orthodox and Catholic peoples in eastern Europe.

MAKE SURE YOU UNDERSTAND THESE KEY POINTS BEFORE MOVING ON

- **The Byzantines were under almost constant attack by Sassanian Persians, Bulgars, Slavs, and western European Christians, but Byzantium survived until it was conquered by the Turks in 1453.**
- **Byzantium's culture and Orthodox Christianity survived because they were spread to many eastern European peoples, including the Russians, the Bulgars, the Serbs, and many Ukrainians.**
- **The Russians, who had adopted Orthodox Christianity, were attacked by the Mongols but emerged as one of the strongest societies in eastern Europe.**

Late Medieval Europe and the Roots of Expansion

What developments between 1300 and 1500 gave Europeans the incentive and means to begin reshaping the world after 1500?

The Late Middle Ages (1300–1500) were a period of transition. A dramatic decrease in population as a result of famine, plague, and warfare contributed to feudalism's gradual end. Royal power increased many places at the expense of the feudal nobility, while the Roman Church also lost influence as questioning of church practices and beliefs increased. Yet, the ferment fostered intellectual and cultural creativity, trade expanded, and brave mariners began exploring the world beyond Europe. These changes eventually led to the resurgence of the West.

The Black Death and Social Change

Late medieval Europe was an unhappy place, ravaged by famine, disease, and war. Europe's climate turned colder about 1300, fostering the "Little Ice Age." Norse farming settlements in Greenland collapsed from deforestation, expanding glaciers, and conflict with the local Inuit. The same cooler temperatures shortened Europe's growing season, causing serious food shortages.

[17]Quoted in Colin Wells, *Sailing from Byzantium: How a Lost Empire Shaped the World* (New York: Delta, 2006), 279.

PRAYING FOR RELIEF This image of survivors carrying away plague victims in Rome was commissioned by a French duke for an illuminated book in the early 1400s. It illustrates the despair and devastating loss of life caused by the Black Death, especially in cities.

Europe also repeatedly suffered from the Black Death, a terrible pandemic, or massive epidemic that crossed many regions, named for the black bruises appearing under the skin. In 1347 a trading ship coming from the Black Sea limped into a Sicilian harbor, the entire crew either dead or dying from a deadly infection spread by fleas living on rats who had scampered aboard ship—probably bubonic plague, perhaps mixed with pneumonic **(noo-MON-ik)** plague. The pandemic caused unprecedented death and suffering as it spread along and disrupted trade networks all over Eurasia and North Africa. During its peak years from 1348 to 1350, it killed a third of all Europeans. Over 65 percent of the population in some congested cities died, greatly reducing commerce; Europe's population in the fourteenth century dropped from around 70 or 75 million to some 45 or 50 million people, most killed by either a fast-acting respiratory infection or by swelling and internal bleeding. Pope Clement VI wrote that "the living were barely sufficient to bury the dead, or so horrified as to avoid the task. So great a terror seized nearly everyone."[18] The horrors endured in nursery rhymes: "Ring around the rosies, a pocketful of posies, ashes, ashes, we all fall down." Those who survived developed some immunities: the Black Death, reoccurring for decades, killed fewer people each time.

The troubles reshaped social patterns, especially for the upper classes. With far fewer peasants alive to till the fields, those remaining asked for more privileges and money. Peasant revolts demanding an end to serfdom increased, most notably in France in 1358 and in England in 1381. Meanwhile, some people challenged social norms. In addition to writing works of history, ethics, and poetry, the French author Christine of Pasan (1364–ca. 1430) proclaimed women equal to men, systematically disproved all negative male stereotypes of women's character, and shrewdly critiqued the patriarchal social structure. She wrote that "those who blame women out of jealousy are those wicked men who have seen many women of greater intelligence and nobler conduct than they themselves possess."[19] Some literature, such as the fiction of the fourteenth-century English writer Geoffrey Chaucer **(CHAW-suhr)** (see Witness to the Past: A Literary View of Late Medieval People), reflected changing social customs and relations.

Death and despair influenced emotional and social life. Many people assumed the pandemic was divine punishment. Hopelessness overwhelmed people digging graves for family members before they too succumbed to death, usually within days. While famine and disease raged, aristocrats enjoyed magnificent banquets, pageants, and ostentatious clothing. The poor sought escape through prayer, meditation, and self-flagellation, imitating the torture of Jesus by beating themselves with whips until their blood flowed. Some places people, looking for scapegoats, blamed outsiders for the troubles. In the mid-1300s thousands of Jews were burned alive or driven out of cities, especially in the German states.

The pandemic affected western and eastern Europe differently. Because eastern Europe had fewer cities and more villages, fewer peasants died. With eastern monarchs weaker, the aristocracy imposed serfdom on many peasants, creating large agricultural estates. In the West, however, nobles were weakened by labor shortages and higher costs. Hence, eastern Europe remained primarily an agricultural area, while western European rulers strengthened their central governments.

Warfare and Political Centralization

Chronic warfare in late medieval western Europe strengthened kings and states (see Map 14.3). For example, the Hundred Years War (1337–1453) involving intermittent English-French conflict enhanced royal power in France and, eventually, England. This war, caused by the English kings' desire to hold on to their feudal lands in France, eventually resulted in French victory. At first the English gained victories by using trained commoners and a new weapon, the longbow, that launched powerful arrows, diminishing the knights

[18] Quoted in Delouche, *Illustrated History*, 168.

[19] Quoted in Brotton, *Renaissance Bazaar*, 75.

WITNESS TO THE PAST

A Literary View of Late Medieval People

The English writer Geoffrey Chaucer (ca. 1340–1400) wrote one of the best-known books of the Late Middle Ages, The Canterbury Tales, *set in the time of the Black Death. A London-born cosmopolitan poet, soldier, and diplomat, Chaucer served in the English Parliament and was familiar with French and Italian intellectual and cultural trends. While strongly influencing spoken and written English,* The Canterbury Tales *also offered a witty and sophisticated picture of English society. This excerpt presents stereotypical and satirical views of various pilgrims on their way to visit Canterbury, the seat of church power in England.*

The knight there was, and he was a worthy man, Who, from the moment that he first began To ride about the world, loved chivalry, Truth, honor, freedom, and all courtesy.... Of mortal battles he had fought fifteen... And always won he sovereign fame for prize... He never yet had any vileness said [about him] in all his life... He was a truly perfect, gentle knight....

There was also a nun, a prioress, Who, in her smiling, modest was and coy... At table she had been well taught withal, And never from her lips let morsels fall, Nor dipped her fingers deep in sauce, but ate With so much care the food upon her plate That never driblet fell upon her breast. In courtesy she had delight and zest....

A monk there was, one made for mastery [and loved hunting]... A manly man, to be an abbot able. Full many a blooded horse had he in stable: And when he rode men might his bridle hear A-jingling in the whistling wind as clear, Aye, and as loud as does the chapel bell Where this brave monk was of the cell.... This said monk let such lowly old things [strict old monastic rules] slowly pace And followed new world manners in their place. What? Should he study as a madman would Upon a book in cloister cell? Or yet, go labor with his hands and... sweat [as Saint Augustine commanded]?...

There was a merchant with forked beard, and girt... Upon his head a Flemish beaver hat; His boots were fastened rather elegantly. He spoke [his opinions] pompously, Stressing the times when he had won, not lost [his profits]... At money changing he could make a crown. This worthy man kept all his wits well set; There was no one could say he was in debt, So well he governed all his trade affairs....

There was a good man of religion, too, A country parson, poor... but rich he was in holy thought and work. He was also a learned man also [a scholar]... who Christ's own Gospel truly sought to preach. Devoutly his parishioner's would he teach... Benign he was and wondrous diligent, Patient in adverse times and well content... But rather would he give... unto those poor parishioners about, Part of his income, even of his goods... That first he wrought and after words he taught [first he practiced, then he preached]....

THINKING ABOUT THE READING

1. What are the various clerical stereotypes presented?
2. How is the merchant portrayed?

Source: General Prologue to Geoffrey Chaucer's *Canterbury Tales*, electronic edition prepared by Edwin Duncan (*http:www.towson.edu/~duncan/chaucer/titlepage.htm*)

as an effective fighting force. However, aided by Jeanne d'Arc **(zhahn DAHRK)** (ca. 1412–1431), a sixteen-year-old peasant who believed saints' voices told her to lead troops into battle, the French broke the English siege of the city of Orleans **(or-lay-AHN)** and slowly recovered most English-held territory in France. Jeanne, captured and burned at the stake, became French nationhood's most famous martyr.

During the conflict's final stages, French monarchs introduced new direct taxes, lessening their dependence on the nobility, while reorganizing royal armies by hiring more mercenary troops. In England, military defeat fostered the War of the Roses (1455–1485) between two rival royal houses. Eventually Henry VII, who founded a new Tudor dynasty, sent armies to reclaim Ireland, followed by English settlers who repressed the Celtic Irish. The Tudors established England as a world power during the 1500s.

Royal power increased during the late 1400s in Spain. In 1085 Iberian Christians began the long reconquest of the peninsula from Muslims, by 1249 reclaiming Portugal and by the 1300s displacing all of the Muslim states except Granada **(gruh-NAH-duh)** in the far south. In 1469 the marriage of King Ferdinand of Aragon **(AR-uh-gon)** to his cousin, Isabella of Castile **(kas-TEEL)**, united the two largest kingdoms. These monarchs finally crushed Granada in 1492 and then, obsessed with religious uniformity, demanded that Spanish Jews and Muslims either convert or be expelled. While many converted, some secretly maintained Jewish or Muslim practices. Jews and Muslims refusing conversion mostly emigrated to Morocco or the Ottoman Empire. Hoping to increase royal wealth, Ferdinand and Isabella also sponsored the first trans-Atlantic voyage by the Italian mariner, Christopher Columbus, in 1492.

Aristocracy remained strong in the Holy Roman Empire, which encompassed many German-speaking lands and parts of Italy. After taking power in 1273, the Habsburg **(HABZ-berg)** family proved unable to create a strong centralized state. In 1356 they reduced the pope's influence over electing Holy Roman Emperors but also ratified aristocratic power. During the coming centuries imperial Habsburg rulers concentrated on increasing their family's personal territorial holdings. In the later 1400s, royal marriage alliances gave them control of the Netherlands and much of southern Italy.

MAP 14.3 **EUROPE, 1400–1500** During this period France became western Europe's strongest kingdom, but Spanish kings gradually reunified much of the Iberian peninsula. The Holy Roman Empire remained decentralized. Meanwhile, Lithuania, Hungary, and Poland controlled much of eastern Europe.

Hemispheric Connections, New Intellectual Horizons, and Technology

The Late Middle Ages fostered new intellectual horizons and technologies, some derived from contacts with Asia and Africa. The Mongols did not conquer western Europe but reenergized Eurasian trade, allowing inventions and ideas to flow to Europe from China and western Asia. Some Chinese inventions, such as printing, gunpowder, and the compass, eventually revolutionized European technology. Meanwhile, Italians imported spices, carpets, silks, porcelain, glassware, and even painting supplies from Muslim Spain, Ottoman Turkey, Mamluk Egypt, and Persia. The cosmopolitan Ottoman ruler Mehmed the Conqueror (1430–1481) read and published Greek and Latin books on history and philosophy while inviting Italian merchants, craftsmen, artists, and architects to work in Istanbul (formerly Constantinople). The magnificent palaces and mosques in Islamic cities influenced some Italians, especially Venetians. By the later 1400s the Portuguese were bringing back artworks and fabrics from West Africa and the Kongo that influenced European artists.

Moral and political corruption fostered decline of papal political power and the Roman Church. Some historians argue that all power tends to corrupt. Church dissidents complained about the buying of church offices, favoritism to relatives, and the absenteeism of bishops who served more than one diocese to collect extra revenue. Detractors of Cardinal Wolsey, archbishop of both Canterbury and York in England, claimed that he entered the cathedral at York only once, for his funeral. Skeptics also viewed practices such as venerating holy relics and making pilgrimages as superstition that encouraged fraud, while defenders argued that relics and pilgrimages gave people something tangible to cling to when seeking God's help.

Papal prestige declined after popes moved to Avignon in southern France (1309–1377). Avignon popes required that candidates for bishop pay a large sum to the papal treasury, hence reserving high church offices for the wealthy. When the papacy finally returned to Rome, two men claimed to be the rightful pope, with Europeans picking sides. Before this "Great Schism" (1378–1417) ended, it badly damaged the papacy's prestige. After a bishop's council tried to replace papal monarchy with church government by such councils, popes refused to call councils on church reform.

Along with church criticism, imported ideas and products contributed to the dramatic flowering of arts and learning, later known as the **Renaissance**, or "rebirth." The Renaissance began in Italian city-states around 1350 and intensified through the 1400s and 1500s, spreading to other societies. In Florence, artists and thinkers rediscovered Classical Greek and Roman ideas. Renaissance philosophy, called **humanism**, emphasized humanity, worldly concerns, and reason rather than religious ideals. The books of Dante Alighieri **(DAHN-tay ah-lee-GYEH-ree)** (1265–1321), especially *The Divine Comedy*, attacked the pope and promoted vernacular language, in this case Italian, rather than Latin. Painters in Italy, such as Sandro Botticelli **(SAHN-dro BOT-i-CHEL-ee)** (1445–1510), and in the Netherlands depicted space and the human figure realistically. Scholars debate whether the Renaissance undermined medieval world-views by fostering individualism, secularism, and scientific inquiry or was mainly a cultural movement among a small privileged elite with little impact on the larger society. Nonetheless, Renaissance artists and writers emphasized tolerance of diverse views and new ideals of beauty, weakening church influence. The Renaissance eventually spread into northern Europe in the 1500s.

Extraordinary technological development, aided by imports from other regions, also characterized late medieval Europe. European scholars translated Arab and Greek scientific writings in Muslim Spain, while Asian and Muslim technologies that reached Europe, such as the Chinese spinning wheel and loom, improved textile manufacturing. During the 1300s and 1400s western Europeans also developed better ships, improving Chinese inventions such as the compass and sternpost rudder and adapting Arab lateen sails. By the 1490s, navigation, sailing, and weaponry advances gave Europeans mastery of the oceans. They also devised time-measuring devices, including mechanical clocks, that allowed people to control and standardize units of time.

Perhaps the most crucial invention, printing by movable type, allowed information to be produced and dispersed in unlimited quantities. Knowledge of Chinese woodblock printing and movable type made of clay and metal, invented centuries earlier (see Chapter 11), may have traveled the trade routes to Europe. By the 1400s Europeans used block printing for books and playing cards, and in 1455 the German goldsmith Johann Gutenberg **(yoh-HAHN GOO-ten-burg)** (1400–1468) introduced the first known metal movable type outside of East Asia, printing a Bible. The printed word became an essential medium of mass communication and no longer the monopoly of the few who could afford expensive hand-copied volumes, undermining both feudalism and the church.

Imported technology, especially Chinese gunpowder, made for more lethal warfare. By the 1200s, the Chinese had developed primitive guns capable of ejecting flame and projectiles 40 yards. This and other weapons, reaching Europe during the Mongol era, were then improved, making warfare far deadlier than before. Gunpowder weapons, while killing many knights and nobles in wars, also gave Europeans a huge military advantage over societies that did not have them, including those in sub-Saharan Africa and the Americas.

Population and Economic Growth

Increased agricultural development spurred a population increase of 40 to 50 percent between the tenth and fourteenth centuries, the world's highest rate. After the Black Death, Europe's population again increased rapidly, grain production doubled, and many peasants moved into eastern Europe to open lands.

Commerce also expanded. Under feudalism and manorialism, merchants mostly dealt in luxury goods for the aristocracy. Indeed, the feudal ethic

Renaissance ("Rebirth") A dramatic flowering in arts and learning that began in the Italian city-states around 1350 and spread through Europe through the 1500s.

humanism The name for the European Renaissance philosophy, which emphasized humanity, worldly concerns, and reason rather than religious ideals.

opposed wealth accumulation and devalued merchants. By the 1300s, however, this feudal ethic was breaking down. As foreign trade expanded, commerce became part of everyday life. Venetian merchants, who had trading posts all around the Middle East and Black Sea, and Genoans distributed valuable spices from India and Southeast Asia. The vast quantity of merchandise, mostly from the East, in fifteenth-century Venice awed observers:

> *It seems as if the whole world flocks here. Who could count the many shops so well furnished that they seem almost warehouses, with so many cloths of every make—tapestry, brocades, carpets of every sort, silks of every kind; and so many warehouses full of spices, groceries and rugs. These things stupefy the beholder.*[20]

West African gold, used in coins, treasuries, and jewelry, also stimulated the economy. European merchants borrowed and used Arab trading practices and mathematics. In the early 1200s Fibonacci **(fee-bo-NACH-ee)**, a merchant from Pisa in Italy, wrote of the Arab and Indian numerals and calculations he studied in Algeria, Egypt, and Syria. Soon Venice, Genoa, and Florence adopted his mathematical and commercial innovations.

Unlike centralized China or the Ottoman Empire, western European cities, located in a politically fragmented region, enjoyed growing political power and were able to bargain with kings for advantages and autonomy. In 1241 various north German cities expanded a trade alliance, the Hanseatic **(han-see-AT-ik)** League, that eventually had over 165 member cities, including some in Holland and Poland, and its own army and navy, making it almost an independent political power. These developments gave European merchants a status and power unique in the world. While Chinese merchants, while often prosperous, had a low ranking in the Confucian social system, were heavily taxed, and faced many restrictions, western European merchants steadily gained influence, becoming city political leaders. Governments now supported merchants and their interests, fostering a social and institutional structure that encouraged profits. Not everyone approved. The Dutch philosopher Erasmus complained about greed, asking, "When did avarice reign more largely and less punished?"[21] Nonetheless, late medieval Europeans sparked an economic revolution that fundamentally altered western European life in the 1500s and later spread its influences around the world.

The Portuguese and Maritime Exploration

In the 1400s a few Europeans, pushed by commercial growth and taking advantage of new maritime and military technologies, began to explore the world beyond Europe by sea. The Portuguese, only recently unified in a kingdom and with a standard of living probably lower than many Africans and Asians, began sailing south seeking slaves, African gold, and other trade goods. Motivated by a missionary desire to outflank Islam and spread Christianity, as well as a compelling appetite for plunder and conquest, they enjoyed the advantage of guns, better ships, and a maritime tradition. They also had a larger strategic purpose: finding a way around Africa and sailing directly to fabled Southeast Asia, the source of spices so valued in Europe. Finally, European legends about a great Christian emperor in Africa, "Prester John," perhaps derived from the Ethiopian king, suggested to the Portuguese that they could find a possible ally against Muslims.

Hence, in search of "Christians and spices," the Portuguese began systematically exploring the West African coast in 1420. Their efforts were sponsored by Prince Henry the Navigator (1394–1460), a shipbuilding design and cartography innovator. Soon Henry's caravels, small ships that could sail on the ocean and into shallow coastal waters and rivers, discovered Madeira **(muh-DEER-uh)** Island and the Azores **(A-zorz)** and Canary Islands in the Atlantic off North Africa. By the 1480s the Portuguese had visited much of Africa's coast as far south as Angola (see Chapter 12). In 1487 Portuguese ships led by Bartolomeu Dias **(DEE-uhsh)** reached the Indian Ocean, intensifying Portuguese interest both in Africa and the world to the east. One of the sailors manning Portuguese ships, a Genoese immigrant to Portugal, Christopher Columbus, later developed an alternative strategy for reaching the East. In 1492 Columbus, under Spanish sponsorship, sailed west across the Atlantic to the Americas, changing world history forever.

MAKE SURE YOU UNDERSTAND THESE KEY POINTS BEFORE MOVING ON

- **The Black Death killed a third of Europe's people and reduced the power of western European nobles while increasing the power of eastern European nobles.**
- **French rulers increased their power in the Hundred Years War, England's Tudor dynasty later made England a world power, and Spanish Christians gradually drove out the Muslims, while in Germany and Italy the nobility remained strong.**
- **The church declined in power and prestige as it came to be seen as corrupt, and the papacy was weakened by the Great Schism.**
- **During the Renaissance, artists and writers rediscovered Classical influences and championed worldly concerns, individualism, and realism rather than spirituality.**
- **Major technological developments, influenced in part by ideas imported from China and the Muslim world, included the printing press, which further undermined the church, and guns, which killed many in European wars.**

[20]Canon Pietro Casola, quoted in ibid., 38.

[21]Quoted in Edith Simon, *The Reformation* (New York: Time-Life Books, 1966), 71.

CHAPTER SUMMARY

European societies changed dramatically between 600 and 1500. By mixing Greco-Roman, Christian, and Germanic legacies between 500 and 1000, western Europeans constructed new societies based on new values and practices. These societies also acquired knowledge from and traded with the Islamic world, especially Muslim Spain. The major medieval institutions of feudalism, manorialism, and the papacy generated conflict between popes and kings, kings and nobles, nobles and merchants, cities and countryside, and Christians and outsiders. The church played a crucial social and political role in European societies. Priests dominated village life, while popes fought heresy and spurred crusades against Muslims.

The social, political, economic, and religious systems of Byzantium were different from those in western Europe. The Byzantine emperors were more powerful and had more control over the church. Eventually the Byzantine Church broke completely with the Roman Church, becoming the Greek Orthodox Church. Byzantium also passed on many traditions to various eastern European societies such as the Russians. Russia later became a strong state with a rival Orthodox Church.

Western Europeans were linked by trade networks to other societies of Eurasia and North Africa. These networks, including those formed by the Mongol expansion, allowed the movement from east to west not only of valuable goods, technologies, and ideas but also of diseases such as the Black Death. Between 1300 and 1500 western European states grew larger and, in some cases, more centralized, the church faced decline as a political force, and warfare became more deadly. Sparked in part by Afro-Asian influences, the Renaissance fostered new humanistic ideas and artistic currents, while economic growth and social change enhanced the influence of merchants. In the fifteenth century, aided by Asian and Islamic seafaring technologies, western Europeans began exploring the world.

KEY TERMS

medieval (p. 311)
feudalism (p. 317)
vassals (p. 318)
benefices (p. 318)
fief (p. 318)
knights (p. 318)
chivalry (p. 318)
manorialism (p. 318)
serfs (p. 318)
guilds (p. 319)
usury (p. 319)
courtly love (p. 320)
excommunicate (p. 321)
simony (p. 321)
Holy Inquisition (p. 321)
Magna Carta (p. 322)
Renaissance (p. 331)
humanism (p. 331)

Eastern Predominance in the Intermediate World

For over a century now the prosperous and powerful nations of North America and western Europe have dominated the world economically and politically. But before 1500 the world looked very different, and various societies in Asia and North Africa were much stronger and more influential than they are today. Some Eastern societies enjoyed power and status far beyond their borders, helping to shape much of the Eastern Hemisphere in these centuries. However, historians debate to what degree we can consider this to have been an era of Eastern predominance in Afro-Eurasia.

The Problem

Some historians believe that the rise to influence and prosperity of the East, especially China, India, and various Islamic societies, was a major theme of the Intermediate Era. In their view, for most of these centuries, these Eastern peoples developed and sustained more dynamic governments, productive economies, and creative technologies than any other societies. Others disagree, contending that after 1000 the advantage shifted to western Europeans, who laid the foundations for rapid growth and eventual world dominance. These arguments are part of a vigorous scholarly debate.

The Debate

Many historians identify Eastern predominance in this era, but they disagree on which society made the greatest contributions to the world. The largest number point to China as the Eurasian leader in the Intermediate Era and offer a variety of factors to explain China's status. S. A. M. Adshead places Tang China at center-stage in the world economy and considers it the world's best-ordered state between 600 and 900. William McNeill identifies Chinese predominance especially from 1000 to 1500, with China as the engine of the Eurasian economy. Various historians of Asia, among them Rhoads Murphey, describe a dynamic and creative Song China enjoying many of the conditions that, in the later eighteenth century, fostered industrialization in northwest Europe: urbanization, commercialization, widening local and overseas markets, rising demand, and mechanical invention. Mary Matossian labels the entire Intermediate Era the "Chinese Millennium," when China was more populous, productive, and wealthy than any other society, enjoying an orderly society and advanced technology.

Many world historians agree that Chinese innovations and commercial expansion energized Eurasian trade and contributed much to the Intermediate world. British scholar Robert Temple credits the Chinese with inventing modern agriculture, shipping, astronomical observatories, oil industries, paper money, decimal mathematics, wheelbarrows, fishing reels, multistage rockets, guns, umbrellas, hot-air balloons, chess, whiskey, and even the essential design of the steam engine. Without Chinese naval technology, he and others argue, Columbus would never have sailed to America. China and India were the two great centers of world manufacturing before 1500, their exports fueling Afro-Eurasian trade.

But China was not the only Asian powerhouse and great source of knowledge. Indians fostered two universal religions, Buddhism and Hinduism, while inventing and exporting scientific, technological, and agricultural techniques to China, the Islamic world, and later Europe in a process the historian Lynda Shaffer terms "southernization." Such innovations as Indian granulated sugar crystals, the decimal system, "Arabic" numerals, and cotton plants had revolutionary implications for Eurasia. Other historians, such as Marshall Hodgson and Richard Eaton, argue for the centrality of the Islamic societies, contending that, before 1600, Islamic culture and economy were the world's most expansive, influential, and integrating force. Islam was cosmopolitan, egalitarian, and flexible, allowing Muslims to rebound from the Mongol conquests and Black Death and reestablish powerful states such as Ottoman Turkey.

Still other historians think China, India, and Islam were all powerhouses in an Eastern-dominated Intermediate world. Robert Marks argues that the Eastern Hemisphere in the 1300s and 1400s had three centers, with dynamic but linked regional systems based on China, India, and Islam. From Ottoman Turkey eastward to Japan, agricultural efficiency, consumer goods, social welfare, and civilian and military technology were generally the equal of, and often superior to, European counterparts. British scholar John Hobson believes that the rise of a dynamic East made possible the later rise of the West, the era's globalization allowing advanced Eastern inventions to flow westward, where they were gradually assimilated by Europe. Many historians describe Europe in this era as economically weak, with small, insignificant states, and not showing renewed vigor until 1400. Nor did Europe have, as some historians suggest, any unique cultural advantages. Jack Goody concludes that there were few decisive cultural differences between East and West in rationality, economic tools, family patterns, and political pluralism. In his view, the Bronze Age urban revolution, affecting China, India, and western Asia well before Europe, fostered a long-term exchange of information between East and West that generated alternating periods of dominance.

Other scholars, doubting that any Eastern societies had a great advantage in this era, strongly contend that medieval Europe was not backward compared to China, India, or Islam. David Landes, while conceding that Europe was well behind China and Islam in many areas of life in 1000, suggests that things had changed considerably 500 years later. With many cultural and geographical advantages, Europeans, argues Landes, caught up to the East with the growth of manufacturing and trade. Landes and others describe an inventive Europe with impressive technological progress using increased nonhuman power, especially in agriculture. Toby Huff favorably contrasts European science with its Chinese counterpart, especially after 1200, when restless human energy, influential merchants, and competing states made late medieval Europe dynamic. Ricardo Duchesne stresses liberal democratic culture as crucial to the rise of the West, and Rodney Stark credits the medieval Catholic Church's emphasis on reason and belief in progress for fostering economic growth, asserting that these ideas were lacking in other religions, a view many scholars have challenged.

THE TANG TRIBUTARY SYSTEM This satirical painting by Yan Liben (600–673) portrays representatives from vassal states bringing tribute to the Tang court.

Landes and Huff also dismissed the notion of Eastern leadership, perceiving China by 1450 as overpopulated, intellectually dormant, indifferent to technology, negating commercial success, and resistant to change. Some historians of China, such as Adshead, concur that the balance of power was shifting toward Europe in the later Intermediate Era.

If several Eastern societies, and especially China, may have had some advantages and great power during much of the Intermediate Era, they lost their status between 1450 and 1800, raising the question of when and how the East declined. Some historians believe the decline of the East preceded and made possible the rise of the West. Janet Abu-Lughod describes a well-integrated hemispheric system linking Afro-Eurasia by trade for several centuries, with no single country dominant. This network declined after 1350, reducing Europe's commercial competition. Other historians blame Eastern decline on the Mongols and their heirs, who devastated western Asia and North India and ended the creative Song dynasty.

Historian L. S. Stavrianos credits what he termed the "Law of the Retarding Lead"—that nothing fails like success—for undermining China and helping underdeveloped Europe. This concept holds that the best-adapted, most successful societies have the most difficulty in changing and retaining their lead in a period of transition, losing their dynamic thrust. Conversely, less successful societies are more likely to eventually adapt and forge ahead. Hence, he argues, in the 1400s China still had an edge, with an advanced technology, efficient government, great regional power, and the world's largest commercial economy. Because these advantages seemed to work so well, they gave China a stake in preserving rather than dramatically altering its system. Indeed, some argue that the leading Eastern societies, especially China, remained successful until overtaken by a rising West between 1600 and 1800.

Evaluating the Debate

China and the Islamic world were two major poles of global trade and technological innovation for much of this era, at least before the 1400s, but any Eastern advantage was eventually lost. We are left with tantalizing questions. What if the Mongols or Ottomans had conquered some of western Europe, or Ming admiral Zheng He had continued his voyages and headed all the way to West Africa, Europe, or the Americas? Had they occurred, these Mongol, Ottoman, or Chinese achievements might have created a world unrecognizable to us today. Perhaps China, with many prerequisites already in place and enriched by greater trade with West Africa and Europe, might have sparked an industrial revolution centuries ahead of England. It did not happen, however. Humanity stood at a crossroads in the middle of the millennium, poised between several very different futures. During the next several centuries Europe gradually forged ahead—what some historians call "the rise of the West"—partly by assimilating Eastern technologies and science, while the Islamic societies,

(Continued)

India, and finally China struggled, making the world after 1500 very different from the world before it.

THINKING ABOUT THE CONTROVERSY

1. Why do some historians emphasize China as the predominant power in this era?
2. What role did India and the Islamic societies play in the Intermediate world?
3. What points support the argument that Europe began its rise to world power in this era?

Exploring the Controversy

Among books making the case for Eastern predominance and leadership are John M. Hobson, *The Eastern Origins of Western Civilisation* (New York: Cambridge University Press, 2004); Robert B. Marks, *The Origins of the Modern World: A Global and Ecological Narrative,* 2nd ed. (Lanham, MD: Rowman and Littlefield, 2006); and Jack Goody, *The East in the West* (Cambridge: Cambridge University Press, 1996) and *The Eurasian Miracle* (Cambridge, United Kingdom: Polity, 2010). On China as the major power, see S. A. M. Adshead, *Tang China: The Rise of the East in World History* (New York: Palgrave, 2004); William H. McNeill, *The Pursuit of Power: Technology, Armed Force, and Society Since* A.D. *1000* (Chicago: University of Chicago Press, 1982); Rhoads Murphey, *East Asia: A New History,* 5th ed. (New York: Pearson, 2009); Mary Kilbourne Matossian, *Shaping World History: Breakthroughs in Ecology, Technology, Science, and Politics* (Armonk, NY: M.E. Sharpe, 1997); and Robert Temple, *The Genius of China: 3,000 Years of Science, Discovery and Invention* (London: Prion Books, 1986). For Indian and Islamic influence, see Lynda Shaffer, "Southernization," *Journal of World History* 5, no.1 (Spring 1994): 1–22; Marshall Hodgson, *Rethinking World History* (Cambridge: Cambridge University Press, 1993); and Richard Eaton, *Islamic History as Global History* (Washington, DC: American Historical Association, 1993). Among books that argue for European superiority are Toby E. Huff, *The Rise of Early Modern Science: Islam, China, and the West* (Cambridge: Cambridge University Press, 1993); David S. Landes, *The Wealth and Power of Nations: Why Some Are So Rich and Some Are So Poor* (New York: Norton, 1998); Ricardo Duchesne, *The Uniqueness of Western Civilization* (Boston: Brill, 2011); and Rodney Stark, *The Victory of Reason: How Christianity Led to Freedom, Capitalism, and Western Success* (New York: Random House, 2005). For a broader study of the rise and demise of the East, see Janet L. Abu-Lughod, *Before European Hegemony: The World System* A.D. *1250–1350* (New York: Oxford University Press, 1989).

Index